Unity 2021 Cookbook
Fourth Edition

Over 140 recipes to take your Unity game development
skills to the next level

Matt Smith
Shaun Ferns

BIRMINGHAM - MUMBAI

Unity 2021 Cookbook
Fourth Edition

Copyright © 2021 Packt Publishing

Associate Group Product Manager: Pavan Ramchandani
Publishing Product Manager: Pavan Ramchandani
Senior Editor: Sofi Rogers
Content Development Editor: Rakhi Patel
Technical Editor: Simran Udasi
Copy Editor: Safis Editing
Project Coordinator: Manthan Patel
Proofreader: Safis Editing
Indexer: Tejal Soni
Production Designer: Shankar Kalbhor

First published: June 2013
Second edition: October 2015
Third edition: August 2018
Fourth edition: September 2021

Production reference: 1030921

Published by Packt Publishing Ltd.
Livery Place
35 Livery Street
Birmingham
B3 2PB, UK.

ISBN 978-1-83921-761-6

www.packt.com

I dedicate this book to my daughter, Charlotte.

– Matt Smith

I dedicate this book to Martina, Tomás, and Sénan.

– Shaun Ferns

Foreword

Not so long ago, developing professional quality games meant licensing an expensive game engine or writing your own from scratch. Then, you needed to hire a small army of developers to use it. Today, game engines like Unity have democratized game development to the point where you can simply download the tools and start making the game of your dreams right away.

Well... kinda. Having a powerful game creation tool is not the same thing as having the technical knowledge and skills to use it effectively.

I started coding games as a kid on my trusty ZX Spectrum, Commodore 64 & later the Amiga. I've been working as a professional game developer since 2003. When I first took the plunge into learning Unity development to create the Fungus storytelling tool, I found a huge amount of online documentation, tutorials, and forum answers available for Unity developers. This makes getting started with Unity development relatively easy, but the information can also be quite fragmented. Often, the last piece of the puzzle you need is buried 40 minutes into an hour-long tutorial video or on the 15th page of a forum thread. The hours you spend looking for these nuggets of wisdom is time that would be better spent working on your game.

The beauty of the Unity Cookbooks is that Matt, Chico, and Shaun have distilled this knowledge into a neat collection of easy-to-follow recipes, and they have provided the scripts and complete working projects so that you can put it to use straight away.

In this latest edition for Unity 2021, Matt and Shaun have updated the recipes from the previous book and added new recipes to introduce many of the latest Unity features. These include topics such as Augmented Reality and XR web publishing, particle systems, 2D physics, the 2021 Unity Starter Assets packages, code coverage, and running Python scripts in Unity.

Getting started with Unity development is free and easy. When you're ready to take your skills to the next level, this book is an effective way to do just that. It covers a great deal in its hundreds of pages, and if you can master even half of what's here, you'll be well on the way to becoming a great Unity developer!

Chris Gregan
Chief Architect, Romero Games: www.romerogames.ie
Author of Fungus: fungusgames.com

Contributors

About the authors

Matt Smith is a computing academic at TU Dublin, the Technological University of Dublin, Ireland, where he leads the **DRIVE** Research Group (**Digital Realities, Interaction, and Virtual Environments**). He has been researching and teaching interactive game and web technologies since he moved to Ireland in 2002. Matt started computer programming on a brand new ZX80 and submitted two games for his computing O-level exam in 1985. After nearly 10 years as a full-time student on a succession of scholarships, he gained several degrees in computing, including a Ph.D. in computational musicology. Since 1994, he has been a full-time computer science lecturer at the University of Winchester (UK), then Middlesex University (UK), and now TU Dublin (Ireland).

In 1985, Matt wrote the lyrics and was in the band whose music appeared on the B-side of the audio cassette carrying the computer game Confuzion (look up the game's Wikipedia page!). Matt is one of the documentation authors for the free, open source Fungus Unity visual scripting and dialogue system. He enjoys sports, martial arts, and music, playing several instruments enthusiastically, if not very well. To get away from the computer completely, he has taken up carpentry and is currently planning to build an oak staircase (with a landing!), which will be his biggest project yet...

Thanks to my family for all their support. Thanks also to the editors, reviewers, and readers who provided feedback and suggestions. Thanks to my students, who continue to challenge and surprise me with their enthusiasm for multimedia and game development. Special thanks to Kris for help with the VR recipes and Nina for the AR recipes. Also thanks to Justin in Limerick for keeping me sane with snooker, golf breaks, and the newly installed full-size table tennis table – and congratulations on getting that first-class degree summa cum laude in 2021! Many thanks to Shaun for coming on board to coauthor this edition; given all the additional challenges this year, I don't think this book would have been completed without him, and I look forward to future collaborations.

Shaun Ferns is an academic at TU Dublin, the Technological University of Dublin, Ireland, where he is a researcher in the **DRIVE** Research Group (**Digital Realities, Interaction, and Virtual Environments**) and an associate researcher at the **Educational Informatics Lab** (**EILab**) at OntarioTechU. Since 2016, he has been primarily researching and teaching multimedia development, and prior to that was involved in the delivery of several engineering programs. He is currently exploring the opportunities transmedia provides in improving user experience and engagement in cultural archive artifacts and serious games for the built environment.

Shaun began to "play" with Unity when designing and building his house in 2010, developing an architectural walk-through to support the development of the design of the new home. Since then, he has been working on several Unity-based cultural projects and hopes to complete one soon!

Since 2011, Shaun has taken up the challenge of playing the Irish tenor banjo and currently enjoys playing in Irish traditional music sessions with his friends. When not practicing, he can be found wandering the cliffs and mountains around Donegal or swimming its Atlantic shores.

Thanks to the students I have been fortunate to work with over the last 20 years; the energy, excitement, and courage in their work have been truly inspirational and continue to have an influence. Thanks also to the editors, reviewers, and readers who provided feedback and suggestions. I began to enjoy our conversations through your comments! Special thanks to Matt, a source of guidance and support throughout this process, and for sharing his love of multimedia development.

About the reviewers

Alessandro Salvati is a bulky, bearded geekbear born in Sardinia, Italy and living in Liverpool. A nerd from the 80s, he is a passionate freelance self-taught Unity game developer and a proud gameplay programmer at Skyhook Games Ltd. He was the lead dev of several top-rated and featured games on mobile stores. His most renowned works are gamification experiences preserving cultural heritage – commissioned by the most prestigious Italian museums. He programmed and led "Father and Son" for The MANN in Naples, thricely praised by the Italian Prime Minister himself on public media, and the first game funded by an international archaeological museum. Alessandro raised awareness about anxiety/panic attacks with his little game "Anxiety Attacks."

I want to thank:

- My mother, Elisa, who's on my side while Covid forcefully keeps dividing us, in two different countries for over a year.
- All the friends in Oristano that I miss so much.
- My dearest Antonio from Pomezia.
- Kinjal Bari (Project Coordinator) and Manthan Patel (Associate Project Manager) from Packt Publishing, for being so patient and understanding during these months of worldwide craziness.
- The UK government in the hope it lets me continue to live in the UK.

Sungkuk Park is a Berlin-based game developer. He majored in art studies at Hongik University in Seoul, Korea but turned into a software engineer in the gaming industry. He is interested in almost everything about gaming. He is now turning into a technical artist!

These are his publications:

- Author of *Seamless Society*, 21 July 2020, in collaboration with an online exhibition platform, DDDD
- Author of *Wallpeckers: Breaking down the barriers between media*, an article in the Korean art magazine Misulsegye, March 2019
- Author of *The Possibility of the Impossibility of the "Art Games"*, an article in the Korean Art magazine Misulsegye, February 2017
- Translator and Editor of *Game Level Generation Using Neural Networks*, a featured post of Gamasutra

Table of Contents

Preface

Game development is a broad and complex task. It is an interdisciplinary field, covering subjects as diverse as artificial intelligence, character animation, digital painting, and sound editing. All these areas of knowledge can materialize as the production of hundreds (or thousands!) of multimedia and data assets. A special software application—the game engine—is required to consolidate all these assets into a single product. Game engines are specialized pieces of software, which used to belong to an esoteric domain. They were expensive, inflexible, and extremely complicated to use. They were for big studios or hardcore programmers only. Then, along came Unity.

Unity represents the true democratization of game development. It is an engine and multimedia editing environment that is user-friendly and versatile. It has free and Pro versions; the latter includes even more features. Unity offers deployment to many platforms, including the following:

- **Mobile:** Android, iOS, Windows Phone, and BlackBerry
- **Web:** WebGL (and WebXR)
- **Desktop:** PC, Mac, and Linux platforms
- **Console:** Nintendo Switch, PS5/4/3, Xbox SeriesX/One/360, PlayStation Mobile, PlayStation Vita, and Wii U
- **Virtual Reality (VR)/Augmented Reality (AR):** Oculus Quest/2 and Rift, Samsung Gear VR, HTC Vive Focus, Google Daydream, and Microsoft Hololens

Today, Unity is used by a diverse community of developers all around the world. Some are students and hobbyists, but many are commercial organizations, ranging from garage developers to international studios, who use Unity to make a huge number of games—you might have already played some on one platform or another.

This book provides over 140 Unity game development recipes. Some recipes demonstrate Unity application techniques for multimedia features, including working with animations and using preinstalled package systems. Other recipes develop game components with C# scripts, ranging from working with data structures and data file manipulation to artificial intelligence algorithms for computer-controlled characters.

If you want to develop quality games in an organized and straightforward way, and you want to learn how to create useful game components and solve common problems, then both Unity and this book are for you.

Who this book is for

This book is for anyone who wants to explore a wide range of Unity scripting and multimedia features and find ready-to-use solutions for many game features. Programmers can explore multimedia features, and multimedia developers can try their hand at scripting. From intermediate to advanced users, from artists to coders, this book is for you, and everyone in your team! It is intended for everyone who has the basics of using Unity and a little programming knowledge in C#.

What this book covers

Chapter 1, *Displaying Data with Core UI Elements*, is filled with **User Interface** (**UI**) recipes to help you increase the entertainment and enjoyment value of your games through the quality of the visual elements displaying text and data. You'll learn a wide range of UI techniques, including displaying text and images, 3D text effects, and an introduction to displaying text and image dialogues with the free Fungus package.

Chapter 2, *Responding to User Events for Interactive UIs*, teaches you about updating displays (for example basic on timers), and detecting and responding to user input actions, such as mouseovers, while the first chapter introduced code UI for displaying values to the user. Among other things, there are recipes for panels in visual layers, radio buttons and toggle groups, interactive text entry, directional radars, countdown timers, and custom mouse cursors.

Chapter 3, *Inventory and Advanced UIs*, relates to the many games that involve the player collecting items, such as keys to open doors, ammo for weapons, or choosing from a selection of items, such as from a collection of spells to cast. The recipes in this chapter offer a range of text and graphical solutions for displaying inventory status to the player, including whether they are carrying an item or not, or the maximum number of items they are able to collect. It also includes an introduction to Unity new input system.

Chapter 4, *Playing and Manipulating Sounds*, suggests ways to use sound effects and soundtrack music to make your game more interesting. The chapter demonstrates how to manipulate sound during runtime through the use of scripts, Reverb Zones, and the Audio Mixer. It also includes recipes for real-time graphics visualizations of playing sounds, a recipe to create a simple 140 bpm loop manager, with visualizations of each playing loop and ends with a recipe on ambisonic sound for 360 video.

Chapter 5, *3D Objects, Terrains, Textures and Materials*, contains recipes that will give you a better understanding of how to create, import and modify 3D objects in scenes, including creating new 3D geometry with Probuilder and the Unity terrain tools. Having worked through this chapter you'll be able to create the large-scale geography of a scene, and also work with inanimate props in that scene.

Chapter 6, *2D Animation and Physics*, introduces some of Unity's powerful 2D animation and physics features. In this chapter, we present recipes to help you understand the relationships between the different animation elements in Unity, exploring the movement of different parts of the body and the use of sprite-sheet image files that contain sequences of sprite frames pictures. In this chapter core Unity Animation concepts are presented, including Animation State Charts, Transitions, and Trigger events, as well as clipping via Sprite Masking. Finally, the use of Tiles and Tilemaps for 2D games are introduced.

Chapter 7, *Characters, GameKits, and Starter Assets*, focuses on character animation and demonstrates how to take advantage of Unity's animation system—Mecanim. It covers a range of subjects, from basic character setup to procedural animation and ragdoll physics. It also offers introductions to some of the newer Unity 3D features, such as the Unity 2D and 3D Gamekits.

Chapter 8, *Web Server Communication and Online Version Control*, explores how games running on devices can benefit from communication with other networked applications. In this chapter, a range of recipes are presented, which illustrate how to set up an online, database-driven leaderboard, how to write Unity games that can communicate with such online systems and ways to protect your games from running on unauthorized servers (to prevent your WebGL games being illegally copied and published on other people's servers). In addition, the recipes illustrate how to structure your projects so that they can be easily backed up using online version control systems such as GitHub, and also how to download projects from online sites to edit and run on our own machine.

Chapter 9, *Controlling and Choosing Positions,* presents a range of recipes for 2D and 3D user- and computer-controlled objects and characters, which can lead to games with a richer and more exciting user experience. Examples of these recipes include spawn-points, checkpoints, and physics-based approaches, such as applying forces when clicking on objects and firing projectiles into the scene.

Chapter 10, *Navigation Meshes and Agents,* explores ways that Unity's Nav Meshes and Nav Mesh Agents offer for the automation of object and character movement and pathfinding in your games. Objects can follow predefined sequences of waypoints, or be controlled by mouse clicks for point-and-click control. Objects can be made to flock together based on the average location and movement of all members of their flock. Additional recipes illustrate how the "cost" of navigation areas can be defined, simulating hard-to-travel areas such as mud and water. Finally, although much navigation behavior is pre-calculated at Design Time (the "baking" process), a recipe is presented illustrating how movable objects can influence pathfinding at runtime, through the use of the NavMesh Obstacle component.

Chapter 11, *Camera and Rendering Pipelines,* presents recipes covering techniques for controlling and enhancing your game's cameras. It offers solutions to work with both single and multiple cameras, illustrates how to apply Post-Processing effects, such as vignettes and grainy grey-scale CCTVs. The chapter introduces ways to work with Unity's powerful Cinemachine components. It concludes with a recipe detailing how to create a project using the **Universal Rendering Pipeline (URP)** and the **High Definition Rendering Pipeline (HDRP)**.

Chapter 12, *Shader Graphs and Video Players,* covers two powerful visual components in Unity: Shader Graphs and the Video Player. Both make it easy to add impressive visuals to your games with little or no programming. It includes recipes on how to simulate CCTV playback, and download and play an online video as well as an introduction to applying Shader Graphs in projects. Several recipes are presented for each of these features in this chapter.

Chapter 13, *Advanced Topics: Gizmos, Automated Testing and More,* explores a range of advanced topics, including creating your own gizmos to enhance design-time work in the scene through visual grid guides with snapping. Automated code and runtime testing is also introduced, in addition to different approaches to saving and loading game data, and a final recipe introducing the new Python for Unity package, allowing scripting in the popular Python programming language.

Chapter 14, *Particle Systems and Other Visual Effects*, offers a hands-on approach to both using and repurposing Unity's particle systems package, and also creating your own particle system from scratch. Other recipes in this chapter introduce visual effects including emissive materials, and "cookie" textures, simulating objects casting shadows between the light source and the surfaces lights shine onto.

Chapter 15, *Virtual and Augmented Reality (VR/AR)*, provides an overview and introduction to VR and AR projects in Unity. Recipes guide you through creating and configuring projects for VR and AR, adding content, and building apps, and deploying them onto devices, or publishing them as WebXR via the web.

Chapter 16, Additional Unity Recipes, this is an additional chapter and contains some nice to know recipes. It presents recipes related to AssetBundles and solutions to create, load, and download them for your project. It also contains recipes to help you implement visual effects. Please note the chapter is not a part of the main book. It can be accessed here: https://github.com/PacktPublishing/Unity-2021-Cookbook-Fourth-Edition/tree/master/Bonus%20Recipes

To get the most out of this book

All you need is a copy of Unity 2021 (and most recipes work in Unity 2020 as well), which can be downloaded for free from unity.com/.

If you wish to create your own image files, for the recipes in *Chapter 14, Particle Systems and Other Visual Effects* you will also need an image editor, such as Adobe Photoshop, which can be found at www.photoshop.com, or GIMP, which is free and can be found at www.gimp.org/.

Download the example code files

You'll find the recipes assets and completed Unity projects for each chapter at: https://github.com/PacktPublishing/Unity-2021-Cookbook-Fourth-Edition.

You can either download these files as Zip archives or use free Git software to download (clone) these files. These GitHub repositories will be updated with any improvements.

We also have other code bundles from our rich catalog of books and videos available at https://github.com/PacktPublishing/. Check them out!

Download the color images

We also provide a PDF file that has color images of the screenshots/diagrams used in this book. You can download it here: https://static.packt-cdn.com/downloads/9781839217616_ColorImages.pdf.

Conventions used

There are a number of text conventions used throughout this book.

CodeInText: Indicates code words in text, database table names, folder names, filenames, file extensions, pathnames, dummy URLs, user input, and Twitter handles. Here is an example: "The playerInventoryDisplay variable is a reference to an instance object of the PlayerInventoryDisplay class."

A block of code is set as follows:

```
using UnityEngine;
using UnityEngine.UI;

[RequireComponent(typeof(PlayerInventoryTotal))]
public class PlayerInventoryDisplay : MonoBehaviour {
   public Text starText;
   public void OnChangeStarTotal(int numStars) {
        string starMessage = "total stars = " + numStars;
        starText.text = starMessage;
   }
}
```

Bold: Indicates a new term, an important word, or words that you see onscreen. For example, words in menus or dialog boxes appear in the text like this. Here is an example: "In the **Inspector** window, set the font of **Text-carrying-star** to **Xolonium-Bold**, and set its color to yellow."

Warnings or important notes appear like this.

Tips and tricks appear like this.

Get in touch

Feedback from our readers is always welcome.

General feedback: If you have questions about any aspect of this book, mention the book title in the subject of your message and email us at customercare@packtpub.com.

Errata: Although we have taken every care to ensure the accuracy of our content, mistakes do happen. If you have found a mistake in this book, we would be grateful if you would report this to us. Please visit www.packt.com/submit-errata, selecting your book, clicking on the Errata Submission Form link, and entering the details.

Piracy: If you come across any illegal copies of our works in any form on the Internet, we would be grateful if you would provide us with the location address or website name. Please contact us at copyright@packt.com with a link to the material.

If you are interested in becoming an author: If there is a topic that you have expertise in and you are interested in either writing or contributing to a book, please visit authors.packtpub.com.

Reviews

Please leave a review. Once you have read and used this book, why not leave a review on the site that you purchased it from? Potential readers can then see and use your unbiased opinion to make purchase decisions, we at Packt can understand what you think about our products, and our authors can see your feedback on their book. Thank you!

For more information about Packt, please visit packt.com.

Displaying Data with Core UI Elements

1

A key element that contributes to the entertainment and enjoyment of most games is the quality of the visual experience, and an important part of this is the **user interface (UI)**. UI elements involve ways for the user to interact with the game (such as buttons, cursors, and text boxes), as well as ways for the game to present up-to-date information to the user (such as the time remaining, current health, score, lives left, or location of enemies). This chapter is filled with UI recipes to give you a range of examples and ideas for creating game UIs.

Every game and interactive multimedia application is different, and so this chapter attempts to fulfill two key roles:

- The first aim is to provide step-by-step instructions on how to create a range of Unity 2021 basic UI elements and, where appropriate, associate them with game variables in code.
- The second aim is to provide a rich illustration of how UI components can be used for a variety of purposes. This will help you get good ideas about how to make the Unity UI set of controls deliver the particular visual experience and interactions for the games that you are developing.

Basic UI components can provide static images and text to just make the screen look more interesting. By using scripts, we can change the content of these images and text objects so that the players' numeric scores can be updated, or we can show stickmen images to indicate how many lives the player has left. Other UI elements are interactive, allowing users to click on buttons, choose options, enter text, and so on. More sophisticated kinds of UI can involve collecting and calculating data about the game (such as percentage time remaining or enemy hit damage; or the positions and types of key GameObjects in the scene and their relationship to the location and orientation of the player), and then displaying these values in a natural, graphical way (such as with progress bars or radar screens).

Core GameObjects, components, and concepts relating to Unity UI development include the following:

- **Canvas**: Every UI element is a child (or sub-child) of a **Canvas**. There can be multiple **Canvas** GameObjects in a single scene. If a **Canvas** is not already present, then one will automatically be created when a new UI GameObject is created, with that UI object as the child of the new **Canvas** GameObject.

- **EventSystem**: An **EventSystem** GameObject is required to manage the interaction events for UI controls. One will automatically be created with the first UI element. Unity generally only allows one **EventSystem** in any scene (some proposed code for multiple event systems can be found at `https://bitbucket.org/Unity-Technologies/ui/pull-requests/18/support-for-multiple-concurrent-event/diff`).

- **Visual UI controls**: The visible UI controls include **Button, Image, Text,** and **Toggle**.

- **The Rect Transform component**: UI GameObjects are special 2D GameObjects that take up a rectangle on a 2D plane. Unity gives all UI GameObjects the special **Rect Transform** component, which has some different properties to the scene's GameObject **Transform** component (with its straightforward X/Y/Z position, rotation, and scale properties). Associated with **Rect Transforms** are pivot points (reference points for scaling, resizing, and rotations) and anchor points.

The following diagram shows the four main categories of UI controls, each in a **Canvas** GameObject and interacting via an **EventSystem** GameObject. UI controls can have their own Canvas, or several UI controls can be in the same **Canvas.** The four categories are **static** (display-only) and **interactive UI** controls, **non-visible** components (such as ones to group a set of mutually exclusive radio buttons), and **C# script** classes to manage UI control behavior through logic written in the program code.

 Note that UI controls that are not a child or descendant of a **Canvas** will not work properly, and interactive UI controls will not work properly if the **EventSystem** GameObject is missing.

Both the **Canvas** and **EventSystem** GameObjects are automatically added to the
Hierarchy window as soon as the first UI GameObject is added to a scene:

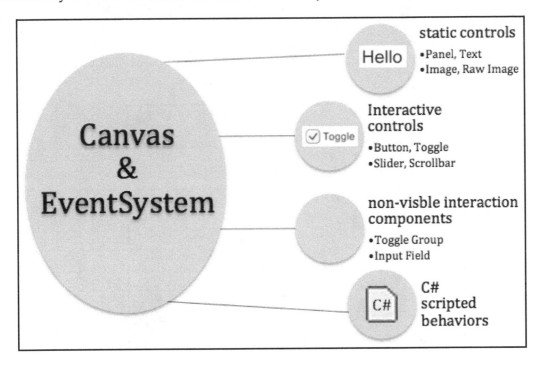

Figure 1.1 – Canvas and EventSystem

Rect Transforms for UI GameObjects represent a rectangular area rather than a single
point, which is the case for scene GameObject transforms. **Rect Transforms** describe
how a UI element should be positioned and sized relative to its parent. Rect
Transforms have a width and height that can be changed without affecting the local
scale of the component. When the scale is changed for the **Rect Transform** of a UI
element, this will also scale font sizes and borders on sliced images, and so on. If all
four anchors are at the same point, resizing Canvas will not stretch the Rect
Transform. It will only affect its position. In this case, we'll see the **Pos X** and **Pos
Y** properties, and the **Width** and **Height** properties of the rectangle in the **Inspector**
window. However, if the anchors are not all at the same point, Canvas resizing will
result in stretching the element's rectangle. So, instead of **Width**, we'll see the values
for left and right – the position of the horizontal sides of the rectangle to the sides of
Canvas, where **Width** will depend on the actual Canvas width (and the same for
top/bottom/height).

Unity provides a set of preset values for pivots and anchors, making the most common values very quick and easy to assign to an element's **Rect Transform**. The following screenshot shows the 3 x 3 grid of the **Anchor Presets** window, which allows you to make quick choices about the left, right, top, bottom, middle, horizontal, and vertical values. Also, the extra column on the right offers horizontal stretch presets, while the extra row at the bottom offers vertical stretch presets. Pressing the *Shift + Alt* keys sets the pivot and anchors when a preset is clicked:

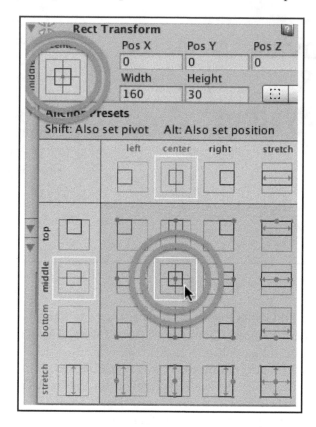

Figure 1.2 – The Rect Transform component in the Inspector window

There are three **Canvas** render modes:

- **Screen Space: Overlay**: In this mode, the UI elements are displayed without any reference to any camera (there is no need for any **Camera** in the scene). The UI elements are presented in front of (overlaying) any sort of camera display of the scene's contents.

- **Screen Space: Camera**: In this mode, **Canvas** is treated as a flat plane in the frustum (viewing space) of a **Camera** scene – where this plane is always facing the camera. So, any scene objects in front of this plane will be rendered in front of the UI elements on **Canvas**. The **Canvas** GameObject is automatically resized if the screen size, resolution, or camera settings are changed.

- **World Space**: In this mode, **Canvas** acts as a flat plane in the frustum (viewing space) of a **Camera** scene – but the plane is not made to always face **Camera**. How the **Canvas** GameObject appears is just as with any other objects in the scene, relative to where (if anywhere), in the camera's viewing frustum, the **Canvas** window is located and oriented.

In this chapter, we are going to use the **Screen Space: Overlay** mode. However, all these recipes can be used with the other two modes as well.

Be creative! This chapter aims to act as a launching pad of ideas, techniques, and reusable C# scripts for your own projects. Get to know the range of Unity UI elements, and try to work smart. Often, a UI component exists with most of the components that you may need for something in your game, but you may need to adapt it somehow. An example of this can be seen in the recipe that makes a UI Slider non-interactive, instead of using it to display a red-green progress bar for the status of a countdown timer. We will take a detailed look at this in *Displaying countdown times graphically with a UI Slider* section in *Chapter 2, Responding to User Events for Interactive UIs*.

Many of these recipes involve C# script classes that make use of the Unity scene-start event sequence of Awake() for all GameObjects, Start() for all GameObjects, and then Update() every frame to every GameObject. Therefore, you'll see many recipes in this chapter (and the whole book) where we cache references to GameObject components in the Awake() method, and then make use of these components in Start() and other methods once the scene is up and running.

In this chapter, we will cover the following recipes:

- Displaying a "Hello World" UI text message
- Displaying a digital clock
- Displaying a digital countdown timer
- Creating a message that fades away
- Displaying a perspective 3D Text Mesh
- Creating sophisticated text with TextMeshPro
- Displaying an image
- Creating UIs with the Fungus open source dialog system
- Creating a Fungus character dialog with images

Technical requirements

For this chapter, you will need Unity 2021.1 or later, plus one of the following:

- Microsoft Windows 10 (64-bit)/GPU: DX10, DX11, and DX12-capable
- macOS Sierra 10.12.6+/GPU Metal-capable Intel or AMD
- Linux Ubuntu 16.04, Ubuntu 18.04, and CentOS 7/GPU: OpenGL 3.2+ or Vulkan-capable, Nvidia or AMD

For each chapter, there is a folder that contains the asset files you will need in this book's GitHub repository at `https://github.com/PacktPublishing/Unity-2021-Cookbook-Fourth-Edition`.

Displaying a "Hello World" UI text message

The first traditional problem to be solved with new computing technology is to display the **Hello World** message, as shown in the following screenshot:

Figure 1.3 – Displaying the "Hello World" message

In this recipe, you'll learn how to create a simple UI text object with this message, in large white text with a selected font, in the center of the screen.

Getting ready

For this recipe, we have prepared the font that you need in a folder named Fonts in the 01_01 folder.

How to do it...

To display a **Hello World** text message, follow these steps:

1. Create a new **Unity 2D project**.
2. Import the provided Fonts folder, as described in the *Getting ready* section. Copy these font files into your Unity project – they need to be in your Assets folder.

3. In the **Hierarchy** window, add a **Text** GameObject to the scene by going to **GameObject | UI | Text**. Name this GameObject Text-hello.

Alternatively, you can use the **Create** menu immediately below the **Hierarchy** tab. To do so, go to **Create | UI | Text**.

4. Ensure that your new Text-hello GameObject is selected in the **Hierarchy** window.
   Now, in the **Inspector** window, ensure the following properties are set:
   - **Text** set to read Hello World
   - **Font** set to Xolonium-Bold
   - **Font Size** as per your requirements (large – this depends on your screen; try 50 or 100)
   - **Alignment** set to horizontal and vertical-center
   - Horizontal and Vertical Overflow set to Overflow
   - **Color** set to white

The following screenshot shows the **Inspector** window with these settings:

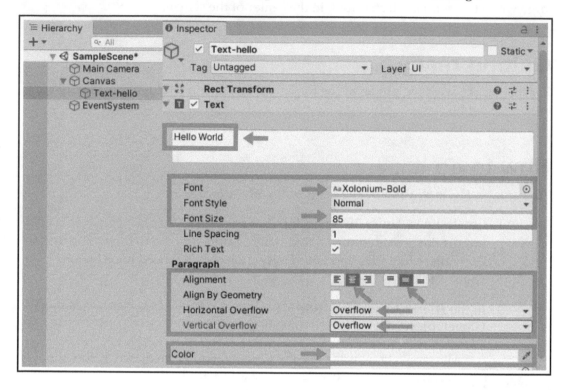

Figure 1.4 – Settings of the Inspector window

5. In the **Inspector** window, click **Rect Transform** to make a dropdown appear, and click on the **Anchor Presets** square icon, which should result in several rows and columns of preset position squares appearing. Hold down *Shift + Alt* and click on the center one (middle row and center column):

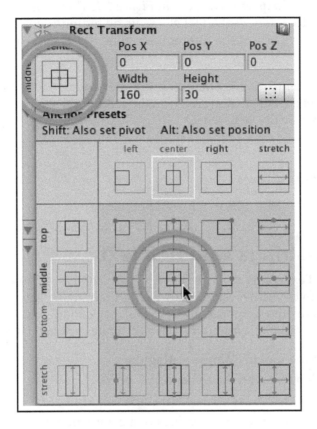

Figure 1.5 – Selecting the center row and column in Rect Transform

6. Your **Hello World** text will now appear, centered nicely in the **Game** window.

How it works...

In this recipe, you added a new `Text-hello` GameObject to the scene. A parent Canvas and UI EventSystem will have also been automatically created. Also, note that by default, a new UI GameObject is added to the UI Layer – we can see this illustrated at the top right of the **Inspector** window in *Figure 1.4*. This is useful since, for example, it is easy to hide/reveal all UI elements by hiding/revealing this layer in the **Culling Mask** property of the **Camera** component of the **Main Camera** GameObject.

You set the text content and presentation properties and used the **Rect Transform** anchor presets to ensure that whatever way the screen is resized, the text will stay horizontally and vertically centered.

There's more...

Here are some more details you don't want to miss.

Styling substrings with rich text

Each separate **UI Text** component can have its own color, size, boldness styling, and so on. However, if you wish to quickly add a highlighting style to the part of a string to be displayed to the user, you can apply HTML-style markups. The following are examples that are available without the need to create separate UI text objects:

- Change the font to **Xolonium-Regular**
- Embolden text with the b markup: I am `<b>bold</b>`
- Italicize text with the i markup: I am `<i>italic</i>`
- Set the text color with hex values or a color name: I am a `<color=green>green text </color>`, but I am `<color=#FF0000>red</color>`

You can learn more by reading the Unity online manual's Rich Text page at `http://docs.unity3d.com/Manual/StyledText.html`.

Displaying a digital clock

Whether it is real-world time or an in-game countdown clock, many games are enhanced by some form of clock or timer display. The following screenshot shows the kind of clock we will be creating in this recipe:

Figure 1.6 – Displaying a digital clock when the scene is run

The most straightforward type of clock to display is a string composed of the integers for hours, minutes, and seconds, which is what we'll create in this recipe.

Getting ready

For this recipe, we have prepared the font that you will need in a folder named `Fonts` in the `01_01` folder.

How to do it...

To create a digital clock, follow these steps:

1. Create a new **Unity 2D project**.
2. Import the provided `Fonts` folder, as described in the *Getting ready* section. Copy these font files into your Unity project – they need to be in your `Assets` folder.
3. In the **Hierarchy** window, add a **UI Text** GameObject to the scene named `Text-clock`.

4. Ensure that the `Text-clock` GameObject is selected in the **Hierarchy** window. Now, in the **Inspector** window, ensure that the following properties are set:

> - **Font Type** set to `Xolonium Bold`
> - **Font Size** set to `20`
> - **Alignment** set to horizontal and vertical-center
> - **Horizontal** and **Vertical Overflow** settings set to `Overflow`
> - **Color** set to white

5. In **Rect Transform**, click on the **Anchor Presets** square icon, which will result in the appearance of several rows and columns of preset position squares. Hold down *Shift + Alt* and click on the top and center column rows.

6. In the **Project** window, create a folder named `_Scripts` and create a C# script class (**Create | C# Script**) called `ClockDigital` in this new folder:

```csharp
using UnityEngine;
using UnityEngine.UI;
using System;

public class ClockDigital : MonoBehaviour {
  private Text textClock;

  void Awake (){
    textClock = GetComponent<Text>();
  }

  void Update (){
    DateTime time = DateTime.Now;
    string hour = LeadingZero( time.Hour );
    string minute = LeadingZero( time.Minute );
    string second = LeadingZero( time.Second );

    textClock.text = hour + ":" + minute + ":" + second;
  }

  string LeadingZero (int n){
    return n.ToString().PadLeft(2, '0');
  }
}
```

It can be useful to prefix important folders with an underscore character so that items appear first in a sequence.
Since **scripts** and **scenes** are things that are most often accessed, prefixing their folder names with an underscore character, as in _Scenes and _Scripts, means they are always easy to find at the top in the **Project** window.

Although the preceding code is useful for illustrating how to access the time component of a DateTime object individually, the Format(...) method of the String class can be used to format a DateTime object all in a single statement. For example, the preceding could be written more succinctly in a single statement; that is, String.Format("HH:mm:ss", DateTime.Now). For more examples, see http://www.csharp-examples.net/string-format-datetime/.

7. Ensure the Text-clock GameObject is selected in the **Hierarchy** window.

8. In the **Inspector** window, add an instance of the ClockDigital script class as a component by clicking the **Add Component** button, selecting **Scripts**, and choosing the ClockDigital script class:

Figure 1.7 – Adding Clock Digital as a component

Add script components through drag and drop.
Script components can also be added to GameObjects via drag and drop. For example, with the `Text-clock` GameObject selected in the **Hierarchy** window, drag your `ClockDigital` script onto it to add an instance of this script class as a component to the `Text-clock` GameObject.

9. When you run the scene, you will now see a digital clock that shows hours, minutes, and seconds in the top-center part of the screen.

How it works...

In this recipe, you added a Text GameObject to a scene. Then, you added an instance of the `ClockDigital` C# script class to that GameObject.

Notice that as well as the standard two C# packages (`UnityEngine` and `System.Collections`) that are written by default for every new script, you added the `using` statements to two more C# script packages, `UnityEngine.UI` and `System`. The **UI package** is needed since our code uses the UI text object, and the `System` package is needed since it contains the `DateTime` class that we need to access the clock on the computer where our game is running.

There is one variable, `textClock`, which will be a reference to the `Text` component, whose text content we wish to update in each frame with the current time in hours, minutes, and seconds.

The `Awake()` method (executed when the scene begins) sets the `textClock` variable to be a reference to the `Text` component in the GameObject, to which our scripted object has been added. Storing a reference to a component in this way is referred to as caching – this means that code that's executed later does not need to repeat the computationally expensive task of searching the GameObject hierarchy for a component of a particular type.

Note that an alternative approach would be to make `textClock` a public variable. This would allow us to assign it via drag and drop in the **Inspector** window.

The Update() method is executed in every frame. The current time is stored in the time variable, and strings are created by adding leading zeros to the number values for the hours, minutes, and seconds properties of the variable. Finally, this method updates the text property (that is, the letters and numbers that the user sees) to be a string, concatenating the hours, minutes, and seconds with colon separator characters.

The LeadingZero(...) method takes an integer as input and returns a string of this number with leading zeros added to the left if the value was less than 10.

Displaying a digital countdown timer

As a game mechanic, countdown clocks are a popular feature in many games:

Figure 1.8 – Countdown clock

This recipe, which will adapt the digital clock shown in the previous recipe, will show you how to display a digital countdown clock that will count down from a predetermined time to zero in *Figure 1.8*.

Getting ready

This recipe adapts to the previous one. So, make a copy of the project for the previous recipe, and work on this copy.

For this recipe, we have prepared the script that you need in a folder named _Scripts inside the 01_03 folder.

How to do it...

To create a digital countdown timer, follow these steps:

1. Import the provided _Scripts folder.

2. In the **Inspector** window, remove the scripted component, ClockDigital, from the Text-clock GameObject. You can do this by choosing **Remove Component** from the 3-dot options menu icon for this component the **Inspector** window.

3. In the **Inspector** window, add an instance of the CountdownTimer script class as a component by clicking the **Add Component** button, selecting **Scripts**, and choosing the CountdownTimer script class.

4. Create a DigitalCountdown C# script class that contains the following code, and add an instance as a scripted component to the Text-clock GameObject:

```
using UnityEngine;
using UnityEngine.UI;

public class DigitalCountdown : MonoBehaviour {
    private Text textClock;
    private CountdownTimer countdownTimer;

    void Awake() {
        textClock = GetComponent<Text>();
        countdownTimer = GetComponent<CountdownTimer>();
    }
    void Start() {
        countdownTimer.ResetTimer( 30 );
    }

    void Update () {
        int timeRemaining =
countdownTimer.GetSecondsRemaining();
        string message = TimerMessage(timeRemaining);
        textClock.text = message;
    }

    private string TimerMessage(int secondsLeft) {
        if (secondsLeft <= 0){
            return "countdown has finished";
        } else {
            return "Countdown seconds remaining = " +
secondsLeft;
```

```
                }
            }
        }
```

5. When you run the scene, you will now see a digital clock counting down from 30. When the countdown reaches zero, a message stating **Countdown has finished** will be displayed.

Automatically add components with [RequireComponent(...)]. The DigitalCountdown script class requires the same GameObject to also have an instance of the CountdownTimer script class. Rather than having to manually attach an instance of a required script, you can use the [RequireComponent(...)] C# attribute immediately before the class declaration statement. This will result in Unity automatically attaching an instance of the required script class.

For example, by writing the following code, Unity will add an instance of CountdownTimer as soon as an instance of the DigitalCountdown script class has been added as a component of a GameObject:

```
using UnityEngine;
using UnityEngine.UI;

[RequireComponent (typeof (CountdownTimer))]
public class DigitalCountdown : MonoBehaviour {
```

You can learn more by reading the Unity documentation at https://docs.unity3d.com/ScriptReference/RequireComponent.html.

How it works...

In this recipe, you added instances of the DigitalCountdown and CountdownTimer C# script classes to your scene's UI Text GameObject.

The Awake() method caches references to the **Text** and **CountdownTimer** components in the countdownTimer and textClock variables. The textClock variable will be a reference to the **UI Text** component, whose text content we wish to update in each frame with a *time-remaining* message (or a *timer-complete* message).

The `Start()` method calls the countdown timer object's `CountdownTimerReset(...)` method, passing an initial value of 30 seconds.

The `Update()` method is executed in every frame. This method retrieves the countdown timer's remaining seconds and stores this value as an integer (whole number) in the `timeRemaining` variable. This value is passed as a parameter to the `TimerMessage()` method, and the resulting message is stored in the string (text) variable message. Finally, this method updates the text property (that is, the letters and numbers that the user sees) of the `textClock` UI Text GameObject to be equal to the string message about the remaining seconds.

The `TimerMessage()` method takes an integer as input, and if the value is zero or less, a message stating the timer has finished is returned. Otherwise (if more than zero seconds remain), a message stating the number of remaining seconds is returned.

Creating a message that fades away

Sometimes, we want a message to only be displayed for a certain time, and then fade away and disappear. This recipe will describe the process for displaying an image and then making it fade away completely after 5 seconds. It could be used for providing instructions or warnings to a player that disappears so as not to take up screen space.

Getting ready

This recipe adapts the previous one. So, make a copy of the project for that recipe and work on this copy.

How to do it...

To display a text message that fades away, follow these steps:

1. In the **Inspector** window, remove the scripted component, `DigitalCountdown`, from the `Text-clock` GameObject.

2. Create a C# script class called `FadeAway` that contains the following code, and add an instance as a scripted component to the `Text-hello` GameObject:

```csharp
using UnityEngine;
using UnityEngine.UI;

[RequireComponent(typeof(CountdownTimer))]
public class FadeAway : MonoBehaviour
{
    private CountdownTimer countdownTimer;
    private Text textUI;

    void Awake()
    {
        textUI = GetComponent<Text>();
        countdownTimer = GetComponent<CountdownTimer>();
    }

    void Start()
    {
        countdownTimer.ResetTimer(5);
    }

    void Update()
    {
        float alphaRemaining =
            countdownTimer.GetProportionTimeRemaining();
        print(alphaRemaining);
        Color c = textUI.color;
        c.a = alphaRemaining;
        textUI.color = c;
    }
}
```

3. When you run the scene, you will see that the message on the screen slowly fades away, disappearing after 5 seconds.

How it works...

In this recipe, you added an instance of the `FadeAway` scripted class to the `Text-hello` GameObject. Due to the `RequireComponent(...)` attribute, an instance of the `CountdownTimer` script class was also **automatically** added.

The `Awake()` method caches references to the **Text** and **CountdownTimer** components in the `countdownTimer` and `textUI` variables.

The `Start()` method reset the countdown timer so that it starts counting down from 5 seconds.

The `Update()` method (executed every frame) retrieves the proportion of time remaining in our timer by calling the `GetProportionTimeRemaining()` method. This method returns a value between `0.0` and `1.0`, which also happens to be the range of values for the alpha (transparency) property of the color property of a UI Text GameObject.

Flexible range of `0.0–1.0`.

It is often a good idea to represent proportions as values between `0.0` and `1.0`. Either this will be just the value we want for something, or we can multiply the maximum value by our decimal proportion, and we get the appropriate value. For example, if we wanted the number of degrees of a circle for a given `0.0–0.1` proportion, we would just multiply by the maximum of 360, and so on.

The `Update()` method then retrieves the current color of the text being displayed (via `textUI.color`), updates its alpha property, and resets the text object to having this updated color value. The result is that each frame in the text object's transparency represents the current value of the proportion of the timer remaining until it fades to fully transparent when the timer gets to zero.

Displaying a perspective 3D Text Mesh

Unity provides an alternative way to display text in 3D via the **Text Mesh** component. While this is really suitable for a text-in-the-scene kind of situation (such as billboards, road signs, and the general wording on the side of 3D objects that might be seen close up), it is quick to create and is another way of creating interesting menus or instruction scenes.

In this recipe, you'll learn how to create scrolling 3D text, simulating the famous opening credits of the movie Star Wars, which looks something like this:

Figure 1.9 – Scrolling 3D text

Getting ready

For this recipe, we have prepared the fonts that you need in a folder named Fonts, and the text file that you need in a folder named Text, both of which can be found inside the 01_05 folder.

How to do it...

To display perspective 3D text, follow these steps:

1. Create a new **Unity 3D project**. This will ensure that we start off with a **Perspective** camera, suitable for the 3D effect we want to create.

 If you need to mix 2D and 3D scenes in your project, you can always manually set any camera's **Camera Projection** property to **Perspective** or **Orthographic** via the **Inspector** window.

2. In the **Hierarchy** window, select the **Main Camera** item and, in the **Inspector** window, set its properties as follows: **Camera Clear Flags** to **Solid color**, **Background color** to **Black**, and **Field of View** to 150.

3. Import the provided Fonts and Text folders.

4. In the **Hierarchy** window, add a UI | Text GameObject to the scene by going to **GameObject** | **UI** | **Text**. Name this GameObject Text-star-wars.

5. Set the UI Text Text-star-wars GameObject's **Text Content** to Star Wars (with each word on a new line). Then, set its **Font** to Xolonium Bold, its **Font Size** to 50, and its **Color** to **White**. Use **Anchor presets** in **Rect Transform** to position this UI text object at the top-center of the screen. Set **Vertical Overflow** to Overflow. Then, set **Alignment Horizontal** to the center (leaving **Alignment Vertical** as **top**).

6. In the **Hierarchy** window, add a 3D Text GameObject to the scene by going to **GameObject** | **3D Object** | **3D Text**. Name this GameObject Text-crawler.

7. In the **Inspector** window, set the **Transform** properties for the Text-crawler GameObject as **Position** (100, -250, 0), **Rotation** (15, 0, 0).

8. In the **Inspector** window, set the **Text Mesh** properties for the Text-crawler GameObject as follows:
   - Paste the content of the provided text file, star_wars.txt, into **Text**.
   - Set **Offset Z** to -20, **Line Spacing** to 1, and **Anchor** to Middle center.
   - Set **Font Size** to 200 and **Font** to SourceSansPro-BoldIt.

9. When the scene is made to run, the Star Wars story text will now appear nicely squashed in a 3D perspective on the screen.

How it works...

In this recipe, you simulated the opening screen of Star Wars, with a flat UI text object title at the top of the screen and a 3D Text Mesh with settings that appear to be disappearing into the horizon with 3D perspective "squashing."

There's more...

There are some details you don't want to miss.

Making the text crawl as it does in the movie

With a few lines of code, we can make this text scroll in the horizon, just as it does in the movie. Add the following C# script class, called ScrollZ, as a component of the Text-crawler GameObject:

```csharp
using UnityEngine;
using System.Collections;

public class ScrollZ : MonoBehaviour
{
  // variable letting us change how fast we'll move text into the
'distance'
  public float scrollSpeed = 20;

  //-----------------
  void Update ()
  {
    // get current position of parent GameObject
    Vector3 pos = transform.position;

    // get vector pointing into the distance
    Vector3 localVectorUp = transform.TransformDirection(0,1,0);

    // move the text object into the distance to give our 3D scrolling
effect
    pos += localVectorUp * scrollSpeed * Time.deltaTime;
    transform.position = pos;
  }
}
```

In each frame, via the Update() method, the position of the 3D text object is moved in the direction of this GameObject's local up direction.

Where to learn more

You can learn more about 3D Text and Text Meshes in the Unity online manual at http://docs.unity3d.com/Manual/class-TextMesh.html.

 An alternative way of achieving perspective text like this would be to use a **Canvas** with the **World Space** render mode.

Creating sophisticated text with TextMeshPro

In 2017, Unity purchased the **TextMeshPro Asset Store** product and has integrated it into Unity as a free core feature. **TextMeshPro** uses a **Signed Distance Field (SDF)** rendering method, resulting in clear and sharply drawn characters at any point size and resolution. You will need them, but it's easy to create them. Just use the ones provided for now and let's focus on something else.

Getting ready

For this recipe, we have prepared the fonts that you need in a folder named Fonts & Materials inside the 01_06 folder.

How to do it...

To display a text message with sophisticated **TextMeshPro** visual styling, follow these steps:

1. Create a new **Unity 3D** project.

2. Add a new UI **TextMeshPro - Text** GameObject in the scene by going to **GameObject | UI | TextMeshPro – Text**. Name this GameObject Text-sophisticated. Choose **Import TMP Essentials** if prompted.

TextMeshPro GameObjects do not have to be part of the UI Canvas. You can add a TextMeshPro GameObject to the scene directly by choosing **Create | 3D Object | TextMeshPro – Text** from the **Scene** window.

3. Ensure that your new Text-sophisticated GameObject is selected in the **Hierarchy** window. In the **Inspector** window for **Rect Transform**, click on the **Anchor Presets** square icon, hold down *Shift + Alt*, and click on the top and stretch rows.

4. Ensure the following properties are set:

Font Settings:

- **Font Asset** set to Anton SDF
- **Material Preset** set to Anton SDF – Outline
- **Font** size set to 200
- **Alignment** set to the horizontal center

Face:

- **Color** set to white
- **Dilate** set to 0

Outline:

- **Color** set to Red
- **Thickness** set to 0.1

Underlay (shadow):

- **Offset X** set to 1
- **Offset Y** set to -1
- **Dilate** set to 1

The following screenshot shows the **Inspector** window with these settings:

Figure 1.10 – Inspector window settings

5. The `Text-sophisticated` GameObject will now be very large with a white inner, red outline, and a drop shadow to the lower right.

How it works...

In this recipe, you added a new UI Text `TextMeshPro` GameObject to a scene. You chose one of the SDF fonts and an outline material preset. You then adjusted the settings for the face (the inner part of each character), outline, and drop shadow (Underlay).

There are hundreds of settings for the **TextMeshPro** component, which means much experimentation may be required to achieve a particular effect.

There's more...

Here are some more details you don't want to miss.

Rich text substrings for colors, effects, and sprites

TextMeshPro offers over 30 HTML-style markups for substrings. The following code illustrates some:

```
<sprite=5> inline sprite graphics

<smallcaps>...</smallcaps> small-caps and colors

<#ffa000>...</color> substring colors
```

One powerful piece of markup is the `<page>` tag, which allows a single set of text to be made interactive and presented to the user as a sequence of pages.

You can learn more by reading the online manual **Rich Text** page at `http://digitalnativestudios.com/textmeshpro/docs/rich-text/`.

Displaying an image

There are many cases where we wish to display an image onscreen, including logos, maps, icons, and splash graphics. In this recipe, we will display an image centered at the top of the screen.

The following screenshot shows Unity displaying an image:

Figure 1.11 – Displaying the Unity logo as an image

Getting ready

For this recipe, we have prepared the image that you need in a folder named Images in the 01_07 folder.

How to do it...

To display an image, follow these steps:

1. Create a new **Unity 2D** project.
2. Set the **Game** window to 400 x 300. Do this by displaying the **Game** window, and then creating a new **Resolution** in the drop-down menu at the top of the panel.
3. Click the plus (+) symbol at the bottom of this menu, setting **Label** to Core UI, **Width** to 400, and **Height** to 300. Click **OK**; the **Game** window should be set to this new resolution:

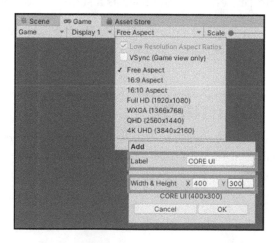

Figure 1.12 – Adding a new screen Resolution to the Game window

Alternatively, you can set the default **Game** window's resolution by going to **Edit | Project Settings | Player** and then the width and height of **Resolution** and **Presentation** in the **Inspector** window (having turned off the **Full-Screen** option).

4. Import the provided `Images` folder. In the **Inspector** window, ensure that the `unity_logo` image has **Texture Type** set to **Default**. If it has some other type, then choose **Default** from the drop-down list and click on the **Apply** button.

5. In the **Hierarchy** window, add a **UI | RawImage** GameObject named `RawImage-logo` to the scene.

6. Ensure that the `RawImage-logo` GameObject is selected in the **Hierarchy** window. In the **Inspector** window for the **RawImage (Script)** component, click the file viewer circle icon at the right-hand side of the **Texture** property and select image `unity_logo`, as shown in the following screenshot:

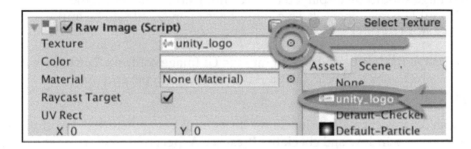

Figure 1.13 – Setting a Texture for a Raw Image UI GameObject

 An alternative way of assigning this **Texture** is to drag the `unity_logo` image from your `Project` folder (`Images`) into the **Raw Image (Script)** public property **Texture**.

7. Click on the **Set Native Size** button to resize the image so that it is no longer stretched and distorted.

8. In **Rect Transform**, click on the **Anchor Presets** square icon, which will result in several rows and columns of preset position squares appearing. Hold down *Shift + Alt* and click on the top row and the center column.

9. The image will now be positioned neatly at the top of the **Game** window and will be horizontally centered.

How it works...

In this recipe, you ensured that an image has its **Texture Type** set to **Default**. You also added a UI RawImage control to the scene. The RawImage control has been made to display the `unity_logo` image file. This image has been positioned at the top-center of the **Game** window.

There's more...

Here are some details you don't want to miss.

Working with 2D sprites and UI Image components

If you simply wish to display non-animated images, then Texture images and UI RawImage controls are the way to go. However, if you want more options regarding how an image should be displayed (such as tiling and animation), the UI Image control should be used instead. This control needs image files to be imported as the **Sprite (2D and UI)** type.

Once an image file has been dragged into the UI Image control's **Sprite** property, additional properties will be available, such as **Image Type**, and options to preserve the aspect ratio.

If you wish to prevent a UI Sprite GameObject from being distorted and stretched, go to the Inspector window and check the **Preserve Aspect** option in its **Image (Script)** component.

See also

An example of tiling a sprite image can be found in the *Revealing icons for multiple object pickups by changing the size of a tiled image* recipe in *Chapter 3, Inventory UIs and Advanced UIs*.

Creating UIs with the Fungus open source dialog system

Rather than constructing your own UI and interactions from scratch each time, there are plenty of UI and dialogue systems available for Unity. One powerful, free, and open source dialog system is called Fungus, which uses a visual flowcharting approach to dialog design:

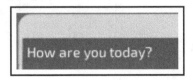

Figure 1.14 – An example of dialogue generated by Fungus

In this recipe, we'll create a very simple, one-sentence piece of dialogue to illustrate the basics of Fungus. The preceding screenshot shows the Fungus-generated dialog for the sentence **How are you today?**.

How to do it...

To create a one-sentence piece of dialog using **Fungus**, follow these steps:

1. Create a new **Unity 2D project** and ensure you are logged into your Unity account in the Unity Editor.

2. Open the Unity asset store in a web browser and log into your Unity account on the Asset Store.

3. On the Asset Store website, search for **Fungus Games** and select this asset. Click on **Add to My Assets**. Then, after the tab changes, click on **Open in Unity**.

4. In your Unity Editor, the **Package Manager** panel should open, and the Fungus assets should be selected in the list of **My Assets**. Click **Download**. Once they've been downloaded, click **Import**.

5. In the **Project** window, you should now see two new folders named Fungus and FungusExamples.

6. Create a new Fungus Flowchart GameObject by going to **Tools** | **Fungus** | **Create** | **Flowchart**.

7. In the **Hierarchy** window, select the new `Flowchart` GameObject. Then, in the **Inspector** window, click the **Open Flowchart Window** button. A new Fungus **Flowchart** window should appear – dock this panel next to the **Game** window.

8. There will be one block in **Flowchart Window**. Click on this block to select it (a green border will appear around the block to indicate that it is selected). In the **Inspector** window, change its **Block Name** to `Start`:

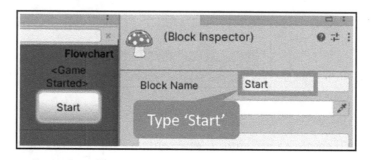

Figure 1.15 – Naming a Fungus block

9. Each block in a **Flowchart** follows a sequence of commands. So, in the **Inspector** window, we are now going to create a sequence of (**Say**) commands to display two sentences to the user when the game runs.

10. Ensure that the **Start** block is still selected in the **Flowchart** window. Click on the plus (**+**) button at the bottom section of the **Inspector** window to display a menu containing commands and select the **Narrative/Say** command:

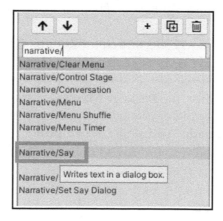

Figure 1.16 – Adding a Say command

Since we only have one command for this block, that command will be automatically selected (highlighted green) in the top part of the **Inspector** window. The bottom half of the **Inspector** window presents the properties for the currently selected command, as shown in the following screenshot. In the bottom half of the **Inspector** window, for the **Story Text** property, enter the text of the question that you wish to be presented to the user, which is How are you today?:

Figure 1.17 – Setting the text for the Say command

11. Create another **Say** command using the same plus (+) button as before, and type in Very well thank you for its **Story Text** property.

12. When you run the game, the user will be presented with the **How are you today?** text (hearing a clicking noise as each letter is typed on the screen). After the user clicks on the **continue** triangle button (at the bottom-right part of the dialog window), they will be presented with the second sentence; that is, **Very well thank you**.

How it works...

In this recipe, you created a new Unity project and imported the **Fungus** asset package, which contains the **Fungus Unity** menus, windows, and commands, as well as the example projects.

Then, you added a **Fungus Flowchart** to your scene with a single block that you named Start. Your block starts to execute when the game begins (since the default for the first block is to be executed upon receiving the **Game Started** event).

In the **Start** block, you added a sequence of two **Say** commands. Each command presents a sentence to the user and then waits for the **continue** button to be clicked before proceeding to the next command.

As can be seen, the **Fungus** system handles the work of creating a nicely presented panel to the user, displaying the desired text and the **Continue** button. **Fungus** offers many more features, including menus, animations, and controls for sounds and music, the details of which can be found in the next recipe and by exploring their provided example projects and their websites:

- http://fungusgames.com/
- https://github.com/FungusGames/Fungus

Creating a Fungus character dialog with images

The **Fungus** dialog system that we introduced in the previous recipe supports multiple characters, whose dialogs can be highlighted through their names, colors, sound effects, and even portrait images. In this recipe, we'll create a two-character dialog between Sherlock Holmes and Watson to illustrate the system:

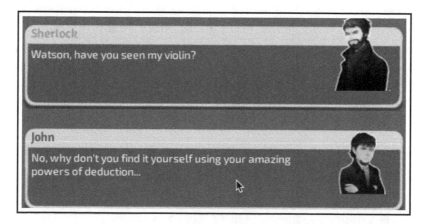

Figure 1.18 – Highlighting the speaking character by name, color, and portrait image

How to do it...

To create a character dialog with portrait images using Fungus, follow these steps:

1. Create a new **Unity 2D project**.
2. Open the **Asset Store** window, **Import** the **Fungus** dialogue asset package (this includes the **Fungus** examples, whose images we'll use for the two characters).
3. Create a new `Fungus Flowchart` GameObject by going to **Tools | Fungus | Create | Flowchart.**
4. Display and dock the **Fungus Flowchart** window.
5. Change the name of the only block in **Flowchart** to `The case of the missing violin.`
6. Create a new character by going to **Tools | Fungus | Create | Character.**
7. You should now see a new `Character` GameObject in the **Hierarchy** window.
8. With the `Character 1` GameObject selected in the **Project** window, edit its properties in the **Inspector** window, like so:
   - Rename this GameObject `Character 1 - Sherlock`.
   - In its **Character(Script)** component, set **Name Text** to `Sherlock` and **Name Color** to green.
   - In the **Inspector** window click the **Add Portrait** button (the plus (+) sign) to get a "slot" that you can add a portrait image to.

- Drag the appropriate image into your new portrait image slot (in this screenshot, we used the **confident** image from the Sherlock example project by going to **Fungus Examples | Sherlock | Portraits | Sherlock**):

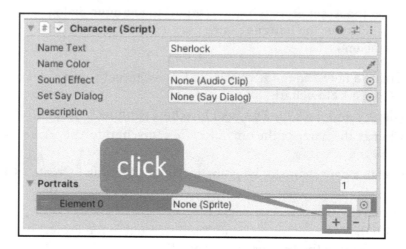

Figure 1.19 – Adding a portrait image to a character

9. Repeat *steps 6* to *8* to create a second character, **John**, using **Name Color** set to blue and **Portrait Image** set to **annoyed**.

10. Select your block in `Fungus Flowchart` so that you can add some commands to be executed.

11. Create a **Say** command for **Character 1 - Sherlock** stating `Watson, have you seen my violin?` and choose the **confident** portrait (since this is the only one we added to the character):

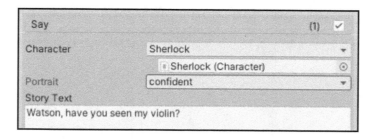

Figure 1.20 – Specifying the portrait image to use with a Say command

12. Add a second **Say** command, this time for **Character 2 – John**, stating `No, why don't you find it yourself using your amazing powers of deduction.` and choose the **annoyed** portrait:

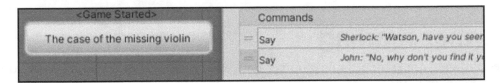

Figure 1.21 – Adding a second Say command

13. Run the scene. You should see a sequence of statements, clearly showing who is saying both with (colored) name text *AND* the portrait image you selected for each **Say** command (after Sherlock's text has finished appearing, click the box to start John's sentence).

How it works...

In this recipe, you created a new Unity project with the **Fungus** asset package.

You then added a **Fungus Flowchart** to your scene, and also added two characters (each with a text color and a portrait image).

For the block in the Flowchart, you added two **Say** commands, stating which character was saying each sentence and which portrait to use (if you had added more portrait images, you could have selected different images to indicate the emotion of the character speaking).

There's more...

Fungus offers a data-driven approach to conversations. The character and portrait (facing direction, movement onto and off the stage, and so on) can be defined through text in a simple format by using the **Say** command's **Narrative | Conversation** option. This recipe's conversation with portrait images can be declared with just two lines of text in a **Conversation**:

```
Sherlock confident: Watson, have you seen my violin?
John annoyed: No, why don't you find it yourself using your amazing
powers of deduction...
```

You can learn more about the Fungus conversation system by reading their documentation pages: `https://github.com/snozbot/fungus/wiki/conversation_system`.

Further reading

The following are some useful resources for learning more about working with core UI elements in Unity:

- The Unity manual provides a very good introduction to UI Basic layout: `http://docs.unity3d.com/Manual/UIBasicLayout.html`.

- The Unity manual also provides an introduction to **Rect Transform:** `https://docs.unity3d.com/ScriptReference/RectTransform.html`.

- In addition, Ray Wenderlich's two-part Unity UI web tutorial also presents a helpful overview of Rect Transform, pivots, and anchors. Both parts of Wenderlich's tutorial make great use of animated GIFs to illustrate the effect of different values for pivots and anchors: `http://www.raywenderlich.com/78675/unity-new-gui-part-1`.

- To learn more about TextMeshPro, take a look at the following link: `https://blogs.unity3d.com/2018/10/16/making-the-most-of-textmesh-pro-in-unity-2018/`.

- Background to how TextMeshPro uses Signed Distance Functions: `https://en.wikipedia.org/wiki/Signed_distance_function`.

Responding to User Events for Interactive UIs

Almost all the recipes in this chapter involve different interactive UI controls. Although there are different kinds of interactive UI controls, the basic way to work with them, as well as to have scripted actions respond to user actions, is all based on the same idea: events triggering the execution of object method functions.

Then, for fun, and as an example of a very different kind of UI, the final recipe will demonstrate how to add sophisticated, real-time communication for the relative positions of objects in the scene to your game (that is, radar!).

The UI can be used for three main purposes:

- To display **static (unchanging) values**, such as the name or logo image of the game, or word labels such as Level and Score, that tell us what the numbers next to them indicate (the recipes for these can be found in Chapter 1, *Displaying Data with Core UI Elements*).
- To display **values that change due to our scripts**, such as timers, scores, or the distance from our **Player** character to some other object (an example of this is the radar recipe at the end of this chapter, *Displaying a radar to indicate the relative locations of objects*).
- **Interactive** UI controls, whose purpose is to allow the player to communicate with the game scripts via their mouse or touchscreen. These are the ones we'll look at in detail in this chapter.

The core concept of working with Unity interactive UI controls is to *register an object's public method so that we're informed when a particular event occurs*. For example, we can add a UI dropdown to a scene named `DropDown1`, and then write a `MyScript` script class containing a `NewValueAction()` public method to perform an action. However, nothing will happen until we do two things:

- We need to add an *instance of the script class as a component* of a GameObject in the scene (which we'll name `go1` for our example – although we can also add the script instance to the UI GameObject itself if we wish to).
- In the UI dropdown's properties, we need to *register the GameObject's public method* of its script component so that it responds to the **On Value Changed** event messages:

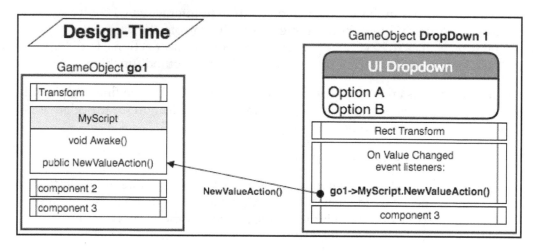

Figure 2.1 – Graphical representation of the UI at design time

The `NewValueAction()` public method of the `MyScript` script will typically retrieve the value that's been selected by the user in the dropdown and do something with it – for example, confirm it to the user, change the music volume, or change the game's difficulty. The `NewValueAction()` method will be invoked (executed) each time the `go1` GameObject receives the `NewValueAction()` message. In the properties of `DropDown1`, we need to register go1's scripted component – that is, MyScript's `NewValueAction()` public method – as an event listener for **On Value Changed** events. We need to do all this at design time (that is, in the Unity Editor before running the scene):

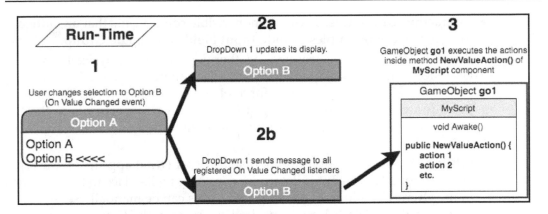

Figure 2.2 – Graphical representation of the runtime of the UI

At runtime (when the scene in the application is running), we must do the following:

1. If the user changes the value in the drop-down menu of the DropDown1 GameObject (*step 1* in the preceding diagram), this will generate an **On Value Changed** event.
2. DropDown1 will update its display on the screen to show the user the newly-selected value (*step 2a*). It will also send messages to all the GameObject components registered as listeners to **On Value Changed** events (*step 2b*).
3. In our example, this will lead to the NewValueAction() method in the go1 GameObject's scripted component being executed (*step 3*).

Registering public object methods is a very common way to handle events such as user interaction or web communications, which may occur in different orders, may never occur, or may happen several times in a short period. Several software design patterns describe ways to work with these event setups, such as the *Observer* pattern and the *Publisher-Subscriber* design pattern.

Core GameObjects, components, and concepts related to interactive Unity UI development include the following:

- **Visual UI controls**: The visible UI controls themselves include Button, Image, Text, and Toggle. These are the UI controls the user sees on the screen and uses their mouse/touchscreen to interact with. These are the GameObjects that maintain a list of object methods that have subscribed to user-interaction events.

- **Interaction UI controls**: These are non-visible components that are added to GameObjects; examples include **Input Field** and **Toggle Group**.
- **Panel**: UI objects can be grouped together (logically and physically) with UI Panels. Panels can play several roles, including providing a GameObject parent in the **Hierarchy** window for a related group of controls. They can provide a visual background image to graphically relate controls on the screen, and they can also have scripted resize and drag interactions added if desired.
- **Sibling Depth**: The bottom-to-top display order (what appears on the top of what) for a UI element is determined initially by its place in the sequence in the **Hierarchy** window. At design time, this can be manually set by dragging GameObjects into the desired sequence in the **Hierarchy** window. At runtime, we can send messages to the Rect Transforms of GameObjects to dynamically change their Hierarchy position (and therefore, the display order) as the game or user interaction demands. This is illustrated in the *Organizing images inside panels and changing panel depths via buttons* recipe.

Often, a UI element exists with most of the components that you may need for something in your game, but you may need to adapt it somehow. An example of this can be seen in the *Displaying a countdown timer graphically with a UI Slider* recipe, which makes a UI Slider non-interactive, instead of using it to display a red-green progress bar for the status of a countdown timer.

In this chapter, we will cover the following recipes:

- Creating UI Buttons to move between scenes
- Animating UI Button properties on mouseover
- Organizing image panels and changing panel depths via UI Buttons
- Displaying the value of an interactive UI Slider
- Displaying a countdown timer graphically with a UI Slider
- Setting custom mouse cursors for 2D and 3D GameObjects
- Setting custom mouse cursors for UI controls
- Interactive text entry with Input Field
- Toggles and radio buttons via toggle groups
- Creating text and image icon UI Drop-down menus
- Displaying a radar to indicate the relative locations of objects

Technical requirements

For this chapter, you will need Unity 2021.1 or later, plus one of the following:

- Microsoft Windows 10 (64-bit)/GPU: DX10, DX11, and DX12-capable
- macOS Sierra 10.12.6+/GPU Metal-capable Intel or AMD
- Linux Ubuntu 16.04, Ubuntu 18.04, and CentOS 7/GPU: OpenGL 3.2+ or Vulkan-capable, NVIDIA or AMD

For each chapter, there is a folder that contains the asset files you will need in this book's GitHub repository at `https://github.com/PacktPublishing/Unity-2021-Cookbook-Fourth-Edition`.

Creating UI Buttons to move between scenes

The majority of games include a menu screen that displays messages to the user about instructions, high scores, the level they have reached so far, and so on. Unity provides UI Buttons to offer users a simple way to indicate their choices:

Figure 2.3 – Example of a Main Menu UI Button

In this recipe, we'll create a very simple game consisting of two screens, each with a button to load the other one, as illustrated in the preceding screenshot.

How to do it...

To create a button-navigable multi-scene game, follow these steps:

1. Create a new **Unity 2D project**.
2. Save the current (empty) scene in a new folder called _Scenes, naming the scene page1.
3. Add a **UI Text** object positioned at the top center of the scene containing large white text that says **Main Menu (page 1)**.

4. Add a **UI Button** to the scene positioned in the middle-center of the screen. In the **Hierarchy** window, click on the show children triangle to display the **Text** child of this GameObject button. Select the `Text` GameObject and, in the **Inspector** window for the **Text** property of the **Text (Script)** component, enter the text `goto page 2`:

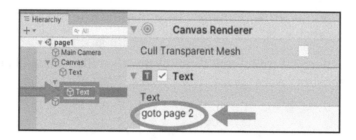

Figure 2.4 – UI Button Text child

5. Create a second scene, named `page2`, with **UI Text = Instructions (page 2)** and a **UI Button** with the goto `page 1` text. You can either repeat the preceding steps or you can duplicate the **page1** scene file, naming the duplicate `page2`, and then edit the UI Text and UI Button Text appropriately.

6. Add both scenes to the build, which is the set of scenes that will end up in the actual application built by Unity. To add **scene1** to the build, open the **page1** scene and go to **File | Build Settings....** Then, click on the **Add Open Scenes** button so that the **page1** scene becomes the first scene in the list of **Scenes** in the build. Now open **page2** and repeat this process so that both scenes have been added to the build.

 We cannot tell Unity to load a scene that has not been added to the list of scenes in the build. This makes sense since when an application is built, we should never try to open a scene that isn't included as part of that application.

7. Ensure you have the **page1** scene open.

8. Create a C# script class called `SceneLoader`, in a new folder called `_Scripts` that contains the following code. Then, add an instance of the `SceneLoader` as a scripted component to **Main Camera**:

```
using UnityEngine;
using UnityEngine.SceneManagement;

public class SceneLoader : MonoBehaviour {
```

```
public void LoadOnClick(int sceneIndex) {
    SceneManager.LoadScene(sceneIndex);
}
}
```

9. Select **Button** in the **Hierarchy** window and click on the plus (+) button at the bottom of the **Button (Script)** component, in the **Inspector** window, to create a new OnClick event handler for this button (that is, an action to perform when the button is clicked).

10. Drag **Main Camera** from the **Hierarchy** window over the **Object** slot immediately below the menu that says **Runtime Only**. This means that when the button receives an OnClick event, we can call a public method from a scripted object inside **Main Camera**.

11. Select the **LoadOnClick** method from the **SceneLoader** drop-down list (initially showing **No Function**). Type 1 (the index of the scene we want to be loaded when this button is clicked) in the text box, below the method's drop-down menu. This integer, **1**, will be passed to the method when the button receives an OnClick event message, as shown here:

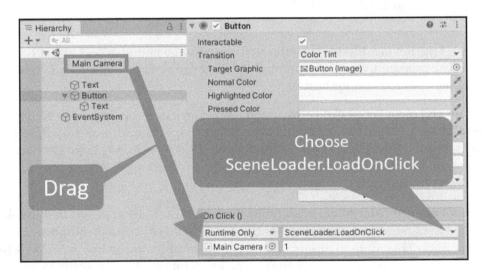

Figure 2.5 – Button (Script) settings

12. Save the current scene (**page1**).

13. Open **page2** and follow the same steps to make the **page2** button load **page1**. That is, add an instance of the `SceneLoader` script class to **Main Camera** and then add an `OnClick` event action to the button that calls `LoadOnClick` and passes an integer of 0 so that **page1** is loaded.

14. Save **page2**.

15. When you run the **page1** scene, you will be presented with your **Main Menu** text and a button that, when clicked, makes the game load the **page2** scene. On **page2**, you'll have a button to take you back to **page1**.

How it works...

In this recipe, you created two scenes and added both of these scenes to the game's build. You added a UI Button and some UI Text to each scene.

 Note that the build sequence of scenes is actually a scripted array that counts from 0, then 1, and so on, so that **page1** has index 0 and **page2** has index 1.

When a UI Button is added to the **Hierarchy** window, a child UI Text object is also automatically created, and the content of the **Text** property of this UI Text child is the text that the user sees on the button.

Here, you created a script class and added an instance as a component to **Main Camera**. In fact, it didn't really matter where this script instance was added, so long as it was in one of the GameObjects of the scene. This is necessary since the `OnClick` event action of a button can only execute a method (function) of a component in a GameObject in the scene.

For the buttons for each scene, you added a new `OnClick` event action that invokes (executes) the `LoadOnClick` method of the `SceneLoader` scripted component in **Main Camera**. This method inputs the integer index of the scene in the project's **Build** settings so that the button on the **page1** scene gives integer **1** as the scene to be loaded and the button for **page2** gives integer **0**.

There's more...

There are several ways in which we can visually inform the user that the button is interactive when they move their mouse over it. The simplest way is to add a **Color Tint** that will appear when the mouse is over the button – this is the default **Transition**. With **Button** selected in the **Hierarchy** window, choose a tint color (for example, red), for the **Highlighted Color** property of the **Button (Script)** component in the **Inspector** window:

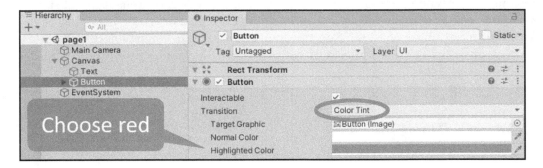

Figure 2.6 – Adjusting the mouseover settings for buttons

Another form of visual **Transition** to inform the user of an active button is **Sprite Swap**. In this case, the properties of different images for Targeted/Highlighted/Pressed/Disabled are available in the **Inspector** window. The default **Targeted Graphic** is the built-in Unity **Button (Image)** – this is the gray rounded rectangle default when GameObject buttons are created. Dragging in a very different-looking image for the **Highlighted s**prite is an effective alternative to setting a **Color Tint**:

Figure 2.7 – Example of an image as a button

We have provided a `rainbow.png` image with the project for this recipe that can be used for the **Button** mouseover's **Highlighted** sprite. You will need to ensure this image asset has its **Texture Type** set to **Sprite (2D and UI)** in the **Inspector** window. The preceding screenshot shows the button with this rainbow background image.

Animating button properties on mouseover

At the end of the previous recipe, we illustrated two ways to visually communicate buttons to users. The animation of button properties can be a highly effective and visually interesting way to reinforce to the user that the item their mouse is currently over is a clickable, active button. One common animation effect is for a button to become larger when the mouse is over it, and then shrink back to its original size when the mouse is moved away. Animation effects are achieved by choosing the **Animation** option for the **Transition** property of a `Button` GameObject, and by creating an animation controller with triggers for the **Normal**, **Highlighted**, **Pressed**, and **Disabled** states.

How to do it...

To animate a button for enlargement when the mouse is over it (the **Highlighted** state), do the following:

1. Create a new **Unity 2D project**.
2. Create a **UI Button**.
3. In the **Inspector Button (Script)** component, set the **Transition** property to **Animation**.
4. Click the **Auto Generate Animation** button (just below the **Disabled Trigger** property) for the **Button (Script)** component:

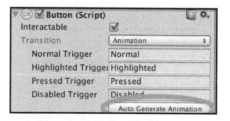

Figure 2.8 – Auto Generate Animation

5. Save the new controller (in a new folder called `Animations`), naming it `button-animation-controller`.

6. Ensure that the `Button` GameObject is selected in the **Hierarchy** window. Open **Window | Animation | Animation**. In the **Animation** window, select the **Highlighted** clip from the drop-down menu:

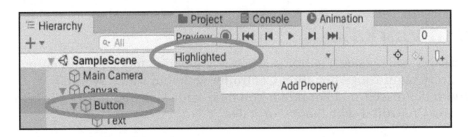

Figure 2.9 – Selecting the Button GameObject in the Hierarchy window

7. In the **Animation** window, click on the red record circle button, and then click on the **Add Property** button, choosing to record changes to the **Rect Transform | Scale** property.

8. Two keyframes will have been created. Delete the second one at **1:00** (since we don't want a "bouncing" button):

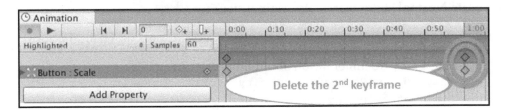

Figure 2.10 – Deleting the keyframe

9. Select the frame at **1:00** by clicking one of the diamonds (both turn blue when selected), and then press the *Backspace/Delete* key.

10. Select the first keyframe at **0:00** (the only one now!). In the **Inspector** window, set the **X** and **Y** scale properties of the **Rect Transform** component to (`1.2, 1.2`).

11. Click on the red record circle button for the second time to stop recording the animation changes.

12. Save and run your scene. You will see that the button smoothly animates and becomes larger when the mouse is over it, and then smoothly returns to its original size when the mouse has moved away.

How it works...

In this recipe, you created a button and set its **Transition** mode to **Animation**. This makes Unity require an **Animation Controller** with four states: **Normal**, **Highlighted**, **Pressed**, and **Disabled**. You then made Unity automatically create an **Animation Controller** with these four states.

Then, you edited the animation for the **Highlighted** (mouseover) state, deleting the second keyframe, and making the only keyframe a version of the button that's larger so that its scale is 1.2.

When the mouse is not hovering over the button, it's unchanged, and the **Normal** state settings are used. When the mouse moves over the button, **Animation Controller** smoothly in-betweens the settings of the button to become those of its **Highlighted** state (that is, bigger). When the mouse is moved away from the button, **Animation Controller** smoothly in-betweens the settings of the button to become those of its **Normal** state (that is, its original size).

The following web pages offer video and web-based tutorials on UI animations:

- The Unity documentation about UI Button Animations: `https://docs.unity3d.com/Packages/com.unity.ugui@1.0/manual/UIAnimationIntegration.html`.

- Ray Wenderlich's great tutorial (part 2), including the available button animations, is available at `http://www.raywenderlich.com/79031/unity-new-gui-tutorial-part-2`.

Organizing image panels and changing panel depths via buttons

UI Panels are provided by Unity to allow UI controls to be grouped and moved together, and also to visually group elements with an image background (if desired). The sibling's depth is what determines which UI elements will appear above or below others. We can see the sibling depth explicitly in the **Hierarchy** window, since the top-to-bottom sequence of UI GameObjects in the **Hierarchy** window sets the sibling depth. So, the first item has a depth of 1, the second has a depth of 2, and so on. The UI GameObjects with larger sibling depths (further down the hierarchy, which means they're drawn later) appear above the UI GameObjects with lower sibling depths:

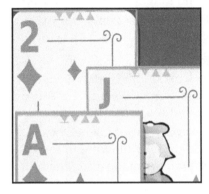

Figure 2.11 – Example of organizing panels

In this recipe, we'll create three UI Panels, each showing a different playing card image. We'll also add four triangle arrangement buttons to change the display order (move to bottom, move to top, move up one, and move down one).

Getting ready

For this recipe, we have prepared the images that you need in a folder named Images in the 02_03 folder.

How to do it...

To create the UI Panels whose layering can be changed by clicking buttons, follow these steps:

1. Create a new **Unity 2D project**.

2. Create a new **UI Panel** GameObject named `Panel-jack-diamonds`. Do the following to this panel:

    - For the **Image (Script)** component, drag the `jack_of_diamonds` playing card image asset file from the **Project** window into the **Source Image** property. Select the **Color** property and increase the **Alpha** value to 255 (so that this background image of the panel is no longer partly transparent).

    - For the **Rect Transform** property, position it in the middle-center part of the screen and set its **Width** to 200 and its **Height** to 300.

3. Create a **UI Button** named `Button-move-to-front`. In the **Hierarchy** window, make this button a child of **Panel-jack-diamonds**. Delete the **Text** child GameObject of this button (since we'll use an icon to indicate what this button does).

4. With the **Button-move-to-front** GameObject selected in the **Hierarchy** window, do the following in the **Inspector** window:

    - In **Rect Transform**, position the button at the top-center of the player card image so that it can be seen at the top of the playing card. Size the image to **Width** = 16 and **Height** = 16. Move the icon image down slightly, by setting **Pos Y** = −5 (to ensure we can see the horizontal bar above the triangle).

    - For the **Source Image** property of the **Image (Script)** component, select the arrangement triangle icon image; that is, `icon_move_to_front`.

    - Add an **OnClick** event handler by clicking on the plus (+) sign at the bottom of the **Button (Script)** component.

    - Drag `Panel-jack-diamonds` from the **Hierarchy** window over to the **Object** slot (immediately below the menu saying **Runtime Only**).

    - Select the **RectTransform.SetAsLastSibling** method from the drop-down function list (initially showing **No Function**):

Figure 2.12: Addition of an OnClick event handler

5. Repeat *step 2* to create a second panel named `Panel-2-diamonds` with its own **move-to-front** button and a **Source Image** of `2_of_diamonds`. Move and position this new panel slightly to the right of `Panel-jack-diamonds`, allowing both **move-to-front** buttons to be seen.

6. Save your scene and run the game. You will be able to click the **move-to-front** button on either of the cards to move that card's panel to the front. If you run the game with the **Game** window not maximized, you'll actually see the panels changing the order in the list of the children of **Canvas** in the **Hierarchy** window.

How it works...

In this recipe, you created two **UI Panels**, each of which contains a background **image** of a playing card and a **UI Button** whose action will make its parent panel move to the front. You set the **Alpha** (transparency) setting of the background image's **Color** to `255` (no transparency).

You then added an `OnClick` event action to the button of each **UI Panel**. This action sends a `SetAsLastSibling` message to the button's **Panel** parent. When the **OnClick** message is received, the clicked **Panel** is moved to the bottom (end) of the sequence of GameObjects in **Canvas**, so this **Panel** is drawn last from the **Canvas** objects. This means that it appears visually in front of all the other GameObjects.

The button's action illustrates how the `OnClick` function does not have to be calling a public method of a scripted component of an object, but it can be sending a message to one of the non-scripted components of the targeted GameObject. In this recipe, we send the `SetAsLastSibling` message to the **Rect Transform** component of the panel where the button is located.

There's more...

There are some details you don't want to miss.

Moving up or down by just one position, using scripted methods

While **Rect Transform** offers SetAsLastSibling (move to front) and
SetAsFirstSibling (move to back), and even SetSiblingIndex (if we knew
exactly what position in the sequence to type in), there isn't a built-in way to make an
element move up or down just one position in the sequence of GameObjects in the
Hierarchy window. However, we can write two straightforward methods in C# to do
this, and we can add buttons to call these methods, providing full control of the top-
to-bottom arrangement of the UI controls on the screen. To implement four buttons
(move-to-front/move-to-back/up one/down one), do the following:

1. Create a C# script class called ArrangeActions containing the following
   code and add an instance as a scripted component to each of your UI
   Panels:

```
using UnityEngine;

public class ArrangeActions : MonoBehaviour {
    private RectTransform panelRectTransform;

    void Awake() {
        panelRectTransform = GetComponent<RectTransform>();
    }

    public void MoveDownOne() {
        int currentSiblingIndex =
panelRectTransform.GetSiblingIndex();
        panelRectTransform.SetSiblingIndex(
currentSiblingIndex - 1 );
    }
    public void MoveUpOne() {
        int currentSiblingIndex =
panelRectTransform.GetSiblingIndex();
        panelRectTransform.SetSiblingIndex(
currentSiblingIndex + 1 );
    }
}
```

2. Add a second **UI Button** to each card panel, this time using the arrangement triangle icon image called `icon_move_to_back`, and set the **OnClick** event function for these buttons to `SetAsFirstSibling`.

3. Add two more **UI Buttons** to each card panel with the up and down triangle icon images; that is, `icon_up_one` and `icon_down_one`. Set the **OnClick** event handler function for the down-one buttons to call the `MoveDownOne()` method, and set the functions for the up-one buttons to call the `MoveUpOne()` method.

4. Copy one of the **UI Panels** to create a third card (this time showing the Ace of diamonds). Arrange the three cards so that you can see all four buttons for at least two of the cards, even when those cards are at the bottom (see the screenshot at the beginning of this recipe).

5. Save the scene and run your game. You will now have full control over how to layer the three card UI Panels.

 Note that we should avoid *negative* sibling depths, so we should probably test for the `currentSiblingIndex` value before subtracting 1 as follows:

```
if(currentsiblingIndex > 0)
        panelRectTransform.SetSiblingIndex( currentSiblingIndex - 1 );
```

Displaying the value of an interactive UI Slider

A UI Slider is a graphical tool that allows a user to set the numerical value of an object:

Figure 2.13 – Example of a UI Slider

This recipe illustrates how to create an interactive **UI Slider** and execute a C# method each time the user changes the **UI Slider** value.

How to do it...

To create a **UI Slider** and display its value on the screen, follow these steps:

1. Create new **Unity 2D project**.

2. Add a `UI Text` GameObject to the scene with a **Font** size of 30 and placeholder text, such as `Slider value here` (this text will be replaced with the slider value when the scene starts). Set **Horizontal-** and **Vertical-Overflow** to **Overflow**.

3. In the **Hierarchy** window, add a `UI Slider` GameObject to the scene by going to **GameObject | UI | Slider**.

4. In the **Inspector** window, modify the settings for the position of the `UI Slider` GameObject's **Rect Transform** to the top-middle part of the screen.

5. In the **Inspector** window, modify the settings of **Position** for the UI Text's **Rect Transform** so that they're just below the slider (top, middle, then **Pos Y** = −30).

6. In the **Inspector** window, set the UI Slider's **Min Value** to 0 and **Max Value** to 20. Then, check the **Whole Numbers** checkbox:

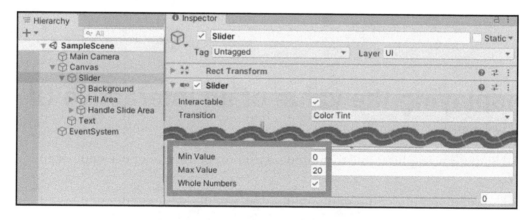

Figure 2.14 – Setting the UI Slider's Min Value and Max Value

7. Create a C# script class called `SliderValueToText` containing the following code and add an instance as a scripted component to the `Text` GameObject:

```
using UnityEngine;
using UnityEngine.UI;

public class SliderValueToText : MonoBehaviour {
```

```
public Slider sliderUI;
private Text textSliderValue;

void Awake() {
    textSliderValue = GetComponent<Text>();
}

void Start() {
    ShowSliderValue();
}

public void ShowSliderValue () {
    string sliderMessage = "Slider value = " +
sliderUI.value;
    textSliderValue.text = sliderMessage;
}
}
```

8. Ensure that the `Text` GameObject is selected in the **Hierarchy** window. Then, in the **Inspector** window, drag the `Slider` GameObject into the public **Slider UI** variable slot for the **Slider Value To Text (Script)** scripted component:

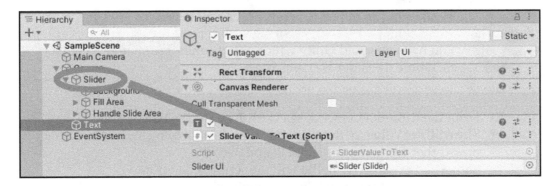

Figure 2.15 – Dragging Slider into the Slider UI variable

9. Ensure that the `Slider` GameObject is selected in the **Hierarchy** window. Then, in the **Inspector** window, drag the `Text` GameObject from the **Hierarchy** window over to the **Object** slot (immediately below the menu that says **Runtime Only**, as shown in the following screenshot:

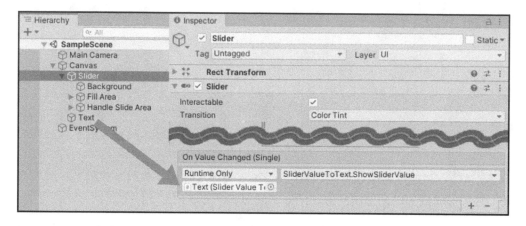

Figure 2.16 – Dragging the Text GameObject into None (Object)

Registering an object to receive UI event messages

You have now told Unity which object a message should be sent to each time the slider is changed.

10. From the drop-down menu, select **SliderValueToText** and the **ShowSliderValue** method, as shown in the following screenshot. This means that each time the slider is updated, the `ShowSliderValue()` method, in the scripted object in the `Text` GameObject, will be executed:

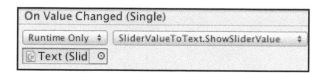

Figure 2.17 – Drop-down menu for On Value Changed (Single)

11. When you run scene, you will see a **UI Slider**. Below it, you will see a text message in the form `Slider value = <n>`.

12. Each time **UI Slider** is moved, the text value that's shown will be (almost) instantly updated. The values should range from `0` (the leftmost of the slider) to `20` (the rightmost of the slider).

How it works...

In this recipe, you created a `UI Slider` GameObject and set it to contain whole numbers in the range of `0` to `20`.

You also added an instance of the `SliderValueToText` C# script class to the `UI Text` GameObject.

The `Awake()` method caches references to the **Text** component in the `textSliderValue` variable.

The `Start()` method invokes the `ShowSliderValue()` method so that the display is correct when the scene begins (that is, the initial slider value is displayed).

The `ShowSliderValue()` method gets the value of the slider and then updates the text that's displayed to be a message in the form of `Slider value = <n>`.

Finally, you added the `ShowSliderValue()` method of the `SliderValueToText` scripted component to the `Slider` GameObject's list of **On Value Changed** event listeners. So, each time the slider value changes, it sends a message to call the `ShowSliderValue()` method so that the new value is updated on the screen.

Displaying a countdown timer graphically with a UI Slider

There are many cases where we wish to inform the player of how much time is left in a game or how much longer an element will take to download; for example, a loading progress bar, the time or health remaining compared to the starting maximum, or how much the player has filled up their water bottle from the fountain of youth. In this recipe, we'll illustrate how to remove the interactive "handle" of a **UI Slider**, and then change the size and color of its components to provide us with an easy to use, general-purpose progress/proportion bar:

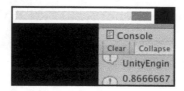

Figure 2.18 – Example of a countdown timer with a UI Slider

In this recipe, we'll use our modified **UI Slider** to graphically present to the user how much time remains on a countdown timer.

Getting ready

For this recipe, we have prepared the script and images that you need in the _Scripts and 02_05 folders, respectively.

How to do it...

To create a digital countdown timer with a graphical display, follow these steps:

1. Create a new **Unity 2D project**.
2. Import the CountdownTimer script and the red_square and green_square images into this project.

3. Add a `UI Text` GameObject to the scene with a **Font** size of 30 and placeholder text such as a `UI Slider` value (this text will be replaced with the slider value when the scene starts). Set **Horizontal-** and **Vertical-Overflow** to **Overflow**.

4. In the **Hierarchy** window, add a `Slider` GameObject to the scene by going to **GameObject | UI | Slider**.

5. In the **Inspector** window, modify the settings for the position of the `Slider` GameObject's **Rect Transform** to the top-middle part of the screen.

6. Ensure that the `Slider` GameObject is selected in the **Hierarchy** window.

7. Deactivate the `Handle Slide Area` child GameObject (by unchecking it).

8. You'll see the "drag circle" disappear in the **Game** window (the user will not be dragging the slider since we want this slider to be display-only):

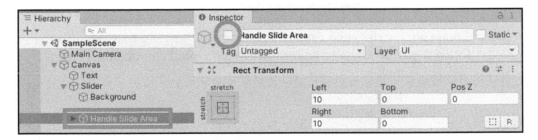

Figure 2.19 – Ensuring Handle Slide Area is deactivated

9. Select the **Background** child and do the following:
   - Drag the `red_square` image into the **Source Image** property of the **Image (Script)** component in the **Inspector** window.

10. Select the **Fill** child of the **Fill Area** child and do the following:
    - Drag the `green_square` image into the **Source Image** property of the **Image (Script)** component in the **Inspector** window.

11. Select the **Fill Area** child and do the following:
    - In the **Rect Transform** component, use the **Anchors** preset position of **left-middle**.
    - Set **Width** to 155 and **Height** to 12:

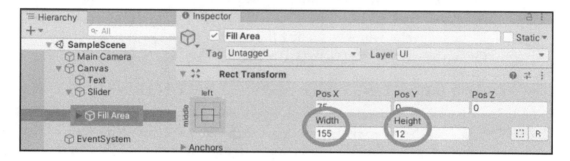

Figure 2.20 – Selections in the Rect Transform component

12. Create a C# script class called `SliderTimerDisplay` that contains the following code and add an instance as a scripted component to the `Slider` GameObject:

```
using UnityEngine;
using UnityEngine.UI;

[RequireComponent(typeof(CountdownTimer))]
public class SliderTimerDisplay : MonoBehaviour {
    private CountdownTimer countdownTimer;
    private Slider sliderUI;

    void Awake() {
        countdownTimer = GetComponent<CountdownTimer>();
        sliderUI = GetComponent<Slider>();
    }

    void Start() {
        SetupSlider();
        countdownTimer.ResetTimer( 30 );
    }

    void Update () {
        sliderUI.value =
countdownTimer.GetProportionTimeRemaining();
        print (countdownTimer.GetProportionTimeRemaining());
    }
```

```
private void SetupSlider () {
    sliderUI.minValue = 0;
    sliderUI.maxValue = 1;
    sliderUI.wholeNumbers = false;
}
}
```

Run your game. You will see the slider move with each second, revealing more and more of the red background to indicate the time remaining.

How it works...

In this recipe, you hid the **Handle Slide Area** child so that the **UI Slider** is for display only, which means it cannot be interacted with by the user. The **Background** color of the **UI Slider** was set to red so that, as the counter goes down, more and more red is revealed, warning the user that the time is running out.

The **Fill** property of the UI Slider was set to green so that the proportion remaining is displayed in green – the more green that's displayed, the greater the value of the slider/timer.

An instance of the provided CountdownTimer script class was automatically added as a component to the UI Slider via [RequireComponent(...)].

The Awake() method caches references to the **CountdownTimer** and **Slider** components in the countdownTimer and sliderUI variables.

The Start() method calls the SetupSlider() method and then resets the countdown timer so that it starts counting down from 30 seconds.

The SetupSlider() method sets up this slider for float (decimal) values between 0.0 and 1.0.

In each frame, the Update() method sets the slider value to the float that's returned by calling the GetProportionRemaining() method from the running timer. At runtime, Unity adjusts the proportion of red/green that's displayed in the UI Slider so that it matches the slider's value.

Setting custom mouse cursors for 2D and 3D GameObjects

Cursor icons are often used to indicate the nature of the interactions that can be done with the mouse. Zooming, for instance, might be illustrated by a magnifying glass; shooting, on the other hand, is usually represented by a stylized target:

Figure 2.21 – Mouse pointer represented as a stylized target

The preceding screenshot shows an example of the Unity logo with the cursor represented as a stylized target. In this recipe, we will learn how to implement custom mouse cursor icons to better illustrate your gameplay – or just to escape the Windows, macOS, and Linux default UI.

Getting ready

For this recipe, we have prepared the folders that you'll need in the `02_06` folder.

How to do it...

To make a custom cursor appear when the mouse is over a GameObject, follow these steps:

1. Create a new **Unity 2D project**.
2. Import the provided folder, called `Images`. Select the `unity_logo` image in the **Project** window. Then, in the **Inspector** window, change **Texture Type** to **Sprite (2D and UI)**. This is because we'll use this image for a `2D Sprite` GameObject and it requires this **Texture Type** (it won't work with the **Default** type).

3. Go to **2D Object | Sprite** to add the necessary GameObject to the scene. Name this `New Sprite`, if this wasn't the default name when it was created:

   - In the **Inspector** window, set the **Sprite** property of the **Sprite Renderer** component to the `unity_logo` image. In the GameObject's **Transform** component, set the scaling to (`3,3,3`) and, if necessary, reposition **Sprite** so that it's centered in the **Game** window when the scene runs.
   - Go to **Physics 2D | Box Collider** to create a **Box Collider** and add it to the `Sprite` GameObject. This is needed for this GameObject to receive `OnMouseEnter` and `OnMouseExit` event messages.

4. Import the provided folder called `IconsCursors`. Select all three images in the **Project** window and, in the **Inspector** window, change **Texture Type** to **Cursor**. This will allow us to use these images as mouse cursors without any errors occurring.

5. Create a C# script class called `CustomCursorPointer` containing the following code and add an instance as a scripted component to the `New Sprite` GameObject:

```csharp
using UnityEngine;

public class CustomCursorPointer : MonoBehaviour {
  public Texture2D cursorTexture2D;
  private CursorMode cursorMode = CursorMode.Auto;
  private Vector2 hotSpot = Vector2.zero;

  public void OnMouseEnter() {
    SetCustomCursor(cursorTexture2D);
  }

  public void OnMouseExit() {
    SetCustomCursor(null);
  }

  private void SetCustomCursor(Texture2D curText){
    Cursor.SetCursor(curText, hotSpot, cursorMode);
  }
}
```

The OnMouseEnter() and OnMouseExit() event methods have been deliberately declared as public. This will allow these methods to also be called from UI GameObjects when they receive the OnPointerEnterExit events.

6. With the **New Sprite** item selected in the **Hierarchy** window, drag the CursorTarget image into the public **Cursor Texture 2D** variable slot in the **Inspector** window for the **Custom Cursor Pointer (Script)** component:

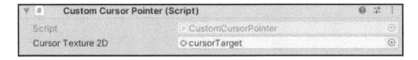

Figure 2.22 – Cursor Texture 2D dragged to the variable slot

7. Save and run the current scene. When the mouse pointer moves over the Unity logo sprite, it will change to the custom **CursorTarget** image that you chose.

How it works...

In this recipe, you created a Sprite GameObject and assigned it the Unity logo image. You imported some cursor images and set their **Texture Type** to **Cursor** so that they can be used to change the image for the user's mouse pointer. You also added a **Box Collider** to the Sprite GameObject so that it would receive OnMouseEnter and OnMouseExit event messages.

Then, you created the CustomCursorPointer script class and added an instance object of this class to the Sprite GameObject. This script tells Unity to change the mouse pointer when an OnMouseEnter message is received; that is, when the user's mouse pointer moves over the part of the screen where the Unity logo's sprite image is being rendered. When an OnMouseExit event is received (the user's mouse pointer is no longer over the cube part of the screen), the system is told to go back to the operating system's default cursor. This event should be received within a few milliseconds of the user's mouse exiting from the collider.

Finally, you selected the CursorTarget image to be the custom mouse cursor image the user sees when the mouse is over the Unity logo image.

Setting custom mouse cursors for UI controls

The previous recipe demonstrated how to change the mouse pointer for 2D and 3D GameObjects receiving OnMouseEnter and OnMouseExit events. Unity UI controls do not receive OnMouseEnter and OnMouseExit events. Instead, UI controls can be made to respond to PointerEnter and PointerExit events if we add a special **Event Trigger** component to the UI GameObject:

Figure 2.23 – Mouse pointer as a magnifying glass cursor

In this recipe, we'll change the mouse pointer to a custom magnifying glass cursor when it moves over a UI Button GameObject.

Getting ready

For this recipe, we'll use the same asset files as we did for the previous recipe, as well as the CustomCursorPointer C# script class from that recipe, all of which can be found in the 02_07 folder.

How to do it...

To set a custom mouse pointer when the mouse moves over a UI control GameObject, do the following:

1. Create a new **Unity 2D project**.
2. Import the provided IconsCursors folder. Select all three images in the **Project** window and, in the **Inspector** window, change **Texture Type** to **Cursor**. This will allow us to use these images as mouse cursors without any errors occurring.
3. Import the provided _Scripts folder containing the CustomCursorPointer C# script class.
4. Add a UI Button GameObject to the scene, leaving this named **Button**.

5. Add an instance of the `CustomCursorPointer` C# script class to the `Button` GameObject.

6. With the `Button` GameObject selected in the **Hierarchy** window, drag the `CursorZoom` image into the public **Cursor Texture 2D** variable slot in the **Inspector** window for the **Customer Cursor Pointer (Script)** component.

7. In the **Inspector** window, add an **Event Trigger** component to the `Button` GameObject by going to **Add Component | Event | Event Trigger**.

8. Add a **PointerEnter** event to your **Event Trigger** component, click on the plus (+) button to add an event handler slot, and drag the `Button` GameObject into the **Object** slot.

9. From the **Function** drop-down menu, choose **CustomCursorPointer** and then choose the **OnMouseEnter** method:

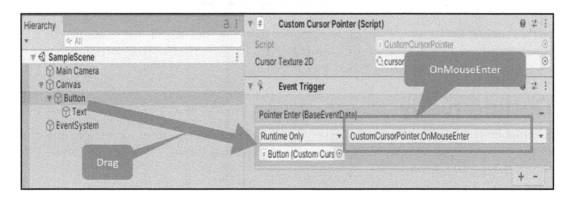

Figure 2.24 – Event Trigger settings

10. Add a **Pointer Exit** event to your **Event Trigger** component, and make it call the `OnMouseExit()` method from **CustomCursorPointer** when this event is received.

11. Save and run the current scene. When the mouse pointer moves over our **UI Button**, it will change to the custom **CursorZoom** image that you chose.

How it works...

In this recipe, you imported some cursor images and set their **Texture Type** to **Cursor** so that they could be used to change the image for the user's mouse pointer. You also created a **UI Button** GameObject and added to it an **Event Trigger** component.

You then added an instance of the `CustomCursorPointer` C# script class to the `Button` GameObject and selected the magnifying glass-style `CursorZoom` image.

After that, you created a `PointerEnter` event and linked it to invoke the `OnMouseEnter` method of the instance of the `CustomCursorPointer` script in the `Button` GameObject (which changes the mouse pointer image to the custom mouse cursor).

Finally, you created a `PointerExit` event and linked it to invoke the `OnMouseExit` method of the instance of the `CustomCursorPointer` C# script class to the `Button` GameObject (which resets the mouse cursor back to the system default).

Essentially, you have redirected `PointerEnter/Exit` events to invoke the `OnMouseEnter/Exit` methods of the `CustomCursorPointer` C# script class so that we can manage custom cursors for 2D, 3D, and UI GameObjects with the same scripting methods.

Interactive text entry with Input Field

While we often just wish to display non-interactive text messages to the user, there are times (such as name entry for high scores) where we want the user to be able to enter text or numbers into our game. Unity provides the UI Input Field component for this purpose. In this recipe, we'll create an Input Field that prompts the user to enter their name:

Figure 2.25 – Example of interactive text entry

Having interactive text on the screen isn't of much use unless we can *retrieve* the text that's entered to be used in our game logic, and we may need to know each time the user changes the text's content and act accordingly. In this recipe, we'll add an event handler C# script that detects each time the user finished editing the text and updates an extra message onscreen, confirming the newly entered content.

How to do it...

To create an interactive text input box for the user, follow these steps:

1. Create a new **Unity 2D project**.
2. In the **Inspector** window, change the background of **Main Camera** to solid white.
3. Add a **UI Input Field** to the scene. Position this at the top center of the screen.
4. Add a **UI Text** GameObject to the scene, naming it `Text-prompt`. Position this to the left of **Input Field**. Change the **Text** property of this GameObject to **Name:**.
5. Create a new **UI Text** GameObject named `Text-display`. Position this to the right of the **Input Text** control, and make its text red.
6. Delete all of the content of the **Text** property of this new GameObject (so that, initially, the user won't see any text onscreen for this GameObject).
7. Add an instance of the `DisplayChangedTextContent` C# script class to the `Text-display` GameObject:

```
using UnityEngine;
using UnityEngine.UI;

public class DisplayChangedTextContent : MonoBehaviour {
    public InputField inputField;
    private Text textDisplay;

    void Awake() {
        textDisplay = GetComponent<Text>();
    }

    public void DisplayNewValue () {
        textDisplay.text = "last entry = '" + inputField.text
+ "'";
    }
}
```

8. With `Text-display` selected in the **Hierarchy** window, from the **Project** window, drag the `InputField` GameObject into the public **Input Field** variable of the **Display Changed Content (Script)** component:

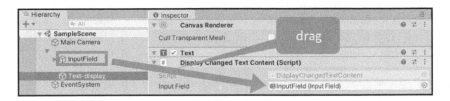

Figure 2.26 – Setting the Input Field variable

9. With `Input Field` selected in the **Hierarchy** window, add an **End Edit (String)** event to the list of event handlers for the **Input Field (Script)** component. Click on the plus (+) button to add an event handler slot and drag the `Text-display` GameObject into the **Object** slot.

10. From the **Function** drop-down menu, choose **DisplayChangedTextContent** and then choose the **DisplayNewValue** method.

11. Save and run the scene. Each time the user types in new text and then presses *Tab* or *Enter*, the **End Edit** event will fire, and you'll see a new content text message displayed in red on the screen.

How it works...

The core of interactive text input in Unity is the responsibility of the **Input Field** component. This needs a reference to a **UI Text** GameObject. To make it easier to see where the text can be typed, **Text Input** (similar to buttons) includes a default rounded rectangle image with a white background.

There are usually three **Text** GameObjects involved in user text input:

- The static prompt text, which, in our recipe, displays the text **Name:**.
- The faint placeholder text, reminding users where and what they should type.
- The editable text object (with the font and color settings) is actually displayed to the user, showing the characters as they type.

First, you created an `InputField` GameObject, which automatically provides two-child `Text` GameObjects, named `Placeholder` and `Text`. These represent the faint placeholder text and the editable text, which you renamed `Text-input`. You then added a third `Text` GameObject, `Text-prompt`, containing **Name:**.

The built-in scripting that is part of **Input Field** components does lots of work for us. At runtime, a **Text-Input** Input Caret GameObject is created, displaying the blinking vertical line to inform the user where their next letter will be typed. When there is no text content, the faint placeholder text will be displayed. As soon as any characters have been typed, the placeholder will be hidden and the characters typed will appear in black text. Then, if all the characters are deleted, the placeholder will appear again.

You then added a fourth **Text** GameObject called `Text-display` and made it red to tell the user what they last entered in **Input Field**. You created the `DisplayChangedTextContent` C# script class and added an instance as a component of the `Text-display` GameObject. You linked the `InputField` GameObject to the **Input Field** public variable of the scripted component (so that the script can access the text content entered by the user).

Finally, you registered an **End Edit** event handler of **Input Field** so that each time the user finished editing text (by pressing *Enter*), the `DisplayNewValue()` method of your `DisplayChangedTextContent` scripted object is invoked (executed), and the red text content of `Text-display` updated to tell the user what the newly edited text contained.

There's more...

Content Type of **Input Field (Script)** can be set (restricted) to several specific types of text input, including email addresses, integer or decimal numbers only, or password text (where an asterisk is displayed for each character that's entered). You can learn more about Input Fields by reading the Unity Manual page: https://docs.unity3d.com/Manual/script-InputField.html.

Toggles and radio buttons via toggle groups

Users make choices and, often, these choices have *one of two* options (for example, sound on or off), or sometimes *one of several* possibilities (for example, difficulty level as easy/medium/hard). Unity **UI Toggles** allows users to turn options on and off; when combined with **toggle groups**, they restrict choices to one of the groups of items. In this recipe, we'll explore the basic **Toggle** and a script to respond to a change in values:

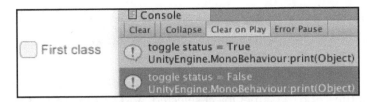

Figure 2.27 – Example showing the button's status changing in the Console window

Then, we'll extend the example to illustrate **toggle groups** and style these with round images to make them look more like traditional radio buttons. The preceding screenshot shows how the button's status changes are logged in the **Console** window when the scene is running.

Getting ready

For this recipe, we have prepared the images that you'll need in a folder named UI Demo Textures in the 02_09 folder.

How to do it...

To display an on/off UI Toggle to the user, follow these steps:

1. Create a new **Unity 2D project**.
2. In the **Inspector** window, change the **Background** color of **Main Camera** to white.
3. Add a **UI Toggle** to the scene.
4. For the **Label** child of the Toggle GameObject, set the **Text** property to **First Class**.
5. Add an instance of the C# script class called ToggleChangeManager to the Toggle GameObject:

```
using UnityEngine;
using UnityEngine.UI;

public class ToggleChangeManager : MonoBehaviour {
    private Toggle toggle;

    void Awake () {
        toggle = GetComponent<Toggle>();
    }
```

```
public void PrintNewToggleValue() {
    bool status = toggle.isOn;
    print ("toggle status = " + status);
}
}
```

6. With the `Toggle` GameObject selected, add an **On Value Changed** event to the list of event handlers for the **Toggle (Script)** component, click on the plus (+) button to add an event handler slot, and drag `Toggle` into the **Object** slot.

7. From the **Function** drop-down menu, choose **ToggleChangeManager** and then choose the **PrintNewToggleValue** method.

8. Save and run the scene. Each time you check or uncheck the `Toggle` GameObject, the **On Value Changed** event will fire, and you'll see a new text message printed into the **Console** window by our script, stating the new Boolean true/false value of `Toggle`.

How it works...

When you create a Unity **UI Toggle** GameObject, it comes with several child GameObjects automatically – `Background`, `Checkmark`, and the text's `Label`. Unless we need to style the look of a `Toggle` in a special way, all we must do is simply edit the text's `Label` so that the user knows what option or feature this `Toggle` is going to turn on/off.

The `Awake()` method of the `ToggleChangeManager` C# class caches a reference to the **Toggle** component in the GameObject where the script instance is located. When the game is running, each time the user clicks on the **Toggle** component to change its value, an **On Value Changed** event is fired. Then, we register the `PrintNewToggleValue()` method, which is to be executed when such an event occurs. This method retrieves, and then prints out to the **Console** window, the new Boolean true/false value of `Toggle`.

There's more...

Unity **UI Toggles** are also the base components if we wish to implement a group of mutually exclusive options in the style of *radio buttons*. We need to group related radio buttons together (**UI Toggles**) to ensure that when one radio button turns on (is selected), all the other radio buttons in the group turn off (unselected).

We also need to change the visual look if we want to adhere to the usual style of radio buttons as circles, rather than the square **UI Toggle** default images:

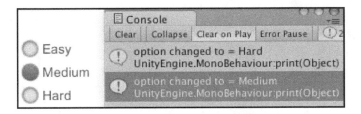

Figure 2.28 – Example of three buttons with Console status

To create a group of related toggles in the visual style of radio buttons, do the following to the project you just created:

1. Import the `UI Demo Textures` folder into the project.
2. Remove the C# script class's **ToggleChangeManager** component from the `Toggle` GameObject.
3. Rename the `Toggle` GameObject `Toggle-easy`.
4. Select the `Canvas` GameObject and, in the **Inspector** window, add a UI | **Toggle Group** component.
5. With the `Toggle-easy` GameObject selected, in the **Inspector** window, drag the `Canvas` GameObject into the **Toggle Group** property of the **Toggle (Script)** component.
6. Change the `Label` text to `Easy` and tag this GameObject with a new tag called `Easy`. Do this by selecting **Add Tag** from the **Tag** drop-down menu in the **Inspector** window, then typing in `Easy`, then selecting the GameObject again and setting its tag to **Easy**.
7. Select the `Background` child GameObject of `Toggle-easy` and, in the **Image (Script)** component, drag the `UIToggleBG` image into the **Source Image** property (a circle outline).

8. Ensure that the **Is On** property of the **Toggle (Script)** component is checked, and then select the `Checkmark` child GameObject of `Toggle-easy`. In the **Image (Script)** component, drag the `UIToggleButton` image into the **Source Image** property (a filled circle).

Of the three choices (easy, medium, and hard) that we'll offer to the user, we'll set the easy option to be the one that is supposed to be initially selected. Therefore, we need its **Is On** property to be checked, which will lead to its checkmark image being displayed.

To make these toggles look more like radio buttons, the background of each is set to the circle outline image of `UIToggleBG`, and the checkmark (which displays the toggles that are on) is filled with the circle image called `UIToggleButton`.

9. Duplicate the `Toggle-easy` GameObject, naming the copy `Toggle-medium`. Set its **Rect Transform** property's **Pos Y** to −25 (so that this copy is positioned below the easy option) and uncheck the **Is On** property of the **Toggle (Script)** component. Tag this copy with a new tag called `Medium`.

10. Duplicate the `Toggle-medium` GameObject, naming the copy `Toggle-hard`. Set its **Rect Transform** property's **Pos Y** to −50 (so that this copy is positioned below the medium option). Tag this copy with a new tag called `Hard`.

11. Add an instance of the `RadioButtonManager` C# script class to the `Canvas` GameObject:

```
using UnityEngine;
using System.Collections;
using UnityEngine.UI;

public class RadioButtonManager : MonoBehaviour {
  private string currentDifficulty = "Easy";

  public void PrintNewGroupValue(Toggle sender){
    // only take notice from Toggle just switched to On
    if(sender.isOn){
      currentDifficulty = sender.tag;
      print ("option changed to = " + currentDifficulty);
    }
  }
}
```

12. Select the `Toggle-easy` GameObject in the **Project** window. Now, do the following:

    - Since we based this on the **First Class** toggle, there is already an **On Value Changed** event for the list of event handlers for the **Toggle (Script)** component. Drag the `Canvas` GameObject in the target object slot (under the drop-down showing **Runtime Only**).
    - From the **Function** drop-down menu, choose **RadioButtonManager**, and then choose the **PrintNewGroupValue** method.
    - In the **Toggle** parameter slot, which is initially **None (Toggle)**, drag the `Toggle-easy` GameObject. Your **On Value Changed** settings in the **Inspector** window should look as follows:

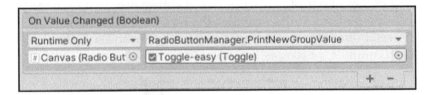

Figure 2.29 – Dragging the Toggle-easy GameObject to the Toggle parameter slot

13. Do the same for the `Toggle-medium` and `Toggle-hard` GameObjects so that each **Toggle** object calls the `PrintNewGroupValue(...)` method of a C# scripted component called `RadioButtonManager` in the `Canvas` GameObject, passing itself as a parameter.

14. Save and run the scene. Each time you check one of the three radio buttons, the **On Value Changed** event will fire, and you'll see a new text message printed into the **Console** window by our script, stating the tag of whichever **Toggle** (radio button) was just set to true (**Is On**).

By adding a **Toggle Group** component to `Canvas`, and having each `Toggle` GameObject link to it, the three radio buttons can tell **Toggle Group** when they have been selected. Then, the other members of the group are deselected. If you had several groups of radio buttons in the same scene, one strategy is to add the **Toggle Group** component to one of the toggles and have all the others link to that one.

We store the current radio button value (the last one switched **On**) in the `currentDifficulty` class property. Since variables declared outside a method are remembered, we could, for example, add a public method, such as `GetCurrentDifficulty()`, which could tell other scripted objects the current value, regardless of how long it's been since the user last changed their option.

Creating text and image icon UI Drop-down menus

In the previous recipe, we created radio-style buttons with a toggle group to present the user with a choice of one of many options. Another way to offer a range of choices is with a drop-down menu. Unity provides the **UI Dropdown** control for such menus. In this recipe, we'll offer the user a drop-down choice for the suit of a deck of cards (hearts, clubs, diamonds, or spades):

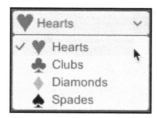

Figure 2.30 – Example showing UI Drop-down menus with text and image

Note that the **UI Dropdown** that's created by default includes a scrollable area, in case there isn't space for all the options. We'll learn how to remove such GameObjects and components to reduce complexity when such a feature is not required. Then, we'll learn how to add icon images with each menu option.

Getting ready

For this recipe, we have prepared the image that you need in a folder named `Images` in the `02_10` folder.

How to do it...

To create a **UI Dropdown** control GameObject, follow these steps:

1. Create a new **Unity 2D project**.
2. Add a **UI Dropdown** to the scene.
3. In the **Inspector** window, for the **Dropdown (Script)** component, change the list of **Options** from **Option A**, **Option B**, and **Option C** to **Hearts**, **Clubs**, **Diamonds**, and **Spades**. You'll need to click the plus (**+**) button to add space for the fourth option; that is, **Spades**.
4. Add an instance of the C# script class called `DropdownManager` to the `Dropdown` GameObject:

```
using UnityEngine;
using UnityEngine.UI;

public class DropdownManager : MonoBehaviour  {
    private Dropdown dropdown;

    private void Awake() {
        dropdown = GetComponent<Dropdown>();
    }

    public void PrintNewValue() {
        int currentValue = dropdown.value;
        print ("option changed to = " + currentValue);
    }
}
```

5. With the `Dropdown` GameObject selected, add an **On Value Changed** event to the list of event handlers for the **Dropdown (Script)** component, click on the plus (**+**) button to add an event handler slot, and drag **Dropdown** into the **Object** slot.
6. From the **Function** drop-down menu, choose **DropdownManager** and then choose the **PrintNewValue** method.

7. Save and run the scene. Each time you change **Dropdown**, the **On Value Changed** event will fire, and you'll see a new text message being printed to the **Console** window by our script, stating the **Integer** index of the chosen **Dropdown** value (0 for the first item, 1 for the second item, and so on):

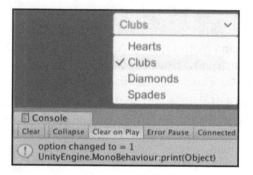

Figure 2.31 – Checking the drop-down menu in the Console window

8. Select the `Template` child GameObject of **Dropdown** in the **Project** window and, in its **Rect Transform**, reduce its height to 50. When you run the scene, you should see a scrollable area, since not all options fit within the template's height:

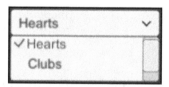

Figure 2.32 – Example of a drop-down menu

9. Delete the `Scrollbar` child of the `Template` GameObject and remove the **Scroll Rect (Script)** component of it. When you run the scene now, you'll only see the first two options (**Hearts** and **Clubs**), with no way to access the other two options. When you are sure your template's height is sufficient for all its options, you can safely remove these scrollable options to simplify the GameObjects in your scene.

How it works...

When you create a Unity **UI DropDown** GameObject, it comes with several components and child GameObjects automatically – Label, Arrow, and Template (as well as ViewPort and Scrollbar, and so on). Dropdowns work by duplicating the Template GameObject for each of the options listed in the **Dropdown (Script)** component. Both the **Text** and **Sprite** image values can be given for each option. The properties of the Template GameObject are used to control the visual style and behavior of the dropdown's thousands of possible settings.

First, you replaced the default options (**Option A**, **Option B**, and so on) in the **Dropdown (Script)** component. You then created a C# script class called DropdownManager that, when attached to your **Dropdown** and having its PrintNewValue method registered for **On Value Changed** events, means that we can see the **Integer** index of the option each time the user changes their choice. Item index values start counting at zero (as with many computing items), so 0 for the first item, 1 for the second item, and so on.

Since the default Dropdown GameObject that was created includes a **Scroll Rect (Script)** component and a Scrollbar child GameObject, when you reduced the height of Template, you could still scroll through the options. You then removed these items so that your dropdown didn't have a scrolling feature anymore.

There's more...

There are some details you don't want to miss.

Adding images to a Dropdown control

There are two pairs of items Unity uses to manage how text and images are displayed:

- The Caption Text and Image GameObjects are used to control how the currently selected item for the dropdown is displayed – this is the part of the dropdown we always see, regardless of whether it is being interacted with.

- The Item Text and Image GameObjects are part of the Template GameObject, and they define how each option is displayed as a row when the **Drop-down** menu items are being displayed – the rows that are displayed when the user is actively working with the Dropdown GameObject.

So, we have to add an image in two places (the **Caption** and **Template** items), in order to get a dropdown working fully with image icons for each option.

To add a **Sprite** image to each **Text** item in the dropdown, do the following:

1. Import the provided Images folder.
2. In the **Inspector** window, for the **Dropdown (Script)** component, for each item in the **Options** list – **Hearts**, **Clubs**, **Diamonds**, and **Spades** – drag the associated **Sprite** image from the card_suits folder into the **Project** window (hearts.png for **Hearts**, and so on).
3. Add a **UI Image** to the **Project** window and make this **Image** a child of the Dropdown GameObject.
4. Drag the hearts.png image from the **Project** window into the **Source Image** property of **Image (Script)** for the **Image** GameObject. Set its size to 25 x 25 in **Rect Transform** and drag it over the letter **H** in **Hearts** in the Label GameObject.
5. Move the Label GameObject to the right of the Hearts image.
6. With **Dropdown** selected in the **Project** window, drag the Image GameObject into the **Caption Image** property of the **Dropdown (Script)** component.
7. Enable the Template GameObject (usually, it is disabled).
8. Duplicate the Image GameObject child of **Dropdown** and name the copy Item Image. Make this image a child of the Item Background and Item Checkmark GameObjects that are in **Dropdown-Template-Content-Item** (Item Image needs to appear below the white Item Background Image; otherwise, it will be covered by the background and not be visible).
9. Since items in the dropdown are slightly smaller, resize Item Image to be 20 x 20 in its **Rect Transform**.
10. Position Item Image over the letter **O** of **Option A** of Item Text, and then move Item Text to the right so that the icon and text are not on top of each other.

11. With **Dropdown** selected in the **Project** window, drag the `Item Image` GameObject into the **Item Image** property of the **Dropdown (Script)** component:

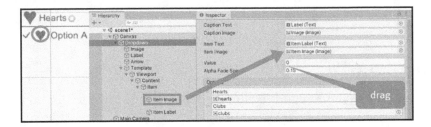

Figure 2.33 – Setting the image for the drop-down menu

12. Disable the `Template` GameObject and then run the scene to see your **Dropdown** with icon images for each menu option.

 Unity UI Dropdowns are powerful interface components. You can learn more about these controls by reading the Unity Manual at `https://docs.unity3d.com/Manual/script-Dropdown.html`.

Displaying a radar to indicate the relative locations of objects

A radar displays the locations of other objects relative to the player, usually based on a circular display, where the center represents the player and each graphical blip indicates how far away and what relative direction objects are to the player. Sophisticated radar displays will display different categories of objects with different colored or shaped blip icons:

Figure 2.34 – Example of a radar

In the preceding screenshot, we can see two red square blips, indicating the relative position of the two red cube GameObjects tagged Cube near the player, and a yellow circle blip indicating the relative position of the yellow sphere GameObject tagged Sphere. The green circle radar background image gives the impression of an aircraft control tower radar or something similar.

Getting ready

For this recipe, we have prepared the images that you need in a folder named Images in 02_11.

How to do it...

To create a radar to show the relative positions of the objects, follow these steps:

1. Create a new **Unity 3D project** with a textured **Terrain**. Download the **Environment** standard asset, which is part of the **Standard Assets** package contents, by going to **Window** | **Asset Store** | **Search Online** | **Standard Assets**.
2. Create a terrain by navigating to the **Create** | **3D Object** | **Terrain** menu.
3. Change the size of **Terrain** to 20 x 20 and position it at (-10, 0, -10) so that its center is at (0, 0, 0):

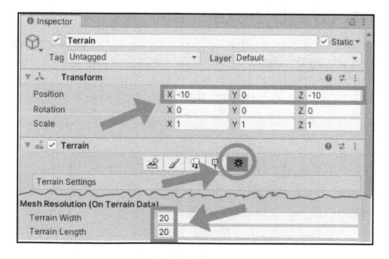

Figure 2.35 – Terrain settings for this recipe

4. Texture paint your **Terrain** with the **SandAlbedo** option, as shown in the following screenshot. You need to select the **Paint Texture** tool in the **Terrain** component, then click **Edit Terrain Layers** and select the **Create Layers** button. After that, you must select the **SandAlbedo** texture from the imported **Environment** assets:

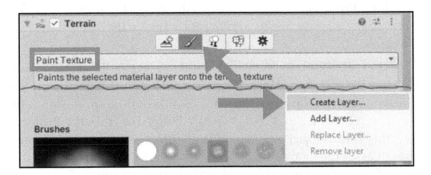

Figure 2.36 – Settings for painting the terrain

5. Import the provided folder; that is, `Images`.

6. Create a **3D Cube** GameObject at **Position** (`2, 0.5, 2`). Create a `Cube` tag and tag this GameObject with this new tag. Texture this GameObject with the yellow image called `icon32_square_red` by dragging the `icon32_square_red` image from the **Project** window over this GameObject in the **Hierarchy** window.

7. Duplicate the `cube` GameObject and move it to **Position** (`6, 0.5, 2`).

8. Create a **3D Sphere** GameObject at **Position** (`0, 0.5, 4`). Create a tag called `Sphere` and tag this GameObject with this new tag. Texture this GameObject with the red image called `icon32_square_yellow`.

9. Import the **Characters** standard asset package into your project.

10. From the `Standard Assets` folder in the **Project** window, drag the `ThirdPersonController` prefab into the scene and position it at (`0, 1, 0`).

11. Tag this `ThirdPersonController` GameObject as `Player` (selecting this built-in tag means that the camera we'll add will automatically track this player object, without us having to manually set the target for the camera).

12. Remove the `Main Camera` GameObject.

13. Import the **Cameras** standard asset package into your project.

14. From the `Standard Assets` folder in the **Project** window, drag the `Multi-PurposeCameraRig` prefab into the scene.

15. In the **Hierarchy** window, add a **UI RawImage** GameObject to the scene named `RawImage-radar`.

16. Ensure that the `RawImage-radar` GameObject is selected in the **Hierarchy** window. From the `Images` folder in the **Project** window, drag the `radarBackground` image into the **Raw Image (Script)** public property's **Texture**.

17. In **Rect Transform**, position `RawImage-radar` at the top left using the **Anchor Presets** item. Then, set both **Width** and **Height** to 200 pixels.

18. Create a new **UI RawImage** named `RawImage-blip`. Assign it the `yellowCircleBlackBorder` texture image file from the **Project** window. Tag this GameObject as `Blip`. In the **Project** window, create a new empty prefab asset file named `blip-sphere` and drag the `RawImage-blip` GameObject into this prefab to store all its properties.

Create a prefab by selecting **Asset | Create Prefab** and then dragging an object from the scene onto the "empty" prefab asset that appears.

19. Set the texture of the `RawImage-blip` GameObject to `redSquareBlackBorder` from the **Project** window. Tag this GameObject as `Blip`. In the **Project** window, create a new empty prefab asset file named `blip-cube` and drag the `RawImage-blip` GameObject into this prefab to store all its properties.

20. Delete the `RawImage-blip` GameObject from the **Hierarchy** window.

21. Create a C# script class called `Radar` containing the following code and add an instance as a scripted component to the `RawImage-radar` GameObject:

```
using UnityEngine;
using UnityEngine.UI;

public class Radar : MonoBehaviour {
    public float insideRadarDistance = 20;
    public float blipSizePercentage = 5;
    public GameObject rawImageBlipCube;
    public GameObject rawImageBlipSphere;
    private RawImage rawImageRadarBackground;
    private Transform playerTransform;
    private float radarWidth;
```

```
        private float radarHeight;
        private float blipHeight;
        private float blipWidth;

    void Start() {
            rawImageRadarBackground = GetComponent<RawImage>();
            playerTransform =
GameObject.FindGameObjectWithTag("Player").transform;
            radarWidth =
rawImageRadarBackground.rectTransform.rect.width;
            radarHeight =
rawImageRadarBackground.rectTransform.rect.height;
            blipHeight = radarHeight * blipSizePercentage / 100;
            blipWidth = radarWidth * blipSizePercentage / 100;
    }

    void Update() {
            RemoveAllBlips();
            FindAndDisplayBlipsForTag("Cube", rawImageBlipCube);
            FindAndDisplayBlipsForTag("Sphere",
rawImageBlipSphere);
    }

    private void FindAndDisplayBlipsForTag(string tag,
GameObject prefabBlip) {
            Vector3 playerPos = playerTransform.position;
            GameObject[] targets =
GameObject.FindGameObjectsWithTag(tag);
            foreach (GameObject target in targets) {
                    Vector3 targetPos = target.transform.position;
                    float distanceToTarget =
Vector3.Distance(targetPos,
                        playerPos);
                    if ((distanceToTarget <= insideRadarDistance))
                     CalculateBlipPositionAndDrawBlip (playerPos,
targetPos,
                        prefabBlip);
            }
    }

    private void CalculateBlipPositionAndDrawBlip (Vector3
playerPos, Vector3
        targetPos, GameObject prefabBlip) {
            Vector3 normalisedTargetPosition =
NormalizedPosition(playerPos,
                targetPos);
            Vector2 blipPosition =
                CalculateBlipPosition(normalisedTargetPosition);
```

```
                DrawBlip(blipPosition, prefabBlip);
    }

    private void RemoveAllBlips() {
        GameObject[] blips =
GameObject.FindGameObjectsWithTag("Blip");
        foreach (GameObject blip in blips)
            Destroy(blip);
    }

    private Vector3 NormalizedPosition(Vector3 playerPos,
Vector3 targetPos) {
        float normalisedyTargetX = (targetPos.x -
playerPos.x) /
            insideRadarDistance;
        float normalisedyTargetZ = (targetPos.z -
playerPos.z) /
            insideRadarDistance;
        return new Vector3(normalisedyTargetX, 0,
normalisedyTargetZ);
    }


    private Vector2 CalculateBlipPosition(Vector3 targetPos) {
        float angleToTarget = Mathf.Atan2(targetPos.x,
targetPos.z) *
            Mathf.Rad2Deg;
        float anglePlayer = playerTransform.eulerAngles.y;
        float angleRadarDegrees = angleToTarget - anglePlayer
- 90;
        float normalizedDistanceToTarget =
targetPos.magnitude;
        float angleRadians = angleRadarDegrees *
Mathf.Deg2Rad;
        float blipX = normalizedDistanceToTarget *
Mathf.Cos(angleRadians);
        float blipY = normalizedDistanceToTarget *
Mathf.Sin(angleRadians);
        blipX *= radarWidth / 2;
        blipY *= radarHeight / 2;
        blipX += radarWidth / 2;
        blipY += radarHeight / 2;
        return new Vector2(blipX, blipY);
    }

    private void DrawBlip(Vector2 pos, GameObject blipPrefab) {
        GameObject blipGO =
(GameObject)Instantiate(blipPrefab);
        blipGO.transform.SetParent(transform.parent);
```

```
        RectTransform rt =
blipGO.GetComponent<RectTransform>();
rt.SetInsetAndSizeFromParentEdge(RectTransform.Edge.Left,
pos.x,
        blipWidth);
rt.SetInsetAndSizeFromParentEdge(RectTransform.Edge.Top,
pos.y,
        blipHeight);
    }
}
```

22. Run your game. You will see two red squares and one yellow circle on the radar, showing the relative positions of the red cubes and the yellow sphere. If you move too far away, the blips will disappear.

At the time of writing, the **Standard Assets** package has not been updated for Unity 2020.1. When using it in recipes, two errors will appear. These need to be resolved before playing your recipe. The solutions for resolving these are as follows:

In `ForcedReset.cs`, add the following code:

```
using UnityEngine.UI;
// change GUITexture to Image
[RequireComponent(typeof (Image))]
```

In `SimpleActivatorMenu.cs`, add the following code:

```
// change GUIText to TEXT
public Text camSwitchButton;
```

These solutions are based on a post at `https://answers.unity.com/questions/ 1638555/guitexture-adn-guitext-are-obsolete-standard-asset.html`, where a complete explanation can be found.

How it works...

A radar background is displayed on the screen. The center of this circular image represents the position of the player's character. In this recipe, you created two prefabs – one for red square images to represent each red cube found within the radar distance, and one for yellow circles to represent yellow sphere GameObjects.

The `Radar` C# script class has been added to the radar **UI Image** GameObject. This class defines four public variables:

- `insideRadarDistance`: This value defines the maximum distance in the scene that an object may be from the player so that it can still be included on the radar (objects further than this distance will not be displayed on the radar).
- `blipSizePercentage`: This public variable allows the developer to decide how large each blip will be, as a proportion of the radar's image.
- `rawImageBlipCube` and `rawImageBlipSphere`: These are references to the prefab UI RawImages that are to be used to visually indicate the relative distance and position of cubes and spheres on the radar.

Since there is a lot happening in the code for this recipe, each method will be described in its own section.

The Start() method

The `Start()` method caches a reference to the **RawImage** of the radar background image. Then, it caches a reference to the **Transform** component of the player's character (tagged as `Player`). This allows the scripted object to know about the position of the player's character in each frame. Next, the width and height of the radar image are cached so that the relative positions for blips can be calculated, based on the size of this background radar image. Finally, the size of each blip (`blipWidth` and `blipHeight`) is calculated using the `blipSizePercentage` public variable.

The Update() method

The `Update()` method calls the `RemoveAllBlips()` method, which removes any old UI **RawImage** GameObjects of cubes and spheres that might currently be displayed. If we didn't remove old blips before creating new ones, then you'd see "tails" behind each blip as new ones are created in different positions – which could actually be an interesting effect.

Next, the `FindAndDisplayBlipsForTag(...)` method is called twice. First, for the objects tagged `Cube`, to be represented on the radar with the `rawImageBlipCube` prefab, and then again for objects tagged `Sphere`, to be represented on the radar with the `rawImageBlipSphere` prefab. As you might expect, most of the hard work of the radar is to be performed by the `FindAndDisplayBlipsForTag(...)` method.

This code is a simple approach to creating a radar. It is very inefficient to make repeated calls to `FindGameObjectWithTag("Blip")` for every frame from the `Update()` method. In a real game, it would be much better to cache all created blips in something such as a `List` or `ArrayList`, and then simply loop through that list each time.

The FindAndDisplayBlipsForTag(...) method

This method inputs two parameters: the string tag for the objects to be searched for, and a reference to the `RawImage` prefab to be displayed on the radar for any such tagged objects within the range.

First, the current position of the player's character is retrieved from the cached player `Transform` variable. Next, an array is constructed, referring to all GameObjects in the scene that have the provided tag. This array of GameObjects is looped through, and for each GameObject, the following actions are performed:

- The position of the target GameObject is retrieved.
- The distance from this target's position to the player's position is calculated.
- If this distance is within the range (less than or equal to `insideRadarDistance`), then the `CalculateBlipPositionAndDrawBlip(...)` method is called.

The CalculateBlipPositionAndDrawBlip (...) method

This method inputs three parameters: the position of the player, the position of the target, and a reference to the prefab of the blip to be drawn.

Three steps are now required to get the blip for this object to appear on the radar:

1. The normalized position of the target is calculated by calling `NormalizedPosition(...)`.
2. The position of the blip on the radar is calculated from this normalized position by calling `CalculateBlipPosition(...)`.
3. The `RawImage` blip is displayed by calling `DrawBlip(...)` and passing the blip's position and the reference to the `RawImage` prefab that is to be created there.

The NormalizedPosition(...) method

The `NormalizedPosition(...)` method inputs the player's character position and the target GameObject's position. It has the goal of outputting the relative position of the target to the player, returning a `Vector3` object (actually, a C# **struct** – but we can think of it as a simple object) with a triplet of X, Y, and Z values. Note that since the radar is only 2D, we ignore the Y-value of the target GameObjects, so the Y-value of the `Vector3` object that's returned by this method will always be 0. So, for example, if a target was at exactly the same location as the player, the X, Y, and Z of the returned `Vector3` object would be (0, 0, 0).

Since we know that the target GameObject is no further from the player's character than `insideRadarDistance`, we can calculate a value in the −1 ... 0 ... +1 range for the X and Z axes by finding the distance on each axis from the target to the player, and then dividing it by `insideRadarDistance`. An X-value of −1 means that the target is fully to the left of the player (at a distance that is equal to `insideRadarDistance`), while +1 means it is fully to the right. A value of 0 means that the target has the same X position as the player's character. Likewise, for −1 ... 0 ... +1 values in the Z-axis (this axis represents how far, in front or behind us, an object is located, which will be mapped to the vertical axis in our radar).

Finally, this method constructs and returns a new `Vector3` object with the calculated X and Z normalized values and a Y-value of zero.

The normalized position

The normalized value is one that has been simplified in some way so that its context has been abstracted away. In this recipe, what we are interested in is where an object is relative to the player. So, our normal form is to get a value of the X and Z position of a target in the −1 to +1 range for each axis. Since we are only considering the GameObjects within our `insideRadarDistance` value, we can map these normalized target positions directly onto the location of the radar image in our UI.

The CalculateBlipPosition(...) method

First, we calculate `angleToTarget`, which is the angle from (0, 0, 0) to our normalized target position.

Next, we calculate `anglePlayer`, which is the angle the player's character is facing. This recipe makes use of the yaw angle of the rotation, which is the rotation about the Y-axis; that is, the direction that a character controller is facing. This can be found in the Y component of a GameObject's `eulerAngles` component of its transform. You can imagine looking from above and down at the character controller and seeing what direction they are facing – this is what we are trying to display graphically with the radar.

Our desired radar angle (the `angleRadarDegrees` variable) is calculated by subtracting the player's direction angle from the angle between the target and player, since a radar displays the relative angle from the direction that the player is facing to the target object. In mathematics, an angle of zero indicates an east direction. To correct this, we need to also subtract 90 degrees from the angle.

The angle is then converted into radians since this is required for these Unity trigonometry methods. We then multiply the `Sin()` and `Cos()` results by our normalized distances to calculate the X and Y values, respectively (see the following diagram):

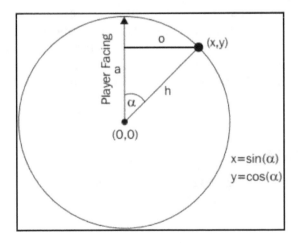

Figure 2.37 – Calculation for the blip method

 In the preceding diagram, alpha is the angle between the player and target object, "a" is the adjacent side, "h" is the hypotenuse, and "o" is the side opposite the angle.

Our final position values need to be expressed as pixel lengths, relative to the center of the radar. So, we multiply our `blipX` and `blipY` values by half the width and the height of the radar; note that we only multiply with half the width since these values are relative to the center of the radar. We then add half the width and the height of the radar image to the `blipX/Y` values so that these values are now positioned relative to the center.

Finally, a new `Vector2` object is created and returned, passing back these final calculated X and Y pixel values for the position of our blip icon.

The DrawBlip() method

The `DrawBlip()` method takes the input parameters of the position of the blip (as a `Vector2` X, Y pair) and the reference to the `RawImage` prefab to be created at that location on the radar.

A new GameObject is created (instantiated) from the prefab and is parented to the `radar` GameObject (of which the scripted object is also a component). A reference is retrieved from the **Rect Transform** component of the new `RawImage` GameObject that has been created for the blip. Calls to the Unity **RectTransform** method, `SetInsetAndSizeFromParentEdge(...)`, result in the `blip` GameObject being positioned at the provided horizontal and vertical locations over the radar image, regardless of where in the **Game** window the background radar image has been located.

There's more...

This radar script scans 360 degrees all around the player and only considers straight-line distances on the X-Z plane. So, the distances in this radar are not affected by any height difference between the player and target GameObjects. The script can be adapted to ignore targets whose height is more than some threshold different from the player's height.

Also, as presented, this recipe's radar sees through *everything*, even if there are obstacles between the player and the target. This recipe can be extended to not show obscured targets by using raycasting techniques. See the Unity scripting reference for more details about raycasting: http://docs.unity3d.com/ScriptReference/Physics.Raycast.html.

Inventory and Advanced UIs

3

Many games involve the player collecting items or choosing from a selection of items. Examples include collecting keys to open doors, collecting ammo for weapons, and choosing from a collection of spells to cast.

The recipes in this chapter provide a range of solutions for displaying to the player whether they are carrying an item or not, whether they are allowed more than one of an item, and how many they have.

The two parts of software design for implementing inventories relate to, first, how we choose to represent the data about inventory items (that is, the data types and structures to store the data) and, second, how we choose to display information about inventory items to the player (the UI).

Also, while not strictly inventory items, player properties such as lives left, health, and time remaining can also be designed around the same concepts that we will present in this chapter.

First, we need to think about the nature of different inventory items for any particular game:

- Single items:
    - Examples: The only key for a level or a suit of magic armor.
    - Data type: `bool` (Boolean – `true`/`false`).
    - UI: Nothing (if not carried) or text/image to show being carried. Or perhaps, if we wish to highlight to the player that there is an **option** to carry this item, we could display a text `string` saying `no key/key` or two images, one showing an empty key outline and the second showing a full-color key.

- Continuous items:
    - Examples: Time left, health, shield strength
    - Data type: `float` (for example, 0.00-1.00) or `int` (Integer) scale (for example, 0% to 100%)
    - UI: Text, number, or image progress bar/pie chart

- Two or more of the same item:
    - Examples: Lives left, number of arrows or bullets left
    - Data type: `int` (Integer – whole numbers)
    - UI: Text count or images

- Collection of related items:
    - Examples: Keys of different colors to open doors of that color, potions of different strength with different titles.
    - Data structure: A `struct` or `class` for the general item type (for example, the `Key` class (color/cost/doorOpenTagString), stored as an array or `List<>`.
    - UI: Text list or list/grid arrangement of icons.

- Collection of different items:
    - Examples: Keys, potions, weapons, and tools, all in the same inventory system.
    - Data structure: `List<>`, `Dictionary<>`, or an array of objects, which can be instances of different classes for each item type.

Each of the preceding representations and UI display methods will be illustrated in the recipes in this chapter. In addition, we'll learn how to create and use custom **sorting layers** so that we have complete control over which objects appear on top of or below other objects – something that is pretty important when scene content can contain background images, pickups, player characters, and so on.

At the time of writing, there is also a new input system named UI Toolkit (formally named UI Elements). A final version hasn't been released, but it looks like a powerful new way to create both runtime game UIs and Editor extension UIs with a single approach, using XML- and CSS-style data descriptions. For highly dynamic UIs, where much of what is to be displayed can change during runtime, a data-driven approach such as UI Toolkit could be a more flexible solution than the standard Unity UI. So, the final recipe in this chapter will introduce UI Toolkit and its UI Builder tool, which we can use to create a dynamically aligned flex row containing multiple buttons.

In this chapter, we will cover the following recipes:

- Creating a simple 2D mini-game – SpaceGirl
- Displaying single object pickups with carrying and not-carrying text
- Displaying single object pickups with carrying and not-carrying icons
- Displaying multiple pickups of the same object with multiple status icons
- Using panels to visually outline the inventory UI area and individual items
- Creating a C# inventory slot UI to display scripted components
- Using UI Grid Layout Groups to automatically populate a panel
- Displaying multiple pickups of different objects as a list of text via a dynamic List<> of scripted PickUp objects
- Displaying multiple pickups of different objects as text totals via a dynamic Dictionary<> of PickUp objects and enum pickup types
- Creating a runtime UI Toolkit interface

Technical requirements

To complete the recipes in this chapter, you will need Unity 2021.1 or later, plus one of the following:

- Microsoft Windows 10 (64-bit)/GPU: DX10, DX11, and DX12-capable
- macOS Sierra 10.12.6+/GPU Metal-capable Intel or AMD

- Linux Ubuntu 16.04, Ubuntu 18.04, and CentOS 7/GPU: OpenGL 3.2+ or Vulkan-capable Nvidia or AMD

For each chapter, there is a folder that contains the asset files you will need in this book's GitHub repository at `https://github.com/PacktPublishing/Unity-2021-Cookbook-Fourth-Edition`.

Creating a simple 2D mini-game – SpaceGirl

This recipe will show you how to create the 2D SpaceGirl mini-game, which almost all the recipes in this chapter are based on. The following figure shows an example of the mini-game we will be creating:

Figure 3.1 – Example of the 2D SpaceGirl mini-game

Getting ready

For this recipe, we have prepared the images you need in a folder named `Sprites` in the `03_01` folder. We have also provided the completed game as a Unity package in this folder, named `Simple2DGame_SpaceGirl`.

How to do it...

To create the simple 2D Space Girl mini-game, follow these steps:

1. Create a new, empty 2D project.
2. Import the supplied `Sprites` folder into your project.

3. Since it's a 2D project, each sprite image should be of the **Sprite (2D and UI)** type. Check this by selecting the sprite in the **Project** panel; then, in the **Inspector** panel, check the **Texture Type** property. If you need to change its type, you can change it from the drop-down menu and then click the **Apply** button.

4. Set the Unity Player's screen size to **800 x 600** by choosing it from the drop-down menu on the **Game** panel. If **800 x 600** isn't an offered resolution, then click the plus (**+**) button and create this as a new resolution for the panel.

5. Display the **Tags and Layers** properties for the current Unity project. Choose menu and go to **Edit | Project Settings | Tags and Layers**. Alternatively, if you are already editing a GameObject, then you can select the **Add Layer...** menu from the **Layer** drop-down menu at the top of the **Inspector** panel, next to the **Static true/false** toggle.

6. Use the expand/contract triangle tools to contract **Tags** and **Layers**, as well as to expand **Sorting Layers**. Use the plus (**+**) button to add two new sorting layers, as shown in the screenshot. First, add one named **Background**, then add one named **Foreground**. The sequence is important since Unity will draw items in layers further down this list on top of the items earlier in the list. You can rearrange the layer sequence by clicking and dragging the position control, the wide equals (**=**) icon to the left of the word **Layer** in each row:

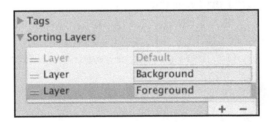

Figure 3.2 – Layer sequence

7. Drag the `background_blue` sprite from the **Project** panel (in the `Sprites` folder) into either the **Game** or **Hierarchy** window to create a GameObject for the current scene. Set **Position** of this GameObject to (0,0,0). It should completely cover the **Game** panel (at a resolution of 800 x 600).

8. Set **Sorting Layer** of the `background_blue` GameObject to **Background** (in the **Sprite Renderer** component):

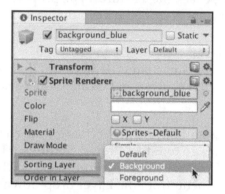

Figure 3.3 – Setting Sorting Layer of the GameObject's background

9. Drag the **star** sprite from the **Project** panel (in the `Sprites` folder) into either the **Game** or **Hierarchy** window to create a GameObject for the current scene:

- Create a new tag called **Star** and assign this tag to the **star** GameObject (tags are created in the same way as sorting layers are).
- Set **Sorting Layer** of the `star` GameObject to **Foreground** (in the **Sprite Renderer** component).
- Add a **Box Collider 2D** (**Add Component I Physics 2D I Box Collider 2D**) to the `star` GameObject and check **Is Trigger**, as shown in the following screenshot:

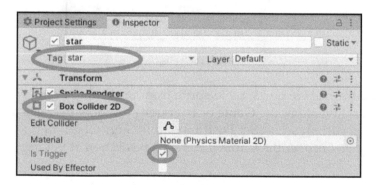

Figure 3.4 – Box Collider 2D trigger setting

10. Drag the **girl1** sprite from the **Project** panel (in the `Sprites` folder) into either the **Scene** or **Hierarchy** window to create a GameObject for the player's character in the current scene. Rename this GameObject `player-girl1`.

11. Set **Sorting Layer** of the `player-girl1` GameObject to **Foreground**.

12. Add a **Physics | Box Collider 2D** component to the `player-girl1` GameObject.

13. Add a **Physics 2D | Rigid Body 2D** component to the `player-girl1` GameObject. Set its **Gravity Scale** to `0` (so that it isn't falling down the screen due to simulated gravity), as shown in the screenshot:

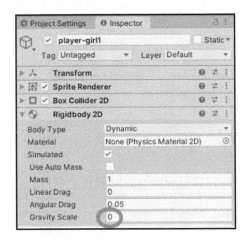

Figure 3.5 – Setting Gravity Scale to zero

14. Create a new folder for your scripts named `_Scripts`.

15. Create a C# script called `PlayerMove` (in the `_Scripts` folder).

16. Add an instance of the `PlayerMove` C# script as a component of the `player-girl1` GameObject in the **Hierarchy** window:

```csharp
using UnityEngine;
using System.Collections;

public class PlayerMove : MonoBehaviour {
  public float speed = 10;
  private Rigidbody2D rigidBody2D;
  private Vector2 newVelocity;

  void Awake(){
    rigidBody2D = GetComponent<Rigidbody2D>();
```

```
  }

  void Update() {
    float xMove = Input.GetAxis("Horizontal");
    float yMove = Input.GetAxis("Vertical");

    float xSpeed = xMove * speed;
    float ySpeed = yMove * speed;

    newVelocity = new Vector2(xSpeed, ySpeed);
  }

  void FixedUpdate() {
    rigidBody2D.velocity = newVelocity;
  }

}
```

17. Save the scene (name it `Main Scene` and save it in a new folder named `_Scenes`).

How it works...

In this recipe, you created a player character in the scene using the **girl1** sprite and added a scripted component instance of the `PlayerMove` class. You also created a `star` GameObject (a pickup), a tagged star with a 2D box collider that will trigger a collision when the player's character hits it. When you run the game, the `player-girl1` character should move around using the *W*, *A*, *S*, and *D* keyboard keys, the arrow keys, or a joystick. There is a `newVelocity` variable that is updated each frame in the `Update()` method based on the inputs. This `Vector2` value is then applied to the `FixedUpdate()` method to become the new velocity for the GameObject.

Unity maps user inputs such as key presses, arrow keys, and game controller controls to its `Input` class. Two special properties of the `Input` class are the **Horizontal** and **Vertical** axes, which can be accessed via the `Input.GetAxis("Horizontal")` and `Input.GetAxis("Vertical")` methods.

 Managing your input mapping: You can map from different user input methods (keys, mouse, controllers, and so on) to the axes via **Edit | Project Settings | Input Manager**.

Currently, nothing will happen if the `player-SpaceGirl` character hits a star because this has yet to be scripted.

With that, you have added a background (the `background_blue` GameObject) to the scene, which will be behind everything since it is in the rearmost sorting layer, called **Background**. Items you want to appear in front of the background (the player character and the star, so far) are placed on the **Foreground** sorting layer.

> You can learn more about Unity tags and layers at `http://docs.unity3d.com/Manual/class-TagManager.html`.

Displaying single object pickups with carrying and not-carrying text

Often, the simplest inventory situation is to display text to tell players whether they are carrying a single item (or not). In this recipe, we'll add the ability to detect collisions with the `star` GameObject and add this to the SpaceGirl mini-game. We will also display an on-screen message stating whether a star has been collected or not:

Figure 3.6 – Example of text for displaying single-object pickups

At the end of the recipe, in the *There's more...* section, we'll learn how to adapt this recipe to maintain the **Integer** total for how many stars have been collected, for a version of the game with lots of stars to collect.

Getting ready

For this recipe, we have prepared a folder named `Fonts`, which can be found in the `03_02` folder.

This recipe assumes that you are starting with the `Simple2Dgame_SpaceGirl` project, which we set up in the previous recipe. So, make a copy of that project and work on that.

How to do it...

To display text to inform the user about the status of carrying a single object pickup, follow these steps:

1. Start with a new copy of the `Simple2Dgame_SpaceGirl` mini-game.

2. Add a UI Text object by going to **GameObject | UI | Text**. Rename it `Text-carrying-star`. Change its text to `Carrying star: false`.

3. Import the provided `Fonts` folder into your project.

4. In the **Inspector** window, set the font of **Text-carrying-star** to **Xolonium-Bold**, and set its color to yellow. Center the text horizontally and vertically, set **Height** to 50, and set **Font Size** to 32.

5. Edit its **Rect Transform** and, while holding down *Shift + Alt* (to set its pivot and position), choose the top stretch box:

Figure 3.7 – Editing Rect Transform

Your text should now be positioned at the top of the Game panel, and its width should stretch to match that of the whole panel, as shown in *Figure 3.6*.

6. Create the following C# script class called `PlayerInventory` in the `_Scripts` folder:

```csharp
using UnityEngine;

public class PlayerInventory : MonoBehaviour {
    private PlayerInventoryDisplay playerInventoryDisplay;
    private bool carryingStar = false;

    void Awake() {
        playerInventoryDisplay =
            GetComponent<PlayerInventoryDisplay();
    }

    void Start() {
        playerInventoryDisplay.OnChangeCarryingStar(
carryingStar);
    }

    void OnTriggerEnter2D(Collider2D hit) {
        if (hit.CompareTag("Star")) {
            carryingStar = true;
            playerInventoryDisplay.OnChangeCarryingStar(
carryingStar);
            Destroy(hit.gameObject);
        }
    }
}
```

7. Create the following C# script class called `PlayerInventoryDisplay` in the `_Scripts` folder:

```csharp
using UnityEngine;
using UnityEngine.UI;

[RequireComponent(typeof(PlayerInventory))]
public class PlayerInventoryDisplay : MonoBehaviour  {
    public Text starText;
    public void OnChangeCarryingStar(bool carryingStar) {
        string starMessage = "no star :-(";
        if(carryingStar)
            starMessage = "Carrying star :-)";
        starText.text = starMessage;
    }
}
```

8. Add an instance of the `PlayerInventoryDisplay` script class to the `player-SpaceGirl` GameObject in the **Hierarchy** window.

   Note that since the `PlayerInventoryDisplay` class contains `RequireComponent()`, an instance of the `PlayerInventory` script class will be automatically added to the `player-SpaceGirl` GameObject.

9. From the **Hierarchy** window, select the `player-SpaceGirl` GameObject. Then, from the **Inspector** window, access the **Player Inventory Display (Script)** component and populate the **Star Text** public field with the `Text-carrying-star` GameObject, as shown in the following screenshot:

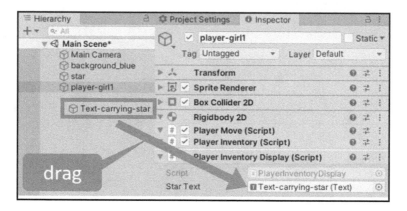

Figure 3.8 – Populating the Star Text public field

10. When you play the scene, after moving the character into the star, the star should disappear, and the onscreen UI Text message should change to **Carrying star :-)**:

Figure 3.9 – Onscreen UI text message example

How it works...

In this recipe, you created a **UI Text** GameObject called `Text-carrying-star` to display a text message stating whether the player is carrying a star. You created two script classes, and an instance of each was added as components of the player's `player-SpaceGirl` character GameObject:

- The `PlayerInventory` script class detects player-star collisions, updates internal variables stating whether a star is being carried, and asks for the UI display to be updated each time a collision is detected.

- The `PlayerInventoryDisplay` script class handles communication with the user by updating the text message that's displayed by the **Text-carrying-star** UI Text GameObject.

A game design pattern (best practice approach) called the **Model-View-Controller** (**MVC**) pattern separates the code that updates the UI from the code that changes player and game variables, such as score and inventory item lists. Although this recipe has only one variable and one method for updating the UI, well-structured game architectures scale up to cope with more complex games, so it is often worth the effort of using a little more code and an extra script class, even at this beginning stage, if we want our final game architecture to be well structured and maintainable.

One additional advantage of this design pattern is that the method that's used to communicate information to the user via the UI can be changed (for example, from text to an icon – see the next recipe!), without any need to change the code in the `PlayerInventory` script class.

The PlayerInventory script class

The `playerInventoryDisplay` variable is a reference to an instance object of the `PlayerInventoryDisplay` class.

The `bool` variable called `carryingStar` represents whether the player is carrying the star at any point in time; it is initialized to `false`.

The `Awake()` method caches a reference to the `playerInventoryDisplay` sibling component.

When the scene begins via the `Start()` method, we call the `OnChangeCarryingStar(...)` method of the `playerInventoryDisplay` script component, passing in the initial value of `carryingStar` (which is `false`). This ensures that we are not relying on text that's been typed into the `Text-carrying-star` UI Text object at **design time**, so that the UI that's seen by the user is always set by our **runtime** methods. This avoids problems where the words to be displayed to the user are changed in code and not in the **Inspector** window, which leads to a mismatch between the onscreen text when the scene first runs and after it has been updated via a script.

 A golden rule in Unity game design is to avoid duplicating content in more than one place so that we avoid having to maintain two or more copies of the same content. Each duplicate is an opportunity for maintenance issues to occur when some, but not all, copies of a value are changed.

Maximizing the use of prefabs is another example of this principle in action. This is also known as the DRY principle – Don't Repeat Yourself.

Each time the player's character collides with any object that has its **Is Trigger** set to `true`, an `OnTriggerEnter2D()` event message is sent to both objects involved in the collision. The `OnTriggerEnter2D()` message is passed as a parameter that is a reference to the `Collider2D` component inside the object that we just collided with.

Our player's `OnTriggerEnter2D()` method tests the tag string of the object that was collided with to see whether it has the **Star** value. Since the `star` GameObject we created has its trigger set and has the **Star** tag, the `if` statement inside this method will detect a collision with the star and complete the following three actions:

- The Boolean (flag) `carryingStar` variable will be set to true.
- The `OnChangeCarryingStar(...)` method of the `playerInventoryDisplay` script component will be called, passing in the updated value of `carryingStar`.
- The GameObject that was just collided with will be destroyed – that is, the star.

Boolean variables are often referred to as flags. The use of a `bool` (`true`/`false`) variable to represent whether some feature of the game state is true or false is very common. Programmers often refer to these variables as flags. So, programmers might refer to the `carryingStar` variable as the star-carrying flag.

The PlayerInventoryDisplay script class

The public `Text` variable known as `starText` is a reference to the `Text-carrying-star` UI Text object. Its value was set via drag-and-drop at design time.

The `OnChangeCarryingStar` (`carryingStar`) method updates the text property of `starText` with the value of the `starMessage` string variable. This method takes a `bool` argument called `carryingStar` as input. The default value of the `starMessage` string tells the user that the player is not carrying the star. However, an `if` statement tests the value of `carryingStar`, and if that is `true`, then the message is changed to inform the player that they are carrying the star.

There's more...

Let's look at some details you won't want to miss.

Collecting multiple items and display the total number carried

Often, there are pickups that the player can collect more than one of. In such situations, we can use an integer to represent the total number collected and use a UI **Text** object to display this total to the user. Let's modify this recipe to allow SpaceGirl to collect lots of stars!

Figure 3.10 – Example of collecting and displaying multiple items

To convert this recipe into one that shows the total number of stars that have been collected, do the following:

1. Make three or four more copies of the star GameObject and spread them around the scene. This gives the player several stars to collect rather than just one.

Use the *Ctrl + D* (Windows) or *Cmd + D* (Mac) keyboard shortcut to quickly duplicate GameObjects.

2. Change the contents of the C# PlayerInventory script class so that it contains the following:

```
using UnityEngine;
public class PlayerInventory : MonoBehaviour {
    private PlayerInventoryDisplay playerInventoryDisplay;
    private int totalStars = 0;

    void Awake() {
        playerInventoryDisplay =
            GetComponent<PlayerInventoryDisplay();
    }

    void Start() {
        playerInventoryDisplay.OnChangeStarTotal(totalStars);
    }

    void OnTriggerEnter2D(Collider2D hit) {
        if (hit.CompareTag("Star")) {
            totalStars++;
playerInventoryDisplay.OnChangeCarryingStar(totalStars);
            Destroy(hit.gameObject);
        }
    }
}
```

3. Change the contents of the C# PlayerInventoryDisplay script class so that it contains the following:

```
using UnityEngine;
using UnityEngine.UI;

[RequireComponent(typeof(PlayerInventoryTotal))]
public class PlayerInventoryDisplay : MonoBehaviour {
```

```
public Text starText;
public void OnChangeStarTotal(int numStars) {
        string starMessage = "total stars = " + numStars;
        starText.text = starMessage;
}
}
```

As you can see, in `PlayerInventory`, we now increment `totalStars` by 1 each time a `star` GameObject is collided with. In `PlayerInventoryDisplay`, we display a simple text message stating `"total stars = "` on-screen, followed by the integer total that was received by the `OnChangeStarTotal(...)` method.

Now, when you run the game, you should see the total stars start at zero and increase by 1 each time the player's character hits a star.

Alternative – combining all the responsibilities into a single script

The separation of the player inventory (what they are carrying) and how to display the inventory to the user is an example of a game design pattern (best practice approach) called **Model-View-Controller** (**MVC**), whereby we separate the code that updates the UI from the code that changes player and game variables, such as score and inventory item lists. Although this recipe has only one variable and one method to update the UI, well-structured game architectures scale up to cope with more complex games, so it is often worth the effort of using a little more code and an extra script class, even at this game's stage of development, if we want our final game architecture to be well structured and maintainable.

However, for *very simple games*, we may choose to display its status in a single script class. For an example of this approach for this recipe, remove the `PlayerInventory` and `PlayerInventoryDisplay` script components, create a C# script class called `PlayerInventoryCombined`, and add an instance of the script to the `player-SpaceGirl` GameObject in the **Hierarchy** window:

```
using UnityEngine.UI;
public class PlayerInventoryCombined : MonoBehaviour {
    public Text starText;
    private bool carryingStar = false;

    void Start() {
        UpdateStarText();
    }
```

```
void OnTriggerEnter2D(Collider2D hit) {
    if (hit.CompareTag("Star")){
        carryingStar = true;
        UpdateStarText();
        Destroy(hit.gameObject);
    }
}

private void UpdateStarText() {
    string starMessage = "no star :-(";
    if (carryingStar)
        starMessage = "Carrying star :-)";
    starText.text = starMessage;
}
}
```

 There is no difference in terms of the experience of the player; the change is simply in the architectural structure of our game code.

This recipe demonstrates how to create a simple inventory that includes display text to tell players whether they are carrying a single item (or not). In addition, you can detect collisions with GameObjects and display an on-screen message stating whether the GameObject has been collected. While it's possible to do all this work in a single script, it's a good idea to break different responsibilities into different script classes whenever we can, since it means at any one time, we are working on a small amount of code that does one key action. Smaller components are easier to debug, more likely to be reused, and less likely to have to be changed.

Displaying single-object pickups with carrying and not-carrying icons

Graphic icons are an effective way to inform the player that they are carrying an item. In this recipe, if no star is being carried, a gray-filled icon in a blocked-off circle will be displayed in the top-left corner of the screen:

Figure 3.11 – Example of a single-object pickup

Then, once a star has been picked up, a yellow-filled star icon will be displayed. In many cases, icons are clearer (they don't require reading and thinking about) and can also be smaller onscreen than text messages that indicate player status and inventory items.

This recipe will also illustrate the benefits of the MVC design pattern, which we described in the previous recipe – we are changing how to communicate with the user (using the **View** via icons rather than text), but we can use, with no changes required, the PlayerInventory script class (the **Model-Controller**), which detects player-star collisions and maintains the Boolean flag that tells us whether a star is being carried.

Getting ready

This recipe assumes that you are starting with the **Simple2Dgame_SpaceGirl** project that we set up in the first recipe of this chapter.

For this recipe, we have prepared a folder named _Scripts in the 03_03 folder.

How to do it...

To toggle carrying and not-carrying icons for a single-object pickup, follow these steps:

1. Start with a new copy of the Simple2Dgame_SpaceGirl mini-game.
2. Import the _Scripts folder from the provided files (this contains a copy of the PlayerInventory script class from the previous recipe, which we can use unchanged for this recipe).
3. Add a **UI Image** object to the scene (**GameObject | UI | Image**). Rename it Image-star-icon.
4. With Image-star-icon selected in the **Hierarchy** window, drag the icon_nostar_100 sprite (in the Sprites folder) from the **Project** window into the **Source Image** field in the **Inspector** window (in the **Image (Script)** component).

5. Click on the **Set Native Size** button for the **Image** component. This will resize the UI image so that it fits the physical pixel's width and height of the `icon_nostar_100` sprite file:

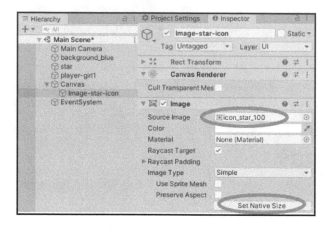

Figure 3.12 – Image source and native size settings

6. Position the image icon at the top, to the left of the **Game** window, in **Rect Transform**. Choose the top-left box component while holding down *Shift + Alt* (to set its pivot and position).

7. Create the following C# `PlayerInventoryDisplay` script class and add an instance of the script to the `player-SpaceGirl` GameObject in the **Hierarchy** window:

```
using UnityEngine;
using UnityEngine.UI;

[RequireComponent(typeof(PlayerInventory))]
public class PlayerInventoryDisplay : MonoBehaviour  {
    public Image imageStarGO;
    public Sprite iconNoStar;
    public Sprite iconStar;

    public void OnChangeCarryingStar(bool carryingStar) {
        if (carryingStar)
            imageStarGO.sprite = iconStar;
        else
            imageStarGO.sprite = iconNoStar;
    }
}
```

8. From the **Hierarchy** window, select the `player-girl1` GameObject. Then, from the **Inspector** window, access the **Player Inventory Display (Script)** component and populate the **Star Image** public field with the **Image-star-icon** UI image object.

9. Populate the **Icon No Star** public field from the **Project** window with the **icon_nostar_100** sprite, and then populate the **Icon Star** public field from the **Project** window with the **icon_star_100** sprite, as shown in the following screenshot:

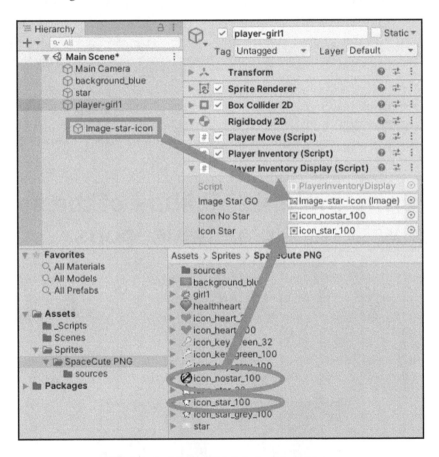

Figure 3.13 – Populating the public fields for Player Inventory Display

10. Play the scene. You should see the no star icon (a gray-filled icon in a blocked-off circle) in the top left until you pick up the star, at which point it will change to show the carrying star icon (yellow-filled star). Note that you might need to reposition either the star or `player-girl1` so that they don't collide on play.

How it works...

In the `PlayerInventoryDisplay` script class, the `imageStarGO` image variable is a reference to the `Image-star-icon` UI image object. The `iconStar` and `iconNoStar` sprite variables are references to the Sprite files in the **Project** window – the sprites that tell the player whether or not a star is being carried.

Each time the `OnChangeCarryingStar(carryingStar)` method is invoked by the `PlayerInventory` object, this method uses an `if` statement to set the UI image to the sprite that corresponds to the value of the `bool` argument that's been received.

Displaying multiple pickups of the same object with multiple status icons

If there is a small, fixed total number of an item to be collected rather than text totals, an effective UI approach is to display placeholder icons (empty or grayed out pictures) to show the user how many of the same item are left to be collected. Each time an item is picked up, a placeholder icon is replaced with a full-color collected icon.

In this recipe, we will use gray-filled star icons as the placeholders and yellow-filled star icons to indicate each collected star, as shown in the following screenshot:

Figure 3.14 – UI showing multiple status icons

Getting ready

This recipe assumes that you are starting with the `Simple2Dgame_SpaceGirl` project, which we set up in the first recipe of this chapter.

How to do it...

To display multiple inventory icons for multiple pickups of the same type of object, follow these steps:

1. Start with a new copy of the `Simple2Dgame_SpaceGirl` mini-game.
2. Create a C# script class called `PlayerInventory` in the `_Scripts` folder:

```csharp
using UnityEngine;

public class PlayerInventory : MonoBehaviour {
    private PlayerInventoryDisplay playerInventoryDisplay;
    private int totalStars = 0;

    void Awake() {
        playerInventoryDisplay =
GetComponent<PlayerInventoryDisplay>
            ();
    }

    void Start() {
        playerInventoryDisplay.OnChangeStarTotal(totalStars);
    }

    void OnTriggerEnter2D(Collider2D hit) {
        if (hit.CompareTag("Star")) {
            totalStars++;
playerInventoryDisplay.OnChangeCarryingStar(totalStars);
            Destroy(hit.gameObject);
        }
    }
}
```

3. Select the `star` GameObject in the **Hierarchy** window and make three more copies of it. There should now be four `star` GameObjects in the scene. Move these new `star` GameObjects to different parts of the screen.

4. Add the following C# script class, called `PlayerInventoryDisplay`, to the `player-girl1` GameObject in the **Hierarchy** window:

```
using UnityEngine;
using System.Collections;
using UnityEngine.UI;

public class PlayerInventoryDisplay : MonoBehaviour {
    public Image[] starPlaceholders;
    public Sprite iconStarYellow;
    public Sprite iconStarGrey;

    public void OnChangeStarTotal(int starTotal){
        for (int i = 0;i < starPlaceholders.Length; ++i){
            if (i < starTotal)
                starPlaceholders[i].sprite = iconStarYellow;
            else
                starPlaceholders[i].sprite = iconStarGrey;
        }
    }
}
```

5. Select **Canvas** in the **Hierarchy** window and add a new **UI Image** object (**Create | UI | Image**). Rename it `Image-star0`.

6. Select **Image-star0** in the **Hierarchy** window.

7. From the **Project** window, drag the `icon_star_grey_100` sprite (in the `Sprites` folder) into the source **Image field** in the **Inspector** window for the **Image (Script)** component.

8. Click on the **Set Native Size** button for the **Image (Script)** component. This will resize the UI image so that it fits the physical pixel width and height of the `icon_star_grey_100` sprite file.

9. Now, we will position our icon at the top left of the **Game** window. Edit the UI image's **Rect Transform** component and, while holding down *Shift + Alt* (to set its pivot and position), choose the top-left box. **UI Image** should now be positioned at the top left of the **Game** window.

10. Make three more copies of `Image-star0` in the **Hierarchy** window, naming them `Image-star1`, `Image-star2`, and `Image-star3`.

11. In the **Inspector** window, change the **Pos X** position (in the **Rect Transform** component) of **Image-star1** to `100`, **Image-star2** to `200`, and **Image-star3** to `300`:

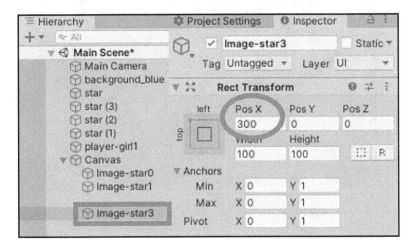

Figure 3.15 – Rect Transform settings

12. In the **Hierarchy** window, select the `player-girl1` GameObject. Then, from the **Inspector** window, access the **Player Inventory Display (Script)** component and set the **Size** property of the **Star Placeholders** public field to `4`.

13. Next, populate the **Element 0/1/2/3** array values of the **Star Placeholders** public field with **UI Image** objects **Image-star0/1/2/3**.

14. Now, populate the **Icon Star Yellow** and **Icon Star Grey** public fields from the **Project** window with the `icon_star_100` and `icon_star_grey_100` sprites, as shown in the following screenshot:

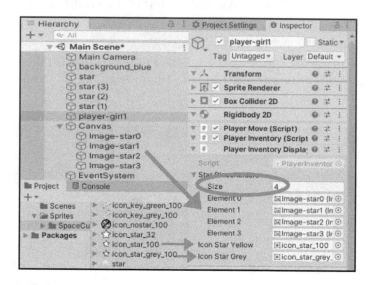

Figure 3.16 – Populating the public fields with sprites

15. Now, when you play the scene, you should see the sequence of four gray placeholder star icons. Then, each time you collide with a star, the next icon at the top should turn yellow.

How it works...

Four **UI Image** objects, **Image-star0/1/2/3**, have been created at the top of the screen and initialized with the gray placeholder icon. The gray and yellow icon sprite files have been resized to be 100 x 100 pixels, which makes positioning them at design time easier, since their positions are $(0,0)$, $(100,0)$, $(200,0)$, and $(300,0)$. In a more complicated game screen or one where screen real estate is precious, the actual size of the icons would probably be smaller – a decision to be made by the game UI designer.

In the `PlayerInventory` script class, the `totalStars` int variable represents how many stars have been collected so far; it is initialized to zero. The `playerInventoryDisplay` variable is a reference to the scripted component that manages our inventory display – this variable is cached before the scene begins in the `Awake()` method.

The `Start()` method that runs at the beginning of the scene calls the `OnChangeStarTotal(...)` method of the `PlayerInventoryDisplay` component, which ensures that the icons on the screen are displayed to match the starting value of `totalStars`.

In the `OnTriggerEnter2D()` method, the `totalStars` counter is incremented by 1 each time the player's character hits an object tagged as **Star**. As well as destroying the **hit** GameObject, the `OnChangeStarTotal(...)` method of the `PlayerInventoryDisplay` component is called, passing the new **star** total integer.

The `OnChangeStarTotal(...)` method of the `PlayerInventoryDisplay` script class contains references to the four UI images and loops through each item in the array of **Image** references, setting the given number of images to yellow and the remaining ones to gray. This method is public, allowing it to be called from an instance of the `PlayerInventory` script class.

There's more...

Let's look at some details you won't want to miss.

Revealing icons for multiple object pickups by changing the size of a tiled image

Another approach that could be taken to show increasing numbers of images is to make use of tiled images. The same visual effect as in the previous recipe can also be achieved by making use of a tiled gray star image with a width of 400 (showing four copies of the gray star icon) behind a tiled yellow star image, whose width is 100 times the number of stars collected.

If the yellow-starred image is less wide than the gray-starred imaged beneath, then we'll see gray stars for any remaining locations. For example, if we are carrying 3 stars, we'll make the width of the yellow-starred image *3 x 100 = 300* pixels wide. This will show 3 yellow stars and reveal 100 pixels; that is, 1 gray star from the gray-starred image beneath it.

To display gray and yellow star icons for multiple object pickups using tiled images, let's adapt our recipe to illustrate this technique:

1. In the **Hierarchy** window, delete the entire **Canvas** GameObject (and therefore delete all four UI images).

2. Add a new **UI Image** object to your scene (**Create | UI | Image**). Rename the GameObject `Image-stars-grey`.

3. Ensure `Image-stars-grey` is selected in the **Hierarchy** window. From the **Project** window, drag the `icon_star_grey_100` sprite (in the `Sprites` folder) into the **Source Image** field in the **Inspector** window (in the **Image (Script)** component).

4. Click on the **Set Native Size** button for the **Image (Script)** component. This will resize the UI image so that it fits the physical pixel width and height of the `icon_star_grey_100` sprite file.

5. Now, position the icon at the top left of the screen. Edit the UI image's **Rect Transform** component and, while holding down *Shift + Alt* (to set its pivot and position), choose the top-left box. The UI image should now be positioned at the top left of the **Game** window.

6. In the **Inspector** window, change **Width** (in the **Rect Transform** component) of `Image-stars-grey` to `400`. Also, set **Image Type** (in the **Image (Script)** component) to `Tiled`, as shown in the following screenshot:

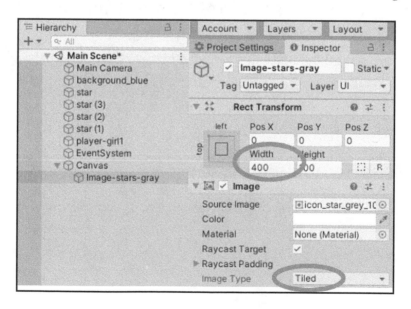

Figure 3.17 – Width and Image settings for Image-stars-grey

For a simple game like this, we are choosing simplicity over memory efficiency. You'll see a notice, suggesting that you use an advanced texture with **Wrap** mode repeated and a cleared packing tag. While more memory efficient, it's more complicated to do for small, simple tiling such as in this recipe.

7. Make a copy of `Image-stars-grey` in the **Hierarchy** window, naming the copy `Image-stars-yellow`.

8. With `Image-stars-yellow` selected in the **Hierarchy** window, from the **Project** window, drag the `icon_star_100` sprite (in the `Sprites` folder) into the **Source Image** field in the **Inspector** window (in the **Image (Script)** component).

9. Set the width of `Image-stars-yellow` to 0 (in the **Rect Transform** component). So, now, we have the yellow stars tiled image above the grey stars tiled image, but since its width is zero, we don't see any of the yellow stars yet.

10. Replace the existing C# script, called `PlayerInventoryDisplay`, with the following code:

```
using UnityEngine;
using UnityEngine.UI;

[RequireComponent(typeof(PlayerInventory))]
public class PlayerInventoryDisplay : MonoBehaviour {
    public Image iconStarsYellow;

    public void OnChangeStarTotal(int starTotal) {
        float newWidth = 100 * starTotal;
        iconStarsYellow.rectTransform.SetSizeWithCurrentAnchors(
            RectTransform.Axis.Horizontal, newWidth );
    }
}
```

11. From the **Hierarchy** window, select the `player-girl1` GameObject. Then, from the **Inspector** window, access the **Player Inventory Display (Script)** component and populate the **Icons Stars Yellow** public field with the `Image-stars-yellow` UI image object.

`Image-stars-gray` is a tiled image, wide enough (`400px`) for the gray sprite, `icon_star_grey_100`, to be shown four times. `Image-stars-yellow` is a tiled image, above the gray one, initially with its width set to zero so that no yellow stars can be seen.

Each time a star is picked up, a call is made from the `PlayerInventory` scripted object to the `OnChangeStarTotal()` method of `PlayerInventoryDisplay`, passing the new integer number of stars collected. By multiplying this by the width of the yellow sprite image (100 px), we get the correct width to set `Image-stars-yellow` so that the corresponding number of yellow stars will now be seen by the user. Any stars that remain to be collected will still be seen as gray stars.

The actual task of changing the width of `Image-stars-yellow` can be completed by calling the `SetSizeWithCurrentAnchors(...)` method. The first parameter is the axis, so we pass the `RectTransform.Axis.Horizontal` constant so that the width will be changed. The second parameter is the new size for that axis, so we must pass a value that is 100 times the number of stars collected so far (the `newWidth` variable).

This recipe has demonstrated two approaches to displaying multiple pickups of the same object with multiple status icons that are commonly used in games, such as health, key collection, or in this case, stars. Both approaches use a placeholder image that is replaced when an item is then collected. The first is best used when the number of items to collect is known, while the second is best for when the number of items is either unknown or there's a large quantity of them. The next recipe will explore improving the UI elements of an inventory.

Using panels to visually outline the inventory UI area and individual items

There are four kinds of objects we see when playing a game:

- GameObjects that have some visual elements, such as 2D and 3D objects.
- UI elements located in **World Space**, so they appear next to GameObjects in the scene.
- UI elements located in **Screen Space - Camera**, so they appear at a fixed distance from the camera (but can be obscured by GameObjects closer to the camera than these UI elements).
- UI elements located in **Screen Space - Overlay**. These always appear above the other three kinds of visual elements and are perfect for **Heads-Up Display (HUD)** elements, such as inventories.

Sometimes, we want to visually make it clear which elements are part of the UI HUD and which are visual objects in the scene. Using Unity UI Panels, along with an opaque or translucent background image, is a simple and effective way to achieve this:

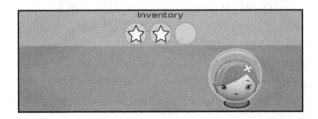

Figure 3.18 – Example of using Unity UI Panels

Panels can also be used to display locations (slots) with shaped or colored backgrounds indicating where items may be placed, or how many may be collected. As shown in the preceding screenshot, in this recipe, we'll create a panel with some title text and three inventory slots, two of which will be filled with star icons, communicating to the player that there is one more star that can be collected/carried.

Getting ready

This recipe assumes that you are starting with the `Simple2Dgame_SpaceGirl` project, which we set up in the first recipe of this chapter. The font you need can be found in the `03_02` folder.

How to do it...

To use panels to visually outline the inventory area and individual items, follow these steps:

1. Start with a new copy of the `Simple2Dgame_SpaceGirl` mini-game.
2. In the **Hierarchy** window, create a **UI Panel (GameObject | UI | Panel)** and rename it `Panel-background`.
3. Now, let's position `Panel-background` at the top of the **Game** window, stretching the horizontal width of the canvas. Edit the UI image's **Rect Transform** component and, while holding down *Shift + Alt* (to set its pivot and position), choose the **top-stretch** box.

4. The panel will still be taking up the whole game window. Now, in the **Inspector** window, change **Height** (in the **Rect Transform** component) of `Panel-background` to `100`.

5. Add a UI **Text** object (**Create** | **UI** | **Text**) and name it `Text-inventory`. For its **Text (Script)** component, change the text to `Inventory`.

6. In the **Hierarchy** window, set the child UI **Text** object, `Text-inventory`, to `Panel-background`.

7. In the **Inspector** window, set the font of `Text-inventory` to **Xolonium-Bold** (this can be found in the `Fonts` folder). Center the text horizontally. Then, for **Alignment**, choose **Vertical center**, set its **Height** to `50`, and set **Font Size** to `23`.

8. Edit **Rect Transform** of `Text-inventory` and, while holding down *Shift + Alt* (to set its pivot and position), choose the **top-stretch** box. The text should now be positioned at the top-center of `Panel-background`, and its width should stretch to match that of the whole panel.

9. Create a new UI Panel (**GameObject** | **UI** | **Panel**) and name it `Panel-inventory-slot`.

10. Edit **Rect Transform** of `Panel-inventory-slot` and, while holding down *Shift + Alt* (to set its pivot and position), choose the **top-center** box. Set both **Width** and **Height** to `70` and **Pos Y** to `-30`, as shown in the following screenshot:

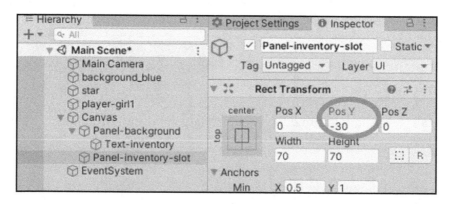

Figure 3.19 – Rect Transform settings for Panel-inventory-slot

11. Ensure that the `Panel-inventory-slot` GameObject is selected in the **Hierarchy** window. In the **Image (Script)** component, change **Source Image** from the UI Panel default of **Background** to the circular **Knob** image (this is one of the built-in images that comes as part of the Unity UI system). As shown in the following screenshot, you should now see a circle centered below the title text in our inventory HUD rectangle. This circle visually tells the user that there is space in the inventory for an item to be collected:

Figure 3.20 – Example of a built-in circular Knob image for the UI

12. Imagine that the player has collected a star. Now, let's add (inside our inventory slot circle panel) a yellow star icon image. Add a UI Image object to the scene (**GameObject | UI | Image**). Rename it `Image-icon`. Make `Panel-inventory-slot` a child of the `Image-icon` GameObject.

Child GameObjects can be hidden, making the GameObject **inactive**. By creating a new **UI Image** GameObject for our star icon and adding it as a child of our `Panel-inventory-slot` GameObject, we can now display the star icon when the image is enabled and hide it by making it inactive. This is a general approach, which means that so long as we have a reference to the **Image** GameObject, we don't have to do extra work swapping images, as we had to do in some of the previous recipes. This means we can start writing more general-purpose code that will work with different inventory panels for keys, stars, money, and so on.

13. With `Image-icon` selected in the **Hierarchy** window, drag the `icon_star_100` sprite (in the `Sprites` folder) from the **Project** window into the **Source Image** field in the **Inspector** window (in the **Image (Script)** component).

14. Edit **Rect Transform** of `Image-icon` and, while holding down *Shift + Alt* (to set its pivot and position), choose the **stretch-stretch** box. The star icon should now be stretched enough that it fits inside the `70x70` parent panel, so that we can see a star inside the circle:

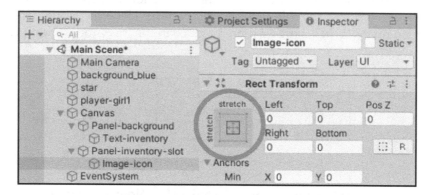

Figure 3.21 – Rect Transform settings of Image-icon

15. Save and run the scene and play the game. You should see a clearly defined rectangle at the top of the screen, with **Inventory** as the title text. Inside the inventory rectangular area, you will see a circular slot, currently showing a star.

16. Let's display three slots to the player. First, change the **Pos X** horizontal position of the `Panel-inventory-slot` panel to -70. This moves it left of center, making space for the next one, and allowing us to center the three slots when we've finished.

17. Duplicate the `Panel-inventory-slot` panel, renaming (if necessary) the copy `Panel-inventory-slot (1)`. Set **Pos X** of this copy to 0.

18. Duplicate `Panel-inventory-slot` again, this time renaming (if necessary) the copy `Panel-inventory-slot (2)`. Set **Pos X** of this copy to 70. Now, select the `Image-star-icon` child of this third panel and make it inactive (at the top of the **Inspector** window, uncheck its active checkbox, to the left of the GameObject's name). The star for this panel should now be hidden so that only the circle background of the slot's panel is visible.

How it works...

In this recipe, we created one simple panel (Panel-background) with the title UI Text as a child GameObject at the top of the game canvas, which shows a grayish background rectangle and the some title text stating **Inventory**. This indicates to the player that this part of the screen is where the inventory HUD will be displayed.

To illustrate how this might be used to indicate a player carrying stars, we added a smaller panel for one slot in the inventory with a circular background image and in that, added a star icon a child GameObject. We then duplicated the slot panel two more times, positioning them 70 pixels apart. After that, we disabled (made inactive) the star icon of the third slot so that an empty slot circle is shown.

Our scene presents the user with a display, indicating that two out of a possible three stars are being carried. This recipe is a good start to a more general-purpose approach to creating inventory UIs in Unity, and we'll build on this in some of the other recipes in this chapter.

We'll learn how to limit the player's movement to prevent their character from moving into the rectangles of HUD items like this in *Chapter 9, Controlling and Choosing Positions*.

Creating a C# inventory slot UI to display scripted components

In the previous recipe, we started to work with UI panels and images to create a more general-purpose GameObject for displaying inventory slots, as well as images to indicate what is stored in them. In this recipe, we will take things a little further with the graphics and also create a C# script class that works with each inventory slot object:

Figure 3.22 – Example showing two items, each with three slots

As shown in the preceding screenshot, in this recipe, we'll create a UI (and scripts) for an inventory that has three locations for stars, and three more for keys, using colored and gray icons to indicate how many have been collected.

Getting ready

This recipe adapts the previous one. So, make a copy of the project from the previous recipe and work on this copy.

For this recipe, we have prepared a folder named _Scripts in the 03_06 folder.

How to do it...

To create a C# inventory slot display script component, follow these steps:

1. Import the _Scripts folder from the provided files (this contains a copy of the PlayerInventory script class from one of the previous recipes, which we can use unchanged for this recipe).

2. Delete two of the three inventory slot GameObjects – that is, Panel-inventory-slot (1) and Panel-inventory-slot (2) – so that only Panel-inventory-slot remains.

3. First, we'll create a panel for three star slots. In the **Hierarchy** window, create a UI Panel (**Create** | **UI** | **Panel**) and rename it Panel-stars.

4. We'll now position Panel-stars at the top-left of the **Game** window and make it fit within the left-hand side of our general inventory rectangle. Edit the UI Image's **Rect Transform** component and, while holding down *Shift* + *Alt* (to set its pivot and position), choose the **top-left** box. Now, set **Width** to 300 and **Height** to 60. We'll nudge this away from the top-left corner by setting **Pos X** to 10 and **Pos Y** to -30.

5. Add a UI Text object (**Create** | **UI** | **Text**) and rename it Text-title. For its **Text (Script)** component, change the text to Stars. Make Panel-stars a child of this.

6. Edit **Rect Transform** of Text-title and, while holding down *Shift* + *Alt* (to set its pivot and position), choose the **left-middle** box. The text should now be positioned to the left of Panel-stars.

7. In the **Inspector** window, set the font of `Text-title` to **Xolonium-Bold** (this can be found in the `Fonts` folder). Center the text horizontally, **center-align** the text vertically, set its **Height** to 50, and set **Font Size** to 32. Choose a **yellow** text color. Set **Vertical-overflow** to **Overflow** and set **Alignment** vertical to **center**. We'll now nudge this away from the very left edge by setting **Pos X** to 10.

8. Make `Panel-stars` a child of `Panel-inventory-slot`. Edit its **Rect Transform** and, while holding down *Shift + Alt* (to set its pivot and position), choose the **left-middle** box.

9. Resize `Panel-inventory-slot` so that its **Width** and **Height** are both 50 x 50 pixels. Set its **Pos X** to 140. It should now appear to the right of the yellow **Stars** text:

Figure 3.23 – Text position in relation to Panel-inventory-slot

10. Rename the `Image-icon` GameObject `Image-icon-grey`. Then, duplicate this GameObject, naming the copy `Image-icon-color`. Both should be child GameObjects of `Panel-inventory-slot`. In the **Hierarchy** window, the sequence should be that the first child is `Image-icon-grey` and the second child is `Image-icon-color`. If this isn't the order, then swap them around.

11. Select `Image-icon-grey` and drag the `icon_star_grey_100` sprite (in the `Sprites` folder) from the **Project** window into the **Source Image** field of the **Inspector** window (in the **Image (Script)** component). Now, if you disable the `Image-icon-color` GameObject, you should see the gray star icon inside the slot panel's circle.

12. Create a C# script called `PickupUI` (a copy can be found in the `_Scripts` folder).

13. Add an instance of the `PickupUI` C# script as a component to the GameObject of `Panel-inventory-slot` in the **Hierarchy** window:

```
using UnityEngine;
using System.Collections;

public class PickupUI : MonoBehaviour {
    public GameObject iconColor;
    public GameObject iconGrey;

    void Awake() {
        DisplayEmpty();
    }

    public void DisplayColorIcon() {
        iconColor.SetActive(true);
        iconGrey.SetActive(false);
    }

    public void DisplayGreyIcon() {
        iconColor.SetActive(false);
        iconGrey.SetActive(true);
    }

    public void DisplayEmpty() {
        iconColor.SetActive(false);
        iconGrey.SetActive(false);
    }
}
```

14. Select `Panel-inventory-slot` in the **Hierarchy** window. In the **Inspector** window, for the **Pickup UI (Script)** component, populate the **Icon Color** public field by dragging `Image-icon-color` from **Hierarchy**. Likewise, populate the **Icon Grey** public field by dragging `Image-icon-grey` from **Hierarchy**. Now, the scripted `PickupUI` component in `Panel-inventory-slot` has references to the colored and gray icons for this inventory slot GameObject.

15. Duplicate `Panel-inventory-slot` and for the new duplicate GameObject, set its **Pos X** to 190.

16. Duplicate `Panel-inventory-slot` for a second time and set its **Pos X** to `240`. You should now see all three star inventory icons lined up nicely spaced to the right of the yellow **Stars** title text:

Figure 3.24 – Panel-inventory-slot showing three star inventory icons lined up

17. Add the following C# script, called `PlayerInventoryDisplay`, to the `player-girl1` GameObject in the **Hierarchy** window:

```
using UnityEngine;
using System.Collections;
using UnityEngine.UI;

[RequireComponent(typeof(PlayerInventory))]
public class PlayerInventoryDisplay : MonoBehaviour
{
  public PickupUI[] slots = new PickupUI[1];

  public void OnChangeStarTotal(int starTotal)
  {
    int numInventorySlots = slots.Length;
    for (int i = 0; i < numInventorySlots; i++)
    {
      PickupUI slot = slots[i];
      if (i < starTotal)
        slot.DisplayColorIcon();
      else
        slot.DisplayGreyIcon();
    }
  }
}
```

18. From the **Hierarchy** window, select the `player-girl1` GameObject. Then, do the following in the **Inspector** window for the **Player Inventory Display (Script)** component:
    - Set **Size** of the **slots** public array to `3`.
    - Populate the **Element 0** public field with the `Panel-inventory-slot` GameObject.
    - Populate the **Element 1** public field with the `Panel-inventory-slot (1)` GameObject.

- Populate the **Element 2** public field with the `Panel-inventory-slot (2)` GameObject:

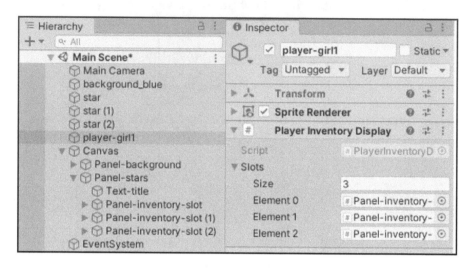

Figure 3.25 – Populating the public fields of Player Inventory Display (Script)

19. Finally, make two more copies of the `star` GameObject in the scene and move them around. So, there are now three GameObjects tagged **Star** for the player to collect.
20. When you run the game and the player's character hits each `star` GameObject, it should be removed from the scene, and the next free inventory star icon should change from gray to yellow.

How it works...

In this recipe, we created a panel (`Panel-stars`) in which to display the large **Stars** title text and three inventory slot panels to show how many stars can be collected, as well as how many have been collected at any point in the game. Each star panel slot is a UI Panel with a circular **Knob** background image and two children, one showing a gray icon image and a second showing a colored icon image. When the colored icon image GameObject is disabled, it will be hidden, which reveals the gray icon. When both the colored and gray images are disabled, then an empty circle will be shown, which could, perhaps, be used to indicate to the user that a general-purpose location is empty and available in the inventory.

The `PickupUI` script class has two public variables that are references to the gray and colored icons for the GameObject they relate to. Before the scene starts (the `Awake()` method is used), the script hides the gray and colored icons and displays an empty circle. This script class declares three public methods (they are public so that they can be invoked from another scripted object when the game is running). These methods hide/reveal the appropriate icons to display the related inventory panel UI object as either empty, gray, or colored. The methods are clearly named `DisplayEmpty()`, `DisplayGreyIcon()`, and `DisplayColorIcon()`.

The `PlayerInventory` script class maintains an integer total, `starTotal`, of how many stars have been collected (initialized to zero). Each time the player character collides with an object, if that object is tagged as **Star**, the `AddStar()` method is invoked. This method increments the total and sends a message, passing the new total to the `OnChangeStarTotal(...)` method of its sibling scripted component, `PlayerInventoryDisplay`.

The `PlayerInventoryDisplay` script class contains a public array of references to `PickupUI` objects, and a single public method called `OnChangeStarTotal(...)`. This method loops through its array of `PickupUI` scripted objects, setting them to display color icons while the loop counter is less than the number of stars carried, and thereafter setting them to display gray icons. This results in the color icons being displayed to match the number of stars being carried.

Note: It might seem that we could make our code simpler by assuming that slots always display gray (no star) and just change one slot to yellow each time a yellow star is picked up. But this would lead to problems if something happens in the game (for example, hitting a black hole or being shot by an alien) that makes us drop one or more stars. The C# `PlayerInventoryDisplay` script class makes no assumptions about which slots may or may not have been displayed as gray, yellow, or empty previously. Each time it is called, it ensures that an appropriate number of yellow stars are displayed, and that all the other slots are displayed with gray stars.

The UI Panel GameObject's slots for the three stars have `PickupUI` scripted components, with each linked to its gray and colored icons.

Several `star` GameObjects are added to the scene (all tagged **Star**). The array of PickupUI object references in the `PlayerInventoryDisplay` scripted component in the `player-SpaceGirl` GameObject is populated with references to the PickupUI scripted components in the three UI Panels for each star.

There's more...

Here are some details you won't want to miss.

Modifying the game for a second inventory panel for keys

We have created a great display panel for collecting star objects. Now, we can reuse what we've done to create a second panel to display the collection of key objects in the game.

To modify the game to make a second inventory panel for key collection, do the following:

1. Duplicate the `Panel-stars` GameObject, naming the copy `Panel-keys`.
2. With `Panel-keys` selected in the **Hierarchy** window, do the following:
     - Change **Text (Script)** of the **Text-title** child from **Stars** to `Keys`.
     - Ensuring `Panel-keys` is still selected, in **Rect Transform**, choose **top-right**, set **Pos X** to -10 (to move away from the right edge), and set **Pos Y** to -30 (to vertically align with `Panel-keys`).
     - For each `Image-icon-grey` GameObject that is a child of all three panel-inventory-slots, change **Image (Script) Source Image** to `icon_key_grey_100`.
     - For each `Image-icon-color` GameObject that is a child of all three panel-inventory-slots, change **Image (Script) Source Image** to `icon_key_green_100`.
     - For all the `Image-icon-grey` GameObjects and the `Image-icon-color` GameObjects that are children of all three panel-inventory-slots, in **Rect Transform**, set **Scale** to (0.75, 0.75, 1). We're doing this to make the key images fit fully inside the background panel circle images.

3. Remove the `PlayerInventory` and `PlayerInventoryDisplay` script components from the `player-girl1` GameObject.

4. Create the following C# script, called `PlayerInventoryKeys`, in the `_Scripts` folder:

```
using UnityEngine;

public class PlayerInventoryKeys : MonoBehaviour {
    private int starTotal = 0;
    private int keyTotal = 0;
    private PlayerInventoryDisplayKeys playerInventoryDisplay;

    void Awake() {
        playerInventoryDisplay =
            GetComponent<PlayerInventoryDisplayKeys>();
    }

    void Start() {
        playerInventoryDisplay.OnChangeStarTotal(starTotal);
        playerInventoryDisplay.OnChangeKeyTotal(keyTotal);
    }

    void OnTriggerEnter2D(Collider2D hit) {
        if(hit.CompareTag("Star")){
            AddStar();
            Destroy(hit.gameObject);
        }

        if(hit.CompareTag("Key")){
            AddKey();
            Destroy(hit.gameObject);
        }
    }

    private void AddStar() {
        starTotal++;
        playerInventoryDisplay.OnChangeStarTotal(starTotal);
    }

    private void AddKey() {
        keyTotal++;
        playerInventoryDisplay.OnChangeKeyTotal(keyTotal);
    }
}
```

5. Add the following C# script, called `PlayerInventoryDisplayKeys`, to the `player-SpaceGirl` GameObject in the **Hierarchy** window:

```csharp
using UnityEngine;

[RequireComponent(typeof(PlayerInventoryKeys))]
public class PlayerInventoryDisplayKeys : MonoBehaviour   {
    public PickupUI[] slotsStars = new PickupUI[1];
    public PickupUI[] slotsKeys = new PickupUI[1];

    public void OnChangeStarTotal(int starTotal) {
        int numInventorySlots = slotsStars.Length;
        for(int i = 0; i < numInventorySlots; i++){
            PickupUI slot = slotsStars[i];
            if(i < starTotal)
                slot.DisplayColorIcon();
            else
                slot.DisplayGreyIcon();
        }
    }

    public void OnChangeKeyTotal(int keyTotal) {
        int numInventorySlots = slotsKeys.Length;
        for(int i = 0; i < numInventorySlots; i++){
            PickupUI slot = slotsKeys[i];
            if(i < keyTotal)
                slot.DisplayColorIcon();
            else
                slot.DisplayGreyIcon();
        }
    }
}
```

6. With `player-girl1` selected in the **Hierarchy** window, for its `PlayerInventoryDisplayKeys` scripted component, set both `slotsKeys` and `slotsStars` to 3 (making the size of each of these arrays 3). Then, drag the corresponding inventory-slot GameObjects from the **Hierarchy** window to populate these arrays.

7. Create a new GameObject called `key` by dragging a copy of the `icon-key-green-100` sprite image from the **Project** window into the scene. Then, add a **Box Collider** component (**Physics 2D**) and tick its **Is Trigger** setting. In its **Sprite Renderer** component, set **Sorting Layer** to **Foreground**. Create a new **Tag** called `Key` and add it to this GameObject.

8. Make two duplicates of the `key` GameObject, moving them to different locations in the scene (so that the player can see all three stars and all three keys).

As you can see, we have duplicated and adjusted the visual UI Panel and components of the star carrying inventory to give us a second one for the key carrying inventory. Likewise, we have added code to detect collisions with objects tagged as `Key` and added this to the inventory display script to update the UI Panel for keys, when notified that a change has been made in terms of the number of keys being carried.

Using UI Grid Layout Groups to automatically populate a panel

So far, the recipes in this chapter have been hand-crafted for each situation. While this is fine, more general and automated approaches to inventory UIs can sometimes save time and effort but still achieve visual and usability results of equal quality.

There can be a lot of dragging slots from the **Hierarchy** window into arrays, such as in the previous recipe for the `PlayerInventoryDisplay` scripted component. This takes a bit of work (and mistakes might be made when dragging items in the wrong order or the same item twice). Also, if we change the number of slots, then we may have to do this all over again or try to remember to drag more slots if we increase the number. A better way of doing things is to make the first task of `PlayerInventoryDisplay`, at runtime, create as many of the panels for the gray-color star (or key or whatever) icon GameObjects as required children of **Panel-slot-grid**, and then populate the array of the scripted component that's displayed:

Figure 3.26 – Example of Unity's Grid Layout Group component for an inventory

In this recipe, we will explore a more engineered approach to inventory UIs by exploiting the automated sizing and layouts offered by Unity's Grid Layout Group component. Some enhancements that we'll look at at the end of this recipe include adding an interactive scroll bar, as shown in the preceding screenshot.

Getting ready

This recipe adapts the previous one. So, make a copy of the project from the previous recipe and work on this copy.

How to do it...

To automatically populate a panel using UI Grid Layout Groups, follow these steps:

1. Create a new folder named `Prefabs`.

2. From the **Hierarchy** window, drag the `Panel-inventory-slot` GameObject into your new empty prefab named **panel-inventory-slot**. This prefab should now turn blue, showing it is populated.

3. In the **Hierarchy** window, delete the three GameObjects; that is, `Panel-inventory-slot / (1) / (2)`.

4. Un-child `Text-title` from `Panel-stars`. Set the **Pos-X** position of `Panel-stars` to `130` so that the panel is now to the right of the **Stars** text.

5. With the **Panel-stars** panel selected in the **Hierarchy** window, add a grid layout group component (**Add Component | Layout | Grid Layout Group**). Set **Cell Size** to `50 x 50` and **Spacing** to `5 x 5`. Also, set **Child Alignment** to **Middle Center** (so that our icons will have even spacing at the far left and right), as shown in the following screenshot:

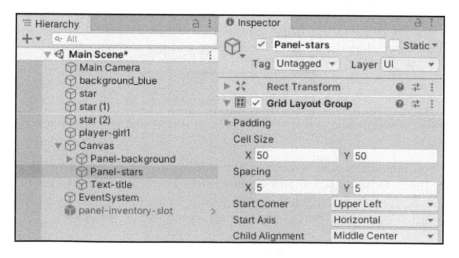

Figure 3.27 – Settings for Grid Layout Group

6. Replace the C# script class called `PlayerInventoryDisplay` in the `player-girl` GameObject with the following code:

```
using UnityEngine;
using System.Collections;
using UnityEngine.UI;

[RequireComponent(typeof(PlayerInventory))]
public class PlayerInventoryDisplay : MonoBehaviour   {
   const int NUM_INVENTORY_SLOTS = 5;
   public GameObject panelSlotGrid;
   public GameObject starSlotPrefab;
   private PickupUI[] slots = new
PickupUI[NUM_INVENTORY_SLOTS];

   void Awake() {
        float width = 50 + (NUM_INVENTORY_SLOTS * 50);
        panelSlotGrid.GetComponent<RectTransform>
            ().SetSizeWithCurrentAnchors(
RectTransform.Axis.Horizontal,
                width );

        for(int i=0; i < NUM_INVENTORY_SLOTS; i++){
            GameObject starSlotGO = (GameObject)
            Instantiate(starSlotPrefab);
starSlotGO.transform.SetParent(panelSlotGrid.transform);
            starSlotGO.transform.localScale = new
Vector3(1,1,1);
            slots[i] = starSlotGO.GetComponent<PickupUI>();
        }
    }

    public void OnChangeStarTotal(int starTotal) {
        for(int i = 0; i < NUM_INVENTORY_SLOTS; i++){
            PickupUI slot = slots[i];
            if(i < starTotal)
                slot.DisplayColorIcon();
            else
                slot.DisplayGreyIcon();
        }
    }
}
```

7. Ensure `player-girl1` is selected in the **Hierarchy** window. Then, from the **Project** window, drag the `Panel-stars` GameObject into the **Player Inventory Display (Script)** variable's **Panel-slot-grid**, in the **Inspector** window.

8. With `player-girl1` selected in the **Hierarchy** window, from the **Project** panel, drag the `panel-inventory-slot` prefab into the **Player Inventory Display (Script)** variable's **Star Slot Prefab**, in the **Inspector** window:

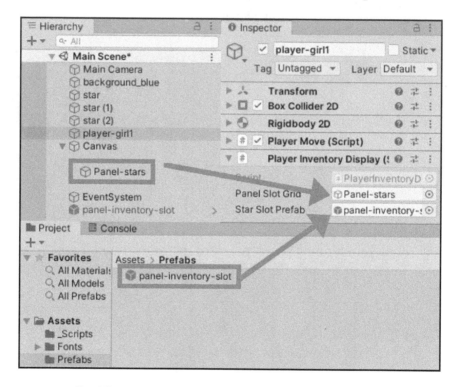

Figure 3.28 – Linking the specified GameObject and Prefab to Player Inventory Display (Script)

9. Edit the `PlayerInventoryDisplay` script class by setting the `NUM_INVENTORY_SLOTS` constant so that it has 10 or 15 slots. This ensures that some can only be seen when using the horizontal scroll bar.

10. Save the scene and play the game. As you pick up stars, you should see more of the gray stars change to yellow in the inventory display.

How it works...

In this recipe, we took one of the panels that contained the **Knob** circle background, as well as the children GameObjects of the gray and colored star images, and used it to create a prefab called `panel-inventory-slot`. We then removed the `Panel-stars` GameObjects from the scene since our `PlayerInventoryDisplay` script class will create as many of these as needed when the scene begins. This approach saves a lot of dragging and dropping, saving **design-time** effort, and also eliminating one possible source of sequence/object reference errors when the design of a scene is changed.

The C# `PlayerInventoryDisplay` script class has two properties:

- A constant integer (`NUM_INVENTORY_SLOTS`) for defining the number of slots in our inventory, which we set to 5 for this game.
- A (`slots`) array of references to `PickupUI` scripted components. Each of these will become a reference to the scripted component in each of the five `Panel-inventory-slot` GameObjects in `Panel-stars`.

The `Awake()` method is used to create instances of the prefab in `PlayerInventoryDispay` so that we know this will be executed before the `Start()` method in `PlayerInventory`. This is because no `Start()` method is executed in a scene until all the `Awake()` methods for all the GameObjects in the scene have been completed. First, the `Awake()` method calculates the width of `Panel-stars` (50 + (50 * the number of inventory slots)). Next, the panel is resized to have that width, using the `SetSizeWithCurrentAnchors()` method. Then, a loop runs for the number of slots in the inventory, each time creating a new star slot GameObject from the prefab, childing the new GameObject to `Panel-stars`, and adding a reference to the icon slot GameObject in array slots. When the `OnChangeStarTotal(...)` method is passed the number of stars we are carrying, it loops through each of the five slots. While the current slot is less than our star total, a yellow star is displayed by calling the `DisplayYellow()` method of the current slot (`PickupUI` scripted component). Once the loop counter is equal to or larger than our star total, all the remaining slots are made to display a gray star via the `DisplayGrey()` method.

Our player character GameObject, `player-girl1`, has a very basic `PlayerInventory` script. This just detects collisions with objects tagged as Star, and when this happens, it removes the `star` GameObject that was collided with and calls the `AddStar()` method of its `playerInventoryModel` scripted component.

Each time the `AddStar()` method is called, it increments (adds 1) to the total number of stars being carried, and then calls the `OnChangeStarTotal(...)` method of the `playerInventoryDisplay` scripted component. Also, when the scene starts, an initial call is made to the `OnChangeStarTotal(...)` method so that the UI display for the inventory is set up to show that we are initially carrying no stars.

The public array has been made private and no longer needs to be populated through manually dragging and dropping. When you run the game, it will play just the same as it did previously, with the process of populating the array of images in our inventory grid panel now automated. The `Awake()` method creates new instances of the prefab (as many as there are defined by the `NUM_INVENTORY_SLOTS` constant) and immediately makes them children of `Panel-slot-grid`. Since we have a grid layout group component, their placement is automatically neat and tidy in our panel.

 The scale property of the transform components of GameObjects is reset when a GameObject changes its parent (to keep the child's size relative to the parent's size). So, it is a good idea to always reset the local scale of GameObjects to (`1`,`1`,`1`) immediately after they have been set as the children of another GameObject. We do this in the `for` loop of `starSlotGO` that follows the `SetParent(...)` statement.

There's more...

Here are some details you won't want to miss.

Automatically inferring the number of inventory slots based on the number of GameObjects tagged Star

Rather than having to manually change the `NUM_INVENTORY_SLOTS` Integer constant in the `PlayerInventoryDisplay` script class to match the number of GameObjects that have been created in the scene for the player to collect, let's have our script count how many GameObjects are tagged Star, and then use this to size and populate our array of references to inventory UI panel slots.

We just need to change from a constant to a variable for our array size and set that variable before anything else in our `Awake()` method. The `GameObject.FindGameObjectsWithTag("Star")` statement gets an array of references to all GameObjects tagged with Star, and its length is the array size we want:

1. Replace the C# `PlayerInventoryDisplay` script class in the `player-SpaceGirl` GameObject with the following code:

```
using UnityEngine;
using System.Collections;
using UnityEngine.UI;

[RequireComponent(typeof(PlayerInventory))]
public class PlayerInventoryDisplay : MonoBehaviour  {
    private int numInventorySlots;
    private PickupUI[] slots;
    public GameObject panelSlotGrid;
    public GameObject starSlotPrefab;

    void Awake() {
        GameObject[] gameObjectsTaggedStar =
            GameObject.FindGameObjectsWithTag("Star");
        numInventorySlots = gameObjectsTaggedStar.Length;
        slots = new PickupUI[numInventorySlots];
        float width = 50 + (numInventorySlots * 50);
        panelSlotGrid.GetComponent<RectTransform>
            ().SetSizeWithCurrentAnchors(
RectTransform.Axis.Horizontal,
                width);

        for(int i=0; i < numInventorySlots; i++){
            GameObject starSlotGO = (GameObject)
            Instantiate(starSlotPrefab);
starSlotGO.transform.SetParent(panelSlotGrid.transform);
            starSlotGO.transform.localScale = new
Vector3(1,1,1);
            slots[i] = starSlotGO.GetComponent<PickupUI>();
        }
    }

    public void OnChangeStarTotal(int starTotal) {
        for(int i = 0; i < numInventorySlots; i++){
            PickupUI slot = slots[i];
            if(i < starTotal)
                slot.DisplayColorIcon();
            else
```

```
                                        slot.DisplayGreyIcon();
                    }
              }
        }
```

2. Add or remove some of the duplicates of the `star` GameObject so that the total is no longer 5.

3. Run the scene. You should see the size and contents of `Panel-star` change to match the number of GameObjects tagged as Star when the scene begins.

Adding a horizontal scroll bar to the inventory slot display

How can we cope with many inventory slots that don't fit in the space provided? One solution is to add a scroll bar so that the user can scroll left and right, viewing five at a time, say, as shown in the following screenshot:

Figure 3.29 – Example game with a horizontal scroll bar

Let's add a horizontal scroll bar to our game. This can be achieved without making any C# code changes; that is, everything can be done through the Unity UI system.

To implement a horizontal scroll bar for our inventory display, we need to do the following:

1. First, increase **Height** of `Panel-background` to `110` pixels.

2. In the **Inspector** window, set the **Child Alignment** property of the **Grid Layout Group (Script)** component of `Panel-slot-grid` to **upper-left**. Then, move this panel to the right a little so that the inventory icons are centered on the screen.

3. Add a UI Panel to **Canvas** and name it `Panel-scroll-container`. Then, give it a red tint by setting the **Color** property of its **Image (Script)** component to red.

4. In the **Hierarchy** window, drag `Panel-slot-grid` so that it is now a child of `Panel-scroll-container`.

5. Set the size and position of `Panel-scroll-container` so that it is just behind our `Panel-slot-grid`. To do this, set its **Rect Transform** to **top-left**, **Pos X** to 130, **Pos Y** to −30, **Width** to 300, and **Height** to 60. You should now see a red rectangle behind the `Panel-slot-grid` inventory panel.

6. Add a **UI Mask** to `Panel-scroll-container` so that you can only see the parts of `Panel-slot-grid` that fit within the rectangle of this red-tinted panel.

> One workflow is to temporarily set this mask component as inactive so that you can see and work on the unseen parts of `Panel-slot-grid` if required.

7. Add a **UI Scrollbar** to **Canvas** and name it `Scrollbar-horizontal`. Move it so that it's just below the red-tinted `Panel-scroll-container` and resize it so that it's the same width, as shown in the following screenshot:

Figure 3.30 – Example of the UI Scrollbar included in Canvas

8. Add a UI **Scroll Rect** component to `Panel-scroll-container`. Uncheck the **Vertical** property of this **Scroll Rect** component.

9. In the **Inspector** window, drag **Scrollbar-horizontal** to the **Horizontal Scrollbar** property of the **Scroll Rect** component of **Panel-scroll-container**.

10. In the **Inspector** window, drag `Panel-slot-grid` to the **Content** property of the **Scroll Rect** component of `Panel-scroll-container`, as shown in the following screenshot:

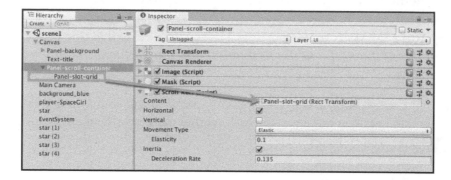

Figure 3.31 – Dragging Panel-slot-grid to the Content property

11. Now, ensure that the mask component of `Panel-scroll-container` is set as active so that we don't see an overflow of `Panel-slot-grid` and uncheck this mask component's option to **Show Mask Graphic** (so that we don't see the red rectangle anymore).

You should now have a working scrollable inventory system.

Automatically changing the grid cell size based on the number of slots in the inventory

Consider a situation where we wish to change the number of slots. An alternative to using scrollbars is changing the cell size in the **Grid Layout Group** component. We can automate this through code so that the cell size is changed to ensure that `NUM_INVENTORY_SLOTS` will fit the width of our panel, at the top of the canvas.

To automatically resize the cell size of **Grid Layout Group** for this recipe, we need to do the following:

1. Comment out the third statement in the `Awake()` method for the C# `PlayerInventoryDisplay` script class:

```
//
panelSlotGrid.GetComponent<RectTransform>().SetSizeWithCurrent
Anchors(
// RectTransform.Axis.Horizontal, width);
```

2. Add the following `Start()` method to `PlayerInventoryDisplay` in the `player-girl1` GameObject with the following code:

```
void Start() {
    float panelWidth = panelSlotGrid.GetComponent<RectTransform>
        ().rect.width;
    print ("slotGrid.GetComponent<RectTransform>().rect = " +
        panelSlotGrid.GetComponent<RectTransform>().rect);
    GridLayoutGroup gridLayoutGroup =
        panelSlotGrid.GetComponent<GridLayoutGroup>();
    float xCellSize = panelWidth / NUM_INVENTORY_SLOTS;
    xCellSize -= gridLayoutGroup.spacing.x;
    gridLayoutGroup.cellSize = new Vector2(xCellSize,
xCellSize);
}
```

We write our code in the `Start()` method, rather than adding it to the `Awake()` method, to ensure that **RectTransform** of the `Panel-slot-grid` GameObject has finished sizing (in this recipe, it stretches based on the width of the **Game** window). While we can't know the sequence in which **Hierarchy** GameObjects are created when a scene begins, we can rely on the Unity behavior that every GameObject sends the `Awake()` message, and that only after all corresponding `Awake()` methods have finished executing all objects does it send the `Start()` message. So, any code in the `Start()` method can safely assume that every GameObject has been initialized:

Figure 3.32 – Example of automatically changing the grid size based on the number of slots

The preceding screenshot shows that the value of NUM_INVENTORY_SLOTS has been changed to 15, and that the cell size has been corresponding changed so that all 15 now fit horizontally in our panel. Note that the spacing between cells is subtracted from what's available, divided by the number of slots (xCellSize `-=` gridLayoutGroup.spacing.x), since that spacing is needed between each item that's displayed as well.

Displaying multiple pickups of different objects as a list of text via a dynamic list of scripted PickUp objects

When working with different kinds of pickups, one approach is to use a C# `List` to maintain a flexible-length data structure containing the items currently in the inventory. In this recipe, we will show you how, each time an item is picked up, a new object is added to such a `List` collection. An iteration through the `List` will show how the text display for items is generated each time the inventory changes. Here, we will introduce a very simple `PickUp` script class, demonstrating how information about a pickup can be stored in a scripted component, extracted upon collision, and stored in our `List`:

Figure 3.33 – Example of the UI displaying multiple pickups of different objects

Getting ready

This recipe assumes that you are starting with the `Simple2Dgame_SpaceGirl` project, which we set up in the first recipe of this chapter.

The font you need can be found in the `03_02` folder.

How to do it...

To display the inventory total text for multiple pickups of different object types, follow these steps:

1. Start with a new copy of the `Simple2Dgame_SpaceGirl` mini-game.

2. Edit the tags, changing `star` to `Pickup`. Ensure that the `star` GameObject now has the **Pickup** tag:

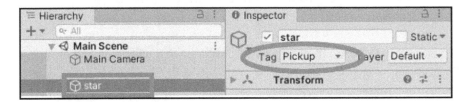

Figure 3.34 – Changing star to Pickup

3. Add the following C# `PickUp` script class to the `star` GameObject in the **Hierarchy** window:

```
using UnityEngine;
using System.Collections;

public class PickUp : MonoBehaviour {
  public string description;
}
```

4. In the **Inspector** window, change the description property of the **PickUp (Script)** component of the `star` GameObject to `star`:

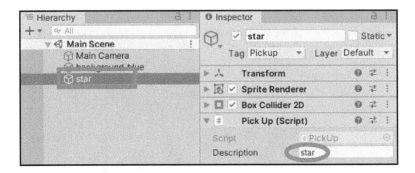

Figure 3.35 – Setting the description property of the PickUp (Script) component to star

5. Select the `star` GameObject in the **Hierarchy** window and make a copy of it, renaming the copy `heart`.

6. In the **Inspector** window, change the description property of the **Pick Up (Script)** component of the heart GameObject to heart. Also, drag the health heart image from the **Project** window (in the Sprites folder) into the **Sprite** property of the heart GameObject. The player should now see the heart image on the screen for this pickup item.

7. Select the star GameObject in the **Hierarchy** window and make a copy of it, renaming the copy key.

8. In the **Inspector** window, change the description property of the **Pick Up (Script)** component of the key GameObject to key. Also, drag the icon_key_green_100 image from the **Project** window (in the Sprites folder) into the **Sprite** property of the key GameObject. The player should now see the key image on the screen for this pickup item.

9. Make two more copies of each pickup GameObject and place them around the screen so that there are two or three each of the star, heart, and key pickup GameObjects.

10. Create the following C# PlayerInventory script class in the _Scripts folder:

```
using UnityEngine;
using System.Collections;
using UnityEngine.UI;
using System.Collections.Generic;

public class PlayerInventory : MonoBehaviour {
    private PlayerInventoryDisplay playerInventoryDisplay;
    private List<PickUp> inventory = new List<PickUp>();

    void Awake() {
        playerInventoryDisplay =
GetComponent<PlayerInventoryDisplay>
            ();
    }

    void Start() {
        playerInventoryDisplay.OnChangeInventory(inventory);
    }

    void OnTriggerEnter2D(Collider2D hit) {
        if(hit.CompareTag("Pickup")){
            PickUp item = hit.GetComponent<PickUp>();
            inventory.Add( item );
playerInventoryDisplay.OnChangeInventory(inventory);
            Destroy(hit.gameObject);
        }
```

```
        }
    }
```

11. Add a UI Text object (**Create | UI | Text**). Rename it `Text-inventory-list`. Change its text to `the quick brown fox jumped over the lazy dog`, or another long list of nonsense words, to test the overflow settings you'll change in the next step.

12. In the **Text (Script)** component, ensure that **Horizontal Overflow** is set to **Wrap**, and set **Vertical Overflow** to **Overflow**. This will ensure that the text will wrap onto a second or third line (if needed) and not be hidden if there are lots of pickups.

13. In the **Inspector** window, set its font to **Xolonium-Bold** (in the `Fonts` folder) and set its color to yellow. For the **Alignment** property, center the text horizontally and ensure that the text is top-aligned vertically. Then, set **Font Size** to 28.

14. Edit its **Rect Transform** and set its **Height** to 50. Then, while holding down *Shift + Alt* (to set its pivot and position), choose the **top-stretch** box. The text should now be positioned at the middle-top of the **Game** window, and its width should stretch to match that of the whole panel.

15. Your text should now appear at the top of the **Game** window.

Figure 3.36 – Example of how the text appears at the top of the Game window

16. Add the following C# `PlayerInventoryDisplay` script class to the `player-girl1` GameObject in the **Hierarchy** window:

```
using UnityEngine;
using System.Collections;
using UnityEngine.UI;
using System.Collections.Generic;

[RequireComponent(typeof(PlayerInventory))]
public class PlayerInventoryDisplay : MonoBehaviour {
    public Text inventoryText;

    public void OnChangeInventory(List<PickUp> inventory) {
        // (1) clear existing display
        inventoryText.text = "";

        // (2) build up new set of items
        string newInventoryText = "carrying: ";
        int numItems = inventory.Count;
        for(int i = 0; i < numItems; i++){
            string description = inventory[i].description;
            newInventoryText += " [" + description+ "]";
        }

        // if no items in List then set string to message
saying inventory is
            empty
        if(numItems < 1)
            newInventoryText = "(empty inventory)";

        // (3) update screen display
        inventoryText.text = newInventoryText;
    }
}
```

17. From the **Hierarchy** window, select the `player-girl1` GameObject. Then, from the **Inspector** window, access the **Player Inventory Display (Script)** component and populate the **Inventory Text** public field with the `Text-inventory-list` UI Text object.

18. Play the game. Each time you pick up a star, key, or heart, the updated list of what you are carrying should be displayed in the form **carrying [key] [heart]**.

How it works...

In the `PlayerInventory` script class, the variable inventory is a C# `List<>`. This is a flexible data structure that can be sorted, searched, and dynamically (at runtime, when the game is being played) have items added to and removed from it. `<PickUp>`, which is in pointy brackets, means that the variable inventory will contain a list of `PickUp` objects. For this recipe, our `PickUp` class just has a single field – a string description – but we'll add more sophisticated data items to the `PickUp` classes we'll look at in later recipes. This variable inventory has been initialized to be a new, empty C# `List` of `PickUp` objects.

Before the scene starts, the `Awake()` method of the `Player` script class caches a reference to the `PlayerInventoryDisplay` scripted component.

When the scene starts, the `Start()` method invokes the `OnChangeInventory(...)` method of the `PlayerInventoryDisplay` scripted component. This is so that the text that's displayed to the user at the beginning of the scene corresponds to the initial value of the variable inventory. (This might, for some games, not be empty. For example, a player might start a game with some money, or a basic weapon, or a map.)

When the `OnTriggerEnter2D(...)` method detects collisions with items tagged as `Pickup`, the `PickUp` object component of the item that's been hit is added to our inventory list. A call is also made to the `OnChangeInventory(...)` method of `playerInventoryDisplay` to update our inventory display to the player, passing the updated inventory `List` as a parameter.

The `playerInventoryDisplay` script class has a public variable that's linked to the `Text-inventory-list` UI Text object. First, the `OnChangeInventory(...)` method sets the UI Text object to empty, and then loops through the inventory list, building up a string of each item's description in square brackets (**[key]**, **[heart]**, and so on). If there were no items in the list, then the string is set to the text (empty inventory). Finally, the text property of `Text-inventory-list` is set to the value of this string representation; that is, what is inside the variable inventory.

There's more...

Here are some details you won't want to miss.

Ordering items in the inventory list alphabetically

It would be nice to alphabetically sort the words in the inventory list, both for neatness and consistency (so that, in a game, if we pick up a key and a heart, it will look the same, regardless of the order they are picked up in), but also so that items of the same type will be listed together so that we can easily see how many of each item we are carrying.

To implement alphabetical sorting for the items in the inventory list, we need to do the following:

1. Add the following C# code to the beginning of the OnChangeInventory(...) method in the PlayerInventoryDisplay script class:

```
public void OnChangeInventory(List<PickUp> inventory){
    inventory.Sort(
        delegate(PickUp p1, PickUp p2){
            return p1.description.CompareTo(p2.description);
        }
    );

    // rest of the method as before ...
}
```

2. You should now see all the items listed in alphabetical order.

This C# code takes advantage of the C# List.Sort(...) method, a feature of collections whereby each item can be compared to the next, and they are swapped if they're in the wrong order (if the CompareTo(...) methods return false). Learn more at https://msdn.microsoft.com/en-us/library/3da4abas(v=vs.110).aspx.

Using a Dictionary and Enums to display text totals for different objects

While the previous recipe worked fine, any old text could have been typed into the description of a pickup or perhaps mistyped (star, Sstar, starr, and so on). A much better way of restricting game properties to one of a predefined (enumerated) list of possible values is to use C# enums. As well as removing the possibility of mistyping a string, it also means that we can write code to deal with the predefined set of possible values. In this recipe, we will improve our general-purpose PickUp class by introducing three possible pickup types (Star, Heart, and Key), and write inventory display code that counts the number of each type of pickup being carried before displaying these totals via a UI Text object on the screen. We will also switch from using a List to using a Dictionary, since the Dictionary data structure is designed specifically for key-value pairs, which is perfect for associating a numeric total with an enumerated pickup type:

Figure 3.37 – Example of multiple pickups being implemented via a dynamic dictionary

In this recipe, we will also manage any additional complexity by separating the controller (user collection event) logic from the stored inventory data by introducing an inventory manager scripted class. By doing this, our player controller will be simplified to just containing two methods (Awake, for getting a reference to the inventory manager, and OnTriggerEnter2D, for responding to collisions by communicating with the inventory manager).

Getting ready

This recipe adapts the previous one. So, make a copy of the project from the previous recipe and work on this copy.

How to do it...

To display multiple pickups of different objects as text totals via a dynamic `Dictionary`, follow these steps:

1. Replace the content of the `PickUp` script class with the following code:

```
using UnityEngine;

public class PickUp : MonoBehaviour
{ public enum PickUpType { Star, Key, Heart }
public PickUpType type; }
```

2. Remove the instance of the `PlayerInventory` script class from the `player-SpaceGirl` GameObject.

3. Create a new C# script class called `PlayerController` containing the following code, and add an instance as a component of the `player-girl1` GameObject:

```
using UnityEngine;

public class PlayerController : MonoBehaviour {
    private InventoryManager inventoryManager;

    void Awake() {
        inventoryManager = GetComponent<InventoryManager>();
    }

    void OnTriggerEnter2D(Collider2D hit) {
        if(hit.CompareTag("Pickup")){
            PickUp item = hit.GetComponent<PickUp> ();
            inventoryManager.Add(item);
            Destroy(hit.gameObject);
        }
    }
}
```

4. Replace the content of the `PlayerInventoryDisplay` script class with the following code:

```
using UnityEngine;
using UnityEngine.UI;
using System.Collections.Generic;

[RequireComponent(typeof(PlayerController))]
[RequireComponent(typeof(InventoryManager))]
```

```
public class PlayerInventoryDisplay : MonoBehaviour {
    public Text inventoryText;

    public void OnChangeInventory(Dictionary<PickUp.PickUpType,
int>
        inventory) {
        inventoryText.text = "";
        string newInventoryText = "carrying: ";

        foreach (var item in inventory) {
            int itemTotal = item.Value;
            string description = item.Key.ToString();
            newInventoryText += " [ " + description + " " +
itemTotal + "
                    ]";
        }

        int numItems = inventory.Count;
        if (numItems < 1)
            newInventoryText = "(empty inventory)";

        inventoryText.text = newInventoryText;
    }
}
```

5. Add an instance of the C# `InventoryManager` script class to the `player-SpaceGirl` GameObject in the **Hierarchy** window:

```
using UnityEngine;
using System.Collections.Generic;

public class InventoryManager : MonoBehaviour {
    private PlayerInventoryDisplay playerInventoryDisplay;
    private Dictionary<PickUp.PickUpType, int> items = new
        Dictionary<PickUp.PickUpType, int>();

    void Awake() {
        playerInventoryDisplay =
GetComponent<PlayerInventoryDisplay>
            ();
    }

    void Start() {
        playerInventoryDisplay.OnChangeInventory(items);
    }

    public void Add(PickUp pickup) {
        PickUp.PickUpType type = pickup.type;
```

```
        int oldTotal = 0;

        if(items.TryGetValue(type, out oldTotal))
            items[type] = oldTotal + 1;
        else
            items.Add (type, 1);

        playerInventoryDisplay.OnChangeInventory(items);
    }
}
```

6. In the **Hierarchy** (or **Scene**) window, select *each pickup* GameObject in turn, and from their drop-down menus, choose their corresponding **Type** in the **Inspector** window. As you can see, public variables that are of the enum type are automatically restricted to the set of possible values as a combo box drop-down menu in the **Inspector** window:

Figure 3.38 – Setting the possible values as a combo box drop-down menu

7. Play the game. First, you should see a message on the screen stating that the inventory is empty. Then, as you pick up one or more items of each pickup type, you'll see text totals for each type you have collected.

How it works...

Each Pickup GameObject in the scene has a scripted component of the PickUp class. The PickUp object for each Pickup GameObject has a single property, a pickup type, which has to be one of the enumerated sets of Star, Key, or Heart. The use of an enumerated type means that the value has to be one of these three listed values, which means no misspelling/mistyping errors that could have happened with a general text string type can happen here, as in the previous recipe.

Previously, the PlayerInventory script class had two sets of responsibilities:

- Maintaining the internal record of items being carried.
- Detecting collisions, updating the state, and asking the display class to inform the player visually of the changed items being carried.

In this recipe, we separate these two sets of responsibilities into separate script classes:

- The InventoryManager script class will maintain the internal record of items being carried (and ask the display class to inform the player visually, each time a change is made to the items being carried).
- The PlayerController script class will detect collisions and ask InventoryManager to update what is being carried.

The addition of this extra software layer separates the player collision detection behavior from how the inventory is internally stored, and it also prevents any single script class from becoming too complex by attempting to handle too many different responsibilities. This recipe is an example of the low coupling of the MVC design pattern. We have designed our code to not rely on or make too many assumptions about other parts of the game, which reduces the likelihood of a change in some other part of our game breaking our inventory display code. The display (view) is separated from the logical representation of what we are carrying (inventory manager model), and changes to the model are made by public methods that are called from the player (controller).

The PlayerController script class gets a reference to the InventoryManager component via its Awake() method, and each time the player's character collides with a Pickup GameObject, it calls the Add(...) method of the inventory manager, passing the PickUp object of the object that was collided with.

In the InventoryManager script class, the inventory being carried by the player is represented by a C# Dictionary. A Dictionary is made up of a sequence of *key-value pairs*, where the key is one of the possible PickUp.PickUpType enumerated **values**, and the value is the integer total of how many of that type of pickup is being carried. This Dictionary states what type will be used for a key, and then what type (or script class) will be stored as the value for that key. The following statement is used to declare our Dictionary variable items:

```
items = new Dictionary<PickUp.PickUpType, int>()
```

C# dictionaries provide a `TryGetValue(...)` method, which receives the parameters of a key and is passed a reference to a variable the same data type as the value for the `Dictionary`. When the `Add(...)` method of the inventory manager is called, the type of the `PickUp` object is tested to see if a total for this type is already in the `Dictionary` items. If an item total is found inside the `Dictionary` for the given type, then the value for this item in the `Dictionary` is incremented. If no entry is found for the given type, then a new element is added to the `Dictionary` with a total of 1.

TryGetValue call-by-reference parameter

 Note the use of the C# `out` keyword before the `oldTotal` parameter in the `items.TryGetValue(type, out oldTotal)` statement. This indicates that a reference to the actual variable, `oldTotal`, is being passed to the `TryGetValue(...)` method, not just a copy of its value. This means that the method can change the value of the variable.

The method returns `true` if an entry is found in the `Dictionary` for the given type, and if so, sets the value of `oldTotal` to the value against this key.

The last action of the `Add(...)` method is to call the `OnChangeInventory(...)` method of the `PlayerInventoryDisplay` scripted component of the `player` GameObject. This will update the text totals that are displayed on the screen.

The `OnChangeInventory(...)` method of the `PlayerInventoryDisplay` script class initializes the `newInventoryText` string variable and then iterates through each item in the `Dictionary`, appending a string of the type name and total for the current item to `newInventoryText`. Finally, the text property of the UI Text object is updated with the completed text inside `newInventoryText`, showing the pickup totals to the player.

You can learn more about using C# lists and dictionaries in Unity in the Unity Technologies tutorial at `https://unity3d.com/learn/tutorials/modules/intermediate/scripting/lists-and-dictionaries`.

Creating a runtime UI Toolkit interface

First, there was **Immediate Mode GUI (IMGUI)**, where code was required for all UI development. For IMGUI, the UI was redrawn every frame. Then came **uGUI**, the current Unity UI system, which is a **retained-mode** system, where UI elements are created and stay in view until they're changed. While uGUI is fine for most **runtime** game requirements, an IMGUI approach is still needed for most **design-time** editor extensions. This is a retained-mode UI system, which can be used for both runtime and design-time UIs. The **UI Toolkit** has an XML file to describe the elements in the UI, and style-sheet files to specify how they will look and be laid out. If you are used to HTML and CSS, then you'll find UXML and USS very familiar. There is even a C# query system based on hierarchy matching that's similar to jQuery and LINQ (`https://docs.microsoft.com/en-us/dotnet/csharp/programming-guide/concepts/linq/`).

In this recipe, you'll learn how to install the **UI Tookit** (formerly UI Elements) runtime and **UI Builder** preview packages and learn how to create and style a simple UI, as well as create a GameObject with a **Panel Renderer** component to display the UI at runtime.

You can learn more about the different features of these three Unity UI systems in the Unity documentation: `https://docs.unity3d.com/2021.1/Documentation/Manual/UI-system-compare.html`.

Getting ready

This recipe requires both the **UI Toolkit** runtime package and **UI Builder** to be installed. At the time of writing, these are preview packages (scheduled for a stable release from Unity 2021.2) and must be installed via their URLs, as described in this recipe:

1. Display the **Package Manager** panel (**Window | Package Manager**).

2. Click the plus (+) button to add a package from files and select **Add package from git URL** from the drop-down menu:

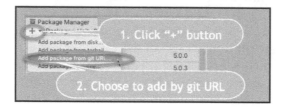

Figure 3.39 – Adding a package via git URL

3. To add the UI Toolkit package, enter `com.unity.ui` for the URL and click the **Add** button:

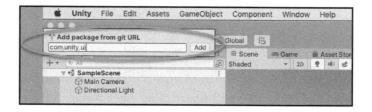

Figure 3.40 – Entering the git URL for the package to be added to the project

4. To add the UI Builder package, follow *step 2* again, but this time, enter `com.unity.ui.builder` for the URL and click the **Add** button.

5. You should now see both UI packages listed as installed for the current project:

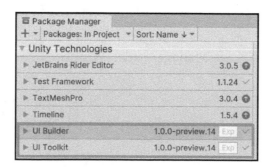

Figure 3.41 – Entering the Git URL for the package to be added to the project

How to do it...

To create a runtime UI Toolkit interface, follow these steps:

1. Create a new, empty 3D project.
2. Add the **UI Toolkit** and **UI Builder** packages to the project using **Package Manager** (see the *Getting ready* section).
3. Open the **UI Builder** panel and go to **Window | UI Toolkit | UI Builder**.
4. Rearrange the panels (personally, I follow the Unite Copenhagen demo layout):

- LEFT HALF: **UI Builder**
- RIGHT HALF: Top: **Scene** + **Game** + **Inspector** + **Console**, with **Game** showing
- RIGHT HALF: Bottom: **Hierarchy** + **Project**, with **Hierarchy** showing:

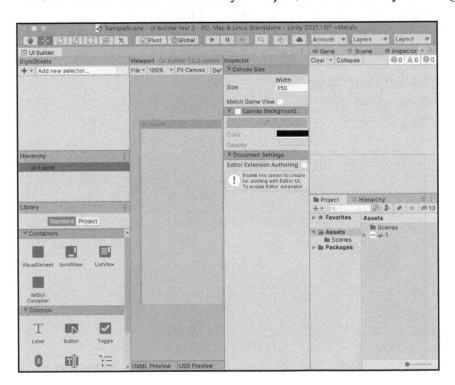

Figure 3.42 – The Unite Copenhagen panel layout for UI Builder workflows

5. **Viewport** is the center panel of the UI Builder. From its **File** menu, choose **Save** and save the current empty new document as `ui-1`. You'll see a `ui-1` UXML document appear in the **Project** window – it will have a child USS named **inline style**:

Figure 3.43 – Saving the current UI Build via its File | Save As menu

6. Add a button to your UI. Do this by dragging a **Button** from **Library Controls** (at the bottom left of the **UI Builder** panel) into **Viewport**.

7. In the **UI Builder Inspector** window (right column), set the following style properties for the button:

- **Background Color**: Yellow
- **Size**: 50% by 50%
- **Text size**: 20:

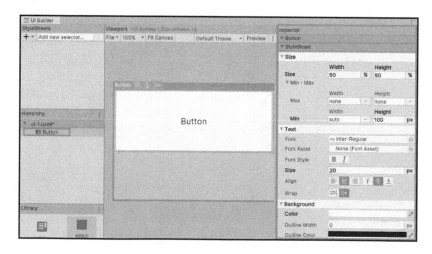

Figure 3.44 – Editing the Button properties in the UI Builder Inspector window

8. Save your UI (**Viewport File** menu: **Save**).

9. In the **Project** window, create a new **Panel Settings** asset file named `PanelSettings1` by going to **Create | UI Toolkit | Panel Settings**.

10. In the **Hierarchy** window, create a new empty GameObject named **GameUI**.

11. Ensure **GameUI** is selected in the **Hierarchy** window. In the **Inspector** window, add a new **UI Document** component. Also, add a new **Input System Event System (UI Toolkit)** component.

12. Ensure **GameUI** is selected in the **Hierarchy** window. Drag the `PanelSettings1` asset file from the **Project** window into the **Inspector** window for the **Panel Settings** variable slot of the GameUI's **UI Document** component.

13. Now, drag the `ui-1` asset file from the **Project** window into the **Inspector** window, for the **Panel Settings** variable slot of the GameUI's **Source Asset** component:

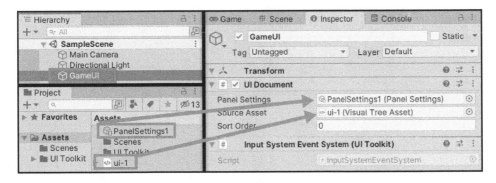

Figure 3.45 – UI Document Panel Settings and the UI asset variables for our scene's GameUI GameObject

14. Save the scene and run the game. You should see your large yellow button at the top left of the screen.

15. Let's add a parent UI element and have two button in a row by using a **Flex** layout.

16. Drag a Visual Element container into **UI Builder Hierarchy** and rename this row (it will appear as **#row** since element names are like HTML IDs) to **#row**.

17. Duplicate **Button** so that there are now two buttons that are children of **#row**.

18. With **#row** selected, set its **Flex** property to go from left to right (third option), set **Alignment: Align Items** to **centered**, and set **Alignment: Justify Content** to **centered**.

19. Since the buttons are now a bit squashed, for each **Button**, set its **Size: Min Height** to 100:

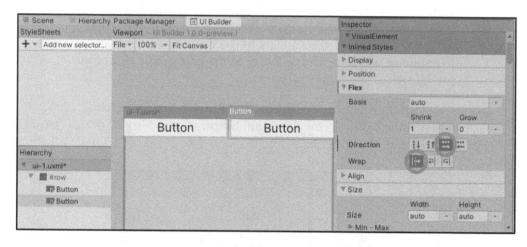

Figure 3.46 – Flex settings for a row with two Button children

20. Run the scene. You should now have a row of two buttons at the top of the **Game** window.

21. Try resizing the **Game** window. The buttons in the row should flex/align nicely.

How it works...

In this recipe, you added preview packages (**UI Toolkit** and **UI Builder)** to your Unity project. You then used UI Builder to create a UXML file describing the elements in your interface – a row containing two buttons. This was saved as a file called ui-1.

UI Toolkit uses a **Panel Settings** asset file (in the **Project** window) to record how a **UI Panel** is to be displayed. So, we created one called PanelSettings1.

To get Unity to display your UI asset in the scene, we had to add a **UI Document** component to a **Scene** GameObject. We did this by creating a new, empty GameObject **GameUI**. Since we want to display clickable buttons, we also needed to add an **Input System Event System (UI Toolkit)** component to this GameObject. We were then able to link our ui-1 and PanelSettings1 asset files from the **Project** window to this **UI Document** component in our **GameUI** GameObject in the scene.

You then added styling to the buttons (yellow background, larger text, center alignment, and so on), which were then placed within a row that allowed flex alignment. These style properties were automatically stored in a USS style sheet that is a child of the ui-1 file. This process is similar to those followed in standard web-based technologies, allowing the UI style and UI content to be separated.

It may seem like this is a lot more work to do to create a UI than just creating a Canvas GameObject and adding UI objects manually to the scene. However, it means that UIs can be defined through data in XML and CSS files, rather than as properties manually created in a scene, which means there is great potential for special-purpose UI editors tools, as well as simpler runtime scripted UIs, based around this new UI system. With the system being part of Unity 2021.2 and later, I think we'll be seeing a lot more use of UI Toolkit in future games.

Further reading

It's an exciting time for Unity UI with the new UI Toolkit stabilizing and the powerful UI Builder tool to make creating and previewing UIs straightforward. The new system is likely to play an important role in Unity 2021 and in the future. The following links will be useful if you wish to learn more about this new UI system:

- The Unity 2021 manual entry about UI Toolkit:
  https://docs.unity3d.com/2020.1/Documentation/Manual/UIElements.html
- Unity blog about UI Elements:
  https://blogs.unity3d.com/2019/04/23/whats-new-with-uielements-in-2019-1/
- Unity forum about the UI Elements Roadmap:
  https://forum.unity.com/threads/uielements-roadmap-update.784388/

- Unite Copenhagen tanks demo video:
  `https://www.youtube.com/watch?v=t4tfgI1XvGs`
- Unite Copenhagen tanks demo code:
  `https://github.com/Unity-Technologies/`
  `UIElementsUniteCPH2019RuntimeDemo`
- Ray Wenderlich UI Elements tutorial:
  `https://www.raywenderlich.com/6452218-uielements-tutorial-for-`
  `unity-getting-started`

The recipes in this chapter demonstrated a range of C# data representations for inventory items and a range of Unity UI interface components for displaying the status and contents of player inventories at runtime. The Inventory UI needs good-quality graphical assets for a high-quality result. Some sources of assets that you might wish to explore include the following:

- The graphics for our SpaceGirl mini-game are from Space Cute art by Daniel Cook; he generously publishes lots of free 2D art for game developers to use:
  - `http://www.lostgarden.com/`
  - `http://www.lostgarden.com/search?q=planet+cute`
- Sethbyrd – lots of fun 2D graphics:
  - `http://www.sethbyrd.com/`
- Royalty-free art for 2D games:
  - `http://www.gameart2d.com/freebies.html`

4
Playing and Manipulating Sounds

Sound is a very important part of the gaming experience. In fact, we can't stress enough how crucial sound is to a player's immersion in a virtual environment. Just think of the engine running in your favorite racing game, the distant urban buzz in a simulator game, or the creeping noises in horror games. Think of how these sounds transport you into the game.

Before we get into the recipes, first, let's review how different sound features work in Unity. A project with audio needs one or more audio files. These are called **AudioClips** in Unity, and they sit in your **Project** folders. At the time of writing, Unity 2021 supports four audio file formats: `.wav`, `.ogg`, `.mp3`, and `.aif`. Files of these types are re-encoded when Unity builds for a target platform (PC, Mac, Linux Standalone, Android, or WebGL, for example). It also supports tracker modules in four formats: `.xm`, `.mod`, `.it`, and `.s3m`.

A scene or prefab GameObject can have an `AudioSource` component, which can either be linked to an `AudioClip` sound file at design time or through scripting at runtime. At any time in a scene, there is one active `AudioListener` component inside a GameObject. When you create a new scene, one is added automatically for you in the main camera. You can think of an `AudioListener` component as a simulated digital "ear," since the sounds Unity plays are based on the relationship between playing `AudioSources` and the active `AudioListener` component.

Simple sounds, such as pickup effects and background soundtrack music, can be defined as **2D sound**. However, Unity supports 3D sounds, which means that the location and distance between playing `AudioSources` and the active `AudioListener` component determine the way the sound is perceived in terms of loudness and left/right balance.

Additionally, you can engineer synchronized sound playing and scheduling through `AudioSettings.dspTime` – this is a value based on the samples in the audio system, so it is far more precise than the `Time.time` value. Also, `dspTime` will pause/suspend with the scene, so no logic is required for rescheduling when using `dspTime`.

In this chapter, we will cover the following recipes:

- Playing different one-off sound effects with a single `AudioSource` component
- Playing and controlling different sounds each with their own `AudioSource` component
- Creating just-in-time `AudioSource` components at runtime through C# scripting
- Delaying before playing a sound
- Preventing an audio clip from restarting if it is already playing
- Waiting for audio to finish playing before auto-destructing an object
- Scheduling a sound to play at a certain time
- Creating audio visualization from sample spectral data
- Synchronizing simultaneous and sequential music to create a simple 140 bpm music-loop manager

Technical requirements

For the recipes in this chapter, you will need access to Unity 2021.1 or later, plus one of the following:

- Microsoft Windows 10 (64-bit)/GPU: DX10, DX11, and DX12-capable
- Mac OS Sierra 10.12.6+/ GPU Metal-capable Intel or AMD
- Linux Ubuntu 16.04, Ubuntu 18.04, and CentOS 7/GPU: OpenGL 3.2+ or Vulkan-capable, Nvidia or AMD

For each chapter, there is a folder with the asset files you need for the recipes. This folder is located in the public **GitHub repository** for the book at `https://github.com/PacktPublishing/Unity-2021-Cookbook-Fourth-Edition`.

Playing different one-off sound effects with a single AudioSource component

The basics of playing a sound are very straightforward in Unity (simply add an AudioSource component to a GameObject and link it to an AudioClip sound file). For simple sound effects, such as short, one-off plays of pickup confirmation noises, it's useful to have a single AudioSource component that you can then reuse to play different sound effects. That is what we'll do in this recipe.

Getting ready

Try out this recipe using any short audio clip that is less than one second in duration. We have included a number of classic Pacman game sound clips inside the 04_01 folder.

How to do it...

To play multiple sounds using the same AudioSource component, perform the following steps:

1. Create a new **Unity 2D** project and import the sound clip files.
2. Create a C# script class, called PlaySounds, in a new folder, _Scripts, that contains the following code. Additionally, add an instance as a scripted component to the **Main Camera**:

```
using UnityEngine;

[RequireComponent(typeof(AudioSource))]
public class PlaySounds : MonoBehaviour
{
    public AudioClip clipEatCherry;
    public AudioClip clipExtraLife;

    private AudioSource audioSource;

    void Awake() {
        audioSource = GetComponent<AudioSource>();
    }

    void Update() {
        if (Input.GetKey(KeyCode.UpArrow))
```

```
                  audioSource.PlayOneShot(clipEatCherry);

            if (Input.GetKey(KeyCode.DownArrow))
                  audioSource.PlayOneShot(clipExtraLife);
        }
    }
```

3. Ensure that the `MainCamera` GameObject is selected in the **Hierarchy** panel. Then, in the **Inspector** panel, drag the **Pacman Eating Cherry** sound clip from the **Project** panel into the public **Pacman Eating Cherry** `AudioClip` variable inside the scripted `PlaySounds` `(Script)` component. Repeat this procedure for the **Pacman Extra Life** sound clip. You can view these steps in the following screenshot:

Figure 4.1 – Dragging sound clips into the scripted component

4. Run the scene, and press the *UP* and *DOWN* arrow keys to play the different sound effects.

How it works...

You have created a C# script class, called `PlaySounds`. The script class includes a `RequireComponent` attribute. It declares that any GameObject containing a scripted object component of this class must have a sibling `AudioSource` component (note that one will be added automatically if such a component does not exist when the scripted component is added).

The `PlaySounds` script class has two public `AudioClip` properties: `Pacman Eating Cherry` and `Pacman Extra Life`. At design time, we associated `AudioClip` sound files from the **Project** panel with these public properties.

At runtime, the `Update()` method is executed in every frame. This method checks whether the *UP* and *DOWN* array keys are being pressed. If so, it plays the **Eat Cherry or Extra Life** sounds, respectively– sending the `AudioSource` component a `PlayOneShot()` message with the appropriate `AudioClip` sound file link.

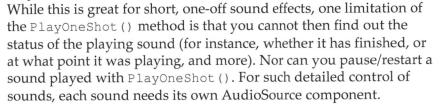

Note: We cannot pause/interrogate sounds played with **PlayOneShot**.
While this is great for short, one-off sound effects, one limitation of the `PlayOneShot()` method is that you cannot then find out the status of the playing sound (for instance, whether it has finished, or at what point it was playing, and more). Nor can you pause/restart a sound played with `PlayOneShot()`. For such detailed control of sounds, each sound needs its own AudioSource component.

You can learn more about the `PlayOneShot()` method in the official Unity documentation
at `https://docs.unity3d.com/ScriptReference/AudioSource.Play OneShot.html`.

There's more...

There are some details that you don't want to miss.

Playing a sound at a static point in 3D world space

Similar to `PlayOneShot()` is the `PlayClipAtPoint()` **AudioSource** method. This allows you to play a sound clip for an `AudioSource` component created at a specific point in 3D world space. Note that this is a static class method – so you don't need an `AudioSource` component to use this method. An `AudioSource` component is created (at the location you provide) and will exist as long as the `AudioClip` sound is playing. The `AudioSource` component will be automatically removed by Unity once the sound has finished playing.

All you need is a Vector3 (*x,y,z*) position object and a reference to the `AudioClip` file that you want to be played:

```
Vector3 location = new Vector3(10, 10, 10);
AudioSource.PlayClipAtPoint(soundClipToPlay, location);
```

Playing and controlling different sounds each with its own AudioSource component

The approach in the previous recipe (using `PlayOneShot(...)` with a single `AudioSource` component) is fine for one-off sound effects. When further control is required over a playing sound, each sound will need to be played in its own `AudioSource` component. In this recipe, we'll create two separate `AudioSource` components and pause/resume each of them with different arrow keys.

Getting ready

Try out this recipe with two audio clips that are several seconds long. We have included two free music clips inside the `04_02` folder.

How to do it...

To play different sounds with their own `AudioSouce` components, perform the following steps:

1. Create a new Unity 2D project and import the sound clip files.
2. Create a GameObject in the scene containing an `AudioSource` component that is linked to the `186772__dafawe__medieval` **AudioClip**. You can do this in a single step by dragging the music clip from the **Project** panel into either the **Hierarchy** panel or the **Scene** panel. Rename this new GameObject as `music1_medieval`.
3. Repeat the previous step to create another GameObject, named `music2_arcade`, containing an `AudioSource` component that is linked to `251461__joshuaempyre__arcade-music-loop`.

4. For both `AudioSource` components that have been created, uncheck the **Play On Awake** property. This is so that the sounds do not begin playing as soon as the scene has been loaded.

5. Create an empty GameObject named `Manager`.

6. Create a C# script class, called `MusicManager`, in a new folder, `_Scripts`, that contains the following code. Also, add an instance as a scripted component to the `Manager` GameObject:

```
using UnityEngine;

public class MusicManager : MonoBehaviour   {
    public AudioSource audioSourceMedieval;
    public AudioSource audioSourceArcade;

    void Update() {
        if (Input.GetKey(KeyCode.RightArrow)){
            if (audioSourceMedieval.time > 0)
                audioSourceMedieval.UnPause();
            else
                audioSourceMedieval.Play();
        }

        if (Input.GetKey(KeyCode.LeftArrow))
            audioSourceMedieval.Pause();
        if (Input.GetKey(KeyCode.UpArrow)){
            if (audioSourceArcade.time > 0)
                audioSourceArcade.UnPause();
            else
                audioSourceArcade.Play();
        }

        if (Input.GetKey(KeyCode.DownArrow))
            audioSourceArcade.Pause();
    }
}
```

7. Ensure that the `Manager` GameObject is selected in the **Hierarchy** panel. In the **Inspector** panel, drag the `music1_medieval` GameObject from the **Scene** panel into the public **Audio Source Medieval** `AudioSource` variable in the scripted `MusicManager (Script)` component. Repeat this procedure by dragging the `music2_arcade` GameObject into the public **Audio Source Arcade** variable.

8. Run the scene, and press the *UP* and *DOWN* arrow keys to start/resume and pause the medieval sound clip. Press the *RIGHT* and *LEFT* arrow keys to start/resume and pause the arcade sound clip.

How it works...

You created a C# script class, called `MusicManager`, and added an instance of this class as a component to the `Manager` GameObject. Additionally, you also created two GameObjects, called `music1_medieval` and `music2_arcade`, in the scene, with each containing an `AudioSource` component linked to a different music clip.

The script class has two public `AudioSource` properties: `Music Medieval` and `Music Arcade`. At design time, we associated the `AudioSource` components of the `music1_medieval` and `music2_arcade` GameObjects with these public properties.

At runtime, the `Update()` method is executed in every frame. This method checks for the *UP/DOWN/RIGHT/LEFT* array keys being pressed. If the *UP* arrow key is detected, the medieval music audio source is sent a `Play()` or `UnPause()` message. The `Play()` message is sent if the clip is not already playing (note that its time property is zero). In comparison, if the *DOWN* arrow key is pressed, the medieval music audio source is sent a `Pause()` message.

The arcade music clip is controlled in a corresponding way through the detection of the *RIGHT/LEFT* arrow keys.

Each `AudioClip` sound file that is associated with its own `AudioSource` component allows you to simultaneously play and manage each sound independently.

Creating just-in-time AudioSource components at runtime through C# scripting

In the previous recipe, for each sound clip that we wanted to manage in the scene, we had to manually create GameObjects with `AudioSource` components at design time. However, using C# scripting, we can create our own GameObjects that contain AudioSources at runtime – just when they are needed.

This method is similar to the built-in AudioSource `PlayClipAtPoint()` method, but the created `AudioSource` component is completely under our programmatic control – though, we are then responsible for destroying this component when it is no longer needed.

 This code was inspired by some of the code posted, in 2011, in the online **Unity Answers** forum, by user Bunny83. Unity has a great online community helping each other and posting interesting ways of adding features to games. You can find out more about that post at `http://answers.unity3d.com/questions/123772/playoneshot-r eturns-false-for-isplaying.html`.

Getting ready

This recipe adapts the previous one. So, make a copy of the project from the previous recipe, and work on this new copy.

How to do it...

To create just-in-time `AudioSource` components at runtime through C# scripting, perform the following steps:

1. Delete the `music1_medieval` and `music2_arcade` GameObjects from the scene – we'll be creating these at runtime in this recipe!

2. Refactor the `MusicManager` C# script class to read as follows (note that the `Update()` method remains unchanged):

```
using UnityEngine;

public class MusicManager : MonoBehaviour {
    public AudioClip clipMedieval;
    public AudioClip clipArcade;

    private AudioSource audioSourceMedieval;
    private AudioSource audioSourceArcade;

    void Awake() {
        audioSourceMedieval = CreateAudioSource(clipMedieval,
true);
        audioSourceArcade = CreateAudioSource(clipArcade,
false);
    }
```

```
        private AudioSource CreateAudioSource(AudioClip audioClip,
bool
        startPlayingImmediately) {
        GameObject audioSourceGO = new GameObject();
            audioSourceGO.transform.parent = transform;
        audioSourceGO.transform.position = transform.position;
        AudioSource newAudioSource =
            audioSourceGO.AddComponent<AudioSource>();
        newAudioSource.clip = audioClip;
        if(startPlayingImmediately)
            newAudioSource.Play();

        return newAudioSource;
    }

    void Update(){
        if (Input.GetKey(KeyCode.RightArrow)){
            if (audioSourceMedieval.time > 0)
                audioSourceMedieval.UnPause();
            else
                audioSourceMedieval.Play();
        }

        if (Input.GetKey(KeyCode.LeftArrow))
            audioSourceMedieval.Pause();
        if (Input.GetKey(KeyCode.UpArrow)){
            if (audioSourceArcade.time > 0)
                audioSourceArcade.UnPause();
            else
                audioSourceArcade.Play();
        }

        if (Input.GetKey(KeyCode.DownArrow))
            audioSourceArcade.Pause();
    }
}
```

3. Ensure that the `Manager` GameObject is selected in the **Hierarchy** panel. In the **Inspector** panel, drag the **AudioClip** `186772__dafawe__medieval` sound clip from the **Project** panel into the public **Clip Medieval AudioClip** variable in the scripted `MusicManager (Script)` component. Repeat this procedure with the `251461__joshuaempyre__arcade-music-loop` **AudioClip** for the **Clip Arcade** variable.

4. Run the scene, and press the *UP* and *DOWN* arrow keys to start/resume and pause the medieval sound clip. Press the *RIGHT* and *LEFT* arrow keys to start/resume and pause the arcade sound clip.

How it works...

The key feature of this recipe is the new `CreateAudioSource(...)` method. This method takes input as a reference to a sound clip file and a Boolean `true/false` value as to whether the sound should start playing immediately. The method does the following:

- It creates a new GameObject (with the same parent and at the same location as the GameObject doing the creating).
- It adds a new `AudioSource` component to the new GameObject.
- It sets the audio clip of the new `AudioSource` component to the provided `AudioClip` parameter.
- If the Boolean parameter is `true`, the `AudioSource` component is immediately sent a `Play()` message so that it starts playing the sound clip.
- A reference to the `AudioSource` component is returned.

The remainder of the `MusicManager` script class is very similar to that of the previous recipe. There are two public `AudioClip` variables, `clipMedieval` and `clipArcade`, which are set through drag and drop at design time to link to the sound clip files inside the `Sounds Project` folder.

The `audioSourceMedieval` and `audioSourceArcade` `AudioSource` variables are now private. These values are set up in the `Awake()` method by calling and storing values returned by the `CreateAudioSource(...)` method with the `clipMedieval` and `clipArcade` AudioClip variables.

To illustrate how the Boolean parameter works, the medieval music `AudioSource` component is created to play immediately, while the arcade music won't start playing until the *UP* arrow key has been pressed. Playing, resuming, and pausing the two audio clips is just the same as in the previous recipe – via the arrow-key detection logic in the (unchanged) `Update()` method.

There's more...

There are some details that you don't want to miss.

Adding the CreateAudioSource(...) method as an extension to the MonoBehavior class

Since the `CreateAudioSource(...)` method is a general-purpose method that could be used by many different game script classes, it doesn't naturally sit within the `MusicManager` class. The best place for general-purpose generative methods such as this is to add them as static (class) methods to the component class they work with. In this case, it would be great if we could add this method to the `MonoBehavior` class itself – so any scripted component could create `AudioSource` GameObjects on the fly.

All we have to do is create a class (usually named `ExtensionMethods`) with a static method, as follows:

```
using UnityEngine;

public static class ExtensionMethods {
    public static AudioSource CreateAudioSource(this MonoBehaviour
parent, AudioClip audioClip, bool startPlayingImmediately)
    {
        GameObject audioSourceGO = new GameObject("music-player");
        audioSourceGO.transform.parent = parent.transform;
        audioSourceGO.transform.position = parent.transform.position;
        AudioSource newAudioSource =
            audioSourceGO.AddComponent<AudioSource>() as AudioSource;
        newAudioSource.clip = audioClip;

        if (startPlayingImmediately)
            newAudioSource.Play();

        return newAudioSource;
    }
}
```

As you can see, we add an additional first parameter to the extension method, stating which class we are adding this method to. Since we have added this to the `MonoBehavior` class, we can now use this method in our scripted classes as though it were built-in. So, our `Awake()` method in our `MusicManager` class appears as follows:

```
void Awake() {
    audioSourceMedieval = this.CreateAudioSource(clipMedieval, true);
    audioSourceArcade = this.CreateAudioSource(clipArcade, false);
}
```

That's it – we can now remove the method from our `MusicManager` class and use this method in any of our `MonoBehavior` scripted classes.

Delaying before playing a sound

Sometimes, we don't want to play a sound immediately but after a short delay. For example, we might want to wait for a second or two before playing a sound to indicate the slightly delayed onset of a poison that has just been drunk or having walked into a spell that weakens the player. For such scenarios, AudioSource offers the `PlayDelayed(...)` method. This recipe illustrates a simple approach for such cases where we do not wish to immediately start playing a sound.

Getting ready

Try out this recipe with two audio clips that are several seconds long. We have included two free music clips inside the `04_01` folder.

How to do it...

To schedule a sound to play after a given delay, perform the following steps:

1. Create a new Unity 2D project and import the sound clip files.
2. Create a GameObject in the scene containing an `AudioSource` component linked to the **Pacman Opening Song AudioClip**. This can be done in a single step by dragging the music clip from the **Project** panel into either the **Hierarchy** panel or the **Scene** panel.
3. Repeat the previous step to create another GameObject, containing an `AudioSource` component linked to the **Pacman Dies** clip.
4. For both `AudioSource` components created, uncheck the **Play Awake** property. This is so that the sounds do not begin playing as soon as the scene is loaded.
5. Create a UI Button named `Button-music` on the screen and change its text to **Play Music Immediately**.
6. Create a UI Button named `Button-dies` on the screen and change its text to **Play Dies Sound After 1 second**.

7. Create an empty GameObject named `SoundManager`.
8. Create a C# script class, called `DelayedSoundManager`, in a new folder, `_Scripts`, that contains the following code. Also, add an instance as a scripted component to the `SoundManager` GameObject:

```
using UnityEngine;

public class DelayedSoundManager : MonoBehaviour {
    public AudioSource audioSourcePacmandMusic;
    public AudioSource audioSourceDies;

    public void ACTION_PlayMusicNow() {
        audioSourcePacmandMusic.Play();
    }

    public void ACTION_PlayDiesSoundAfterDelay() {
        float delay = 1.0F;
        audioSourceDies.PlayDelayed(delay);
    }
}
```

9. With the `SoundManager` GameObject selected in the **Hierarchy** panel, drag the two audio clips to the audio sources.
10. With the `Button-music` GameObject selected in the **Hierarchy** panel, create a new on-click event-handler. You can do this by dragging the `SoundsManager` GameObject into the **Object** slot and selecting the **ACTION_PlayMusicNow()** method.
11. With the `Button-dies` GameObject selected in the **Hierarchy** panel, create a new on-click event-handler. You can do this by dragging the `SoundsManager` GameObject into the **Object** slot and selecting the **ACTION_PlayDiesSoundAfterDelay()** method.

How it works...

In this recipe, you added two GameObjects to the scene that contain `AudioSource` components linked to music and dying sound clips. Additionally, you created a C# script class, called `DelayedSoundManager`, and added an instance to an empty GameObject. You associated the two `AudioSource` components in your GameObjects with the two public variables in your scripted component.

You created two buttons, as follows:

- `Button-music`, with a click action to invoke the `DelayedSoundManager.ACTION_PlayMusicNow()` method
- `Button-dies`, with a click action to invoke the `DelayedSoundManager.PlayDiesSoundAfterDelay()` method

The `DelayedSoundManager.ACTION_PlayMusicNow()` method immediately sends a `Play()` message to the audio source linked to the **Pacman Opening Song AudioClip**. However, the `DelayedSoundManager.PlayDiesSoundAfterDelay()` method sends a `PlayDelayed(...)` message to the audio source linked to the **Pacman Dies AudioClip**, passing a value of `1.0`. This makes Unity wait one second before playing the sound clip.

Preventing an audio clip from restarting if it is already playing

In a game, there might be several different events that cause a particular sound effect to start playing. If the sound is already playing, then in almost all cases, we won't want to restart the sound. This recipe includes a test so that an `AudioSource` component is only sent a `Play()` message if it is currently not playing.

Getting ready

Try out this recipe with any audio clip that is one second or longer in duration. We have included the `engineSound` audio clip inside the `04_05` folder.

How to do it...

To prevent an audio clip from restarting, perform the following steps:

1. Create a new Unity 2D project and import the sound clip file.
2. Create a GameObject in the scene containing an `AudioSource` component that is linked to the `engineSound` AudioClip. You can do this in a single step by dragging the music clip from the **Project** panel into either the **Hierarchy** panel or the **Scene** panel.

3. Uncheck the **Play Awake** property for the `AudioSource` component of the `engineSound` GameObject. This is to ensure the sound does not begin playing as soon as the scene has been loaded.

4. Create a UI button named `Button-play-sound` and change its text to `Play Sound`. Position the button in the center of the screen by setting its **Rect Transform** property position to the middle center.

5. Create a C# script class, called `WaitToFinishBeforePlaying`, in a new folder, `_Scripts`, that contains the following code. Also, add an instance as a scripted component to the `MainCamera` GameObject:

```
using UnityEngine;
using UnityEngine.UI;

public class WaitToFinishBeforePlaying : MonoBehaviour  {
    public AudioSource audioSource;
    public Text buttonText;

    void Update() {
        string statusMessage = "Play sound";
        if(audioSource.isPlaying )
            statusMessage = "(sound playing)";

        buttonText.text = statusMessage;
    }

    public void ACTION_PlaySoundIfNotPlaying() {
        if( !audioSource.isPlaying )
            audioSource.Play();
    }
}
```

6. With the **Main Camera** selected in the **Hierarchy** panel, drag `engineSound` into the **Inspector** panel for the public `AudioSource` variable. Then, drag the **Text** child of `Button-play-sound` for the public **ButtonText**.

7. With `Button-play-sound` selected in the **Hierarchy** panel, create a new on-click event-handler. You can do this by dragging the **Main Camera** into the **Object** slot and selecting the `ACTION_PlaySoundIfNotPlaying()` function.

How it works...

AudioSource components have a public readable property, isPlaying, which is a Boolean true/false flag that indicates whether the sound is currently playing. In this recipe, the text of the button is set to display **Play Sound** when the sound is not playing and **sound playing** when it is. When the button is clicked on, the ACTION_PlaySoundIfNotPlaying() method is called. This method uses an if statement, ensuring that a Play() message is only sent to the AudioSource component if its isPlaying is false, and it updates the button's text as appropriate.

Waiting for the audio to finish playing before auto-destructing an object

An event might occur (such as an object pickup or the killing of an enemy) that we wish to notify the player of by playing an audio clip and an associated visual object (such as an explosion particle system or a temporary object in the location of the event). However, as soon as the clip has finished playing, we will want the visual object to be removed from the scene. This recipe provides a simple way in which to link the ending of a playing audio clip with the automatic destruction of its containing object.

Getting ready

Try out this recipe with any audio clip that is one second or more in duration. We have included the engineSound audio clip inside the 04_06 folder.

How to do it...

To wait for audio to finish playing before destroying its parent GameObject, perform the following steps:

1. Create a new Unity 2D project and import the sound clip file.

2. Create a GameObject in the scene containing an AudioSource component that is linked to the engineSound AudioClip. This can be done in a single step by dragging the music clip from the **Project** panel into either the **Hierarchy** panel or **Scene** the panel. Rename this as the AudioObject GameObject.

3. Uncheck the **Play Awake** property for the AudioSource component of the engineSound GameObject. This is to ensure the sound does not begin playing as soon as the scene has been loaded.

4. Create a C# script class, called AudioDestructBehaviour, in a new folder, _Scripts, that contains the following code. Also, add an instance as a scripted component to the AudioObject GameObject:

```
using UnityEngine;
using UnityEngine;

public class AudioDestructBehaviour : MonoBehaviour {
    private AudioSource audioSource;

    void Awake() {
        audioSource = GetComponent<AudioSource>();
    }

    private void Update() {
        if( !audioSource.isPlaying )
            Destroy(gameObject);
    }
}
```

5. In the **Inspector** panel, disable (uncheck) the scripted AudioDestructBehaviour component of AudioObject (when needed, it will be re-enabled via C# code):

Figure 4.2 – Disabling (unchecking) the scripted component of AudioObject

6. Create a C# script class called `ButtonActions` in the `_Scripts` folder that contains the following code. Also, add an instance as a scripted component to the `MainCamera` GameObject:

```
using UnityEngine;

public class ButtonActions : MonoBehaviour {
    public AudioSource audioSource;

    public AudioDestructBehaviour audioDestructScriptedObject;

    public void ACTION_PlaySound() {
        if( !audioSource.isPlaying )
            audioSource.Play();
    }

    public void ACTION_DestroyAfterSoundStops(){
        audioDestructScriptedObject.enabled = true;
    }
}
```

7. With the **Main Camera** selected in the **Hierarchy** panel, drag `AudioObject` into
the **Inspector** panel for the public **Audio Source** variable.

8. With the **Main Camera** selected in the **Hierarchy** panel, drag `AudioObject` into the **Inspector** panel for the public **Audio Destruct Scripted Object** variable.

9. Create a UI button named `Button-play-sound` and change its text to **Play Sound**. Position the button in the center of the screen by setting its **Rect Transform** property to the middle center.

10. With `Button-play-sound` selected in the **Hierarchy** panel, create a new on-click event-handler. You can do this by dragging the **Main Camera** into the **Object** slot and selecting the `ACTION_PlaySound()` function.

11. Create a second UI button named `Button-destroy-when-finished-playing`, and change its text to **Destroy When Sound Finished**. Position the button in the center of the screen (just below the other button) by setting its **Rect Transform** property to the middle center and then dragging the button down a little.

12. With `Button-destroy-when-finished-playing` selected in the **Hierarchy** panel, create a new on-click event-handler. You can do this by dragging the **Main Camera** into the **Object** slot and selecting the `ACTION_DestroyAfterSoundStops()` function.

13. Run the scene. Clicking on the **Play Sound** button will play the engine sound each time. However, once the **Destroy When Sound Finished** button has been clicked on, as soon as the `engineSound` audio clip has finished playing, you'll see the `AudioObject` GameObject disappear from the **Hierarchy** panel. This is because the GameObject has destroyed itself.

How it works...

In this recipe, you created a `ButtonActions` script class and added an instance as a component to the **Main Camera** GameObject. This has two public variables, one to an `AudioSource` component and one to an instance of the scripted `AudioDestructBehaviour` component.

The GameObject named `AudioObject` contains an `AudioSource` component, which stores and manages the playing of the audio clip. Interestingly, `AudioObject` also contains a scripted component, which is an instance of the `AudioDestructBehaviour` class. This script is initially disabled. When enabled, every frame in this object (via its `Update()` method) tests whether the audio source is playing (`!audio.isPlaying`). As soon as the audio is found to be not playing, the GameObject is destroyed.

Two UI buttons are created. The `Button-play-sound` button calls the `ACTION_PlaySound()` method of the scripted component in the **Main Camera**. This method will start playing the audio clip if it is not already playing.

The second button, `Button-destroy-when-finished-playing`, calls the `ACTION_DestoryAfterSoundStops()` method of the scripted component in the **Main Camera**. This method enables the scripted `AudioDestructBehaviour` component in the `AudioObject` GameObject. This is so that the `AudioObject` GameObject will be destroyed once its `AudioSource` sound has finished playing.

See also

Please refer to the *Preventing an audio clip from restarting if it is already playing* recipe in this chapter.

Scheduling a sound to play at a certain time

You might want to schedule a sound to play at a certain time, for example, after a specific event occurs. Alternatively, you might want to schedule a series of audio clips to be played back to back. This recipe provides a simple way to schedule a sound to play at a certain time:

Figure 4.3 – Setting the time for a scheduled sound to play

Getting ready

This recipe works with any sound clip file. For example, you could use one of the **Pacman Opening Song.mp3** files from the classic Pacman game sound clips inside the 04_01 folder.

How to do it...

To schedule a sound to play at a certain time, perform the following steps:

1. Create a new 2D project and import the audio clip files you wish to use.
2. Create a new empty GameObject named SoundManager. Add an AudioSource component that is linked to the **Pacman Opening Song AudioClip**. You can do this by ensuring the SoundManager GameObject is selected and dragging the clip to either the **Hierarchy** panel or the **Scene** panel.
3. Uncheck the **Play Awake** property of the AudioSource component.
4. Create a C# script class, called ScheduledSoundManager, that contains the following code. Also, add an instance as a scripted component to the SoundManager GameObject:

```csharp
using UnityEngine;
using System;
using UnityEngine.UI;

public class ScheduledSoundManager : MonoBehaviour
{
    public Text textScheduledMessage;
    private AudioSource audioSource;
    private bool activated = false;
    private float secondsUntilPlay = 0;
    private DateTime scheduledPlayTime;

    private void Awake() {
        audioSource = GetComponent<AudioSource>();
    }

    public void PlayMusic(int hours, int minutes, int seconds)
    {
        scheduledPlayTime = DateTime.Today.Add(new TimeSpan(hours, minutes,
            seconds));
        UpdateSecondsUntilPlay();
```

```
        audioSource.PlayDelayed(secondsUntilPlay);
        activated = true;
    }

    private void Update() {
        // default message
        String message = "played!";

        if(activated){
            UpdateSecondsUntilPlay();
            if(secondsUntilPlay > 0){
                message = "scheduled to play in " +
secondsUntilPlay + "
                    seconds";
            } else {
                activated = false;
            }
            textScheduledMessage.text = message;
        }
    }

    private void UpdateSecondsUntilPlay() {
        TimeSpan delayUntilPlay = scheduledPlayTime -
DateTime.Now;
        secondsUntilPlay = delayUntilPlay.Seconds;
    }
}
```

5. Create a C# script class, called `ButtonActions`, that contains the following code. Also, add an instance as a scripted component to the `SoundManager` GameObject:

```
using UnityEngine;
using System;
using UnityEngine.UI;

public class ButtonActions : MonoBehaviour {
    public Text clockText;
    public Text hoursText;
    public Text minutesText;
    public Text secondsText;

    private ScheduledSoundManager _scheduledSoundManager;

    private void Awake() {
        _scheduledSoundManager =
GetComponent<ScheduledSoundManager>();
    }
```

```
public void ACTION_PlayMusic() {
    int hours = int.Parse(hoursText.text);
    int minutes = int.Parse(minutesText.text);
    int seconds = int.Parse(secondsText.text);

    _scheduledSoundManager.PlayMusic(hours, minutes,
seconds);
}

private void Update() {
    clockText.text = "Time = " +
DateTime.Now.ToString("HH:mm:ss");
}
}
```

6. Add a UI Text object to the **Scene** named clock. In the **Inspector** panel, make this text a larger size and color it red (it will become our digital clock display). Set its **Horizontal Overflow** and **Vertical Overflow** to **Overflow**.

7. Add a UI Input Field object to the **Scene** named InputField-hours. Rename the **Text** child of this object to Text-hours. Set the placeholder text to hours.

8. Make two duplicates of the UI Input GameObject InputField-hours object and name the copies InputField-minutes and InputField-seconds. Rename the **Text** children of these objects as Text-minutes and Text-seconds, respectively. Likewise, change their placeholder texts to minutes and seconds. Space out the three InputText objects vertically, as shown in *Figure 4.4*.

9. Add a UI Button to the **Scene** named Button-music. Set the text of this button to **Play Music At Scheduled Time**.

10. Add a UI Text object to the **Scene** named Text-scheduled-message. In the **Inspector** panel, make this text a medium size and color it red (it will become our countdown display). In its Text component, set the initial text message to **(not scheduled)**. Set its **Horizontal Overflow** and **Vertical Overflow** to **Overflow**.

11. Select the SoundManager GameObject in the **Hierarchy** panel. As illustrated in *Figure 4.5*, drag the **Text-scheduled-message** text object to its corresponding variable slot in the **Scheduled Sound Manager (Script)** component.

12. With the `SoundManager` GameObject still selected in the **Hierarchy** panel, drag the four remaining text objects to their corresponding variable slots in the **Button Actions (Script)** component. The UI Text objects to drag are **clock**, **Text-hours**, **Text-minutes**, and **Text-seconds**:

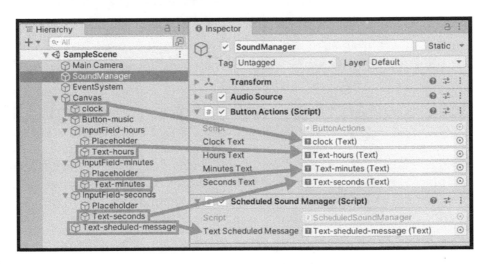

Figure 4.4 – Dragging the input text GameObjects to the **ButtonAction** script component

13. With `Button-music` selected in the **Hierarchy** panel, create a new **On Click** event handler. You can do this by dragging the `SoundManager` GameObject into the **Object** slot and then by selecting **ButtonsActions | ACTION_PlayMusic()** from the drop down menu.

14. Play the scene.

15. Enter numeric values for the hour/minute/seconds, and then click on the **Play Music At Scheduled Time** button. You should hear the sound play when that time is reached.

How it works...

In this recipe, you created a `SoundManager` GameObject with an `AudioSource` component attached. Then, you added an instance of the `ScheduledSoundManager` and `ButtonActions` scripts.

Additionally, you created a UI Text object, `clock`, which has been linked to the `clockText` variable in the `ButtonActions` script. Once per frame, via the `Update()` method, the current time is displayed to the user, in 24-hour clock format as hours/minutes/sections:

```
clockText.text = "Time = " + DateTime.Now.ToString("HH:mm:ss");
```

You created three UI Input Field objects, `InputField-hours`, `InputField-minutes`, and `InputField-seconds`. The user can type integer values for the hours/minutes/seconds into these input fields.

Additionally, you created a UI button, called **Play Music At Scheduled Time**, and added an `OnClick()` event to invoke the `ACTION_PlayMusic()` method of the scripted `ButtonActions` component of `SoundManager` when the button is clicked on. When the `ACTION_PlayMusic()` method is invoked, it retrieves the values of the hours/minutes/seconds input fields, and in turn, passes these values as parameters to the `PlayMusic(...)` method of the `SoundManager` component.

The `PlayMusic(hours, minutes, seconds)` method of the `SoundManager` script updates the `scheduledPlayTime` **DateTime** object based on the current date – that is, `DateTime.Today` – plus the number of received hours, minutes, and seconds. Next, the `UpdateSecondsUntilPlay()` method is invoked – this updates the `secondsUntilPlay` variable. The `secondsUntilPlay` variable refers to the number of seconds from the current time to the scheduled sound play time. This number of seconds is passed to the `PlayDelayed(...)` method of the `AudioSource` component of the `SoundManager` GameObject, and our **Boolean** flag of `activated` is set to true:

```
audioSource.PlayDelayed(secondsUntilPlay);
activated = true;
```

The `Update()` method of the `SoundManager` script class is involved in every frame. The logic in this method tests the `activated` **Boolean** flag. If this flag is `false`, we do nothing, which leaves the default **(not scheduled)** message on the screen for the `Text-scheduled-message` UI Text GameObject. However, if the `activated` **Boolean** flag is `true`, we invoke the `UpdateSecondsUntilPlay()` method. Then, we perform the following logic:

- If `secondsUntilPlay` has not reached zero, then we update the scheduled message UI Text on screen with a message in the form of "**scheduled to play in** " + secondsUntilPlay + " **seconds**".

- If `secondsUntilPlay` is not greater than zero, then the sound is about to play, so we display the **Played** message, and set our `activated` **Boolean** flag to `false`.

Audio visualization from sample spectral data

The Unity audio systems allow us to access music data via the `AudioSource.GetSpectrumData(...)` method. This gives us the opportunity to use that data to present a runtime visualization of the overall sound being heard (from the `AudioListener`) or the individual sound being played by individual `AudioSource` components.

The following screenshot shows lines drawn using a sample script provided by Unity at `https://docs.unity3d.com/ScriptReference/AudioSource.GetSpectrumData.html`:

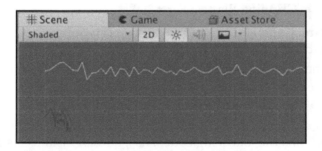

Figure 4.5 – An example of an audio visualization recipe

Note that, in the preceding sample code, the use of `Debug.DrawLine()` only appears in the **Scene** panel when running the game in the Unity Editor (not for final builds). Therefore, it cannot be seen by the game player. In this recipe, we'll take that same spectral data and use it to create a runtime audio spectral visualization in the **Game** panel. We'll do this by creating a row of 512 small cubes and then changing the heights of each frame based on 512 audio data samples for the playing `AudioSource` component.

Getting ready

For this recipe, we have provided several free 140 bpm music clips inside the `04_13` folder.

How to do it...

To create audio visualization from the sample spectral data, perform the following steps:

1. Create a new 3D project and import the provided sound clip files.
2. In the **Inspector** panel, set the background of the **Main Camera** to black.
3. Set the **Main Camera Transform Position** to (224, 50, −200).
4. Set the **Main Camera Camera** component to have the following settings:
   - **Projection = Perspective**
   - **Field of View 60**
   - **Clipping Planes: Near = 0.3**
   - **Clipping Planes: Far = 300**
5. Add **DirectionalLight** to the scene. You can do this by navigating to **GameObject | Light | Directional Light**.
6. Add a new empty GameObject, named `visualizer`, to the scene. Add an `AudioSource` component to this GameObject, and set its **AudioClip** to one of the 140 bpm loops provided. Check the **Loop** option.
7. Create a C# script class, called `SpectrumCubes`, in a new folder, `_Scripts`, that contains the following code. Also, add an instance as a scripted component to the `visualizer` GameObject:

```
using UnityEngine;

public class SpectrumCubes : MonoBehaviour
{
    const int NUM_SAMPLES = 512;
    public Color displayColor;
    public float multiplier = 5000;
    public float startY;
    public float maxHeight = 50;
    private AudioSource audioSource;
    private float[] spectrum = new float[NUM_SAMPLES];
    private GameObject[] cubes = new GameObject[NUM_SAMPLES];

    void Awake() {
```

```csharp
        audioSource = GetComponent<AudioSource>();
        CreateCubes();
    }

    void Update() {
        audioSource.GetSpectrumData(spectrum, 0,
FFTWindow.BlackmanHarris);
        UpdateCubeHeights();
    }

    private void UpdateCubeHeights() {
        for (int i = 0; i < NUM_SAMPLES; i++)
        {
            Vector3 oldScale = cubes[i].transform.localScale;
            Vector3 scaler = new Vector3(oldScale.x,
                HeightFromSample(spectrum[i]), oldScale.z);
            cubes[i].transform.localScale = scaler;
            Vector3 oldPosition = cubes[i].transform.position;
            float newY = startY +
cubes[i].transform.localScale.y / 2;
            Vector3 newPosition = new Vector3(oldPosition.x,
newY,
                oldPosition.z);
            cubes[i].transform.position = newPosition;
        }
    }

    private float HeightFromSample(float sample) {
        float height = 2 + (sample * multiplier);
        return Mathf.Clamp(hcight, 0, maxIleight);
    }

    private void CreateCubes() {
        for (int i = 0; i < NUM_SAMPLES; i++) {
            GameObject cube =
GameObject.CreatePrimitive(PrimitiveType.Cube);
            cube.transform.parent = transform;
            cube.name = "SampleCube" + i;

            Renderer cubeRenderer =
cube.GetComponent<Renderer>();
            cubeRenderer.material = new
Material(Shader.Find("Specular"));
            cubeRenderer.sharedMaterial.color = displayColor;

            float x = 0.9f * i;
            float y = startY;
            float z = 0;
```

```
                        cube.transform.position = new Vector3(x, y, z);

                        cubes[i] = cube;
                }
        }

    }
```

8. With the `visualizer` GameObject selected in the **Hierarchy** panel, click to choose a visualization color from the public **Display Color** variable for the **SpectrumCubes (Script)** component in the **Inspector** panel.

9. Run the scene. You should see the cubes jump up and down, presenting a runtime visualization of the sound data spectrum for the playing sound.

How it works...

In this recipe, you created a C# script class, called `SpectrumCubes`. You created a GameObject with an `AudioSource` component and an instance of your scripted class. All the work is done by the methods of the `SpectrumCubes` C# script class. Here is an explanation of each of these methods:

- **The void Awake() method**: This method caches references to the sibling `AudioSource` component and then invokes the `CreateCubes()` method.

- **The void CreateCubes() method**: This method loops for the number of samples (the default is 512) to create a 3D Cube GameObject, in a row along the *x* axis. Each cube is created with the name of `SampleCube<i>` (where "i" is from 0 to 511) and then parented to the `visualizer` GameObject (since the scripted method is running in this GameObject). Then, each cube has the color of its renderer set to the value of the public `displayColor` parameter. The cube is then positioned on the *x* axis according to the loop number, the value of the public `startY` parameter (so that multiple visualizations can be viewed in different parts of the screen), and $Z = 0$. Finally, a reference to the new cube GameObject is stored in the `cubes[]` array.

- **The void Update() method**: Each frame in this method updates the values inside the `spectrum[]` array through a call to `GetSpectrumData(...)`. In our example, the `FFTWindow.BlackmanHarris` frequency window technique is used. Then, the `UpdateCubeHeights()` method is invoked.

- **The void UpdateCubeHeights() method**: This method loops for each cube to set its height to a scaled value of its corresponding audio data value in the `spectrum[]` array. The cube has its *y* value scaled by the value returned by the `HeightFromSample(spectrum[i])` method. Then, the cube is moved up (that is, its transform position is set) from the value of `startY` by half its height so that all the scaling appears upward (rather than up and down). This is to ensure there is a flat line along the base of our spectrum of cubes.
- **The float HeightFromSample(float) method**: The `HeightFromSample(float)` method does a simple calculation (sample value times the public parameter multiplier) with a minimum value of two added to it. The value returned from the function is this result, limited to the `maxHeight` public parameter (via the `Mathf.Clamp(...)` method).

There's more...

There are some details that you don't want to miss.

Adding visualizations to a second AudioSource component

The script has been written so that it is easy to have multiple visualizations in a scene. So, to create a second `visualizer` for a second audio clip in the scene, perform the following steps:

1. Duplicate the `visualizer` GameObject.
2. Drag a different audio clip from the **Project** panel into the `AudioSource` component of your new GameObject.
3. Set the `startY` public parameter in the **Inspector** panel to 60 (so that the new row of cubes will be above the original row).

4. In the **Inspector** panel, choose a different **Display Color** public variable for the **SpectrumCubes (Script)** component:

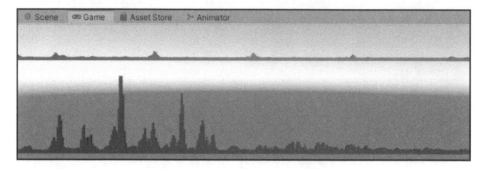

Figure 4.6 – Two visualizer GameObjects in play mode

Trying out different Fast Fourier Transform (FFT) window types

There are several different approaches to the frequency analysis of audio data; our recipe currently uses the FFTWindow.BlackmanHarris version. You can learn about (and try out!) some of the others from the Unity FFTWindow documentation page at `https://docs.unity3d.com/ScriptReference/FFTWindow.html`.

Synchronizing simultaneous and sequential music to create a simple 140 bpm music-loop manager

There are times when we need to precisely schedule audio start times to ensure a smooth transition from one music track to another or to ensure simultaneous music tracks play in time together.

In this recipe, we'll create a simple 4-track 140 bpm music manager that starts playing a new sound after a fixed time – the result of which is that the tracks fit together perfectly, and those that do overlap do so in synchronicity.

Getting ready

For this recipe, we have provided several free 140 bpm music clips inside the `04_14` folder.

How to do it...

To create a music-loop manager, perform the following steps:

1. Create a new Unity 3D project and import the provided sound clip files.
2. Create four GameObjects in the scene that contain an `AudioSource` component linked to a different **AudioClip** loop from the 140 bpm files provided. You can do this in a single step by dragging the music clip from the **Project** panel into either the **Hierarchy** panel or the **Scene** panel.

3. In the **Inspector** panel, uncheck the **Play On Awake** parameter for all four `AudioSource` components (so that they don't start playing until we tell them to).
4. Add a new empty **GameObject** named `musicScheduler` to the scene.
5. Create a C# script class, called `LoopScheduler`, in a new folder, `_Scripts`, that contains the following code. Also, add an instance as a scripted component to the `musicScheduler` GameObject:

```
using UnityEngine;

public class LoopScheduler : MonoBehaviour {
    public float bpm = 140.0F;
    public int numBeatsPerSegment = 16;
    public AudioSource[] audioSources = new AudioSource[4];
    private double nextEventTime;
    private int nextLoopIndex = 0;
    private int numLoops;
    private float numSecondsPerMinute = 60F;
    private float timeBetweenPlays;

    void Start() {
        numLoops = audioSources.Length;
        timeBetweenPlays = numSecondsPerMinute / bpm *
numBeatsPerSegment;
        nextEventTime = AudioSettings.dspTime;
    }

    void Update() {
```

```
            double lookAhead = AudioSettings.dspTime + 1.0F;
            if (lookAhead > nextEventTime)
                StartNextLoop();

            PrintLoopPlayingStatus();
        }

        private void StartNextLoop() {
    audioSources[nextLoopIndex].PlayScheduled(nextEventTime);
            nextEventTime += timeBetweenPlays;

            nextLoopIndex++;
            if (nextLoopIndex >= numLoops)
                nextLoopIndex = 0;
        }

        private void PrintLoopPlayingStatus(){
            string statusMessage = "Sounds playing: ";
            int i = 0;

            while (i < numLoops) {
                statusMessage += audioSources[i].isPlaying + " ";
                i++;
            }

            print(statusMessage);
        }
    }
```

6. With the `musicScheduler` GameObject selected in the **Hierarchy** panel, drag each of the music-loop GameObjects into the four available slots for the **AudioSources** public array variable inside the **Loop Scheduler (Script)** component:

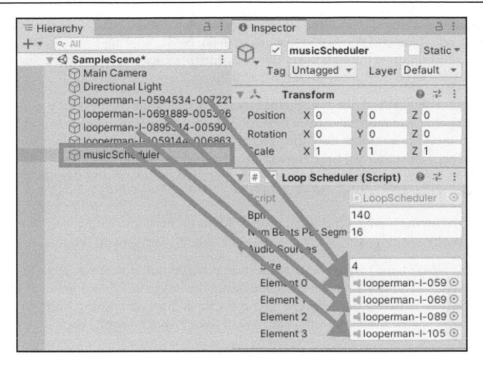

Figure 4.7 – Connecting each music-loop GameObject to the AudioSources

7. Run the scene. Each clip should start, in turn, after the same time delay. If you chose one or two longer clips, they will continue playing while the next clip begins – all overlapping perfectly since they are all 140 bpm sound clips.

How it works...

In this recipe, you added four GameObjects to the scene, each containing **AudioSources** linked to 140 bpm music clips. You created a C# script class, called LoopScheduler, and added an instance to an empty GameObject. You associated the four **AudioSources** in your GameObjects with the four slots in the public AudioSource array variable in your scripted component.

The number of music clips you use can easily be changed by changing the size of the public array variable.

The `Start()` method counts the length of the array to set the `numLoops` variable. Then, it calculates the number of seconds to delay before starting each clip (this is fixed according to the beats-per-minute and beats-per-measure). Finally, it sets the current time to be the time to start the first loop.

The `Update()` method decides whether it's time to schedule the next loop. It does this by testing whether the current time, plus a one-second look-ahead, is past the time to start the next loop. If so, the `StartNextLoop()` method is invoked. Regardless of whether we have started the next loop, the `PrintLoopPlayingStatus()` method is printed to the console, displaying to the user which loops are playing or not.

The `PrintLoopPlayingStatus()` method loops for each `AudioSource` reference in the array, creating a string of `true` and `false` values to be printed out.

The `StartNextLoop()` method sends a `PlayScheduled(...)` message to the next `AudioSource` component to be played, passing the `nextEventTime` value. It then adds the time between plays for the next event time. Then, the next value of the loop index is calculated (add one, if past the end of the array, then reset this to zero again).

There's more...

There are some details that you don't want to miss.

Adding visualizations to the four playing loops

It's great fun to watch the visualization of the loop sounds as they play together. To add visualizations to the four AudioSources, perform the following steps:

1. Import the `SpectrumCubes.cs` C# script file from the previous recipe into this project.
2. Select the **Main Camera** in the **Hierarchy** panel. Then, in the **Inspector** panel, set the **Transform Position** to (224, 50, -200).
3. With the **Main Camera** still selected, set the **Camera** in the **Inspector** panel to have the following settings: **Projection = Perspective**, **Field of View 60**, and **Clipping Planes 0.3 - 300**.
4. Add a `DirectionalLight` GameObject to the scene.
5. For each of the four **GameObjects** containing your **AudioSources**, add an instance of the `SpectrumCubes` script class.

6. In the **Inspector** panel for the **Spectrum Cubes (Script)** component, change the `displayColors` variable for each `AudioSource` GameObject.

7. Set the `startY` values of the **Spectrum Cubes (Script)** components for the four GameObjects to -50, 0, 50, and 100. For most screen sizes, this should allow you to see all four visualization spectrums.

Further reading

The recipes in this chapter demonstrate both scripted and Unity audio system approaches to help you manage audio and introduce dynamic effects at runtime. Games can become far more engaging when the audio environment of effects and music subtly change based on the context of what is happening in the game. You may wish to explore further with the Unity Audio Mixer, for example. Please refer to the following:

- https://docs.unity3d.com/2020.2/Documentation/Manual/AudioMixer.html

What is possible with special audio is now becoming even more interesting with the introduction of ambisonic audio when playing 3D VR games. This allows listeners to enjoy rich audio experiences based on whether sounds are above or below the listener, as well as their distance from an audio source. To find out more about ambisonic audio, please view the following references:

- Rode offers some information on the history of ambisonics: https://www.rode.com/blog/all/what-is-ambisonics.
- You can learn about Unity and ambisonic audio from the official Unity documentation: https://docs.unity3d.com/Manual/AmbisonicAudio.html.
- Google's reference pages regarding special audio and ambisonics can be found at https://developers.google.com/vr/concepts/spatial-audio.
- Oculus' reference pages regarding special audio and ambisonics can be found at https://developer.oculus.com/downloads/package/oculus-ambisonics-starter-pack/.
- Robert Hernadez has published a great article on *Medium.com* disambiguating how to record and edit ambisonic audio: https://medium.com/@webjournalist/spatial-audio-how-to-hear-in-vr-10914a41f4ca.

5
Creating 3D Objects, Terrains, Textures, and Materials

3D games need 3D objects in their scenes! In this chapter, we will explore different ways of adding 3D objects to our scenes, including the following:

- Using and adapting the built-in 3D primitives that Unity offers, such as cubes and cylinders
- Importing 3D models from third parties, and converting other modeling formats into .fbx format, the easiest format to use in Unity
- Creating our own 3D object geometry from scratch using the ProBuilder tools that are now built into the Unity Editor
- Creating and customizing 3D **Terrain** objects using the built-in Unity Terrain tools

In addition to this, the use of textures and materials changes how a 3D object is displayed to the user. In this chapter, we will also explore the use of image textures and materials for customizing the look of 3D objects, including examples of how to dynamically change GameObject materials at runtime, such as responding to when the user clicks a GameObject with the mouse.

In this chapter, we will cover the following recipes:

- Creating 3D primitives and adding materials and textures
- Converting and importing 3D models into a project
- Highlighting GameObject materials on mouseover
- Fading the transparency of a material
- Creating geometry with ProBuilder

- Creating a house with ProBuilder
- Creating and texture-painting terrains
- Height painting terrains
- Adding Terrain holes

Technical requirements

For this chapter, you will need Unity 2021.1 or later, as well as one of the following:

- Microsoft Windows 10 (64-bit)/GPU: DX10, DX11, or DX12-capable
- macOS Sierra 10.12.6+/GPU Metal-capable Intel or AMD
- Linux Ubuntu 16.04, Ubuntu 18.04, and CentOS 7/GPU: OpenGL 3.2+ or Vulkan-capable, NVIDIA or AMD

For each chapter, there is a folder that contains the asset files you will need in this book's GitHub repository at `https://github.com/PacktPublishing/Unity-2021-Cookbook`.

Creating 3D primitives and adding materials and textures

In this recipe, we'll create a simple signpost using an image containing text, as well as a combination of 3D cubes, cylinders, and plane primitives.

While in some cases we'll use complex 3D models that have been imported from modeling apps or third parties, there are several cases where 3D primitives are quick, simple, and sufficient for a game task. Examples of 3D primitives in games include invisible objects with trigger colliders (such as to open doors or to signal a checkpoint), the use of spheres as projectiles, the use of scaled cubes and planes for signposts, and so on. The speed and simplicity of using 3D primitives also make them perfect for fast prototyping, where the objects act as placeholders that can be replaced with more sophisticated models at a later stage in the production of the game. Materials can be quickly created that reference images to textured 3D primitives:

Figure 5.1 – A signpost created with 3D primitives

Getting ready

For this recipe, you'll need an image. Either use one of your own or use the `beware.png` image that we've provided in the `05_01` folder.

How to do it...

To create elements in a scene using 3D primitives, follow these steps:

1. Create a new 3D project.
2. Import the `beware.png` image (or your own) into the newly created 3D project.
3. Add a 3D Cube to the scene by going to **GameObject** | **3D Object** | **Cube**. In the **Hierarchy** window, rename this `Cube-signpost`.
4. Set **Position** of the `Cube-signpost` GameObject to (0,0,0) and its **Scale** to (2, 1, 0.1) by selecting it in the **Hierarchy** window and then setting these coordinates in the **Inspector** window. This should make it a portrait-style rectangle shape that only has a little depth (like a big, flat piece of wood for a signpost...):

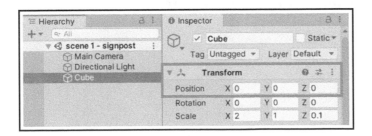

Figure 5.2 – Setting the properties of the 3D Cube primitive

5. Create a 3D plane named `Plane-sign` by going to **GameObject | 3D Object | Plane**. Then, in the **Hierarchy** window, make it a child of `Cube-signpost` (that is, drag **Plane-sign** onto `Cube-signpost`). This means its properties will be relative to `Cube-signpost`. Don't worry about its size, orientation, and so on – we'll fix that soon.

6. Drag the `beware` material asset file from the **Project** window onto the `Plane-sign` GameObject in the **Hierarchy** window. You'll now see the image painted on the panel (don't worry that it's in mirror writing – we'll fix that soon), and that a new folder has been created named `Materials` in the **Project** window. This folder contains the new **Material** asset files with the same name as the image asset file; that is, `beware`:

Figure 5.3 – Setting the properties of the 3D Cube primitive

7. Set **Position** of the `Plane-sign` GameObject to `(0, 0, -0.51)`, its **Rotation** to `(-90, 0, 0)`, and its **Scale** to `(-0.08, 1, -0.08)` by selecting it in the **Hierarchy** window and then setting these coordinates in the **Inspector** window. This should now display the textured panel on the front of our cube, fixing the mirror-writing issue and showing a nice border for the cube around the textured panel:

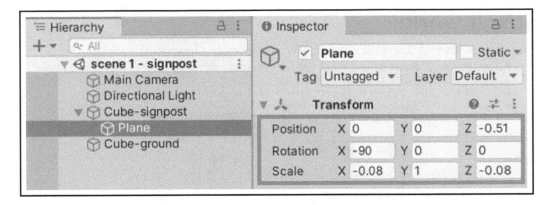

Figure 5.4 – Setting the properties of the 3D Plane primitive as a child of the cube

8. Now, use a 3D **Cylinder** as a pole to hold our signpost. Create a new 3D cylinder named `Cylinder-pole` with **Position** set to (0, -0.4, 0.05), **Rotation** set to (0, 0, 0), and **Scale** set to (0.1, 1, 0.1):

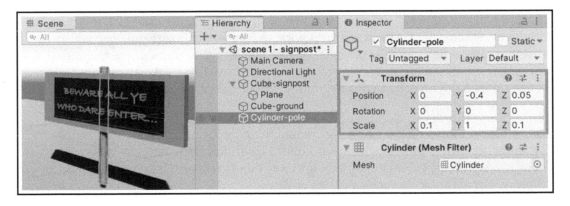

Figure 5.5 – Setting the properties of Cylinder-pole for the pole of our signpost

9. Finally, let's add the ground. Again, we can use a scaled and positioned 3D Cube for this. Create a new 3D **Cube** named `Cube-ground` with its **Position** set to (0, -2, 0) and its **Scale** set to (20, 1, 20).

10. If you like, you can add a spotlight to highlight the signpost.

How it works...

Unity offers several different 3D primitives objects, as shown in the following screenshot of the **GameObject | 3D Object** menu:

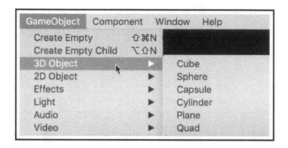

Figure 5.6 – The list of 3D primitives you can create from the GameObject | 3D Object menu

Perhaps the most versatile is **Cube** since it can be stretched and flattened into many useful rectangular polyhedrons. We used a **Cube** to create the main part of our signpost.

However, when a 3D **Cube** is textured with an image, the image will appear, in different orientations, on all six sides. For the text image of our signpost, we used a **Plane**, since a **Plane** has only two sides (front and back) and only displays a textured image on its front face. In fact, we cannot even see the plane at all from the side or behind.

As we found in this recipe when we created the pole for our signpost with a 3D **Cylinder**, cylinders are straight, round objects with flat circle ends, which makes them useful for approximating metal and wooden poles, or when making very shallow, circular objects such as plates or discs.

Some game developers have a set of Prefabs for quickly prototyping a scene. However, as we've seen in this recipe, Unity's 3D primitives can be quite effective for testing or providing placeholders with recognizable approximations of objects in a scene.

There's more...

Here are some ways to enhance this recipe.

Enhancing the scene – adding a spotlight and wood material

Let's enhance the scene a little more by creating a long shadow effect:

1. Change **Rotation** of **Directional Light** in the scene to (10, 20, 40).

2. Add a new **Spot Light** to the scene (**Create** | **Light** | **Spot Light**) and set its **Position** to (0, 0, -2), its **Range** to 5, its **Spot Angle** to 50, and its **Intensity** to 10:

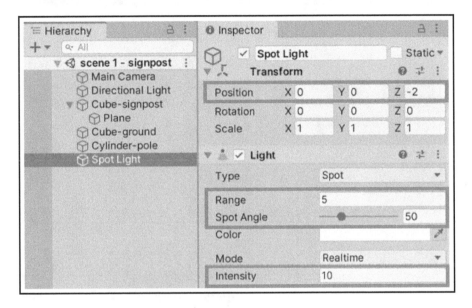

Figure 5.7 – Spot Light settings to add atmosphere to our signpost scene

Make our signpost and pole look like they're made of wood. You can download a free wood texture from the following web page (thanks to Free Stock Textures for sharing this image for free): https://freestocktextures.com/texture/wood-plank-weathered,310.html.

3. Download the wood texture image file and import it into your Unity project.

4. Then, drag the image asset file from the **Project** window onto the `Cube-signpost` GameObject in the **Hierarchy** window. You'll see a wood effect on the signpost, and you'll also see a new `Material` asset file appear in the `Materials` folder in the **Project** window, with the same name as the image file:

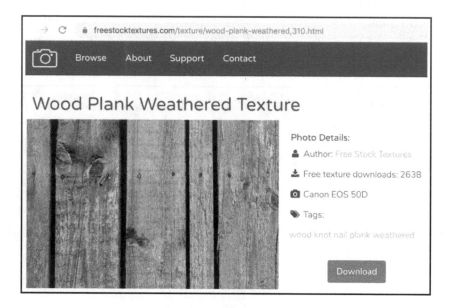

Figure 5.8 – Downloading the free wood texture from freestocktextures.com

5. Select the new material in the **Project** window and, in the **Inspector** window, explore the different tiling settings. For example, try setting its tiling to **X** = 5, **Y** = 5.

6. Also, drag the new `Material` asset file from the **Project** window onto the `Cylinder-pole` GameObject in the **Hierarchy** window, to also make that appear to be made of wood.

Creating a new Material asset file in the Project window and then setting its Albedo to a texture

Another way to make a material is to directly create a `Material` asset file in the **Project** window. To do this, follow these steps:

1. Click the plus (+) sign of the **Project** window and choose **Material**:

Figure 5.9 – Creating a new Material asset file in the Project window

2. Select the new material in the **Project** window. Then, in the **Inspector** window, set the **Albedo** property to the **beware** image:

Figure 5.10 – Setting the beware image as the material's Albedo property

This is what happens automatically if an image is dragged onto a GameObject – a new `Material` asset file with the Albedo of that image is created in the `Materials` folder.

Converting and importing 3D models into a project

There are times where, to get the visual effect we want, we need a complex 3D object. One option is to create our own using the ProBuilder modeling tools built into Unity, which we will explore later in the *Creating geometry with ProBuilder* recipe. However, another option is to use a 3D model that's been created by a third party. The Unity Asset Store is just one source for models, and they are already prepared for importing into Unity as FBX models or even Unity Prefabs. However, there are thousands of free 3D models available online that have been made with third-party 3D modeling applications, and all we need to do is open them in their applications and export them as FBX models, ready to be imported into Unity.

In this recipe, we'll convert a free 3D model of some pumpkin Jack-o'lanterns and other items into an .fbx file, which we can then import and use in a Unity project:

Figure 5.11 – Closeup of the pumpkin model in the free Blender 3D modeling application

Getting ready

In the first part of this recipe, we will use the free Blender 3D modeling application to convert a `.blend` 3D scene file into an `.fbx` format model that can be imported into Unity. We have provided a file called `pumpkin.blend` in the `05_02` folder. Thanks to Oltsch for posting this model free on the TurboSquid website. You can download the installer (for Windows, Mac, or Linux) for Blender from the following URL: `https://www.blender.org/download/`.

However, if you can't install or use the Blender application, we have also provided the `.fbx` format model, `pumpkin.fbx`, in the `05_02` folder.

How to do it...

To convert a Blender 3D model into an `FBX` model for use in Unity, follow these steps:

1. Locate and download the free `pumpkin` and `candlesBlender` models from TurboSquid at `https://www.turbosquid.com/3d-models/3d-pumpkins-candles-model-1484325`.

2. Open the Blender file in the Blender application. You'll see that there are four main objects – some flames and candles and a glass jar. For this recipe, we only want the pumpkin with the face and its lid. Keep `Plane.003` and `Plane.011`, and then right-click to delete the other objects. Rename `Plane.003` to `Pumpkin` by right-clicking the menu and going to **ID Data |
Rename**. Then, rename `Plane.011` to `Pumpkin-lid`:

Figure 5.12 – Deleting the Bottle.001 object in Blender

3. Now, go to **File**, choose **Export**, and select the **FBX (.fbx)** format. Save the exported model as pumpkin. You can now quit the Blender application:

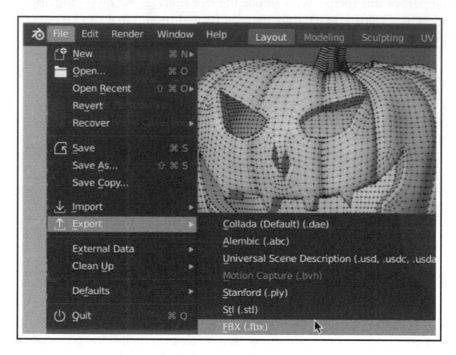

Figure 5.13 – Exporting the edited model in Blender as an FBX file

4. Create a new 3D project.
5. In the **Project** window, create a folder named Models. Import your pumpkin.fbx model into the Models folder.
6. Create a GameObject by dragging the pumpkin asset file from the **Project** window into the scene.
7. Select the pumpkin asset file in the Models folder in the **Project** window.
8. In the **Inspector** window, ensure the **Model** tab is selected. Then, change **Scale Factor** to 5 and click **Apply**. Now, the model is 5 times larger, and so too will be any other GameObjects that are created using this model:

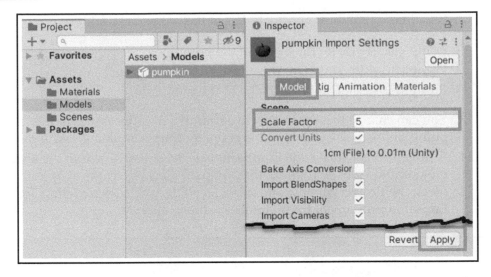

Figure 5.14 – Increasing the Scale Factor property of our pumpkin mode in the Inspector window

9. Create a new folder named `Materials` in the **Project** window.

10. Select the `pumpkin` asset file in the `Models` folder in the **Project** window.

11. In the **Inspector** window, ensure the **Materials** tab is selected. Then, click the **Extract Materials...** button and select your `Materials` folder:

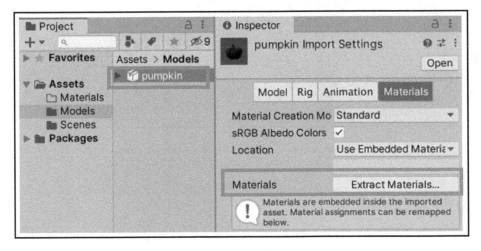

Figure 5.15 – Extracting the materials of the pumpkin model

12. You'll now find three new materials in the `Materials` folder:

- **Pumpkin**: This is for the inside of the pumpkin.
- **Pumpkin_skin**: This is for the outside of the pumpkin.
- **Pumpkin_stem**: This is for the lid of the pumpkin.

13. You can change these materials to customize the appearance of the pumpkin, such as by making the gray lid of the pumpkin green and so on.

14. A fun effect is to make the **Pumpkin** material emissive so that the inside of the pumpkin glows. To make the pumpkin glow, select the `Pumpkin` asset file in the **Project** window and select an HDR color such as yellow for the **Emission** property of the material, as shown here:

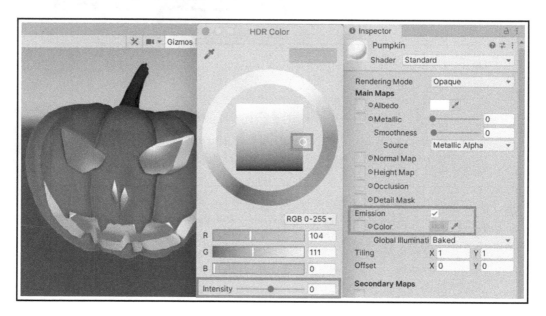

Figure 5.16 – Making the inside of the pumpkin an emissive glowing material

How it works...

For third-party 3D models already in `FBX` format, we can just import them directly into our Unity project. For models in other formats, if we have the same application that we used to create the model, then we can do what we did in this recipe; that is, we can open the model in the modeling application, remove any unwanted elements, and then export it in `FBX` format.

3D modeling applications are complex, sophisticated applications. However, as demonstrated in this recipe, all we really need to know is how to view, select, and delete elements, as well as how to export the model in FBX format.

In this recipe, we removed the unwanted elements of the model in the Blender application. It is also possible to remove some elements after a model has been imported into Unity – some elements will appear as child GameObjects when the model has been added to a scene.

Different modeling applications work at different scales, so Unity has made it easy for us to adjust a **Scale Factor** for models we have imported. For this recipe, the pumpkin seemed about one-fifth the size of a 1 x 1 x 1 cube, so we applied a **Scale Factor** of 5 to make the pumpkin a size that was easier to work with in our project.

If the model we wish to use requires no editing before being converted into FBX format, then there are some online converters that will do this for us, such as Aspose's **X-to-FBX** and Green Token's **onlineconv**.

These two online converters can be found at the following links:

- **Free online X to FBX Converter**: https://products.aspose.app/3d/conversion/x-to-fbx
- **Online 3D Model Converter**: http://www.greentoken.de/onlineconv/

Highlighting GameObject materials on mouseover

Changing the look or color of an object at runtime can be a very effective way of letting players know that they can interact with it. This is very useful in a number of game genres, such as puzzles and point-and-click adventures, and it can also be used to create 3D user interfaces.

In this recipe, we'll swap materials when the mouse is over an object by using a second material showing a border:

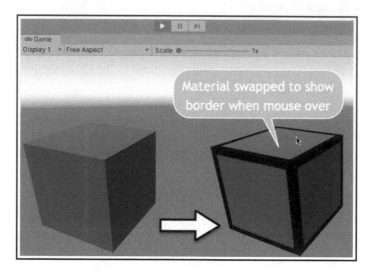

Figure 5.17 – The interactive cube rollover highlight effect we'll create in this recipe

Getting ready

For this recipe, you'll need an image of a white square with a black border. We have provided such an image, called border.png, in the 05_03 folder.

How to do it...

To highlight a material at mouseover, follow these steps:

1. Create a new 3D project.
2. Import the border.png image into your project.
3. Create a 3D **Cube** in the scene (**Create | 3D Object | Cube**).
4. In the **Project** window, create a new **Material** asset named m_cube. Set its **Albedo** color to red.
5. Duplicate your material, naming the copy m_cubeHighlighed. Set the **Albedo** image for this new material to **border**:

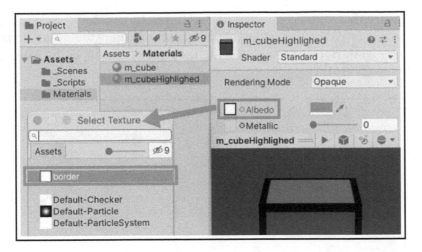

Figure 5.18 – Assigning the border image to the Albedo texture

6. In the **Hierarchy** window, select the **Cube** GameObject and assign it **m_cube Material**. To do so, drag the asset file from the **Project** window onto the GameObject.

7. Create a new C# script class called MouseOverSwap and add an instance object as a component to the cube:

```csharp
using UnityEngine;

public class MouseOverSwap : MonoBehaviour
{
  public Material mouseOverMaterial;
  private Material _originalMaterial;
  private MeshRenderer _meshRenderer;

  void Start()
  {
    _meshRenderer = GetComponent<MeshRenderer>();
    _originalMaterial = _meshRenderer.sharedMaterial;
  }
  void OnMouseOver()
  {
    _meshRenderer.sharedMaterial = mouseOverMaterial;
  }
  void OnMouseExit()
  {
    _meshRenderer.sharedMaterial = _originalMaterial;
  }
}
```

8. Ensure that **Cube** is selected in the **Hierarchy** window. Then, drag the m_cubeHighlighed asset file from the **Project** window into the **Mouse Over Material** variable slot in the **Inspector** window of the **Mouse Over Swap (Script)** component:

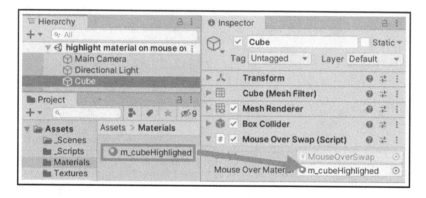

Figure 5.19 – Assigning the highlighted material to the public scripted component variable of the cube

9. Run the scene. **Cube** will be red initially; then, when the mouse hovers over it, you'll see a black border on each edge.

How it works...

The Start() method performs two actions:

- Stores a reference to the MeshRenderer component in the _meshRenderer variable
- Stores a reference to the original material of the GameObject in the _originalMaterial variable

The cube is automatically sent the mouse enter/exit events as the user moves the mouse pointer over and away from the part of the screen where the cube is visible. Our code has added a behavior to the cube to change the material when these events are detected.

We can change the material for the cube by changing which material is referred to by the `sharedMaterial` property of the `MeshRenderer` GameObject.

When the `OnMouseOver` message is received, the method with that name is invoked, and the GameObject's material is set to `mouseOverMaterial`.
When the `OnMouseExit` message is received, the GameObject's material is returned to `_originalMaterial`.

> If the material of a GameObject is shared by several objects, we must be careful when changing the material properties so that we only change those we want to. If we wish to only change the values of a particular GameObject, we can use the `.material` property of `Renderer` since a separate clone is created if there is more than one object that uses the same material. If we want all GameObjects using the same material to be affected by changes, we should use the `.sharedMaterial` property of `Renderer`. Since there was only one GameObject in this recipe, either could have been used.
> Read more at https://docs.unity3d.com/ScriptReference/Renderer-material.html.

There's more...

Here are some ways to enhance this recipe.

Collider needed for custom meshes

In this recipe, we created a primitive 3D **Cube**, which automatically has a **Box Collider** component. If you were to use the preceding script with a custom 3D mesh object, ensure the GameObject has a **Physics | Collider** component so that it will respond to mouse events.

Changing the material's color in response to mouse events

Another way to indicate a GameObject can be interacted with using the mouse is to just change the **Albedo** color of the material, rather than swapping to a new material. To illustrate this, we can have one color for mouseover and a second color for a mouse click.

Do the following:

1. Remove the scripted MouseOverSwap from the Cube GameObject.
2. Create a new C# script class called MouseOverDownHighlighter and add an instance object as a component to Cube:

```csharp
using UnityEngine;

public class MouseOverDownHighlighter : MonoBehaviour {
  public Color mouseOverColor = Color.yellow;
  public Color mouseDownColor = Color.green;

  private Material _originalMaterial;
  private Material _mouseOverMaterial;
  private Material _mouseDownMaterial;
  private MeshRenderer _meshRenderer;

  private bool _mouseOver = false;

  void Awake()
  {
    _meshRenderer = GetComponent<MeshRenderer>();
    _originalMaterial = _meshRenderer.sharedMaterial;
    _mouseOverMaterial = NewMaterialWithColor(mouseOverColor);
    _mouseDownMaterial = NewMaterialWithColor(mouseDownColor);

  }

  void OnMouseEnter()
  {
    _mouseOver = true;
    _meshRenderer.sharedMaterial = _mouseOverMaterial;
  }

  void OnMouseDown()
  {
    _meshRenderer.sharedMaterial = _mouseDownMaterial;
  }

  void OnMouseUp()
  {
    if (_mouseOver)
      OnMouseEnter();
    else
      OnMouseExit();
  }
  void OnMouseExit()
```

```
    {
      _mouseOver = false;
      _meshRenderer.sharedMaterial = _originalMaterial;
    }

    private Material NewMaterialWithColor(Color newColor)
    {
      Material material = new
Material(_meshRenderer.sharedMaterial);
      material.color = newColor;

      return material;
    }
  }
```

There are two public colors: one for mouseover and one for mouse click highlighting.

3. Run the scene. You should now see different highlight colors when the mouse pointer is over the `Cube` GameObject, and when you click the mouse button when the mouse pointer is over the `Cube` GameObject.

Since we are creating two new materials, the reusable `NewMaterialWithColor(...)` C# method is included here to simplify the content of the `Start()` method. A `Boolean` (true/false) variable has been introduced so that the correct behavior occurs once the mouse button is released, depending on whether the mouse pointer is still over the object (`mouseOver = true`) or has moved away from the object (`mouseOver = false`).

Fading the transparency of a material

A feature of many games is for objects to fade away so that they're invisible, or so that they appear gradually until they're fully visible. Unity provides a special **Rendering Mode** called **Fade** for this purpose.

In this recipe, we will create an object that, once clicked, fades out and disappears. We'll also look at how to enhance the code so that it takes the GameObject's own initial alpha value into account. This will make it self-destruct and destroy the GameObject completely when the object has faded out.

How to do it...

Follow these steps:

1. Create a new Unity 3D project.
2. Create a new 3D **Sphere** by going to **Create** | **3D Object** | **Sphere**.
3. Select the Sphere GameObject in the **Hierarchy** window and confirm that it has a **Collider** component. It will since it's a Unity 3D primitive.

Note
If you are using a custom 3D object in this recipe, you'll have to add a **Collider**. To do this, in the **Inspector** window, go to **Add Component** | **Physics** | **Mesh Collider**.

4. Create a new material named `m_fade`.
5. With the `m_fade` asset file selected in the **Project** window, change its **Rendering Mode** to **Fade** in the **Inspector** window:

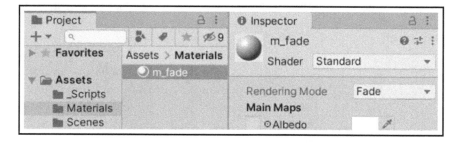

Figure 5.20 – Setting Rendering Mode of a material to Fade

The **Fade** rendering mode is specifically designed for situations such as this recipe.
Other rendering modes, such as **Transparent**, will turn the Albedo color transparent, but not the specular highlights nor the reflections, in which case the object will still be visible.

6. Apply the `m_fade` asset file to the `Sphere` GameObject by dragging it from the **Project** window into the `Sphere` GameObject in the **Hierarchy** window.

7. Create a new C# script class called `FadeAway.cs` and add an instance object as a component to `Sphere`:

```csharp
using UnityEngine;
using System.Collections;

public class FadeAway: MonoBehaviour {
  public float fadeDurationSeconds = 1.0f;
  public float alphaStart = 1.0f;
  public float alphaEnd = 0.0f;
  private float startTime;
  private MeshRenderer meshRenderer;
  private Color fadeColor;
  private bool isFading = false;

  void Start () {
    meshRenderer = GetComponent<MeshRenderer>();
    fadeColor = meshRenderer.material.color;
    UpdateMaterialAlpha(alphaStart);
  }
  void Update() {
    if (isFading)
      FadeAlpha();
  }

  void OnMouseUp() {
    StartFading();
  }

  private void StartFading() {
    startTime = Time.time;
    isFading = true;
  }

  private void FadeAlpha() {
    float timeFading = Time.time - startTime;
    float fadePercentage = timeFading / fadeDurationSeconds;
    float alpha = Mathf.Lerp(alphaStart, alphaEnd,
fadePercentage);
    UpdateMaterialAlpha(alpha);

    if (fadePercentage >= 1)
      isFading = false;
  }

  private void UpdateMaterialAlpha(float newAlpha) {
    fadeColor.a = newAlpha;
    meshRenderer.material.color = fadeColor;
```

```
    }
  }
```

> **Note**
> There are many parts to this code. A fully commented listing of this code is available in the folder for this chapter. See the *Technical requirements* section at the beginning of this chapter for the URL.

8. Play your **Scene** and click on the `Sphere` GameObject to see it fade away.

How it works...

The opaqueness of the material that's using a **Fade Shader** is determined by the alpha value of its main **color**. This recipe is based on changing the **Alpha** value of the color of **MeshRenderer**.

There are three public variables:

- `fadeDurationSeconds`: The time in seconds we want our fading to take
- `alphaStart`: The initial **Alpha** (transparency) value we want the GameObject to start with (1 = fully visible, 0 = invisible)
- `alphaEnd`: The **Alpha** value we want to fade the GameObject into

The `UpdateMaterialAlpha(...)` method updates the **Alpha** value of the GameObject's color object with the given value by updating the **Alpha** value of the `fadeColor` color variable and then forcing the **MeshRenderer** material to update its color value to match those in `fadeColor`.

When the scene begins, the `Start()` method caches a reference to the **MeshRenderer** component (the `meshRenderer` variable), and also the `Color` object of the material of **MeshRenderer** (the `fadeColor` variable). Finally, the GameObject's **Alpha** variable is set to match the value of the `alphaStart` variable, which it does by invoking the `UpdateMaterialAlpha(...)` method.

The `OnMouseUp()` method is invoked when the user clicks the GameObject with their mouse. This invokes the `StartFading()` method.

The actions to start fading weren't put in this method since we may also wish to start fading due to some other events (such as keyboard clicks, a timer hitting some value, or an NPC going into a mode such as dying). So, we separated the logic that detects that the event that we are interested in has taken place from the logic for the actions we wish to perform – in this case, to start the fading process.

The `StartFading()` method records the current time since we need that to know when to finish fading (the time when we started fading, plus `fadeDurationSeconds`). Also, the `isFading` Boolean flag is set to `true` so that logic elsewhere related to fading will know it's time to do things.

The `Update()` method, which is called each frame, tests whether the `isFading` flag is `true`. If it is, the `FadeAlpha()` method is invoked for each frame.

The `FadeAlpha()` method is where the majority of our alpha-fading logic is based:

- `timeFading` is calculated: The time since we started fading.
- `fadePercentage` is calculated: How far we are from the start (0) to the finish (1) of our fading.
- Alpha is calculated: The appropriate **Alpha** value for our fade percentage, using the `Lerp(...)` method to choose an `intermedia` value based on a `0..1` percentage.
- The `UpdateMaterialAlpha(...)` method with the new **Alpha** value.
- If fading has finished (`fadePercentage >= 1`), we set the `isFading` Boolean flag to `false` to indicate this.

There's more...

Here are some ways to enhance our fading features.

Destroying objects when fading is complete

If fading to invisible is how a GameObject communicates to the player that it is leaving the scene (completed/dying), then we may want that GameObject to be destroyed after the fading process is completed. Let's add this feature to our code.

Do the following:

1. Add a new public Boolean variable to our script (default to `false`):

```
public bool destroyWhenFadingComplete = true;
```

2. Add a new `EndFade()` method that sets `isFading` to `false` and then tests whether the public `destroyWhenFadingComplete` variable was set to `true` and, if so, destroys the GameObject:

```
private void EndFade() {
  isFading = false;

  if(destroyWhenFadingComplete)
  Destroy (gameObject);
  }
```

3. Refactor the `FadeAlpha()` method so that it invokes `EndFade()` when the fading is completed (`fadeProgress >= fadeDurationSeconds`):

```
private void FadeAlpha()
 {
     float fadeProgress = Time.time - startTime;
     float alpha = Mathf.Lerp(alphaStart, alphaEnd,
fadeProgress
          / fadeDurationSeconds);
     UpdateMaterialAlpha(alpha);

     if (fadeProgress >= fadeDurationSeconds)
         EndFade();
 }
```

Using the GameObject's alpha as our starting alpha value

It may be that the game designer has set the alpha value of a GameObject in the **Inspector** window to the initial value they want. So, let's enhance our code to allow this to be indicated by checking a public Boolean flag variable in the **Inspector** window and adding code to read and use the GameObject's alpha if that option is chosen.

Do the following:

1. In the **Inspector** window, click **Color picker** for the **Albedo** material and set the **Alpha** value to something other than 255 (for example, set it to 32, which is almost transparent):

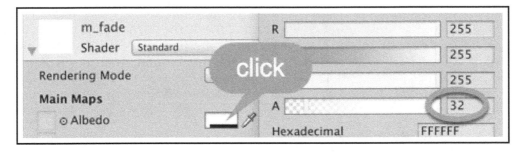

Figure 5.21 – Setting Rendering Mode of a material to Fade

2. Add a new public Boolean variable to our script (default to `false`):

```
public bool useMaterialAlpha = false;
```

3. Add logic to the `Start()` method so that if this flag is `true`, we use the **Alpha** value of the color that was read from the GameObject's material as the scene begins (`fadeColor.a`):

```
void Start () {
        meshRenderer = GetComponent<MeshRenderer>();

        // set object material's original color as fadeColor
        fadeColor = meshRenderer.material.color;

        // IF using material's original alpha value, THEN use
            //material's alpha value for alphaStart
        if (useMaterialAlpha)
            alphaStart = fadeColor.a;

        // start object's alpha at our alphaStart value
        UpdateMaterialAlpha(alphaStart);
    }
```

Using a coroutine for our fading loop

Where possible, we should avoid adding code to the `Update()` method since this is invoked every frame, which means it can reduce the performance of our games, especially if many objects have scripted components with `Update()` methods, all testing flags every frame.

One very effective solution is to invoke a coroutine when we want some actions to be performed over several frames. This is because a coroutine can perform some actions, then yield control back to the rest of the scene, and then resume its actions from where it left off, and so on until its logic is completed.

Do the following:

1. Remove the `Update()` method.
2. Add a new `using` statement at the top of the script class since coroutines return an `IEnumerator` value, which is part of the `System.Collections` package:

   ```
   using System.Collections;
   ```

3. Add a new method:

   ```
   private IEnumerator FadeFunction() {
           while (isFading)
           {
               yield return new WaitForEndOfFrame();
               FadeAlpha();
           }
       }
   ```

4. Refactor the `StartFading()` method, so that it starts our coroutine:

   ```
   private void StartFading() {
           startTime = Time.time;
           isFading = true;
           StartCoroutine(FadeFunction());
       }
   ```

That's it – once the coroutine has been started, it will be called each frame until it completes its logic, temporarily suspending its execution each time a yield statement is executed.

Creating geometry with ProBuilder

A recent addition to the 3D Unity tools is **ProBuilder**, which allows you to create and manipulate geometry inside the Unity Editor. Much more powerful than the existing **Terrain** editor, **ProBuilder** allows you to create 3D primitives and then manipulate them, such as by extruding or moving vertices, edges, or faces, and then painting with colors or texturing with materials.

In this recipe, we'll create some geometry that might be useful for an original game, or to add to a 3D **Gamekit Scene**.

If you've not used a 3D modeling package before (such as Blender, 3D Studio Max, or Maya), then it is well worth exploring the different features of **ProBuilder**. By doing so, you'll learn about some key concepts, including the following:

- **Vertex**: A point where lines touch – a corner where the edges touch
- **Edges**: A straight line between two vertices
- **Faces**: Flat 2D surfaces, usually a rectangle or triangle:

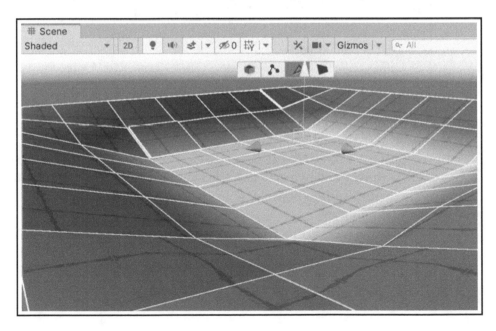

Figure 5.22 – Example of the two-colored mesh we'll create in this recipe

How to do it...

To create geometry with ProBuilder, follow these steps:

1. Create a new Unity 3D project.
2. Ensure **Unity Grid Snapping** is active (the button icon should be dark when selected). Set the **X** grid size and movement to 1 by going to **Edit | Grid and Snap Settings ...** and setting these values to 1:

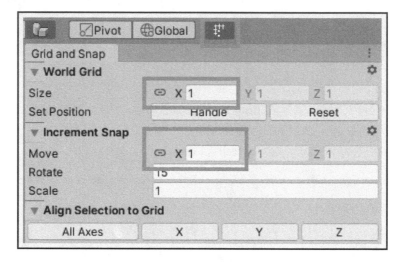

Figure 5.23 – Unity Grid Snapping set to 1

3. Use **Package Manager** to install the **ProBuilder** package by going to **Window** | P**ackage Manager**. Set this to **Packages: ALL**, click **Advanced**, and click **Show preview packages**. Click on **ProBuilder** and click **Install**.
4. Display the **ProBuilder** panel by going to **Tools | Probuilder | ProBuilder Window**.
5. Dock the panel (next to the **Hierarchy** window works well). Choose **Text Mode** or **Icon Mode**, as you prefer, by right-clicking the context menu:

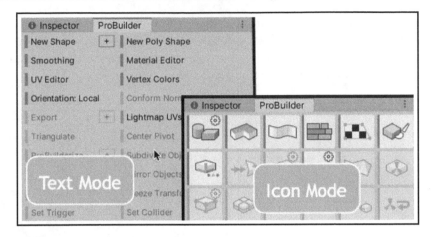

Figure 5.24 – Text Mode versus Icon Mode for the ProBuilder window

6. Create a new **ProBuilder Plane** by clicking **New Shape** and choosing
    the **Plane** shape from the **Create Shape** pop-up panel (its icon is a simple
    square). In this pop-up panel, for **Plane Settings**, set both **Height Cuts** and
    Width Cuts to 3:

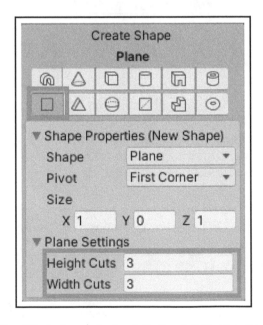

Figure 5.25 – Creating a new plane from the New Shape ProBuilder pop-up window

7. In the **Scene** panel you can now use the mouse (click and drag) to draw your ProBuilder **Plane** GameObject – in the **Inspector** window, you should see a ProBuilder **MeshFilter** component and a **ProBuilder Shape (Script)** component. Drag the plane until its size is (4, 0, 4):

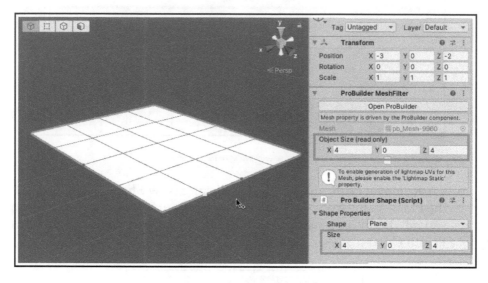

Figure 5.26 – Dragging the new plane so that it's 4 x 4 units in size

8. Click the **New Shape** ProBuilder tool icon again to hide the **Create Shape** pop-up panel.

9. You should now see that a **Plane** GameObject has been created in the **Hierarchy** and **Scene** windows. This **Plane** should consist of 16 faces in a 4 x 4 grid (since we set the height and width cuts to 4 each). The default material for **ProBuilder** is off-white with lines, so it may not immediately be clear where each face begins and ends.

10. Note that when a **ProBuilder** GameObject is selected, there is a small **ProBuilder** tool icon bar displayed in the **Scene** panel, allowing the **Object**, **Vertex**, **Edge**, and **Face** selection modes to be used:

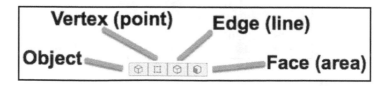

Figure 5.27 – The ProBuilder Scene panel selection mode menu

11. Choose the **Face** selection (the rightmost of the four **ProBuilder** section icons) and move the mouse over the plane that's the closest to the 16 faces highlighted in yellow.

12. Let's make a depression in the middle of our plane. Choose the **Face** selection (the rightmost of the four **ProBuilder** section icons) and, using the *Shift* key to make multiple sections, select the four inner faces (the selected faces will turn yellow). Then, use the Y-axis arrow to move these four selected faces downward:

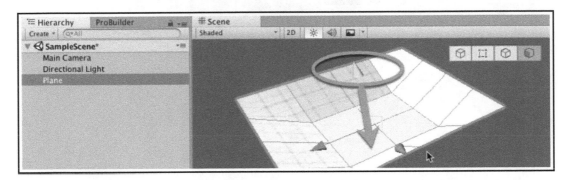

Figure 5.28 – Moving multiple faces using ProBuilder's Face mode selection

13. Let's paint all the faces red and then add some yellow to the center. Ensure you are still in the **Face** selection mode.

14. Click **ProBuilder Vertex Colors**. The **ProBuilder Vertex Colors** pop-up window should be displayed – dock this next to the **ProBuilder** window. Select all the faces of the plane and then click the red color in the **ProBuilder Vertex Colors** pop-up window.

15. Select **Vertex** selection mode (the second icon – the square with four dots). Now, select the vertex in the center of the four lower faces and click the **Apply** button by the yellow vertex. Repeat this for the eight vertices around the four lower faces. You should now see yellow nicely blending upward from the lower four faces.

16. Let's **Vertex Paint** some color on the object. This is easier to do carefully when there are more faces. First, in the **ProBuilder** window, click the **Subdivide** tool. This divides each **Face** into four faces (2 x 2). Moving your mouse over the faces, you'll see that there are now 8 x 8 = 64 faces in our plane:

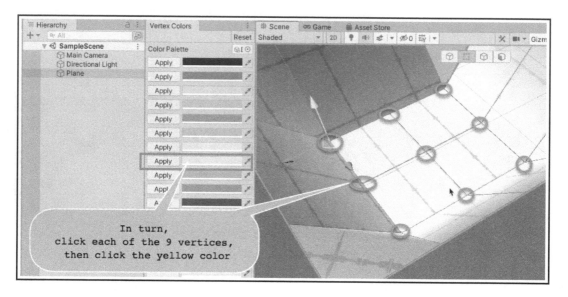

Figure 5.29 – Coloring the nine vertices (points) of the lower part of the Plane mesh

17. Save your **Scene**.

How it works...

By adding the **ProBuilder** package to a new 3D project, we can enable ProBuilder's features.

ProBuilder allows a mesh to be added to the scene. Dragging faces using the ProBuilder **Face-selection** tool allows you to select and then move some of the faces to create a depression. The meshes next to those faces are then deformed, creating a slope so that there are no holes in the mesh.

Once the whole mesh has been colored with one color, selecting only some of the vertices (points) and applying another color results in smoothly painted areas around those vertices.

ProBuilder offers many more features, including creating objects by drawing a line-by-line polygon and texturing surfaces rather than just painting around vertices, as we did in this recipe. You can find links regarding the documentation of **ProBuilder** in the *Further reading* section.

Creating a house with ProBuilder

If you quickly want to create a more detailed prototype, maybe based on an actual building, we can combine the techniques that we used in the previous recipe to extrude a complex building. In this recipe, we will demonstrate how to make a square room that includes a window and a door. Following the same process, a building of any shape can be made using ProBuilder:

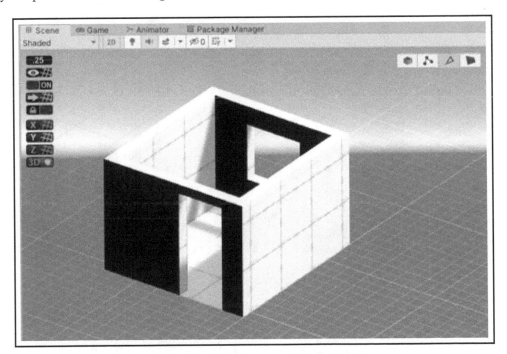

Figure 5.30 – Example of a room being created

How to do it...

To create a house with ProBuilder, follow these steps:

1. Create a new 3D project.
2. As with the previous recipe, ensure the ProBuilder package is installed and that **Unity Grid Snapping** is active and set to 1.
3. Select the top view and set the projection to orthographic view.
4. Choose the **New Poly Shape** tool from the **ProBuilder** window and draw 12 points in a kind of *C* shape, representing the walls and a doorway for a small, one-room building:

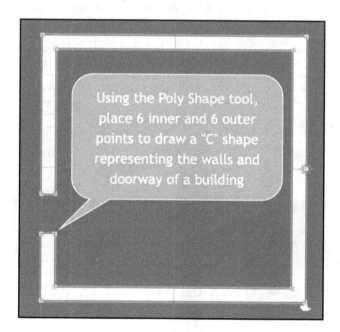

Figure 5.31 – Poly Shape tool creating a wall footprint for our room

5. Choose **Face Selection** mode and, while holding *Shift*, move the face upward 10 steps to extrude the walls of our room:

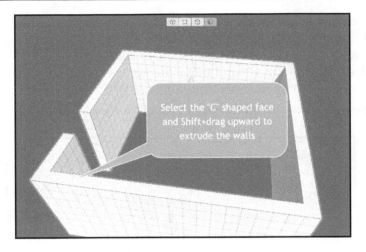

Figure 5.32 – Extruding the walls upward

6. Choose **Edge Selection** mode (this is the third icon – the 3D Cube with three lines selected).

7. Select one of the top-outside edges of a wall that doesn't have the door gap. Add an **Edge Loop** from the **ProBuilder** window. Select the top-outside wall edge again and add a second **Edge Loop**. Move the edge loops so that each is 5 units from the corner of the room:

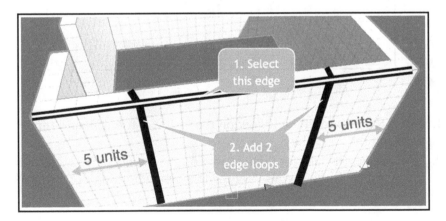

Figure 5.33 – The two evenly spaced edge loops

8. Choose **Face Selection** mode (this is the fourth icon – the 3D Cube with one face selected). Select the middle face between your two edge loops.

9. Choose the **Unity Scale** tool (the keyboard shortcut key for this is *R*). While holding down the *Shift* key, reduce the size of the selected face so that it's approximately two units smaller above/below/left/right. Now, change to **Vertex selection** mode and move the vertices of the four corners of this inner face to snap them to Unity units.

10. Repeat this process on the inner face of this wall:

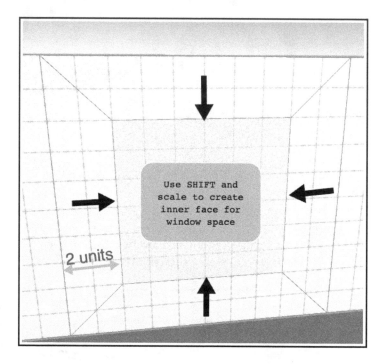

Figure 5.34 – Adding inner faces for the window location

11. Select the face for the window on the inside of the wall and remove it by pressing the *Delete* key.

12. Now, select the face for the window on the outside of the wall, and extrude it inward by 1 unit, by moving the face while holding down the *Shift* key. Now, select and delete this face:

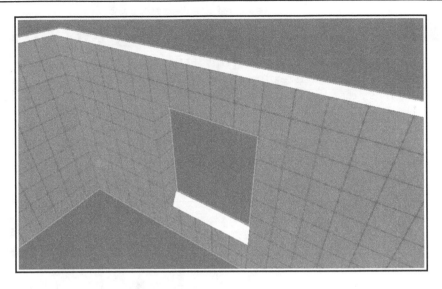

Figure 5.35 – The completed window gap in our wall

How it works...

In this recipe, you used several ProBuilder techniques to create a room with a doorway and a window in a wall. The **Poly Shape** tool is a great way to create a *footprint* of a shape quickly, which we did for our room. We then extruded this face upward to create the walls of our room. By leaving a gap in our **Poly Shape**, we left a gap for a doorway.

Edge loops are useful if we want to subdivide things such as walls. By creating an inner face with the scale tool, we were able to create two faces for on the inside and outside of the wall where we wanted our window gap to be created.

By extruding one face from the other for the window gap, when we removed the two faces, there was no gap between the faces of our inner and outer walls.

Creating and texture-painting terrains

After ProBuilder, perhaps the most powerful 3D feature of Unity is its terrains and their associated tools. Through texture and height painting, and the addition of trees and details such as grass and plants, complete environments can be modeled in a Unity scene.

In this recipe, we will introduce terrains by creating, sizing, positioning, and **Texture** (image) painting a flat **Terrain**. Later recipes will enhance this **Terrain** with heights, trees, and other details:

Figure 5.36 – Our flat Terrain texture painted with sand and grass around a cube

How to do it...

To create a **Terrain**, follow these steps:

1. Create a new 3D project.
2. Open **Package Manager**, select **All Packages**, and open the **Standard Assets** package import window.
3. Deselect all the assets and scroll through, selecting only **Environment** | **Terrain Assets** | **Surface Textures**. Click **Import** to add these **Texture** image asset files to your project:

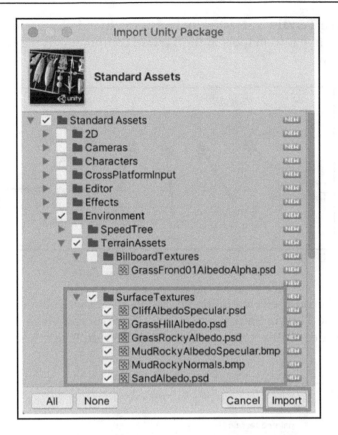

Figure 5.37 – Importing the Terrain texture images from the Standard Assets package

4. Add a 3D **Cube** to the scene by going to **Create | 3D Object | Cube**. In the **Inspector** window, set its **Position** to (0, 0, 0).

5. Add a **Terrain** to the scene by going to **Create | 3D Object | Terrain**. In the **Inspector** window, set its **Position** to (0, 0, 0).

6. You'll notice that the cube appears at one of the **corners** of the terrain! This is because Unity terrains are positioned by a corner and not their center, as with 3D primitives such as cubes.

7. To make the center of the terrain (0, 0, 0), we need to position it at (-width/2, 0, -length/2). Let's set the size of this **Terrain** to **100 x 100**; then, we can center it by setting its **Position** to (-50, 0, -50).

8. When a **Terrain** is selected in the **Hierarchy** window, you'll see the icons for the five terrain tools in the **Terrain** component in the **Inspector** window:

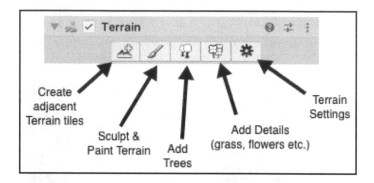

Figure 5.38 – The five terrain tools in the Inspector window

9. With **Terrain** selected in the **Hierarchy** window, in the **Inspector** window, click the **Terrain Settings** gear icon. Then, for the **Mesh Resolution** properties of this component, set both **Terrain Width** and **Terrain Length** to 100:

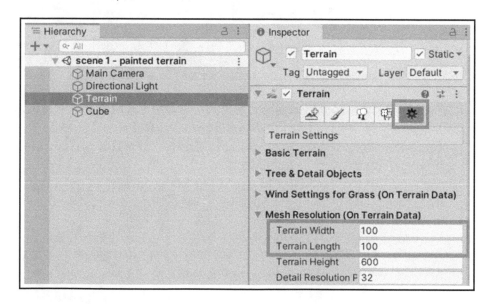

Figure 5.39 – Setting both Terrain Width and Terrain Length to 100

10. Now, for the **Transform** component in the **Inspector** window, set its **Position** to (-50, 0, -50). You should see that our **Cube** at (0, 0, 0) is sitting in the center of our **Terrain**.

11. Perhaps the most powerful way to make terrains feel like natural outdoor surfaces is by texturing different parts of them with environmental images such as sand, grass, stones, moss, and so on. The **Standard Assets** textures we imported at the beginning of this recipe are a great place to start.

12. In the **Inspector** window, select the **Sculpt and Paint Terrain** tool (the second icon, which looks like a paintbrush). Click the **Edit Terrain Layers...** button, choose **Create Layer...**, and, from the **Select Texture 2D** panel, select the **SandAlbedo** texture:

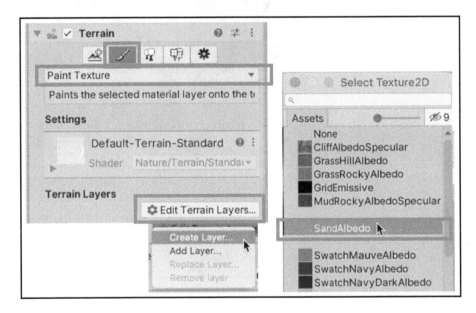

Figure 5.40 – Adding SandAlbedo as the first Terrain Layer

13. When there is only a single **Terrain Layer**, this **Texture** will be painted over the entire **Terrain**. Follow the same steps you did previously to add a second **Terrain Layer**, this time choosing **GrassHillAlbedo**.

14. Ensure your **GrassHillAlbedo** layer is selected and select the second brush (white-centered but with a fuzzy outline). Set **Brush Size** to 50. Now, use your brush to *paint* half of the terrain with grass:

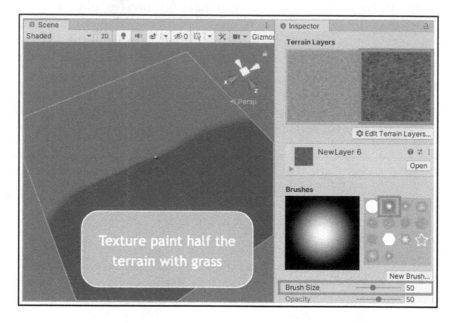

Figure 5.41 – Setting the gradient edged grass brush's size to 50

15. Save your scene.
16. Your scene should now contain a large, flat terrain that is half sand and half grass looking, meeting near the cube at the center.

How it works...

Terrains are sophisticated 3D object meshes in Unity. Since the position of terrains is based on a corner, if we want the terrain to be centered on a particular point such as (0, 0, 0), we have to subtract half the width from the X-coordinate and half the length from the Z-coordinate. So, for our 100 x 100 terrain, we set its corner position to (-50, 0, -50) so that its center is (0, 0, 0), which is where our **Cube** was located.

Textures are painted onto terrains through **Terrain Layers**. When there is only one **Terrain Layer**, the texture is used to paint the entire terrain, as it did when we set the first **Terrain Layer** to the **SandAlbedo** image. Once there are two or more terrain layers, we can use the brushes to paint different parts of the terrain with different textures.

The "softer" the edge of a brush, the more mixing there is between the texture that was present and the new texture of the brush being applied. The softer outline brushes create soft edges where two different textures meet on a painted terrain. When painting with vegetation such as grass and moss, it is effective for simulating where the vegetation at the edges of the rocky areas and fully green areas begin. The opacity of a brush affects the *mix* of textures all over the **Brush** area.

Height painting terrains

Using a combination of textures and terrains with variations in height enables sophisticated and realistic physical environments to be created. In this recipe, we'll build on the previous texture-painted terrain by varying the height to create an interesting landscape in our scene:

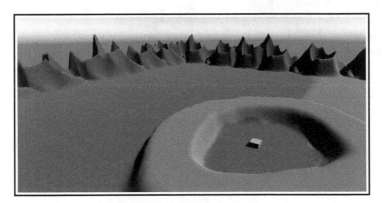

Figure 5.42 – A smooth, raised circle of Terrain around our Cube location

Getting ready

This recipe builds on the previous one, so make a copy of that and work on this copy. We have also provided a Unity package that contains the completed recipe in the 05_07 folder.

How to do it...

To height paint **Terrain**, follow these steps:

1. Open your copy of the Unity project from the previous recipe.
2. Select **Terrain** in the **Hierarchy** window.
3. In the **Inspector** window, select the **Sculpt and Paint Terrain** tool (the second icon, which looks like a paintbrush).
4. From the drop-down menu in the **Inspector** window, immediately below the five terrain tool icons, select **Set Height**:

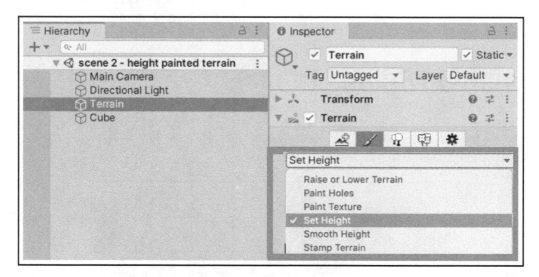

Figure 5.43 – Choosing the Set Height option from the terrain tools in the Inspector window

5. Set the painting's **Height** to 2 and select the first brush (the large white circle with a well-defined border). In the **Scene** window, paint a raised area with a **Height** of 2 around the cube at the center of the terrain:

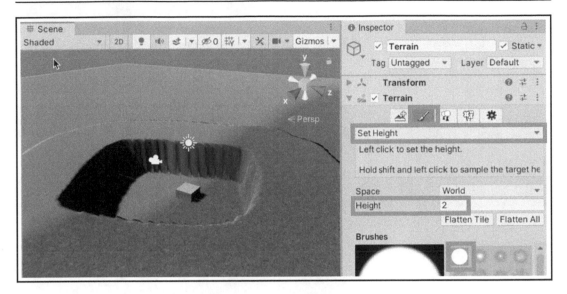

Figure 5.44 – Choosing the Set Height option from the terrain tools in the Inspector window

6. This isn't a very natural **Terrain** shape but it nicely illustrates this brush.

 If we wanted to remove raised areas, we can set the height to **zero** and return the height of **Terrain** to **0**.

7. From the drop-down menu in the **Inspector** window, immediately below the five terrain tool icons, select **Smooth Height**. Now, paint with the same brush – the steep edges of our raised circle around the cube should be smoothed into more natural slopes.

8. Now, texture paint all the low areas inside the circle with green grass and all the raised areas with yellow sand. We have made an interesting location for our **Cube**, which might be a special pickup or location in a game.

9. Finally, let's reduce the chance of our player falling off the edge of the world by creating a range of spiky high mountains all around the edge of our **Terrain**. Using the **Paint** tool, select the first menu item; that is, **Raise or Lower Terrain**.

10. Choose one of the star-like brushes with white star-shaped areas and a large brush size of 15. Now, click the mouse along the edge of each side of the terrain. Each click should raise the terrain into spikes. If you raise it too much, you can **lower** the terrain's height by holding the *Shift* key:

Figure 5.45 – Raising the terrain's height using a complex brush to create spiky mountains

How it works...

In this recipe, we explored three height painting tools. The first areas were raised straight up to a height of 2 using the **Set Height** tool. The **Set Height** tool is useful for quickly raising or lowering areas to a **specific** height. However, it leaves very steep *walls* between areas of different heights. It's also great for returning areas of the terrain back to zero.

The second tool we used was **Smooth Height**. This tool is used for finessing the final quality of the areas of the terrain where the height changes are too steep, so it is often used in combination with the **Set Height** tool.

Finally, we used the **Raise or Lower Terrain** height painting tool. This incrementally adds (or with *Shift* pressed, subtracts) to the height of the **Terrain** areas being painted upon. In combination with complex brushes, it allows us to quickly add complex details to areas of the terrain.

Adding Terrain holes

A limitation of terrains is that they are a single mesh, with points raised or lowered. Sometimes, we want more complex, concave geometry for effects such as caves, tunnels, or just simple holes in the terrain. In this recipe, we'll build on the previous one to add a **Terrain** hole that leads to another piece of terrain:

Figure 5.46 – A third-person controller character falling down our Terrain hole to a bonus level

Getting ready

This recipe builds on the previous one, so make a copy of that and work on that copy. We have also provided a Unity package containing the completed recipe in the 05_08 folder.

How to do it...

To paint and make use of a hole in a **Terrain**, follow these steps:

1. Open your copy of the Unity project from the previous recipe.
2. Add a **Spot Light** that shines on where the cube is sitting by going to **Create | Light | Spot Light**. In the **Inspector** window, set its **Position** to (0, 0.5, 0), its **Range** to 50, its **Spot Angle** to 125, and its **Intensity** to 2. This will allow this light to light up a bonus level we'll create beneath our **Terrain**.

3. Delete the cube from the scene – in a full game, this cube will be removed when a goal has been achieved, revealing the entrance to the bonus level we are going to create.

4. Select **Terrain** in the **Hierarchy** window.

5. In the **Inspector** window, select the **Sculpt and Paint Terrain** tool (the second icon, which looks like a paintbrush).

6. From the drop-down menu in the **Inspector** window, immediately below the five terrain tool icons, select **Paint Holes**.

7. Select the first brush (the large white circle with a well-defined border) and set **Brush Size** to 1:

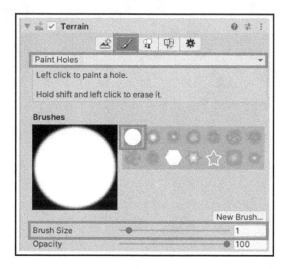

Figure 5.47 – Choosing the Paint Holes option from the terrain tools in the Inspector window

8. Now, paint a hole in the **Terrain** for the white circle lit by our **Spot Light**. This is the area that would have been beneath the cube we just deleted:

Figure 5.48 – The ragged-edged hole in our Terrain

9. Let's tidy up the edges of this hole. For something sophisticated, we could use **ProBuilder** tools, but for speed, we'll use four squashed cubes. Create a **Cube** named `Cube-wall` and scale it to (`1.7, 1.7. 0.25`). Make three more copies (`Cube-wall2/3/4`), rotating two of them by 90 degrees about the Y-axis (`0, 90, 0`). Move these squashed cubes to make a neat edge for the hole:

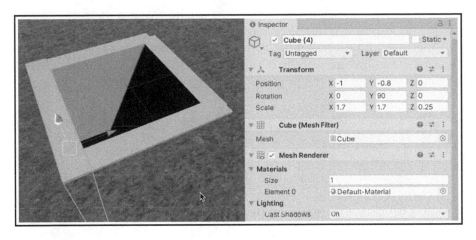

Figure 5.49 – Four cubes squashed and positioned to make an entrance near the Terrain hole

10. Now, let's create a simple, flat level beneath this hole. Create a **Cube** named `Cube-bonus-level` (**Create | 3D Object | Cube**) and set its **Position** to (`0, -10, 0`) and **Scale** to (`30, 1, 30`).

11. With that, we have created a scene containing a **Terrain**, and a neat hole in that **Terrain** leading to a subterranean lit level where we could place some bonus items or a bonus challenge:

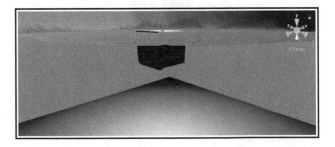

Figure 5.50 – The bonus level Cube and drop through the Terrain hole, as seen from below

How it works...

As we have seen, holes can be painted in **Terrain** meshes, as simply as we can height- and texture-paint terrains. Adding holes opens up a wide range of features we can add to scenes, allowing us to make complex combinations of one or more terrains with other scene objects and geometry.

When created, the edges of holes in terrains are unsightly, and in most games, they will need tidying up. In this recipe, we used four cubes positioned and scaled to form a neat entrance and channel from the surface of the terrain, down to the bonus **Cube** level. For a more natural entrance to a **Terrain** hole, you could use a pre-existing 3D model or a custom mesh that's been textured using the ProBuilder Unity tools.

There's more...

If you quickly want to explore the terrain and visit the bonus level via the **Terrain** hole, a quick and easy way of getting a working third-person controller is to visit the Asset Store and get the free Invector LITE package. Once imported, remove **Main Camera** from your scene, and drag **ThirdPersonController_LITE** and **vThirdPersonCamera_LITE Prefs** into it. Select **ThirdPersonController_LITE** and, in the **Inspector** window, set **Jump Height** to 10. This should be sufficient to allow the character to jump up and over the raised circle around the entrance to the **Terrain** hole so that they can get to the bonus level:

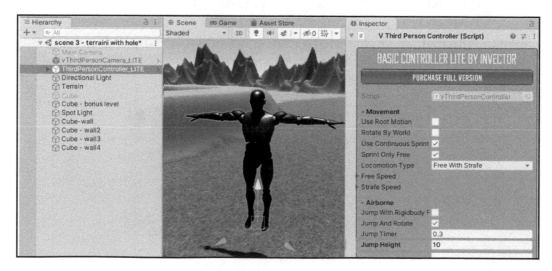

Figure 5.51 – Adding the Invector LITE free third-person controller to the scene

Further reading

This section contains some sources that provide more information about the topics that were covered in this chapter.

Every game needs textures. Here are some sources of free textures that are suitable for many games:

- textures.com: `https://www.textures.com/`
- GAMETEXTURES: `https://gametextures.com/`

Take a look at the following links for importing models into Unity:

- Importing models: `https://docs.unity3d.com/Manual/ImportingModelFiles.html`
- Limitations of importing models: `https://docs.unity3d.com/Manual/HOWTO-ImportObjectsFrom3DApps.html`
- Maxon's Free Cinema3D Importer on the Asset Store: `https://assetstore.unity.com/packages/tools/integration/cineware-by-maxon-158381`

You can learn more about modeling in Unity with ProBuilder:

- Unity blog post in 2018 outlining core ProBuilder features: `https://blogs.unity3d.com/2018/02/15/probuilder-joins-unity-offering-integrated-in-editor-advanced-level-design/`
- Unity Technology ProBuilder documentation manual: `https://docs.unity3d.com/Packages/com.unity.probuilder@3.0/manual/index.html`
- Unity Technology ProBuilder videos: `https://www.youtube.com/user/Unity3D/search?query=Probuilder`

To learn more about Unity terrains, take a look at the following links:

- Creating and editing terrains: `https://docs.unity3d.com/Manual/terrain-UsingTerrains.html`
- A Unity blog post outlining the Terrain tools: `https://blogs.unity3d.com/2019/05/28/speed-up-your-work-with-the-new-terrain-tools-package/`

- A Unit blog post about using Terrain tools to sculpt a volcano: `https://blogs.unity3d.com/2019/08/15/accelerate-your-terrain-material-painting-with-the-2019-2-terrain-tools-update/`
- A Unity blog post with tips about adding features by adding Terrain holes: `https://blogs.unity3d.com/2020/01/31/digging-into-terrain-paint-holes-in-unity-2019-3/`

2D Animation and Physics

6

Since Unity 4.6 in 2014, Unity has shipped with dedicated 2D features, and Unity 2021 continues to build on these. In this chapter, we will present a range of recipes that introduce the basics of 2D animation in Unity 2021 to help you understand the relationships between the different animation elements.

In Unity 2D, animations can be created in several different ways – one way is to create many images, each slightly different, which give the appearance of movement frame by frame. A second way to create animations is by defining keyframe positions for individual parts of an object (for example, the arms, legs, feet, head, and eyes) and getting Unity to calculate all the in-between positions when the game is running:

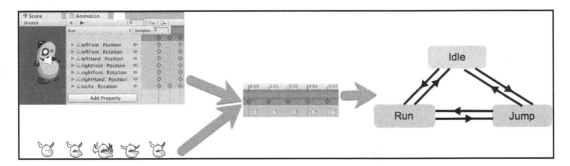

Figure 6.1 – Overview of animation in Unity

Both sources of animations become animation clips in the **Animation** panel. Each **Animation Clip** then becomes a **State** in **Animator Controller State Machine**. We can also duplicate **States** based on animation clips, or create new states and add scripted behaviors. We can also define sophisticated conditions, under which the GameObject will **Transition** from one animation **State** to another.

In this chapter, we will look at the animation system for 2D game elements. The PotatoMan2D character is from Unity's **2D Platformer**, which you can download yourself from the Unity Asset Store. This project is a good place to see lots more examples of 2D game and animation techniques:

Figure 6.2 – Unity 2D Platformer Game Kit

In this chapter, we will cover the following recipes:

- Flipping a sprite horizontally – the DIY approach
- Flipping a sprite horizontally – using Animator State Chart and transitions
- Animating body parts for character movement events
- Creating a three-frame animation clip to make a platform continually animate
- Making a platform start falling once stepped on using a Trigger to move the animation from one state to another
- Creating animation clips from sprite sheet sequences
- Creating a platform game with tiles and tilemaps
- Using sprite placeholders to create a simple physics scene
- Editing polygon Colliders for more realistic 2D physics
- Creating an explosionForce method for 2D physics objects
- Clipping via Sprite Masking

Technical requirements

For this chapter, you will need Unity 2021.1 or later, plus one of the following:

- Microsoft Windows 10 (64-bit)/GPU: DX10, DX11, and DX12-capable
- MacOS Sierra 10.12.6+/GPU Metal-capable Intel or AMD
- Linux: Ubuntu 16.04, Ubuntu 18.04, and CentOS 7/GPU: OpenGL 3.2+ or Vulkan-capable, NVIDIA or AMD

For each chapter, there is a folder that contains the asset files you will need in this book's GitHub repository at `https://github.com/PacktPublishing/Unity-2021-Cookbook-Fourth-Edition`.

Flipping a sprite horizontally – the DIY approach

Perhaps the simplest 2D animation is a simple flip, from facing left to facing right, facing up to facing down, and so on. In this recipe, we'll add a cute bug sprite to the scene and write a short script to flip its horizontal direction when the *Left* and *Right* arrow keys are pressed:

Figure 6.3 – Example of flipping a sprite horizontally

Getting ready

For this recipe, we have prepared the image you need in a folder named `Sprites` in the `06_01` folder.

How to do it...

To flip an object horizontally with arrow key presses, follow these steps:

1. Create a new Unity 2D project.

 If you are working on a project that was originally created in 3D, you can change the default project behavior (for example, new **Sprite Texture** additions and **Scene** mode) to 2D by going to **Edit | Project Settings | Editor** and then choosing **2D** for **Default Behavior Mode** in the **Inspector** window:

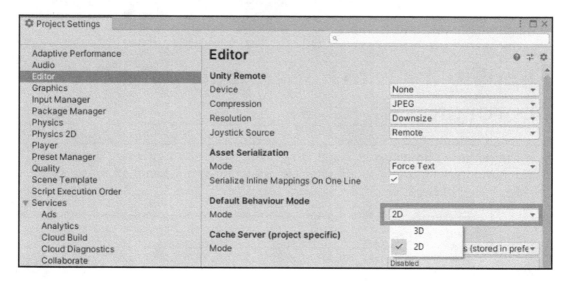

Figure 6.4 – Setting Default Behaviour Mode to 2D

2. Import the provided image; that is, `EnemyBug.png`.
3. Drag an instance of the red **Enemy Bug** image from the **Project | Sprites** folder into the scene. Position this GameObject at (0, 0, 0) and scale it to (2, 2, 2).
4. Create a C# script class called `BugFlip` and add an instance object as a component of **Enemy Bug**:

```
using UnityEngine;
using System.Collections;

public class BugFlip : MonoBehaviour {
  private bool facingRight = true;
```

```
        void Update() {
            if (Input.GetKeyDown(KeyCode.LeftArrow) &&
facingRight)
                Flip ();
            if (Input.GetKeyDown(KeyCode.RightArrow) &&
!facingRight)
                Flip();
        }

        void Flip (){
            // Switch the way the player is labelled as facing.
            facingRight = !facingRight;

            // Multiply the player's x local scale by -1.
            Vector3 theScale = transform.localScale;
            theScale.x *= -1;
            transform.localScale = theScale;
        }
    }
```

5. When you run your scene, pressing the *Left* and *Right* arrow keys should make the bug face left or right.

How it works...

The C# class defines a Boolean variable, `facingRight`, that stores a `true`/`false` value that corresponds to whether the bug is facing right. Since our bug sprite was initially facing right, we set the initial value of `facingRight` to `true` to match this.

Every frame, the `Update()` method checks whether the *Left* or *Right* arrow keys have been pressed. If the *Left* arrow key is pressed and the bug is facing right, then the `Flip()` method is called; likewise, if the *Right* arrow key is pressed and the bug is facing left (that is, facing right is `false`), the `Flip()` method is called.

The `Flip()` method performs two actions; the first simply reverses the `true`/`false` value in the `facingRight` variable. The second action changes the +/- sign of the X-value of the `localScale` property of the transform. Reversing the sign of `localScale` results in the 2D flip that we desire. Look inside the `PlayerControl` script for the `PotatoMan` character in the next recipe – you'll see that the same `Flip()` method is used.

There's more...

As an alternative to changing the X-component of the local scale, we could change the flipX Boolean property of the GameObject's SpriteRenderer component by changing the contents of our BugFlip script to the following:

```
using UnityEngine;
using System.Collections;

public class BugFlip : MonoBehaviour {
    private bool facingRight = true;
    private SpriteRenderer _spriteRenderer;

    void Awake() {
        _spriteRenderer = GetComponent<SpriteRenderer>();
    }

    void Update() {
        if (Input.GetKeyDown(KeyCode.LeftArrow) &&
facingRight) {
            _spriteRenderer.flipX = facingRight;
            facingRight = false;
        }

        if (Input.GetKeyDown(KeyCode.RightArrow) &&
!facingRight){
            _spriteRenderer.flipX = facingRight;
            facingRight = true;
        }
    }
}
```

Once again, we are basing our code on the assumption that the sprite begins by facing right.

Flipping a sprite horizontally – using Animator State Chart and transitions

In this recipe, we'll use the Unity animation system to create two states corresponding to two animation clips, and a script that changes localScale according to which animation state is active. We'll use a second script, which will map the arrow keys to the **Horizontal** input axis values as a **Parameter** in the state chart, which will drive the transition from one state to the other.

While this may seem like a lot of work, compared to the previous recipe, such an approach illustrates how we can map from input events (such as key presses or touch inputs) to parameters and triggers in a **State Chart**.

Getting ready

For this recipe, we have prepared the image you need in a folder named `Sprites` in the `06_02` folder.

How to do it...

To flip an object horizontally using **Animator State Chart** and transitions, follow these steps:

1. Create a new Unity 2D project.
2. Import the provided image; that is, `EnemyBug.png`.
3. Drag an instance of the red **Enemy Bug** image from the `Project` | `Sprites` folder into the scene. Position this GameObject at `(0, 0, 0)` and scale it to `(2, 2, 2)`.
4. With the `Enemy Bug` GameObject selected in the **Hierarchy** window, open the **Animation** window (**Window** | **Animation** | **Animation**) and click the **Create** button to create a new **Animation Clip** asset. Save the new **Animation Clip** asset as `beetle-right`. You will also see that an `Animator` component has been added to the `Enemy Bug` GameObject:

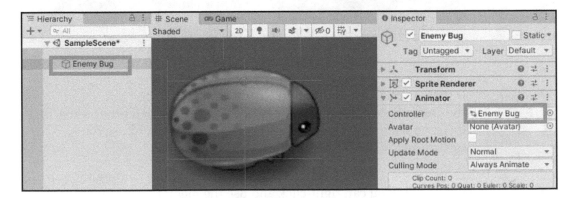

Figure 6.5 – Animator component added to the Enemy Bug GameObject

5. If you look in the **Project** window, you'll see that two new asset files have been created: an **Animation Clip** called `beetle-right` and an **Animator Controller** named `Enemy Bug`:

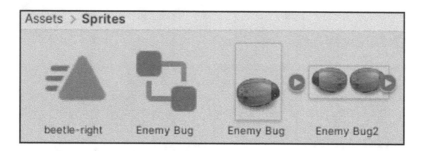

Figure 6.6 – Two new asset files included as part of the project

6. Close the **Animation** window and double-click **Enemy Bug Animator Controller** to start editing it – it should appear in a new **Animator** window. You should see four *states*; the **Any State** and **Exit** states should be unlinked, and **Entry** should have a **Transition** arrow connecting to the `beetle-right` state. This means that as soon as **Animator Controller** starts to play, it will enter the `beetle-right` state. `beetle-right` is tinted orange to indicate that it is in the **Default** state:

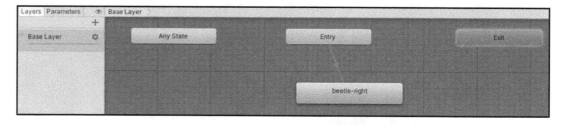

Figure 6.7 – Animation controller for Enemy Bug

 If there is only one **Animation Clip** state, that will be the **Default** state automatically. Once you have added other states to the state chart, you can right-click a different state and use the context menu to change which state is entered first.

7. Select the `beetle-right` state and make a copy of it, renaming the copy `beetle-left` (you can right-click and use the menu that appears or the *Ctrl + C*/*Ctrl + V* keyboard shortcuts). It makes sense to position `beetle-left` to the **left** of `beetle-right`:

Figure 6.8 – Adding a Transition to beetle-right

8. Move your mouse pointer over the `beetle-right` state. Then, in the right-click context menu, choose **Make Transition** and drag the white arrow that appears into the `beetle-left` state.

9. Repeat this step with `beetle-left` to create a **Transition** back from `beetle-left` to `beetle-right`:

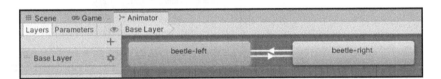

Figure 6.9 – Creating the beetle-left to beetle-right Transition

10. We want an instant **Transition** between the left- and right-facing beetles. So, for **each Transition**, uncheck the **Has Exit Time** option. Click the **Transition** arrow to select it (it should turn blue) and then uncheck this option in the **Inspector** window:

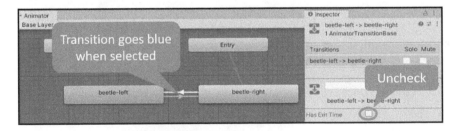

Figure 6.10 – Unchecking the Has Exit Time option for an instant transition

 To delete a **Transition**, select it and then use the *Delete* key (**Windows**) or press *Fn + Backspace* (**macOS**).

11. To decide when to change the active state, we need to create a parameter indicating whether the *Left/Right* arrow keys have been pressed. *Left/Right* key presses are indicated by the Unity input system's **Horizontal** axis value. Create a state chart float parameter named `axisHorizontal` by selecting **Parameters** (rather than **Layers**) from the top left of the **Animator** window, clicking the plus (**+**) button, and choosing **Float**. Name it `axisHorizontal`:

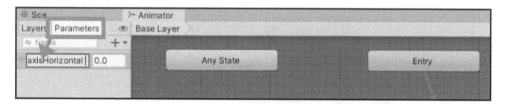

Figure 6.11 – Adding a Float as a parameter and naming it axisHorizontal

12. With our parameter, we can define the conditions for changing between the left- and right-facing states. When the *Left* arrow key is pressed, the Unity input system's **Horizontal** axis value is negative, so select the **Transition** from `beetle-right` to `beetle-left` and in the **Inspector** window, click the plus (**+**) symbol in the **Conditions** section of the **Transition** properties. Since there is only one parameter, this will automatically be suggested, with defaults of **Greater** than **zero**. Change **Greater** to **Less** so that we get our desired condition:

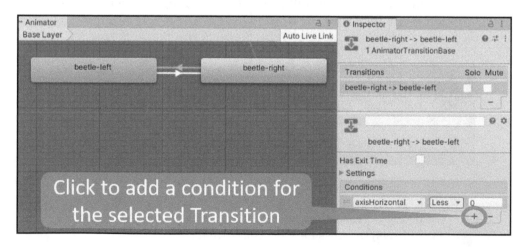

Figure 6.12 – Changing the condition of Transition to Less

13. Now, select the **Transition** from `beetle-left` to `beetle-right` and add a **Condition**. In this case, the defaults for `axisHorizontal` **Greater** than **zero**, are just what we want (since a positive value is returned by the Unity input system's **Horizontal** axis when the *Right* arrow key is pressed).

14. We need a method to actually map from the Unity input system's **Horizontal** axis value (from the *Left/Right* arrow keys) to our **Animator** state chart parameter, called `axisHorizontal`. We can do this with a short script class, which we'll create shortly.

15. Create a C# script class named `InputMapper` and add an instance object as a component to the `Enemy Bug` GameObject:

```
using UnityEngine;

public class InputMapper : MonoBehaviour {
    Animator animator;

    void Start() {
        animator = GetComponent<Animator>();
    }

    void Update() {
        animator.SetFloat("axisHorizontal",
Input.GetAxisRaw("Horizontal"));
    }
}
```

16. Now, we need to change the local scale property of the GameObject when we switch to the left- or right-facing state. Create a C# script class named `LocalScaleSetter`:

```
using UnityEngine;

public class LocalScaleSetter : StateMachineBehaviour {
    public Vector3 scale = Vector3.one;

    override public void OnStateEnter(Animator animator,
AnimatorStateInfo stateInfo, int layerIndex) {
        animator.transform.localScale = scale;
    }

}
```

17. In the **Animator** window, select the `beetle-right` state. In the **Inspector** window, click the **Add Behaviour** button and select **LocalScaleSetter**. The default public `Vector3` value of (`1, 1, 1`) is fine for this state.

18. In the **Animator** window, select the `beetle-left` state. In the **Inspector** window, click the **Add Behaviour** button and select **LocalScaleSetter**. Change the public `Vector3` scale to a value of (`-1, 1, 1`) – that is, we need to swap the X-scaling to make our **Sprite** face to the left:

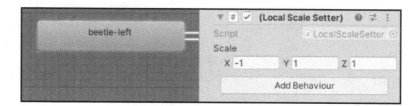

Figure 6.13 – Setting the public Vector3 scale to a value of (-1,1,1) for beetle-left

 Adding instance objects of C# script classes to **Animator** states is a great way to link the logic for actions when entering into/exiting a state with the **Animator** states themselves.

19. When you run your scene, pressing the *Left* and *Right* arrow keys should make the bug face left or right.

How it works...

Each frame of the `Update()` method of the `InputMapper` C# script class reads the Unity input system's **Horizontal** axis value and sets the **Animator** state chart's `axisHorizontal` parameter to this value. If the value is less than (left arrow) or greater than (right arrow) zero, if appropriate, the **Animator** state system will switch to the other state.

The `LocalScaleSetter` C# script class actually changes the `localScale` property (with an initial value of `1, 1, 1`, or reflected horizontally to make it face left at `-1, 1, 1`). For each state, the public `Vector3` variable can be customized to the appropriate values.

The `OnStateEnter(...)` method is involved each time you enter the state that an instance object of this C# class is attached to. You can read about the various event messages for the `StateMachineBehaviour` class at `https://docs.unity3d.com/ScriptReference/StateMachineBehaviour.html`.

When we press the *Left* arrow key, the value of the Unity input system's **Horizontal** axis value is negative, and this is mapped to the **Animator** state chart's `axisHorizontal` parameter, causing the system to **Transition** to the `beetle-left` state and `OnStateEnter(...)` of the `LocalScaleSetter` script class instance to be executed. This sets the local scale to `(-1, 1, 1)`, making **Texture** flip **Horizontally** so that the beetle faces left.

There's more...

Here are some suggestions for enhancing this recipe.

Instantaneous swapping

You may have noticed a delay, even though we set **Exit Time** to **zero**. This is because there is a default blending when transitioning from one state to another. However, this can be set to **zero** so that the state machine switches instantaneously from one state to the next.

Do the following:

1. Select each **Transition** in the **Animator** window.
2. Expand the **Settings** properties.
3. Set both **Transition Duration** and **Transition Offset** to 0:

Figure 6.14 – Setting both Transition Duration and Transition Offset to zero

Now, when you run the scene, the bug should immediately switch left and right as you press the corresponding arrow keys.

Animating body parts for character movement events

In the previous recipe, we used the Unity animation tool to alter the transition of a sprite based on input. In this recipe, we'll learn how to animate the hat of the Unity potato-man character in response to a jumping event using a variety of animation techniques, including keyframes and transforms.

Getting ready

For this recipe, we have prepared the files you need in the 06_03 folder.

How to do it...

To animate body parts for character movement events, follow these steps:

1. Create a new Unity 2D project.
2. Import the provided PotatoManAssets package into your project.
3. Increase the size of **Main Camera** to 10.
4. Set up the 2D gravity setting for this project – we'll use the same setting that's provided in Unity's 2D platform tutorial – that is, a setting of **Y=** -30. Set 2D gravity to this value by going to **Edit** | **Project Settings** | **Physics 2D** and changing the Y value to -30:

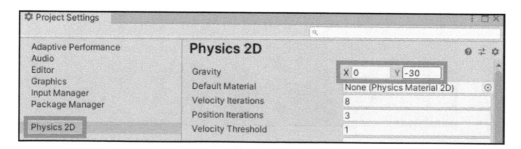

Figure 6.15 – Setting up 2D gravity for this project

5. Drag an instance of the **PotatoMan hero** character from the **Project |
Prefabs** folder into the scene. Position this GameObject at (0, 3, 0).

6. Drag an instance of the platformWallBlocks sprite from the **Project |
Sprites** folder into the scene. Position this GameObject at (0, -4, 0).

7. Add a **Box Collider 2D** component to
the platformWallBlocks GameObject by going to **Add Component |
Physics 2D | Box Collider 2D**.

8. We now have a stationary platform that the player can land on and walk
left and right on. Create a new **Layer** named Ground and assign
the platformWallBlocks GameObject to this new layer, as shown in the
following screenshot. Pressing the spacebar when the character is on the
platform will now make him jump:

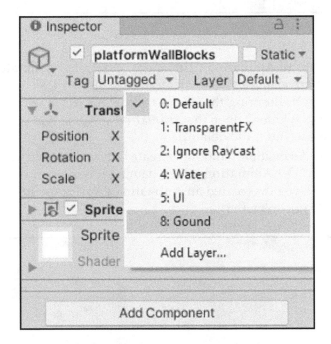

Figure 6.16 – Adding a new Layer called Ground

9. Currently, the **PotatoMan hero** character is animated (arms and legs moving) when we make him jump. Let's remove the **Animation Clip** components and **Animator Controller** and create our own from scratch. Delete the **Clips** and **Controllers** folders from **Project | Assets |PotatoMan2DAssets | Character2D | Animation**, as shown here:

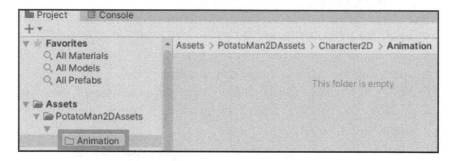

Figure 6.17 – Animation folder with Clips and Controllers removed

10. Let's create an **Animation Clip** (and its associated **Animator Controller**) for our **hero** character. In the **Hierarchy** window, select the hero GameObject. Ensuring that the hero GameObject is selected in the **Hierarchy** window, open the **Animation** window and ensure it is in **Dope Sheet** view (this is the default).

11. Click the **Animation** window's **Create** button and save the new clip in the **Character2D | Animation** folder, naming it character-potatoman-idle. You've now created an **Animation Clip** for the **Idle** character state (which is not animated):

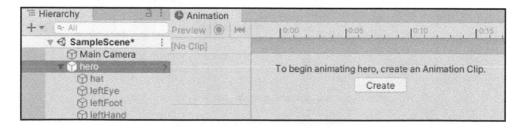

Figure 6.18 – Animation panel for the potatoman character

 Your final game may end up with dozens, or even hundreds, of animation clips. Make things easy to search for by prefixing the names of the clips with the object's type, name, and then a description of the animation clip.

12. Looking at the **Character2D** | **Animation** folder in the **Project** window, you should see both animation clips you have just created (`character-potatoman-idle`) and a new **Animator Controller**, which has defaulted to the name of your **hero** Character2D GameObject:

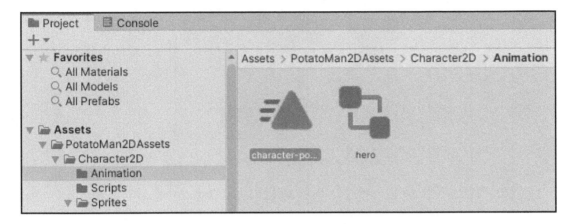

Figure 6.19 – Animation clips and Animator Controller for the potatoman character

13. Ensuring the `hero` GameObject is selected in the **Hierarchy** window, open the **Animator** window. You'll see a **State Machine** for controlling the animation of our character. Since we only have one **Animation Clip** (`character-potatoman-idle`), upon entry, **State Machine** immediately enters this state:

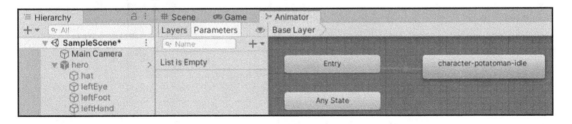

Figure 6.20 – State Machine for controlling the animation of the character

14. Run your scene. Since the character is always in the "idle" state, we see no animation yet when we make it jump.

15. Create a jump **Animation Clip** that animates **hat**. Ensure that the `hero` GameObject is still selected in the **Hierarchy** window. Click the empty drop-down menu in the **Animation** window (next to the word **Samples**) and create a new clip in your **Animation** folder, naming it `character-potatoman-jump`:

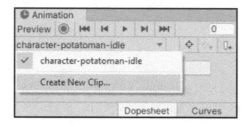

Figure 6.21 – Creating a new clip in your Animation folder

16. Click the **Add Property** button and choose **Transform | Position** for the **hat** child object, by clicking its plus + button. We are now ready to record changes that are made to the (X, Y, Z) position of the **hat** GameObject in this Animation Clip:

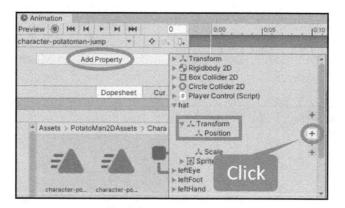

Figure 6.22 – Adding the Position property

17. You should now see two keyframes at 0.0 and 1.0. These are indicated by diamonds in the **Timeline** area in the right-hand section of the **Animation** window.

18. Click to select the first keyframe (at time 0.0) – the diamond should turn blue to indicate it is selected.

19. Let's record a new position for **hat** for this first frame. Click the red **Record** circle button once to start recording in the **Animation** window. Now, in the **Scene** window, move **hat** up and left a little, away from the head. You should see that all three X, Y, and Z values have a red background in the **Inspector** window – this is to inform you that the values of the **Transform** component are being recorded in **Animation Clip**:

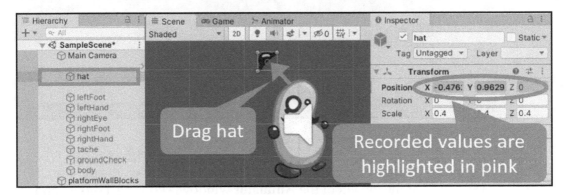

Figure 6.23 – Recording a new position for hat

20. Click the red **Record** circle button again to stop recording in the **Animation** window.

21. Since 1 second is perhaps too long for our jump animation, drag the second keyframe diamond to the left to a time of 0.5:

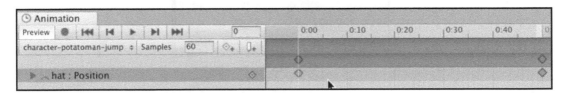

Figure 6.24 – Adjusting the second keyframe to a time of 0.5

22. We need to define when the character should **Transition** from the **Idle** state to the **Jump** state. In the **Animator** window, select the `character-potatoman-idle` state and create a **Transition** to the `character-potatoman-jump` state by right-clicking and choosing the **Make Transition** menu. Then, drag the **Transition** arrow to the `character-potatoman-jump` state, as shown in the following screenshot:

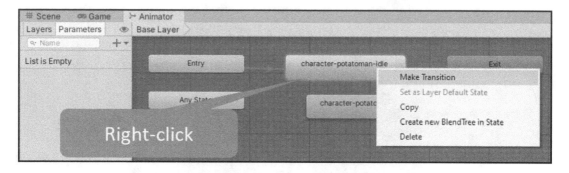

Figure 6.25 – Making a transition for character-potatoman-idle

23. Let's add a **Trigger** parameter named **Jump** by clicking on the plus (+) button at the top left of the **Animator** window, choosing **Trigger**, and typing in `Jump`:

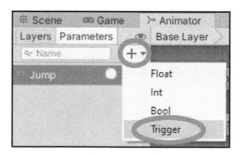

Figure 6.26 – Adding a Trigger parameter named Jump

24. We can now define the properties for when our character should **Transition** from **Idle** to **Jump**. Click the **Transition** arrow to select it, set the following two properties, and add one condition to the **Inspector** window:

- **Has Exit Time**: Uncheck this option.
- **Transition Duration(s)**: Set to `0.01`.
- **Conditions**: Add **Jump** (click the plus (+) button at the bottom):

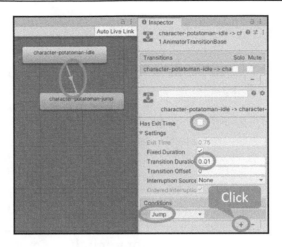

Figure 6.27 – Inspector window for character Transition properties

25. Save and run your scene. Once the character has landed on the platform and you press the *spacebar* to jump, you'll see the character's hat jump away from his head and slowly move back. Since we haven't added a **Transition** to leave the **Jump** state, this **Animation Clip** will loop so that **hat** keeps on moving, even when the jump is completed.

26. In the **Animator** window, select the `character-potatoman-jump` state and add a new **Transition** to the `character-potatoman-idle` state. Select this **Transition** arrow and in the **Inspector** window, set its properties as follows:

    - **Has Exit Time**: (leave checked).
    - **Exit Time**: 0.5 (this needs to have the same time value as the second keyframe of our `Jump` animation clip):

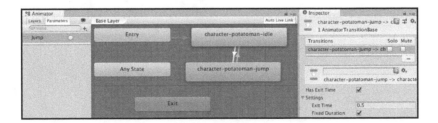

Figure 6.28 – The character-potatoman-jump state and character-potatoman-idle state Transition properties

27. Save and run your scene. Now, when you jump, **hat** should animate once, after which the character will immediately return to its **Idle** state.

How it works...

In this recipe, you added an **Animation Controller State Machine** to the hero GameObject. The two animation clips you created (**idle** and **jump**) appear as states in the **Animator** window. You created a **Transition** from **Idle** to **Jump** when the **JumpTrigger** parameter is received by **State Machine**. You then created a second **Transition**, which transitions back to the **Idle** state after waiting 0.5 seconds (the same duration between the two keyframes in our **Jump Animation Clip**).

The player makes the character jump by pressing the *spacebar*. This causes the code in the PlayerControl C# scripted component of the hero GameObject to be invoked, which makes the sprite move upward on the screen and also sends a SetTrigger(...) message to the **Animator Controller** component for the **Jump** trigger.

The difference between a **Boolean Parameter** and a **Trigger** is that a **Trigger** is temporarily set to **True**. Once the SetTrigger(...) event has been consumed by a state transition, it automatically returns to **False**. So, triggers are useful for actions we wish to complete once and then revert to a previous state. A **Boolean Parameter** is a variable that can have its value set to **True** or **False** at different times during the game. So, different **Transitions** can be created to fire, depending on the value of the variable at any time. Note that Boolean parameters have to have their values explicitly set back to **False** with SetBool(...).

The following screenshot highlights the line of code that sends the SetTrigger(...) message:

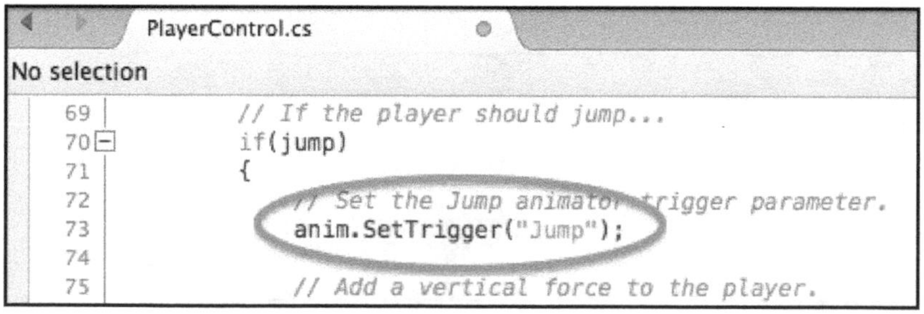

```
      PlayerControl.cs
No selection
    69          // If the player should jump...
    70 □       if(jump)
    71          {
    72              // Set the Jump animator trigger parameter.
    73              anim.SetTrigger("Jump");
    74
    75              // Add a vertical force to the player.
```

Figure 6.29 – Example of the code that sends the trigger message

The state machines of animations with a range of motions (running/walking/jumping/falling/dying) will have more states and transitions. The Unity-provided potatoman `hero` character has a more complex **State Machine**, and more complex animations (for its hands and feet, eyes and hat, and so on for each **Animation Clip**), which you may wish to explore.

You can learn more about the **Animation** view at `http://docs.unity3d.com/Manual/AnimationEditorGuide.html`.

Creating a three-frame animation clip to make a platform continually animate

In this recipe, we'll make a wooden-looking platform continually animate, moving upward and downward. This can be achieved with a single three-frame **Animation Clip** (starting at the top, then positioned at the bottom, and finally back at the top position). Note that each frame is a static position and that we will employ the animation technique known as **in-betweening** to create the necessary movement:

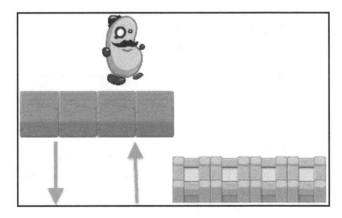

Figure 6.30 – Example of a moving platform game

Getting ready

This recipe builds on the previous one, so make a copy of that project and work on the copy for this recipe.

How to do it...

To create a continually moving animated platform, follow these steps:

1. Drag an instance of the `platformWoodBlocks` sprite from the **Project |
Sprites** folder into the scene. Position this GameObject at `(-4, -5, 0)` so
that these wood blocks are neatly to the left and slightly below the wall
blocks platform.

2. Add a **Box Collider 2D** component to
the `platformWoodBlocks` GameObject so that the player's character can
stand on this platform too. To do this, go to **Add Component | Physics 2D
| Box Collider 2D**.

3. Create a new folder named `Animations` to store the controller
and **Animation Clip** we'll create next.

4. Ensuring the `platformWoodBlocks` GameObject is still selected in the
Hierarchy window, open an **Animation** window and ensure it is in **Dope
Sheet** view (this is the default).

5. Click the **Animation** window's **Create** button and save the new clip in your
new `Animation` folder, naming it `platform-wood-moving-up-down`.

6. Click the **Add Property** button, choose **Transform**, and then click the plus
(+) button by **Position**. We are now ready to record changes to the (X, Y, Z)
position of the `platformWoodBlocks` GameObject in this **Animation Clip**:

Figure 6.31 – Animation setting for Transform | Position of platformWoodBlocks

7. You should now see two keyframes at **0.0** and at **1.0**. These are indicated by
diamonds in the **Timeline** area in the right-hand section of the **Animation**
window.

8. We need three keyframes, with the new one at 2:00 seconds. Click at **2:00** in
the **Timeline** area, along the top of the **Animation** window, so that the red
line for the current playhead time is at **2:00**. Then, click the diamond +
button to create a new keyframe at the current playhead time:

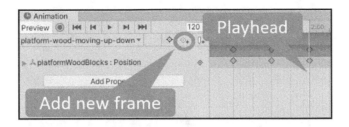

Figure 6.32 – Adding a new keyframe at 2:00 seconds

9. The first and third keyframes are fine – they record the current height of the wood platform at **Y** = -5. We need to make the middle keyframe record the height of the platform at the top of its motion, and Unity **in-betweening** will do the rest of the animation work for us.

10. Select the middle keyframe (at time **1:00**) by clicking on the diamond at time 1:00 (they should both turn blue, and the red playhead vertical line should move to **1:00** to indicate that the middle keyframe is being edited).

11. Click the red **Record** circle button to start recording changes.

12. In the **Inspector** window, change the Y-position of the platform to 0. You should see that all three X, Y, and Z values have a red background in the **Inspector** window – this is to inform you that the values of the **Transform** component are being recorded in **Animation Clip**.

13. Click the red **Record** circle button again to finish recording your changes.

14. Save and run your scene. The wooden platform should now be animating continuously, moving smoothly up and down the positions we set up.

 If you want the potato-man character to be able to jump when on the moving wooden block, you'll need to select the `block` GameObject and set its layer to **Ground**.

How it works...

In this recipe, you added an animation to the `platformWoodBlocks` GameObject. This animation contains three keyframes. A keyframe represents the values of the properties of the object at a point in time. The first keyframe stores a Y-value of -4, the second keyframe a Y-value of 0, and the final keyframe -4 again. Unity calculates all the in-between values for us, and the result is a smooth animation of the Y-position of the platform.

There's more...

Here are some suggestions for enhancing this recipe.

Copying the animation relative to a new parent GameObject

If we wanted to duplicate the moving platform, simply duplicating the platformWoodBlocks GameObject in the **Hierarchy** window and moving the copy won't work. When you run the scene, each duplicate would be animated back to the location of the original animation frames (that is, all the copies would be positioned and moving from the original location).

The solution is to create a new, empty GameObject named movingBlockParent, and then a platformWoodBlocks parent for this GameObject. Once we've done this, we can duplicate the movingBlockParent GameObject (and its platformWoodBlocks child) to create more moving blocks in our scene that each move relative to where the parent GameObject is located at design time.

Making a platform start falling once stepped on using a Trigger to move the animation from one state to another

In many cases, we don't want an animation to begin until some condition has been met, or some event has occurred. In these cases, a good way to organize an **Animator Controller** is to have two animation states (clips) and a **Trigger** on the transition between the clips. We can use code to detect when we want the animation to start playing, and at that time, we send the **Trigger** message to the **Animation Controller**, causing a **Transition** to start.

In this recipe, we'll create a water platform block in our 2D platform game. Such blocks will begin to slowly fall down the screen as soon as they have been stepped on, and so the player must keep on moving; otherwise, they'll fall down the screen with the blocks too!

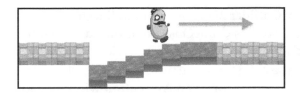

Figure 6.33 – Example of a falling platform

Getting ready

This recipe builds on the previous one, so make a copy of that project and work on the copy for this recipe.

How to do it...

To construct an animation that only plays once a **Trigger** has been received, follow these steps:

1. In the **Hierarchy** window, create an empty GameObject named `water-block-container`, positioned at `(2.5, -4, 0)`. This empty GameObject will allow us to make duplicates of animated water blocks that will animate relative to their parent GameObject's position.

2. Drag an instance of the `Water Block` sprite from the **Project | Sprites** folder into the scene and make it a child of the `water-block-container` GameObject. Ensure the position of your new child `Water Block` GameObject is `(0, 0, 0)` so that it appears neatly to the right of the wall blocks platform:

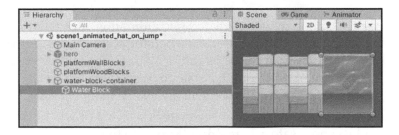

Figure 6.34 – Dragging the Water Block sprite to the scene and ensuring its position is (0,0,0)

3. Add a **Box Collider 2D** component to the child `Water Block` GameObject. Set the layer of this GameObject to **Ground** so that the player's character can stand and jump on this water block platform.

4. Ensuring the child `Water Block` GameObject is selected in the **Hierarchy** window, open an **Animation** window and create a new clip named `platform-water-up`, saving it in your `Animations` folder. Click the **Add Property** button, choose **Transform** and **Position**, and delete the second keyframe at **1:00**.

5. Create a second **Animation Clip** named `platform-water-down`. Again, click the **Add Property** button, choose **Transform** and **Position**, and delete the second keyframe at **1:00**.

6. With the first keyframe at **0:00** selected, click the red **Record** button once to start recording changes and set the Y-value of the GameObject's **Transform Position** to −5. Press the red **Record** button again to stop recording changes. You have now created the `water-block-down` **Animation Clip**.

7. You may have noticed that as well as the up/down animation clips that you created, another file was created in your `Animations` folder – an **Animator Controller** named `Water Block`. Select this file and open the **Animator** window to be able to view and edit the **State Machine** diagram:

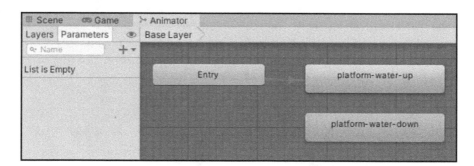

Figure 6.35 – Animation Controller for the Water Block GameObject

8. Currently, although we've created two animation clips (states), only the **Up** state is ever active. This is because when the scene begins (**Entry**), the object will immediately go into the `platform-water-up` state, but since there are no **Transition** arrows from this state to `platform-water-down`, at present, the `Water Block` GameObject will always be in its **Up** state.

9. Ensure the `platform-water-up` state is selected (it will have a blue border around it) and create a **Transition** (arrow) to the `platform-water-down` state by choosing **Make Transition** from the right-click menu.

10. If you run the scene now, the default **Transition** settings will be provided after 0.75 seconds (default **Exit Time**), and `Water Block` will **Transition** into its **Down** state. We don't want this – we only want them to animate downward after the player has walked onto them.

11. Create a **Trigger** named `Fall` by choosing the **Parameters** tab in the **Animator** window, clicking the + button and selecting **Trigger**, and then selecting **Fall**.

12. Do the following to create the transition to wait for our **Trigger**:
    - In the **Animator** window, select **Transition**.
    - In the **Inspector** window, uncheck the **Has Exit Time** option.
    - Set **Transition Duration** to `3.0` (so that `Water Block` slowly transitions to its **Down** state over a period of 2 seconds).
    - In the **Inspector** window, click the + button to add a **Condition**. This should automatically suggest the only possible **Condition Parameter**, which is our `Fall` **Trigger**:

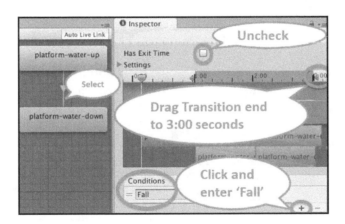

Figure 6.36 – Fall Trigger settings for the Down state of the platform

An alternative to setting **Transition Duration** numerically is to drag the **Transition** end time to **3:00** seconds in the **Animation Timeline**, under **Transition Settings** in the **Inspector** window.

13. We need to add a `Collider` trigger just above `Water Block`, and a C# script class called `behaviour` to send our **Animator Controller Trigger** when the player enters the Collider.

14. Ensure the child `Water Block` GameObject is selected, add a (second) **2D Box Collider** with a **Y-Offset** of 1, and tick its **Is Trigger** checkbox:

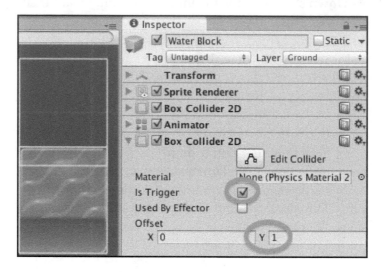

Figure 6.37 – Box Collider 2D settings for Water Block

15. Create a C# script class called `WaterBlock` and add an instance object as a component to the child `Water Block` GameObject:

```
using UnityEngine;
using System.Collections;

public class WaterBlock : MonoBehaviour {
    const string TAG_PLAYER = "Player";
    const string ANIMATION_TRIGGER_FALL = "Fall";

    private Animator animatorController;

    void Start(){
        animatorController = GetComponent<Animator>();
    }

    void OnTriggerEnter2D(Collider2D hit){
        if(hit.CompareTag(TAG_PLAYER)){
animatorController.SetTrigger(ANIMATION_TRIGGER_FALL);
        }
    }
}
```

16. Make six more copies of the `water-block-container` GameObject, with their X-positions increasing by 1 each time; that is, `3.5`, `4.5`, `5.5`, and so on.

17. Run the scene. As the player's character runs across each water block, they will start falling down, so they had better keep running!

How it works...

In this recipe, you created an empty GameObject called `water-block-container` to act as a container for a `WaterBlock`. By adding a `WaterBlock` to this parent GameObject, you made it possible to make copies and move them in the scene so that the animations were **relative** to the location of each parent (container) GameObject.

By adding a **Box Collider** and setting the layer of `WaterBlock` to **Ground**, you enabled the player's character to walk on these blocks.

You created a two-state **Animator Controller** state machine. Each state was an **Animation Clip**. The **Up** state is for `WaterBlock` at normal height (**Y** = 0), while the **Down** state is for `WaterBlock` further down the screen (**Y** = −5). You created a **Transition** from the **Water Block Up** state to its **Down** state that will take place when **Animator Controller** receives a `Fall` **Trigger** message.

After that, you added a second **Box Collider 2D** with a **Trigger** to `WaterBlock` so that our script could detect when the player (tagged **Player**) enters its Collider. When the player triggers the Collider, the `Fall` **Trigger** message is set, which makes the `Water Block` GameObject start gently transitioning into its **Down** state further down the screen.

You can learn more about animation controllers at `http://docs.unity3d.com/Manual/class-AnimatorController.html`.

Creating animation clips from sprite sheet sequences

The traditional method of animation involved hand-drawing many images, each slightly different, which were displayed quickly frame by frame to give the appearance of movement. For computer game animation, the term **sprite sheet** is given to an image file that contains one or more sequences of sprite frames. Unity provides tools to break up individual sprite images into large sprite sheet files so that individual frames, or sub-sequences of frames, can be used to create animation clips that can become states in **Animator Controller** state machines. In this recipe, we'll import and break up an open source monster sprite sheet into three animation clips for **Idle**, **Attack**, and **Death**, as follows:

Figure 6.38 – An example of a sprite sheet

Getting ready

For all the recipes in this chapter, we have prepared the sprite images you need in the 06_04 folder. Many thanks to Rosswet Mobile for making these sprites available as open source.

How to do it...

To create a frame-by-frame animation using a sprite sheet, follow these steps:

1. Create a new Unity 2D project.
2. Import the provided image; that is, monster1.
3. With the monster1 image selected in the **Project** window, change its sprite mode to **Multiple** in the **Inspector** window. Then, click the **Apply** button at the bottom of the window:

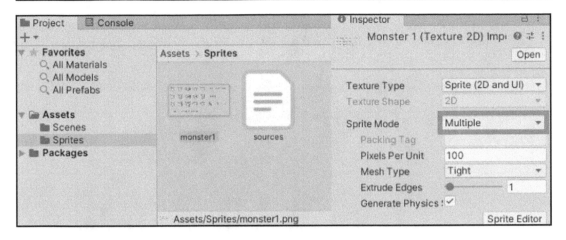

Figure 6.39 – Setting for changing Sprite mode to Multiple

4. In the **Inspector** window, open the **Sprite Editor** panel by clicking the **Sprite Editor** button.

5. In **Sprite Editor**, open the **Slice** drop-down dialog. For **Type**, choose the **Grid** by **CellSize** drop-down option and set **X** and **Y** to 64. Click the **Slice** button, and then the **Apply** button in the bar at the top right of the **Sprite Editor** panel:

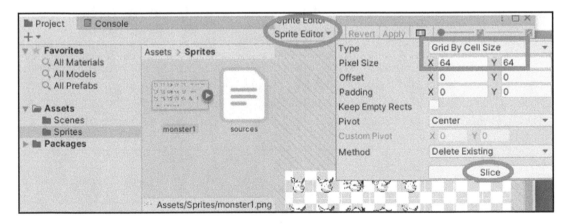

Figure 6.40 – Sprite Editor settings for splicing the sprite sheet

6. In the **Project** window, you can now click the triangle button on the right-hand side of the sprite. You'll see all the different child frames for this sprite (as highlighted in the following screenshot):

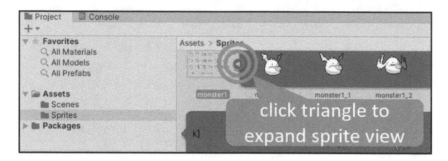

Figure 6.41 – Clicking the triangle to expand the sprite view to access each individual sprite

7. Create a folder named `Animations`.

8. In your new folder, create an **Animator Controller** asset file named `monster-animator` by going to the **Project** window and selecting **Create | Animator Controller**.

9. In the scene, create a new empty GameObject named `monster1` (at position `0, 0, 0`) and drag your `monster-animator` into this GameObject.

10. With the `monster1` GameObject selected in the **Hierarchy** window, open the **Animation** window and create a new **Animation Clip** named `monster1-idle`.

11. Select the `monster1` image in the **Project** window (in its expanded view) and select and drag the first five frames (frames `monster1_0` to `monster1_4`) into the **Animation** window. Change the sample rate to `12` (since this animation was created to run at 12 frames per second):

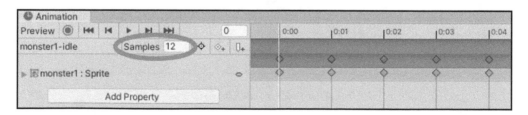

Figure 6.42 – Setting up the Animation window with the sample rate set to 12

12. If you look at **State Chart** for `monster-animator`, you'll see that it has a default state (clip) named `monster-idle`.

13. When you run your scene, you should see the `monster1` GameObject animating in its `monster-idle` state. You may wish to make the size of **Main Camera** a bit smaller (size 1) since these are quite small sprites:

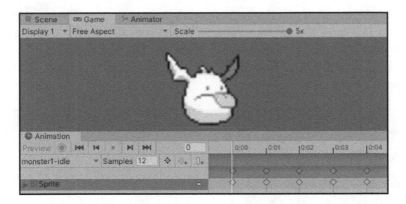

Figure 6.43 – Animation panel for the sprite animation of monster1

How it works...

Unity's **Sprite Editor** knows about sprite sheets, and once the correct Grid size has been entered, it treats the items in each Grid square inside the sprite sheet image as an individual image, or frame, of the animation. In this recipe, you selected sub-sequences of sprite animation frames and added them to several animation clips. You added an **Animation Controller** to your GameObject so that each **Animation Clip** appears as a state in **Animation Controller State Machine**.

You can now repeat this process, creating an **Animation Clip** called `monster-attack` that uses frames 8-12, and a third clip called `monster-death` that uses frames 15-21. You can then create triggers and transitions to make the `monster` GameObject transition into the appropriate states as the game is played.

You can learn more about the Unity Sprite Editor by looking at the Unity video tutorials at `https://unity3d.com/learn/tutorials/modules/beginner/2d/sprite-editor`.

You can learn more about 2D animation with sprite sheets by reading the following article by John Horton on GameCodeSchool.com: `http://gamecodeschool.com/unity/simple-2d-sprite-sheet-animations-in-unity/`.

Creating a platform game with tiles and tilemaps

Unity has introduced a set of **Tile** features that makes creating tile-based scenes quick and easy. A `Tile Grid` GameObject acts as the parent to tilemaps. These are the GameObjects that tiles are painted on, from the **Tile Palette** panel. Sprites can be made into **Tile** assets, and a collection of tiles can be added to form a **Tile Palette**, which we can use to paint a scene:

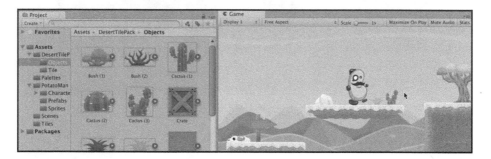

Figure 6.44 – Example of using Tilemapper and GameArt2D supplied sprites

It also offers powerful, scripted **Rule Tiles** that enhance the **Tile** brush tools, automatically adding top, left, right, and bottom edge **Tiles** as more **Grid** elements are painted with tiles. **Rule Tiles** can even randomly choose from a selection of tiles under defined conditions. You can learn more at `https://unity3d.com/learn/tutorials/topics/2d-game-creation/using-rule-tiles-tilemap`.

In this recipe, we'll create a simple 2D platformer by building a Grid-based scene using some free **Tile** sprite images.

Getting ready

For this recipe, we have prepared the Unity package and images you need in the `08_07` folder.

Special thanks to GameArt2D.com for publishing the Desert image sprites under the **Creative Commons Zero** license: `https://www.gameart2d.com/free-desert-platformer-tileset.html`.

How to do it...

To create a platform game with tiles and tilemaps, follow these steps:

1. Create a new Unity 2D project.
2. Import the provided images.
3. The tile sprites we're using for this recipe are 128 x 128 pixels in size. It's important to ensure that we set the pixels per unit to `128` so that our **Sprite** images will map to a Grid of 1 x 1 Unity units. Select all the sprites in the **Project | DesertTilePack | Tile** folder and in the **Inspector** window, set **Pixels per Unit** to `128`:

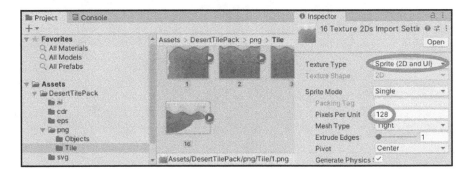

Figure 6.45 – Import settings for DesertTilePack

4. Display **Tile Palette** by going to **Window | 2D | Tile Palette**.
5. In the **Project** window, create a new folder named `Palettes` (this is where you'll save your `TilePalette` assets).
6. Click the **Create New Palette** button in **Tile Palette** and create a new **Tile Palette** named `DesertPalette`:

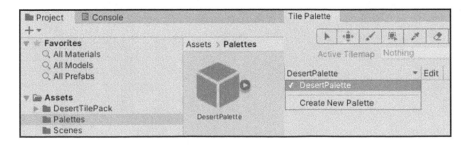

Figure 6.46 – Creating a new Tile Palette named DesertPalette

7. In the **Project** window, create a new folder named `Tiles` (this is where you'll save your `Tile` assets).

8. Ensure that `DesertPalette` is selected in the **Tile Palette** panel. Then, select all the sprites in the `Project | DesertTilePack | Tile` folder and drag them into the **Tile Palette** window. When asked where to save these new `Tile` asset files, select your new `Assets | Tiles` folder. You should now have 16 `Tile` assets in your `Tiles` folder, and these tiles should be available so that you can work with them in your `DesertPalette` in the **Tile Palette** window:

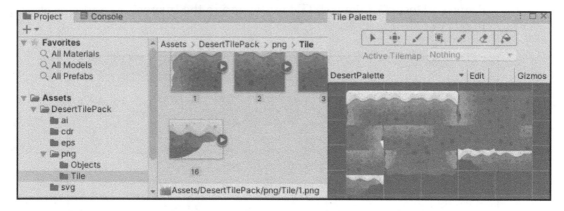

Figure 6.47 – DesertPalette created, which includes 16 tile assets

9. Drag **Sprite BG** (included in `DesertTilePack`) into the scene. Resize `Main Camera` (it should be **Orthographic** since this is a 2D project) so that the desert background fills the entire **Game** window.

10. Add a `Tilemap` GameObject to the scene by going to **2D Object | Tilemap | Rectangular**. You'll see a `Grid` GameObject added, and as a child of that, you'll see a `Tilemap` GameObject. Rename the `Tilemap` GameObject `Tilemap-platforms`. Select the `Tilemap` GameObject and ensure **TileMap renderer | Additional Settings | Sorting Layer** is set to **Background**:

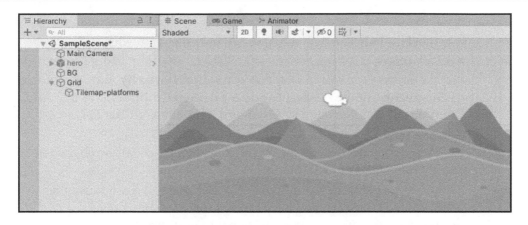

Figure 6.48 – Adding a Rectangular Tilemap Grid named Tilemap-platforms

 Just as **UI** GameObjects are children of a **Canvas**, **Tilemap** GameObjects are children of a **Grid**.

11. We can now start *painting* tiles onto our `Tilemap`. Ensure `Tilemap-platforms` is selected in the **Hierarchy** window and that you can see the **Tile Palette** window. In the **Tile Palette** window, select the **Paint with active brush** tool (the *paintbrush* icon). Now, click on a **Tile** in the **Tile Palette** panel. Then, in the **Scene** window, each time you click the mouse, button you'll be adding a `Tile` to `Tilemap-platforms` that's automatically aligned with the Grid:

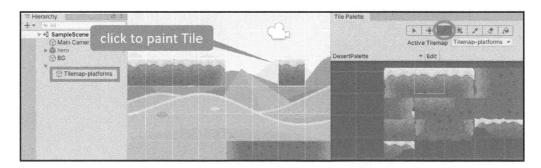

Figure 6.49 – Painting tiles onto an active Tilemap by selecting the active brush tool

12. If you want to delete a `Tile`, *Shift* + click over that Grid position.

13. Use the **Tile Palette** brush to paint two or three platforms.

14. Add a suitable `Collider` to the `Tilemap-platforms` GameObject. Select the `Tilemap-platforms` GameObject in the **Hierarchy** window and, in the **Inspector** window, select to add a **Tilemap Collider 2D**. Click **Add Component** and then choose **Tilemap | Tilemap Collider 2D**.

15. Create a new **Layer** named `Ground` and set the `Tilemap-platforms` GameObject to be on this **Layer** (this will allow characters to jump when standing on a platform).

16. Let's test our platform scene with a 2D character – we can reuse the potatoman character from Unity's free tutorials. Import the provided `PotatoManAssets` package into your project.

17. Let's set up the 2D gravity setting for this project since the size of the potatoman character is big with respect to the platforms. We'll make the character move slowly by using a heavy gravity setting of **Y** = -60. Set 2D gravity to this value by going to **Edit | Project Settings | Physics 2D** and then, at the top, changing the **Y** value to -60.

18. Drag an instance of the potatoman `hero` character from the `Project |` `Prefabs` folder into the scene. Position him somewhere above one of your platforms.

19. Play the scene. The 2D `hero` character should fall down and land on the platform. You should be able to move the character left and right, and make him jump using the spacebar.

20. You may wish to decorate the scene by dragging some of the object sprites onto the scene (in the **Project** window, go to the **Project |** **DesertTilePack | Object** folder).

How it works...

By having a set of platform sprites that are all a regular size (128 x 128), it is straightforward to create a **Tile Palette** from those sprites, and then to add a `Grid` and `Tilemap` to the scene, allowing the **Tile Palette** brush to paint tiles into the scene. By doing this, we added platforms to this scene that are all well-aligned with each other, both horizontally and vertically.

You had to set the **Sprite** pixels per unit to `128`, matching the size of these sprites, so that each **Tile** maps to a 1 x 1 Unity Grid unit. If we were to use different size sprites (say, 256 x 256), then the pixels per unit must be set to that size, again to achieve a 1 x 1 Unity Grid.

You added a **Tilemap Collider 2D** to the `Tilemap` GameObject so that characters (such as the potatoman) can interact with the platforms. Without a Collider 2D, these tiles would have seemed just part of the background graphics. By adding a **Layer Ground** and setting the `Tilemap` GameObject to this **Layer**, the jumping code in the potatoman `character-controller` script can test the layer of the object being stood on so that the jump action will only be possible when standing on a platform **Tile**.

There's more...

Here are some suggestions for enhancing this recipe.

Tile palettes for objects and walls

The sprite objects in the `Desert` free pack are all different sizes, and certainly not consistent with the 128 x 128 sprite size for the platform tiles.

However, if the sprites for the objects and walls in your game *are* the same size as your platform sprites, you can create a **Tile Palette** for your objects and paint them into the scene using the **Tile Palette** brush.

Using sprite placeholders to create a simple physics scene

Unity offers physics for 2D scenes by providing Colliders, rigid bodies, gravity, and so on, just as it does for 3D scenes. In this recipe, we'll create a 2D mountain-style landscape made up of some colored triangles, and then have some square blocks fall down due to gravity into one of the low dips where two triangles overlap. Rather than using images for our sprites, we'll learn how to use 2D geometric **sprite placeholders**, a feature in Unity allowing for quick prototyping and scene layouts, where the placeholder sprites can easily be replaced with texture images later. The following screenshot illustrates the starting and ending locations of the square blocks as they fall down and collide with the triangular landscape sprites:

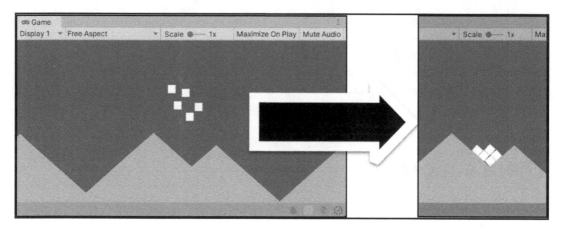

Figure 6.50 – A physics scene where 2D squares fall into a dip in the landscape

Getting ready

We'll create everything from scratch in Unity for this recipe, so no preparation is required.

How to do it...

To use sprite placeholders to create a simple physics scene, follow these steps:

1. Create a new Unity 2D project.
2. Create a new `Sprite Placeholder` asset file named `Triangle` by going to **Assets** | **Create** | **Sprites** | **Triangle**. You should now see an asset file in the **Project** window named `Triangle`.
3. Create a folder in the **Project** window named `Sprites` and move your `Triangle` sprite file into it:

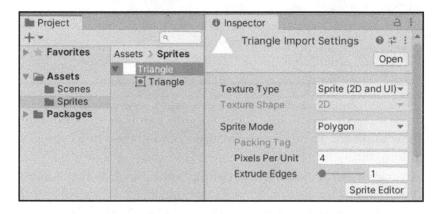

Figure 6.51 – The new Triangle Sprite asset file in the Project window

4. Drag the `Triangle` Sprite file into the scene to create a GameObject named `Triangle`.
5. Ensure the `Triangle` GameObject is selected in the **Hierarchy** window. Then, in the **Inspector** window, set the **Color** property of the **Sprite Renderer** component to a red-pink color.
6. In the **Inspector** window, add a **Polygon Collider 2D** component by clicking the **Add Component** button).
7. Then, add a **Rigidbody 2D** component.

8. We don't want our triangles to move at all (they are mountains!), so we will freeze their X, Y, and Z positions. In the **Inspector** window, for the **Rigidbody 2D** component, check **Freeze Position** for **X** and **Y** and **Freeze Rotation** for **Z**:

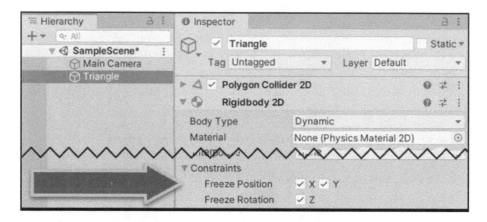

Figure 6.52 – Freeze position and rotation for our Triangle GameObject landscape

9. Now make the `Triangle` sprite larger, and make 4 or 5 copies, which will automatically be named `Triangle 1`, `Triangle 2`, and so on.

10. Arrange them at the lower part of the scene panel, so they look like pointy mountains at the bottom of the **Game** panel. See *Figure 6.52* for the effect you are trying to achieve. The aim is to have no *gap* at the bottom of the screen, so our square sprites will fall down onto this *landscape* of triangle mountains. See *Figure 6.53*:

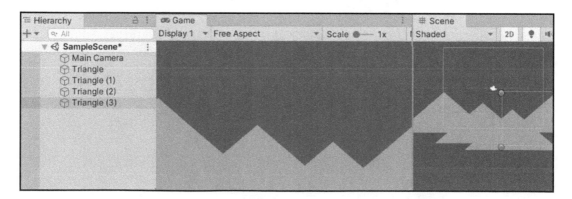

Figure 6.53 – Our landscape of Triangle GameObjects

11. Create a new `Square` **Sprite Placeholder** in the **Project** window and move it into the `Sprites` folder.

12. Drag the `Square` sprite asset file from the **Project** window into the scene to create a GameObject.

13. Ensure the `Square` GameObject is selected in the **Hierarchy** window. Then, in the **Inspector** window, add a **Polygon Collider 2D** component and a **Rigidbody 2D** component.

14. Duplicate the `Square` GameObject four times so that you have five GameObjects named `Square`, `Square 1`, `Square 2`, `Square 3`, and `Square 4`.

15. Then, arrange these `Square` GameObjects so that they are no overlapping in the middle of the scene. This will ensure that when they fall down due to gravity, they'll end up rolling down into one of the dips in our `Triangle` landscape:

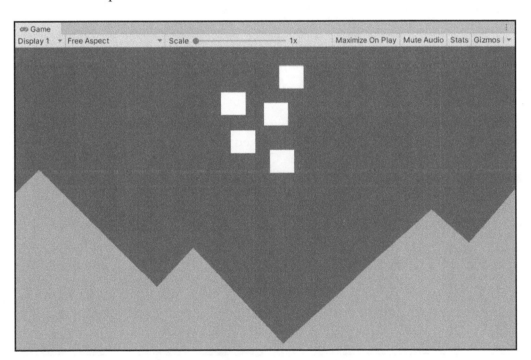

Figure 6.54 – Our collection of Square GameObjects, ready to fall down into the Triangle landscape

16. Play the scene. You should see the `Square` GameObjects fall downward due to gravity and roll down into one of the low points where two triangles overlap.

How it works...

In this recipe, you created `Triangle` and `Square` **Sprite Placeholder** asset files in the **Project** window. Then, you dragged them into the scene to create GameObjects. For each GameObject, you added 2D **Polygon Collider** components (following the shape of the `Triangle` and `Square` sprites), as well as **Rigidbody 2D** components, which make these GameObjects behave as if they have mass, gravity, and so on. The Colliders indicate that the objects will hit each other with force and behave accordingly.

Then, you froze the position and rotation of the `Triangle` GameObjects so that they will be solid and immobile, as if they were made from solid rock mountains. The `Square` GameObjects were positioned in the middle of the **Scene** window – as if they were starting in the air, above the ground of `Triangle`. So. when the scene is played, gravity is applied by the Unity 2D physics system, making the `Square` GameObjects fall downward until they hit each of the immobile `Triangle` mountains. Then, they roll around until they end up being collected in the low points where the two triangles overlap.

There's more...

Once a scene has been successfully prototyped with GameObjects based on sprite placeholders, it's easy to replace the 2D geometric shape with an actual image. For example, we could select all the `Square` GameObjects and, in their **Sprite Renderer** components, select the **Enemy Bug** sprite to replace the `Square` GameObjects:

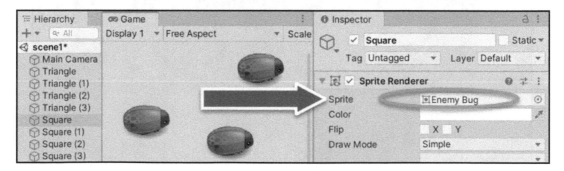

Figure 6.55 – Enemy Bug sprite replacing the Square sprite placeholder

Editing polygon Colliders for more realistic 2D physics

In this recipe, we will address the issue of simple geometric polygon Colliders from sprite placeholders not matching the final image sprite that replaces the placeholder. This will allow you to use polygon Colliders to approximate the shape of any image outline you might use in your game.

Getting ready

This recipe builds on the previous one, so make a copy of that project and work on the copy for this recipe. We'll also be using the Enemy Bug image from the first recipe in this chapter, which can be found in a folder named Sprites in the 06_01 folder.

How to do it...

To edit polygon Colliders for more realistic 2D physics, follow these steps:

1. Copy the project from the previous recipe and use this copy for this recipe.
2. If you haven't done so already, import the Enemy Bug image from the provided assets. Then, in the **Inspector** window, for each Square GameObject, change the sprite in the **Sprite Renderer** component to the Enemy Bug sprite (replacing Square).
3. Run the scene. You should see all the Enemy Bug GameObjects fall down into a pile at a low point where two triangles meet:

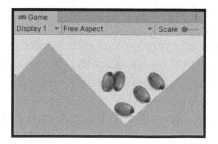

Figure 6.56 – Bugs falling into a pile. There's space in-between them due to the Square polygon Collider

4. However, looking at the screen, there is some space between the `Enemy Bug` GameObjects, and looking at the Colliders in the **Scene** window, we can see that there are `Square` Colliders with lots of space around each oval `Enemy Bug` image:

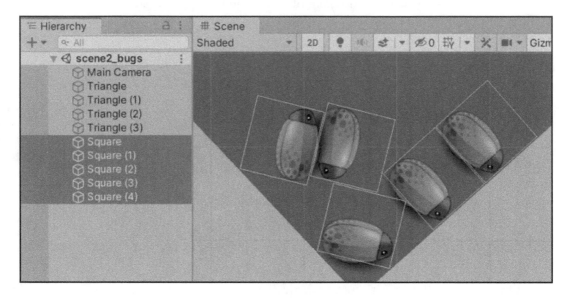

Figure 6.57 – Square Colliders around oval Enemy Bug images

5. Select the `Square` GameObject in the **Hierarchy** window. Then, in the **Inspector** window, for the **Polygon Collider 2D** component, click the **Edit Collider** icon. In the **Scene** window, you'll now have a small square on the Collider lines, which you can drag to deform the Collider polygon so that it matches the oval outline of the `Enemy Bug` image.

6. When your Collider polygon approximates the outline of `Enemy Bug`, stop editing by clicking the **Edit Collider** icon again.

7. Delete the `Square (1)`, `Square (2)`, `Square (3)`, and `Square (4)` GameObjects. Now, duplicate `Square` four times and arrange them so that they are not overlapping. You now have five GameObjects with polygon Colliders that match what the user can see.

8. Run the scene. You should see all the `Enemy Bug` GameObjects fall down into a pile at a low point where two triangles meet.

9. This time, they should be almost touching the Collider and each other based on the polygon Collider that matches the oval shape of the **Enemy Bug** icon:

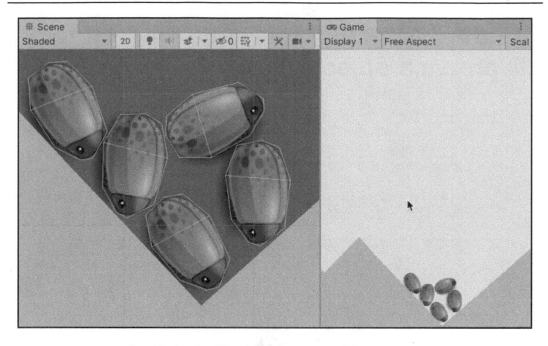

Figure 6.58 – Enemy bugs falling and colliding based on a more realistic bug polygon shape

How it works...

Since the GameObjects that were created with the `Square` sprite placeholders had a polygon Collider added to them, although the Collider was created to match the geometric **Square** shape of the `Square` sprite placeholders, it can be edited and made a different shape.

In this recipe, you replaced the `Square` sprite with the `Enemy Bug` sprite image, then edited the **Polygon Collider 2D** component so that it matches the oval shape of the outline of the `Enemy Bug` image. By removing the GameObjects with the `Square` polygon Colliders, and then duplicating the one containing the oval bug-shaped polygon, all the falling GameObjects collided to match the visible shape of the `Enemy Bug` images.

This approach can be used to create polygon Colliders to approximate the shape of any image outline you might wish to use in your game.

Creating an explosionForce method for 2D physics objects

For 3D games, the **Rigidbody** component has a useful method called `AddExlosionForce(...)` that will cause an object to look as if it's exploded from a given position. However, there is no such method for **Rigidbody2D** components. In this recipe, we'll write an extension method for the `Rigidbody2D` class so that we can add an `explosionForce` method for 2D objects.

Thanks to Swamy for posting the code for the `Rigidbody2D` extension class's explosion force on Unity Forum (Nov 21, 2013), which this recipe is based on:

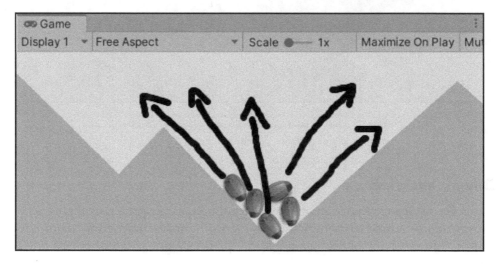

Figure 6.59 – Bugs being violently forced away from an invisible explosion point

Getting ready

This recipe builds on the previous one, so make a copy of that project and work on the copy for this recipe.

How to do it...

To create an `explosionForce` method for 2D physics objects, follow these steps:

1. Copy the project from the previous recipe, and use this copy for this recipe.
2. We can add a method to the `Rigidbody2D` script class by creating the following C# script class called `Rigidbody2DExtension`:

```
using UnityEngine;

public static class Rigidbody2DExtension{
    public static void AddExplosionForce(this Rigidbody2D
body, float explosionForce, Vector3 explosionPosition, float
explosionRadius){
        Vector3 forceVector = (body.transform.position -
explosionPosition);
        float wearoff = 1 - (forceVector.magnitude /
explosionRadius);
        body.AddForce(forceVector.normalized * explosionForce
* wearoff);
    }
}
```

3. Create a new empty GameObject named `explosion`.
4. Create a C# script class called `ExplodeCircle` and add an instance object as a component to the child `explosion` GameObject:

```
using System.Collections;
using System.Collections.Generic;
using UnityEngine;

public class ExplodeCircle : MonoBehaviour{
    public float power = 800f;
    public float radius = 3f;
    void Update(){
        if (Input.GetKeyUp(KeyCode.Space)){
            print("Exploding ...");
            Explode();
        }
    }
    void Explode(){
        Vector2 explosionPos = transform.position;
        Collider2D[] Colliders =
Physics2D.OverlapCircleAll(explosionPos, radius);
        foreach (Collider2D hit in Colliders){
```

```
                    Rigidbody2D rigidbody =
          hit.GetComponent<Rigidbody2D>();

                 if (rigidbody != null)
                     rigidbody.AddExplosionForce(power,
          explosionPos, radius);
                }
            }
        void OnDrawGizmosSelected(){
            // Draw a red circle to show range of explosion radius
            Gizmos.color = Color.red;
            Gizmos.DrawWireSphere(transform.position, radius);
        }
    }
```

5. Move the `explosion` GameObject just below the low point where the bugs will fall down to when the scene runs.

6. In the **Inspector** window, you can change the radius of the explosion. In the **Scene** window, you'll see the red circle resize to indicate the extent of the explosion's radius:

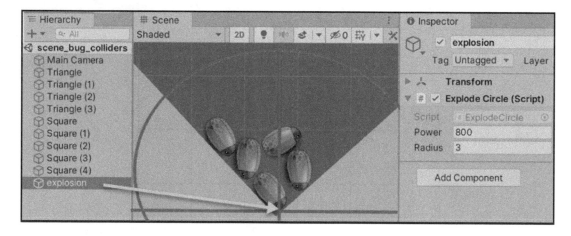

Figure 6.60 – Circle in the Scene window showing the radius of the explosion's force

7. Run the scene. The bugs should fall down toward the low point, inside the explosion circle. Each time you press the spacebar, an explosion force will be applied to all the bugs inside the explosion radius.

How it works...

The C# `Rigidbody2DExtension` script class adds a new method
called `AddExlosionForce(...)` to all **Rigidbody2D** components in the project. The
advantage of using an extension class method is that this method now becomes
available to use by all other scripts in the project, with no need to refer to this
extension class explicitly – it's as if Unity provided this extra method as part of its
core code library.

This `AddExlosionForce(...)` method takes three parameters when called:

- `float explosionForce`: The magnitude of the force to be applied (the
  larger the value, the more force will be applied)
- `Vector3 explosionPosition`: The center (origin) point of where the
  explosion is to take place (the further a GameObject is from this position,
  the less force it will receive)
- `float explosionRadius`: The furthest point beyond which no force will
  be applied by the simulated explosion

This method will apply a force to **Rigidbody2D** based on the direction and position it
is from `explosionPosition`, the force will be applied to move the object away from
`explosionPosition`. The `wearoff` variable reduces the force that's applied based
on how far away **Rigidbody2D** is from `explosionPosition` – objects closer to this
position will have more force applied to them, simulating how an explosion works in
the real world.

The C# `ExplodeCircle` script class has two public variables called `power` and
`radius` that will be passed to `AddExlosionForce(...)` when applied to a
Rigidbody2D. The `Update()` method checks each frame to see if the user has pressed
the spacebar and when detected, the `Explosion()` method is invoked. However, you
could have some other way to decide when to apply an explosion, such as when a
timer has finished, when a Collider has been triggered, and so on.

The `OnDrawGizmosSelected()` method of the `ExplodeCircle` class draws a red
circle in the **Scene** window, which indicates the extent of the radius value for where
the explosion force will be applied. It uses the **Gizmos** wire sphere drawing
command.

The `Explosion()` method of the `ExplodeCircle` class uses the Physics2D `OverlapCircleAll()` method to return an array of all **Rigidbody2D** components of GameObjects within a circle of the value of the radius from the position of the GameObject. Each of these Colliders is looped through, and the `AddExlosionForce(...)` method is invoked on them so that all the GameObjects within the circle for the current radius value will have the explosion force applied to them.

There's more...

Rather than using a Physics2D circle to decide which GameObjects are to be affected by the explosion, another game situation might be to apply an explosion force to all the objects of a particular tag. In this case, you would replace the `explodedCircle` scripted component of the `explosion` GameObject with an instance of the following script class, setting the `tagName` string to the desired tag in the **Inspector** window:

```
using UnityEngine;

public class ExplodeTagged : MonoBehaviour {
    public string tagName = "Bug";
    public float force = 800f;
    public float radius = 3f;

    private GameObject[] _gameObjects;

    private void Awake(){
        _gameObjects = GameObject.FindGameObjectsWithTag(tagName);
    }

    void Update(){
        if (Input.GetKeyUp(KeyCode.Space))
        {
            Explode();
        }
    }
    private void Explode(){
        foreach(var gameObject in _gameObjects){
            Rigidbody2D rigidbody2D =
gameObject.GetComponent<Rigidbody2D>();
            rigidbody2D.AddExplosionForce(force, transform.position,
radius);
        }
    }
}
```

Clipping via Sprite Masking

Clipping is the computer graphics term for choosing which parts of a graphical object to display or hide. In 2D graphics, it's very common to have one image to define parts of a screen to either only show other images, or to never show other images. Such an image is known as an **image mask**. In this recipe, we'll use two related images. One is an image of the inside of a room, showing a window out to a night skyscape. The second image is transparent, except for the rectangle where the window is. We'll use the second image to only allow other sprites to be seen when they pass by the window rectangle. The following figure shows how we can only see the parts of the moving blue bird sprite when it is overlapping with the window rectangle:

Figure 6.61 – Image mask being used to only show the bird when it flies through the window rectangle area of the screen

Getting ready

For this recipe, we have prepared the files you need in the 06_10 folder.

How to do it...

To clip images via **Sprite Masking**, follow these steps:

1. Create a new Unity 2D project.
2. Create a folder named Images and import the three provided images into it; that is, GAME_ROOM.png, GAME_ROOM_windowMask.png, and blueBird.png.

3. Drag the GAME_ROOM image into the scene and resize it so that it completely fills the **Game** window. For its **Sprite Renderer** component, set **Order in Layer** to -1 (so that this room image will be behind other images in the scene).

4. With the GAME_ROOM GameObject selected, from the **Create** menu in the **Hierarchy** window, go to **2D Object | Sprite Mask**. A GameObject named New Sprite Mask should now appear in the **Hierarchy** window as a child of the GAME_ROOM GameObject:

Figure 6.62 – Adding a Sprite Mask child to the GAME_ROOM GameObject

5. Select the New Sprite Mask GameObject in the **Hierarchy** window. Then, in the **Inspector** window, for its **Sprite Mask** component, click the **Sprite** selection circle icon. Then, from the list of sprites, choose **GAME_ROOM_windowMask**. If you look in the **Scene** window carefully, you'll see an orange border around the rectangle of the window of the **GAME_ROOM** image:

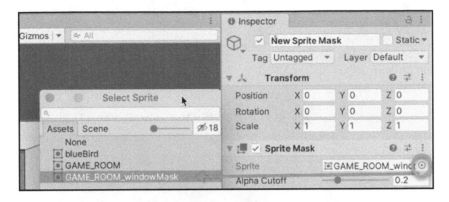

Figure 6.63 – Selecting the image to use as the mask for the Sprite Mask child of GAME_ROOM

6. Drag the `blueBird` image from the **Project** window into the scene to create a `blueBird` GameObject. Make the newly created `blueBird` GameObject a child of the `GAME_ROOM` GameObject in the **Hierarchy** window.

7. Resize and reposition the `blueBird` GameObject so that its right-hand side is just inside the window's night skyscape.

8. In the **Inspector** window, for the **Sprite Renderer** component, set the **Mask Interaction** property to **Visible Inside Mask**. You should now only see the parts of the `blueBird` image that are inside the rectangle of the night skyscape window:

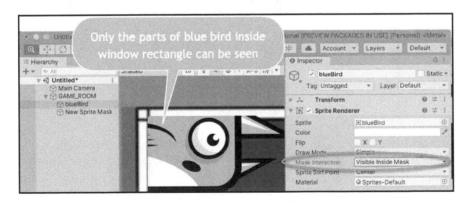

Figure 6.64 – Setting blueBird to only be visible inside the window rectangle mask

9. Run the scene to confirm that the `blueBird` sprite is masked (unseen) except for the parts inside the night skyscape window rectangle.

How it works...

In this recipe, you added the GAME_ROOM sprite to the scene, then added a GameObject containing a **Sprite Mask** component as a child of the GAME_ROOM GameObject.

You set the sprite of **SpriteMask** to **GAME_ROOM_windowMask**. This was a special image that only contained the rectangular area of the night skyscape:

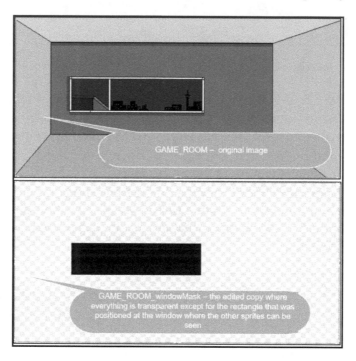

Figure 6.65 – Original GAME_ROOM and mask images

The black rectangle in the **GAME_ROOM_windowMask** image defines the only places where a masked sprite will be displayed – that is, the rectangle where the window appears in the GAME_ROOM image.

By adding the blueBird GameObject to the scene as a child of GAME_ROOM and setting its relationship to **Sprite Mask**, only the parts of the blueBird image that appear inside the rectangular mask image of **GAME_ROOM_windowMask** will be seen by the user.

You can think of a sprite mask as a piece of cardboard with a hole cut out of it – we can only see images behind the mask that pass by the cut-out hole.

There's more...

If you wanted to have the `blueBird` GameObject fly from left to right, you could add a scripted component to `blueBird` based on a new C# script class called `MoveBird` containing the following code:

```
using UnityEngine;

public class MoveBird : MonoBehaviour
{
    public float speed = 1f;

    void Update()
    {
        transform.Translate(speed * Vector3.right * Time.deltaTime);
    }
}
```

As can be seen in the last line of the scripted component, when the public `speed` variable is changed, it adjusts the speed at which the sprite moves.

You can learn more about sprite masks at the following links:

- **Sprite masks in the Unity manual**: https://docs.unity3d.com/Manual/class-SpriteMask.html
- **InScope Studios video (it's a few years old but still useful)**: https://www.youtube.com/watch?v=1QktsHJwXCQ

Further reading

Take a look at the following links for useful resources and sources of information regarding the 2D features provided by Unity:

- Overview of 2D features in Unity: https://unity.com/solutions/2d
- Unity's 2D rogue-like tutorial series: https://unity3d.com/learn/tutorials/s/2d-roguelike-tutorial

- Platform sprites from Daniel Cook's Planet Cute game
  resources: `http://www.lostgarden.com/2007/05/dancs-miraculously-flexible-game.html`
- Creating a basic
  2D platformer game: `https://www.unity3d.com/learn/tutorials/modules/beginner/live-training-archive/creating-a-basic-platformer-game`
- Hat Catch 2D game
  tutorial: `https://www.unity3d.com/learn/tutorials/modules/beginner/live-training-archive/2d-catch-game-pt1`
- Unity games from a 2D
  perspective: `https://www.unity3d.com/learn/tutorials/modules/beginner/live-training-archive/introduction-to-unity-via-2d`
- A fantastic set of modular 2D characters released under the free Creative Commons license from Kenny. These assets would be perfect for animating body parts in a similar way to the PotatoMan example in this chapter and in the Unity 2D platformer
  demo: `http://kenney.nl/assets/modular-characters`
- Joe Strout's illuminating Gamasutra article on three approaches to 2D character animation with Unity's scripting and animation
  states: `https://www.gamasutra.com/blogs/JoeStrout/20150807/250646/2D_Animation_Methods_in_Unity.php`

Here are some learning resources about tilemapping:

- Unity TileMap tutorial: `https://learn.unity.com/tutorial/introduction-to-tilemaps`
- Lots of 2D extra resources, free from Unity
  Technologies: `https://github.com/Unity-Technologies/2d-extras`
- Sean Duffy's great tutorial on tilemapping on the Ray Wenderlich site: `https://www.raywenderlich.com/188105/introduction-to-the-new-unity-2d-tilemap-system`

Characters, Game Kits, and Starter Assets

/*nity has developed several special collections of assets and common game features such as the **2D Game Kit** and the **3D Game Kit** (and its Lite version). These bring together several powerful Unity features for constructing 2D and 3D games, including the following:

- **Character Controller 2D** (and **Input Mapper** and **Player Character** components)
- **Cinemachine** intelligent camera control
- The Unity **Event** system
- Many prefabricated common 2D game components, including doors, teleporters, dialog panels, switches, inventory, melee, collectables and inventory, damageables, enemies, and much more
- **Tilemaps** and **Rule Tiles**, especially for 2D games

The first two recipes in this chapter introduce the **2D and 3D Game Kits**, and the other recipes in this chapter cover several ways to import and work with game characters and models. The gamekits make many core game mechanics very straightforward, including interactivity (such as pressure pads to open doors), walking into items to have them added to a player's inventory, and many more game features. One way in which games have a unique identity is their 3D human character models.

In this chapter, you'll learn how to import characters and animations from Mixamo and the **Unity Multipurpose Avatar** (**UMA**), and also how to change the character for the Unity Standard Assets Third-Person Controller scripts. The final recipe introduces the Starter Assets packages released by Unity Technologies mid-2021; these assets provide a great starting point to try out content and characters with first- and third-person cameras.

In this chapter, we'll learn how to do the following:

- Creating a game with the 3D Game Kit
- Creating a game with the 2D Game Kit
- Importing third-party 3D models and animations from Mixamo
- Swapping the Standard Assets Ethan for a different character
- Importing a 3D model and adding an Animation Controller
- Using scripts to control 3D animations
- Importing and using a UMA free character
- Getting started with the 2021 Starter Assets package

Technical requirements

To complete this chapter, Unity 2021.1 or later is required, plus the following:

- Microsoft Windows 10 (64-bit)/GPU: DX10-, DX11-, and DX12-capable
- macOS Sierra 10.12.6+/GPU Metal-capable Intel or AMD
- Linux Ubuntu 16.04, Ubuntu 18.04, and CentOS 7/GPU: OpenGL 3.2+ or Vulkan-capable, NVIDIA, or AMD

For each chapter, there is a folder with the asset files you require for the recipes at the book's public GitHub repository: `https://github.com/PacktPublishing/Unity-2021-Cookbook`.

Creating a game with the 3D Game Kit

A collection of Unity 3D tools has been combined to become the Unity **3D GameKit**. In this recipe, we'll create a new Scene and make use of some of the kit's Prefabs and Scripts to illustrate how characters can interact with objects such as doors and pickups. In this recipe, we'll explore how we can add interactivity, such as a character walking onto a pressure pad that opens a door. We'll also learn how to declare that an item should be collectable, and so when the player walks into it, they can add a crystal to their inventory. Note that if your system cannot handle the gigabytes of rich assets for the main 3D Game Kit, then we have added steps in the *There's more...* section for working with the 3D Game Kit Lite that Unity released:

Figure 7.1 – The interactable door Scene we'll create with the 3D Game Kit

How to do it...

To create a game with the 3D GameKit, follow these steps:

1. Start a new 3D project and ensure that you are logged in to your Unity account in the Unity Editor.
2. Open the Unity Asset Store in a web browser and log in to your Unity account in the Asset Store.
3. Search for and select the free 3D Game Kit in the Asset Store:

Figure 7.2 – The Unity 3D Game Kit asset in the Asset Store

4. Click **Add to My Assets**, and then, after the button changes, click **Open in Unity**.

5. In your Unity Editor, the **Package Manager** panel should open, and the **3D Game Kit** assets should be selected in the list of **My Assets**.
Click **Download**, and when downloaded, click **Import**. Say **Yes** to any popup about losing saved work by importing a complete project.

 Note: This is a large set of assets (over 2 GB), so could take 10-20 minutes to download and import onto your computer. Additional required packages, including **Cinemachine**, should also be added to your project.

6. In the **Project** panel, you should now see a new folder named **3DGameKit**. You should also see menus for **Cinemachine** and **Kit Tools**.

7. First, open the example Scene (**Project** panel: **3DGameKit | Scenes | Start**) provided and explore the 3D world by controlling the 3D Ellen character:

Figure 7.3 – Exploring the fully populated demo Start Scene

 Movement is standard *WASD/spacebar/*arrow keys. Camera control is via the mouse pointer. Click the left mouse button to use a weapon.

8. Create a new 3D GameKit Scene named `myScene` by choosing **Kit Tools |
Create New Scene**. You'll be asked to name the Scene, and a
new **Scene** asset file will be created in your **Project | Assets** folder. You'll
see that there are quite a few special GameObjects in
the **Hierarchy** window of your new Scene:

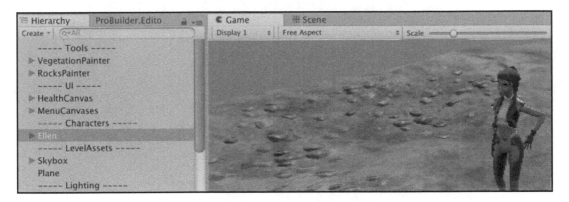

Figure 7.4 – Our new 3D Game Kit Scene

9. As you can see, the new Scene starts off by containing an animated 3D
character **(Ellen)** on a ProBuilder 3D Plane that forms the ground she is
standing on.

10. Add a small door to the Scene. Drag a clone of the **DoorSmall** Prefab from
the **Project** panel (**Assets | 3DGamekit | Prefabs | Interactables**) to the
middle of the 3D Plane Scene.

11. Add a crystal to the Scene, on the opposite side of the door from where
the **Ellen** character starts. Drag a clone of the **Crystal** Prefab from
the **Project** panel (**Assets | 3DGamekit | Prefabs | Interactables**) to
the Scene behind the door.

12. Now, add some walls on either side of the door so that the door must be
opened in order for Ellen to reach the crystal. Drag two clones of
the **Wall2x** Prefab from the **Project** panel (**Assets | 3DGamekit | Prefabs |
Environment | Structures**) into the Scene.

13. Finally, add an interactive pressure pad to the Scene near Ellen. Drag a clone of the **PressurePad** Prefab from the **Project** panel (**Assets | 3DGamekit | Prefabs | Interactables**) to the middle of the 3D Plane Scene:

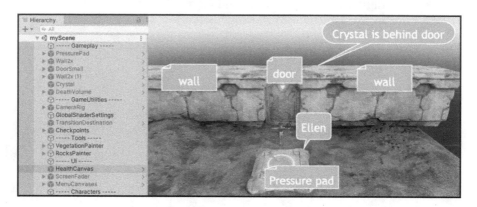

Figure 7.5 – Our new Scene content of walls, door, crystal, and pressure pad

We now need to connect the pressure pad to the door, so when Ellen steps on the pressure pad, it sends a message to open the door. This is very straightforward since the door has a **GameCommandReceiver** component, which can be linked to the **Send on Trigger Enter (Script)** component of the pressure pad.

14. Select the PressurePad GameObject in the **Hierarchy** window and drag DoorSmall into the public **Interactive Object** slot of its **Send on Trigger Enter (Script)** component:

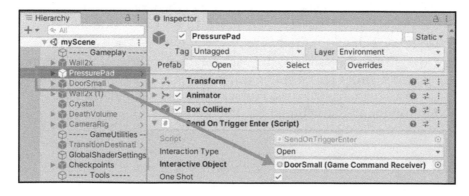

Figure 7.6 – Linking the pressure pad to the door's GameObject

15. Save and run the Scene. When Ellen steps onto the pressure pad, the door should open.

16. We now need to make the crystal collidable by adding a Box Collider. Add a **Box Collider** component to the `Crystal` GameObject and check its **On Trigger** option.

17. The 3D Game Kit has inventory features. Let's make the crystal collectible by the player by adding an **Inventory Item (Script)** component.

18. With the crystal still selected in the **Hierarchy** window, in the **Inspector** window, click **Add Component**, then type inven, and choose the **Inventory Item** scripted component. Once you have added the component, type Crystal as the **Inventory Key** name:

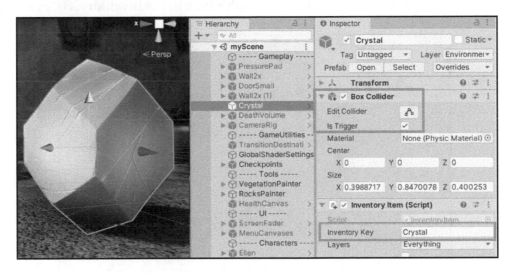

Figure 7.7 – Making the crystal an inventory item

19. Now, we can add an **Inventory Controller (Script)** component to **Ellen**, with a slot for a crystal. In the **Hierarchy** window, select the `Ellen` GameObject. In the **Inspector** window, click **Add Component**, then type inven, and choose the **Inventory Controller (Script)** scripted component.

20. We now need to configure the properties of the **Inventory Controller (Script)** component in the **Inspector** window as follows:

- Change the size from 0 to 1.
- For its key, type `Crystal`.
- For the **On Add()** events, click the plus sign, **+**, to create a new event.
- Drag **Ellen** into the **Object** slot for the new event (below **Runtime Only**).
- Change the function from **No Function** to **InventoryController Add Item**.
- Finally, type the name of this item in the **Inventory** as `Crystal`:

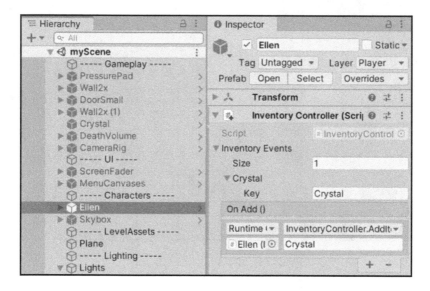

Figure 7.8 – Setting up the Crystal Inventory Controller (Script) for the Ellen character

 For the Gamekit inventory system to work, we must ensure that the **Inventory Key** names match, so we have to use exactly the same string, `Crystal`, for both the inventory key in the **Inventory Item (Script)** component (*step 16* above), and the key of the **Inventory Event** added to the **Inventory Controller (Script)** component (*step 20* above).

21. Run the Scene. Ellen can now open the door via the pressure pad and walk into the crystal, which is added to her inventory.

How it works...

Although a small number of elements, the core of a game has been created. We have a goal – to collect the crystal and add it to our inventory. We have a challenge – to get through the door. **Interactables**, such as the pressure pad, which we added to the Scene, send a message to a **GameCommandReceiver** component in the GameKit. The door can receive commands, so we were able to link the pressure pad to our door.

The inventory system works by having inventory items, such as our crystal, have a **Key** text inventory – this is like a tag for a GameObject. Characters can have an **Inventory Controller** component, which has a maximum size, which we set to 1 for our crystal. They also have a list of the text keys permitted for the character's inventory (so we added the **Crystal** text key to Ellen's **Inventory Controller**.

We have dipped our toes into the wide range of features of the 3D Game Kit. Hopefully, this recipe gave you an idea of how to work with the Prefabs provided, and how 3D Game Kit components could be added to custom GameObjects.

There's more...

If you want to get started quickly with the 3D Game Kit, but do not need all the rich (and very large) sets of asset files, then the 3D Game Kit Lite is a good choice. Follow these steps to get started:

1. Start a new 3D project and ensure that you are logged in to your Unity account in the Unity Editor.
2. Open the Unity Asset Store in a web browser and log in to your Unity account in the Asset Store.

3. Search for and select the free 3D Game Kit Lite in the Asset Store:

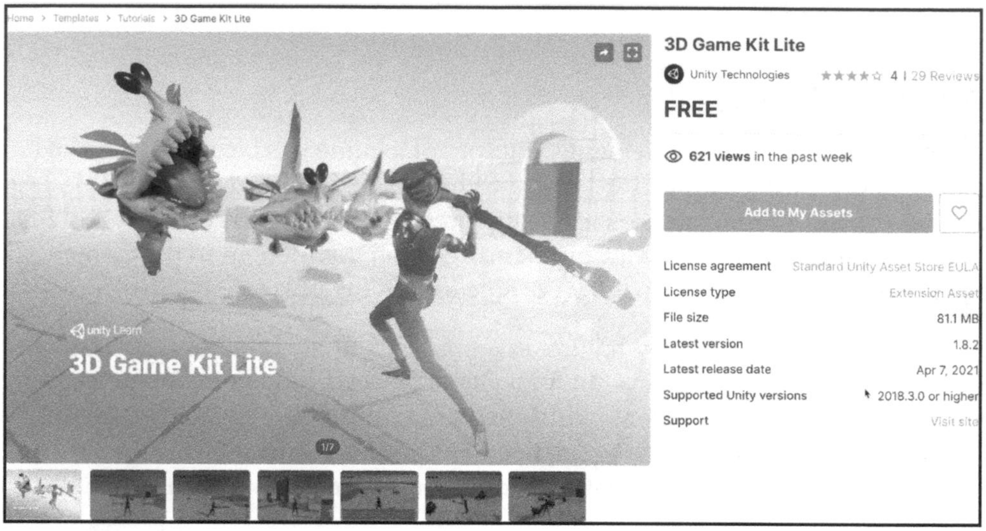

Figure 7.9 – The Unity 3D Game Kit Lite asset in the Asset Store

4. Click **Add to My Assets**, and then, after the button changes, click **Open in Unity**.

5. In your Unity Editor, the **Package Manager** panel should open, and the **3D Game Kit Lite** assets should be selected in the list of **My Assets**. Click **Download**, and when downloaded, click **Import**. Say **Yes** to any popup about losing saved work by importing a complete project.

6. In the **Project** panel, you should now see a new folder named **3DGameKit Lite**. You should also see menus for **Cinemachine** and **Kit Tools**.

7. First, open the example Scene (**Project** panel: **Assets | ExampleScene**) provided and explore the 3D world by controlling the 3D Ellen character.

8. You can create a new Scene from the menu just as with the full 3D Game Kit. You'll notice that the floor is a simple ProBuilder plane. You can use the ProBuilder tools to add/modify geometry in the Scene – refer to the ProBuilder recipes in *Chapter 5, 3D Objects, Terrains, Textures, and Materials*.

9. You can add **Interactable** Prefabs such as doors and pressure pads, and collectables such as crystals. Again, all these have simple shapes and colors to keep the size of the assets and project small:

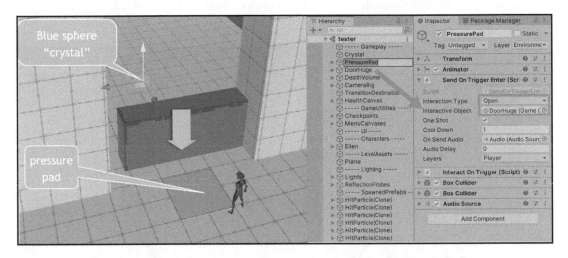

Figure 7.10 – A simple pressure pad and door interaction Scene made with the Unity 3D Game Kit Lite

You can learn more about the 3D Game Kit Lite from the Unity Learn tutorial: https://learn.unity.com/project/3d-game-kit-lite.

Creating a game with the 2D Game Kit

A collection of Unity 2D tools has been combined to become the Unity **2D Game Kit**. In this recipe, we'll create a simple 2D platformer to explore some of the features offered by the 2D Game Kit, including pressure plates, doors, and falling objects that damage enemies. You'll learn how to paint additional platform files into the Scene, add a wall of spikes, and how to add enemies. In this recipe, we'll give our Ellen character an **Interactable** teleporter to allow her to bypass the Chomper enemy in the Scene:

Figure 7.11 – Example Scene built with the Unity 2D Game Kit

Getting ready

This recipe uses the free Unity **Asset Store** and **Package Manager** packages.

How to do it...

To create a game with the **2D Game Kit**, follow these steps:

1. Create a new Unity 2D project.

2. Import **2D Game Kit** (free from Unity Technologies) from the Asset Store by following the same steps as in the previous recipe. So first, open the Unity Asset Store in a web browser and log in to your Unity account in the Asset Store.

3. Search for and select the free 2D Game Kit in the Asset Store. Click **Add to My Assets**, and then, after the button changes, click **Open in Unity**. Click **Download**, and when downloaded, click **Import**. Say **Yes** to any popup about losing saved work by importing a complete project.

4. Create a new **2D Game Kit** Scene by choosing **Kit Tools | Create New Scene**. You'll then be asked to name the Scene (enter `2D_gameKit_example`) and a new **Scene** asset file will be created in your **Project | Assets** folder. You'll see that there are quite a few special GameObjects in the **Hierarchy** window of your new Scene:

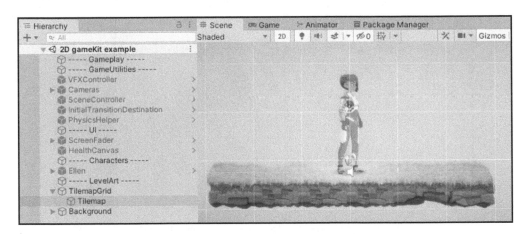

Figure 7.12 – New Scene created with an animated 2D character on a platform

5. As you can see, the new Scene starts off by containing an animated 2D character (Ellen), and a small platform.

6. In the **Inspector** window, select the `Tilemap` child of the `TilemapGrid` GameObject. We are getting ready to paint some tiles onto this `Tilemap` GameObject.

7. Display the tile palette by going to **Window | 2D | Tile Palette**. Select **TilesetGameKit**, and then click on the green-topped grass platform tile. Select the **Paint with active Brush** tool (the *paintbrush* icon).

8. Start painting grass-topped platforms onto the Scene. This is a **Rule Tile**, so it cleverly ensures that only the top tiles in a touching group are painted with the grass-topped tile. The other touching tiles (left/right/below) are painted with a brown, earthy tile.

9. Create a wide, flat area, and then, to the right of where Ellen starts, create a very tall wall of earth, too tall for Ellen to jump over.

10. Close the **Tile Palette** panel to exit tile painting mode.

11. Add four spikes between Ellen and the earth wall, meaning she would get hurt trying to jump over them. To create these GameObjects, drag instances of the **Spikes** Prefab from the **2DGameKit | Prefabs | Environment** project folder.

12. To make things even harder, add a **Chomper** enemy between the spikes and the earth wall! Drag an instance of the **Chomper** Prefab from the **2DGameKit | Prefabs | Enemies** project folder:

Figure 7.13 – Chomper, four spikes, and a wall of earth added to the Scene

13. Run the Scene. Ellen cannot get past the spikes, and even if she could, we have not yet given Ellen some way to get past the earth wall and Chomper obstacles.

14. Let's add a **Teleporter**, to the left of where Ellen starts. Drag an instance of the **Teleporter** Prefab from the **2DGameKit | Prefabs | Interactables** project folder.

15. Let's create a destination point for the teleporter using a custom sprite. Import the **EnemyBug** sprite into this project, and drag an instance from the **Project** panel into the Scene somewhere to the right of the earth wall.

16. Teleporters require a **Transition Point** component in the GameObject that is to be the destination of the teleportation. Add a **Collider 2D** to **Enemy Bug**, and choose **Add Component | Physics 2D | Box Collider 2D**. Check its **Is Trigger** option.

17. Add a **Transition Point** component to **Enemy Bug**, choose **Add Component**, search for **Transition**, and then add **Transition Point**.

18. We can now set up the teleporter. With the teleporter selected in the **Hierarchy** window, in the **Inspector** window for the **Transition Point (Script)** component, perform the following steps:

   - **Transitioning Game Object**: Drag **Ellen** into this slot.
   - **Transition Type**: Choose **Same Scene** from the drop-down menu.
   - **Destination Transform**: Drag **Enemy Bug** into this **Transition Point** slot.
   - **Transition When**: Choose **On Trigger Enter** from the drop-down menu:

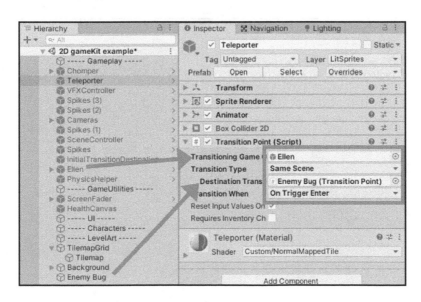

Figure 7.14 – Settings for the Teleporter Transition Point (Script)

19. Run the Scene. Ellen can now safely avoid the spikes and Chomper by using the teleporter.

20. Let's make it a bit more interesting by having the teleporter GameObject initially inactive (not visible or able to be interacted with), and adding a switch that Ellen has to hit to make the teleporter active.

21. Select the `Teleporter` GameObject in the **Hierarchy** window and uncheck its active box at the top-left of the **Inspector** window. The GameObject should be invisible and appear grayed out in the **Hierarchy** window.

22. Add a single-use switch to the game, to the left of where Ellen starts. Drag an instance of **Single Use Switch** from the **2DGameKit | Prefabs | Interactables** project folder.

23. With **Single Use Switch** selected in the **Hierarchy** window, in the **Inspector** window, set the following:

- **Layers**: Add **Player** to **Interactable Layers** (so the switch can be enabled by the player colliding or firing a bullet).

- **On Enter**: Drag **Teleporter** into a free **RunTime Only** GameObject slot, and change the action drop-down menu from **No Function** to **GameObject | Set Active (bool)**, and then **check** the checkbox that appears:

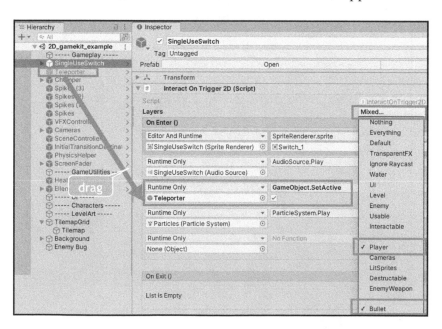

Figure 7.15 – The SingleUseSwitch settings for the Interact on Trigger 2D (Script) component

24. Run the Scene. Ellen now has to travel over to the switch, to reveal the teleporter, which then leads her to safely transport to the **Enemy Bug** location, beyond the earth wall and away from danger.

How it works...

We have dipped our toes into the wide range of features of the 2D Game Kit. Hopefully, this recipe gives you an idea of how to work with the Prefabs provided, and also how to explore how custom artwork can be used, with appropriately added components to create your own GameObjects using the features of the 2D Game Kit.

If you look at the Ellen 2D character, you'll see some scripted components that manage the character's interaction with the 2D Game Kit. These include the following:

- **CharacterController 2D**: Movement and physical interactions
- **Player Input**: Keyboard/input control mapping, so you can change which keys/controller buttons control movement, jumping, and so on
- **Player Character**: How characters interact with the 2D Game Kit, including fighting (melee), damage, and bullet pools

Learn more about Ellen and her component in the reference guide: `https://unity3d.com/learn/tutorials/projects/2d-game-kit/ellen?playlist=49633`.

Importing third-party 3D models and animations from Mixamo

While there are many 3D models and animations available and ready to use in Unity from the Asset Store, there are many more sources of 3D assets from third-party organizations. **Mixamo** (now part of **Adobe)** offers a fantastic range of characters and animations via their web-based system.

In this recipe, we'll select and download a character and some animations. We will also format them for use with Unity and control the animations with an Animation Controller state chart:

Figure 7.16 – The Adobe Mixamo website for characters and animations

Getting ready

This recipe uses the free **Adobe Mixamo** system, so you'll need to sign up for an account with them if you don't have one already.

How to do it...

To import third-party **3D models** and animations from **Mixamo**, follow these steps:

1. Open a web browser and visit Mixamo.com.
2. Sign up/log in with your **Mixamo/Adobe** account.
3. Select the **Characters** section (from the navigation bar in the top-left corner of the web page).
4. Select your character, such as **Lola B Styperek**. You'll see this character appear in the right-hand preview panel.
5. Download your character, choosing **FBX For Unity (.fbx)** and **T-pose**:

Figure 7.17 – Download settings for a character via the Adobe Mixamo website

6. Create a new 3D Unity project, and in the **Project** panel, create a folder named `Models`.

7. Import the downloaded FBX file into the `Models` folder.

8. Select the asset file in the **Project** panel and, in the **Inspector** window, select the **Materials** section.

9. Click the **Extract Textures...** button and extract the model's **Textures** into your `Models` folder. If asked to fix an issue with a Material using a texture as a normal map, choose **Fix Now**:

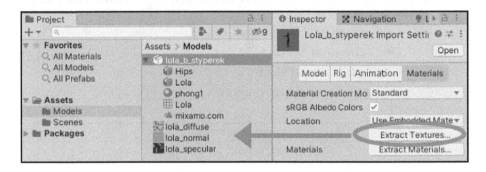

Figure 7.18 – Extracting textures for the imported character model

10. Drag the clone of the character from the **Project** panel into the Scene:

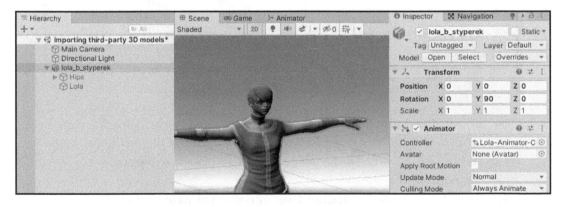

Figure 7.19 – Inspector view of the imported character with the addition of the Animator Controller

11. We need an Animator Controller to manage animations. In the **Project** panel, create a folder named `Animation`. Create a new Animator Controller file in the `Animation` folder named `Lola-Animator-Controller`.

12. Select **Lola B Styperek** in the **Hierarchy** window. Drag the `Lola-Animator-Controller` file from the **Project** panel into the **Animator | Controller** slot in the **Inspector** window.

13. Now, let's animate this model. Go back to the `Mixamo.com` web page and select an animation, such as **Golf Drive**. Click the **Download** button and choose these options:
    - **Format: FBX for Unity (.fbx)**
    - **Frames per Second: 30**
    - **Skin: Without skin**
    - **Keyframe Reduction: none**:

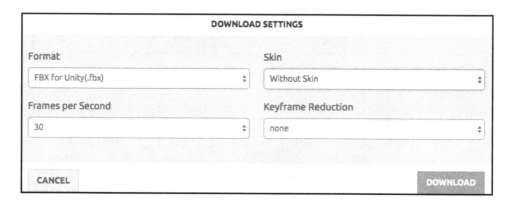

Figure 7.20 – Download settings for a character animation via the Adobe Mixamo website

14. Import the **Animation Clip** FBX file (`lola_b_styperek@Golf Drive.fbx` in this case) into the `Animation` folder of your Unity project.

15. Double-click the `Lola-Animator-Controller` file to open the **Animator** (state machine) editor panel.

16. Drag **Golf Drive Animation Clip** into the **Animator** panel; it should appear as an orange state, with a transition from **Entry** to it (that is, this one state becomes the default state):

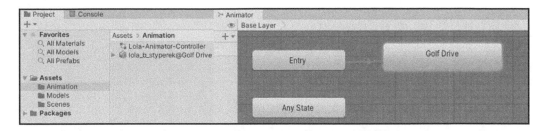

Figure 7.21 – Downloaded animation added to the Animator panel

17. Run the Scene. You should now see **Lola** practicing her golf swing. If you have the character selected in the **Hierarchy** window and can view the **Animator** panel, you'll see that **Golf Swing Animation Clip (State)** is playing:

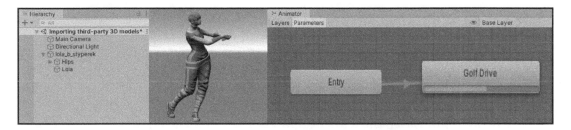

Figure 7.22 – Example of animation running in Game view with the golf drive animation status visible in the Animator panel

How it works...

Mixamo exports 3D rigged character models and animation clips in FBX format. The Materials for models are embedded in the **FBX** file, so we had to extract them once the model was imported into Unity.

Unity controls the animation of models with an Animator Controller, so we had to create one for our character model and then drag in the animation clip we wished to use to animate our model.

There's more...

Here are some ways to go further with this recipe.

Looping the animation

Select **Animation Clip** in the **Project** panel and, in the **Inspector** window, check its **Loop Time** option, and then click the **Apply** button to make the change to this asset file. When you run the scene, **Lola** will now repeat the animation indefinitely.

Scripting events to control when animation clips are played

Additional animation clips can be added to the state chart in the character's Animator Controller. You can then define variables and triggers, to define when animations transition from one clip to another. Many of the recipes in this chapter illustrate ways to allow scripts to influence the transition from one **Animation Clip (State)** to another.

Swapping the Standard Assets Ethan for a different character

The Unity Standard Assets are a great source of useful prefabs, scripts, textures, and so on when getting to know Unity. The Ethan `ThirdPersonController` prefab, along with `MultipurposeCameraRig`, are a fast and easy way to add a character and dynamic camera to test a scene you've just created.

However, over time, you'll want to replace the Standard Assets with other assets. Rather than learning how to create alternatives from scratch, a useful skill, and a good way to learn, is to incrementally change components of an existing asset. In this recipe, we'll learn how to replace the Ethan 3D character with an import from the Asset Store, while re-using the scripting and the Animation Controller that are part of `ThirdPersonController`. In the next recipe, we'll learn how to start creating our own character controller scripts to complete the replacement process:

Figure 7.23 – The MaleDummy 3D character moving around a textured plane

Getting ready

A useful source of free textures (such as the hex pattern used in this recipe) are websites such as `http://www.texturise.club/`. Our thanks to websites such as **Texturise** for making these resources available.

How to do it...

To swap the Ethan character from the Unity Standard Assets package with a different 3D model of your choosing, follow these steps:

1. Start a new 3D project and ensure you are logged in to your Unity account in the Unity Editor.
2. Open the Unity Asset Store in a web browser and log in to your Unity account in the Asset Store.
3. In the Asset Store, search for `Standard Assets`, and import the **Asset Package** into your project. Click on **Open in Unity** | **Import**.

4. You should now have a `Standard Assets` folder in your **Project** panel, containing the `Cameras` and `Characters` folders (and possibly some others, such as `CrossPlatformInput` and `Editor`).

 At the time of writing, the Standard Assets package has not been updated for Unity 2020.1. When using it in recipes, two errors will appear, and these need to be resolved before playing your recipe. The solution can be found in the first recipe in *Chapter 11, Cameras and Rendering Pipelines*.
Alternatively, a Unity package named `StandardAssets_fixedFor2020.unitypackage` has also been prepared containing all the resources for this recipe. The package can found in the `07_00` folder.

5. Create a 3D **Plane** in your Scene.
6. Add an instance of the **ThirdPersonController** Prefab to your Scene. Do this by dragging the **ThirdPersonController** Prefab from the **Standard Assets | Characters | ThirdPersonController | Prefabs** folder into the Scene. Tag this **Player** GameObject.
7. With the **ThirdPersonController** GameObject selected in the **Hierarchy** window, in the **Inspector** window, tag this GameObject with the **Player** tag.
8. Add a clone of the **MultipurposeCameraRig** prefab to your scene. Do this by dragging the **MultipurposeCameraRig** prefab from the **Standard Assets | Cameras | Prefabs** folder into the scene.
9. Delete the **MainCamera** GameObject from the **Hierarchy** window.
10. Run the scene. As you move the character around the scene with the arrow keys, the camera should smoothly follow behind. You may wish to add a texture to the plane, to make it easier to see how the character is moving (such as a free tileable texture from `http://www.texturise.club/`):

Figure 7.24 – Ethan character moving around a textured plane

11. Now, go back to the Asset Store and locate the free **3D Character Dummy** published by Kevin Iglesias (thanks for making this free!). Import this asset package into your project:

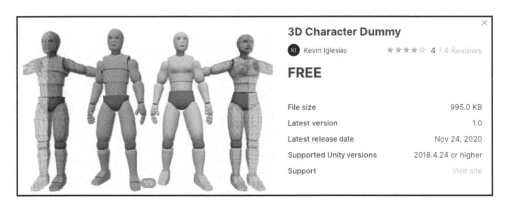

Figure 7.25 – The free 3D Character Dummy from the Asset Store

12. Duplicate the **ThirdPersonController** Prefab from the **Standard Assets | Characters | ThirdPersonController | Prefabs** folder, and rename the duplicate `MyThirdPersonController`. Open this prefab for editing by double-clicking the file in the **Project** panel.

13. Disable the three Ethan child GameObejcts (`EthanBody`, `EthanGlasses`, and `EthanSkeleton`).

14. Replace the 3D model we see by dragging a clone of the **MaleDummy** prefab from **Assets | Kevin Iglesias | Prefabs** into the **Hierarchy** window as a child of the **MyThirdPersonController** Prefab's GameObject.

15. With **MyThirdPersonController** selected in the **Hierarchy** window, in the **Inspector** window for the **Animator** component, change the **Avatar** property to **MaleDummyAvatar**:

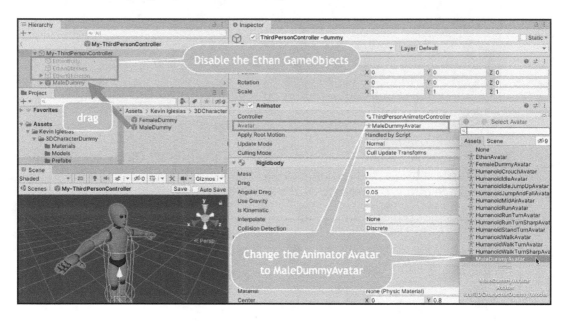

Figure 7.26 – Creating a third person controller with the MaleDummy model

16. Save your changed Prefab.

17. In the Scene, delete the **ThirdPersonController** GameObject, and instead add a new GameObject character by dragging your **MyThirdPersonController** Prefab from the **Project** panel into the Scene.

18. Save and run the Scene. You should now have a blue **MaleDummy** character moving around the Scene using the arrow keys.

How it works...

First, we created a scene containing the **ThirdPersonController** Standard Assets with the Ethan character. We were able to make use of the scripts and Animator Controller from the standard **ThirdPersonController** assets, but we changed the character the player sees to **MaleDummy**, which we imported from the Asset Store. Deleting or disabling the Ethan components in the Prefab meant that we don't see the Ethan 3D character model.

Adding a GameObject based on **MaleDummy** to our **MyThirdPersonController** Prefab placed a 3D character model in our Prefab. In order for the **MaleDummy** model to be correctly animated, we needed to ensure that the Animator Controller is targeting the Avatar (virtual skeleton) of the **MaleDummy** model, which we updated in the **Inspector** window.

The Animator Controller was then able to apply the animations (idle, walking, turning, running, and so on) to the **MaleDummy** character when directed to do so by its scripted components.

Importing a 3D model and adding an Animation Controller

Sometimes, we may get a 3D model from a third party that has no animations. Unity makes it straightforward to import models (and their textures if available) and create an avatar for use in our games. In this recipe, we'll import a free detailed 3D character model with its image textures, add an avatar, create an Animation Controller by re-using some animations from the Standard Assets, and write a simple controller script:

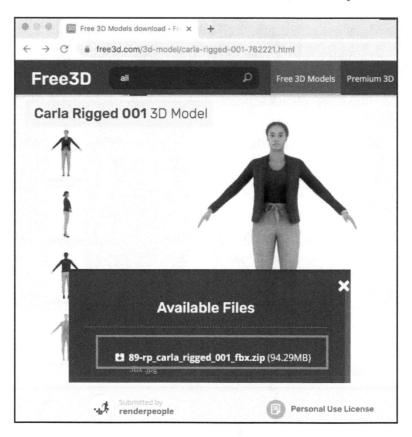

Figure 7.27 – The free Carla human model by RenderPeople on Free3D.com

How to do it...

To import and animate a 3D human model, follow these steps:

1. Start a new 3D project and ensure you are logged in to your Unity account in the Unity Editor.
2. Download, unzip, and import the FBX version of the free Carla model from www.free3d.com (or use some other FBX human model).

 If any files have a forward or backslash character (for example /) in them, such as tex/imagename.jpg, then remove this character. Otherwise, Unity may not be able to import all the files. If there are multiple versions of the model, then choose the Y-up version for use in Unity.

3. Select the **Carla** model in the **Project** panel.
4. In the **Inspector** window, select the **Rig** tab, change the animation type to **Humanoid**, and then click the **Apply** button:

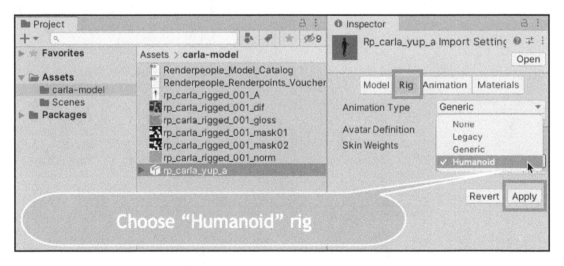

Figure 7.28 – Setting the model's rig type to Humanoid

5. You'll now see a new file in the folder for your character, ending with the word `Avatar`. If you select this file in the **Project** panel and then, in the **Inspector** window, click the **Configure Avatar** button, you can see how the virtual skeleton "rig" that was imported as part of the model has been mapped to a Unity Human avatar, which can be affected by animations:

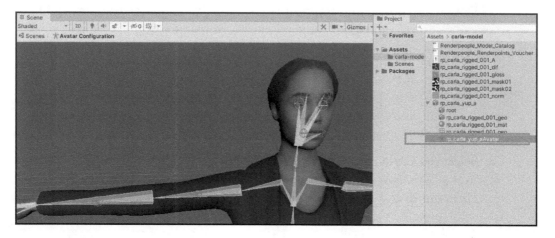

Figure 7.29 – Viewing the automatically created Unity Avatar for our Humanoid model

6. Drag your **Carla** 3D model from the **Project** panel into the Scene.
7. Add a 3D **Plane** to the Scene (**GameObject | 3D Object | Plane**). In the **Inspector** window for the **Transform** component, set the scale of **Plane** to (20, 1, 20).
8. You may also wish to texture the plane, such as with the free hexagonal pattern, at `http://www.texturise.club/2013/09/tileable-hexagonal-stone-pavement.html`:

Figure 7.30 – The 3D model in the scene

9. Now that we have a 3D human model with an avatar, we can control and animate it. Let's get the Ethan animations from the Unity **Standard Assets** package. First, open the Unity Asset Store in a web browser and log in to your Unity account in the Asset Store.

10. In the Asset Store, search for **Standard Assets,** and then import **Asset Package** into your project. Click on **Open in Unity | Import**.

11. You should now have a `Standard Assets` folder in your **Project** panel, containing the `Cameras` and `Characters` folders (and possibly some others, such as `CrossPlatformInput` and `Editor`).

> At the time of writing, the Standard Assets package has not been updated for Unity 2020.1. When using it in recipes, two errors will appear, and these need to be resolved before playing your recipe. The solution can be found in the first recipe in *Chapter 11, Cameras and Rendering Pipelines*.
> Alternatively, a Unity package named `StandardAssets_fixedFor2020.unitypackage` has also been prepared containing all the resources for this recipe. The package can found in the `07_00` folder.

12. In the **Project** panel, create a new Animator Controller (**Create | Animator Controller**), and rename it `Carla Animator Controller`. Double-click this asset file to open up the **Animator** panel. You should see a green state, **Entry**, a red state, **Exit**, and a dirty blue state, **Any State**.

13. In the **Project** panel, locate the **Animation** folder for **ThirdPersonController** from the **StandardAssets** (**Standard Assets | Characters | ThirdPersonController | Animation**). From this folder, drag the **HumanoidIdle** animation into the **Animator** panel. You should now see a new orange state named **HumanoidIdle**, and a faint orange **Transition** arrow from the green **Start** state to this new state.

14. In the **Hierarchy** window, select your Carla character. In the **Inspector** window for the **Avatar** property of the **Animator** component, select **Carla Animator Controller**.

15. Save and run the Scene. You should see your character performing the idling animation if you have the character selected in the **Hierarchy** window, and the **Animator** panel is visible when running the Scene:

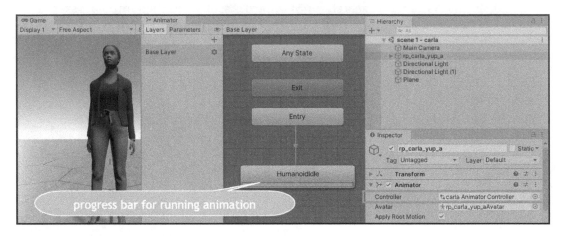

Figure 7.31 – The running idle animation in the Animator Controller when you play the Scene

16. Now, drag the **HumanoidWalk** animation from the **Project** panel into the **Animator** panel.
17. In the **Animator** panel, select the **HumanoidIdle** animation state, and right-mouse-click to create a new **Transition** arrow from this state to the **HumanoidWalk** state.
18. You now have an Animator Controller containing two humanoid animations. Save and run the scene. You should see your character performing the idling animation for a second or so, and then the walk animation – and the character will actually move in the scene when walking.

How it works...

The model we imported was textured and *rigged*, so it came with a virtual 3D skeleton and images. Once we set the animation type to **Humanoid**, Unity was able to create an avatar linked to the rig.

The power of the Unity Mechanism animation system is that animations are related to avatars, not to the 3D models specifically. Therefore, we can apply the same animation to different avatars in different 3D models. If one character model is short or tall or fat or thin, or has long arms, and so on, it does not matter. As long as the rig has been appropriately created to match the locations of the 3D model, animation can be applied to the 3D model.

A GameObject Scene containing a character model has an animator component, and its two most important properties are linked to the avatar, and to the Animation Controller. We created a simple Animation Controller that starts with the idle animation from the Unity Standard Assets and uses the defaults for a transition over a short period to a walk animation.

The character actually moves in the scene when the **HumanoidWalk** animation is playing, because we kept the default option of **Apply Root Motion** in the **Animator** component for our Carla GameObject character in the scene. If this option was unchecked, the character would appear to be walking on the spot:

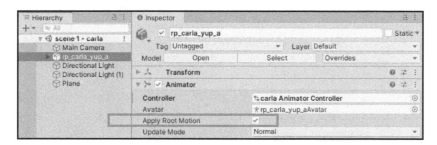

Figure 7.32 – The default Apply Root Motion option checked for the GameObject character's Animator component

In the next recipe, we'll take things further to use scripts to control when to change animations.

Using scripts to control 3D animations

In the previous recipe, we created a simple transition in our Animator Controller from the Idle to the Walk animation. The default settings mean that the transition will fire after a set exit time, and the model will transition into the next animation state. However, in many situations, we don't want animations to change automatically, we want animations to correspond to events and changes to in-game values. Therefore, we need to be able to trigger animation transitions and parameters through our scripted code.

In this recipe, we'll create a very simple controller script for our human model and its Animator Controller. After learning the basics in this recipe, you'll have the knowledge and skills to understand third-party character controllers, such as those from the Unity Standard Assets and Asset Store assets.

Getting ready

This recipe builds upon the previous one, so make a copy of that and use this copy.

How to do it...

To use scripts to control 3D animations, perform the following steps:

1. Start a new 3D project and ensure you are logged in to your Unity account in the Unity Editor.
2. Since we're going to be moving our character around the scene, let's get rid of the fixed main camera and use the AI-controller camera rig from **Standard Assets**, so our character is always in view. Delete the main camera.
3. Tag the **Carla** GameObject with the preset tag **Player**.
4. Add to the scene an instance of the multi-purpose camera rig from **Standard Assets**. Drag the Prefab asset file, MultiPurposeCameraRig, into the **Hierarchy** window from the **Project** panel folder: **Standard Assets | Cameras | Prefabs**.

   Now, when you run the Scene, the camera should smoothly reposition itself above and behind the player's character.

5. Select the **Carla** Animator Controller in the **Project** panel.
6. Simplify the state names in our controller. In the **Animator** panel, rename the HumanIdle animation state to just Idle, and the HumanWalk animation state to just Walk.

7. Select the **Parameters** tab at the top-left of the **Animator** panel, and then click the plus (+) button to add a new **Float** parameter named **Speed**:

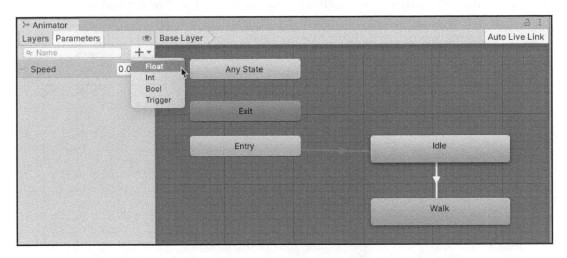

Figure 7.33 – Creating the Speed Float parameter in the Animator Controller

8. Now, select the **Transition** arrow from **Idle** to **Walk**. In the **Inspector** window, uncheck the **Has Exit Time** option.

9. Then, at the bottom of this component, add a new condition by clicking the plus (+) button. Since we only have one parameter, **Speed**, this is automatically chosen for the Condition variable. The default values of **Greater** for operator and **zero** for value are also what we want, so we have no more work to do here. We now have a conditional transition from **Idle** to **Walk** that will only fire when the **Speed** parameter is greater than zero:

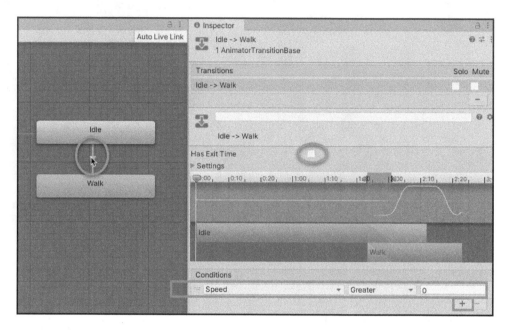

Figure 7.34 – Making the Idle to Walk transition conditional on the value of the Speed parameter

Let's now write a script that allows the *Up/Down* arrows (and *W/S* keys) to change the **Speed** parameter in our Animator Controller.

10. In the **Project** panel, create a new C# script class named PlayerMove.cs containing the following:

```
using UnityEngine;

public class PlayerMove : MonoBehaviour {
    private float vertical = 0;
    private Animator animator;
    private void Awake() {
        animator = GetComponent<Animator>();
    }

    private void Update() {
```

```
        vertical = Input.GetAxis("Vertical");
    }

    void FixedUpdate() {
        animator.SetFloat("Speed", vertical);
    }
}
```

11. Add an instance object of this script class to the character in the scene by dragging the **PlayerMove** script asset file from the **Project** panel onto the **Carla** GameObject character in the **Hierarchy** window.

12. Save and run your Scene. The character should begin in the **Idle** animation state. If you press the *Up arrow* or *W* keys, you should see the character start walking. If you arrange your panels so you can see the **Animator** panel when the Scene is running, then you'll see the value of the **Speed** parameter being changed. However, if you release the keys, while the value of the **Speed** parameter returns to zero, the character stays in the **Walk** state.

13. Add a conditional transition with no exit time (**Has Exit Time** option unchecked) from the **Walk** state to the **Idle** state, with the condition that the **Speed** parameter has to be less than 0.1 for the character to return to the **Idle** state:

Figure 7.35 – Returning to Idle when Speed is less than 0.1

14. Let's make our character transition from **Walk** to **Run** when a *Shift* key is pressed. In the **Animator** panel, click the plus (+) button and add a new **Bool** parameter named **Run**.

15. Drag the `HumanoidRun` animation clip asset file from the **Project** panel (**Standard Assets** | **Characters** | **ThirdPersonController** | **Animation**) into the **Animator** panel. Rename this animation state simply `Run`.

16. Add a transition with no exit time (**Has Exit Time** option unchecked) from **Walk** to **Run** with the condition that the **Run** parameter is `true`.

17. Add a transition with no exit time (**Has Exit Time** option unchecked) from **Run** to **Walk** with the condition that the **Run** parameter is `false`.

We now need to add to our script class to detect the *Shift* key and set the **Run** Boolean parameter in the Animator accordingly.

18. Update the C# script class, `PlayerMove.cs`, to now contain the following:

```
using UnityEngine;

public class PlayerMove : MonoBehaviour {
    private float vertical = 0;
    private bool runKeyDown = false;
    private Animator animator;
    private void Awake() {
        animator = GetComponent<Animator>();
    }

    private void Update() {
        vertical = Input.GetAxis("Vertical");
        runKeyDown = Input.GetKey(KeyCode.LeftShift) ||
            Input.GetKey(KeyCode.RightShift);
    }

    void FixedUpdate() {
        animator.SetFloat("Speed", vertical);
        animator.SetBool("Run", runKeyDown);
    }
}
```

19. Save and run the Scene. Now, when you have the character walking and if you press the *Shift* key, you'll see the character start running, and if you release the *Shift* key, the character returns to a walk.

How it works...

By making transitions between animation states conditional, we enable the whole animation of a character to be driving through in-game events and scripting. Unity Animation Controllers provide a range of different types of parameter, from simple integer and float numeric values to true/false **Boolean** variables, and consumable Boolean "triggers."

While sometimes we do want an automatic, timed transition from one animation state to another, in many cases, we need to uncheck the **Exit Time** property for **Transitions** and define the appropriate condition for when we wish the **Animation State** change to take place.

In this recipe, we created a parameter named **Speed**, whose value we set in our script based on the **vertical** input axis. Unity's default input setup means that the *W/S* and *Up/Down* keyboard keys affect the vertical axis values in the range -1 ... 0 .. +1. Our scripted variable, vertical, is set based on this Unity input axis: vertical = Input.GetAxis("Vertical"). Therefore, our code has two functions:

- Get values from the user/game events.
- Set the corresponding parameter in the Animator Controller.

It's best to process user input in Update() methods (each frame), and to communicate with Animator Controllers in FixedUpdate() (in-sync with the Physics and Animation engines). So we declare variables in our script that can be accessed by any method.

Since running is a true/false property of our game, we defined a Boolean parameter in our Animator Controller, and used the Input.GetKey(...) method to detect whether a *Shift* key is currently pressed. Note that we didn't use GetKeyDown(...) since that only fires once when the key is first pressed down. Since we want our character to keep running while the key is pressed down, we interrogate the *Shift* key status every frame using Input.GetKey(...).

Since our players may be left- or right-handed, we can detect either left or right *Shift* keys with the Boolean OR statement:

```
runKeyDown = Input.GetKey(KeyCode.LeftShift) ||
    Input.GetKey(KeyCode.RightShift);
```

There's more...

We can use the left-right arrow keys (or *A* and *D*) to turn by adding a few more lines to our script:

- We can add a new public variable for the rotation speed: `rotateSpeed`.
- We can add a new private variable, `horizontal`, and set its value in `Update()` based on the `Input.GetAxis(...)` method.
- We can then perform a `Rotate(...)` operation on the character's `transform` component in `FixedUpdate()`:

```
using UnityEngine;

public class PlayerMoveTurn : MonoBehaviour {
    public float rotateSpeed = 1;

    private float vertical = 0;
    private float horizontal = 0;
    private bool runKeyDown = false;
    private Animator animator;
    private void Awake() {
        animator = GetComponent<Animator>();
    }

    private void Update() {
        vertical = Input.GetAxis("Vertical");
        horizontal = Input.GetAxis("Horizontal");
        runKeyDown = Input.GetKey(KeyCode.LeftShift) ||
            Input.GetKey(KeyCode.RightShift);
    }

    void FixedUpdate()
    {
        animator.SetFloat("Speed", vertical);
        animator.SetBool("Run", runKeyDown);
        // turn
        transform.Rotate(0, horizontal * rotateSpeed, 0);
    }
}
```

Importing and using a UMA free character

A powerful free Unity asset is the **UMA** system – the **Unity Multipurpose Avatar**. This asset provides two key benefits:

- Clothes and the character model can be combined into a small number of textures and meshes, reducing the workload for the game engine (and thereby improving performance).
- UMA offers many customizable physical features of the character model, including height, muscle size, and facial features.

So, UMA offers the possibility of creating many different kinds of characters from a single asset. In this recipe, we'll learn how to add the UMA package to a project, use the runtime editor, save new prefabs based on our customizations, and create a scene that loads a character from a prefab:

Figure 7.36 – A scene full of random UMA characters

How to do it...

To import and use a UMA character in your games, follow these steps:

1. Start a new 3D project and ensure you are logged in to your Unity account in the Unity Editor.
2. Open the Unity Asset Store in a web browser and log in to your Unity account in the Asset Store.

3. Search for and select the free UMA 2 asset in the Asset Store:

Figure 7.37 – The UMA 2 asset in the Asset Store

4. Click **Add to My Assets**, and then, after the button changes, click **Open in Unity**.

5. In your Unity Editor, the **Package Manager** panel should open, and the **UMA** assets should be selected in the list of **My Assets**. Click **Download**, and when downloaded, click **Import**. Say **Yes** to any popup about losing saved work by importing a complete project.

 Note: This is a relatively large set of assets (over 0.5 GB), so could take some minutes to download and import onto your computer.

6. In the **Project** panel, you should now see a new folder named **UMA**.

7. To quickly see what UMA can do, open the **UMA DCS Demo - Random Characters** Scene (**UMA | Examples | DynamicCharacterSystem Examples**). Run the Scene, and you'll see many randomly generated UMA characters. Stop and run the Scene again and you will see a new set of characters.

8. To get hands-on experience of how the customization of UMA characters works, open the **UMA DCS Tool - DNAConverterBehaviour Customizer** Scene (**UMA | Examples | DynamicCharacterSystem Examples**). Run the Scene, click on a character, and then click the large category buttons at the top to get a set of properties for customizing your character:

Figure 7.38 – Customizing a character in the UMA Runtime character editor

9. Start a new Scene, containing just the two default basic GameObjects of a **Main Camera** and **Directional Light**.

10. Drag the **UMA_GLIB** prefab into this Scene from the **UMA | Getting Started** folder.

11. Create a cube by choosing **GameObject | 3D Object | Cube**. Edit its **Transform Position** (if required) to position this cube at (0, 0, 0).

12. Drag the **UMADynamicCharacterAvatar** Prefab into this Scene from the **UMA | Getting Started** folder. Set the position of this GameObject character to (0, 0.5, 0), so it is just above our cube and won't fall down into the abyss when we run the Scene.

13. Save and run the Scene, and you should see a male character, just wearing underwear, with an **Idle** animation, standing on the cube.

14. Stop the Scene. In the **Hierarchy** window, select the **UMADynamicCharacterAvatar** GameObject. In the **Inspector** window, you should see **XX**.

15. Locate the **UMA | Examples | Physics Examples | Assets | Recipe** folder in the **Project** panel. Now, making sure that the **UMADynamicCharacterAvatar** GameObject is selected in the **Hierarchy** window, drag the ClothRobeRecipe asset file from the **Project** panel into the **Drag Wardrobe Recipes Here** area in the **Inspector** window.

16. Save and run the Scene. Now, the man should be wearing a medieval-style robe. Note how the robe cloth sways around his legs like real cloth, illustrating cloth physics:

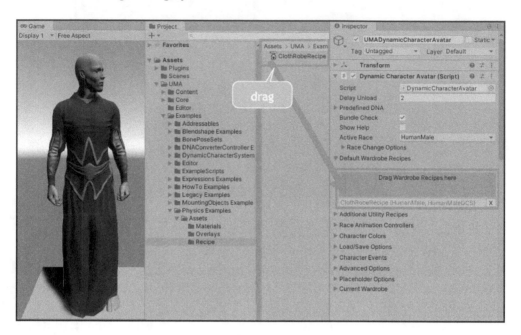

Figure 7.39 – Creating a robed man UMA character in your Scene

How it works...

The UMA Unity package contains many components for editing and combining 3D characters and clothing textures. The **UMA DCS Demo - Random Characters** Scene illustrated how, at runtime, the properties of a UMA character can be changed through the interactive sliders. The UMA Unity package provides a way to customise core sets of properties related to the DNA (character type: male, female, car!), dimensions of parts of the body, colors of character components, and clothing items.

Your custom Scene required the core **UMA_GLIB** GameObject. This contains the core character generator and mesh combination components.
The **UMADynamicCharacterAvatar** GameObject is what the character becomes in the Scene. By adding `ClothRobeRecipe` to the public recipes slot in the **Inspector** window for this GameObject, the UMA system combined the character model with the robe model and textures to create an optimized GameObject character at runtime.

Through code or the creation of Prefabs, an amazing range of characters can be created once you get to know the UMA assets. PDF guides are included in the **UMA** folder when you add this asset package to a project.

There's more...

A fun feature of the UMA character is how easy it is to make the mode act as a rag doll. Perform the following steps:

1. Select the **UMADynamicCharacterAvatar** GameObject in the **Hierarchy** window.

2. Increase the number of slots for **Additional Utility Recipes** to 2, and drag the **Physics HD Recipe** UMA recipe into the new slot (from the **UMA | Content | Example | Additional Slots | Physics | HD** project folder):

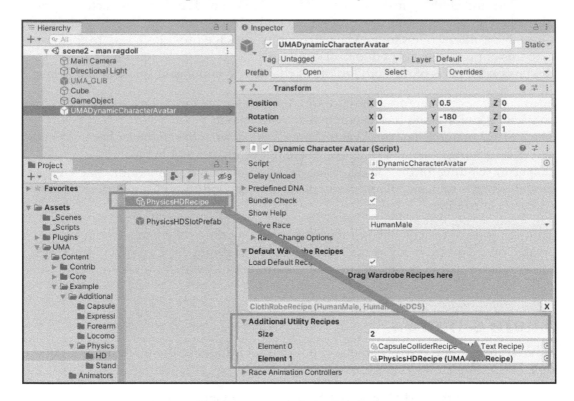

Figure 7.40 – Adding the Physics HD recipe to the character

3. Create the following C# script class and add it as a component to the **UMADynamicCharacterAvatar** GameObject in your Scene:

```csharp
using UnityEngine;
using UMA.Dynamics;

public class SpaceKeyRagDoll : MonoBehaviour {
    void Update() {
        if (Input.GetKeyDown(KeyCode.Space))
        {
            MakeRagDoll();
        }
    }
    private void MakeRagDoll() {
        Transform avatar =
```

```
GetComponent<Rigidbody>().transform.root;
        UMAPhysicsAvatar physicsAvatar =
avatar.GetComponent<UMAPhysicsAvatar>
            ();
        physicsAvatar.ragdolled = true;
    }
}
```

4. Now, when you press the *Spacebar*, you'll turn your character into a rag doll!

You can see how this could be effective in a first-person shooter in the **UMA | Examples | Physics Examples | RagDollExample** example Scene:

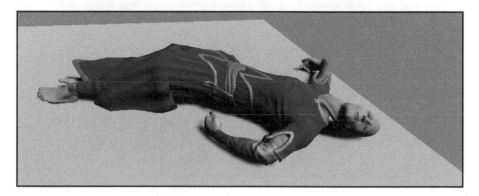

Figure 7.41 – Adding the RagDoll physics recipe to the UMA character

Getting started with the 2021 Starter Assets package

In June 2021, Unity published two new collections of starter assets, for third-person and first-person games. These new assets are relatively lightweight and will work with Unity 2021 with no fixing required (which is now needed for some of the older **Standard Assets** packages from Unity). So, these assets make a great starting point for trying out new techniques with pre-made controllers. In this recipe, we'll explore the ready-made Scene and work with some of the prefabs provided in the **Third Person Starter Assets** package:

Figure 7.42 – The pyramid of tunnels Prefabs Scene that we'll make in this recipe

How to do it...

To get started with the 2021 third-person Starter Assets from Unity, follow these steps:

1. Start a new 3D project and ensure you are logged in to your Unity account in the Unity Editor.
2. Open the Unity Asset Store in a web browser and log in to your Unity account in the Asset Store.
3. Search for and select the free **Starter Assets - Third Person Character Controller** from Unity Technologies in the Asset Store:

Figure 7.43 – Starter Asserts in the Asset Store

4. Click **Add to My Assets,** and then, after the button changes, click **Open in Unity**.

5. In your Unity Editor, the **Package Manager** panel should open, and the **Starter Assets - Third Person Character Controller** assets should be selected in the list of **My Assets**. Click **Download**, and when downloaded, click **Import**. Say **Yes** to any popup about resetting the project to use the new input system.

6. In the **Project** panel, you should now see a new folder named **StarterAssets**.

7. Open the **Playground** Scene provided, which you can find in the **Project** panel: **Assets | StarterAssets | ThirdPersonController | Scenes**.

8. Run and explore the Scene. You have a robot-style **Third-Person Character** and a Scene with stairs, ramps, blocks, tunnels, and other objects to explore. The character controller uses the standard *WASD | Spacebar* (jump) + *Shift* (run). The mouse changes the way the camera is facing – the camera stays near the character since it is controlled by a **CineMachine** Virtual Camera:

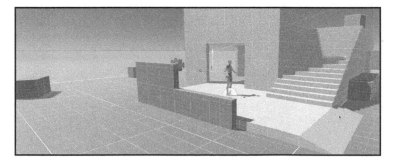

Figure 7.44 – The Playground Scene that comes with the third-person starter assets

9. Let's create a pyramid of tunnels. You'll find the tunnel Prefab in the **Project** panel (**Assets** | **StarterAssets** | **Environment** | **Prefabs** | **Tunnel_prefab**). Drag four Prefabs to form the base, then three more sitting on top of them, then two, and then the final one.

10. Let's make one of the **Tunnel_prefab** GameObjects blue by changing its material. Select a **Tunnel_prefab** object and, in the **Inspector** window, drag **Blue_Mat Material** into its **Mesh Renderer** component. You will find this material in the **Project** panel folder: **Assets** | **StarterAssets** | **Environment** | **Art** | **Materials**.

How it works...

Unity have provided two Starter Asset packages, with many useful prefabs. One of the packages provides a ready-made third-person character controller and camera, which we explored in this recipe. The other one does the same, but with a first-person character controller.

We added to the Scene provided by creating GameObjects from the **Environment** Prefabs provided. We were able to change the color of one of the **Tunnel** objects by using one of the **Art Material** asset files provided.

Further reading

Here are some links to further reading/resources regarding the topics covered in the chapter.

The Unit 3D Game Kit:

- The 3D Game Kit reference guide: https://unity3d.com/learn/tutorials/projects/3d-game-kit/introduction-3d-reference-guide?playlist=51061
- The Unity 3D Game Kit walk-through pages: https://unity3d.com/learn/tutorials/projects/3d-game-kit/introduction-walkthrough?playlist=51061

- Download the 3D Game Kit, including a sample Scene, from the Asset Store: `https://assetstore.unity.com/packages/essentials/tutorial-p rojects/3d-game-kit- beta-115747?_ga=2.127077645.1823824032.1533576706-1834737598.1481 552646`

The Unity 2D Game Kit:

- Unity's 2D Game Kit online tutorials/reference guide/advanced topics: `https://unity3d.com/learn/tutorials/s/2d-game-kit`
- Unity's official 2D Game Kit forum: `https://forum.unity.com/threads/2d-game-kit-official-threa d.517249/`
- Asset Store 2D Game Kit tutorial project: `https://assetstore.unity.com/packages/essentials/tutorial- projects/2d-game-kit-107098`
- Series of YouTube video tutorials from Unity Technologies entitled *Getting Started with 2D Game Kits*:
    - Overview and Goals [1/8]: `https://www.youtube.com/watch?v=cgqIOWu8W1c`
    - Ellen and Placing Hazards [2/8] Live 2018/2/21: `https://www.youtube.com/watch?v=V2_vj_bbB4M`
    - Adding Moving Platforms [3/8]: `https://www.youtube.com/watch?v=SfC3qYz4gAI`
    - Doors and Destructible Objects [4/8]: `https://www.youtube.com/watch?v=-hj6HnbI7PE`
    - Adding and Squishing Enemies [5/8]: `https://www.youtube.com/watch?v=WRKG_DDlUnQ`
    - Controlling Platforms With Switches [6/8]: `https://www.youtube.com/watch?v=YCy3PTVLGQA`
    - Using the Inventory System [7/8]: `https://youtu.be/LYQz-mtr90U`
    - Teleporting and Dialog Boxes [8/8]: `https://www.youtube.com/watch?v=gZ_OZL57c0g`

Learn more about 3D models and animation importing from the following sources:

- Unity docs on importing **3D Models**: `https://docs.unity3d.com/Manual/HOWTO-importObject.html`
- Unity docs about the **Model Import Settings** window: `https://docs.unity3d.com/Manual/class-FBXImporter.html`
- Unity docs about the **Model** tab: `https://docs.unity3d.com/Manual/FBXImporter-Model.html`
- Unity docs about **Model** file formats: `https://docs.unity3d.com/Manual/3D-formats.html`
- Samples of **Mixamo** free assets in the Asset Store:
  - `https://assetstore.unity.com/packages/3d/animations/melee-axe-pack-35320`
  - `https://assetstore.unity.com/packages/3d/animations/magic-pack-36269`
- A great tutorial by Tom Bozon based on the Ethan model for learning about Animator Controllers: `https://gamedevacademy.org/unity-animator-tutorial/`

Learn more about Unity Animator Controllers and scripting animations from the following sources:

- Unity video tutorial about Animator Controllers: `https://www.youtube.com/watch?v=JeZkctmoBPw`
- Unity video tutorial about using scripting to influence Animator Controllers: `https://www.youtube.com/watch?v=s7EIp-OqVyk`
- Invector offers a free version of its powerful human player controller in the Asset Store. It is well worth checking out if you are writing a third-person controller game: `https://assetstore.unity.com/packages/tools/utilities/third-person-controller-basic-locomotion-free-82048`.

Web Server Communication and Online Version Control

8

A server waits for messages requesting something for a client, and when one is received, it attempts to interpret and act upon the message, and send back an appropriate response to the client. A client is a computer program that can communicate with other clients and/or servers. Clients send requests, and receive responses in return.

It is useful to keep the following four concepts in mind when thinking about and working with client-server architectures:

- Client
- Server
- Request
- Response

The world is networked, which involves many different clients communicating with other clients, and also with servers.

Each of the Unity deployment platforms illustrates an example of a client:

- WebGL (running in a web browser)
- Windows and Mac applications
- Nintendo Switch
- Microsoft Xbox
- Sony Playstation
- Mobile devices, such as tablets and smartphones

The servers that these games can communicate with include dedicated multiplayer game servers, regular web servers, and online database servers. Multiplayer game development is a topic for a whole book of its own.

Web and database servers can play many roles in game development and runtime interaction. One form of Unity game interaction with web servers involves a game communicating with an online server for data, such as high scores, inventories, player profiles, and chat forums.

Another kind of client-server relationship involves **Distributed Version Control Systems** (**DVCS**), where content on a local computer (laptop or desktop) can be synchronized with an online server, both for backup and historical change purposes, and also to allow the sharing, and collaborative authoring, of code projects with other people. Private repositories are used within commercial game companies, and public repositories are used for open source projects, allowing anyone access to the contents.

The recipes in this chapter explore a range of these client-server communication scenarios in relation to Unity game development, online runtime communication, and cloud code version control and sharing.

In this chapter, we will cover the following recipes:

- Setting up a leaderboard using PHP and a database
- Unity game communication with a web server leaderboard
- Creating and cloning a GitHub repository
- Adding a Unity project to a local Git repository, and pushing files up to GitHub
- Unity project version control using GitHub for Unity
- Creating an asset bundle
- Loading an AssetBundle from a local StreamingAssets folder
- Downloading an asset bundle from a web server

Technical requirements

To complete this chapter, Unity 2021.1 or later is required, plus the following:

- Microsoft Windows 10 (64-bit) / GPU: DX10-, DX11-, and DX12-capable
- macOS Sierra 10.12.6+ / GPU: Metal-capable Intel or AMD
- Linux Ubuntu 16.04, Ubuntu 18.04, and CentOS 7 / GPU: OpenGL 3.2+ or Vulkan-capable, NVIDIA, or AMD

For each chapter, there is a folder with the asset files you require for the recipes at the book's public GitHub repository: `https://github.com/PacktPublishing/Unity-2021-Cookbook-Fourth-Edition`.

Since some of the recipes in this chapter make use of web servers and a database, for those recipes, you will require either the PHP language (which comes with its own web server and SQLite database features) or an AMP package.

If you are installing the PHP language, refer to the installation guide and download links:

- `https://www.php.net/manual/en/install.php`
- `https://www.php.net/downloads`

 If you do want to install a web server and database server application, a great choice is XAMPP. It is a free, cross-platform collection of everything you need to set up a database and web server on your local computer. The download page also contains FAQs and installation instructions for Windows, Mac, and Linux: `https://www.apachefriends.org/download.html`.

Setting up a leaderboard using PHP and a database

Games are more fun when there is a leaderboard of high scores that the players have achieved. Even single-player games can communicate with a shared web-based leaderboard. This recipe creates the web server-side (PHP) scripts to set and get player scores from a SQL database. The recipe after this one then sees us creating a Unity game client that can communicate with this web leaderboard's server.

Getting ready

This recipe assumes that you either have your own web hosting, or are running a local web server. You could use the built-in PHP web server, or a web server such as Apache or Nginx. For the database, you could use a SQL database Server such as MySQL or MariaDB. However, we've tried to keep things simple using SQLite—a file-based database system. So all you actually need on your computer is PHP 7, since it has a built-in web server and can talk to SQLite databases, which is the setup on which this recipe was tested.

All the PHP scripts for this recipe, along with the SQLite database file, can be found in the `08_01` folder.

How to do it...

To set up a leaderboard using PHP and a database, perform the following steps:

1. Copy the PHP project provided to where you will be running your web server:

   - **Live website hosting**: Copy the files to the live web folder on your server (often `www` or `htdocs`).
   - **Running on a local machine**: At the command line, you can use the Composer script shortcut to run the PHP built-in web server by typing `composer serve` or `php -S localhost:8000 -t public`:

Figure 8.1 – Running a web server in a macOS command-line Terminal using the shortcut composer serve

2. Open a web browser to your website location:

   - **Live website hosting**:Visit the URL for your hosted domain.
   - **Running on a local machine**: Visit the `localhost:8000` URL:

Figure 8.2 – Viewing the high score website home page in a web browser

3. Create/reset the database by clicking the last bulleted link: **reset database**. You should see a page with the message **database has been reset**, and a link back to the **home** page (click that link).

4. To view the leaderboard scores as a web page in your web browser, click the second link: **list players (HTML)**:

Figure 8.3 – Viewing scores as HTML

5. Try the fifth link – **list players (TXT)** – to retrieve the leaderboard data as a text file. Note how it looks different when viewed in the web browser (which ignores line breaks) compared to how it looks when you view the actual source file returned from the server:

Figure 8.4 – Viewing the source page to see raw text data

6. Do the same with the JSON and XML options – to see how our server can return the contents of the database wrapped up as HTML, plain text (TXT), XML, or JSON.

7. Click the sixth link – **create (username = mattilda, score=800)**. When you next retrieve the contents, you'll see that there is a new database record for player **mattilda** with a score of **800**. This shows that our server can receive data and change the contents of the database, as well as just return values from it.

How it works...

The player's scores are stored in a SQLite database. Access to the database is facilitated through the PHP scripts provided. In our example, all the PHP scripts were placed in a folder on our local machine, from which we'll run the server (it can be anywhere when using the PHP built-in server). So, the scripts are accessed via `http://localhost:8000`.

All access is facilitated through the PHP file called `index.php`. This is called a Front Controller, acting like a receptionist in a building, interpreting requests and asking the appropriate function to execute some actions and return a result in response to the request.

There are five actions implemented, and each is indicated by adding the action name at the end of the URL. (This is the GET HTTP method, which is sometimes used for web forms. Take a look at the address bar of your browser next time you search Google for example). The actions and their parameters (if any) are as follows:

- action = list & format = HTML / TXT / XML / JSON: This action asks for a listing of all player scores to be returned. Depending on the value of the second variable format (html/txt/xml/json), the list of users and their scores are returned in different text file formats.

- action = reset: This action asks for a set of default player names and score values to replace the current contents of the database table. This action takes no argument. It returns some HTML stating that the database has been reset, and a link to the home page.

- action = get & username = & format = HTML / TXT: This action asks for the integer score of the named player that is to be found. It returns the score integer. There are two formats: HTML, for a web page giving the player's score, and TXT, where the numerical value is the only content in the HTTP message returned.

- action = update & username = <usermame> & score = <score>: This action asks for the provided score of the named player to be stored in the database (but only if this new score is greater than the currently stored score). It returns the word *success* (if the database update was successful), otherwise -1 (to indicate that no update took place).

There's more...

Here are some ways to go further with this recipe.

SQLite, PHP, and database servers

The PHP code in this recipe used the PDO data object functions to communicate with a SQLite local file-based database. Learn more about PHP and SQLite at http://www.sqlitetutorial.net/sqlite-php/.

When SQLite isn't a solution (not supported by a web-hosting package), you may need to develop locally with a SQL Server, such as MySQL Community Edition or MariaDB, and then deploy with a live database server from your hosting company.

A good solution for trying things out on your local machine can be a combined web application collection, such as XAMP/WAMP/MAMP. Your web server needs to support PHP, and you also need to be able to create the MySQL databases:

- XAMP: `https://www.apachefriends.org/index.html`
- WAMP: `https://www.wampserver.com/`
- MAMP: `https://www.mamp.info/`

phpLiteAdmin

When writing code that talks to database files and database servers, it can be frustrating when things are not working to not be able to see inside the database. Therefore, database clients exist to allow you to interact with database servers without having to use code.

A lightweight (single file!) solution when using PHP and SQLite is phpLiteAdmin, which is free to use (although you may consider donating if you use it a lot). It is included in the `phpLiteAdmin` folder with this recipe's PHP scripts. It can be run using the Composer script shortcut command—`composer dbadmin`—and will run locally at `localhost:8001`. Once running, just click on the link for the player table to see the data for each player's score in the database file:

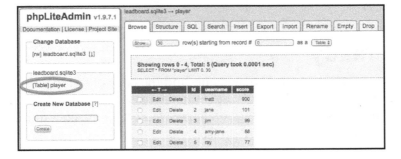

Figure 8.5 – Using phpLiteAdmin in a web browser

See also

Learn more about phpLiteAdmin at the project's GitHub repository and website:

- `https://github.com/phpLiteAdmin/pla`
- `https://www.phpliteadmin.org/`

Unity game communication with a web server leaderboard

In this recipe, we create a Unity game client that can communicate, via UI buttons, with our web server leaderboard from the previous recipe:

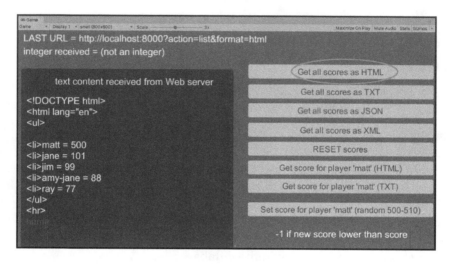

Figure 8.6 – Screenshot showing a Unity game retrieving scores from a web server

Getting ready

Since the Scene contains several UI elements and the code of the recipe is the communication with the PHP scripts and SQL database, in the 08_02 folder, we have provided a Unity package called UnityLeaderboardClient, containing a Scene with everything set up for the Unity project.

How to do it...

To create a Unity game that communicates with the web server leaderboard, perform the following steps:

1. Import the Unity package provided, UnityLeaderboardClient.
2. Run the Scene provided.

3. Ensure that your PHP leaderboard is up and running.

4. If you are not running locally (`localhost:8000`), you'll need to update the URL by selecting **Main Camera** in the **Hierarchy** window, and then editing the **Leader Board URL** text for the **Web Leader Board (Script)** component in the **Inspector** window:

Figure 8.7 – Setting a website URL public variable in the Inspector window

5. Click on **UI Buttons** to make Unity communicate with the PHP scripts that have access to the high-score database.

How it works...

The player's scores are stored in a SQL database. Access to the database is facilitated through the PHP scripts provided by the web server project that was set up in the previous recipe.

In our example, all the PHP scripts were placed in a web server folder for a local web server. So, the scripts are accessed via `http://localhost:8000/`. However, since the URL is a public string variable, this can be set to the location of your server and site code before running the scene.

There are buttons in the Unity Scene (corresponding to the actions the web leaderboard understands) that set up the corresponding action and the parameters to be added to the URL, for the next call to the web server, via the `LoadWWW()` method. The `OnClick()` actions have been set up for each button to call the corresponding methods of the `WebLeaderBoard` C# script of **Main Camera**.

There are also several **UI Text** objects. One displays the most recent URL string sent to the server. Another displays the integer value that was extracted from the Response message that was received from the server (or a **not an integer** message if some other data was received).

The third **UI Text** object is inside a UI panel, and has been made large enough to display a full, multi-line text string received from the server (which is stored inside the `textFileContents` variable).

We can see that the contents of the HTTP text Response message are simply an integer when a random score is set for player *Matt*, when the **Get score for player 'matt' (TXT)** button is clicked, and a text file containing `506` is returned:

Figure 8.8 – Score of 506 retrieved for player Matt from the web server

The **UI Text** objects have been assigned to public variables of the `WebLeaderBoard` C# script for the main camera. When any of the UI buttons are clicked, the corresponding method of the `WebLeaderBoard` method is called, which builds the URL string with parameters, and then calls the `LoadWWW()` method. This method sends the request to the URL, and waits (by virtue of being a coroutine) until a response is received. It then stores the content, received in the `textFileContents` variable, and calls the `UpdateUI()` method. There is a prettification of the text received, inserting newline characters to make the JSON, HTML, and XML easier to read.

There's more...

Here are some ways to go further with this recipe.

Extracting the full leaderboard data for display within Unity

The XML/JSON text that can be retrieved from the PHP web server provides a useful method for allowing a Unity game to retrieve the full set of the leaderboard data from the database. Then, the leaderboard can be displayed to the user in the Unity game (perhaps, in a nice 3D fashion, or through a game-consistent UI).

Using secret game codes to secure your leaderboard scripts

The Unity and PHP code that is presented illustrates a simple, unsecured web-based leaderboard. To prevent players from hacking into the board with false scores, we should encode some form of secret game code (or key) into the communications. Only update requests that include the correct code will actually cause a change to the database.

 Note: The example here is an illustration using the MD5 hashing algorithm. For protecting a personal game, this is fine, but it's quite old and would not be suitable for sensitive or valuable data, such as financial or personal details. Some links to articles on more secure approaches can be found at the end of this topic.

The Unity code will combine the secret key (in this example, the harrypotter string) with something related to the communication – for example, the same MySQL/PHP leaderboard may have different database records for different games that are identified with a game ID:

```
// Unity Csharp code
  string key = "harrypotter";
  string gameId = 21;
  string gameCode = Utility.Md5Sum(key + gameId);
```

The server-side PHP code will receive both the encrypted game code, and the piece of game data that is used to create that encrypted code. In this example, it is the game ID and MD5 hashing function, which is available in both Unity and in PHP. You can learn more about MD5 hashing on PracticalCryptography.com: http://practicalcryptography.com/hashes/md5-hash/.

The secret key (harrypotter) is used with the game ID to create an encrypted code that can be compared with the code received from the Unity game (or whatever user agent or browser is attempting to communicate with the leaderboard **Server** scripts). The database actions will only be executed if the game code created on the **Server** matches that sent along with the request for a database action:

```
// PHP - security code
$key = "harrypotter";
$game_id =  $_GET['game_id'];
$provided_game_code =  $_GET['game_code'];
$server_game_code = md5($key.$game_id);
if( $server_game_code == $provided_game_code ) {
  // codes match - do processing here
}
```

See also

If you really want to get serious about web server security, then a proper **API key strategy** is probably the way to go. Here are two articles on sophisticated approaches to securing game data:

- *Creating API keys using Okta in PHP* was published in May 2019 by Krasimir Hristozov:
  https://dev.to/oktadev/build-a-simple-rest-api-in-php-2k0k
- *Securing Unity Games with DexGuard and iXGuard* from GuardSquare, March 2020:
  https://www.guardsquare.com/en/blog/securing-unity-games-dexguard-and-ixguard-how-it-works

Creating and cloning a GitHub repository

Distributed Version Control Systems (**DVCSes**) are becoming a bread-and-butter everyday tool for software developers. One issue with Unity projects can be the many binary files in each project. There are also many files in a local system's Unity project directory that are not needed for archiving/sharing, such as OS-specific thumbnail files and trash files. Finally, some Unity project folders themselves do not need to be archived, such as Temp and Library.

While Unity provides its own **Unity Teams** online collaboration, many small game developers chose not to pay for this extra feature. Also, Git and Mercurial (the most common DVCSes) are free and work with any set of documents that are to be maintained (programs in any programming language, text files, and so on). So, it makes sense to learn how to work with a third-party, industry-standard DVCS for Unity projects. In fact, the documents for this very book were all archived and version-controlled using a private GitHub repository!

In this project, we'll create a new online project repository using the free GitHub server, and then clone (duplicate) a copy onto a local computer. The recipe that follows will then transfer a Unity project into the local project repository, and use the stored link from the cloning to push the changed files back up to the GitHub online server.

Note: **All** the projects from this cookbook have been archived on GitHub in public repositories for you to read, download, edit, and run on your computer. Despite a hard disk crash during the authoring of this book, no code was lost, since the steps of this recipe were being followed for every part of this book.

Note: Git is a version-control system, and GitHub is one of several online systems that host projects archived in the Git format. Popular alternatives to GitHub include **Bitbucket**, which can host both Git and Mercurial version-control project formats, and also **GitLab**.

Getting ready

Since this recipe illustrates hosting code on GitHub, you'll need to create a (free) GitHub account at GitHub.com if you do not already have one.

If not already installed, you'll need to install Git on your local computer as part of this recipe. Learn how to do this and download the client from the following links:

- http://git-scm.com/book/en/Getting-Started-Installing-Git
- http://git-scm.com/downloads/guis

The screenshots for this recipe were created on a Mac. On Windows, you would use the Git Bash (see `https://gitforwindows.org/`) or PowerShell (see `https://docs.microsoft.com/en-us/powershell/`) Terminal windows for command-line Git operations.

How to do it...

To create and clone a GitHub repository, perform the following steps:

1. Install Git for the command line on your computer. As usual, it is good practice to do a system backup before installing any new application: `https://git-scm.com/book/en/v2/Getting-Started-Installing-Git`.

2. Test that you have Git installed by typing `git` at the command line in a terminal window. You should see text help displayed, showing a list of possible command options:

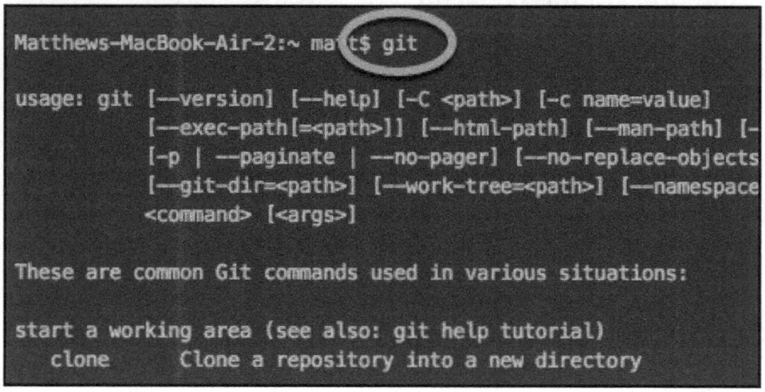

```
Matthews-MacBook-Air-2:~ matt$ git

usage: git [--version] [--help] [-C <path>] [-c name=value]
           [--exec-path[=<path>]] [--html-path] [--man-path] [-
           [-p | --paginate | --no-pager] [--no-replace-objects
           [--git-dir=<path>] [--work-tree=<path>] [--namespace
           <command> [<args>]

These are common Git commands used in various situations:

start a working area (see also: git help tutorial)
   clone      Clone a repository into a new directory
```

Figure 8.9 – Testing Git at the command line

3. Open a web browser and navigate to your GitHub **Repositories** page:

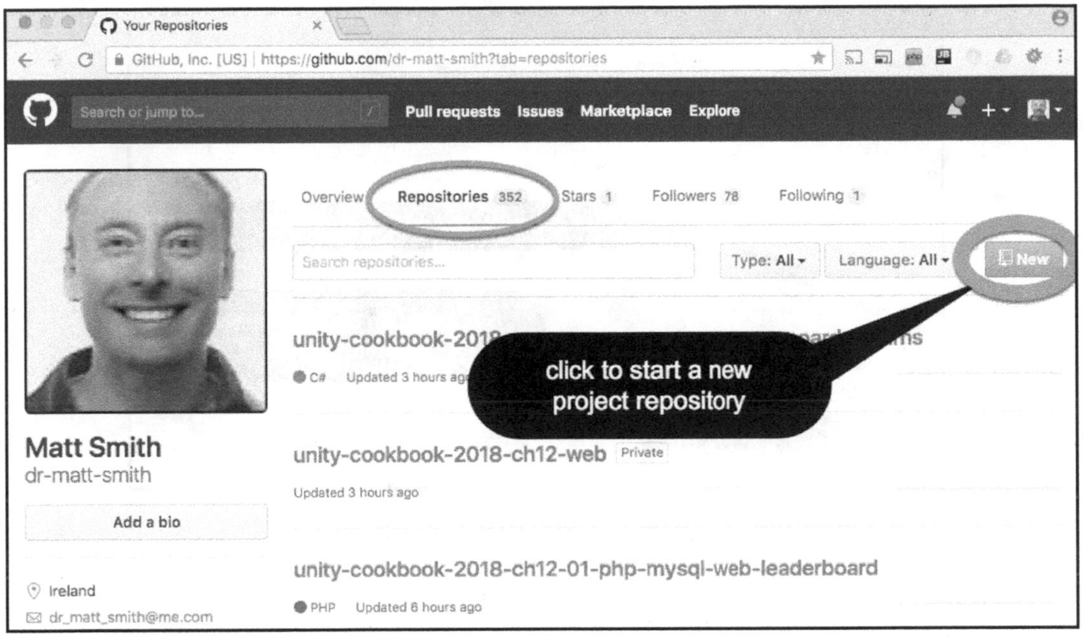

Figure 8.10 – Creating new GitHub repository

4. Click the green button to start creating a new repository (such as my-github-demo):
    - Enter a name for the new repository, such as my-github-demo.
    - Click the option to create a README file (important, so you can clone the files to a local computer).

- Add a `.gitignore` file – choose the Unity one:

Figure 8.11 – Adding a README and .gitignore file

The `.gitignore` file is a special file; it tells the version control system which files do not need to be archived. For example, we don't need to record the Windows or Mac image thumbnail files (`DS_STORE` or `Thumbs.db`).

5. With the options selected, click the green **Create Repository** button.
6. You should now be taken to the repository contents page. Click the green dropdown named **Clone or download**, and then click the URL copy-to-clipboard tool button. This copies the special GitHub URL required for connecting to GitHub and copying the files to your local computer:

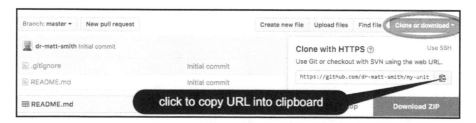

Figure 8.12 – Copying the URL repository into the clipboard

7. Open a command-line Terminal window, and navigate to the location where you wish to clone your GitHub project repository (such as desktop or Unity-projects).

8. At the **Command-Line Interface (CLI)**, type `git clone`, and then paste the URL from your clipboard. It will be something like `https://github.com/dr-matt-smith/my-unity-github-demo.git`:

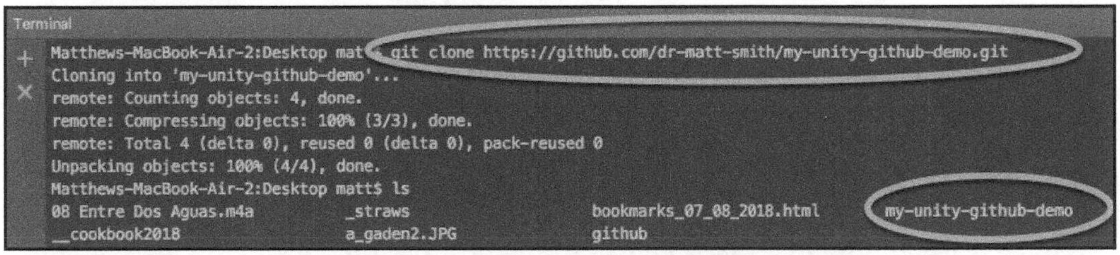

Figure 8.13 – Cloning the repository to the local computer at the command line

9. Change into your cloned directory, such as `cd my-unity-github-demo`.

10. List the files. You should see your `README.md`, and if you have enabled the option to see hidden folders and files, you'll also see `.git` and `.gitignore`:

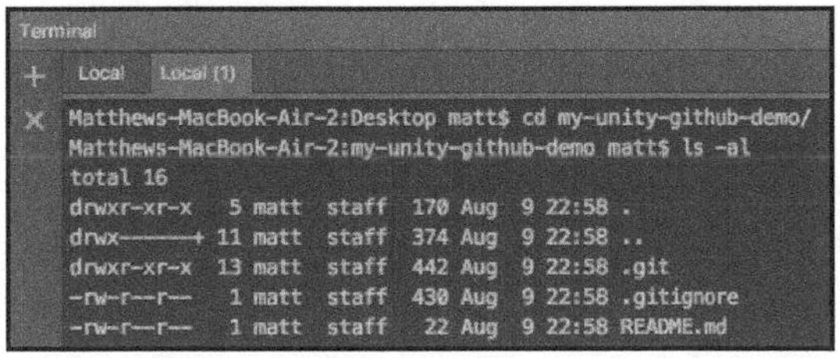

Figure 8.14 – Viewing the hidden files and README that have been downloaded

11. Use the `git remote -v` command to see the stored link from this copy of the project files on your computer, and then back them up to the GitHub online repository:

```
$ git remote -v
    origin
https://github.com/dr-matt-smith/my-unity-github-demo.git
(fetch)
    origin
https://github.com/dr-matt-smith/my-unity-github-demo.git
(push)
```

How it works...

You have learned how to create a new empty repository on the GitHub web server. You then cloned it to your local computer.

You also checked to see that this clone had a link back to its remote origin.

 If you have simply downloaded and decompressed the ZIP file, you would not have the `.git` folder, nor would you have the remote links back to its GitHub origin.

The `.git` file actually contains the entire history of changes to the project repository files, and using different Git commands, you can update the folder to re-instance any of the committed snapshots for the project repository contents.

The special file called `.gitignore` lists all the files and directories that are **not** to be archived. At the time of writing, here are the contents of files that do not need to be archived (they are either unnecessary or can be regenerated when a project is loaded into Unity):

```
[Ll]ibrary/
[Tt]emp/
[Oo]bj/
[Bb]uild/
[Bb]uilds/
Assets/AssetStoreTools*
# Visual Studio cache directory
.vs/
# Autogenerated VS/MD/Consulo solution and project files
ExportedObj/
.consulo/
```

```
*.csproj
*.unityproj
*.sln
*.suo
*.tmp
*.user
*.userprefs
*.pidb
*.booproj
*.svd
*.pdb
*.opendb
# Unity3D generated meta files
*.pidb.meta
*.pdb.meta
# Unity3D Generated File On Crash Reports
sysinfo.txt
# Builds
*.apk
*.unitypackage
```

As we can see, folders such as `Library` and `Temp` are not to be archived. Note that if you have a project with a lot of resources (such as those using the 2D or 3D Game Kits), rebuilding the library may take a few minutes depending on the speed of your computer.

Note that the recommended files to ignore for Git change from time to time as Unity changes its project folder structure. GitHub has a master recommended `.gitignore` for Unity, and it is recommended that you review it from time to time, especially when upgrading to a new version of the Unity Editor:
`https://github.com/github/gitignore/blob/master/Unity.gitignore`.

> If you are using an older (pre-2020) version of Unity, you may need to look up what the appropriate `.gitignore` contents should be. The details given in this recipe were up to date for the 2020.2b version of the Unity Editor.

There's more...

Here are some ways to go further with this recipe.

Learn more about DVCS

Here is a short video introduction to DVCS: `http://youtu.be/1BbK9o5fQD4`.

Note that the Fogcreek Kiln Harmony feature now allows seamless work between Git and Mercurial with the same Kiln repository:
`http://blog.fogcreek.com/kiln-harmony-internals-the-basics/`.

Learn more about Git at the command line

If you are new to working with a CLI, it is well worth following up with the help of some online resources to improve your skills. Any serious software development will probably involve some work at a command line at some point.

Since both Git and Mercurial are open source, there are lots of great, free online resources available. The following are some good sources to get you started:

- Learn all about Git, download free GUI clients, and even get free online access to *The Pro Git book* (by Scott Chacon), available through a Creative Commons license: `http://git-scm.com/book`.
- You will find an online interactive Git command line to practice on at `https://try.github.io/levels/1/challenges/1`.

Using Bitbucket and Sourcetree visual applications

Unity offers a good tutorial on version control using the Bitbucket website and the Sourcetree application:

- `https://unity3d.com/learn/tutorials/topics/cloud-build/creating-your-first-source-control-repository`

Sourcetree is a free Mercurial and Git GUI client, available at the following link:

- `http://www.sourcetreeapp.com/`

Learning about Mercurial rather than Git

The main Mercurial website, including free online access to *Mercurial: The Definitive Guide* (by Bryan O'Sullivan), is available through the Open Publication License at `http://mercurial.selenic.com/`.

Adding a Unity project to a local Git repository, and pushing files up to GitHub

In the previous recipe, you created a new online project repository using the free GitHub server, and then cloned (duplicated) a copy onto a local computer.

In this recipe, we will transfer a Unity project to the local project repository and use the stored link from the cloning to push the changed files back up to the GitHub online server.

Getting ready

This recipe follows on from the previous one, so ensure that you have completed that recipe before beginning this one.

How to do it...

To add a Unity project to a local Git repository, and push the files up to GitHub, perform the following steps:

1. Create a new Unity project (or make use of an old one), save the Scene, and quit Unity. For example, we created a project named `project-for-version-control` that contains the default `SampleScene` and a Material named `m_red`. It is the asset files in the **Project** panel that are the files that are stored on disk, and these are the ones you'll be version controlling with Git and GitHub.

 It is important that all work has been saved and the Unity application is not running when you are archiving your Unity project since, if Unity is open, there may be unsaved changes that will not get correctly recorded.

2. On your computer, copy the following folders into the folder of your cloned GitHub repository:

```
/Assets
/Plugins (if this folder exists - it may not)
/ProjectSettings
/Packages
```

3. The folder after copying these contents is illustrated here:

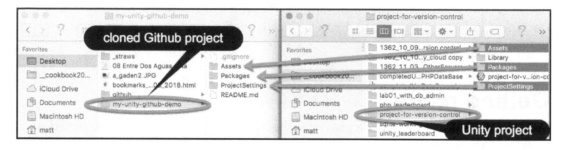

Figure 8.15 – Copying files into the GitHub project folder

4. At the CLI, type `git status` to see a list of folders/files that have changed and need to be committed to the next snapshot of project contents for our Git version control system.

5. Add all these files by typing `git add`.

6. Commit our new snapshot with the `git commit -m "files added to project"` command:

```
matt$ git commit -m "files added to project"

[master 1f415a3] files added to project
 23 files changed, 1932 insertions(+)
 create mode 100644 Assets/Scenes.meta
 create mode 100644 Assets/Scenes/SampleScene.unity
 ...
```

7. We have created a snapshot of the new files and folders, so now we can push this new committed snapshot up to the GitHub cloud servers. Type `git push`:

```
matt$ git push

Counting objects: 29, done.
Delta compression using up to 4 threads.
Compressing objects: 100% (27/27), done.
```

```
        Writing objects: 100% (29/29), 15.37 KiB | 0 bytes/s,
done.
        Total 29 (delta 0), reused 0 (delta 0)
        To
https://github.com/dr-matt-smith/my-unity-github-demo.git
        1b27686..1f415a3  master -> master
        matt$
```

 Note: The first time you do this, you'll be asked for your GitHub username and password.

8. Visit **GitHub**. You should see that there is a new commit and that your Unity files and folders have been uploaded to the GitHub online repository:

Figure 8.16 – Viewing the updated files on the GitHub website

How it works...

In the previous recipe, you created a project repository on the GitHub cloud server and then cloned it to your local machine. You then added the files from a (closed) Unity application to the cloned project repository folder. These new files were added and committed to a new snapshot of the folder, and the updated contents pushed up to the GitHub server.

Due to the way Unity works, it creates a new folder when a new project is created. Therefore, we had to turn the contents of the Unity project folder into a Git repository. There are two ways to do this:

1. Copy the files from the Unity project to a cloned GitHub repository (so it has remote links set up for pushing back to the GitHub server).
2. Make the Unity project folder into a Git repository, and then either link it to a remote GitHub repository or push the folder contents to the GitHub server and create a new online repository at that point in time.

For people new to Git and GitHub, the first procedure, which we followed in this recipe, is probably the simplest to understand. Also, it is the easiest to fix if something goes wrong – since a new GitHub repository can be created, cloned to the local machine, and the Unity project files copied there, and then pushed up to GitHub (and the old repository deleted), by pretty much following the same set of steps.

Interestingly, the second approach is recommended when using the **Open Source GitHub for Unity** package, which is explored in the next recipe.

Unity project version control using GitHub for Unity

GitHub has released an open source tool integrating Git and GitHub into Unity, which we'll explore in this recipe.

Getting ready

You will need Git installed at the command line on your computer:

- `https://git-scm.com/book/en/v2/Getting-Started-Installing-Git`

You may need to install Git **Large File Storage** (**LFS**) in order for the GitHub for Unity package to work correctly:

- `https://git-lfs.github.com/`

You may wish to create a .gitattributes file to specify which files should be used with Git LFS. For some guidance, check out Rob Reilly's useful article, *How to Git With Unity*: https://robots. thoughtbot.com/how-to-git-with-unity.

How to do it...

To manage Unity project version control using GitHub for Unity, perform the following steps:

1. Create a new Unity project.
2. Open the **Asset Store** panel (choose **Window** | **Asset Store**).
3. Search for the keyword GitHub, and then select **GitHub for Unity**.
4. Click the **Add to My Assets** button (it's free!):

Figure 8.17 – GitHub for Unity on the Asset Store website

5. Click the blue **Import** button, and when the **Import Unity Package** window appears, click the **Import** button.
6. If a popup appears regarding a newer version, accept it and download the newer version. This will download as a Unity package (probably in your **Downloads** folder), which you can then import into your Unity project.

7. Once imported, you should see a **Plugins | GitHub** folder in your **Project** panel. You will also now see two new items on your **Window** menu, for **GitHub** and **GitHub Command Line**:

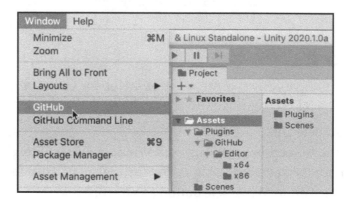

Figure 8.18 – New GitHub menu, plus the GitHub folder in Assets | Plugins

8. Choosing the **Window | GitHub Command Line** menu item allows you to use the Git commands listed in the previous two recipes (it will open at the directory of your Unity project).

9. Choosing the **Window | GitHub** menu item will result in a **GitHub** panel being displayed. Initially, this project is not a Git repository, so it will need to be initialized as a new Git project, which can be performed by clicking the **Initialize a git repository for this project** button:

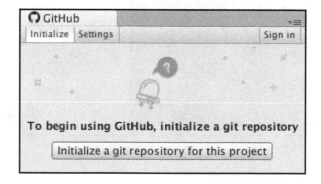

Figure 8.19 – Initializing a Unity project as a new Git repository

10. You will be able to see that there is one commit for the snapshot for this initialization of the Git version control tracking for this project:

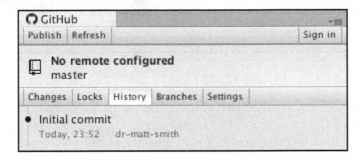

Figure 8.20 – Viewing the commit history

11. Click the **Sign in** button at the top-right of the panel and log in with your GitHub username and password:

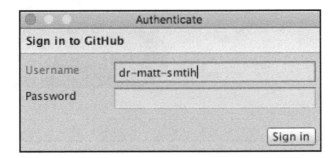

Figure 8.21 – Logging in with a GitHub username and password

12. Open a web browser, log in to your GitHub account, and create a new empty repository (with no extra files, that is, no README, .gitignore, or Licence file):

Figure 8.22 – New repository created on the GitHub website

13. Copy the URL for the new repository to your clipboard:

Figure 8.23 – Copying a new GitHub URL repository to the clipboard

14. Back in Unity, for the **GitHub** panel, click the **Settings** button, paste the URL for the `Remote: origin` property, and click the **Save Repository** button to save this change. Your Unity project is now linked to the remote GitHub cloud repository:

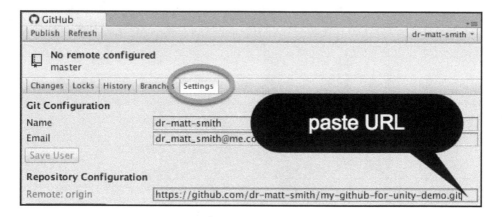

Figure 8.24 – Adding the GitHub repo URL to the Unity project GitHub settings

15. You may now commit and push changes from your Unity project up to GitHub.

16. Add some new assets (such as a new C# script and a Material named
    `m_red`). Click the **Changes** tab in the **GitHub** panel, ensure that the
    complete `Assets` folder is checked (and all its contents), write a brief
    summary of the changes, and click the **Commit to [master]** button:

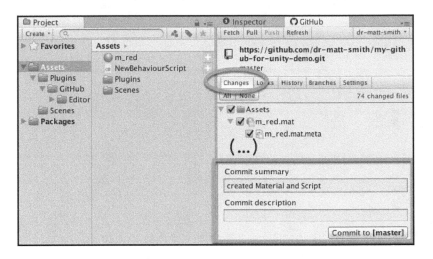

Figure 8.25 – Committing changes to the project as a new project snapshot locally

17. You now have a committed snapshot of the new Unity project contents on
    your computer. Push this new committed snapshot up to the GitHub server
    by clicking the **Push (1)** button. The (1) indicates that there is one new
    committed snapshot locally that has not yet been pushed. This shows that
    the local machine is one commit ahead of the master on the GitHub server:

Figure 8.26 – Pushing a committed snapshot to the GitHub web server

18. Visit the repository on GitHub in your web browser, and you'll see that the new committed snapshot of the Unity project contents have been pushed up from your computer to the GitHub cloud servers:

Figure 8.27 – Viewing changes that have been pushed up to the GitHub website repository

How it works...

The **GitHub for Unity** package adds a special panel with functionality for the following Git/GitHub actions:

- Initializing a new Git project repository for the current Unity project
- Signing in with your GitHub username and password credentials
- Linking your Unity project's Git history to a remote GitHub online repository
- Committing a snapshot of the changes in the Unity project you wish to record
- Pushing committed changes to the remote GitHub online repository

In this recipe, you've installed the **GitHub For Unity** plugin. You've committed changes to the project contents as a local "snapshot" Git archive. You created an empty repository on the GitHub.com website, and then linked your Unity project to this repository. This allowed you to push the committed project snapshot up to the GitHub cloud server.

Having followed these steps with any project, you can then ensure that your project is archived on the GitHub web server by following these steps:

1. Make changes to the project.
2. Use the **GitHub for Unity** changes tab to commit these changes to the current local snapshot.
3. Click the **Push** button in **GitHub for Unity** to push the snapshot up to the GitHub web server.

There's more...

Here are some ways to go further with this recipe.

Further reading on GitHub for Unity

Check out the following links for more information:

- The GitHub for Unity project website: `https://unity.github.com/`.
- The Quick Start guide: `https://github.com/github-for-unity/Unity/blob/master/docs/using/quick-guide.md`.

Pulling down updates from other developers

The GitHub plugin also provides the feature of being able to pull down changes from the remote GitHub repository to your computer (useful if you are working on multiple computers, or a fellow game developer is helping add features to your game).

 If you are working with other game developers, it is very useful to learn about Git branches. Also, before starting work on a new feature, perform a pull to ensure you are then working with the most up-to-date version of the project.

Unity Collaborate from Unity Technologies

Although Git and GitHub are used for many Unity projects, they are general-purpose version control technologies. Unity Technologies offers its own online system for developers and teams to collaboratively work on the same Unity projects. However, this is a feature that is no longer in the free Unity licence plan.

Learn more about **Unity Collaborate** and **Unity Teams** on the Unity website:

- https://unity3d.com/unity/features/collaborate
- https://unity3d.com/teams

Further reading

The following are good sources of further reading and guides for working with asset bundles:

- Unity Asset Bundle documentation:
  https://docs.unity3d.com/2020.1/Documentation/Manual/
  AssetBundlesIntro.html
- Unity Learn Asset Bundle tutorial:
  https://learn.unity.com/tutorial/introduction-to-asset-bundles
- One Game Foundation Asset Bundle tutorial:
  https://onegamefoundation.github.io/docs/asset-bundle-laughing-
  panda-tutorial.html

Controlling and Choosing Positions

In this chapter, we will introduce a few recipes and demonstrate a selection of approaches to character control, spawn points, and checkpoints. In the next chapter, we'll look at waypoints for AI-controlled characters traversing Unity navigation meshes.

Many **GameObjects** in games move! Movement can be controlled by the player, by the (simulated) laws of physics in the environment, or by **Non-Player Character** (**NPC**) logic. For example, objects follow the path of a waypoint, or seek (move toward) or flee (away) from the current position of a character. Unity provides several controllers for first- and third-person characters, and for vehicles such as cars and airplanes. **GameObject** movement can also be controlled through the state machines of the Unity **Mecanim** animation system.

However, there may be times when you wish to tweak the player character controllers from Unity or write your own. You might wish to write directional logic – simple or sophisticated **artificial intelligence** (**AI**) to control the game's NPC and enemy characters – which we'll explore in *Chapter 10, Navigation Meshes and Agents*. Such AI might involve your computer program making objects orient and move toward or away from characters or other game objects.

This chapter (and the chapter that follows) presents a range of such directional recipes, from which many games can benefit in terms of a richer and more exciting user experience.

Unity provides sophisticated classes and components, including the Vector3 class and rigid body physics for modeling realistic movements, forces, and collisions in games. We will make use of these game engine features to implement some sophisticated NPC and enemy character movements in the recipes of this chapter.

For 3D games (and to some extent, 2D games as well), a fundamental data object (struct) is the `Vector3` class, whose objects store and manipulate the **X**, **Y**, and **Z** values, representing locations in a 3D space. If we draw an imaginary arrow from the origin (0, 0, 0) to a point on the space, then the direction and length of this arrow (vector) can represent a velocity or force – that is, a certain amount of magnitude in a certain direction. In most cases, we can think of 1 Unity unit (X, Y, or Z) modeling 1 meter in the real world.

If we ignore all the character controller components, colliders, and the physics system in Unity, we can write code that **teleports** objects directly to a particular **(x, y, z)** location in our scene. Sometimes, this is just what we want to do; for example, we may wish to spawn or teleport an object at a location. However, in most cases, if we want objects to move in more physically realistic ways, then we either apply a force to the object's **RigidBody** or change its velocity component. Or, if it has a **Character Controller** component, then we can send it a `Move()` message. Teleporting objects directly to a new location increases the chance that a collision with another object is missed, which can lead to frustrating game behavior for players.

Some important concepts we must understand for NPC object movement and creation (instantiation) include the following:

- **Spawn points**: Specific locations in the scene where objects are to be created or moved to.
- **Checkpoints**: Locations (or colliders) that, once passed through, change what happens later in the game (for example, extra time, or if a player's character gets killed, they respawn to the last checkpoint they crossed, and so on).
- **Waypoints**: A sequence of locations to define a path for NPCs or, perhaps, the player's character to follow.

You can learn more about the Unity 2D character controllers at `http://unity3d.com/learn/tutorials/modules/beginner/2d/2d-controllers`.
You can learn about the Unity 3D character component and its controls at `http://docs.unity3d.com/Manual/class-CharacterController.html` and `http://unity3d.com/learn/tutorials/projects/survival-shooter/player-character`, respectively.

In this chapter, we will cover the following recipes:

- Using a rectangle to constrain 2D Player object movement
- Player control of a 3D GameObject (and limiting the movement within a rectangle)
- Choosing destinations – finding a random spawn point
- Choosing destinations – finding the nearest spawn point
- Choosing destinations – respawning to the most recently passed checkpoint
- Moving objects by clicking on them
- Firing projectiles in the direction of movement

Technical requirements

For this chapter, you will need Unity 2021.1 or later, plus one of the following:

- Microsoft Windows 10 (64-bit)/GPU: DX10, DX11, and DX12-capable
- macOS Sierra 10.12.6۱/GPU Metal-capable Intel or AMD
- Linux Ubuntu 16.04, Ubuntu 18.04, and CentOS 7/GPU: OpenGL 3.2+ or Vulkan-capable, Nvidia or AMD

For each chapter, there is a folder that contains the asset files you will need in this book's GitHub repository at `https://github.com/PacktPublishing/Unity-2021-Cookbook-Fourth-Edition`.

Using a rectangle to constrain 2D Player object movement

Basic character movement in 2D (within a bounding rectangle) is a core skill for many 2D games, so this first recipe will illustrate how to achieve these features for a 2D game. The remaining recipes will then build on this approach for 3D games.

Since in Chapter 3, *Inventory and Advanced UIs*, we created a basic 2D game template, we'll adapt this game to restrict the movement to a bounding rectangle:

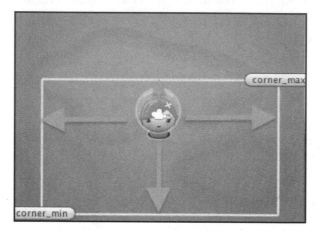

Figure 9.1 – Movement of the character within the rectangular area

Getting ready

This recipe builds on the simple 2D mini-game called Simple2DGame_SpaceGirl from the first recipe of Chapter 3, *Inventory and Advanced UIs*. Start with a copy of this game, or use the provided completed recipe project as the basis for this recipe.

How to do it...

To create a 2D sprite controlled by the user with movement that is limited to within a rectangle, follow these steps:

1. Create a new, empty GameObject named corner_max and position it somewhere above and to the right of player_spaceGirl. With this GameObject selected in the **Hierarchy** window, choose the large yellow oblong icon in the **Inspector** window:

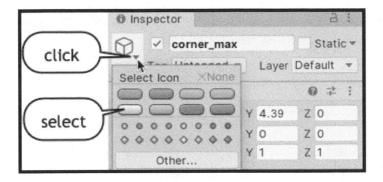

Figure 9.2 – Setting a colored design time icon for a GameObject

2. Duplicate the `corner_max` GameObject by naming the copy `corner_min` and position this clone somewhere below and to the left of the `player-spaceGirl` GameObject. The coordinates of these two GameObjects will determine the maximum and minimum bounds of movement that are permitted for the player's character.

3. Modify the C# script called `PlayerMove` to declare some new variables at the beginning of the class:

```
public Transform corner_max;
public Transform corner_min;

private float x_min;
private float y_min;
private float x_max;
private float y_max;
```

4. Modify the C# script called `PlayerMove` so that the `Awake()` method now gets a reference to `SpriteRenderer` and uses this object to help set up the maximum and minimum X and Y movement limits:

```
void Awake(){
    rigidBody2D = GetComponent<Rigidbody2D>();
    x_max = corner_max.position.x;
    x_min = corner_min.position.x;
    y_max = corner_max.position.y;
    y_min = corner_min.position.y;
}
```

5. Modify the C# script called `PlayerMove` to declare a new method called `KeepWithinMinMaxRectangle()`:

```
private void KeepWithinMinMaxRectangle(){
   float x = transform.position.x;
   float y = transform.position.y;
   float z = transform.position.z;
   float clampedX = Mathf.Clamp(x, x_min, x_max);
   float clampedY = Mathf.Clamp(y, y_min, y_max);
   transform.position = new Vector3(clampedX, clampedY, z);
}
```

6. Modify the C# script called `PlayerMove` so that, after having updated the velocity in the `FixedUpdate()` method, a call will be made to the `KeepWithinMinMaxRectangle()` method:

```
void FixedUpdate(){
   rigidBody2D.velocity = newVelocity;

   // restrict player movement
   KeepWithinMinMaxRectangle();
}
```

7. With the `player-spaceGirl` GameObject selected in the **Hierarchy** window, drag the `corner_max` and `corner_min` GameObjects into the **Corner_max** and **Corner_min** public variables in the **Inspector** window:

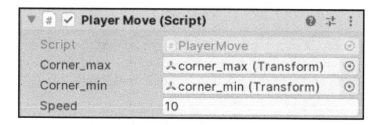

Figure 9.3 – Populating the public Corner_max and Corner_min variables with our GameObjects

Before running the scene in the **Scene** window, try repositioning the `corner_max` and `corner_min` GameObjects. When you run the scene, the positions of these two GameObjects (**max** and **min**, and **X** and **Y**) will be used as the limits of movement for the player's `player-spaceGirl` character.

How it works...

In this recipe, you added the empty GameObjects called `corner_max` and `corner_min` to the scene. The **X** and **Y** coordinates of these GameObjects will be used to determine the bounds of movement that we will permit for the player-controlled character; that is, `player-spaceGirl`. Since these are empty GameObjects, they will not be seen by the player when in **play-mode**. However, we can see and move them in the **Scene** window and since we added the yellow oblong icons, we can see their positions and names very easily.

When the `Awake()` method is executed for the `PlayerMoveWithLimits` object inside the `player-spaceGirl` GameObject, the maximum and minimum **X** and **Y** values of the `corner_max` and `corner_min` GameObjects are recorded. Each time the physics system is called via the `FixedUpdate()` method, the velocity of the `player-spaceGirl` character is updated to the value set in the `Update()` method, which is based on the horizontal and vertical keyboard/joystick inputs. However, the final action of the `FixedUpdate()` method is to call the `KeepWithinMinMaxRectangle()` method, which uses the `Math.Clamp(...)` function to move the character back inside the **X** and **Y** limits. This happens so that the player's character is not permitted to move outside the area defined by the `corner_max` and `corner_min` GameObjects.

We have kept to a good rule of thumb:

> *"Always listen for **input** in `Update()`.*
> *Always apply **physics** in `FixedUpdate()`."*

You can learn more about why we should not check for inputs in `FixedUpdate()` in the Unity Answers thread (which is also the source for the preceding quote from user Tanoshimi) at `https://answers.unity.com/questions/1279847/getaxis-being-missed-in-fixedupdate-work-around.html`.

There's more...

There are some details that you don't want to miss out on.

Drawing a gizmo yellow rectangle to visually show a bounding rectangle

As developers, it is useful to *see* elements such as bounding rectangles when **run-testing** our game. Let's make the rectangular bounds of the movement visually explicit in yellow lines in the **Scene** window by drawing a yellow "gizmo" rectangle. Add the following method to the C# script class called `PlayerMove`:

```
void OnDrawGizmos(){
    Vector3 top_right = Vector3.zero;
    Vector3 bottom_right = Vector3.zero;
    Vector3 bottom_left = Vector3.zero;
    Vector3 top_left = Vector3.zero;

    if(corner_max && corner_min){
      top_right = corner_max.position;
      bottom_left = corner_min.position;

      bottom_right = top_right;
      bottom_right.y = bottom_left.y;

      top_left = top_right;
      top_left.x = bottom_left.x;
    }

    //Set the following gizmo colors to YELLOW
    Gizmos.color = Color.yellow;

    //Draw 4 lines making a rectangle
    Gizmos.DrawLine(top_right, bottom_right);
    Gizmos.DrawLine(bottom_right, bottom_left);
    Gizmos.DrawLine(bottom_left, top_left);
    Gizmos.DrawLine(top_left, top_right);
  }
```

The `OnDrawGizmos()` method tests that the references to the `corner_max` and `corner_min` GameObjects are not `null`, and then sets the positions of the four `Vector3` objects, representing the four corners defined by the rectangle, with `corner_max` and `corner_min` at the opposite corners:

Figure 9.4 – Use of design time gizmos to show the game creator the rectangular boundaries of player movement

As we can see, the gizmo's color is set to yellow and draws lines, connecting the four corners in the **Scene** window to show the bounding rectangle.

Player control of a 3D GameObject (and limiting movement within a rectangle)

Many of the 3D recipes in this chapter are built on this basic project, which constructs a scene with a textured terrain, a **Main Camera**, and a red cube that can be moved around by the user with the four directional arrow keys:

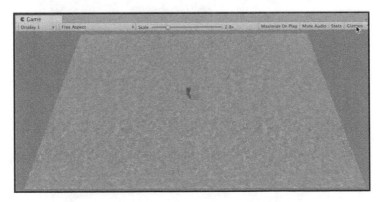

Figure 9.5 – Basic 3D scene with a player-controlled cube

The bounds of movement of the cube will be constrained using the same technique that we used in the previous 2D recipe.

How to do it...

To create a basic 3D cube controlled game, follow these steps:

1. Create a new, empty **Unity 3D project**.

2. Import the single **Terrain Texture** named **SandAlbedo** from Unity's Standard Assets. To do this, open the **Asset Store** window, search for **Standard Assets**, and click **Import**. When importing, click the **None** button to deselect everything, and then locate and tick the `SandAlbedo.psd` asset in the `Standard Assets/Environment/TerrainAssets/SurfaceTextures` folder. Finally, click the **Import** button; the **SandAlbedo** texture file should be downloaded into the project files in your **Project** window:

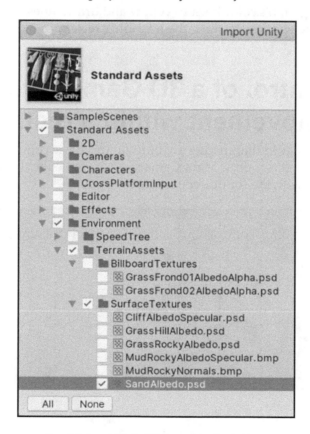

Figure 9.6 – Importing the SandAlbedo texture from Standard Assets

3. Create a new terrain by going to **GameObject | 3D Object | Terrain**.

4. With this new **Terrain** GameObject selected in **Hierarchy** window, in its **Inspector** window, set its **Transform Position** to (−15, 0, −10).

5. In the **Inspector** window for the **Terrain | Mesh Resolution** settings, set the terrain's **Width** and **Length** to 30 x 20:

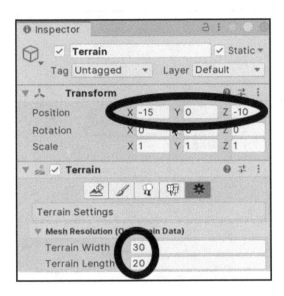

Figure 9.7 – Setting the position and size of the terrain

The transform position for terrains relates to the near-left **corner**, not their **center**.

Since the **Transform** position of terrains relates to the corner of the object, we center such objects at (0, 0, 0) by setting the X coordinate equal to (*-1 times width*/2) and the Z-coordinate equal to (*-1 times length*/2). In other words, we slide the object by half its width and half its height to ensure that its center is just where we want it.

In this case, the width is 30 and the length is 20, so we get −15 for **X** (*-1 * 30/2*) and −10 for **Z** (*-1 * 20/2*).

6. Texture paint this terrain with the texture we imported earlier; that is, **SandAlbedo**. First, click the paintbrush tool for **Terrain texture painting**, choose **Paint Texture** from the dropdown menu, click the **Edit Terrain Textures...** button, click **Create Layer...**, and choose **SandAlbedo** from the pop-up **Select Texture2D** window:

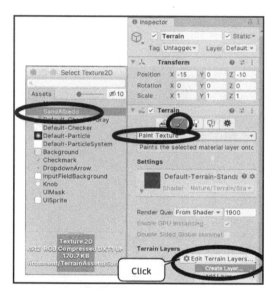

Figure 9.8 – Texture painting the terrain with the SandAlbedo texture

7. In the **Inspector** window, make the following changes to the properties of **Main Camera**:
    - **Position**: (0, 20, -15)
    - **Rotation**: (60, 0, 0)

8. Change **Aspect Ratio** of the **Game** window from **Free Aspect** to 4 : 3. You will now see all the terrain in the **Game** window.

9. Create a new empty GameObject named corner_max and position it at (14, 0, 9). With this GameObject selected in the **Hierarchy** window, choose the large, yellow oblong icon highlighted in the **Inspector** window.

10. Duplicate the corner_max GameObject, naming the clone corner_min, and position it at (-14, 0, -9). The coordinates of these two GameObjects will determine the maximum and minimum bounds of the movement permitted for the player's character.

11. Create a new cube GameObject by going to **Create** | **3D Object** | **Cube**. Name this `Cube-player` and set its position to (0, 0.5, 0) and its size to (1, 1, 1).

12. With `Cube-player` selected in the **Hierarchy** window, in the **Inspector** window, for the **Box Collider** component, check the **Is Trigger** option.

13. Add a **RigidBody** component to the `Cube-player` GameObject (**Physics** | **RigidBody**) and uncheck the **RigidBody** property called **Use Gravity**.

14. Create a red **Material** named `m_red` and apply it to `Cube-player`.

15. Create a C# script class called `PlayerControl` and add an instance object as a component of the `Cube-player` GameObject:

```
using UnityEngine;

public class PlayerControl : MonoBehaviour {
 public Transform corner_max;
 public Transform corner_min;
 public float speed = 40;
 private Rigidbody rigidBody;
 private float x_min;
 private float x_max;
 private float z_min;
 private float z_max;
 private Vector3 newVelocity;

 void Awake() {
 rigidBody = GetComponent<Rigidbody>();
 x_max = corner_max.position.x;
 x_min = corner_min.position.x;
 z_max = corner_max.position.z;
 z_min = corner_min.position.z;
 }

private void Update() {
  float xMove = Input.GetAxis("Horizontal") * speed * Time.deltaTime;
  float zMove = Input.GetAxis("Vertical") * speed * Time.deltaTime;
  float xSpeed = xMove * speed;
  float zSpeed = zMove * speed;
  newVelocity = new Vector3(xSpeed, 0, zSpeed);
}

void FixedUpdate() {
 rigidBody.velocity = newVelocity;
 KeepWithinMinMaxRectangle();
}
```

```
private void KeepWithinMinMaxRectangle() {
float x = transform.position.x;
float y = transform.position.y;
float z = transform.position.z;
float clampedX = Mathf.Clamp(x, x_min, x_max);
float clampedZ = Mathf.Clamp(z, z_min, z_max);
transform.position = new Vector3(clampedX, y, clampedZ);
}
}
```

16. With the `Cube-player` GameObject selected in the **Hierarchy** window, drag the `corner_max` and `corner_min` GameObjects over the `corner_max` and `corner_min` public variables in the **Inspector** window.

When you run the scene, the positions of the `corner_max` and `corner_min` GameObjects will define the bounds of movement for the player's `Cube-player` character.

How it works...

The scene contains a positioned terrain so that its center is at $(0, 0, 0)$. The red cube is controlled by the user's arrow keys through the `PlayerControl` script.

Just as with the previous 2D recipe, a reference to the (3D) **RigidBody** component is stored when the `Awake()` method executes, and the maximum and minimum **X** and **Z** values are retrieved from the two corner GameObjects and are stored in the `x_min`, `x_max`, `z_min`, and `z_max` variables. Note that for this basic 3D game, we won't allow any Y-movement, although such movement (and bounding limits by adding a third `max-height` corner GameObject) can be easily added by extending the code in this recipe.

The `KeyboardMovement()` method reads the horizontal and vertical input values (which the Unity default settings read from the four directional arrow keys). Based on these left-right and up-down values, the velocity of the cube is updated. The distance it will move depends on the speed variable.

The `KeepWithinMinMaxRectangle()` method uses the `Math.Clamp(...)` function to move the character back inside the X and Z limits so that the player's character is not permitted to move outside the area defined by the `corner_max` and `corner_min` GameObjects.

There's more...

There are some details that you don't want to miss out on.

Drawing a gizmo yellow rectangle to visually show a bounding rectangle

As developers, it is useful to *see* elements such as bounding rectangles when test-running our game. Let's make the rectangular bounds of the movement visually explicit by using yellow lines in the **Scene** window by drawing a yellow "gizmo" rectangle. Add the following method to the C# script class called `PlayerMove`:

```csharp
void OnDrawGizmos (){
        Vector3 top_right = Vector3.zero;
        Vector3 bottom_right = Vector3.zero;
        Vector3 bottom_left = Vector3.zero;
        Vector3 top_left = Vector3.zero;

        if(corner_max && corner_min){
          top_right = corner_max.position;
          bottom_left = corner_min.position;

          bottom_right = top_right;
          bottom_right.z = bottom_left.z;

          top_left = bottom_left;
          top_left.z = top_right.z;
        }

        //Set the following gizmo colors to YELLOW
        Gizmos.color = Color.yellow;

        //Draw 4 lines making a rectangle
        Gizmos.DrawLine(top_right, bottom_right);
        Gizmos.DrawLine(bottom_right, bottom_left);
        Gizmos.DrawLine(bottom_left, top_left);
        Gizmos.DrawLine(top_left, top_right);
    }
```

The `OnDrawGizmos()` method tests that the references to the `corner_max` and `corner_min` GameObjects are not null, and then sets the positions of the four `Vector3` objects, representing the four corners defined by the rectangle, with the `corner_max` and `corner_min` GameObjects at the opposite corners. It then sets the gizmo's color to yellow and draws lines that connect the four corners in the **Scene** window.

Drawing thick gizmo lines

The Unity gizmos `DrawLine(...)` method only draws lines that are a single pixel in width. For 3D projects, this can be hard to see. In the Unity forums, in March 2019, **Jozard** kindly suggested the following method to draw multiple single-pixel lines to create lines of greater thickness that are easier to see. Here is the updated code to do this:

```
void OnDrawGizmos (){
    ... (as before)

    // draw thick lines ...
    DrawThickLine(top_right, bottom_right, 5);
    DrawThickLine(bottom_right, bottom_left, 5);
    DrawThickLine(bottom_left, top_left, 5);
    DrawThickLine(top_left, top_right, 5);

}

// from
//
https://answers.unity.com/questions/1139985/gizmosdrawline-thickens.ht
ml
public static void DrawThickLine(Vector3 p1, Vector3 p2, float width)
{
    int count = 1 + Mathf.CeilToInt(width); // how many lines are
needed.
    if (count == 1)
    {
        Gizmos.DrawLine(p1, p2);
    }
    else
    {
        Camera c = Camera.current;
        if (c == null)
        {
            Debug.LogError("Camera.current is null");
            return;
```

```
        }
        var scp1 = c.WorldToScreenPoint(p1);
        var scp2 = c.WorldToScreenPoint(p2);

        Vector3 v1 = (scp2 - scp1).normalized; // line direction
        Vector3 n = Vector3.Cross(v1, Vector3.forward); // normal
vector

        for (int i = 0; i < count; i++)
        {
            Vector3 o = 0.99f * n * width * ((float)i / (count - 1) -
0.5f);
            Vector3 origin = c.ScreenToWorldPoint(scp1 + o);
            Vector3 destiny = c.ScreenToWorldPoint(scp2 + o);
            Gizmos.DrawLine(origin, destiny);
        }
    }
}
```

The code works by looping to draw multiple lines next to each other, giving the appearance of a thick line.

Choosing destinations – finding a random spawn point

Many games make use of spawn points and waypoints. This recipe will show you how to choose a random spawn point, and then the instantiation of an object at that chosen point:

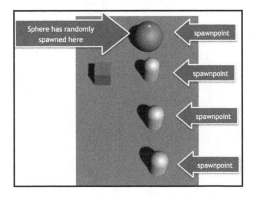

Figure 9.9 – Sphere randomly spawned at one of the spawn point capsules

As shown in the preceding figure, the sphere has been spawned at one of the four capsule spawn points.

Getting ready

This recipe builds upon the previous recipe. So, make a copy of this project, open it, and then follow the steps in the next section.

How to do it...

To find a random spawn point, follow these steps:

1. In the **Scene** window, create a sphere (by navigating to **GameObject | 3D Object | Sphere**) sized as (2, 2, 2) at position (2, 2, 2) and apply the m_red material.

2. In the **Project** window, create a new prefab based on your sphere by dragging the Sphere GameObject from the **Hierarchy** window into the **Project** window. Rename this new prefab Prefab-ball.

3. Delete the sphere from the **Hierarchy** window (we don't need it now we've made our prefab).

4. In the **Scene** window, create a new capsule (by navigating to **GameObject | 3D Object | Capsule**) named Capsule-spawnPoint at (3, 0.5, 3), and give it a tag of **Respawn** (this is one of the default tags that Unity provides):

For testing, we'll leave these **Respawn** points visible. For the final game, we would usually uncheck the **Mesh Rendered** property of each Respawn GameObject so that they are not visible to the player.

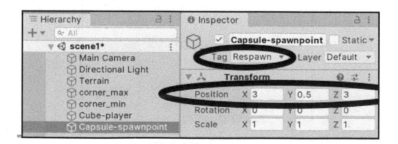

Figure 9.10 – Capsule GameObject tagged as "Respawn" and positioned at (3, 0.5, 3)

5. Make several copies of your `Capsule-spawnPoint` (use *Ctrl + D/Cmd + D*) and move them to different locations on the terrain.

6. Create a C# script class called `BallSpawner` and add an instance object as a component to the `Cube-player` GameObject:

```csharp
using UnityEngine;

public class BallSpawner : MonoBehaviour {
    public GameObject prefabBall;
    private SpawnPointManager spawnPointManager;
    private float timeBetweenSpawns = 1;

    void Start () {
        spawnPointManager = GetComponent<SpawnPointManager> ();
        InvokeRepeating("CreateSphere", 0, timeBetweenSpawns);
    }

    private void CreateSphere() {
        GameObject spawnPoint =
        spawnPointManager.RandomSpawnPoint();

        GameObject newBall = (GameObject)Instantiate(
            prefabBall, spawnPoint.transform.position,
                Quaternion.identity);
        Destroy(newBall, timeBetweenSpawns/2);
    }
}
```

7. Create a C# script class called `SpawnPointManager` and add an instance object as a component to the `Cube-player` GameObject:

```csharp
using UnityEngine;

public class SpawnPointManager : MonoBehaviour {
    private GameObject[] spawnPoints;

    void Start() {
        spawnPoints =
GameObject.FindGameObjectsWithTag("Respawn");
    }

    public GameObject RandomSpawnPoint() {
        int r = Random.Range(0, spawnPoints.Length);
        return spawnPoints[r];
    }
}
```

8. Ensure that `Cube-player` is selected. Then, in the **Inspector** window of the `BallSpawner` scripted component, drag `Prefab-ball` over the `Prefab Ball` public variable.

9. Now, run your game. Once per second, a red ball should be spawned and disappear after half a second. The location where each ball is spawned should be randomly chosen from the four capsules tagged **Respawn**.

How it works...

The `Capsule-spawnPoint` objects represent candidate locations, where we might wish to create an instance of our ball prefab. When our `SpawnPointManager` object, inside the `Cube-player` GameObject, receives the `Start()` message, it creates an array called `spawnPoints` of all the GameObjects in the scene that have the **Respawn** tag. This can be achieved through a call to the built-in `FindGameObjectsWithTag("Respawn")` method. This creates an array of all the objects in the scene with the **Respawn** tag – that is, the four `Capsule-spawnPoint` objects we created in our scene.

When our `BallSpawner` GameObject, `Cube-player`, receives the `Start()` message, it sets the `spawnPointManager` variable to be a reference to its sibling `SpawnPointManager` script component. Next, we used the `InvokeRepeating(...)` method to schedule the `CreateSphere()` method to be called every **1 second**.

 Note that invoke repeating can be a dangerous action to perform in a scene since it means the named method will be continually invoked at a set interval, so long as the scene is running. So, be very careful when using the `InvokeRepeating(...)` statement.

The `SpawnPointManager` method, `RandomSpawnpoint(...)`, chooses and returns a reference to a randomly chosen member of `spawnPoints` – the array of GameObjects in the scene with the **Respawn** tag. This method was declared as `public` so that our `BallSpawner` component instance can invoke this method of the `SpawnPointManager` instance-object component. Note that the second parameter for the `Random.Range(...)` method is the exclusive limit – so, if it's set to `10`, we'll get numbers up to, but not including, 10. This makes it perfect for getting random array indexes since they start at zero and will be up to, but not including, the number of items in the array (`.Length`).

The `BallSpawner` method, `CreateSphere()`, assigns the `spawnPoint` variable to the GameObject that's returned by a call to the `RandomSpawnpoint(...)` method of our `spawnPointManager` object. Then, it creates a new instance of `prefab_ball` (via the `public` variable) at the same position as the `spawnPoint` GameObject. Finally, the built-in `Destroy(...)` method is used to tell Unity to remove the newly created GameObject after half a second (`timeBetweenSpawns / 2`).

See also

The same techniques and code can be used for selecting waypoints. Please refer to the *NPC NavMeshAgent control for following waypoints in sequence* recipe in *Chapter 10, Navigation Meshes and Agents*) for more information about waypoints.

Choosing destinations – finding the nearest spawn point

Rather than just choosing a random spawn point or waypoint, sometimes, we want to select the one that's closest to an object (such as the player's GameObject). In this recipe, we will modify the previous recipe to find the nearest spawn point to the player's cube, and then use that location to spawn a new red ball prefab:

Figure 9.11 – Spawning a sphere at the spawn point capsule that is nearest the player cube

Getting ready

This recipe builds upon the previous recipe. So, make a copy of that project, open it, and then follow the steps in the next section.

How to do it...

To find the **nearest** spawn point, follow these steps:

1. Add the following method to the C# script class called `SpawnPointManager`:

```
public GameObject GetNearestSpawnpoint (Vector3 source){
    GameObject nearestSpawnPoint = spawnPoints[0];
    Vector3 spawnPointPos = spawnPoints[0].transform.position;
    float shortestDistance = Vector3.Distance(source,
spawnPointPos);

    for (int i = 1; i < spawnPoints.Length; i++){
      spawnPointPos = spawnPoints[i].transform.position;
      float newDist = Vector3.Distance(source, spawnPointPos);
      if (newDist < shortestDistance){
        shortestDistance = newDist;
        nearestSpawnPoint = spawnPoints[i];
      }
    }

    return nearestSpawnPoint;
  }
```

2. We now need to change the first line in the C# `SpawnBall` class so that the `spawnPoint` variable is set by a call to our new method; that is, `NearestSpawnpoint(...)`:

```
 private void CreateSphere(){
    GameObject spawnPoint =
    spawnPointManager.GetNearestSpawnpoint(transform.position);

    GameObject newBall = (GameObject)Instantiate (prefabBall,
    spawnPoint.transform.position, Quaternion.identity);
    Destroy(newBall, timeBetweenSpawns/2);
  }
```

3. Now, run your game. Every second, a red ball should be spawned and disappear after half a second. Use the arrow keys to move the player's red cube around the terrain.

4. Each time a new ball is spawned, it should be at the spawn point **closest** to the player.

How it works...

In the `NearestSpawnpoint(...)` method, we set `nearestSpawnpoint` to the first (array index 0) GameObject in the array as our default. We then looped through the rest of the array (array index 1 up to `spawnPoints.Length`). For each GameObject in the array, we checked the distance from the current spawnpoint position (`Vector3 spawnPointPos`) to the provided `Vector3 source` parameter position is less than the shortest distance so far, and if it is, we updated the shortest distance, and also set `nearestSpawnpoint` to the current element. Once we'd searched the arrray, we returned the GameObject that the `nearestSpawnpoint` variable refers to.

 Note that to keep the code simple, we are not performing a test for the `NearestSpawnpoint(...)` method – production code would require that a test be made in case the received parameter was null, in which case the code would exit the method without taking any action.

There's more...

There are some details that you don't want to miss out on.

Avoiding errors due to an empty array

Let's make our code a little more robust so that it can cope with the issue of an empty `spawnPoints` array; that is, when no objects are tagged as `Respawn` in the scene.

To cope with no objects being tagged as `Respawn`, we need to do the following:

1. Improve our `Start()` method in the C# script class called `SpawnPointManager` so that an *error* is logged if the array of the objects tagged as `Respawn` is empty:

```
void Start() {
    spawnPoints = GameObject.FindGameObjectsWithTag("Respawn");

    // logError if array empty
    if(spawnPoints.Length < 1)
      Debug.LogError ("SpawnPointManagaer - cannot find any objects
      tagged 'Respawn'!");
}
```

2. Improve the `RandomSpawnPoint()` and `NearestSpawnpoint()` methods in the C# script class called `SpawnPointManager` so that they still return a value (that is, `null`), even if the array is empty:

```
public GameObject RandomSpawnPoint (){
    // return current GameObject if array empty
    if(spawnPoints.Length < 1)
        return null;

    // the rest as before ...
```

3. Improve the `CreateSphere()` method in the C# class called `SpawnBall` so that we only attempt to instantiate a new GameObject if the `RandomSpawnPoint()` and `NearestSpawnpoint()` methods have returned a non-null object reference:

```
private void CreateSphere(){
    GameObject spawnPoint = spawnPointManager.RandomSpawnPoint ();

    if(spawnPoint){
        GameObject newBall = (GameObject)Instantiate (prefabBall,
            spawnPoint.transform.position, Quaternion.identity);
        Destroy(newBall, destroyAfterDelay);
    }
}
```

See also

The same techniques and code can be used for selecting waypoints. Please refer to the *NPC NavMeshAgent control for following waypoints in sequence* recipe in *Chapter 10, Navigation Meshes and Agents*.

Choosing destinations – respawning to the most recently passed checkpoint

A checkpoint usually represents a certain distance through the game (or perhaps a race track) in which an agent (user or NPC) has succeeded reaching. Reaching (or passing) checkpoints often results in bonus awards, such as extra time, points, ammo, and so on. Also, if a player has multiple lives, then a player will often only be respawned back as far as the most recently passed checkpoint, rather than right to the beginning of the level.

This recipe will demonstrate a simple approach to checkpoints, whereby once the player's character has passed a checkpoint if they die, they are moved back to the most recently passed checkpoint:

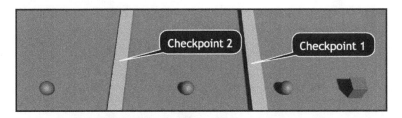

Figure 9.12 – The three kill spheres, separated by two checkpoints

In the preceding screenshot, we can see a player-controlled cube on the right. The game area contains three spheres that will kill the player when hit. The game area is divided into three areas by the two elongated cubes specified as checkpoint 1 and checkpoint 2. The player starts on the right, and if they hit the sphere in the right-hand area, they will die and be respawned to where they started. Once the player moves through checkpoint 1 into the middle section, if they hit the middle sphere, they will die, but be respawned into the middle section. Finally, if the player moves through checkpoint 2 into the left-hand side of the game area, if they hit the leftmost sphere, they will die, but be respawned into the right-hand section of the game area.

Getting ready

This recipe builds upon the player-controlled 3D cube Unity project that you created at the beginning of this chapter. So, make a copy of that project, open it, and then follow the steps for this recipe.

How to do it...

To have the respawn position change upon losing a life, depending on the checkpoints that have been passed, follow these steps:

1. Move the `Cube-player` GameObject to **Position** (12, 0.5, 0).

2. Select `Cube-player` in the **Inspector** window and add a **Character Controller** component by clicking on **Add Component | Physics | Character Controller** (this is to enable the **OnTriggerEnter** collision messages to be received).

3. Create a cube named `Cube-checkpoint-1` at `(5, 0, 0)`, scaled to `(1, 1, 20)`.

4. Create a `CheckPoint` tag and assign this tag to `Cube-checkpoint-1`.

5. Duplicate `Cube-checkpoint-1`, name the clone `Cube-checkpoint-2`, and position it at `(-5, 0, 0)`.

6. Create a sphere named `Sphere-Death` at `(7, 0.5, 0)`. Assign the `m_red` material to this sphere to make it red.

7. Create a `Death` tag and assign it to `Sphere-Death`.

8. Duplicate `Sphere-Death` and position the clone at `(0, 0.5, 0)`.

9. Duplicate `Sphere-Death` a second time and position the second clone at `(-10, 0.5, 0)`.

10. Add an instance of the following C# script class, called `CheckPoint`, to the `Cube-player` GameObject:

```csharp
using UnityEngine;

public class CheckPoint : MonoBehaviour {
    private Vector3 respawnPosition;
    void Start () {
        respawnPosition = transform.position;
    }

    void OnTriggerEnter (Collider hit) {
        if(hit.CompareTag("Checkpoint"))
            respawnPosition = transform.position;

        if(hit.CompareTag("Death")){
            transform.position = respawnPosition;
        }
    }
}
```

Run the scene. If the cube runs into a red sphere before crossing a checkpoint, it will be respawned back to its starting position. Once the red cube has passed a checkpoint, if a red sphere is hit, then the cube will be moved back to the location of the most recent checkpoint that it passed through.

How it works...

The C# script class called `CheckPoint` has one variable called `respawnPosition`, which is a `Vector3` object that refers to the position the player's cube is to be moved to (respawned) if it collides with a `Death` tagged object. The default setting for this is the position of the player's cube when the scene begins. This default position is set in the `Start()` method; we set `respawnPosition` to the player's position before the scene started running.

Each time an object tagged as `Checkpoint` is collided with, the value of `respawnPosition` is updated to the current position of the player's red cube at this point in time (that is, where it is when it touches a stretched cube tagged as `CheckPoint`). The next time an object tagged as `Death` is hit, the cube will be respawned back to where it last touched the object tagged as `CheckPoint`.

Moving objects by clicking on them

Sometimes, we want to allow the user to interact with objects through mouse pointer clicks. In this recipe, we will allow the user to move an object in a random direction by clicking on it.

Getting ready

This recipe builds upon the player-controlled 3D cube Unity project that you created at the beginning of this chapter. So, make a copy of that project, open it, and then follow the steps for this recipe. The result of this recipe should look as follows:

Figure 9.13 – A pyramid of cubes falling down after being clicked on

How to do it...

To move objects by clicking on them, follow these steps:

1. Delete the `Cube-player` GameObject.
2. Set the position of **Main Camera** to (0, 3, -5) and its rotation to (25, 0, 0).
3. Create a C# script class called `ClickMove`:

```
using UnityEngine;
[RequireComponent(typeof(Rigidbody))]
public class ClickMove : MonoBehaviour {

 public float multiplier = 500f;
 private Rigidbody rigidBody;

 private void Awake() {
   rigidBody = GetComponent<Rigidbody>();
 }

 void OnMouseDown() {
   float x = RandomDirectionComponent();
   float y = RandomDirectionComponent();
   float z = RandomDirectionComponent();
   Vector3 randomDirection = new Vector3(x,y,z);
   rigidBody.AddForce(randomDirection);
 }

 private float RandomDirectionComponent() {
   return (Random.value - 0.5f) * multiplier;
 }
}
```

4. Create a Cube GameObject and add an instance object of the `ClickMove` script class as a component.

You should see that a **RigidBody** component is automatically added to the new cube since the script class has the `RequireComponent(typeof(Rigidbody))` directive. This only works if the directive is in the code **before** the script class is added to a GameObject.

5. Make four more duplicates of the cube and arrange the six cubes into a pyramid by setting their positions like so:

```
(0, 2.5, 0)
  (-0.75, 1.5, 0), (0.75, 1.5, 0)
  (-1.5, 0.5, 0), (0, 0.5, 0), (1.5, 0.5, 0)
```

6. Run the scene. Each time you use the mouse pointer to click on a cube, that cube will have a random directional force applied to it. So, with a few clicks, you can knock down the pyramid!

How it works...

The public **float** variable multiplier allows you to change the maximum magnitude of the force by changing the value in the `ClickMove` scripted component of each cube.

The `ClickMove` script class has a private variable called `rigidBody` set as a reference to the **RigidBody** component in the `Awake()` method.

Each time a cube receives a `MouseDown()` message (such as when it has been clicked with the user's mouse pointer), this method creates a random directional `Vector3` object and applies this as a force to the object's `rigidBody` reference.

The `RandomDirectionComponent()` method returns a random value between –`multiplier` and +`multiplier`.

Firing projectiles in the direction of movement

Another common use of force is to apply a force to a newly instantiated object, making it a projectile traveling in the direction that the Player's GameObject is facing. That's what we'll create in this recipe. The result of this recipe should look as follows:

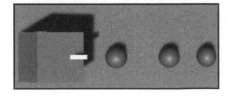

Figure 9.14 – Projectiles being fired by the player's object

In the preceding screenshot, on the left, we can see a player-controlled tank, while on the right, we can see three sphere projectiles that have been fired from the player's character.

Getting ready

This recipe builds upon the player-controlled 3D cube Unity project that you created at the beginning of this chapter. So, make a copy of that project, open it, and then follow the steps for this recipe.

How to do it...

To fire projectiles in the direction of movement, follow these steps:

1. Create a new Sphere GameObject (by navigating to **Create | 3D Object | Sphere**). Set its size as (0.5, 0.5, 0.5).

2. In the **Inspector** window, add a **RigidBody** component to Sphere (go to **Physics | RigidBody**).

3. In the **Project** window, create a new blue material named m_blue (go to **Create | Material**).

4. Apply the m_blue material to your sphere.

5. Use your Sphere GameObject to create a new prefab in the **Project** window named prefab_projectile. First, create a new folder in the **Project** window named **Prefabs**, then drag the Sphere GameObject from the **Hierarchy** window into the folder in the **Project** window. Rename this new prefab file prefab_projectile.

6. Now, delete the Sphere GameObject from the scene (that is, delete it from the **Hierarchy** window).

7. Ensure set the position of the Cube-player GameObject to (0, 0.5, 0).

8. Create a new cube named Cube-launcher. Disable its **Box Collider** component and set its transform as follows:
   - **Position:** (0, 1, 0.3)
   - **Rotation:** (330, 0, 0)
   - **Scale:** (0.1, 0.1, 0.5)

9. In the **Hierarchy** window, make `Cube-launcher` a child of `Cube-player` by dragging `Cube-launcher` onto `Cube-player`. This means that both objects will move together when the user presses the arrow keys:

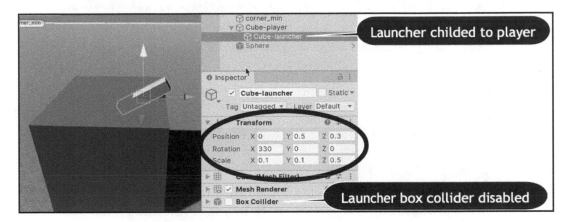

Figure 9.15 – The Cube-launcher Gamebject's Transform settings (childed to Cube-player)

10. Create a C# script class called `FireProjectile` and add an instance object as a component to `Cube-launcher`:

```csharp
using UnityEngine;

public class FireProjectile : MonoBehaviour {
 const float FIRE_DELAY = 0.25f;
 const float PROJECTILE_LIFE = 1.5f;


 public Rigidbody projectilePrefab;
 public float projectileSpeed = 500f;

 private float nextFireTime = 0;

 void Update() {
   if (Time.time > nextFireTime)
     CheckFireKey();
 }

 private void CheckFireKey() {
   if(Input.GetButton("Fire1")) {
     CreateProjectile();
     nextFireTime = Time.time + FIRE_DELAY;
   }
 }
```

```
private void CreateProjectile() {
  Vector3 position = transform.position;
  Quaternion rotation = transform.rotation;

  Rigidbody projectileRigidBody = Instantiate(projectilePrefab,
position,
      rotation);
  Vector3 projectileVelocity = transform.TransformDirection(
    Vector3.forward * projectileSpeed);

  projectileRigidBody.AddForce(projectileVelocity);

  GameObject projectileGO = projectileRigidBody.gameObject;
  Destroy(projectileGO, PROJECTILE_LIFE);
  }
}
```

11. With `Cube-launcher` selected in the **Inspector** window, from the **Project** wiondow, drag `prefab_projectile` into the **Projectile Prefab** public variable in the **Fire Projectile (Script)** component in the **Inspector** window.

12. Run the scene. You can move around the terrain with the arrow keys, and each time you click the mouse button, you should see a blue sphere projectile be launched in the direction that the player's cube is facing.

How it works...

In this recipe, you created a blue sphere as a prefab (containing a **RigidBody**). You then created a scaled and rotated cube for the projectile launcher called `Cube-launcher` and then made this object a child of `Cube-player`.

A common issue is for projectiles to collide with their launcher object, so for this reason, we disabled the **Box Collider** component of the `Cube-launcher` GameObject. An alternative solution would be to create separate layers and remove the physics interaction between the layer of the launcher object and the layer of the projectiles.

The `FireProjectile` script class contains a constant called `FIRE_DELAY` – this is the minimum time between firing new projectiles, set to `0.25` seconds. There is also a second constant called `PROJECTILE_LIFE` – this is how long each projectile will "live" until it is automatically destroyed; otherwise, the scene and memory would fill up quickly with lots of old projectiles!

There are also two public variables. The first is for the reference to the sphere prefab, while the second is for the initial speed of newly instantiated prefabs.

There is also a private variable called `nextFireTime` – this is used to decide whether enough time has passed to allow a new projectile to be fired.

The `Update()` method tests the current time against the value of `nextFireTime`. If enough time has passed, then it will invoke the `CheckFireKey()` method.

The `CheckFireKey()` method tests to see if the **Fire1** button has been clicked. This is usually mapped to the left mouse button, but it can be mapped to other input events via **Project Settings** (**Edit | Project Settings | Input Manager**). If the `Fire1` event is detected, then the next fire time is reset to be `FIRE_DELAY` seconds in the future, and a new projectile is created by invoking the `CreateProjectile()` method.

The `CreateProjectile()` method gets the current position and rotation of the parent GameObject. Remember that the instance object of this class has been added to `Cube-launcher`, so our scripted object can use the position and rotation of this launcher as the initial settings for each new projectile. A new instance of `projectilePrefab` is created with these position and rotation settings.

Next, a `Vector3` object called `projectileVelocity` is created by multiplying the `projectileSpeed` variable by the standard forward vector **(0, 0, 1)**. In Unity, for 3D objects, the Z-axis is usually the direction in which the object is facing.

The special `TransformDirection(...)` method is used to turn the local-space forward direction into a world-space direction so that we have a vector representing a forward motion relative to the `Cube-launcher` GameObject. This world-space directional vector is then used to add force to the projectile's **RigidBody**.

Finally, a reference is made to the parent GameObject of the projectile, and the `Destroy(...)` method is used so that the projectile will be destroyed after `1.5` seconds – the value of `PROJECTILE_LIFE`.

You can learn more about `Transform.TransformDirection()` at `https://docs.unity3d.com/ScriptReference/Transform.TransformDirection.html`.

10
Navigation Meshes and Agents

Unity provides **navigation meshes (NavMeshes)** and **artificial intelligence (AI)** agents that can plan pathways and move objects along those calculated paths. **Pathfinding** is a classic AI task, and Unity has provided game developers with fast and efficient pathfinding components that work out of the box.

Having objects that can automatically plot and follow paths from their current location to the desired destination point (or a moving object) provides the components for many different kinds of interactive game characters and mechanics. For example, we can create point-and-click games by clicking on a location or object, toward which we wish one or more characters to travel. Or, we can have enemies that "wake up" when our player's character is nearby, and move toward (seek) our player, then perhaps going into combat or dialogue mode once they are within a short distance of our player's character. In other situations, we can create objects that collectively flock together, moving as a swarm toward a common destination.

This chapter will explore ways to exploit Unity's navigation-based AI components to control game character pathfinding and movement.

At the core of Unity's navigation system are two concepts/components:

- **Navigation meshes**
- **Navigation mesh agents**

A navigation **mesh** defines the areas of the world that are navigable. It is usually represented as a set of polygons (2D shapes) so that a path to a destination is plotted as the most efficient sequence of adjacent polygons to follow, taking into account the need to avoid non-navigable obstacles.

The **agent** is the object that needs to calculate (plot) a path through the mesh from its current position to its desired destination position. **NavMesh Agents** have properties such as a stopping distance, so that they aim to arrive at a point that's a certain distance from the target coordinates, and auto braking, so that they gradually slow down as they get close to their destination.

A **navigation mesh** can be made up of **areas** that have different "costs." The default cost for an area is **1**. However, to make a more realistic path calculation by AI agent-controlled characters, we might want to model the additional effort it takes to travel through water, mud, or up a steep slope. Therefore, Unity allows us to define custom areas with names that we choose (such as **Water** or **Mud**) and associated costs, such as **2** (that is, water is twice as tiring to travel through).

Different navigable areas can be connected via **NavMesh links**: https://docs.unity3d.com/Manual/class-NavMeshLink.html.

The most efficient way for games to work with navigation meshes is to pre-calculate the costs of polygons in the game world; this is known as **baking** and is performed at **design time**, before we run the game.

However, sometimes, there will be features in the game that we wish to use to influence navigation decisions and route planning differently at different times in the game; that is, dynamic **runtime** navigation obstacles. Unity provides a **NavMesh Obstacle** component that can be added to GameObjects and has features such as "carving out" (temporarily removing) areas of a **NavMesh** to force AI agents to recalculate paths that avoid areas blocked by GameObjects with **NavMesh Obstacle** components.

In this chapter, you'll learn how to add **NavMesh Agents** to control characters and how to work with your game environment to specify and bake **navigation meshes** for a scene. Some recipes will explore how to create point-and-click style games, where you indicate where you want a character to navigate by clicking on an object or point in the game world.

You'll create "swarms" of objects that move and flock together, and you'll also learn how to add **NavMesh Obstacle** components to moving GameObjects, forcing AI agents to dynamically recalculate their paths at runtime due for objects moving in their way.

In this chapter, we will cover the following recipes:

- NPC to travel to destination while avoiding obstacles
- NPC to seek or flee from a moving object
- Point-and-click move to object
- Point-and-click move to tile
- Point-and-click raycast with user-defined, higher-cost navigation areas
- NPC to follow waypoints in sequence
- Controlling object group movement through flocking
- Creating a movable NavMesh Obstacle

Technical requirements

For this chapter, you will need Unity 2021.1 or later, plus one of the following:

- Microsoft Windows 10 (64-bit)/GPU: DX10, DX11, and DX12-capable
- macOS Sierra 10.12.6+/GPU Metal-capable Intel or AMD
- Linux Ubuntu 16.04, Ubuntu 18.04, and CentOS 7/GPU: OpenGL 3.2+ or Vulkan-capable, Nvidia or AMD

For each chapter, there is a folder that contains the asset files you will need in this book's GitHub repository at `https://github.com/PacktPublishing/Unity-2021-Cookbook-Fourth-Edition`.

NPC to travel to destination while avoiding obstacles

The introduction of Unity's **NavMeshAgent** has greatly simplified the coding for **non-player character** (**NPC**) and enemy agent behaviors. In this recipe, we'll add some wall obstacles (scaled cubes) and generate a **NavMesh** so that Unity knows not to try to walk through walls. We'll then add a `NavMeshAgent` component to our NPC GameObject and tell it to head to a stated destination location by intelligently planning and following a path while avoiding the wall obstacles.

When the **Navigation** window is visible, the **Scene** window displays the blue-shaded walkable areas, as well as unshaded, non-walkable areas at the edge of the terrain and around each of the two wall objects:

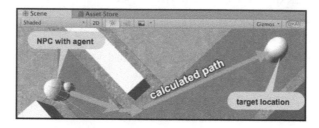

Figure 10.1 – Example of an NPC avoiding obstacles

Getting ready

The required **TextureSandAlbedo** terrain can be found in the 10_01 folder. Alternatively, you can go to **Assets | Import Package | Standard Assets | Environments**, deselect everything, and then locate and tick the **Assets/Environment/TerrainAssets/SurfaceTextures/SandAlbedo.psd** asset.

How to do it...

To make an NPC travel to a destination while avoiding obstacles, follow these steps:

1. Create a new, empty **Unity 3D project**.
2. Create a new 3D **Terrain** by going to **Create | 3D Object | Terrain**. With this new Terrain GameObject selected in the **Hierarchy** window, in the **Inspector** window's properties, set its scale to 30 x 20 and its position to (-15, 0, -10) so we have this GameObject centered at (0, 0, 0).
3. Texture paint this terrain with the **SandAlbedo** texture.
4. Create a 3D **Capsule** named Capsule-destination at (-12, 0, 8). This will be the target destination for our NPC self-navigating GameObject.
5. Create a sphere named Sphere-arrow that is positioned at (2, 0.5, 2). Scale it to (1, 1, 1).
6. Create a second sphere named Sphere-small. Scale it to (0.5, 0.5, 0.5).

7. In the **Hierarchy** window, make `Sphere-small` a child of `Sphere-arrow` and position it at (0, 0, 0.5):

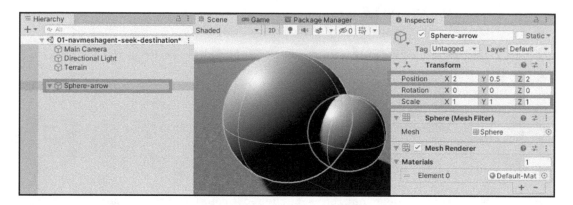

Figure 10.2 – Setting Sphere-small as a child of Sphere-arrow in the Hierarchy window

8. In the **Inspector** window, add a new **NavMeshAgent** to **Sphere-arrow**. Do this by going to **Add Component | Navigation | Nav Mesh Agent**.

9. Set the **Stopping Distance** property of the **NavMeshAgent** component to 2:

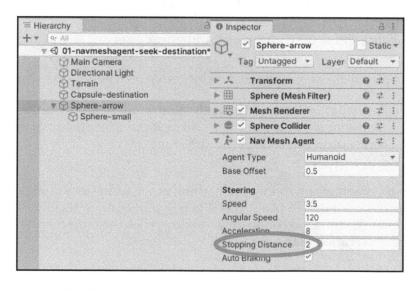

Figure 10.3 – Setting the Stopping Distance property of the NavMeshAgent component to 2

10. Create the `ArrowNPCMovement` C# script class, and add an instance object to the `Sphere-arrow` GameObject:

```
using UnityEngine;
 using UnityEngine.AI;

public class ArrowNPCMovement : MonoBehaviour {
 public GameObject targetGo;
 private NavMeshAgent navMeshAgent;

void Start() {
 navMeshAgent = GetComponent<NavMeshAgent>();
 HeadForDestintation();
 }

private void HeadForDestintation () {
 Vector3 destination = targetGo.transform.position;
 navMeshAgent.SetDestination (destination);
 }
 }
```

11. Ensure that **Sphere-arrow** is selected in the **Inspector** wndow. For the **ArrowNPCMovement** scripted component, drag **Capsule-destination** over the **Target Go** variable.

12. Create a 3D **Cube** named **Cube-wall** at (−6, 0, 0) and scale it to (1, 2, 10).

13. Create another 3D **Cube** named **Cube-wall2** at (−2, 0, 6) and scale it to (1, 2, 7).

14. Display the **Navigation** window by going to **Window | AI |Navigation**.

 A great place to dock the **Navigation** window is next to the **Inspector** window since you will never be using the **Inspector** and **Navigation** windows at the same time.

15. In the **Hierarchy** windows, select both of the **Cube-wall** objects (we select the objects that are not supposed to be a part of the walkable parts of our scene). Then, in the **Navigation** window, click the **Object** button and check the **Navigation Static** checkbox:

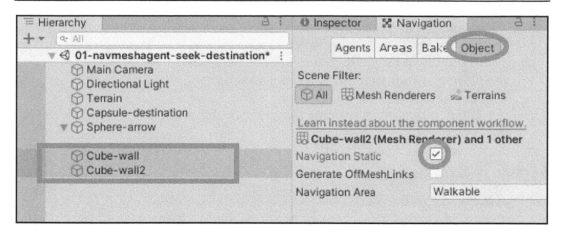

Figure 10.4 – Ticking the Navigation Static checkbox for both Cube-wall objects

16. In the **Inspector** window, click on the **Bake** button at the top for baking options. Then, click on the **Bake** button at the bottom right to create your **Navigation Mesh** asset:

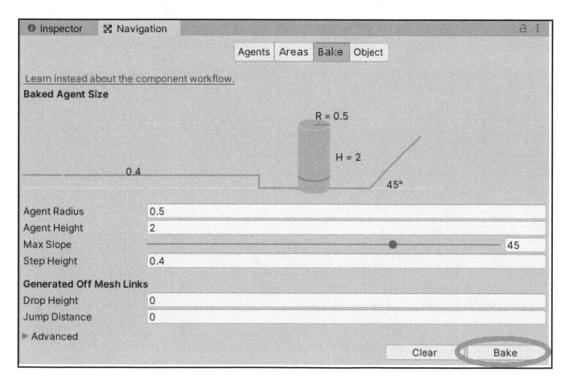

Figure 10.5 – Creating the Navigation Mesh asset with the Bake settings

17. When the **Navigation** window is displayed, you'll see a blue tint on the parts of the scene that are areas for a `NavMeshAgent` to consider for its navigation paths.

18. Now, run your game. You will see that the `Sphere-arrow` GameObject automatically move toward the `Capsule-destination` GameObject, following a path that avoids the two wall objects.

How it works...

The **NavMeshAgent** component that we added to the `Sphere-arrow` GameObject does most of the work for us. **NavMeshAgents** need two things:

- A destination location to head toward
- A **NavMesh** component of the terrain with walkable/non-walkable areas so that it can plan a path by avoiding obstacles

We created two obstacles (the **Cube-wall** objects), and these were selected when we created the NavMesh for this scene in the **Navigation** window. When the **Navigation** window is displayed, at the same time in the **Scene** window (and the **Game** window with **Gizmos** enabled), we can see walkable areas forming a blue navigation mesh.

 Note that the blue areas are the default NavMesh area. Later in this chapter, we'll look at different, custom named, costed, and color-coded NavMesh areas.

The location for our NPC object to travel toward is the position of the `Capsule-destination` GameObject at (-12, 0, 8); but, of course, we could just move this object in the **Scene** window at design time, and its new position would be the destination when we run the game.

The `ArrowNPCMovement` C# script class has two variables: one is a reference to the destination GameObject, while the second is a reference to the `NavMeshAgent` component of the GameObject, in which our instance of the `ArrowNPCMovement` class is also a component. When the scene starts, the `NavMeshAgent` sibling component is found via the `Start()` method, and the `HeadForDestination()` method is called, which sets the destination of `NavMeshAgent` to the position of the destination GameObject.

Once `NavMeshAgent` has a target to head toward, it will plan a path there and will keep moving until it arrives (or gets within the stopping distance, if that parameter has been set to a distance greater than zero).

In the **Scene** window, if you select the GameObject that contains `NavMeshAgent` and choose **Show Avoidance Gizmo**, you can view the candidate local target positions the agent is considering. The lighter the squares are, the better the position ranks.

The darker red the squares are, the less desirable the position; so, dark red squares indicate positions to avoid since they might, for instance, cause the agent to collide with a **NavMesh Static** obstacle:

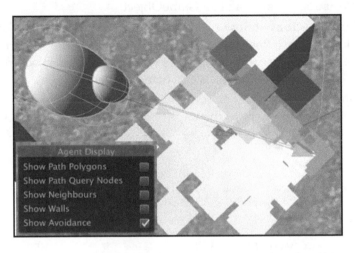

Figure 10.6 – Show Avoidance Gizmo showing candidate local target positions the agent is considering

Ensure that the object with the **NavMeshAgent** component is selected in the **Hierarchy** window at runtime to be able to see this navigation data in the **Scene** window.

NPC to seek or flee from a moving object

Rather than a destination that is fixed when the scene starts, let's allow the **Capsule-destination** object to be moved by the player while the scene is running. In every frame, we'll get our NPC arrow to reset the destination of **NavMeshAgent** to wherever **Capsule-destination** has been moved to.

Getting ready

This recipe adds to the previous one, so make a copy of that project folder and do your work for this recipe with that copy.

How to do it...

To make an NPC seek or flee from a moving object, follow these steps:

1. In the **Inspector** window, add a **Rigid Body Physics** component to the `Capsule-destination` GameObject.

2. In the **Inspector** window for the `Capsule-destination` GameObject, check the **Freeze Position** constraint for **Y-axis** in the **Constraints** options of the **RigidBody** component. This will prevent the object from moving in the Y-axis due to collisions when being moved.

3. Create the `SimplePlayerControl` C# script class and add an instance object as a component to the `Capsule-destination` GameObject:

```csharp
using UnityEngine;

public class SimplePlayerControl : MonoBehaviour {
public float speed = 1000;
private Rigidbody rigidBody;
private Vector3 newVelocity;

private void Start() {
rigidBody = GetComponent<Rigidbody>();
}

void Update() {
    float xMove = Input.GetAxis("Horizontal") * speed *
Time.deltaTime;
    float zMove = Input.GetAxis("Vertical") * speed *
Time.deltaTime;
    newVelocity = new Vector3(xMove, 0, zMove);
}

void FixedUpdate() {
    rigidBody.velocity = newVelocity;
}
}
```

4. Update the `ArrowNPCMovement` C# script class so that we call the `HeadForDestintation()` method every frame – that is, from `Update()` rather than just once in `Start()`:

```
using UnityEngine;
using UnityEngine.AI;

public class ArrowNPCMovement : MonoBehaviour
{
  public GameObject targetGo;
  private NavMeshAgent navMeshAgent;
  void Start()
  {
    navMeshAgent = GetComponent<NavMeshAgent>();
  }

  private void Update()
  {
    HeadForDestintation();
  }

  private void HeadForDestintation()
  {
    Vector3 destination = targetGo.transform.position;
    navMeshAgent.SetDestination(destination);

  }
}
```

How it works...

The `SimplePlayerControl` script class detects arrow key presses and translates them into a force to apply to move the `Capsule-destination` GameObject in the desired direction.

The `Update()` method of the `ArrowNPCMovement` script class makes `NavMeshAgent` update its path **every** frame, based on the current position of the `Capsule-destination` GameObject. As the user moves `Capsule-destination`, `NavMeshAgent` calculates a new path to the object.

There's more...

Here are some details that you don't want to miss.

Using a Debug Ray to show a source-to-destination line

It's useful to use a visual **Debug Ray** to show us the straight line from the NPC with `NavMeshAgent` to the current destination it is trying to navigate toward. Since this is a common thing we may wish to do for many games, it's useful to create a static method in a general-purpose class; then, the ray can be drawn with a single statement.

To use a **Debug Ray** to draw a source-to-destination line, follow these steps:

1. Create a `UsefulFunctions.cs` C# script class containing the following code:

```
using UnityEngine;

public class UsefulFunctions : MonoBehaviour {
 public static void DebugRay(Vector3 origin, Vector3
destination, Color c) {
 Vector3 direction = destination - origin;
 Debug.DrawRay(origin, direction, c);
 }
 }
```

2. Now, add a statement at the end of the `HeadForDestination()` method in the `ArrowNPCMovement` C# script class:

```
using UnityEngine;
using UnityEngine.AI;

public class ArrowNPCMovement : MonoBehaviour
{
 public GameObject targetGo;
 private NavMeshAgent navMeshAgent;

 void Start()
 {
 navMeshAgent = GetComponent<NavMeshAgent>();
 }
```

```
private void Update()
{
HeadForDestintation();
}

private void HeadForDestintation()
{
Vector3 destination = targetGo.transform.position;
navMeshAgent.SetDestination(destination);
// show yellow line from source to target
UsefulFunctions.DebugRay(transform.position, destination,
Color.yellow);
 }
}
```

We can now see a yellow line in the **Scene** window when the scene is running. We can also see this in the **Game** window if the **Gizmos** option is selected (at the top right of the **Game** window's title bar):

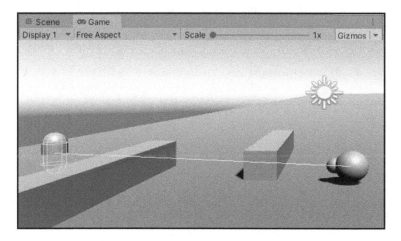

Figure 10.7 – Yellow line illustrating the Debug Ray source to destination

Constantly updating the NavMeshAgent's destination to flee from the player's current location

There are times when we want an AI-controlled NPC character to move **away** from another character, rather than go toward it. For example, an enemy with very low health might run away, and so gain time to regain its health before fighting again. Or, a wild animal might flee from any other character moving near it.

To instruct our **NavMeshAgent** component to flee from the player's location, we need to replace the ArrowNPCMovement C# script class with the following:

```
using UnityEngine;
using UnityEngine.AI;

public class ArrowNPCMovement : MonoBehaviour {
public float runAwayDistance = 10;
public GameObject targetGO;
private NavMeshAgent navMeshAgent;

void Start() {
navMeshAgent = GetComponent<NavMeshAgent>();
}

void Update() {
 Vector3 targetPosition = targetGO.transform.position;
 float distanceToTarget = Vector3.Distance(transform.position,
targetPosition);
 if (distanceToTarget < runAwayDistance)
 FleeFromTarget(targetPosition);
 }

private void FleeFromTarget(Vector3 targetPosition) {
 Vector3 destination = PositionToFleeTowards(targetPosition);
 HeadForDestintation(destination);
 }

private void HeadForDestintation (Vector3 destinationPosition) {
 navMeshAgent.SetDestination (destinationPosition);
 }

private Vector3 PositionToFleeTowards(Vector3 targetPosition) {
  transform.rotation = Quaternion.LookRotation(transform.position -
targetPosition);
  Vector3 runToPosition = targetPosition + (transform.forward *
runAwayDistance);
  return runToPosition;
  }
 }
```

There is a public variable here called runAwayDistance. When the distance to the enemy is less than the value of this runAwayDistance variable, we'll instruct the computer-controlled object to flee in the opposite direction.

The Start() method caches a reference to the **NavMeshAgent** component.

The `Update()` method calculates whether the distance to the enemy is within `runAwayDistance` and if so, it calls the `FleeFromTarget(...)` method, which passes the location of the enemy as a parameter.

The `FleeFromTarget(...)` method calculates a point that is `runAwayDistance` in Unity units away from the player's cube, in a direction that is directly away from the computer-controlled object. This is achieved by subtracting the enemy's position vector from the current transform's position.

Finally, the `HeadForDestintation(...)` method is called, passing the flee-to position, which results in **NavMeshAgent** being told to set the location as its new destination.

Unity units are arbitrary since they are just numbers on a computer. However, in most cases, it simplifies things to think of distances in terms of meters (1 Unity unit = 1 meter) and mass in terms of kilograms (1 Unity unit = 1 kilogram). Of course, if your game is based on a microscopic world or pan-galactic space travel, then you need to decide what each Unity unit corresponds to for your game context. For more information on units in Unity, check out this post about Unity measurements: `http:/ /forum.unity3d.com/threads/best-units-of-measurement-in-unity.284133/ #post-1875487`.

Debug Ray shows the point the NPC is aiming for, whether it be to flee from the player's character or to catch up and maintain a constant distance from it.

> You might need to ensure that the **ArrowNPCMovement** scripted component is still connected to **Sphere-arrow** by dragging **Capsule-destination** over the **Target Go** variable.

Maintaining a constant distance from the target ("lurking" mode!)

It is simple to adapt the previous code to have an NPC try to maintain a constant distance from a target object. It involves always moving toward a point that is `runAwayDistance` away from the target, regardless of whether this point is toward or away from the target.

Just remove the `If` statement in the `Update()` method:

```
void Update() {
  Vector3 targetPosition = targetGO.transform.position;
```

```
    float distanceToTarget = Vector3.Distance(transform.position,
  targetPosition);
   FleeFromTarget(targetPosition);
    }
```

However, with this variation, it might be better to have the method named something like `MoveTowardsConstantDistancePoint()` rather than `FleeFromTarget()`, since our NPC is sometimes fleeing and sometimes following.

Point-and-click move to object

Another way to choose the destination for our `Sphere-arrow` GameObject is by the user clicking on an object on the screen, and then the `Sphere-arrow` GameObject moving to the location of the clicked object:

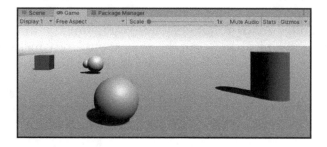

Figure 10.8 – Example of point-and-click move to object

Getting ready

This recipe adds to the first recipe in this chapter, so make a copy of that project folder and do your work for this recipe with that copy.

How to do it...

To create an object-based point-and-click mini-game, do the following:

1. In the **Inspector** window, add the **Player** tag to the `Sphere-arrow` GameObject.

2. Delete the two 3D Cubes and the 3D **Capsule-destination** from the scene.

3. Create three GameObjects – a 3D Cube, a 3D Sphere, and a 3D Cylinder.

4. Create a `ClickMeToSetDestination` C# script class containing the following code:

```
using UnityEngine;

public class ClickMeToSetDestination : MonoBehaviour
  {
  private UnityEngine.AI.NavMeshAgent playerNavMeshAgent;

void Start() {
  GameObject playerGO =
GameObject.FindGameObjectWithTag("Player");
  playerNavMeshAgent =
playerGO.GetComponent<UnityEngine.AI.NavMeshAgent>();
  }

private void OnMouseDown() {
  playerNavMeshAgent.SetDestination(transform.position);
  }
  }
```

5. Add instance objects of the `ClickMeToSetDestination` C# script class as components to your 3D **Cube**, **Sphere**, and **Cylinder**.

6. Run the scene. When you click on one of the 3D objects, the Sphere-arrow GameObject should navigate toward the clicked object.

How it works...

The `OnMouseDown()` method of the `ClickMeToSetDestination` C# script class changes the destination of `NavMeshAgent` in the Sphere-arrow GameObject to be the position of the clicked 3D object.

The `Start()` method of the `ClickMeToSetDestination` C# script class gets a reference to the `NavMeshAgent` component of the GameObject tagged as **Player** (that is, the Sphere-arrow GameObject).

Each time a different object is clicked, the `NavMeshAgent` component inside the Sphere-arrow GameObject is updated to make the GameObject move toward the position of the clicked object.

There's more...

There are some details that you don't want to miss.

Creating a mouseover yellow highlight

A good **user experience** (**UX**) feedback technique is to visually indicate to the user when an object can be interacted with via the mouse. A common way to do this is to present an audio or visual effect when the mouse is moved over an interactable object.

We can create a **Material** object with a yellow color, which can make an object appear yellow while the mouse is over it, and then make it return to its original material when the mouse is moved away.

Create the MouseOverHighlighter C# script class with the following contents. Then, add an instance object as a component to each of the three 3D GameObjects:

```
using UnityEngine;

public class MouseOverHighlighter : MonoBehaviour
 {
 private MeshRenderer meshRenderer;
 private Material originalMaterial;

void Start() {
 meshRenderer = GetComponent<MeshRenderer>();
 originalMaterial = meshRenderer.sharedMaterial;
 }

void OnMouseOver() {
 meshRenderer.sharedMaterial = NewMaterialWithColor(Color.yellow);
 }

void OnMouseExit() {
 meshRenderer.sharedMaterial = originalMaterial;
 }

private Material NewMaterialWithColor(Color newColor) {
 Shader shaderSpecular = Shader.Find("Specular");
 Material material = new Material(shaderSpecular);
 material.color = newColor;

 return material;
```

```
    }
}
```

Now, when running the game, when your mouse is over one of the three objects, that object will be highlighted in yellow. If you click on the mouse button when the object is highlighted, the `Sphere-arrow` GameObject will make its way up to (but stop just before) the clicked object.

Point-and-click move to tile

Rather than clicking specific objects to indicate the target for our AI-controlled agent, we can create a grid of 3D **Plane** (tile) objects to allow the player to click any tile to indicate a destination for the AI controller character. So, any location can be clicked, rather than only one of a few specific objects:

Figure 10.9 – Example of point-and-click move to tile with a 3D Plane grid

Getting ready

This recipe adds to the previous one, so make a copy of that project folder and do your work for this recipe with that copy.

For this recipe, we have prepared a red-outlined black square **Texture** image named `square_outline.png` in a folder named `Textures` in the `10_04` folder.

How to do it...

To create a point-and-click game by setting GameObjects to a selected tile, do the following:

1. Delete your 3D **Cube**, **Sphere**, and **Cylinder** GameObjects from the scene.

2. Create a new 3D **Plane** object scaled to (0.1, 0.1, 0.1).

3. Create a new **Material** object with the **Texture** image provided; that is, square_outline.png (a black square with a red outline). Apply this **Material** object to your 3D **Plane**.

4. Add an instance object of the ClickMeToSetDestination script class as a component to your 3D **Plane**.

5. In the **Project** window, create a new, empty **Prefab** named tile.

6. Populate your tile prefab with the properties of your 3D Plane GameObject by dragging the Plane GameObject over your tile prefab (it should change from white to blue to indicate that the prefab now has the properties of your GameObject).

7. Delete your 3D Plane GameObject from the scene.

8. Create a new TileManager C# script class containing the following and add an instance object as a component to the **Main Camera** GameObject:

```
using UnityEngine;

public class TileManager : MonoBehaviour {
    public int rows = 50;
    public int cols = 50;
    public GameObject prefabClickableTile;

    void Start () {
        for (int r = 0; r < rows; r++) {
            for (int c = 0; c < cols; c++) {
                float y = 0.01f;
                Vector3 pos = new Vector3(r - rows/2, y, c -
cols/2);
                Instantiate(prefabClickableTile, pos,
Quaternion.identity);
            }
        }
    }
}
```

9. Select **Main Camera** in the **Hierarchy** window and, in the **Inspector** window for the **Tile Manager (Script)** component, populate the **Prefab Clickable Tile** public property with your `tile` prefab from the **Project** window.

10. Run the scene. You should now be able to click on any of the small square tiles to set the destination of the **NavMeshAgent** controlled `Sphere-arrow` GameObject.

How it works...

In this recipe, you created a prefab containing the properties of a 3D **Plane** named `tile`, which contained a component instance object of the `ClickMeToSetDestination` C# script class.

The `TileManager` script class loops to create `50 x 50` instances of this `tile` Gameobject in the scene.

When you run the game, if you click on the mouse button when the mouse pointer is over a tile, the **NavMeshAgent** component inside the `Sphere-arrow` GameObject is set to that tile's position. So, the `Sphere-arrow` GameObject will move toward, but stop just before reaching, the clicked tile position.

The **Y** value of `0.01` means the plane will be just above the terrain, so we avoid any kind of Moire interference pattern due to meshes being at the same location. By subtracting `rows/2` and `cols/2` from the **X** and **Z** positions, we center our grid of tiles at `(0, Y, 0)`.

 Moire patterns or large-scale interference patterns occur when two similar patterns are overlaid in an offset, rotated, or altered pitch position. In Unity 3D, Moire patterns can be commonly identified by texture flicker.

There's more...

There are some details that you don't want to miss.

Using a yellow debug ray to show the destination of the AI agent

We can show a debug ray from a moving object to its destination tile by creating the `MouseOverHighlighter` C# script class with the following contents. We then add an instance object as a component to the **NavMeshAgent** component's controlled `Sphere-arrow` GameObject:

```
using UnityEngine;
 using UnityEngine.AI;

public class DebugRaySourceDestination : MonoBehaviour {
 void Update() {
 Vector3 origin = transform.position;
 Vector3 destination = GetComponent<NavMeshAgent>().destination;
 Vector3 direction = destination - origin;
 Debug.DrawRay(origin, direction, Color.yellow);
 }
 }
```

The preceding code uses the current position of the character (`transform.position` – our moment **origin**) and the destination point (`GetComponent<NavMeshAgent>().destination`) as the two endpoints to display a yellow debug ray.

Point-and-click raycast with user-defined, higher-cost navigation areas

Rather than indicating a desired destination by clicking an object or tile, we can use Unity's built-in `Physics.Raycast(...)` method to identify which Vector3 (*x*,*y*,*z*) position relates to the object surface in the game.

This involves translating from the 2D (*x*,*y*) screen position to an imagined 3D "ray" from the user's point of view, through the screen, into the game world, and identifying which object (polygon) it **hits** first.

This recipe will use `Physics.Raycast` to set the position of the location that's clicked on as the new destination for a **NavMeshAgent** controller object. The actual route that's followed can be influenced by defining navigation mesh areas of different costs. For example, walking through mud or swimming through water can have a higher cost, since they would take longer, so the AI **NavMeshAgent** can calculate the lowest-cost route, which may not be the shortest distance route in the scene:

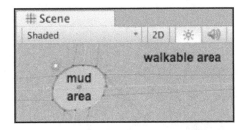

Figure 10.10 – Example of using a raycast and navigation areas

Getting ready

This recipe adds to the previous one, so make a copy of that project folder and do your work for this recipe with that copy.

How to do it...

To create a point-and-click game using a **Raycast**, do the following:

1. Remove the **Tile Manager (Script)** component from the **Main Camera** GameObject.

2. Create a new 3D **Sphere**, named `Sphere-destination`, scaled to (`0.5`, `0.5`, `0.5`).

3. Create a new **Material** object that's red and assign it to the `Sphere-destination` GameObject.

4. Create a new `MoveToClickPoint` C# script class containing the following and add an instance object as a component to the `Sphere-arrow` GameObject:

```
using UnityEngine;
using UnityEngine.AI;

public class MoveToClickPoint : MonoBehaviour {
```

```
        public GameObject sphereDestination;
        private NavMeshAgent navMeshAgent;
        private RaycastHit hit;

        void Start() {
           navMeshAgent = GetComponent<NavMeshAgent>();
           sphereDestination.transform.position =
transform.position;
        }

       void Update() {
           Ray rayFromMouseClick =
Camera.main.ScreenPointToRay(Input.mousePosition);

           if (FireRayCast(rayFromMouseClick)){
              Vector3 rayPoint = hit.point;
              ProcessRayHit(rayPoint);
           }
       }

       private void ProcessRayHit(Vector3 rayPoint) {
           if(Input.GetMouseButtonDown(0)) {
              navMeshAgent.destination = rayPoint;
              sphereDestination.transform.position = rayPoint;
           }
       }

       private bool FireRayCast(Ray rayFromMouseClick) {
           return Physics.Raycast(rayFromMouseClick, out hit,
100);
       }
     }
```

5. Select the `Sphere-arrow` GameObject in the **Hierarchy** window and, in the **Inspector** window for the **MoveToClickPoint (Script)** component, populate the **Sphere Destination** public property with your red `Sphere-destination` GameObject.

6. Run the scene. You should now be able to click anywhere on the terrain to set the destination of the **NavMeshAgent** controlled `Sphere-arrow` GameObject. As you click, the red `Sphere-destination` GameObject should be positioned at this new destination point, toward which the `Sphere-arrow` GameObject will navigate.

How it works...

In this recipe, you created a small red 3D **Sphere** named **Sphere-destination**.

There is one public variable for the `MoveToClickPoint` scripted component of the `Sphere-arrow` GameObject. This public `sphereDestination` variable has been linked to the red `Sphere-destination` GameObject in the scene.

There are two private variables:

- `navMeshAgent`: This will be set to refer to the **NavMeshAgent** component of the `Sphere-arrow` GameObject so that its destination can be reset when appropriate.
- `hit`: This is a `RaycastHit` object that is passed in as the object to be set by `Physics.Raycast(...)`. Various properties of this object are set after a raycast has been created, including the position in the scene where the raycast hits the surface of an object.

The `Start()` method caches a reference to the **NavMesh** component of the `Sphere-arrow` GameObject and also moves the `Sphere-destination` GameObject to the current object's location.

Each frame, in the `Update()` method, a ray is created based on **Main Camera** and the $(2,y)$ point that's clicked on the screen. This ray is passed as a parameter to the `FireRayCast(...)` method. If that method returns `true`, then the position of the object that's hit is extracted and passed to the `ProcessRayHit(...)` method.

The `FireRayCast(...)` method receives a `Ray` object. It uses `Phyics.Raycast(...)` to determine whether the raycast collides with part of an object in the scene. If the raycast hits something, the properties of the `RaycastHit` `hit` object are updated. A `true/false` output for whether `Physics.Raycast(...)` hit a surface is returned by this method.

Each time the user clicks on the screen, the corresponding object in the scene is identified with the raycast, the red sphere is moved there, and the **NavMeshAgent** component begins to navigate toward that location.

You can learn more about the Unity raycast C# script class at https://docs.unity3d.com/ScriptReference/RaycastHit.html.

There's more...

Here are some details that you won't want to miss.

More intelligent pathfinding by setting different costs for custom-defined navigation areas such as mud and water

We can create objects whose meshes are defined as more expensive for **NavMeshAgents** to travel across, helping AI agent behavior be more realistic in terms of choosing faster paths that avoid water, mud, and so on.

To create a custom **NavMesh Area** (we'll pretend it's mud) with a higher traveling cost, do the following:

1. In the **Navigation** window, reveal the areas by clicking the **Areas** button. Then, define a new area named **Mud** with a cost of **2**:

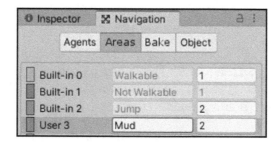

Figure 10.11 – Defining Mud as a NavMesh area

2. Create a new 3D **Cylinder** named `Cylinder-mud` positioned at (0, -4.9, 0) and scaled to (5,5,5).

3. Ensure that the `Cylinder-mud` GameObject is selected in the **Hierarchy** window and that the **Navigation** window is displayed.

4. In the **Navigation** window, click the **Object** button, check **Navigation Static**, and choose **Mud** from the **Navigation Area** drop-down list:

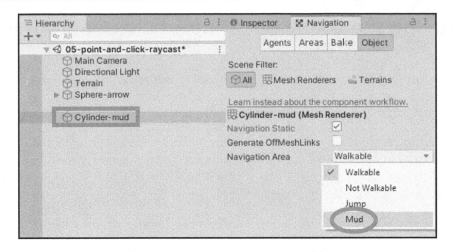

Figure 10.12 – Setting Mud as our Navigation Area in the Navigation window

5. Now, click the **Bake** button to show the **NavigationBake** sub-panel. Then, in this sub-panel, click the **Bake** button to regenerate the navigation mesh with the new object.

Click to move the `Sphere-arrow` GameObject near the edge of the `Cylinder-mud` area. Now, click on the opposite side; you will see **NavMeshAgent** make the `Sphere-arrow` GameObject follow a semi-circular (lowest cost) path around the edge of the `Cylinder-mud` area. We are doing this rather than following a direct line (as the crow flies) path as the mud area (higher cost) would take longer to traverse.

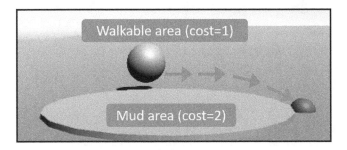

Figure 10.13 – Path of the Sphere-arrow GameObject bypassing the high-cost mud area

Improving the UX by updating a "gaze" cursor each frame

It's nice to know what our destination will be set to **before** we click the mouse. So, let's add a yellow sphere to show the "candidate" destination for where our raycast is hitting a surface, updating each frame as we move the mouse.

So, we need to create a second, yellow sphere. We also need to create a **Layer** to ignore; otherwise, if we move the yellow sphere to the point where a raycast hits a surface, then in the next frame, our raycast will hit the surface of our yellow sphere – moving it closer and closer to us each frame!

To improve the UX by updating a "gaze" cursor each frame, do the following:

1. Create a new yellow **Material** object named `m_yellow`.
2. Create a second 3D **Sphere** named `Sphere-destination-candidate` that's textured with `m_yellow`.
3. Create a new **Layer** called `UISpheres`.
4. Set this **Layer** for both the `Sphere-destination` and `Sphere-destination-candidate` GameObjects as **LayerUISpheres**.
5. Modify the `MoveToClickPoint` C# script class as follows to add a new public variable called `sphereDestinationCandidate`:

   ```
   public class MoveToClickPoint : MonoBehaviour {
   public GameObject sphereDestination;
   public GameObject sphereDestinationCandidate;
   ```

6. Modify the `MoveToClickPoint` C# script class as follows to add an `Else` clause to the logic in the `ProcessRayHit(...)` method so that if the mouse is not clicked, the yellow `sphereDestinationCandidate` object is moved to where the raycast hit a surface:

   ```
   private void ProcessRayHit(Vector3 rayPoint) {
      if(Input.GetMouseButtonDown(0)) {
         navMeshAgent.destination = rayPoint;
         sphereDestination.transform.position = rayPoint;
      } else {
         sphereDestinationCandidate.transform.position =
   rayPoint;
      }
   }
   ```

7. Modify the `MoveToClickPoint` C# script class as follows so that a `LayerMask` is created to ignore the `UISpheres` layer and to pass it as a parameter when `Physics.Raycast(...)` is invoked:

```
private bool FireRayCast(Ray rayFromMouseClick) {
    LayerMask layerMask = ~LayerMask.GetMask("UISpheres");
    return Physics.Raycast(rayFromMouseClick, out hit, 100,
layerMask.value);
}
```

8. Select the `Sphere-arrow` GameObject in the **Hierarchy** window and, in the **Inspector** window for the **MoveToClickPoint (Script)** component, populate the **Sphere Destination Candidate** public property with your yellow `Sphere-destination-candidate` GameObject.

9. Run the scene. You should now be able to click anywhere on the terrain to set the destination of the **NavMeshAgent** controlled `Sphere-arrow` GameObject. As you click, the red `Sphere-destination` GameObject should be positioned at this new destination point, toward which the `Sphere-arrow` GameObject will navigate.

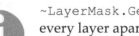

We have set a `LayerMask` using the `~LayerMask.GetMask("UISpheres")` statement, which means every layer apart from the named one. This is passed to the `Raycast(...)` method so that our red and yellow spheres are ignored when casting the ray and looking to see which surface the ray hits first.

NPC NavMeshAgent to follow waypoints in a sequence

Waypoints are often used as guides for helping autonomously moving NPCs and enemies follow a path in a general way, but be able to respond with other directional behaviors, such as flee or seek, if friends/predators/prey are sensed nearby. The waypoints are arranged in a sequence so that when the character reaches or gets close to a waypoint, it will select the next waypoint in the sequence as the target location to move toward. This recipe will demonstrate an arrow object moving toward a waypoint. Then, when it gets close enough, it will choose the next waypoint in the sequence as the new target destination. When the last waypoint has been reached, it will start heading toward the first waypoint once more.

Since Unity's **NavMeshAgent** has simplified coding NPC behavior, our work in this recipe basically becomes finding the position of the next waypoint and then telling **NavMeshAgent** that this waypoint is its new destination:

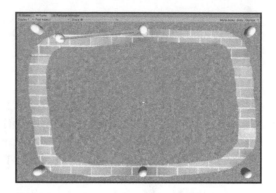

Figure 10.14 – Example with six waypoints along a "yellow brick road"

Getting ready

This recipe adds to the first recipe in this chapter, so make a copy of that project folder and do your work for this recipe with that copy.

For this recipe, we have prepared the yellow brick texture image that you need in a folder named `Textures` in the `10_06` folder.

How to do it...

To instruct an object to follow a sequence of waypoints, follow these steps:

1. Replace the contents of the `ArrowNPCMovement` C# script class with the following:

```
using UnityEngine;
 using UnityEngine.AI;

public class ArrowNPCMovement : MonoBehaviour {
  private GameObject targetGo = null;
  private WaypointManager waypointManager;
  private NavMeshAgent navMeshAgent;

void Start () {
```

```
      navMeshAgent = GetComponent<NavMeshAgent>();
      waypointManager = GetComponent<WaypointManager>();
      HeadForNextWayPoint();
   }

   void Update () {
     float closeToDestinaton = navMeshAgent.stoppingDistance * 2;
     if (navMeshAgent.remainingDistance < closeToDestinaton) {
       HeadForNextWayPoint ();
      }
   }

   private void HeadForNextWayPoint () {
     targetGo = waypointManager.NextWaypoint (targetGo);
       navMeshAgent.SetDestination (targetGo.transform.position);
      }
   }
```

2. Create a new 3D **Capsule** object named `Capsule-waypoint-0` at `(-12, 0, 8)`.

3. Copy `Capsule-waypoint-0`, name the copy `Capsule-waypoint-3`, and position this copy at `(8, 0, -8)`.

 We are going to add some intermediate waypoints numbered 1 and 2 later on. This is why our second waypoint here is numbered 3, in case you were wondering.

4. Create the `WaypointManager` C# script class with the following contents and add an instance object as a component to the `Sphere-arrow` GameObject:

```
using UnityEngine;

public class WaypointManager : MonoBehaviour {
   public GameObject wayPoint0;
   public GameObject wayPoint3;

   public GameObject NextWaypoint(GameObject current) {
      if(current == wayPoint0)
          return wayPoint3;

      return wayPoint0;
   }
}
```

5. Ensure that **Sphere-arrow** is selected in the **Inspector** window for the `WaypointManager` scripted component. Drag `Capsule-waypoint-0` and `Capsule-waypoint-3` over the public variable projectiles called `WayPoint 0` and `WayPoint 3`, respectively.

6. Now, run your game. The arrow object will move toward one of the waypoint capsules. Then, when it gets close to it, it will slow down, turn around, head toward the other waypoint capsule, and keep doing that continuously.

How it works...

The **NavMeshAgent** component that we added to the `Sphere-arrow` GameObject does most of the work for us. NavMeshAgent needs two things:

- A destination location to head toward
- A **NavMesh** so that it can plan a path and avoid obstacles

We created two possible waypoints as the locations for our NPC to move toward; that is, `Capsule-waypoint-0` and `Capsule-waypoint-3`.

The C# script class called `WaypointManager` has one job: to return a reference to the next waypoint that our NPC should head toward. There are two variables, `wayPoint0` and `wayPoint3`, that reference the two waypoint GameObjects in our scene. The `NextWaypoint(...)` method takes a single parameter named `current`, which is a reference to the current waypoint that the object is moving toward (or `null`). This method's task is to return a reference to the next waypoint that the NPC should travel toward. The logic for this method is simple: if `current` refers to `waypoint0`, then we'll return `waypoint3`; otherwise, we'll return `waypoint0`. Note that if we pass this method as `null`, then we'll get `waypoint0` back (this is our default first waypoint).

The `ArrowNPCMovement` C# script class has three variables. One is a reference to the destination GameObject named `targetGo`. The second is a reference to the **NavMeshAgent** component of the GameObject in which our instance of the class called `ArrowNPCMovement` is also a component. The third variable, called `waypointManager`, is a reference to the sibling scripted component, which is an instance of our `WaypointManager` script class.

When the scene starts via the `Start()` method, the `NavMeshAgent` and `WaypointManager` sibling components are found, and the `HeadForDestination()` method is called.

The `HeadForDestination()` method sets the variable called `targetGO` to refer to the GameObject that is returned by a call to `NextWaypoint(...)` of the scripted component called `WaypointManager` (that is, `targetGo` is set to refer to either `Capsule-waypoint-0` or `Capsule-waypoint-3`). Next, it instructs **NavMeshAgent** to make its destination the position of the `targetGO` GameObject.

Each frame method called `Update()` is called. A test is performed to see whether the distance from the NPC arrow object is close to the destination waypoint. If the distance is smaller than twice the stopping distance that was set in our **NavMeshAgent**, then a call is made to `WaypointManager.NextWaypoint(...)` to update our target destination to be the next waypoint in the sequence.

There's more...

Here are some details that you won't want to miss.

Working with arrays of waypoints

Having a separate `WaypointManager` C# script class to simply swap between `Capsule-waypoint-0` and `Capsule-waypoint-3` may have seemed to be a bit heavy duty and a case of over-engineering, but this was actually a very good move. An instance object of the `WaypointManager` script class has the job of returning the next waypoint. It is now very straightforward to add the more sophisticated approach of having an array of waypoints, without us having to change any code in the `ArrowNPCMovement` C# script class. We can choose a random waypoint to be the next destination; for example, see the *Choosing destinations – finding the nearest (or a random) spawnpoint* recipe in `Chapter 14`, *Choosing and Controlling Positions*. Or, we can have an array of waypoints and choose the next one in the sequence.

To improve our game so that it works with an array of waypoints to be followed in sequence, we need to do the following:

1. Copy `Capsule-waypoint-0`, name the copy `Capsule-waypoint-1`, and position this copy at (0, 0, 8).

2. Make four more copies (named `Capsule-waypoint-1, 2, 4, 5`) and position them as follows:

- `Capsule-waypoint-1`: Position = (-2, 0, 8)
- `Capsule-waypoint-2`: Position = (8, 0, 8)
- `Capsule-waypoint-4`: Position = (-2, 0, -8)
- `Capsule-waypoint-5`: Position = (-12, 0, -8):

Figure 10.15 – Position of the waypoints to create a rectangular path

3. Replace the `WaypointManager` C# script class with the following code:

```
using UnityEngine;
using System;

public class WaypointManager : MonoBehaviour {
    public GameObject[] waypoints;

    public GameObject NextWaypoint (GameObject current) {
        if( waypoints.Length < 1)
            Debug.LogError ("WaypointManager:: ERROR - no
waypoints have been added to array!");

        int currentIndex = Array.IndexOf(waypoints, current);
        int nextIndex = (currentIndex + 1) % waypoints.Length;

        return waypoints[nextIndex];
    }
}
```

4. Ensure that `Sphere-arrow` is selected. In the **Inspector** window for the `WaypointManager` scripted component, set the size of the `Waypoints` array to 6. Now, drag in all six capsule waypoint objects called `Capsule-waypoint-0/1/2/3/4/5`.

5. Run the game. Now, the `Sphere-arrow` GameObject will move toward waypoint 0 (top left), and then follow the sequence around the terrain.

6. Finally, you can make it look as if the `Sphere` GameObject is following a yellow brick road. Import the provided yellow brick texture, add this to your terrain, and paint the texture to create an oval-shaped path between the waypoints. You may also uncheck the **Mesh Renderer** component for each waypoint capsule so that the user does not see any of the waypoints, just the arrow object following the yellow brick road.

In the `NextWaypoint(...)` method, we check whether the array is empty, in which case an error is logged. Next, the array index for the current `waypoint` GameObject is found (if present in the array). Finally, the array index for the next waypoint is calculated using a modulus operator to support a cyclic sequence, returning to the beginning of the array after the last element has been visited.

Increased flexibility with the WayPoint class

Rather than forcing a GameObject to follow a single rigid sequence of locations, we can make things more flexible by defining a `WayPoint` class where each waypoint GameObject has an array of possible destinations, and each of these has its own array. In this way, a **directed graph** (`digraph`) can be implemented, of which a linear sequence is just one possible instance.

To improve our game and make it work with a digraph of waypoints, do the following:

1. Remove the scripted `WayPointManager` component from the `Sphere-arrow` GameObject.

2. Replace the `ArrowNPCMovement` C# script class with the following code:

```
using UnityEngine;
using System.Collections;

public class ArrowNPCMovement : MonoBehaviour {
    public Waypoint waypoint;
    private bool firstWayPoint = true;
    private NavMeshAgent navMeshAgent;
```

```
        void Start (){
           navMeshAgent = GetComponent<NavMeshAgent>();
           HeadForNextWayPoint();
        }

        void Update () {
            float closeToDestinaton = navMeshAgent.stoppingDistance
* 2;
            if (navMeshAgent.remainingDistance <
closeToDestinaton){
                HeadForNextWayPoint ();
            }
        }

        private void HeadForNextWayPoint (){
           if(firstWayPoint)
              firstWayPoint = false;
           else
              waypoint = waypoint.GetNextWaypoint();

           Vector3 target = waypoint.transform.position;
           navMeshAgent.SetDestination (target);
        }
    }
```

3. Create a new `WayPoint` C# script class containing the following code:

```
using UnityEngine;
using System.Collections;

public class WayPoint: MonoBehaviour {
   public WayPoint[] waypoints;

   public WayPoint GetNextWayPoint () {
      return waypoints[ Random.Range(0, waypoints.Length) ];
   }
}
```

4. Select all six GameObjects called `Capsule-waypoint –0/1/2/3/4/5` and add an instance object component of the `WayPoint` C# class to them.

5. Select the `Sphere-arrow` GameObject and add to it an instance object component of the `WayPoint` C# class.

6. Ensure that the `Sphere-arrow` GameObject is selected. In the **Inspector** window for the `ArrowNPCMovement` scripted component, drag `Capsule-waypoint-0` into the `Waypoint` public variable slot.

7. Now, we need to link `Capsule-waypoint-0` to `Capsule-waypoint-1`, `Capsule-waypoint-1` to `Capsule-waypoint-2`, and so on. Select `Capsule-waypoint-0`, set its **Waypoints** array size to 1, and drag in `Capsule-waypoint-1`. Next, select `Capsule-waypoint-1`, set its **Waypoints** array size to 1, and drag in `Capsule-waypoint-2`. Continue in this way until you finally link `Capsule-waypoint-5` back to `Capsule-waypoint-0`.

You now have a much more flexible game architecture, allowing GameObjects to randomly select one of several different paths at each waypoint that's reached. In this recipe variation, we implemented a waypoint sequence, since each waypoint has an array of just one linked waypoint. However, if you change the array size to 2 or more, you will be creating a graph of linked waypoints, adding random variations in the sequence of waypoints that a computer-controlled character follows for any given run of your game.

Controlling object group movement through flocking

A realistic, natural-looking flocking behavior (for example birds, antelope, or bats) can be developed by creating collections of objects with the following four simple rules:

- **Separation**: Avoid getting too close to neighbors.
- **Avoid obstacles**: Turn away from an obstacle immediately ahead.
- **Alignment**: Move in the general direction the flock is heading.
- **Cohesion**: Move toward a location in the middle of the flock.

Each member of the flock acts independently but needs to know about the current heading and location of the members of its flock. This recipe will show you how to create a scene with two flocks of cubes: one flock of green cubes and one flock of yellow cubes.

To keep things simple, we won't worry about separation in this recipe:

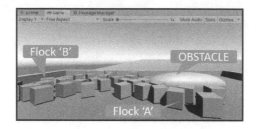

Figure 10.16 – Example of controlling object group movement through flocking

Getting ready

This recipe builds upon the player-controlled 3D Cube Unity project that you created in the first recipe. So, make a copy of this project, open it, and then follow the steps for this recipe.

The required script to control the movement of the red **Cube** (PlayerControl.cs) is provided in the 10_07 folder.

How to do it...

To make a group of objects flock together, please follow these steps:

1. Create a **Material** object in the **Project** window and name it m_green, with **Main Color** tinted green.

2. Create a **Material** object in the **Project** window and name it m_yellow, with **Main Color** tinted yellow.

3. Create a 3D **Cube** GameObject named Cube-drone at (0, 0, 0). Drag the m_yellow material into this object.

4. Add a **Navigation | NavMeshAgent** component to Cube-drone. Set the **Stopping Distance** property of the **NavMeshAgent** component to 2.

5. Add a **Physics RigidBody** component to Cube-drone with the following properties:
   - **Mass** is 1
   - **Drag** is 0
   - **Angular Drag** is 0.05

- **Use Gravity** and **Is Kinematic** are both unchecked
- **Constraints Freeze Position:** Check the **Y-axis**

6. Create the following `Drone` C# script class and add an instance object as a component to the `Cube-drone` GameObject:

```
using UnityEngine;
using UnityEngine.AI;

public class Drone : MonoBehaviour {
    private NavMeshAgent navMeshAgent;

    void Start() {
        navMeshAgent = GetComponent<NavMeshAgent>();
    }

    public void SetTargetPosition(Vector3 swarmCenterAverage,
Vector3 swarmMovementAverage) {
        Vector3 destination = swarmCenterAverage +
swarmMovementAverage;
        navMeshAgent.SetDestination(destination);
    }
}
```

7. Create a new, empty **Prefab** named `dronePrefabYellow` and, from the **Hierarchy** window, drag your `Cube-drone` GameObject into this prefab.

8. Now, drag the `m_green` material object into the `Cube-drone` GameObject.

9. Create a new, empty **Prefab** named `dronePrefabGreen` and, from the **Hierarchy** window, drag your `Cube-drone` GameObject into this prefab.

10. Delete the `Cube-drone` GameObject from the **Scene** window.

11. Create the following `Swarm` C# script class and add an instance object as a component to **Main Camera**:

```
using UnityEngine;
using System.Collections.Generic;

public class Swarm : MonoBehaviour {
    public int droneCount = 20;
    public GameObject dronePrefab;

    private List<Drone> drones = new List<Drone>();

    void Awake() {
        for (int i = 0; i < droneCount; i++)
            AddDrone();
```

```
        }

        void FixedUpdate() {
            Vector3 swarmCenter = SwarmCenterAverage();
            Vector3 swarmMovement = SwarmMovementAverage();

            foreach(Drone drone in drones )
                drone.SetTargetPosition(swarmCenter,
swarmMovement);
        }

        private void AddDrone() {
            GameObject newDroneGo = Instantiate(dronePrefab);
            Drone newDrone = newDroneGo.GetComponent<Drone>();
            drones.Add(newDrone);
        }

        private Vector3 SwarmCenterAverage() {
            Vector3 locationTotal = Vector3.zero;
            foreach(Drone drone in drones )
                locationTotal += drone.transform.position;

            return (locationTotal / drones.Count);
        }

        private Vector3 SwarmMovementAverage() {
            Vector3 velocityTotal = Vector3.zero;
            foreach(Drone drone in drones )
                velocityTotal +=
drone.GetComponent<Rigidbody>().velocity;

            return (velocityTotal / drones.Count);
        }
    }
```

12. With **Main Camera** selected in the **Hierarchy** window, drag `dronePrefabYellow` from the **Project** window over the **Drone Prefab** public variable.

13. With **Main Camera** selected in the **Hierarchy** window, add a second instance object of the `Swarm` script class to this GameObject, and then drag `dronePrefabGreen` from the **Project** window over the **Drone Prefab** public variable.

14. Create a new 3D **Cube** named `wall-left` with the following properties:
    - **Position**: (-15, 0.5, 0).
    - **Scale**: (1, 1, 20).

- Duplicate the `wall-left` object by naming the new object `wall-right` and change the position of `wall-right` to (15, 0.5, 0).

15. Create a new 3D **Cube** named `wall-top` with the following properties:
    - **Position:** (0, 0.5, 10)
    - **Scale:** (31, 1, 1)

16. Duplicate the `wall-top` object by naming the new object `wall-bottom` and change the position of `wall-bottom` to (0, 0.5, -10).

17. Create a new 3D **Sphere** named `Sphere-obstacle` with the following properties:
    - **Position:** (5, 0, 3)
    - **Scale:** (10, 3, 3)

18. In the **Hierarchy** window, select the `Sphere-obstacle` GameObject. Then, in the **Navigation** window, check the **Navigation Static** checkbox. Then, click on the **Bake** button at the bottom of the **Navigation** window.

19. Create the following `PlayerControl` C# script class:

```csharp
using UnityEngine;

public class PlayerControl : MonoBehaviour
{
  public float y;

  public const float MIN_X = -15;
  public const float MAX_X - 15;
  public const float MIN_Z = -10;
  public const float MAX_Z = 10;

  private float speed = 20;

  private void Awake()
  {
    y = transform.position.y;
  }

  private void Update()
  {
    KeyboardMovement();
    CheckBounds();
  }

  private void KeyboardMovement()
  {
```

```
        float dx = Input.GetAxis("Horizontal") * speed *
Time.deltaTime;
        float dz = Input.GetAxis("Vertical") * speed *
Time.deltaTime;
        transform.Translate(new Vector3(dx, y, dz));
    }

    private void CheckBounds()
    {
        float x = transform.position.x;
        float z = transform.position.z;
        x = Mathf.Clamp(x, MIN_X, MAX_X);
        z = Mathf.Clamp(z, MIN_Z, MAX_Z);
        transform.position = new Vector3(x, y, z);
    }
}
```

20. Finally, add an instance object of the `PlayerControl` C# script class provided as a component to the `Sphere-arrow` GameObject. Ensure that you remove the **Arrow NPC movement** script component.

How it works...

The `Swarm` class contains three variables:

1. `droneCount`: This is an integer referencing the number of `Swarm` class members that have been created.
2. `dronePrefab`: This references the prefab to be cloned to create swarm members.
3. `drones`: This is a list of objects that reference drones; a list of all the scripted `Drone` components inside all the `Swarm` objects that have been created.

Upon creation, as the scene starts, the `Swarm` script class's `Awake()` method loops to create `droneCount` swarm members by repeatedly calling the `AddDrone()` method. This method instantiates a new GameObject from the prefab and then sets the `newDrone` variable to be a reference to the `Drone` scripted object inside the new `Swarm` class member. In each frame, the `FixedUpdate()` method loops through the list of `Drone` objects by calling their `SetTargetPosition(...)` method, and passes in the `Swarm` center's location and the average of all the swarm member's velocities.

The rest of this `Swarm` class is made up of two methods: one (`SwarmCenterAverage`) returns a `Vector3` object representing the average position of all the `Drone` objects, while the other (`SwarmMovementAverage`) returns a `Vector3` object representing the average velocity (movement force) of all the `Drone` objects:

- `SwarmMovementAverage()`:
    - What is the general direction that the swarm is moving in?
    - This is known as alignment: A swarm member is attempting to move in the same direction as the swarm average.
- `SwarmCenterAverage()`:
    - What is the center position of the swarm?
    - This is known as cohesion: a swarm member is attempting to move toward the center of the swarm.

The core work is undertaken by the `Drone` class. Each drone's `Start(...)` method finds and caches a reference to its `NavMeshAgent` component.

Each drone's `UpdateVelocity(...)` method takes two `Vector3` arguments as input: `swarmCenterAverage` and `swarmMovementAverage`. This method then calculates the desired new velocity for this `Drone` by simply adding the two vectors, and then uses the result (a `Vector3` location) to update the NavMeshAgent's target location.

Most of the flocking models in modern computing owe much to the work of Craig Reynolds in the 1980s. You can learn more about Craig and his boids program on his website: `http://www.red3d.com/cwr/`.

Creating a movable NavMesh Obstacle

Sometimes, we want a moving object to slow down or prevent an AI **NavMeshAgent** controlled character from passing through an area of our game. Or, perhaps we want something such as a door or drawbridge to sometimes permit travel, and not at other times. We can't "bake" these objects into the NavMesh at design time since we want to change them during runtime.

While computationally more expensive (that is, they slow down your game more than static, non-navigable objects), NavMesh Obstacles are components that can be added to GameObjects, and these components can be enabled and disabled like any other component.

A special property of NavMesh Obstacles is that they can be set to "carve out" areas of the NavMesh, causing **NavMeshAgents** to then recalculate routes that avoid these carved out parts of the mesh.

In this recipe, you'll create a player-controlled red **Cube** that you can move to obstruct an AI **NavMeshAgent** controlled character. Also, if your cube stays in one place for half a second or longer, it will carve out part of the NavMesh around it, causing the NavMeshAgent to stop bumping into the obstacle and calculate and follow a path that avoids it:

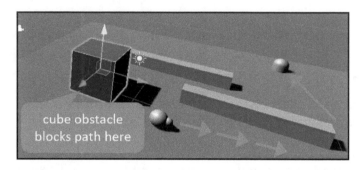

Figure 10.17 – Example of the red Cube blocking the path of the AI NavMeshAgent

Getting ready

This recipe adds to the first recipe in this chapter, so make a copy of that project folder and do your work for this recipe with that copy.

The required script to control the movement of the red Cube (`PlayerControl.cs`) is provided in the `10_08` folder.

How to do it...

To create a movable **NavMesh Obstacle**, please follow these steps:

1. Create a **Material** object in the **Project** window and name it `m_green`, with **Main Color** tinted green.

2. Create a red 3D **Cube** for the player to control called `Cube-player`, making it red by adding a `m_red` material to it and making it large by setting its scale to (3, 3, 3).

3. Add an instance of the provided `PlayerControl` C# script class as a component to this GameObject.

4. In the **Inspector** window, add a **Navigation | NavMesh Obstacle** component to `Cube-player` and check its **Carve** property.

5. Run the game. You can move the player-controlled red **Cube** so that it gets in the way of the moving `Sphere-arrow` GameObject. When 0.5 of a second of the **Obstacles Time-to-stationary** NavMesh is reached and with **Gizmos** displayed, you'll see the carving out of the NavMesh so that the area occupied by `Cube-player`, and a little way around it, is removed from the NavMesh. Then, the `Sphere-arrow` GameObject will recalculate a new route, avoiding the carved out area where `Cube-player` is located.

How it works...

At runtime, the AI **NavMeshAgent** controlled `Sphere-arrow` GameObject heads toward the destination point but stops when the player-controlled red **Cube** is in its way. Once the cube is stationary for 0.5 seconds or more, the NavMesh is carved out so that the AI **NavMeshAgent** controlled `Sphere-arrow` GameObject no longer even attempts to plan a path through the space occupied by the cube. It then calculates a new path to completely avoid the obstacle, even if it means backtracking and heading away from the target for part of its path.

Further reading

The following are sources that provide further information about Unity and AI navigation.

Some NavMesh features (such as NavMesh Links and dynamic mesh baking at runtime) are not part of the standard Unity installation and require additional installation. You can learn more about these components, their APIs, and how to install them at the following links:

- https://docs.unity3d.com/Manual/NavMesh-BuildingComponents.html
- https://docs.unity3d.com/Manual/NavMesh-BuildingComponents-API.html

You can learn more about Unity NavMeshes from the Unity Technologies tutorial, which is available here: `https://youtu.be/OccDZCndmnA`.

You can learn lots about computer-controlled moving GameObjects from the classic paper entitled *Steering Behaviors For Autonomous Characters* by Craig W. Reynolds, presented at the GDC-99 (Game Developer's Conference): `http://www.red3d.com/cwr/steer/gdc99/`.

While the Unity development community has been asking for 2D NavMeshes for some years now, they've not yet been released as a core feature. There is a lot of online information about how to write your own pathfinding system that would work in 2D. A good thread with plenty of links can be found at **TIGForums**: `https://forums.tigsource.com/index.php?topic=46325.0`.

11
Cameras and Rendering Pipelines

We should always pay attention to **Cameras**. They are the windows through which our players see our games. In this chapter, we will explore a range of methods for using **Cameras** to enhance a player's experience.

A **Scene** can contain multiple cameras. Often, we have one **Main Camera** (by default, we're given one with a new **Scene**). For **First-Person** viewpoint games, we control the position and rotation of the **Camera** directly, since it acts as our eyes. In **Third-Person** viewpoint games, our main camera follows an animated 3D character (usually from above, behind, or over the shoulder). It can slowly and smoothly change its position and rotation as if a person were holding the camera and moving to keep us in view.

Perspective **Cameras** have a triangular pyramid-shaped volume of space in front of them, called a **frustrum**. Objects inside this space are projected onto a plane, which determines what we see from the **Camera**. We can control this volume of space by specifying the clipping planes and the **Field of View**. The clipping planes define the minimum and maximum distances that objects have to be between in order to be considered viewable. The Field of View is decided by how wide or narrow the pyramid shape is, as shown in the following diagram:

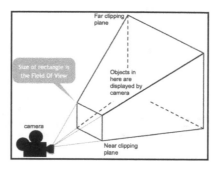

Figure 11.1 – A diagram depicting the Field of View of a camera

Cameras can be customized in many ways. Cameras can do the following:

- They can be set to render in **Orthographic** mode (that is, without **Perspective**).
- They have their **Field of View** manipulated to simulate a wide- or narrow-angle lens.
- They can be rendered on top of other cameras or within specific rectangular sub-areas of the screen (viewports).
- They send their output to **RenderTexture** asset files (this output can potentially be used to texture other objects in the scene).
- They include/exclude objects on specific layers for/from rendering (using Mulling Masks).

Cameras have a `depth` property. This is used by Unity to determine in what sequence **Cameras** are rendered. Unity renders **Cameras** starting with the lowest depth number and working up to the highest. This is necessary to ensure that **Cameras** that are not rendered to fill the whole screen are rendered after **Cameras** that are.

Cinemachine is a powerful automated system for camera control. It was developed by Adam Myhill and is now a free Unity package. It offers much to Unity developers, both for **runtime** in-game camera control and in cinematic creation for cutscenes or creating fully animated films. In this chapter, we will present examples of how to add some runtime camera controls to your games using Cinemachine.

At the core of Cinemachine is the concept of a set of virtual cameras in a scene and a Cinemachine `Brain` component, which decides what virtual camera's properties should be used to control the scene's **Main Camera**.

Unity now offers several different **Rendering Pipelines**. These are related to how Unity computes what we see, based on the visible objects in the scene, their materials, the lighting system, and more. Photo-realistic games are now possible on computers with powerful graphics cards, using the **High Definition Rendering Pipeline (HDRP)**. Cubemap assets can be used for skyboxes and to provide environmental visual effects to a scene. Additionally, Unity offers (by default) a **Universal Rendering Pipeline** (**URP**), which can be used on all platforms.

Additionally, Unity offers many powerful postprocessing visual effects, such as *film grain, depth of field blurring, wet surface style reflections,* and more. A postprocessing **Volume** can be added to a scene, which will affect how the output of a camera will be rendered and seen by the user.

In this chapter, we will cover the following recipes:

- Creating the basic scene for this chapter
- Working with a fixed **Main Camera**
- Changing how much of the screen a camera renders to
- Using Render Textures to send camera output to places other than the screen
- Working with Unity's multipurpose camera rig
- Using Cinemachine ClearShot to switch cameras to keep the player in shot
- Letting the player switch to a Cinemachine FreeLook camera
- Creating a project with the URP
- Adding a vignette effect with postprocessing
- Creating an HDRP project with a **High Dynamic Range Imaging** (**HDRI**) skybox

Technical requirements

For the recipes in this chapter, you will need Unity 2021.1 or later, plus one of the following:

- Microsoft Windows 10 (64-bit)/GPU: DX10, DX11, and DX12-capable
- Mac OS Sierra 10.12.6+/GPU Metal-capable Intel or AMD

- Linux Ubuntu 16.04, Ubuntu 18.04, and CentOS 7/GPU: OpenGL 3.2+ or Vulkan-capable, Nvidia or AMD

For each chapter, there is a folder with the asset files that you need for these recipes. This can be found inside the public **GitHub repository** for the book at `https://github.com/PacktPublishing/Unity-2021-Cookbook-Fourth-Edition`.

Creating the basic scene for this chapter

All of the recipes in this chapter start off with the same basic scene, featuring a modern house layout, some objects, and a keyboard-controllable 3D character. In this recipe, you'll create a project with this scene that can be duplicated and adapted for each recipe that follows:

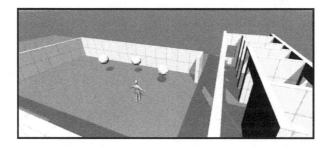

Figure 11.2 – An example of the basic scene for this chapter

Getting ready

We have prepared a Unity package named `BasicSceneSetup.unitypackage` that contains all the resources for this recipe. The package can be found in the `11_01_basic_scene` folder.

How to do it...

To create the basic scene for this chapter, simply perform the following steps:

1. Create a new 3D project.

2. Import the `BasicSceneSetup.unitypackage` package into your Unity project.

3. Also, ensure your project has the `ProBuilder` package. Navigate to **Window | Package Manager**, set **Packages** to **ALL**, search for `ProBuilder`, click on **ProBuilder** when it appears in the list, and finally, click on **Install.**

4. Open the **BasicScene** scene.

5. In the **Hierarchy** panel, select the `modernHouse` GameObject. Then, in the **Inspector** panel, ensure its position is **(7, 0, 20)**.

6. You should now see a house that includes red floors and white walls, as shown in *Figure 11.3*. Note that there is also a second directional light to reduce shadows.

Let's now add a third-person controller to the scene. To do so, we can use the one provided in the Unity `Standard Assets` package.

7. Click on **Asset Store | Search Online**. Once the website opens in your browser, search for `Standard Assets`, and when you find it, click on the **Open in Unity** button.

Inside the Unity app, you should now see **Standard Assets** listed in the **Package Manager** panel; you should be able to import this just like any other package. Once imported into your project, you should see a new folder in the **Project** panel named `Standard Assets`:

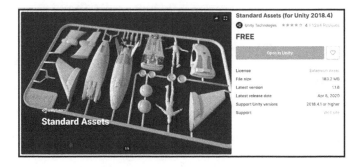

Figure 11.3 – Searching for Unity Standard Assets on the Asset Store website

8. In the **Project** panel, locate the `Prefabs` folder in **Standard Assets | Characters | ThirdPersonCharacter**. Then, drag the **ThirdPersonController** prefab into the scene and position it at `(0, 0, 0)`.

9. Let's attach the scene's **Main Camera** to the character so that you'll be able to view this third-person controller character all the time as you move it around the house. Child the **Main Camera** to the **ThirdPersonController** character, and in the **Inspector** panel, set its **Position** to (0, 3, -4) and **Rotation** to (5, 0, 0).

10. Save and run the scene.

11. As you use the arrow keys to move the character around the house, the **Main Camera** should move and rotate automatically with the character, and you should be able to see the back of the character at all times.

How it works...

By cloning prefabs, you have added a house and some objects to an empty scene. Additionally, you have added a keyboard-controller character to the scene.

By childing the **Main Camera** to the character GameObject, the **Main Camera** maintains the same position and rotation that is relative to the character at all times. Therefore, as the character moves, so does the **Main Camera**, giving a simple, over-the-shoulder type of viewpoint for the game action.

Remember, because the **Main Camera** is now a child of the **ThirdPersonController** character, the values of the `Transform` component's **Position** and **Rotation** are relative to the **Position** and **Rotation** of its parent. For example, the **Main Camera** position of **(0, 3, -4)** means that it is **3** Unity units **above** the **ThirdPersonController** (**Y = 3**) and **4** Unity units **behind** (**Z = -4**).

There's more...

There are some details that you don't want to miss.

At the time of writing (that is, early 2021), the **Standard Assets** package has not been updated for Unity 2021 (it still uses the 2018 version). When using it in recipes, we find that two errors appear, and these need to be resolved before playing your recipe. The solution to resolving these errors is as follows:

In the `ForcedReset.cs` file, add the following:

```
// add UI using statement
using UnityEngine.UI;
```

```
// change GUITexture to Image
[RequireComponent(typeof (Image))]
```

In the `SimpleActivatorMenu.cs` file, add the following:

```
// add UI using statement
using UnityEngine.UI;

// change GUIText to TEXT
public Text camSwitchButton;
```

We would like to thank **ktduffyinc_unity** and others for posting solutions to these issues on the Unity forums. The full discussion thread can be found at `https://answers.unity.com/questions/1638555/guitexture-adn-guitext-are-obsolete-standard-asset.html`.

We have also prepared a Unity package, named `StandardAssets_fixedFor2020.unitypackage`, that contains all the resources for this recipe. The package can be found in the `11_01_basic_scene` folder.

Working with a fixed Main Camera

A quick way to begin creating a scene where the player controls a third-person character is to use a fixed **Main Camera** that faces the area the character will start moving around in. We can position and orient the camera to view most of the area that the player's character will be moving around in, and we can change the amount of what is in front of a camera, which the camera "sees," by changing its **Field Of View**. In this recipe, we'll use the basic 3D scene from the previous recipe and work with the **Main Camera** so that we can see our character moving around. We'll delete the **Main Camera** from the existing scene and learn how to create a new camera, which we will then turn into the **Main Camera** for a scene. Then, we'll work with the **Position**, **Rotation**, and **Field of View** properties so that the player can see much of the house scene from a single, fixed perspective.

In later recipes, we'll learn how to use more dynamic cameras with our third-person characters.

Getting ready

This recipe follows on from the previous one. So, make a copy of that and work on the copy. Alternatively, we have prepared a Unity package, named `BasicScene_completed.unitypackage`, that was completed as per the instructions in the previous recipe. The package can be found in the `11_02` folder.

How to do it...

To enable a fixed **Main Camera** look at our third-person character, simply perform the following steps:

1. Either work from the copy of the previous recipe or create a new 3D project, import the `BasicScene_completed.unitypackage` package, and, finally, add the `ProBuilder` package to your project.
2. Open the **BasicScene** scene.
3. In the **Hierarchy** panel, delete the **Main Camera**. This is a child inside the `ThirdPersonController` GameObject:

Figure 11.4 – Tagging our new camera as the Main Camera

4. Now, create a new **Camera** in the scene, naming it **Main Camera**. In the **Inspector** panel, give this GameObject the preset tag of **Main Camera**.
5. In the **Inspector** panel, set the position of our new **Main Camera** to (`-3`, `7`, `-7`). Additionally, set the rotation to (`35`, `0`, `0`). This positions the camera above and behind the main room, in which the `ThirdPersonController` character is located:

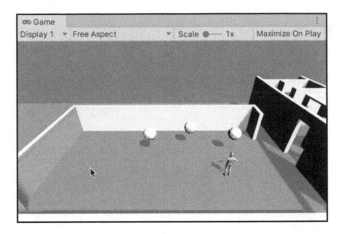

Figure 11.5 – Positioning the fixed Main Camera above and behind the main room, angled slightly downward

6. The default **Field Of View** for a new camera is 60. However, we can change this to a larger value, for example, 120. This is so that our camera can "see" much more of the scene. In the **Inspector** panel, change the **Field of View** to `120`, the **Position** to (`-3, 8, -6`), and the **Rotation** to (`50, 0, 0`). When you run the scene, it should look something similar to the following diagram. Here, we can see our character move between rooms from this bird's-eye view camera setup:

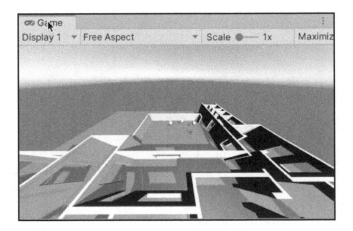

Figure 11.6 – Using a larger Field of View and higher camera for a bird's-eye view

How it works...

We have created a **Main Camera** by simply adding a new camera Game Object to the scene, then tagging this GameObject with the preset tag of **Main Camera**. It is important that the **Main Camera** of the scene is tagged with this special predefined tag.

 Some scripts explicitly search for the **Main Camera** of a scene using the `Camera.main` C# expression. So, we should always have the **Main Camera** in scenes using such scripts.

You can learn more about this in the Unity manual at `https://docs.unity3d.com/ScriptReference/Camera-main.html`.

By changing the **Position** and **Rotation** of this camera, we positioned it so that the player can see most of the main room where the `ThirdPersonController` character starts off. This fixed **Main Camera** might be sufficient if all the action for a scene is inside a single room. However, by making the camera's **Field of View** larger, more of the scene can be seen in the camera's rendering to the **Game** panel. Additionally, by adjusting the **Position** and **Rotation** of the camera, many of the different rooms of the house in this scene can be seen from this single fixed **Main Camera**.

While it might not enough for a finished game, there are times when we might want the user to benefit from an unchanging camera view, perhaps even augmented with a minimap or a top-down view.

Changing how much of the screen a camera renders to

Often, we want different parts of the screen to display different things to the player. For example, the top of the screen might be game statistics, such as scores, lives, or pickups. The main area of the screen might show a first- or third-person view of the gameplay, and we also might have a part of the screen showing additional information, such as radars and minimaps.

In this recipe, we'll create three cameras to add to our player's view:

- The **Main Camera**: This is childed to the third-person-controller character. This shows the main gameplay to the player.

- **Camera 2**: This is the elapsed time display that covers the top 15% of the screen. Note that there is no gameplay going on behind the text.
- **Camera 3**: This is a simple minimap located at the bottom left of the screen, created from a top-down **Orthographic** (non-perspective) camera:

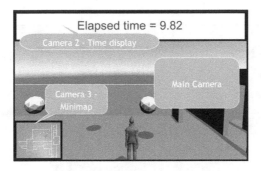

Figure 11.7 – Cameras rendering to different parts of the screen

Getting ready

This recipe builds on the basic scene created in the first recipe of this chapter. So, make a copy of that and work on the copy. Alternatively, we have prepared a Unity package, named `BasicScene_completed.unitypackage`, that was completed in the previous recipe. The package can be found in the `11_02` folder.

How to do it...

To change how much of the screen a camera renders to, simply perform the following steps:

1. Either work from the copy of the first recipe in this chapter or create a new 3D project, import the `BasicScene_completed.unitypackage` package, and, finally, add the **ProBuilder** package to your project.
2. Open the **BasicScene** scene.

3. First, let's reduce the amount of the screen that the **Main Camera** renders to. In the **Hierarchy** panel, select the **Main Camera**, which is a child of the `ThirdPersonController` GameObject. Then, in the **Inspector** panel for the **Camera** component, set the **H** (**Height**) value for the camera's **Viewport Rect** to `0.85`:

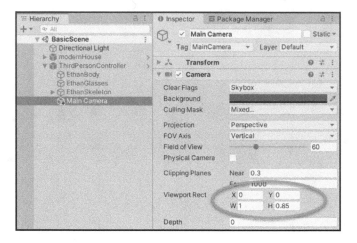

Figure 11.8 – Changing the Viewport Rect of the Main Camera

4. Let's now create a second **Camera** in the scene to display a rectangle in the top 15% of the screen. In the **Hierarchy** panel, create a new **Camera** called `Camera 2 - timer`. You can do this by navigating to **GameObject | Camera** and renaming it. Delete its **AudioListener** component (since we should only have one in a scene, and there is already one in the **Main Camera**).

5. For this new **Camera**, in the **Inspector** panel for the **Camera** component, set its **Y** value to **0.85**. It should have the values of **X** = 0, **W** = 1, **Y** = `0.85`, **H** = 1. This means it will render to the full width of the screen, for the top 15% (from `0.85` to `1.0`).

6. Additionally, for the **Camera** component, set the **Clear Flags** to **Solid Color** and the **Background** to a **White** color. This is so that the black timing text will now stand out within the bright white rectangle (rather than get lost in the **Skybox** gradients).

7. Now, let's create **Canvas** and UI **Text** GameObjects to display our game timings. In the **Hierarchy** panel, create a new **Canvas** GameObject (you can do this by navigating to **UI | Canvas**).

8. With this **Canvas** selected, in the **Inspector** panel for the **Canvas** component, set its **Render Mode** to **Screen Space - Camera**. A **Render Camera** property slot should appear in the **Inspector** panel. For this property, choose Camera 2 - timer:

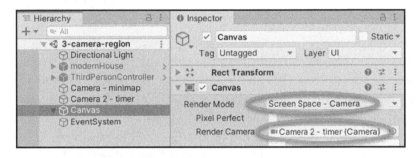

Figure 11.9 – Setting Camera 2 - timer for the Render Camera UI Canvas

9. With the **Canvas** GameObject selected in the **Hierarchy** panel, add a new UI **Text** GameObject (you can do this by navigating to **UI | Text**). Rename this GameObject Text-timer. Increase the font size of its text component to 40, and set the **Horizontal** and **Vertical Overflows** to **Overflow**.

10. In the **Project** panel, create a new C# script, called GameTime.cs, that contains the following code:

```csharp
using UnityEngine;
using UnityEngine.UI;

public class GameTime : MonoBehaviour {
    private Text _textUITime;
    private float _startTime;
    void Awake() {}
        _textUITime = GetComponent<Text>();
        _startTime = Time.time;
    }

    void Update() {
        float elapsedSeconds = (Time.time - _startTime);
        string timeMessage = "Elapsed time = " +
elapsedSeconds.ToString
            ("F");
        _textUITime.text = timeMessage;
    }
}
```

11. Add an instance of our script class to our `Text-timer` UI Text GameObject by dragging the `GameTime.cs` C# script onto the `Text-timer` GameObject in the **Hierarchy** panel.

    Now, we'll add a third **Camera** to the scene; this one will display a simple minimap at the bottom-left of the screen.

12. In the **Hierarchy** panel, create a new **Camera** and name it `Camera 3 - minimap`. Delete its **AudioListener** component (since we should only have one in a scene, and there is already one in the **Main Camera**).

13. In the **Inspector** panel, set the **Camera Depth** to `1`. This is so that the camera will display whatever is being displayed by the **Main Camera**.

14. Make `Camera 3 - minimap` render to the bottom-left corner of the screen. You can do this by setting its **Viewport Rect** values in the **Inspector** panel to **X** = 0, **W** = 0.2, **Y** = 0.0, and **H** = 0.2. This means it will render a small rectangle (that is, 20% of the screen size) at the bottom-left corner of the screen, from (0,0) to (0.2, 0.2).

15. Now, set this camera's **Project** property to **Orthographic** (non-perspective), its **Size** to 14, its **Position** to (-5.5, 20, -4), and its **Rotation** to (90, 0, 0). So, this camera is above the scene and is looking down at its contents (GameObjects):

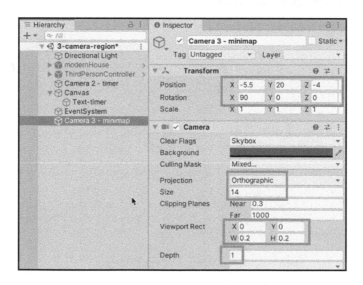

Figure 11.10 – Setting up the properties for Camera 3 - minimap

16. The final thing we'll do is a little trick that will make it easier to see an indication of the player's character on the minimap, that is, a large blue floating **Sphere** above the head of `ThirdPersonController`! In the **Project** panel, create a new blue **Material** asset named `m_blue`.

17. Now, in the **Hierarchy** panel, create a new **Sphere** 3D object primitive (**Create | 3D Object | Sphere**). Drag the `m_blue` **Material** asset from the **Project** panel on the **Sphere** GameObject, and child this **Sphere** GameObject to the `ThirdPersonController` GameObject.

18. Finally, set the **Position** of the **Sphere** to (0, 10, 0) and its **Scale** to (2, 2, 2).

19. When you run the scene, you should now be able to view a neat minimap in the bottom-left corner of the screen and a moving blue circle indicating where in the scene your player's character is located.

How it works...

Setting the **Main Camera**'s **Viewport Rect** height to **0.85** means that the gameplay will only be rendered for 85% of the screen, leaving the top 15% unchanged by the camera.

We had to delete the `AudioListener` components in our extra two cameras. This is because, for the Unity 3D sound system to work effectively, there should only be one listener in a scene (at one location). This is so that the reproduction of the distance from and angle to the listener can be simulated.

By setting our UI Canvas' **Render Mode** to **Screen Space - Camera** and its **Render Camera** to **Camera 2 - timer**, our UI Text is automatically centered in the camera's view, and so, our timing text appears clearly displayed in the top 15% of the screen. The `GameTime.cs` C# script class gets a reference to the UI Text component of the GameObject that the script has been added to (`_textUITime`). It records the time the scene begins (in the `_startTime` variable), and each frame subtracts this from the current time, giving an elapsed time. This value is formatted to one decimal place, and a string message is displayed by updating the value in the `_textUITime` variable's `text` property.

The default **Depth** value for a camera is **0**. Cameras with larger depth values are displayed *closer* to the viewer, so a camera with **Depth** = 1 will be seen in front of anything displayed by a camera with **Depth** = 0. So, by setting the **Depth** of Camera 3 - minimap to 1, we ensured that this minimap rendering will appear in front of whatever the **Main Camera** (**Depth = 0**) is rendering.

We see a blue **circle** showing the location of the ThirdPersonController. This is because the large blue **Sphere** is first seen by this top-down camera since it's above (that is, a higher **Y** value than) the player's character. Because the sphere is **childed** to the ThirdPersonController, each time the player's character moves, so does the sphere floating above its head.

There's more...

There are some details that you don't want to miss.

Another tweak we can make to our simple minimap is for an **arrow** rather than a **circle** to indicate the location of our player's character. This is so that we can view the direction that the player is facing in the minimap. In some parts of some games, players do much of their gameplay by simply looking at the minimap for things such as solving mazes and avoiding enemies.

We can create an arrow effect by using three scaled cubes. Delete the blue sphere that is a child of the ThirdPersonController. Create three blue cubes, and child them to the ThirdPersonController. Set the properties of the three cubes as follows:

- Cube 1: **Position** (0, 10, -1.2), **Rotation** (0, 0, 0), and **Scale** (0.3, 1, 3)
- Cube 2: **Position** (-0.5, 10, -0.24), **Rotation** (0, 45, 0), and **Scale** (0.3, 1, 1.5)
- Cube 2: **Position** (0.44, 10, -0.2), **Rotation** (0, -45, 0), and **Scale** (0.3, 1, 1.5)

Figure 11.11 – The giant floating "arrow" above the ThirdPersonController

Using Render Textures to send camera output to places other than the screen

Cameras do not have to output directly to the screen all the time. Different effects can be achieved by having the cameras send their output to a Render Texture asset file. In the scene, 3D objects can be linked to a Render Texture asset file, and so the output of a camera can be directed to 3D objects such as **Planes** and **Cubes**.

In this recipe, first, we'll duplicate the over-the-shoulder **Main Camera** child of the ThirdPersonController, and send the output of this duplicate camera (via a RenderTexture asset file) to a plane on one of the house walls. Then, we'll add a different camera facing out from the wall. This is so that our plane will act just like a mirror, rather than duplicating the over-the-shoulder **Main Camera**:

Figure 11.12 – A copy of Main Camera rendering to Render Texture, which is being displayed on a Plane in the scene

Getting ready

This recipe builds on the basic scene created in the first recipe of this chapter. So make a copy of that recipe, and work on the copy. Alternatively, we have prepared a Unity package, named BasicScene_completed.unitypackage, that was completed in the previous recipe. The package can be found in the 11_02 folder.

How to do it...

To send camera output to places other than the screens, simply perform the following steps:

1. Either work from the copy of the first recipe in this chapter or create a new 3D project, import the `BasicScene_completed.unitypackage` package, and, finally, add the `ProBuilder` package to your project.

2. Open the **BasicScene** scene.

   All the work of this recipe requires a special `RenderTexture` asset file to be created, so let's do that next.

3. In the **Project** panel, create a new `RenderTexture` file and rename it `MyRenderTexture` (**Create | Render Texture**).

4. Duplicate the **Main Camera** child inside the `ThirdPersonController` GameObject, naming the copy `Main Camera CLONE`. Delete its `AudioListener` component (since we should only have one in a scene, and there is already one in the **Main Camera**).

5. With `Main Camera CLONE` selected in the **Hierarchy** panel, drag the `MyRenderTexture` asset file from the **Project** panel to the **Target Texture** property slot of the **Camera** component inside the **Inspector** panel:

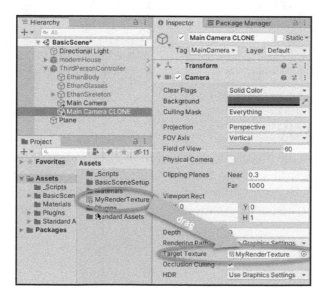

Figure 11.13 – Sending the Main Camera CLONE output to the MyRenderTexture asset file

Now our cloned camera is sending its output to `MyRenderTexture`; we need to create a 3D object to display this output.

6. Add a new 3D **Plane** to the scene. Set its **Position** to (-0.4, 1, 4.6), its **Rotation** to (-270, -90, 90), and its **Scale** to (0.1, 0.2, 0.18). It should now be positioned like a mirror on the wall of the house facing the player's character when the game runs.

7. Now we can assign the `MyRenderTexture` file to be the **Texture** to be displayed on the **Plane**. Select the plane in the **Hierarchy** panel, and drag the `MyRenderTexture` asset file from the **Project** panel to **Element 0** of the **Materials** array of the **Mesh Renderer** component inside the **Inspector** panel:

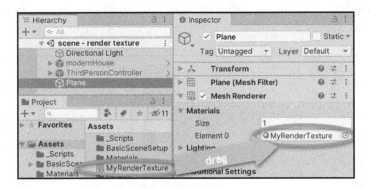

Figure 11.14 – Texturing the 3D Plane with the MyRenderTexture asset file

8. Run the scene. As your character approaches the **Plane** on the wall, you should also be able to view a rendering of the screen displayed in the plane.

9. Now, let's get a better mirror effect. Delete the `Main Camera CLONE` inside the `ThirdPersonController` GameObject.

10. Create a new camera in the scene, naming it `Camera 2 - mirror`. Delete its `AudioListener` component (since we should only have one in a scene, and there is already one in the **Main Camera**).

11. Just as we did with the cloned camera, we want this camera to send its output to our `MyRenderTexture` asset file. With `Main Camera 2 - mirror` selected in the **Hierarchy** panel, drag the `MyRenderTexture` asset file from the **Project** panel into the **Target Texture** property slot of the **Camera** component inside the **Inspector** panel.

12. Now, all we have to do is locate the new camera to face out from where our plane is located. Set its **Position** to (-0.4, 1, 4.6), its **Rotation** to (0, 180, 0), and its **Scale** to (1, 1, 1). **Main Camera 2 - mirror** should now be positioned so that it is facing the player's character when the game runs.

13. Let's also add a spotlight, so we can see the player's character when it is close to the mirror. Add a new **Spot Light** to the scene (**Create | Light | Spotlight**).

14. In the **Inspector** panel, set the properties of the spotlight as follows: its **Position** to (0.06, 1.8, 4.6), its **Rotation** to (155, 0, 0), its **Rand** to 100, and its **Spot Angle** to 65.

15. Run the scene. Now, when your character gets close to the plane, it works like a mirror – except that things are not reversed left-to-right (please refer to the *There's more...* section to learn how to flip the image to be like a real-world mirror):

Figure 11.15 – Our simulated mirror using a Render Texture

How it works...

A Render Texture asset file is a special asset file that can store images sent from cameras. Cameras usually render (that is, send their images) to all or part of the screen. However, as we've seen in this recipe, interesting effects are possible when we send a camera output to a Render Texture and then have a 3D object in our scene that displays the current image in the Render Texture asset file.

In this recipe, we've simulated a kind of mirror effect. Another common use of cameras and `Render Texture` asset files are simulated closed-circuit TVs, where a **Cube** (or a more detailed model of a TV monitor) can display what is being viewed in some other part of the scene by a camera. So, you might have a game where a player is in a control room, changing between which cameras they are looking at, to find out the location of enemies or teammates.

There's more...

There are some details that you don't want to miss.

Inverting our mirror camera horizontally

Let's fix that mirror effect. We need to flip the image rendered by **Camera 2 - mirror** for the *x* axis (horizontally). We can do that by writing a C# script class that multiplies the camera's project matrix by a Vector3 of (**-1, 1, 1**). Note that the first -1 means the *x* values are flipped horizontally:

Figure 11.16 – Our mirror effect working after a horizontal flip

Write the following in a new C# script class, called `FlipCamera.cs`. Then, add an instance as a component to **Camera 2 - mirror**:

```
using UnityEngine;

public class FlipCamera : MonoBehaviour
```

```
    {
        private Camera _camera;

        void Awake() {
            _camera = GetComponent<Camera>();
        }
        void OnPreCull () {
            _camera.ResetWorldToCameraMatrix ();
            _camera.ResetProjectionMatrix ();
            _camera.projectionMatrix = _camera.projectionMatrix *
Matrix4x4.Scale(new
                Vector3 (-1, 1, 1));
        }
        void OnPreRender () {
            GL.invertCulling = true;
        }
        void OnPostRender () {
            GL.invertCulling = false;
        }
    }
```

This code was adapted from the following script in Unity Wiki:

- `http://wiki.unity3d.com/index.php?title=InvertCamera`

A simple snapshot of a scene at runtime

By the way, if you simply want to be able to take a snapshot of the game screen during the game as a PNG file, this is something Unity has made really easy. Create a script class such as the following, and add an instance as a component to any GameObject (or create a new Empty GameObject to hold the script instance):

```
using UnityEngine;
using System;

public class Snapshot : MonoBehaviour {
    void Update() {
        if (Input.GetKeyUp(KeyCode.P)) {
            print("taking snapshot");
            string timeStamp = DateTime.Now.ToString("HH_mm_ss");
            ScreenCapture.CaptureScreenshot("snapshot_" + timeStamp +
".png");
        }
    }
}
```

Of course, you can change which `KeyCode` and what filename your image is saved as by editing the script. The PNG snapshot file will be created outside your `Assets` folder where your Unity project is stored:

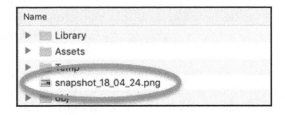

Figure 11.17 – A PNG snapshot image taken while playing the game

Working with Unity's multipurpose camera rig

Unity provides some **Camera** rigs, which can make setting up scenes much faster and help you to test out ideas. In this recipe, you'll use a **Third-Person Character** and the multipurpose camera rig from the default Unity asset packages to quickly create a scene with a camera that automatically follows a character as it moves, smoothing the rotation behind the character as the character changes direction:

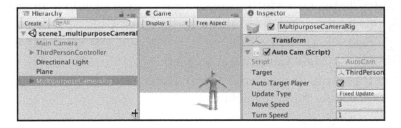

Figure 11.18 – The MultipurposeCameraRig GameObject from Unity's Standard Assets

How to do it...

To work with Unity's multipurpose camera rig, simply perform the following steps:

1. Create a new Unity 3D scene.

2. Import the **Standard Assets** asset package. You can do this by navigating to **Asset Store | Search Online search for Standard Assets | Open in Unity | Import.**

3. You should now have a `Standard Assets` folder in your **Project** panel that contains the `Cameras` and `Characters` folders (and possibly some others, such as `CrossPlatformInput`, `Editor`, and more).

 At the time of writing, the **Standard Assets** package has not been updated for Unity 2020.1. When using it in recipes, two errors will appear, and these need to be resolved before playing your recipe. The solution can be found in the *Creating the basic scene for this chapter* recipe. Alternatively, we have also prepared a Unity package, named `StandardAssets_fixedFor2020.unitypackage`, that contains all of the resources for this recipe. The package can be found in the `11_01` folder.

4. Create a 3D **Plane** inside your scene.

5. Add an instance of the **ThirdPersonController** prefab to your scene. You can do this by dragging the **ThirdPersonController** prefab from the `Standard Assets | Characters | ThirdPersonController | Prefabs` folder into the scene.

6. With the `ThirdPersonController` GameObject selected in the **Hierarchy** panel, tag this GameObject with the **Player** tag inside the **Inspector** panel.

7. Add a clone of the **MultipurposeCameraRig** prefab to your scene. You can do this by dragging the **MultipurposeCameraRig** prefab from the `Standard Assets | Cameras | Prefabs` folder into the scene.

8. Disable the **Main Camera** GameObject.

9. Run the scene. As you move the character around the scene, the **Camera** should follow smoothly behind.

How it works...

You added a **ThirdPersonController** to the scene and gave it a **Player** tag. Additionally, you added a **MultipurposeCameraRig** to the **Scene.** The code attached to the camera rig automatically looks for a target GameObject that is tagged **Player** and positions itself to follow from above and behind this GameObject.

You can adjust the speed at which the camera follows and turns by changing the public properties for the **MultipurposeCameraRig** inside its **Inspector** component, **Auto Cam (Script)**.

Using Cinemachine ClearShot to switch cameras to keep the player in shot

Cinemachine is a suite of tools that sets up a suite of cameras that improves player capture for dynamic view or improved cutscenes. This recipe implements Cinemachine ClearShot to switch cameras to keep the player within shot. We'll do this by specifying the spine of the human character, which should be kept in the center of the shot as much as possible, and the AI system will decide which camera to select that meets these criteria:

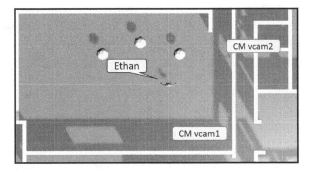

Figure 11.19 – An example of the recipe with the Cinemachine ClearShot component

Getting ready

This recipe builds on the basic scene created in the first recipe of this chapter. So, make a copy of that, and work on the copy. Alternatively, we have prepared a Unity package, named `BasicScene_completed.unitypackage`, that was completed in the previous recipe. The package can be found in the `11_02` folder.

How to do it...

To use **Cinemachine ClearShot** to switch cameras to keep the player in the shot, simply perform the following steps:

1. Either work from the copy of the first recipe in this chapter or create a new 3D project, import the `BasicScene_completed.unitypackage` package, and, finally, add the `ProBuilder` package to your project.
2. Open the scene provided, containing **modernHouse** and **Ethan** – the **ThirdPersonController** from the **Standard Asset** package.
3. Un-child the **Main Camera** from **Ethan.** This is because we need this camera free for **Cinemachine** to take control of it.
4. Install the **Cinemachine** package using the Unity Package Manager (to get the most up-to-date version).

> Important note: If you are upgrading from the Asset Store version of Cinemachine, delete the Cinemachine asset from your project BEFORE installing the version from the Package Manager.

5. Add a **Cinemachine ClearShot** camera GameObject to the scene (navigate to **Cinemachine I Create ClearShot Camera**). You should see a new GameObject in the **Hierarchy** panel named `CM Clearshot 1`. Set the position of this new GameObject to $(0,0,0)$.
6. The `CM Clearshot 1` GameObject should have a child GameObject: a Cinemachine virtual camera called **CM vcam 1**. Set the **Position** of this virtual camera, **CM vcam 1**, to $(3, 2, -3)$.
7. You will also see that a Cinemachine **Brain** component has been added to the **Main Camera**, and in the **Hierarchy** panel, you'll see the Cinemachine **Brain** icon next to the **Main Camera** name (the half-gray cog and the half-red camera):

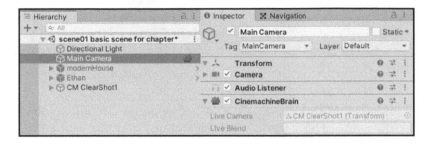

Figure 11.20 – The Main Camera with Cinemachine Brain added

8. Locate the `mixamorig:neck` GameObject in the **Hierarchy** panel inside the **Ethan** character. We'll use this part of **Ethan** to be the part that our **Cinemachine** cameras will use to orient toward.

9. Select `CM Clearshot 1`, and in the **Inspector** panel, populate the **Look At** property of the **Cinemachine ClearShot** component with a reference to the `EthanSpine1` GameObject (drag the GameObject from **Hierarchy** into the **Look At** property inside the **Inspector** panel):

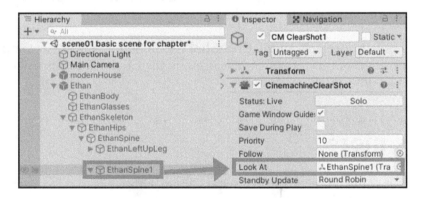

Figure 11.21 – Drag the EthanSpine1 GamObject inside the Look At property

10. Run the scene. As you move **Ethan** around the scene, the Main Camera (which is controlled by **Cinemachine Brain**) should rotate to always look at the character. However, sometimes, a wall obscures the view.

11. Create a second child virtual camera by selecting `CM Clearshot 1` in the **Hierarchy** panel, and then in the **Inspector** panel, click on the plus (**+**) button for the **Virtual Camera Children** property of the Cinemachine **Clear Shot** component. You should be able to see that a new child virtual camera, named `CM vcam 2`, has been created. Set the **Position** of `CM vcam 2` to (`5.5, 2.25, 2.5`).

12. Run the scene. Initially, CM vcam 1 has the best shot, and so this camera's position will be used to direct the **Main Camera**. However, if you move **Ethan** along the corridor toward CM vcam 2, **Cinemachine** will then switch control to CM vcam 2.

If you find that the CM vcam 2 is displaying, initially, you can set the priority by selecting **CM Clearshot 1** and increasing the priority of CM vcam 1.

How it works...

A Cinemachine **Brain** component was added to the scene. This takes control of the **Main Camera** and uses properties of one or more **Virtual Cinemachine** cameras to decide what properties to apply to the **Main Camera**. You added a **Cinemachine ClearShot** GameObject, whose purpose is to tell the **Cinemachine Brain** which of its **Virtual Camera** children has the best shot.

You set the **Look At** property of the **ClearShot** component to the spine component of **Ethan**. The position of this GameObject is used by the **ClearShot** component to rank each virtual camera's quality of the shot.

There's more...

We've only just touched the surface of what **Cinemachine** has to offer. Here are some suggestions regarding how to learn more.

Unity Cinemachine tutorials

In the *Learn* section of the Unity website, you'll find many video tutorials introducing the different animation features of Unity. There is a special category for **Cinemachine** tutorials, which provide a great overview of the features and uses of **Cinemachine**. You can access this at https://unity3d.com/learn/tutorials/s/animation.

Will Goldstone's ClearShot tutorial

This recipe was inspired by Will Goldstone's **ClearShot** tutorial. It is available on YouTube at `https://www.youtube.com/watch?v=kLcdrDljakA`.

Adam Myhill's Cinemachine blog posts

Adam Myhill's blog posts (he is the creator of **Cinemachine**) have lots of information and video links about many different Cinemachine features. You can access the posts at `https://blogs.unity3d.com/2017/08/25/community-stories-cinemachine-and-timeline/`.

Reading the installed Cinemachine documentation

Later versions of **Cinemachine (2.4+)** have release notes installed with the package. Display the **Cinemachine About** panel (navigate to **Cinemachine | About**), then view the release notes:

Figure 11.22 – The built-in About page of the Cinemachine suite of tools

You can also find the documentation online
at `https://docs.unity3d.com/Packages/com.unity.cinemachine@2.1/manual/index.html`.

Cinemachine and Timeline

A popular use of Cinemachine is in conjunction with Timeline for creating cutscenes and game trailers. The following resources will be useful when you are developing your elements:

- Unity Timeline documentation: `https://docs.unity3d.com/Packages/com.unity.timeline@1.5/manual/tl_about.html`
- Uriel Carrillo's Unity Cinemachine and Timeline tutorial: `https://medium.com/@carrillouriel/unity-cinemachine-timeline-tutorial-348576861a8e`
- CG Auro's CutScene in Unity 3D video can be found at `https://www.youtube.com/watch?v=w6lc8svzBms`. This works well with the *Importing third-party 3D models and animations from Mixamo* recipe of *Chapter 7, Characters, GameKits, and Starter Assests*.

Letting the player switch to a Cinemachine FreeLook camera

It's always good to give players choices and control over their gaming experience. In this recipe, we'll set up a mouse-controllable **Cinemachine FreeLook** camera and let the player switch to it.

Getting ready

This recipe adds to the previous one. So, make a copy of that project folder, and do your work for this recipe using that copy.

How to do it...

To explore **Cinemachine FreeLook**, perform the following steps:

1. Ensure that the **Default Blend** property of the **Cinemachine Brain** component, inside the **Main Camera**, is set to **Ease In Out**. This means we'll have a smooth transition when switching between cameras.

2. Add a **Cinemachine FreeLook** camera GameObject to the scene (you can do this by navigating to **Cinemachine | Create FreeLook Camera**). You should be able to view a new GameObject in the **Hierarchy** panel, named `CM FreeLook 1`. Set the **Priority** property of the **Cinemachine Free Look** component to 0.

3. Locate the `EthanSpine1` GameObject in the **Hierarchy** panel inside **Ethan**. We'll use this part of the **Ethan** character to be the part that our **Cinemachine** cameras use to orient toward and follow at a steady distance.

4. Select **CM FreeLook 1**. Then, in the **Inspector** panel, populate the **Look At** and **Follow** properties of the **Cinemachine Free Look (Script)** component with a reference to the `EthanSpine1` GameObject (drag the GameObject from **Hierarchy** to the properties inside the **Inspector** panel):

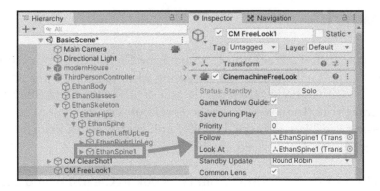

Figure 11.23 – Settings for the Cinemachine FreeLook1 camera

5. Create a new `FreeLookSwitcher.cs` C# script class that contains the following code. Then, add an instance object of `FreeLookSwitcher` as a component for the `CM FreeLook 1` GameObject:

```
using UnityEngine;
using Cinemachine;
```

```
public class FreeLookSwitcher : MonoBehaviour {
    private CinemachineFreeLook cinemachineFreeLook;

    private void Start() {
        cinemachineFreeLook =
GetComponent<CinemachineFreeLook>();
    }

    void Update() {
        if (Input.GetKeyDown("1"))
            cinemachineFreeLook.Priority = 99;

        if (Input.GetKeyDown("2"))
            cinemachineFreeLook.Priority = 0;
    }
}
```

6. Run the scene. When moving around the maze, initially, the **Cinemachine ClearShot** cameras will be chosen by the **Cinemachine Brain**. However, pressing the *1* key will make it switch to the **FreeLook** camera following the player's character. Pressing *2* will switch it back to the **ClearShot** cameras.

How it works...

In this recipe, you added a **FreeLook Cinemachine** GameObject, but with a priority of zero. So, initially, it will be ignored. When the *1* key is pressed, the script increases the **Priority** to 99 (much higher than the default of 10 for the **ClearShot** cameras), so then the **Cinemachine Brain** will make the **FreeLook** virtual camera control the **Main Camera**. Pressing the *2* key reduces the **FreeLook** component's **Priority** back to 0. So, the **ClearShot** cameras will be used again.

There should be a smooth transition from **FreeLook** to **ClearShot** and back again since you set the **Default Blend** property of the **Cinemachine Brain** component in the **Main Camera** to **Ease In Out**.

Creating a project with the URP

The URP is a scriptable render pipeline that replaces Unity's built-in Render Pipeline. URP provides workflows that let you quickly and easily create optimized graphics that improve the visual effect of your project. In this recipe, we'll use the basic scene created in the first recipe to add **Film Grain** as a postprocessing effect to our scene. The **Film Grain** effect simulates the random (grainy!) texture of a photographic film:

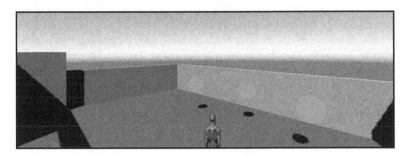

Figure 11.24 – An example of the recipe with the Film Grain visual effect applied

Getting ready

This recipe builds on the basic scene created in the first recipe of this chapter. So, make a copy of that and work on the copy. Alternatively, we have prepared a Unity package, named `BasicScene_completed.unitypackage`, that was completed in the previous recipe. The package can be found in the `11_02` folder.

How to do it...

Perform the following steps:

1. Either work from the copy of the first recipe in this chapter or create a new 3D project, import the `BasicScene_completed.unitypackage` package, and add the **ProBuilder** package to your project.

2. Install the URP from the Package Manager. To do this, navigate to **Package Manager | All Packages | Universal RP**, and make sure it is installed and up to date:

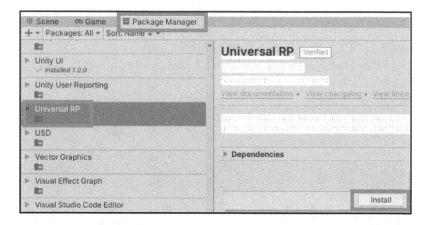

Figure 11.25 – Settings for installing the URP

3. Create a URP asset. To do this, right-click on the **Project** window. Select the menu by navigating to **Create | Rendering | Universal Render Pipeline | Pipeline Asset**. Name the `PostProcessing` asset.

4. Open the **Project Settings** panel by navigating to **Edit | Project settings**. For the **Graphics** tab, select the `PostProcessing` rendering asset we just created:

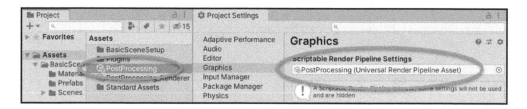

Figure 11.26 – Setting the project to use our PostProcessing asset

5. The objects in the scene might have changed color to pink. So, next, we will upgrade the project materials to URP materials. Navigate to **Edit | Render Pipeline | Universal Render Pipeline | Upgrade Project Materials to UniversalRP Materials**.

Tip: If you are using Probuilder, just as we did in the creation of the `modernHouse` prefab, the wall might still be pink. Create a new material menu by navigating to **Assets | Create | Material**. Rename the material as `white`, and drag it onto the walls of the GameObject `modernHouse.prefab` in the **Project** panel.

6. Enable postprocessing on the camera. With the **Main Camera** selected in the **Hierarchy** panel, check the **Post Processing** option for the **Camera** component inside the **Inspector** panel.

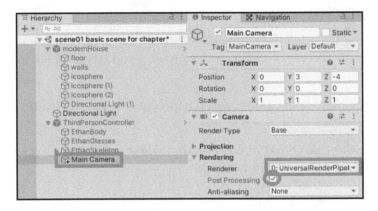

Figure 11.27 – Enabling postprocessing for the camera component of the Main Camera

7. Create an empty **GameObject** and name it `Post Processing`.
8. We will now add a postprocessing **Volume** component to this GameObject. Ensure `Post Processing` is selected in the **Hierarchy** panel. Then, in the **Inspector** panel, click on **Add Component** and search for **Volume**.
9. Next, create a postprocessing profile by clicking on **New**:

Figure 11.28 – Adding a new postprocessing profile

10. With `Post Processing` selected inside the **Inspector** panel, add an override by clicking on **Add Override**. Then, click on `Post Processing` and select an override.

11. Select **Film Grain** and set the **type** to `Medium 4`, the **Intensity** to `0.7`, and the **response** to `0.4`.

12. Run the game; you should be able to view a grain effect across the gameplay screen.

How it works...

In this recipe, you installed the URP package into your project, created a `Post Processing` asset, and then set the render pipeline to **Universal RP** in the **Project Settings**.

Additionally, the Main Camera enabled postprocessing visual effects through its **Volume** component.

The `Post Processing` GameObject contains a **Volume** profile component with the **PostProcessing | Film Grain** override.

The rendering of the **Main Camera** is affected by the **Film Grain** volume, and so we see the film grain effect globally applied to everything that is rendered by the **Main Camera** to the screen.

Adding a vignette effect

In the previous recipe, we set up a volumetric postprocessing effect for a scene on a **Global** basis, for example, the whole scene. This recipe will build on the previous one by creating a second postprocessing effect within a **Local** area of a scene. In this recipe, we will apply a visual *vignette*:

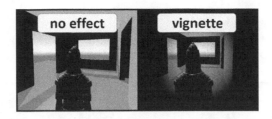

Figure 11.29 – An example of the recipe demonstrating the effect of adding a vignette

 Vignetting refers to the darkening of image corners when compared to the center. In photography, vignetting can be caused by optics. In Unity, you can use URP postprocessing to draw the viewer's eye away from the distractions in the corner and, instead, toward the center of the image. In games, vignetting can be used to add suspense or atmosphere to a scene.

Getting ready

This recipe builds on the previous recipe. So, make a copy of that project folder, and do your work for this recipe using that copy.

How to do it...

To add a vignette effect, perform the following steps:

1. Work with your copy of the project for the previous recipe.
2. Create an empty GameObject by navigating to **GameObject | Create Empty**. Name it `PostProcessingHall`, set the **Position** to `(6, 2, -11)`, and attach a postprocessing volume to it.
3. With **PostProcessingHall** selected in the **Hierarchy** panel, click on **Add Component** and search for **Volume**.
4. Next, create a **PostProcessing** profile by clicking on **New**.
5. With **PostProcessingHall** selected in the **Inspector** panel, add an override by clicking on **Add Override**. Then, click on **PostProcessing**, and select an override.

6. Select **Vignette** and set the **Color** to
black, **Intensity** to 1, **Smoothness** to 0.6, and then select **Rounded**. You
should be able to view a darkening effect around the edges of the scene:

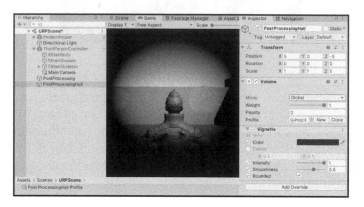

Figure 11.30 – Settings for the postprocessing volume

7. Now, we need this to only apply to the position within the scene that we
select. With **PostProcessingHall** selected, switch **Global** to **Local** and click
on **Add Collider | box.**

8. Set the center of the Box Collider to (0, 0, 0) and the size to (3.5, 4,
9). Then, check the **Is Trigger** option:

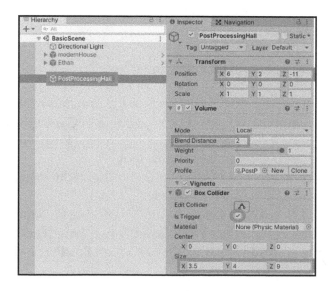

Figure 11.31 – Setting the Box Collider to trigger the vignette effect

9. Set **Blended Distance** to 2.

10. Adjust the **Main Camera Position** to `(0, 1.5, -1)`. The Main Camera is a child of the `ThirdPersonController` GameObject.

11. Run the game. Move the player through the hall and room using the **Box Collider**, and you should be able to view a vignette effect across the gameplay screen.

How it works...

In this recipe, similar to creating the postprocessing volume in both the URP and HDRP, we create an additional URP asset with a unique postprocessing profile, called **PostProcessingHall**.

Then, we added a volumetric effect called a vignette that creates the darker edges around the scene.

In the previous example, the postprocessing was set to **global**, so the effects were added to the whole scene. In this recipe, we only want to activate the effect when the character enters a specific location in the scenes. So, we created a **Box Collider** that triggers the vignette effect when the player's character enters the collider.

There's more...

You can find out more about vignettes via the following references:

- `https://docs.unity3d.com/Packages/com.unity.render-pipelines.high-definition@7.3/manual/Post-Processing-Vignette.html`

- `https://www.youtube.com/watch?v=cuvx9tWGlHc`

Creating an HDRP project with an HDRI skybox

HDRI is a method of representing images with a high range of luminosity (human-perceived color brightnesses). In this recipe, we'll use a Creative Commons-licensed HDRI image to create a high-quality skybox in an HDRP project:

Figure 11.32 – The rocky landscape we see from the Koppenheim HRDI skybox

We'd like to thank Geg Zaal (`http://gregzaal.com/`) for publishing the Kloppenheim 06 HDRI assets under the CCO license at HDRI Haven.

Getting ready

For this recipe, we have prepared the image that you need in a folder, named `HDRI_Kloppenheim06`, inside the `11_08` folder.

How to do it...

To create an HDRP project with an HDRI skybox, perform the following steps:

1. Create a new **HDRP** project.

Note: You might be asked about upgrading materials for the HDRP. If so, agree and wait for the project to finish initializing.

2. Open the **Package Manager** (you can do this by navigating to **Window | Package Manager**), and ensure that you have the most up-to-date version of the **HDRP** package.

3. In the **Project** panel, create a new folder called HDRI_sky.

4. In this new folder, create a new scene named **HDRI sky scene**.

5. Import the provided HDRI_ Kloppenheim06 folder. Then, in the **Project** panel, select the kloppenheim_06_4k asset file inside that folder.

6. In the **Inspector** panel, change the **Texture Shape** to **Cube**, the **Max Size** to **4096**, and then click on the **Apply** button. Depending on the speed of your computer, it might take a few seconds for these properties to be applied to the asset file:

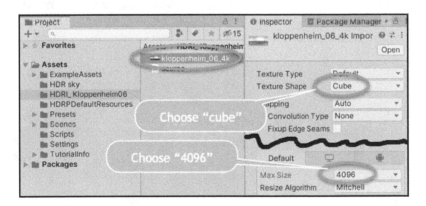

Figure 11.33 – Setting Texture Shape to Cube and Max Size to 4096

7. In the **Project** panel, create a new **Volume Profile** asset file named sky profile. In the **Inspector** panel, add an **HDRI Sky override**. You can do this by clicking on **Override**, selecting **Sky**, and then selecting **HDRI Sky**.

8. Select the `sky profile` asset file. Then, in the **Inspector** panel, check the **Hdri Sky** property. Finally, drag this property slot into the `kloppenheim_06_4k` asset file:

Figure 11.34 – Setting up the sky profile asset properties

9. Select the **Main Camera** in the **Hierarchy** panel.

10. In the **Inspector** panel, add a new **Volume** component to the **Main Camera** by clicking on the **Add Component** button and selecting the **Volume** component. Drag the `sky profile` asset file from the **Project** panel into the **Profile** property of this new **Volume** component:

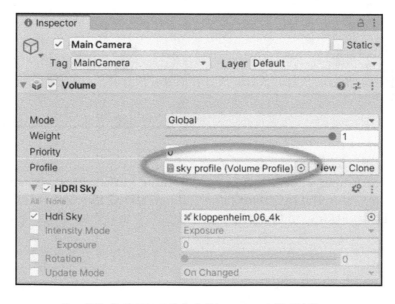

Figure 11.35 – Creating a new profile for the Volume component of the Main Camera

11. Run the game. You should be able to see a view of some rocks in a green grass landscape.
12. If you want to really get a feeling of being in this landscape, drag the `SimpleCameraController` script from the `Scripts` folder onto the **Main Camera**. You can now use the right mouse button to rotate the view to look all around the HDRI landscape image.

How it works...

In an **HDRP** project, you created a new empty scene. You imported an HDRI image asset and set it to be a **CubeMap**. Then, you created a **Volume Profile** set with an **HDRI Sky** override, and set it to your HDRI image asset.

Additionally, you added a **Volume** component to the **Main Camera** GameObject, this set its **Volume Profile** to your `HDRI Sky` asset file.

All of the **Main Camera** renderings are now affected by this **Volume** and are displayed in the HDRI image as a skybox.

Further reading

Projects made using URP are not compatible with the HDRP or the built-in render pipeline. Before you start development, you must decide which render pipeline you want to use in your project. The Unity manual provides some information on how to choose a render pipeline:

- `https://docs.unity3d.com/Manual/render-pipelines.html`

A complete list of postprocessing volume effects can be found here:

- `https://docs.unity3d.com/Packages/com.unity.render-pipelines.universal@7.1/manual/EffectList.html`

You can learn more about the URP from the Unity manual and video:

- `https://docs.unity3d.com/Packages/com.unity.render-pipelines.universal@9.0/manual/index.html`
- `https://www.youtube.com/watch?v=m6YqTrwjpP0`

YouTube also has some useful tutorials, as follows:

- `https://blogs.unity3d.com/2020/08/26/learn-how-to-bring-your-game-graphics-to-life/`
- `https://youtu.be/oXNy9mszKxw`
- `https://youtu.be/HqaQJfuK_u8`

Another Unity feature is **Camera Stacking**. This allows you to layer the output of multiple cameras and create a single combined output. Unity Technologies have published a short video tutorial about camera stacking, which you can view here:

- `https://youtu.be/OmCjPctKkjw`

12
Shader Graphs and Video Players

Two powerful features of Unity are the Video Player API and the Shader Graph tool. Between them, they offer easier and more configurable ways to work with visual content in games. For example, they help with loading and playing videos on different visible objects, and they also provide a comprehensive way for non-shader programmers to construct sophisticated shader transformations using a visual graphing approach. This chapter explores Unity Shader Graphs and Video Player components.

The Shader Graph tool

Shader Graph is a tool that allows us to visually build shaders by creating and connecting the inputs and output of nodes.

Some great Shader Graph features include the following:

- An instant, visual preview of each node in the graph is provided so that you can see how different nodes are contributing to the final Master output node.
- Properties can be publicly exposed in the graph (via the Blackboard) so that they become customizable values in the **Inspector** window for the material using the Shader Graph.
- Publicly exposed properties can also be accessed and changed via scripts.

- The output of one node can become one of the inputs to another node, so a sophisticated shader can be created from many combined, simple component nodes:

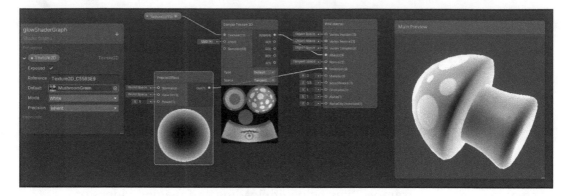

Figure 12.1 – Illustration of how Shader Graphs are composed

As shown in the preceding screenshot, Shader Graphs are composed of a graph of connected nodes, where the output of one node becomes the input of another node. Node input/outputs can be numeric values, Textures, noise, Boolean `true`/`false` values, colors, and other Shader Graph files are created in the **Project** window and can be selected as a graph shader in the **Shader** property of a **Material** component.

Unity uses a **physically based rendering** (PBR) approach that attempts to render images that model the flow of light in the real world. This is achieved by using Shader Graph and several recipes will be presented in this chapter to introduce some of the powerful features of Shader Graph and its workflow.

Playing videos with the Video Player API

Playing videos is as simple as manually adding a `VideoPlayer` component in the **Inspector** window to a GameObject at design time and associating a `VideoClip` asset file from the **Project** window, or providing the URL of an online resource.

Videos can be played on the camera's far plane (appearing behind the scene content) or near plane (appearing in front of content – often with semi-transparency). Video content can also be directed to a `RenderTexture` asset, which can then be displayed on a 2D or 3D object in the scene, via a **Material** component. The internal texture that's used by a `VideoPlayer` can also be mapped to a texture on screen – such as a UI RawImage.

Scripting can be used to manage video playback for single videos and arrays (sequence) of video clips. Several recipes will be presented in this chapter to introduce these different ways of working with `VideoPlayer`.

In this chapter, we will cover the following recipes:

- Playing videos by manually adding a `VideoPlayer` component to a GameObject
- Using scripting to control video playback on scene textures
- Ensuring a movie is prepared before playing it
- Outputting video playback to a RenderTexture
- Using scripting to play a sequence of videos back to back
- Creating and using a simple Shader Graph
- Using a Shader Graph to create a color glow effect
- Toggling a Shader Graph color glow effect through C# code

Technical requirements

For this chapter, you will need Unity 2021.1 or later, plus one of the following:

- Microsoft Windows 10 (64-bit)/GPU: DX10, DX11, and DX12-capable
- macOS Sierra 10.12.6+/GPU Metal-capable Intel or AMD
- Linux Ubuntu 16.04, Ubuntu 18.04, and CentOS 7/GPU: OpenGL 3.2+ or Vulkan-capable, Nvidia or AMD

For each chapter, there is a folder that contains the asset files you will need in this book's GitHub repository at `https://github.com/PacktPublishing/Unity-2021-Cookbook-Fourth-Edition`.

Playing videos by manually adding a VideoPlayer component to a GameObject

TV sets, projectors, monitors... If you want complex animated materials in your level, you can play video files as texture maps. In this recipe, we will learn how to add and use `VideoPlayer` components to the `Main Camera` GameObject. By default, `Main Camera` fills the entire visible game window and has a renderer component, making it an ideal location for adding a `VideoPlayer` component when we want the video images to fill the whole screen.

Getting ready

If you need a video file so that you can follow this recipe, please use the `54321TestVideo.mov` file included in the `12_01` folder.

How to do it...

To place videos manually with a `VideoPlayer` component, follow these steps:

1. Create a new **Unity 3D project**.
2. Import the provided `54321TestVideo.mov` file.
3. Add a 3D Cube to the scene by going to **GameObject | 3D Object | Cube**.
4. Select the `Main Camera` GameObject and, in the **Inspector** window, add a `VideoPlayer` component by clicking **Add Component** and choosing **Video | Video Player**. Unity will have noticed that we are adding the `VideoPlayer` component to a camera, so it will have set up the default properties correctly for us:
   - **Play On Awake** (Checked)
   - **Wait For First Frame** (Checked)
   - **Render Mode: Camera Far Plane**
   - **Camera: Main Camera (Camera)**

5. Drag the video clip asset file called `videoTexture` from the **Project** window into the **Video Clip** property slot in the **Inspector** window, like so:

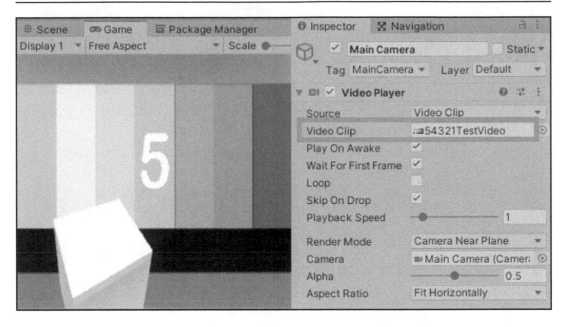

Figure 12.2 The Inspector window of Main Camera showing the source Video Clip

6. Test your scene.

You should be able to see the movie being played behind the scene content. Notice that there are a variety of options for how the video should be displayed on the screen. For example, you can choose whether to stretch the video content by changing the **Aspect Ratio** property in the **Inspector** window.

How it works...

We gave the `VideoPlayer` component a reference to a `VideoClip` asset file. Since we added the `VideoPlayer` component to a camera (`Main Camera`, in this example), it automatically chose **Camera Far Play Render Mode**, which is linked to the `Main Camera` GameObject.

The default setting is **Play On Awake**, so as soon as the first frame has loaded (since **Wait For First Frame** is also checked by default), the video will start playing. The video is displayed behind all main camera content (the far plane). Because of this, we can see our 3D Cube in the scene, with the video playing in the background.

There's more...

Sometimes, we may want to play a video so that it's the user's main focus, but allow them to see scene objects in the background.

To achieve this with the `VideoPlayer` component, we just need to make two changes:

- Change **Render Mode** to **Near Camera Plane** (so that the video content is played in front of the scene content).
- To allow the user to partially see through the video, we need to make **Video Player** semi-transparent. To do so, change its **Alpha** property to `0.5`.

Now, when you run the scene, you'll see the video playing in front of scene content, but you will also be able to see the 3D Cube in the background.

 At the time of writing this book, there seem to be issues with the **Direct** option for **Audio Output Mode** audio playback for some non-Apple systems. One solution is to add an `AudioSource` component to the same GameObject that has the `VideoPlayer` component and to set **Audio Output Mode** to `AudioSource`.

Using scripting to control video playback on scene textures

While the previous recipe demonstrated how we can place videos using the `VideoPlayer` component, which is set up at design time, much more is possible when controlling video playback through scripting – for example, allowing the user to interactively pause/play/stop video playback:

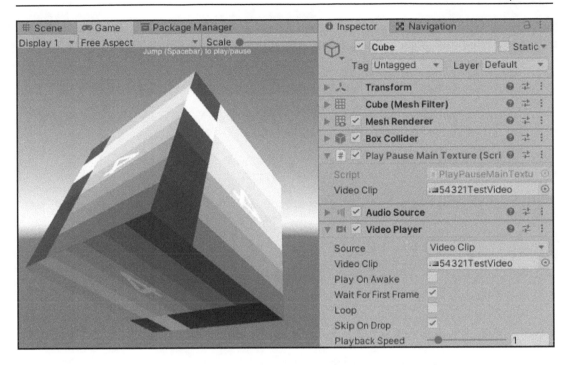

Figure 12.3 – Example of using a script to control the video

In this recipe, we'll use scripting to play/pause the playback of a video rendered onto a 3D Cube.

Getting ready

If you need a video file to follow this recipe, please use the `54321TestVideo.mov` file included in the `12_01` folder.

How to do it...

To use scripting to control video playback, follow these steps:

1. Create a new **Unity 3D project**.
2. Import the provided `videoTexture.mov` file.
3. Create a 3D Cube by going to **GameObject | 3D Object | Cube**.

4. Create a C# script class named `PlayPauseMainTexture` and attach an instance object as a component to your 3D Cube GameObject:

```csharp
using UnityEngine;
using UnityEngine.Video;

[RequireComponent(typeof(VideoPlayer))]
[RequireComponent(typeof(AudioSource))]

public class PlayPauseMainTexture : MonoBehaviour {
  public VideoClip videoClip;

  private VideoPlayer videoPlayer;
  private AudioSource audioSource;

  void Start() {
    videoPlayer = GetComponent<VideoPlayer>();
    audioSource = GetComponent<AudioSource>();

    // disable Play on Awake for both vide and audio
    videoPlayer.playOnAwake = false;
    audioSource.playOnAwake = false;

    // assign video clip
    videoPlayer.source = VideoSource.VideoClip;
    videoPlayer.clip = videoClip;

    // setup AudioSource
    videoPlayer.audioOutputMode =
VideoAudioOutputMode.AudioSource;
    videoPlayer.SetTargetAudioSource(0, audioSource);

    // render video to main texture of parent GameObject
    videoPlayer.renderMode = VideoRenderMode.MaterialOverride;
    videoPlayer.targetMaterialRenderer =
GetComponent<Renderer>();
    videoPlayer.targetMaterialProperty = "_MainTex";
  }

  void Update() {
    // space bar to start / pause
    if (Input.GetButtonDown("Jump"))
      PlayPause();
  }

  private void PlayPause() {
    if (videoPlayer.isPlaying)
      videoPlayer.Pause();
```

```
        else
            videoPlayer.Play();
    }
}
```

5. Ensure that your 3D Cube is selected in the **Project** window. Then, drag the `Video Clip` asset file called `videoTexture` from the **Project** window into the **Video Clip** property slot of the `PlayPauseMainTexture` component (script) in the **Inspector** window.

6. Run your scene. Pressing the *Spacebar* should play/pause playback of the video on the surfaces of the 3D Cube. You should also hear the beeping audio for video.

How it works...

We have explored the basics of using scripting and the `VideoPlayer` component. As well as defining and setting up where `VideoPlayer` will render, as we need to each time, in the steps above we have completed the following:

1. Create or get references to the `VideoPlayer` and `AudioSource` components (we will automatically have both components for this recipe since we have the `RequireComponent(...)` script instructions immediately before our class declaration):

```
videoPlayer = GetComponent<VideoPlayer>();
audioSource = GetComponent<AudioSource>();
```

2. Set their **Play On Awake** properties to `true`/`false`:

```
videoPlayer.playOnAwake = false;
audioSource.playOnAwake = false;
```

3. Define where the `VideoPlayer` will find a reference to the video clip to play:

```
videoPlayer.source = VideoSource.VideoClip;
videoPlayer.clip = videoClip
```

4. Define the audio settings (so that you can output to the `AudioSource` component):

```
videoPlayer.audioOutputMode =
VideoAudioOutputMode.AudioSource;
videoPlayer.setTargetAudioSource(0, audioSource);
```

In this recipe, we followed these four steps by adding the instance object of our `PlayPauseMainTexture` scripted class to the 3D Cube and dragging a reference to a `Video Clip` asset file to the public slot. In the following code, we're telling the `VideoPlayer` component to override the material of the object it is a component of (in this case, the 3D Cube) so that `VideoPlayer` will render (display) on the main texture of the 3D Cube:

```
videoPlayer.renderMode = VideoRenderMode.MaterialOverride;
videoPlayer.targetMaterialRenderer = GetComponent<Renderer>();"
videoPlayer.targetMaterialProperty = "_MainTex";
```

There's more...

Here are some additional ways to work with video player scripting. Sometimes, the video we want is not available as a video clip file on the computer we are using – instead, it is available online via a URL. In this section, we will examine how to adapt our script so that the source of the video can be provided as a URL.

Downloading an online video (rather than a clip)

Rather than dragging an existing `Video Clip` asset file to specify which video to play, `VideoPlayer` can also download video clips from an online source. To do this, we need to assign a string URL to the video player's URL property.

To download a video, do the following:

1. Declare a public array of strings, in which one or more URLs can be defined:

```
public string[] urls = {
"http://mirrors.standaloneinstaller.com/video-sample/grb_2.mov
",
"http://mirrors.standaloneinstaller.com/video-sample/lion-samp
le.mov"
    };
```

2. Declare a new method that returns one URL string, randomly chosen from the array:

```
public string RandomUrl(string[] urls)
{
    int index = Random.Range(0, urls.Length);
    return urls[index];
}
```

3. Finally, in the `SetupVideoAudioPlayers()` method, we need to get the random URL string and assign it to the video player's `url` property:

```
private void SetupVideoAudioPlayers()
{
    ... as before

    // assign video clip
    string randomUrl = RandomUrl(urls);
    videoPlayer.url = randomUrl;

    ... as before
}
```

Ensuring a movie is prepared before playing

In the preceding recipe, the movie has time to prepare since the game waits until we press the jump/*Spacebar* key. If we are using scripting to set up a video player for a video clip, we need to do some initial work before the video is ready to play. Unity provides the `prepareCompleted` event for this, which allows us to register a method to be invoked once a `VideoPlayer` is ready to play.

Getting ready

This recipe follows on from the previous one, so make a copy of that and work on the copy.

How to do it...

To ensure a movie is prepared before it's played by subscribing to a `prepareCompleted` event, do the following:

1. Add a UI RawImage to the scene by going to **GameObject | UI | Raw Image**.

2. Create a new, empty GameObject named `video-object`.

3. Create a C# script class named `PrepareCompleted` and attach an instance of the script as a component to the `video-object` GameObject:

```csharp
using UnityEngine;
using UnityEngine.UI;
using UnityEngine.Video;

public class PrepareCompleted: MonoBehaviour {
  public RawImage image;
  public VideoClip videoClip;

  private VideoPlayer videoPlayer;
  private AudioSource audioSource;

  void Start() {
    SetupVideoAudioPlayers();
    videoPlayer.prepareCompleted += PlayVideoWhenPrepared;
    videoPlayer.Prepare();
    Debug.Log("A - PREPARING");
  }

  private void SetupVideoAudioPlayers() {
    videoPlayer = gameObject.AddComponent<VideoPlayer>();
    audioSource = gameObject.AddComponent<AudioSource>();

    videoPlayer.playOnAwake = false;
    audioSource.playOnAwake = false;

    videoPlayer.source = VideoSource.VideoClip;
    videoPlayer.clip = videoClip;

    videoPlayer.audioOutputMode =
VideoAudioOutputMode.AudioSource;
    videoPlayer.SetTargetAudioSource(0, audioSource);
  }

  private void PlayVideoWhenPrepared(VideoPlayer
theVideoPlayer) {
```

```
        Debug.Log("B - IS PREPARED");
        image.texture = theVideoPlayer.texture;
        Debug.Log("C - PLAYING");
        theVideoPlayer.Play();
    }
}
```

4. Ensure that the `video-object` GameObject is selected in the **Project** window. Now, drag the `Raw Image` GameObject from the **Hierarchy** window into the **Raw Image** slot. Then, drag the `Video Clip` asset file called `videoTexture` from the **Project** window into the **Video Clip** property slot of the `PrepareCompleted` component (script) in the **Inspector** window.

5. Test your scene. You should be able to see the movie being played behind the scene's content.

How it works...

As you can see, in the `Start()` method, we register a method named `PlayVideoWhenPrepared` with the `videoPlayer.prepareCompleted` event, before invoking the `Prepare()` method of the `videoPlayer` component:

```
videoPlayer.prepareCompleted += PlayVideoWhenPrepared;
videoPlayer.Prepare();
```

The `PlayVideoWhenPrepared(...)` method has to accept a parameter as a reference to a `VideoPlayer` object. A UI GameObject was added to the scene displaying a **RawImage** texture.

We directly assigned the `VideoPlayer` object's texture property to the UI GameObject's RawImage's texture. Then, we sent the `Play()` message.

You can track the progress of clip preparation and so on through the **Log** messages in the **Console** window.

There's more...

Here is an alternative to event subscription to ensure a movie has been prepared before playing it.

Ensuring that the movie has been prepared before playing it with coroutines

Many Unity programmers are very used to working with coroutines, so instead of using the `prepareCompleted` event, we can rewrite the preceding script by using a coroutine.

Do the following:

1. Remove the `PlayVideoWhenPrepared()` method.
2. Add a new `using` statement at the top of the script (so that we can refer to the `IEnumerator` interface):

```
using System.Collections;
```

3. Replace the existing `Start()` method with the following:

```
private IEnumerator Start() {
    SetupVideoAudioPlayers();
    videoPlayer.Prepare();

    while (!videoPlayer.isPrepared)
        yield return null;

    videoPlayer.Play();
}
```

As you can see, our `Start()` method has become a coroutine (returning an `IEnumerator`), which means that it can yield control back to Unity during its execution. In the next frame, it will resume execution at that same statement.

There is also a while loop that will continue running until the `isPrepared` property is `true` for `VideoPlayer`. So, each frame of Unity will return to this `while` loop, and if `VideoPlayer` is still not prepared, it will enter the loop again and yield execution until the next frame. When `VideoPlayer isPrepared` is finally `true`, the loop condition will be `false` so that the statement after the loop (`videoPLayer.Play()`) is executed and the method finally completes its execution.

For a single video, there is little to choose between the `isPrepared` event and the preceding coroutine. However, for a sequence of videos, the use of the `isPrepared` and `loopPointReached` events helps us make much simpler logic for preparing and then waiting to play the next video in a sequence (see the next recipe for more information).

Outputting video playback to a RenderTexture asset

Directly working with the `VideoPlayer` texture works for this example, but usually, setting up a separate `RenderTexture` is more reliable and flexible. This recipe will build on the previous one to demonstrate this approach. A flexible way to work with video players is to output their playback to a `RenderTexture` asset file. A material can be created to get input from `RenderTexture` and. Using that material, GameObjects will display the video. Also, some GameObjects can directly have `RenderTexture` assigned to their texture.

Getting ready

This recipe follows on from the previous one, so make a copy of that and work on the copy.

How to do it...

To output video playback to a `RenderTexture`, do the following:

1. In the **Project** window, create a new `Render Texture` asset file named `myRenderTexture` by going to **Create | Render Texture**.
2. Select the UI RawImage in the **Hierarchy** window, and assign its **Raw Image (Script)** texture property to the `myRenderTexture` asset file.
3. In the **Project** window, create a new `Material` asset file named `m_video`. For this material, in the **Inspector** window, set its **Albedo Texture** property to `myRenderTexture` (drag it from the **Project** window into the **Inspector** window).
4. Create a new 3D Capsule in the scene and assign the `m_video` material to it.
5. Edit the C# script class called `PrepareCompleted` by replacing the public `rawImage` variable with a public `renderTexture` variable:

   ```
   public VideoClip videoClip;
   public RenderTexture renderTexture;
   ```

6. Edit the C# script class called `PrepareCompleted` by adding the following statements at the end of the `SetupVideoAudioPlayers()` method to output video to `RenderTexture`:

```
videoPlayer.renderMode = VideoRenderMode.RenderTexture;
videoPlayer.targetTexture = renderTexture;
```

7. Edit the C# script class called `PrepareCompleted` in the `PlayVideoWhenPrepared()` method. Remove the statement that directly assigns the `VideoPlayer` component's texture property to the RawImage's **Texture**:

```
private void PlayVideoWhenPrepared(VideoPlayer
theVideoPlayer) {
    Debug.Log("B - IS PREPARED");

    // Play video
    Debug.Log("C - PLAYING");
    theVideoPlayer.Play();
}
```

8. Ensure that the `video-object` GameObject is selected in the **Project** window. Now, drag the `myRenderTexture` asset from the **Project** window into the **Render Texture** public property of **Prepare Completed (Script)** in the **Inspector** window:

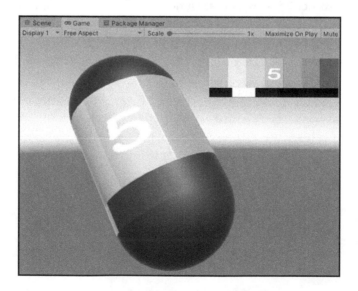

Figure 12.4 – Example of a video being rendered onto a capsule

9. Run the scene. You should now see the video playing both in the UI RawImage and also rendered over the 3D Capsule object.

How it works...

A `Render Texture` is an asset file (in the **Project** window). This file can be written to with the current frame of a video being played. In this recipe, you created a `Render Texture` asset file named `myRenderTexture`. We had to set two properties of the `VideoPlayer` object in order to write the video to our `myRenderTexture`:

- `renderMode` was set to a public constant value called `VideoRenderMode.RenderTexture`
- `targetTexture` was set to a new public variable called `renderTexture`

We created a new UI RawImage in **Canvas** and set its **Raw Image (Script)** texture property to the `myRenderTexture` asset file. This means that whatever image is currently in `myRenderTexture` will be displayed on the screen as a flat, rectangular image in the UI RawImage.

Finally, we had to assign our asset file to the public variable. We did this by dragging `myRenderTexture` from the **Hierarchy** window into the public variable named `renderTexture` in the **Inspector** window. Having made these changes, the video plays both as the texture on the `capsule` GameObject and also via the `Render Texture` asset file called `myRenderTexture` to the UI RawImage in **Canvas**.

Using scripting to play a sequence of videos back to back

One of the advantages of scripting is that it allows us to easily work with multiple items through loops, arrays, and so on. In this recipe, we'll work with an array of `Video Clip` assets and use scripting to play them back to back (one starts as soon as the previous clip finishes), illustrating the use of the `isPrepared` and `loopPointReached` events to avoid complicated loops and coroutines.

Getting ready

If you need video files to follow this recipe, please use
the `54321TestVideo.mov` file included in the `12_01` folder.

 The Standalone Installer website is a good online source of test
videos: `http://standaloneinstaller.com/blog/big-list-of-`
`sample-videos-for-testers-124.html`.

How to do it...

To play a sequence of videos using scripting, follow these steps:

1. Create a new **Unity 3D project**.
2. Import the provided `54321TestVideo.mov` file, and perhaps a second
   video clip, so that we can have a sequence of two different videos to test
   (although you can run the same one twice if you wish).
3. In the **Project** window, create a new `Render Texture` asset file
   named `myRenderTexture` by going to **Create | Render Texture**.
4. Add a UI RawImage to the scene by going to **Create | UI | Raw Image**.
5. Select the UI RawImage in the **Hierarchy** window and assign its **Raw
   Image (Script) Texture** property to the `myRenderTexture` asset file.
6. In the **Project** window, create a new `Material` asset file named `m_video`.
   For this material, in the **Inspector** window, set its **Albedo Texture** property
   to `myRenderTexture` (drag it from the **Project** window into
   the **Inspector** window).
7. Create a 3D Cube by going to **Create | 3D | Cube**.
   Assign the `m_video` material to your 3D Cube.
8. Create a new, empty GameObject named `video-object`.
9. Create a C# script class named `VideoSequenceRenderTexture` and attach
   an instance of the script as a component to the GameObject's `video-`
   `object`:

```
using UnityEngine;
using UnityEngine.Video;

public class VideoSequenceRenderTexture : MonoBehaviour {
    public RenderTexture renderTexture;
    public VideoClip[] videoClips;
```

```
        private VideoPlayer[] videoPlayers;
        private int currentVideoIndex;

        void Start() {
            SetupObjectArrays();
            currentVideoIndex = 0;
            videoPlayers[currentVideoIndex].prepareCompleted +=
PlayNextVideo;
            videoPlayers[currentVideoIndex].Prepare();
            Debug.Log("A - PREPARING video: " + currentVideoIndex);
        }

        private void SetupObjectArrays() {
            videoPlayers = new VideoPlayer[videoClips.Length];
            for (int i = 0; i < videoClips.Length; i++)
                SetupVideoAudioPlayers(i);
        }

        private void PlayNextVideo(VideoPlayer theVideoPlayer) {
            VideoPlayer currentVideoPlayer =
videoPlayers[currentVideoIndex];

            Debug.Log("B - PLAYING Index: " + currentVideoIndex);
            currentVideoPlayer.Play();

            currentVideoIndex++;
            bool someVideosLeft = currentVideoIndex <
videoPlayers.Length;

            if (someVideosLeft) {
                VideoPlayer nextVideoPlayer =
videoPlayers[currentVideoIndex];
                nextVideoPlayer.Prepare();
                Debug.Log("A - PREPARING video: " +
currentVideoIndex);
                currentVideoPlayer.loopPointReached += PlayNextVideo;
            } else {
                Debug.Log("(no videos left)");
            }
        }

        private void SetupVideoAudioPlayers(int i) {
            string newGameObjectName = "videoPlayer_" + i;
            GameObject containerGo = new
GameObject(newGameObjectName);
            containerGo.transform.SetParent(transform);
            containerGo.transform.SetParent(transform);
```

```
                    VideoPlayer videoPlayer =
containerGo.AddComponent<VideoPlayer>();
                    AudioSource audioSource =
containerGo.AddComponent<AudioSource>();

            videoPlayers[i] = videoPlayer;

            videoPlayer.playOnAwake = false;
            audioSource.playOnAwake = false;

            videoPlayer.source = VideoSource.VideoClip;
            videoPlayer.clip = videoClips[i];

            videoPlayer.audioOutputMode =
VideoAudioOutputMode.AudioSource;
            videoPlayer.SetTargetAudioSource(0, audioSource);

            videoPlayer.renderMode = VideoRenderMode.RenderTexture;
            videoPlayer.targetTexture = renderTexture;
        }
    }
```

10. Ensure that the `video-object` GameObject is selected in
    the **Project** window. Now, drag the `myRenderTexture` asset from
    the **Project** window into the **Render Texture** public property
    of **PrepareCompleted (Script)** in the **Inspector** window. For the **Video
    Clips** property, set its size to 2. You should now see two video
    clip elements (elements 0 and 1). From the **Project** window, drag a video
    clip into each slot:

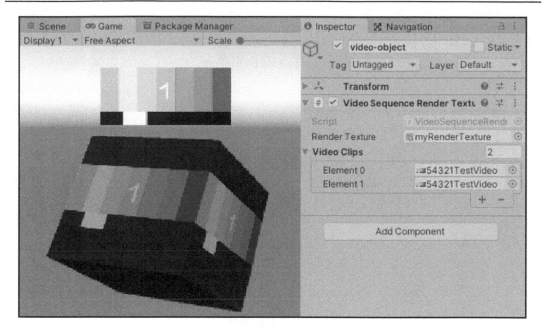

Figure 12.5 – Settings for Video Sequence Render Texture of video-object

11. Run the scene. You should now see the first video clip playing both for the UI RawImage and the 3D Cube surface. Once the first video clip has finished playing, the second video clip should immediately start playing.

You can track the progress of clip preparation and so on through the **Log messages** section of the **Console** window.

How it works...

This script class makes the `Video Player` objects output their videos to the Render Texture's asset file, `myRenderTexture`. This is used by both the 3D Cube and the UI RawImage for their surface displays.

The `videoClips` variable is a public array of video clip references.

The instance object of the C# script class called `VideoSequenceRenderTexture` was added as a component to the GameObject's `video-object`. This script will create child GameObjects of the `video-object` GameObject, each containing a `VideoPlayer` and `AudioSource` component, ready to play each of the video clips that have been assigned in the public array's `videoClips` variables.

The `SetupObjectArrays()` method initializes `videoPlayers` to be an array that's the same length as `videoClips`. It then loops for each item, invoking `SetupVideoAudioPlayers(...)` by passing the current integer index.

The `SetupVideoAudioPlayers(...)` method creates a new child GameObject for the GameObject's `video-object` and adds the `VideoPlayer` and `AudioSource` components to that GameObject. It sets the `Video Player` clip property to the corresponding element in the public `videoClips` array variable. It also adds a reference to the new `VideoPlayer` component to the appropriate location in the `videoPlayers` array. It then sets the video player to output audio to the new `AudioSource` component, and to output its video to the `renderTexture` public variable.

The `Start()` method does the following:

- It invokes `SetupObjectArrays()`.
- It sets the `currentVideoIndex` variable to 0 (for the first item in the arrays).
- It registers the `PlayNextVideo` method for the `prepareCompleted` event of the first `videoPlayers` object (`currentVideoIndex = 0`).
- It invokes the `Prepare()` method for the `videoPlayers` object (`currentVideoIndex = 0`).
- It logs a debug message stating that the item is being prepared.

The `PlayNextVideo(...)` method gets a reference to the `Video Player` element of the `videoPlayers` array that corresponds to the `currentVideoIndex` variable.

This method ignores the reference to the `videoPlayer` argument it receives – this parameter is required in the method declaration since it is the required signature to allow this method to register for the `prepareCompleted` and `loopPointReached` events. It performs the following steps:

1. First, it sends a `Play()` message to the current video player.
2. Then, it increments the value of `currentVideoIndex` and tests whether there are any remaining video clips in the array.

3. If there are remaining clips, then it gets a reference to the next clip and sends it a `Prepare()` message. Also, the video player that's currently being played has its `loopPointReached` event registered for the `PlayNextVideo` method
(if there are no videos left, then a simple debug log message is printed and the method ends).

The clever bit is when the currently playing video player has its `loopPointReached` event registered for the `PlayNextVideo` method. The `loopPointReached` event occurs when a video clip has finished playing and will start to look again for the next video to play (if its loop property is `true`). What we are doing with this script is saying that when the video player's video clip has finished, the `PlayNextVideo(...)` method should be invoked again – once again using the value of `currentVideoIndex` to send a `Play()` message to the next video player, and then testing for any remaining video players, and so on until the end of the array has been reached.

This is a good example of conditions (`if` statements) being used with events, rather than coroutine while loops. So long as you're happy with how methods can be registered with C# events, then this approach allows our code to be less complex by avoiding loops and coroutine yield `null` statements.

In the following screenshot, we can see how our `video-object` GameObject, at runtime, ends up with `videoPlayer_0` and `videoPlayer_1` child GameObjects – one for each element in the array. This allows one `VideoPlayer` to be playing while the next is preparing, and so on:

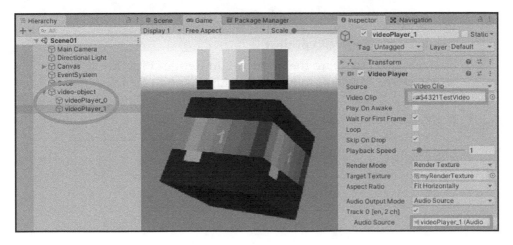

Figure 12.6 – Example highlighting the child elements at runtime, one for each element in the array

Creating and using a simple Shader Graph

The Shader Graph feature in Unity 2020 is a powerful and exciting feature that opens up shader creation and editing to everyone, without any need for complex mathematics or coding skills. In this recipe, we'll create a simple Shader Graph to generate a checkerboard pattern, create a material that uses that shader, and then apply it to a 3D Cube. The end result will be as follows:

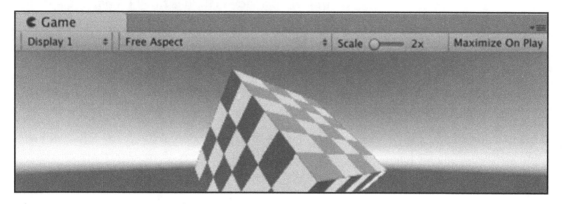

Figure 12.7 – Example of a checkerboard pattern being applied to a 3D Cube

How to do it...

To create and use a simple Shader Graph, follow these steps:

1. Create a new **Unity 3D project**.
2. First, we need to set up the **Lightweight Render Pipeline** (LWRP). Use **Package Manager** to import the **Lightweight Render Pipeline** package.
3. In the **Project** window, create a new Lightweight Pipeline asset file named `myLightweightAsset` by going to **menu: Create | Rendering | Lightweight Pipeline Asset**.

4. In the **Inspector** window, display the project's graphics settings by going to **Edit | Project Settings | Graphics**. Then, drag `myLightweightAsset` from the **Project** window into the **Scriptable Render Pipeline Settings** property:

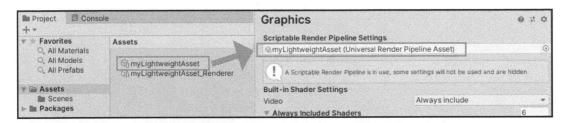

Figure 12.8 – Dragging myLightweightAsset into Scriptable Render Pipeline Settings

5. In the **Project** window, create a new **Physically-Based Rendering (PBR)** Shader Graph named `myShaderGraph` by going to **Create | Shader | PBR Graph**.

6. In the **Project** window, create a new material named `m_cube` by going to **Create | Material**.

7. With `m_cube` selected, in the **Inspector** window, set its **Shader** property to `myShaderGraph`. For the material's Shader property, choose **graphs | myShaderGraph**:

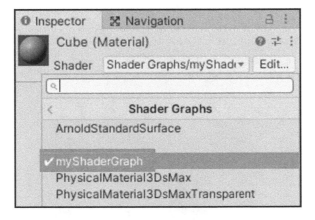

Figure 12.9 – Setting m_cube's Shader property to myShaderGraph

8. Add a 3D Cube to the scene by going to **GameObject | 3D Object | Cube**. Set the material for this 3D Cube to `m_Cube`.

9. In the **Project** window, double-click `myShaderGraph` to open the Shader Graph editing panel. A new PRB Shader Graph will open with three components; that is, (1) the BlackBoard (for publicly exposing parameters), (2) the Master PRB node, and (3) the output previewer node:

Figure 12.10 – The Shader Graph panel

 When editing a Shader Graph, you should maximize the **Shader Graph** panel so that it's easier to see.

10. Right-click the output previewer and select **Cube**:

 You can zoom in and rotate the preview mesh. You can also choose a custom mesh from within your project, allowing you to preview the Shader Graph on the intended destination's 3D object.

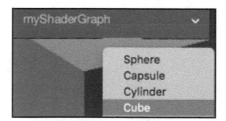

Figure 12.11 – Selecting Cube in the output previewer

11. Let's flood the shader with a red color. Choose red from the color picker for the top property of the **PRB Master** node; that is, **Albedo**.

12. Create a new graph node by right-clicking and going to **Create Node** |
    Procedural | **Checkerboard**. You'll see the checkerboard pattern in the
    preview for this node. Set the **X** property to 2 and the **Y** property to 3.

13. Now, drag a link from the checkerboard's note output, **Out(3)**, to the
    Emission (3) input for the **PRB Master** node. You should now see a
    red/pink checkerboard pattern in the **PBR Master** node preview. You'll also
    see that the following output has been applied to the **Cube** mesh in the
    output previewer node:

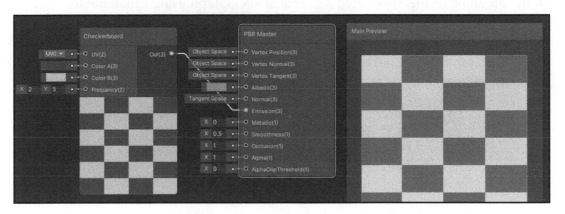

Figure 12.12 – Linking from the checkerboard's note output Out(3) to the Emission (3) input for the PRB Master node

14. You must save the changes for your Shader Graph before they will be
    applied to the scene. Click the **Save Asset** button at the top left of the
    Shader Graph window to do so.

15. Save and run your scene. You should see a red/pink checkerboard 3D
    Cube being displayed.

How it works...

In this recipe, you enabled the Lightweight Rendering Pipeline by installing the
package, creating an asset, and choosing that asset for the project's **Scriptable
Rendering Pipeline Graphics** property.

You then created a new Shader Graph asset file and a new material that uses your
shader.

Your Shader Graph feeds a procedurally generated checkerboard into the **Emission** property of the **PBR Master** output node and also tints the output by choosing a red **Color** value for the **Albedo** property. You saved the changes to your Shader Graph asset so that they will be available when the scene runs.

Creating a glow effect with Shader Graph

In the previous recipe, we created a simple Shader Graph using a material for a primitive 3D Cube mesh. In this recipe, we'll take things further by creating a Shader Graph that applies a parameterized glow effect to a 3D object. The end result will look as follows:

Figure 12.13 – Example demonstrating a blue glow effect

Getting ready

This recipe builds on the previous one, so make a copy of that project and use the copy for this recipe.

How to do it...

To create a glow effect with a Shader Graph, follow these steps:

1. In the **Project** window, create a new PBR Shader Graph named glowShaderGraph by going to **Create | Shader | PBR Graph**.
2. In the **Project** window, create a new material named m_glow by going to **Create | Material**.
3. With m_glow selected, in the **Inspector** window, set its **Shader** property to glowShaderGraph by going to **graphs | glowShaderGraph**.

4. We now need a 3D mesh object in the scene that uses m_glow. While we could just use a 3D Cube again, it's more fun to add a low-polygon textured character to the scene. For this recipe, we've used the free Unity Asset Store character pack called *Fantasy Mushroom Mon(ster)* from *AmusedArt*. Once the package has been added, drag **Mushroom Monster Prefab** into the scene from the **Project** window folder; that is, **amusedART | Mushroom Monster | Prefab**:

Figure 12.14 – Free Fantasy Mushroom Mon(ster) asset from AmusedArt

5. In the **Project** window, double-click glowShaderGraph to open the **Shader Graph** editing panel.
6. Right-click the output previewer, select **Custom Mesh**, and choose **MushroomMon** from the selection dialog.
7. Add a new **Texture exposed** property to your Shader Graph by creating a new property texture in **Shader Graph Blackboard**. Click the plus (+) button and choose the **Texture** property type.
8. In **Blackboard**, change the **Default value** setting of the **Texture** property from **None** to **Mushroom Green**.
9. To use a publicly exposed **Blackboard** property in our Shader Graph, we need to drag a reference to the property from **Blackboard** into the **Graph** area.

10. Drag the **Blackboard** property's **Texture** into the **Graph** area. You should see a new node with a title and value of **Texture2D**:

Figure 12.15 – Dragging the Blackboard property's Texture to create a new node

11. There is no **Texture** input to the **Master PDB** Node, so we need to add a converter node that can take sample data from a 2D texture image and turn it into RBG values that can be sent to the **Albedo** input of the **PBR Master** node. Create a new **Sample Texture 2D** node in your Shader Graph by right-clicking and going to **Create Node | Input | Texture | Sample Texture 2D**.

12. Now, let's send the **Mushroom Green** texture into the **PBR Master** node via the **Sample Texture 2D converter** node. Link the **Texture (T)** output from the **Property** node to the **Texture (T)** input of the **Sample Texture 2D** node. You should now see the **Mushroom Green** texture image appear in the 2D rectangular preview at the bottom of the **Sample Texture 2D** node.

13. Next, link the **RGBA (4)** output of the **Sample Texture 2D** node to the **Albedo (3)** input of the **PBR Master** node (Unity will intelligently just ignore the **4th Alpha (A)** values). You should now see the **Mushroom Green** texture image appear in the preview at the bottom of the **PBR Master** node. You should also see the **Mushroom Green** texture being applied to **3D Mushroom Monster Mesh** in the Shader Graph output previewer node:

Figure 12.16 – Shader Graph showing connections between Sample Texture 2D and PBR Master

14. One way to create a glow effect is by applying a **Fresnel Effect**. (By adjusting the viewing angle, it adjusts the reflection. For more, see the following information box.) Create a new **Fresnel Effect** node in our Shader Graph. Link the **Out (1)** output from the **Fresnel Effect** node to the **Emission (3)** input of the **PBR Master** node. You should now see a brighter glow outline effect in the Shader Graph output previewer node.

> Augustin-Jean Fresnel (1788-1827) studied and documented how an object's reflection depends on the viewing angle – for example, looking straight down into still water, little sunlight is reflected and we can see into the water clearly. But if our eyes are closer to the level of the water (for example, if we are swimming), then much more light is reflected by the water. Simulating this effect in a digital shader is one way to make the edges of an object lighter, since light is glancing off the edges of the object and reflected in our game camera.

15. Let's tint our **Fresnel Effect** by combining it with a publicly exposed **Color** property, which can be set either in the **Inspector** window or through C# code.

16. First, delete the link of the **Out (3)** output from the **Fresnel Effect** node for the **Emission (3)** input of the **PBR Master** node.

17. Add a new **Color** property to your Shader Graph by creating a new property called `Color` in **Blackboard**. Click the plus (**+**) button and choose the **Color** property type.

18. In **Blackboard**, set **Default value** of the **Color** property to red (using the color picker).

19. Drag the Blackboard's **Color** property into the **Graph** area. You should see a new node called **Property** with a value of **Color(4)**.

20. Create a new **Multiply** node in your Shader Graph by right-clicking and going to **Create Node | Math | Basic | Multiply**.

The mathematical **Multiply** node is an easy way to combine values from two nodes, which are then to be passed to a single input of a third node.

21. Let's combine the **Color** property and **Fresnel Effect** by making both inputs of the **Multiply** node. Link the **Color (4)** output from the **Property (Color)** node to the **A (4)** input of the **Multiply** node. Next, link the **Out (3)** output from the **Fresnel Effect** node to the **B (4)** input of the **Multiply** node. Finally, link the **Out (3)** output from the **Fresnel Effect** node to the **Emission(3)** input of the **PBR Master** node. You should now see a red-tinted glow outline effect in the Shader Graph output previewer node. The following screenshot shows these node connections for our Shader Graph:

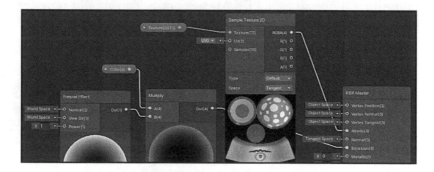

Figure 12.17 – Final Shader Graph with connections for the glow effect

22. Save your updated Shader Graph by clicking the **Save Asset** button at the top right of the **Shader Graph** window.

23. Save and run your scene. You should see a red glow around the character:

Figure 12.18 – Adjusting the Color property to blue using the color picker

24. In the **Project** window, locate the material that your 3D GameObject uses (for **Green Mushroom Monster**, it is in **Project** | **amusedART** | **Mushroom_Monster** | **Materials** | **MusroomMonGreen**). The publicly exposed properties of the Shader Graph Blackboard should appear in the **Inspector** window as customizable properties. Change the **Color** property to blue and run the scene again. The glow effect around the 3D GameObject should now be blue.

How it works...

In this recipe, you created a new Shader Graph that had several connected nodes. The output(s) of one node becomes the input(s) of another node.

You created publicly exposed properties for **Color** and **Texture** using the Shader Graph Blackboard and introduced those properties as inputs in your Shader Graph. By publicly exposing these properties, you allow them to be edited via the **Inspector** window when a **Material** that's been assigned to a Shader Graph is selected.

You used a **Sample Texture 2D** node to convert the **2D Texture** image into RBG values suitable for the **Albedo** input for the **PBR Master** node.

You then created a **Fresnel Effect** node and combined this, via a **Multiply** node, with the publicly exposed **Color** property, sending the output into the **Emission** input of the **PBR Master** node. Multiply nodes can be used to combine different elements of a Shader Graph.

To apply a Shader Graph to a GameObject in a scene, you needed to create a **Material** asset file named `m_glow`. Once this **Material** had its Shader assigned to the Shader Graph that we'd created, when this **Material** is assigned to a GameObject, the rendering of the GameObject will be influenced by the Shader Graph.

Finally, you changed the publicly exposed property for **Color** in the **Inspector** window via the material's properties.

Toggling a Shader Graph color glow effect through C# code

Effects such as the glow effect from the previous recipe are often features we wish to toggle on and off under different circumstances. The effect can be turned on or off during a game to visually communicate the status of a GameObject – for example, an angry character might glow red, while a happy monster might glow green, and so on.

We'll add to the previous recipe to create a new publicly exposed Shader Graph Blackboard property named `Power`. Then, we'll write some code that can be used to set this value to 0 or 5 in order to turn the glow effect on and off. We'll also access the **Color** property so that we can set what color the glow effect displays.

Getting ready

This recipe builds on the previous one, so make a copy of that project and use the copy for this recipe.

How to do it...

To toggle the glow effect from the Shader Graph, follow these steps:

1. First, delete the link from the **Out(4)** output from the **Multiply** node to the **Emission(3)** input of the **PBR Master** node. We are doing this because the output of this **Multiply** node will become the input for a second **Multiply** node that we are about to create.

2. Create a new **Multiply** node in your Shader Graph by right-clicking and going to **Create Node | Math | Basic | Multiply**.

3. Link the **Out(4)** output from the original **Multiply** node to the **A (4)** input of your new **Multiply** node. Also, link the **Out(4)** output from the new **Multiply** node to the **Emission(3)** input of the **PBR Master** node.

4. Add a new float (decimal number), exposed to the **Power** property, to your Shader Graph by creating a new property in the Shader Graph Blackboard. Click the plus (+) button, choose the **Vector 1** property type, and rename this `Power`.

5. In **Blackboard**, set **Default value** of the **Power** property to 5. Also, set **Display mode** to **Slider** with the values of `Min 0` and `Max 5`.

6. Drag the Blackboard **Power** property into the **Graph** area. You should see a new node with a title of **Property** and a value of **Power(1)**.

7. Finally, link the **Power(1)** output from the **Property** node (Power) to the **B (4)** input of the new **Multiply** node:

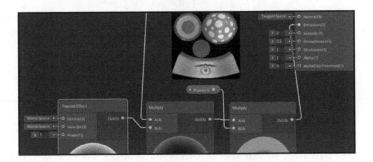

Figure 12.19 – Settings of the Shader Graph with an additional Multiply node

8. Save your updated Shader Graph by clicking the **Save Asset** button at the top left of the **Shader Graph** window.

9. Create a new C# script class named GlowManager containing the following code:

```csharp
using UnityEngine;

public class GlowManager : MonoBehaviour {
    private string powerId = "Vector1_AA07C639";
    private string colorId = "Color_466BE55E";

    void Update () {
        if (Input.GetKeyDown("0"))
            GetComponent<Renderer>().material.SetFloat(powerId,
0);

        if (Input.GetKeyDown("1"))
            SetGlowColor(Color.red);

        if (Input.GetKeyDown("2"))
            SetGlowColor(Color.blue);
    }

    private void SetGlowColor(Color c) {
        GetComponent<Renderer>().material.SetFloat(powerId, 5);
        GetComponent<Renderer>().material.SetColor(colorId, c);
    }
}
```

10. Select `glowShaderGraph` in the **Project** window and view its properties in the **Inspector** window:

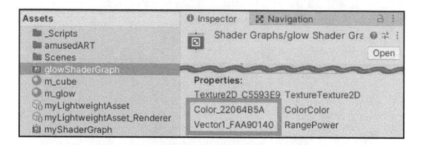

Figure 12.20 – The properties of glowShaderGraph shown in the Inspector window

11. Find the internal IDs of the publicly exposed **Power** and **Color** properties – they will be something like `Vector1_AA07C639` and `Color_466BE55E`. Copy these IDs into C# script statements by setting the ID strings:

```
private string powerId = "Vector1_AA07C639";
private string colorId = "Color_466BE55E";
```

12. In the **Hierarchy** window, locate the component of your 3D GameObject that contains the `Mesh Renderer` component (for our Mushroom Monster example, this is the `Mushroom Mon` child of the `Mushroom Monster` GameObject). Add an instance object of the `GlowManager` script class as a component to this GameObject.

13. Save and run your Scene. Pressing the *1* key should turn on the red glow effect, pressing the *2* key should turn on the blue glow effect, and pressing the *0* key should turn off the glow effect.

How it works...

In this recipe, you created a new **Power** property for your Shader Graph that combined with the Fresnel color effect so that a value of 0 will turn off the effect. You looked up the internal IDs of the **Power** and **Color** properties and updated the C# script so that it can update these properties.

The script class checks for the 0/1/2 keys and turns the effect off, to a red glow, or to a blue glow, respectively. The script class can influence the Shader Graph because we found the internal IDs that referred to the **Power** and **Glow** color variables.

By combining publicly exposed properties with code, we can change Shader Graph values at runtime through events detected by code.

At the time of writing this book, the current version of Shader Graph doesn't provide a convenient way to access exposed properties using the names chosen in the Shader Graph Blackboard, hence the need to look up the internal ID needed for the `material.SetFloat(powerId, power)` statement when changing the value. It is likely that Unity will soon update the Shader Graph scripting API to make this action more straightforward.

There's more...

Here are some ways to take your Shader Graph features even further.

You could use **Sine Time** to create a pulsating glow effect, as follows:

- You could make the glow effect pulse by creating a **Time** node and then link the **Sine Time (1)** output to the **Fresnel Effect** node's input of **Power (1)**. As the **Sine Time** value changes between - 1/0/+1, it will influence how strong the Fresnel Effect is, changing the brightness of the glow effect.

Another way to find exposed property IDs (and to get more of an idea of how Unity internally sees Shader Graphs) is to use the **Compile and Show Code** button.

When you are viewing the properties of a Shader Graph asset in the **Inspector** widow, you'll see a button entitled **Compile and Show Code**. If you click this, you'll see a generated `ShaderLab` code file in your script editor.

This isn't the actual code used by Unity, but it provides a good idea of the code that is generated from your Shader Graph. The internal IDs for your publicly exposed Blackboard properties are listed in the `Properties` section, which is at the beginning of the generated code:

```
Shader "graphs/glowShaderGraph" {
    Properties {

        [NoScaleOffset]  Texture_C5AA766B ("Texture", 2D) = "white" { }
        Vector1_AA07C639 ("Power", Range(0.000,5.000)) = 5.000

        Color_466BE55E ("Color", Color) = (1.000,0.000,0.038368,0.000)
    }

    etc.
```

Shader graphs are very powerful ways to influence the visual output of your games. We've explored a few of their features in this chapter. Spending some time getting to know them better will result in increased ways to add visual effects to your games.

Further reading

The following are some useful sources for the topics that were covered in this chapter.

Shader Graph online resources

The Unity documentation and third-party articles about Shader Graphs can be found online at the following links:

- Introduction to Shader Graph: `https://blogs.unity3d.com/2018/02/27/introduction-to-shader-graph-build-your-shaders-with-a-visual-editor/`
- Unity Shader Graph Overview: `https://unity3d.com/shader-graph`
- The Unity GitHub Shader Graph Wiki: `https://github.com/Unity-Technologies/ShaderGraph/wiki`
- The Shader Graph Example Library on GitHub: `https://github.com/UnityTechnologies/ShaderGraph_ExampleLibrary`
- Video Tutorial of Shader Graph from Unity Technology's Andy Tough at GDC 2018: `https://www.youtube.com/watch?v=NsWNRLD-FEI`
- Unity's Manual Page for the Scriptable Render Pipeline: `https://docs.unity3d.com/Manual/ScriptableRenderPipeline.html`

Video player online resources

The Unity documentation and third-party articles about the `VideoPlayer` component can be found online at the following links:

- The Unity Video Player Manual Page: `https://docs.unity3d.com/Manual/class-VideoPlayer.html`
- The Unity Scripting Reference for the VideoPlayer Class: `https://docs.unity3d.com/ScriptReference/Video.VideoPlayer.html`

Advanced Topics - Gizmos, Automated Testing, and More

13

This chapter will put together four sets of advanced recipes:

- Gizmos
- Saving and loading game data
- Automated testing
- An introduction to Unity Python

Let's take a look at each in this introduction!

Gizmos

Gizmos are another kind of Unity editor customization. Gizmos are visual aids for game designers that are provided in the **Scene** window. They can be useful as setup aids (to help us know what we are doing) or for debugging (understanding why objects aren't behaving as expected).

Gizmos are not drawn through Editor scripts, but as part of the Monobehaviour class, so they only work for GameObjects in the current scene. Gizmo drawing is usually performed in two methods:

- `OnDrawGizmos()`: This is executed every frame or editor window repaint, for every GameObject in the **Hierarchy** window.
- `OnDrawGizmosSelect()`: This is executed every frame, for just the/those GameObject(s) that are currently selected in the **Hierarchy** window.

Gizmo graphical drawing makes it simple to draw lines, cubes, and spheres. More complex shapes can also be drawn with meshes, and you can also display 2D image icons (located in the **Project** folder: `Assets | Gizmos`).

Several recipes in this chapter will illustrate how Gizmos can be useful. Often, new GameObjects created from editor extensions will have helpful Gizmos associated with them.

Saving/loading data at runtime

When loading/saving data, it is important to keep in mind the data types that can be used. When writing C# code, our variables can be of any type permitted by the language, but when communicated by the web interface, or to local storage using Unity's `PlayerPrefs` class, we are restricted in the types of data that we can work with. When using the `PlayerPrefs` class, we are limited to saving and loading integers, floats, and strings. We will provide several recipes illustrating ways to save and load data at runtime, including the use of static variables, `PlayerPrefs`, and a public class called `TextAsset` containing text-format data for a 2D game level.

 `PlayerPrefs` offers a great, cross-platform way to store persistent data locally for Unity games. However, it is also very easy to hack into, so sensitive or confidential data should not be stored using this technique. For securely storing data online in hashed/encrypted format, data storage methods should be used. But for data such as lives left, checkpoints reached, scores and time remaining, and so on, it is an easy and simple way to implement memory after a scene has been exited.

Automated testing

For a very simple computer program, we can write code, run it, enter a variety of valid and invalid data, and see whether the program behaves as we expect it to. This is known as a code-then-test approach. However, this approach has several significant weaknesses:

- Each time we change the code, as well as run new tests relating to the code we are improving, we have to run all the old tests to ensure that no unexpected modified behaviors have been introduced (in other words, our new code has not **broken** another part of our program)
- Running tests manually is time-consuming.
- We are relying on a human to rerun the test each time. However, this test may be run using different data, some data may be omitted, or different team members may take a different approach to run tests.

Therefore, even for simple programs (and most are not simple), some kind of fast, automated testing system makes a lot of sense.

There is an approach to software development called **test-driven development (TDD)**, whereby code is **only** written until all tests pass. So, if we want to add or improve the behavior of our game program, we must specify what we want in terms of tests, and then the programmers write code to pass the tests. This avoids a situation whereby programmers write code and features that are not needed, spend time over-optimizing things that would have been fine, and so on. This means that the game development team directs its work toward agreed goals understood by all since they have been specified as tests.

The following diagram illustrates the basic TDD in that we only write code until all tests pass. Then, it's time to write more tests:

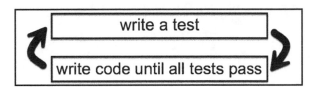

Figure 13.1 – Test then code to the test

Another way that TDD is often summarized is as **red-green-refactor**:

- **Red:** We write a new test for which code is needed, so initially, our test fails (in other words, we write a test for the new feature/improved behavior we wish to add to our system).
- **Green:** We write code that passes the new test (and all the existing ones).
- **Refactor:** We (may) choose to improve the code (and ensure that the improved code passes all the tests).

Two kinds of software tests exist, as follows:

- **Unit tests**
- **Integration tests**

A **unit test** tests a "unit" of code, which can be a single method, but which may include some other computer work being executed between the method being tested and the end result(s) being checked.

> *"A unit test is a piece of code that invokes a unit of work and checks one specific end result of that unit of work. If the assumptions on the end result turn out to be wrong, the unit test has failed."*
> — *Roy Oshergrove (p. 5, The Art of Unit Testing (Second edition)*

Unit tests should be as follows:

- Automated (runnable at the "push of a button")
- Fast
- Easy to implement
- Easy to read
- Executed in isolation (tests should be independent of one another)
- Assessed as either having passed or failed
- Relevant tomorrow
- Consistent (the same results each time!)
- Able to easily pinpoint what was at fault for each test that fails

Most computer languages have a xUnit unit testing system available; for example:

- **C#**: NUnit
- **Java**: JUnit
- **PHP**: PHPUnit

Unity offers an easy way to write and execute NUnit tests in its editor (and at the command line).

Typically, each unit test will be written in three sections, like so:

- **Arrange**: Set any initial values needed (sometimes, we are just giving a value to a variable to improve code readability)
- **Act**: Invoke some code (and, if appropriate, store the results)
- **Assert**: Make assertions for what should be true about the code that's been invoked (and any stored results)

Observe that the naming of a unit test method (by convention) is quite verbose – it is made up of lots of words that describe what it does. For example, you might have a unit test method named `TestHealthNotGoAboveOne()`. The idea is that if a test fails, the name of the test should give a programmer a very good idea of what behavior is being tested and, therefore, how to quickly establish whether the test is correct, If so, it tells you where to look in your program code for what was being tested. Another part of the convention of naming unit tests is that numerals are not used, just words, so we write "one," "two," and so on, in the name of the test method.

An **integration test** (PlayMode tests in Unity) involves checking the behavior of interacting software components, for example, ones that are real time, or a real filesystem, or that communicate with the web or other applications running on the computer. Integration tests are usually not as fast as unit tests, and may not produce consistent results (since the components may interact in different ways at different times).

Both unit and integration yests are important, but they are different and should be treated differently.

Unity offers **PlayMode** testing, allowing integration testing as Unity scenes execute with testing code in them.

Unity Python

As part of Unity 2021, Unity Technologies published the **Unity Python** package, which allows Python code to be executed as part of a Unity project. The final recipe in this chapter will help you install and begin using this scripting tool in a Unity project.

In this chapter, we will cover the following recipes:

- Using Gizmo to show the currently selected object in the Scene window
- Creating an editor snap-to-grid drawn by a Gizmo
- Saving and loading player data – using static properties
- Saving and loading player data – using `PlayerPrefs`
- Loading game data from a text file map
- Saving data to a file while the game is running
- Generating and running a default test script class
- A simple unit test
- Parameterizing tests with a data provider

- Unit testing a simple health script class
- Creating and executing a unit test in PlayMode
- PlayMode testing a door animation
- PlayMode and unit testing a player health bar with events, logging, and exceptions
- Reporting Code Coverage testing
- Running simple Python scripts inside Unity

Technical requirements

For this chapter, you will need Unity 2021.1 or later, plus one of the following:

- Microsoft Windows 10 (64-bit)/GPU: DX10, DX11, and DX12-capable
- macOS Sierra 10.12.6+/GPU Metal-capable Intel or AMD
- Linux Ubuntu 16.04, Ubuntu 18.04, and CentOS 7/GPU: OpenGL 3.2+ or Vulkan-capable, Nvidia or AMD

For each chapter, there is a folder that contains the asset files you will need in this book's GitHub repository at `https://github.com/PacktPublishing/Unity-2021-Cookbook-Fourth-Edition`.

Using Gizmo to show the currently selected object in the Scene window

Gizmos are visual aids that are provided to game designers in the **Scene** window. In this recipe, we'll highlight the GameObject that is currently selected in the **Hierarchy** window in the **Scene** window:

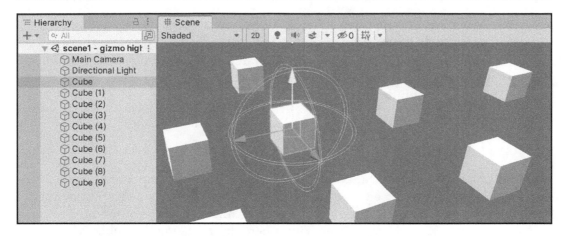

Figure 13.2 – Wireframe spheres around the selected GameObject

How to do it...

To create a Gizmo to show the selected object in the **Scene** window, follow these steps:

1. Create a new **Unity 3D project**.
2. Create a 3D **Cube** by going to **Create | 3D Object | Cube**.
3. Create a C# script class called `GizmoHighlightSelected` and add an instance object as a component to the 3D **Cube**:

```
using UnityEngine;

public class GizmoHighlightSelected : MonoBehaviour {
    public float radius = 5.0f;

    void OnDrawGizmosSelected() {
        Gizmos.color = Color.red;
        Gizmos.DrawWireSphere(transform.position, radius);

        Gizmos.color = Color.yellow;
        Gizmos.DrawWireSphere(transform.position, radius - 0.1f);

        Gizmos.color = Color.green;
        Gizmos.DrawWireSphere(transform.position, radius - 0.2f);
    }
}
```

4. Make lots of duplicates of the 3D **Cube**, distributing them randomly around the scene.

5. When you select one cube in the **Hierarchy** window, you should see three colored wireframe spheres drawn around the selected GameObject in the **Scene** window.

How it works...

When an object is selected in a scene, if it contains a scripted component that includes the `OnDrawGizmosSelected()` method, then that method is invoked. Our method draws three concentric wireframe spheres in three different colors around the selected object. You can change the size of the wire spheres by changing the public radius property of the scripted component of a cube.

See also

You can learn more from the Gizmos Unity manual entry at `https://docs.unity3d.com/ScriptReference/Gizmos.html`.

Creating an editor snap-to-grid drawn by a Gizmo

If the positions of objects need to be restricted to specific increments, it is useful to have a grid drawn in the **Scene** window to help ensure that new objects are positioned based on those values, as well as code to snap objects to that grid.

In this recipe, we'll use Gizmos to draw a grid with a customizable grid size, color, number of lines, and line length. The result of following this recipe will look as follows:

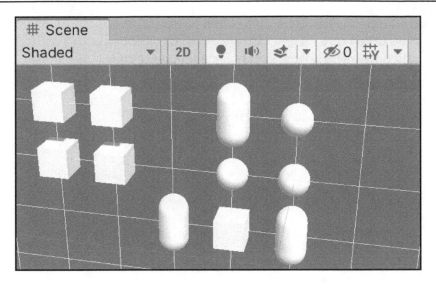

Figure 13.3 – Example of a visible grid that objects snap to

How to do it...

To create a design-time snap-to-grid drawn by a Gizmo in the **Scene** window, follow these steps:

1. Create a new **Unity 3D project**.
2. In the **Scene** window, turn off the **Skybox** view (or simply toggle off all the visual settings) so that you have a plain background for your grid:

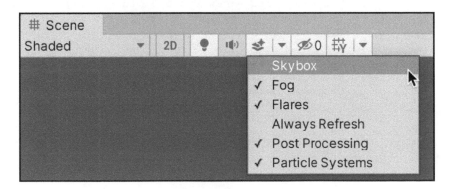

Figure 13.4 – Turning off the Skybox view in the Scene window

3. Updating the display and the child objects will be performed by a script class called `GridGizmo`. Create a new C# script class called `GridGizmo` that contains the following code:

```csharp
using UnityEngine;

public class GridGizmo : MonoBehaviour {
    public int grid = 2;

    public void SetGrid(int grid) {
        this.grid = grid;
        SnapAllChildren();
    }

    public Color gridColor = Color.red;
    public int numLines = 6;
    public int lineLength = 50;

    private void SnapAllChildren() {
        foreach (Transform child in transform)
            SnapPositionToGrid(child);
    }

    void OnDrawGizmos() {
        Gizmos.color = gridColor;

        int min = -lineLength;
        int max = lineLength;

        int n = -1 * RoundForGrid(numLines / 2);
        for (int i = 0; i < numLines; i++) {
            Vector3 start = new Vector3(min, n, 0);
            Vector3 end = new Vector3(max, n, 0);
            Gizmos.DrawLine(start, end);

            start = new Vector3(n, min, 0);
            end = new Vector3(n, max, 0);
            Gizmos.DrawLine(start, end);

            n += grid;
        }
    }

    public int RoundForGrid(int n) {
        return (n/ grid) * grid;
    }

    public int RoundForGrid(float n) {
```

```
        int posInt = (int) (n / grid);
        return posInt * grid;
    }

    public void SnapPositionToGrid(Transform transform) {
        transform.position = new Vector3 (
            RoundForGrid(transform.position.x),
            RoundForGrid(transform.position.y),
            RoundForGrid(transform.position.z)
        );
    }
}
```

4. Let's use an **Editor Script** to add a new menu item to the **GameObject** menu. Create a folder named `Editor` and, in that folder, create a new C# script class called `EditorGridGizmoMenuItem` that contains the following code:

```
using UnityEngine;
using UnityEditor;

public class EditorGridGizmoMenuItem : Editor {
    const string GRID_GAME_OBJECT_NAME = "___snap-to-grid___";
    [MenuItem("GameObject/Create New Snapgrid", false, 10000)]
    static void CreateCustomEmptyGameObject(MenuCommand menuCommand)
{
        GameObject gameObject = new
GameObject(GRID_GAME_OBJECT_NAME);

        gameObject.transform.parent = null;
        gameObject.transform.position = Vector3.zero;
        gameObject.AddComponent<GridGizmo>();
    }
}
```

5. Now, let's add another **Editor Script** for a custom **Inspector** display (and updater) for the `GridGizmo` components. Also, in your `Editor` folder, create a new C# script class called `EditorGridGizmo` that contains the following code:

```
using UnityEngine;
using UnityEditor;


[CustomEditor(typeof(GridGizmo))]
public class EditorGridGizmo : Editor {
    private GridGizmo gridGizmoObject;
```

```
            private int grid;
            private Color gridColor;
            private int numLines;
            private int lineLength;

            private string[] gridSizes = {
                "1", "2", "3", "4", "5"
            };

            void OnEnable() {
                gridGizmoObject = (GridGizmo)target;
                grid = serializedObject.FindProperty("grid").intValue;
                gridColor =
serializedObject.FindProperty("gridColor").colorValue;
                numLines =
serializedObject.FindProperty("numLines").intValue;
                lineLength =
serializedObject.FindProperty("lineLength").intValue;
            }

            public override void OnInspectorGUI() {
                serializedObject.Update ();

                int gridIndex = grid - 1;
                gridIndex =  EditorGUILayout.Popup("Grid size:",
gridIndex, gridSizes);
                gridColor = EditorGUILayout.ColorField("Color:",
gridColor);
                numLines =  EditorGUILayout.IntField("Number of grid
lines",  numLines);
                lineLength =  EditorGUILayout.IntField("Length of grid
lines",  lineLength);

                grid = gridIndex + 1;
                gridGizmoObject.SetGrid(grid);
                gridGizmoObject.gridColor = gridColor;
                gridGizmoObject.numLines = numLines;
                gridGizmoObject.lineLength = lineLength;
                serializedObject.ApplyModifiedProperties ();
                sceneView.RepaintAll();
            }
        }
```

6. Add a new `GizmoGrid` GameObject to the scene by going to **GameObject** | **Create New Snapgrid**. You should see a new **GameObject** named ___`snap-to-grid`___ added to the **Hierarchy** window:

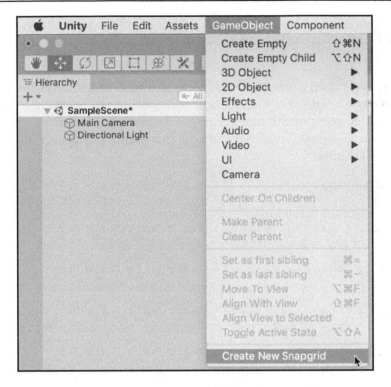

Figure 13.5 – Our new menu item at the bottom of the GameObject menu

7. Select the ___**snap-to-grid**___ GameObject and modify some of its properties in the **Inspector** window. You can change the grid's size, the color of the grid's lines, the number of lines, and their length:

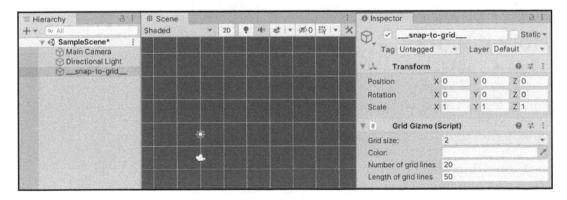

Figure 13.6 – Changing the properties of the snap grid

8. Create a 3D **Cube** by going to **Create | 3D Object | Cube**. Now, drag the 3D **Cube** into the **Hierarchy** window and make it a child of ___**snap-to-grid**___.

9. We now need a small script class so that each time the GameObject is moved (in Editor mode), it asks for its position to be snapped by the parent scripted component; that is, `SnapToGizmoGrid`. Create a C# script class called `SnapToGizmoGrid` and add an instance object as a component to the 3D **Cube**:

```
using UnityEngine;

[ExecuteInEditMode]
public class SnapToGridGizmo : MonoBehaviour {
    public void Update()
    {
#if UNITY_EDITOR
transform.parent.GetComponent<GridGizmo>().SnapPositionToGrid(transform);
#endif
    }
}
```

10. Make lots of duplicates of the 3D **Cube**, distributing them randomly around the scene – you'll find that they snap to the grid.

11. Select ___**snap-to-grid**___ again and modify some of its properties in the **Inspector** window. You'll see that the changes are instantly visible in the scene and that all the child objects that have a scripted component of `SnapToGizmoGrid` are snapped to any new grid size changes.

How it works...

Scripts that we place in a folder named `Editor` are known as Editor scripts, and in such scripts, we can customize and extend the features and look-and-feel of the Unity Editor. In this recipe, we've created Editor scripts to display and limit the movement of scene objects in a grid.

The `EditorGridGizmoMenuItem` script class adds a new item to the **GameObject** menu. When selected, a new GameObject is added to the **Hierarchy** window named ___snap-to-grid___, positioned at (0, 0, 0), and containing an instance object component of the `GridGizmo` script class.

`GridGizmo` draws a 2D grid based on public properties for grid size, color, number of lines, and line length. Regarding the `SetGrid(...)` method, as well as updating the integer grid size variable grid, it also invokes the `SnapAllChildren()` method so that each time the grid size is changed, all child GameObjects are snapped into the new grid positions.

The `SnapToGridGizmo` script class includes an Editor attribute called `[ExecuteInEditMode]` so that it will receive `Update()` messages when its properties are changed at design time in the Editor. Each time `Update()` is invoked, it calls the `SnapPositionToGrid(...)` method in its parent `GridGizmo` instance object so that its position is snapped based on the current settings of the grid. To ensure this logic and code is not compiled into any final build of the game, the contents of `Update()` are wrapped in an `#if UNITY_EDITOR` compiler test. Such content is removed before a build is compiled for the final game.

The `EditorGridGizmo` script class is a custom Editor **Inspector** component. This allows us to both control which properties are displayed in the **Inspector** window and how they are displayed, and it allows actions to be performed when any values are changed. So, for example, after changes have been saved, the `sceneView.RepaintAll()` statement ensures that the grid is redisplayed since it results in an `OnDrawGizmos()` message being sent.

There's more...

The preceding implementation works fine when the only objects we want to tie to the grid are children of our ___snap-to-grid___ GameObject. However, if we don't want to require affected objects to be such children, then we can use the singleton pattern to allow a GameObject anywhere in the **Hierarchy** window to get a reference to the **GridGizmo** component. Do the following to adapt this recipe to use this approach:

1. Update the contents of the `GridGizmo.cs` #C script class so that it matches the following:

```
using System.Collections;
using System.Collections.Generic;
using UnityEngine;

public class GridGizmo : MonoBehaviour
{
    private static GridGizmo _instance = null;
```

```
    public static void SetInstance(GridGizmo instance) {
      _instance = instance;
    }

    public static GridGizmo GetInstance() {
      if(_instance == null){
        throw new System.Exception("error - no GameObject has
GridGizmo component to snap to ...");
      }

      return _instance;
    }

    public int grid = 2;

    public void SetGrid(int grid) {
      this.grid = grid;
      SnapAllChildren();
    }
    ... the rest of the script is unchanged ...
```

2. Update the contents of the `Update()` method of the `SnapToGizmoGrid.cs` C# script class so that it matches the following:

```
using System.Collections;
using System.Collections.Generic;
using UnityEngine;

[ExecuteInEditMode]
public class SnapToGridGizmo : MonoBehaviour
{
    /**
     * we've moved!
     * snap position to its grid
     */
    public void Update()
    {
#if UNITY_EDITOR
        GridGizmo.GetInstance().SnapPositionToGrid(transform);
#endif
    }
}
```

3. Update the contents of the `EditorGridGizmoMenuItem.cs` C# script class to match the following:

```csharp
using UnityEngine;
using UnityEditor;
using System.Collections;

public class EditorGridGizmoMenuItem : Editor
{
    const string GRID_GAME_OBJECT_NAME = "___snap-to-grid___";

    /**
     * menu item to create a GridSnapper
     */
    [MenuItem("GameObject/Create New Snapgrid", false, 10000)]
    static void CreateCustomEmptyGameObject(MenuCommand menuCommand)
    {
        GameObject gameObject = new GameObject(GRID_GAME_OBJECT_NAME);
        // ensure not a child of any other object
        gameObject.transform.parent = null;
        // zero position
        gameObject.transform.position = Vector3.zero;

        // add Scripted component
        GridGizmo newInstance = gameObject.AddComponent<GridGizmo>();
        GridGizmo.SetInstance(newInstance);
    }
}
```

When the menu item is chosen, the method in the `EditorGridGizmoMenuItem` C# script class creates the game grid GameObject, adds a `GridGizmo` scripted component, and also uses the new `SetInstance(...)` method of the `GridGizmo` script class to store the reference to the `GridGizmo` scripted component in its static variable, called `_instance`. This means that when we add GameObjects such as cubes or cylinders anywhere in the **Hierarchy** window, we can add to them a `SnapToGizmoGrid` scripted component that can call the `GridGizmo.GetInstance()` public state method. To summarize what we have done, by using the singleton pattern, we have allowed any GameObject, anywhere in the **Hierarchy** window, to access the `GridGizmo` component.

Saving and loading player data – using static properties

Keeping track of the player's progress and user settings during a game is vital to give your game a greater feeling of depth and content. In this recipe, we will learn how to make our game remember the player's score between the different levels (scenes).

Note that this game is rigged, in that higher will always win and lower will always lose, but we can build on this to count, store, and retrieve the number of wins and games that have been played.

Getting ready

We have included a complete project in a Unity package named `game_HigherOrLower` in the `13_03` folder. To follow this recipe, we will import this package as the starting point.

How to do it...

To save and load player data, follow these steps:

1. Create a new **Unity 2D project** and import the `game_HigherOrLower` package.
2. Remove the default scene from the build and add each of the scenes from the imported package to the build in their name sequence (`scene0_mainMenu`, then `scene1_gamePlaying`, and so on).
3. Make yourself familiar with the game by playing it a few times and examining the content of the scenes. The game starts on the `scene0_mainMenu` scene, inside the `Scenes` folder.

4. Let's create a class to store the number of correct and incorrect guesses made by the user. Create a new C# script called `Player` with the following code:

```
using UnityEngine;

public class Player : MonoBehaviour {
  public static int scoreCorrect = 0;
  public static int scoreIncorrect = 0;
}
```

5. In the lower-left corner of the `scene0_mainMenu` scene, create a **UI Text** GameObject named **Text - score** containing the placeholder text **Score: 99 / 99**. Change the font color to a light gray:

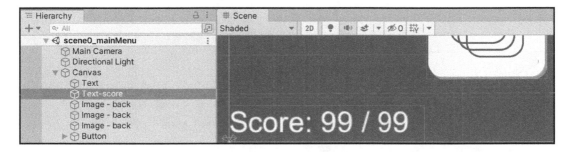

Figure 13.7 – Creating a UI Text GameObject to display the score

6. Next, attach the following C# script to **Text—score**:

```
using UnityEngine;
using System.Collections;

using UnityEngine.UI;

public class UpdateScoreText : MonoBehaviour {
  void Start(){
    Text scoreText = GetComponent<Text>();
    int totalAttempts = Player.scoreCorrect +
Player.scoreIncorrect;
    string scoreMessage = "Score = ";
    scoreMessage += Player.scoreCorrect + " / " +
totalAttempts;

    scoreText.text = scoreMessage;
  }
}
```

7. In the `scene2_gameWon` scene, attach the following C# script to **Main Camera**:

```
using UnityEngine;

public class IncrementCorrectScore : MonoBehaviour {
  void Start () {
    Player.scoreCorrect++;
  }
}
```

8. In the `scene3_gameLost` scene, attach the following C# script to **Main Camera**:

```
using UnityEngine;

public class IncrementIncorrectScore : MonoBehaviour {
  void Start () {
    Player.scoreIncorrect++;
  }
}
```

9. Save your scripts and play the game. As you progress from level (scene) to level, you will find that the score and the player's name are remembered, until you quit the application.

How it works...

The `Player` class uses static (class)
properties called `scoreCorrect` and `scoreIncorrect` to store the current total number of correct and incorrect guesses, respectively. Since these are public static properties, any object from any scene can access (set or get) these values, since the static properties are remembered from scene to scene. This class also provides the public static method called `ZeroTotals()`, which resets both values to zero.

When the `scene0_mainMenu` scene is loaded, all the GameObjects with scripts will have their `Start()` methods executed. The **UI Text** GameObject called **Text-score** has an instance of the `UpdateScoreText` class as a script component so that the script's `Start()` method will be executed, which retrieves the correct and incorrect totals from the `Player` class, creates a `scoreMessage` string about the current score, and updates the text property so that the user sees the current score.

When the game is running and the user guesses correctly (higher), then the `scene2_gameWon` scene is loaded. When the `scene2_gameWon` scene is loaded, the `Start()` method of the `IncrementCorrectScore` script component of **Main Camera** will be invoked, which adds 1 to the `scoreCorrect` variable of the `Player` class.

When the game is running and the user guesses incorrectly (lower), then the `scene3_gameLost` scene is loaded. When the `scene3_gameLost` scene is loaded, the `Start()` method of the `IncrementIncorrectScore` script component of **Main Camera** will be invoked, which adds 1 to the `scoreIncorrect` variable of the `Player` class.

The next time the user visits the main menu scene, the new values of the correct and incorrect totals will be read from the `Player` class, and the UI Text on the screen will inform the user of their updated total score for the game.

There's more...

There are some details that you don't want to miss.

Hiding the score before the first attempt is completed

Showing a score of zero out of zero isn't very professional. Let's add some logic so that the score is only displayed (a non-empty string) if the total number of attempts is greater than zero:

```
void Start(){
    Text scoreText = GetComponent<Text>();
    int totalAttempts = Player.scoreCorrect + Player.scoreIncorrect;

    // default is empty string
    string scoreMessage = "";
    if( totalAttempts > 0){
      scoreMessage = "Score = ";
      scoreMessage += Player.scoreCorrect + " / " + totalAttempts;
    }

    scoreText.text = scoreMessage;
}
```

See also

Refer to the *Saving and loading player data – using PlayerPrefs* recipe in this chapter for more information about alternative ways to save and load player data.

Saving and loading player data – using PlayerPrefs

While the previous recipe illustrates how the static properties allow a game to remember values between different scenes, these values are forgotten once the game application is exited. Unity provides the PlayerPrefs feature to allow a game to store and retrieve data between the different game-playing sessions:

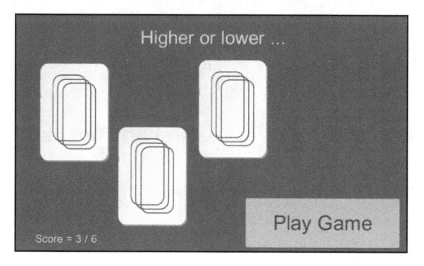

Figure 13.8 – Our higher-or-lower game, with the score being remembered between scenes

Getting ready

This recipe builds upon the previous recipe, so make a copy of that project and work on the copy.

How to do it...

To save and load the player data using `PlayerPrefs`, follow these steps:

1. Delete the C# script called `Player`.
2. Edit the C# script called `UpdateScoreText` by replacing the `Start()` method with the following code:

    ```
    void Start(){
        Text scoreText = GetComponent<Text>();

        int scoreCorrect = PlayerPrefs.GetInt("scoreCorrect");
        int scoreIncorrect = PlayerPrefs.GetInt("scoreIncorrect");

        int totalAttempts = scoreCorrect + scoreIncorrect;
        string scoreMessage = "Score = ";
        scoreMessage += scoreCorrect + " / " + totalAttempts;

        scoreText.text = scoreMessage;
    }
    ```

3. Now, edit the C# script called `IncrementCorrectScore` by replacing the `Start()` method with the following code:

    ```
    void Start () {
        int newScoreCorrect = 1 +
    PlayerPrefs.GetInt("scoreCorrect");
        PlayerPrefs.SetInt("scoreCorrect", newScoreCorrect);
    }
    ```

4. Now, edit the C# script called `IncrementIncorrectScore` by replacing the `Start()` method with the following code:

    ```
    void Start () {
        int newScoreIncorrect = 1 +
    PlayerPrefs.GetInt("scoreIncorrect");
        PlayerPrefs.SetInt("scoreIncorrect", newScoreIncorrect);
    }
    ```

5. Save your scripts and play the game. Quit Unity and then restart the application. You will find that the player's name, level, and score are now kept between the game sessions.

How it works...

We had no need for the `Player` class since this recipe uses the built-in runtime class called `PlayerPrefs`, which is provided by Unity.

Unity's `PlayerPrefs` runtime class is capable of storing and accessing information (the `string`, `int`, and `float` variables) in the user's machine. Values are stored in a `plist` file (Mac) or the registry (Windows), in a similar way to web browser cookies, which means they are remembered between game application sessions.

Values for the total correct and incorrect scores are stored by the `Start()` methods in the `IncrementCorrectScore` and `IncrementIncorrectScore` classes. These methods use the `PlayerPrefs.GetInt("")` method to retrieve the old total, add 1 to it, and then store the incremented total using the `PlayerPrefs.SetInt("")` method.

These correct and incorrect totals are then read each time the `scene0_mainMenu` scene is loaded, and the score totals are displayed via the **UI Text** object on the screen.

For more information on `PlayerPrefs`, see Unity's online documentation at `http://docs.unity3d.com/ScriptReference/PlayerPrefs.html`.

See also

Refer to the *Saving and loading player data – using static properties* recipe in this chapter for more information about alternative ways to save and load player data.

Loading game data from a text file map

Rather than having to create and place every GameObject on the screen by hand for every level of a game, a better approach can be to create the text files of rows and columns of characters, where each character corresponds to the type of GameObject that is to be created in the corresponding location.

In this recipe, we'll use a text file and a set of prefab sprites to display a graphical version of a text data file for a screen from the classic game *NetHack*:

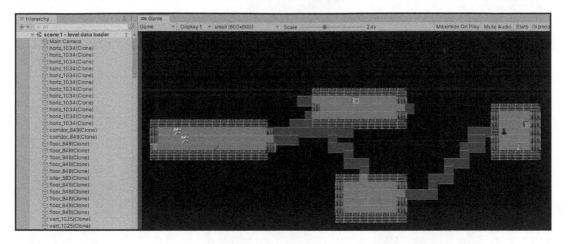

Figure 13.9 – The level we've created from a text file level description

Getting ready

In the 13_05 folder, we have provided the following two files for this recipe:

- level1.txt: A text file representing a level
- absurd128.png: A 128 x 128 sprite sheet for NetHack

The level data came from the NetHack Wikipedia page, while the sprite sheet came from SourceForge:

- http://en.wikipedia.org/wiki/NetHack
- http://sourceforge.net/projects/noegnud/files/tilesets_nethack-3. 4.1/absurd%20128x128/

Note that we also included a Unity package with all the prefabs set up, since this can be a laborious task.

How to do it...

To load game data from a text file map, do the following:

1. Create a new **Unity 2D project**.
2. Import the level1.txt text file and the absurd128.png image file.

3. Select `absurd128.png` in the **Inspector** window and set **Texture Type** to **Sprite (2D and UI)** and **Sprite Mode** to **Multiple**. Then, click the **Sprite Editor** button to open **Sprite Editor**.

4. In **Sprite Editor**, click the **Slice** dropdown option, then for **Type** choose **Grid by Cell Size** and set **Pixel Size** to `128 x 128`. Then, click the **Slice** button to apply these settings:

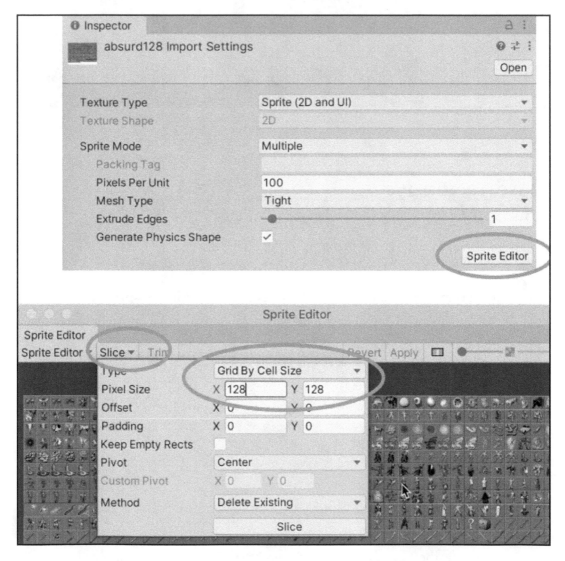

Figure 13.10 – Slicing the sprite sheet into a grid of 128 x 128 pixel images

5. In the **Project** window, click on the right-facing white triangle to explode the icon to show all the sprites in this sprite sheet individually:

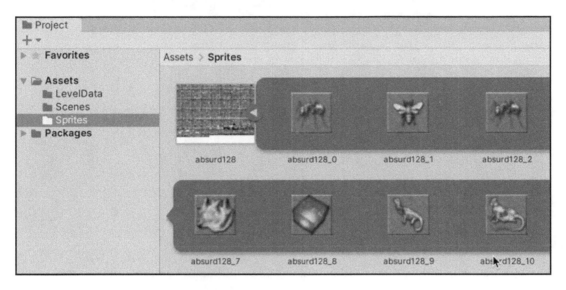

Figure 13.11 – All the individual 128 x 128 sprites in the Project window

6. Drag the sprite called **absurd128_175** onto the scene. Rename this GameObject `corpse_175`. So, the **Sprite** asset file named **absurd128_175** gives us a **Scene** GameObject named `corpse_175`.

7. In the **Project** window, create a folder named `Prefabs` and create a new prefab by dragging the `Sprite 175` GameObject into this `Prefabs` folder. Finally, delete `corpse_175`. You have now created a prefab containing `Sprite 175`.

8. Repeat this process for the following sprites (that is, create GameObjects, rename them, and then create prefabs for each one). The default name for each sprite will be **absurd128_<n>**, where **<n>** is the number for each sprite in the list. You can quickly find an asset file in the **Project** window by typing part of its name in the search box – see *Figure 13.12*. The sprites include the following:

- `floor_848`
- `corridor_849`
- `horiz_1034`
- `vert_1025`
- `door_844`

- potion_675
- chest_586
- alter_583
- stairs_up_994
- stairs_down_993
- wizard_287:

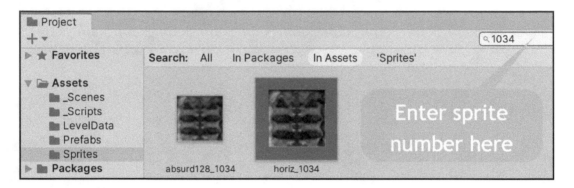

Figure 13.12 – Using the Project window asset name search tool to find absurd128_1034 and rename it horiz_1043

9. Select **Main Camera** in the **Inspector** window and ensure that it is set to an orthographic camera, sized **20**, with **Clear Flags** set to **Solid Color** and **Background** set to **Black**.

10. Attach the following C# code to **Main Camera** in a script class called LoadMapFromTextfile:

```
using UnityEngine;
using System.Collections.Generic;

public class LoadMapFromTextfile : MonoBehaviour
{
  public TextAsset levelDataTextFile;

  public GameObject floor_848;
  public GameObject corridor_849;
  public GameObject horiz_1034;
  public GameObject vert_1025;
  public GameObject corpse_175;
  public GameObject door_844;
  public GameObject potion_675;
  public GameObject chest_586;
  public GameObject alter_583;
```

```
      public GameObject stairs_up_994;
      public GameObject stairs_down_993;
      public GameObject wizard_287;

      public Dictionary<char, GameObject> dictionary = new
Dictionary<char, GameObject>();

      void Awake(){
        char newlineChar = '\n';

        dictionary['.'] = floor_848;
        dictionary['#'] = corridor_849;
        dictionary['('] = chest_586;
        dictionary['!'] = potion_675;
        dictionary['_'] = alter_583;
        dictionary['>'] = stairs_down_993;
        dictionary['<'] = stairs_up_994;
        dictionary['-'] = horiz_1034;
        dictionary['|'] = vert_1025;
        dictionary['+'] = door_844;
        dictionary['%'] = corpse_175;
        dictionary['@'] = wizard_287;

        string[] stringArray =
levelDataTextFile.text.Split(newlineChar);
        BuildMaze( stringArray );
      }

    private void BuildMaze(string[] stringArray){
        int numRows - stringArray.Length;

        float yOffset = numRows / 2;

        for(int row=0; row < numRows; row++){
          string currentRowString = stringArray[row];
          float y = -1 * (row - yOffset);
          CreateRow(currentRowString, y);
        }
      }

    private void CreateRow(string currentRowString, float y) {
        int numChars = currentRowString.Length;
        float xOffset = numChars / 2;

        for(int charPos = 0; charPos < numChars; charPos++){
          float x = charPos - xOffset;
          char prefabCharacter = currentRowString[charPos];
```

```
            if (dictionary.ContainsKey(prefabCharacter)){
               CreatePrefabInstance( dictionary[prefabCharacter], x,
    y);
            }
         }
      }

      private void CreatePrefabInstance(GameObject objectPrefab,
    float x, float y){
         float z = 0;
         Vector3 position = new Vector3(x, y, z);
         Quaternion noRotation = Quaternion.identity;
         Instantiate (objectPrefab, position, noRotation);
      }
   }
```

11. With **Main Camera** selected, drag the appropriate prefabs onto the prefabs slots in the **Inspector** window for the **Load Map From Textfile (Script)** component.

12. When you run the scene, you will see that a sprite-based NetHack map will appear, using your prefabs.

If you want to have a bit of fun, you could replace the image prefabs with 3D mesh objects and adapt this recipe to create a 3D scene from a 2D map file.

How it works...

The sprite sheet was automatically sliced up into hundreds of 128 x 128-pixel sprite squares. We created the prefab objects from some of these sprites so that the copies can be created at runtime when needed.

The text file called level1.txt contains the lines of text characters. Each non-space character represents where a sprite prefab should be instantiated (column = x; row = y). These characters have been chosen so that the text file is human-readable. As shown in the following screenshot, when displayed in a text editor with a fixed-width (typewriter) font, the text file gives us a good idea of how the actual sprite-based graphical 2D map will look:

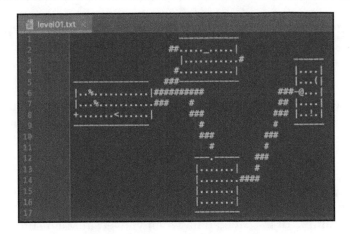

Figure 13.13 – The text-level data viewed in a code editor

In the `LoadMapFromTextfile` script class, a C# dictionary variable named `dictionary` is declared and initialized in the `Start()` method to associate the specific prefab GameObjects with some particular characters in the text file.

The `Awake()` method splits the string into an array using the newline character as a separator. So, now, we have `stringArray` with an entry for each row of the text data. The `BuildMaze(...)` method is called with `stringArray`.

The `BuildMaze(...)` method interrogates the array to find its length (the number of rows of data for this level) and sets `yOffSet` to half this value. This is done to allow the prefabs to be placed half above *y = 0* and half below, so (0, 0, 0) is the center of the level map. A `for` loop is used to read each row's string from the array. It passes it to the `CreateRow(...)` method, along with the *y*-value corresponding to the current row.

The `CreateRow(...)` method extracts the length of the string and sets `xOffSet` to half this value. This is done to allow the prefab to be placed one half to the left of *x = 0* and the other half to the right, so (0, 0, 0) is the center of the level map. A `for` loop is used to read each character from the current row's string, and (if there is an entry in our dictionary for that character) then the `CreatePrefabInstance (...)` method is called, passing the prefab reference in the dictionary for that character, as well as the *x* and *y* values.

The `CreatePrefabInstance(...)` method instantiates the given prefab at a position of *x, y, z*, where *z* is always zero, and there is no rotation (`Quarternion.identity`).

Saving data to a file while the game is running

Sometimes, we want to save data from our game into our local computer, whether for debugging, recording game testing experiments, and so on. The **comma-separated variable (CSV)** text file format is a good format to save data in since it is easily read into rows and columns by almost all spreadsheet applications.

In this recipe, we'll write a script that offers a method that can be called from anywhere in our game, from any scene, that will add a row of text to a log file. The following is an example of the saved data when viewed in Microsoft Excel:

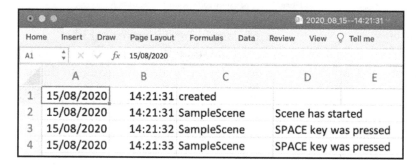

Figure 13.14 – Log data viewed in a spreadsheet application

How to do it...

To save data to a file while a game is running, follow these steps:

1. Create a new 3D project.
2. Create a new `AddToLogFile.cs` C# script class containing the following code:

```
using UnityEngine;
using System.IO;
using System;
using UnityEngine.SceneManagement;

public class AddToLogFile : MonoBehaviour {
  private static string _fileName = "";
  private static string _folderName = "Logs";
```

```
    private static string _filePath = "(no file path yet)";

  private static void CreateNewLogFile() {
    _fileName = DateTime.Now.ToString("yyy_MM_dd--HH:mm:ss") +
".csv";
    _filePath = Path.Combine(Application.dataPath,
_folderName);
    _filePath = Path.Combine(_filePath, _fileName);

    // Create a file to write to
    using (StreamWriter sw = File.CreateText(_filePath)) {
      sw.WriteLine(TimeStamp() + ",created");
    }
  }

  private static string TimeStamp() {
    return DateTime.Now.ToString("yyyy/MM/dd") + "," +
DateTime.Now.ToString("HH:mm:ss");
  }
  public static void LogLine(string textLine) {
    // the first time we try to log a line, we need to create
the file
    if (!File.Exists(_filePath)) {
      CreateNewLogFile();
    }

    string sceneName = SceneManager.GetActiveScene().name;
    textLine = TimeStamp() + "," + sceneName + "," + textLine;
    using (StreamWriter sw = File.AppendText(_filePath)) {
      sw.WriteLine(textLine);
    }
  }
}
```

3. Attach the following C# code to **Main Camera** as a script class
   called SimpleLogging:

```
using UnityEngine;

public class SimpleLogging : MonoBehaviour
{
    void Start() {
        AddToLogFile.LogLine("Scene has started");
    }

    void Update() {
        if (Input.GetKeyUp(KeyCode.Space)) {
            AddToLogFile.LogLine("SPACE key was pressed");
```

```
            }
        }
    }
```

4. Run the scene. Press the *spacebar* key a few times, then end the game.

5. You should now see a new timestamped CSV log file in the Logs folder:

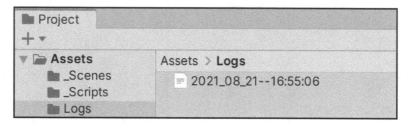

Figure 13.15 – The CSV log file in the Logs folder

How it works...

In this recipe, you created a C# script class called AddToLogFile.cs . This contains a public method called LogLine(...), which takes in a string message and adds a new line at the end of the CSV file. This method is static, which means it can be called from any script in any scene through a single line of code since it is not a component of a GameObject. This method creates a new text file if one does not already exist (by executing CreateNewLogFile()). Then, it creates a timestamp of the current date and time (with TimeStamp()), adds the name of the scene that is currently running, and appends this long, comma-separated string to the text file.

To illustrate how to use our file logging script, we created a second C# script class called SimpleLogging. An instance of this class was added as a component to **Main Camera**. This script will add a line to the log file when its Start() method is invoked (when the scene begins), and also each time the user presses and releases the *spacebar*.

This example logged events such as the scene starting when the *spacebar* is pressed. However, the events resulting in data being appended to the log file could be anything, such as the user passing a checkpoint or losing a life, completing a level, and so on. This type of live game logging can be useful for recording data about whatever aspects of gameplay we might want to record and analyze for debugging, gameplay testing, and so on.

See also

This concept can also be used to log data to a live web database. For an example of this, see this open source Unity user action logging project: `https://github.com/dr-matt-smith/unity-user-action-logger-web`.

Generating and running a default test script class

Unity can create a default C# test script for you, thereby enabling you to quickly start creating and executing tests on your project. In this recipe, we will add the Unity Test Framework to a project and use it to automatically generate a default test script for us. This will be the basis for several of the following recipes:

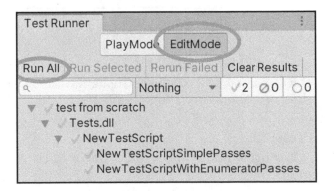

Figure 13.16 – Passing the test (indicated by green ticks)

How to do it...

To generate a default test script class, follow these steps:

1. Create a new **3D Unity project**.
2. Display the **Test Runner** window by going to **Window | General | Test Runner.**

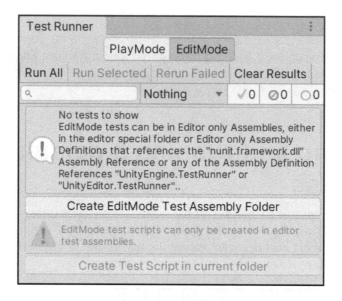

Figure 13.17 – The **Test Runner** panel

3. Ensure that the **EditMode** button is selected in the **Test Runner** window.
4. In the **Test Runner** window, click the **Create EditMode Test Assembly Folder** button. You'll now see a folder called `Tests` that's been created in the **Project** window.
5. Select the **Tests** folder.
6. In the **Test Runner** window, click the **Create Test Script in Current Folder** button.
7. You should now have a new C# script named `NewTestScript` inside your **Tests** folder.
8. To run the tests in your script class, click the **Run All** button in the **Test Runner** window.
9. You should now see all green ticks (check marks) in the panel, as shown in *Figure 13.16*.

How it works...

Unity checks that you have a folder named **Editor** selected in the **Project** window, and then creates a `NewTestScript` C# script class for you containing the following:

```
using System.Collections;
using System.Collections.Generic;
using NUnit.Framework;
using UnityEngine;
using UnityEngine.TestTools;

namespace Tests {
    public class NewTestScript {
        // A Test behaves as an ordinary method
        [Test]
        public void NewTestScript1SimplePasses() {
            // Use the Assert class to test conditions
        }

        // A UnityTest behaves like a coroutine in Play Mode. In Edit
Mode you can use
        // `yield return null;` to skip a frame.
        [UnityTest]
        public IEnumerator NewTestScriptWithEnumeratorPasses() {
            // Use the Assert class to test conditions.
            // Use yield to skip a frame.
            yield return null;
        }
    }
}
```

In the **Test Runner** window, you should see the script class and its two methods listed. Note that the first line in the **Test Runner** window is the Unity project name; the second line will say `<projectName>.dll`, followed by your script class's `namespace`, which is `Tests`, followed by the script class called `NewTestScript`, and, finally, each of the test methods. The generated default script creates two methods:

- `NewTestScriptSimplePasses()`: This is a simple, empty test method (since it's empty, it will always pass).

- `NewTestScriptWithEnumeratorPasses()`: This is a coroutine test method that always yields a null return so, again, it will not create a failed event and always pass.

The generated script and two methods are a basic skeleton that we can populate with simple methods and coroutine methods as appropriate for each project's testing requirements.

There are three symbols to indicate the status of each test/class:

- **Empty circle**: The test hasn't been executed since the script class was last changed.
- **Green tick** (checkmark): The test passed successfully.
- **Red cross**: The test failed.

There's more...

Here are some details that you won't want to miss.

Creating a default test script from the Project window's Create menu

Another way of creating a default **Unit Test** script is by going to the **Project** window and going to **Create | Testing | C# Test Script.**

Edit mode minimum skeleton unit test script

Be aware that if you are only going to use this script class for testing in **EditMode**, you can delete the second method using statements such as the following to give you a minimal skeleton to work from:

```
using NUnit.Framework;

public class UnitTestSkeleton
{
    [Test]
    public void NewTestScriptSimplePasses()
    {
        // write your assertion(s) here
    }
}
```

This simpler skeleton testing class is for when we are writing code-only unit tests.

A simple unit test

In the same way as printing "hello world" is most programmers' first program statement, asserting that 1 + 1 = 2 is perhaps the most common first test that's executed for those learning unit testing. That's what we'll create in this recipe:

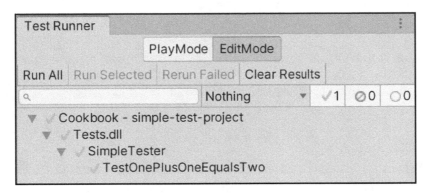

Figure 13.18 – Our simple numeric test method passing with a green tick

How to do it...

To create and execute a simple unit test, follow these steps:

1. Create a new **3D Unity project**.
2. In the **Package Manager** window, ensure you have the latest version of the **Test Framework** package installed.
3. Display the **Test Runner** window by going to **Window | General | Test Runner**.
4. Ensure that the **EditMode** button is selected in the **Test Runner** window.
5. In the **Test Runner** window, click the **Create EditMode Test Assembly Folder** button. You'll now see a folder called **Tests** in the **Project** window.
6. Select the **Tests** folder.
7. In the **Test Runner** window, click the **Create Test Script in Current Folder** button. Rename the script class `SimpleTester.cs` and replace its contents with the following:

```
using NUnit.Framework;

class SimpleTester
{
```

```
[Test]
public void TestOnePlusOneEqualsTwo()
{
    // Arrange
    int n1 = 1;
    int n2 = 1;
    int expectedResult = 2;

    // Act
    int result = n1 + n2;

    // Assert
    Assert.AreEqual(expectedResult, result);
}
}
```

8. Click **Run All**.
9. You should see the results of your unit test being executed – if the test concluded successfully, it should have a green "tick" next to it.

How it works...

In this recipe, you declared that the `TestOnePlusOneEqualsTwo()` method in the `SimpleTester.cs` C# script class is a test method. When executing this test method, **Unity Test Runner** executes each statement in sequence, so variables n1, n2, and `expectedResult` are set, then the calculation of 1 + 1 is stored in the variable result, and finally (the most important bit), we make an assertion of what should be true after executing that code. Our assertion states that the value of the `expectedResult` variable should be equal to the value of the variable result.

If the assertion is `true`, the test passed; otherwise, it failed. Generally, as programmers, we expect our code to pass, so we inspect each fail very carefully, first to see whether we have an obvious error, then perhaps to check whether the test itself is correct (especially if it's a new test), and then to begin to debug and understand why our code behaved in such a way that it did not yield the anticipated result.

There's more...

Here are some details that you won't want to miss.

Shorter tests with values in the assertion

For simple calculations, some programmers prefer to write less test code by putting the values directly into the assertion. So, as shown here, our 1 + 1 = 2 test could be expressed in a single assertion, where the expected value of 2 and the expression 1 + 1 are entered directly into an `AreEqual(...)` method's invocation:

```
using NUnit.Framework;

class SimpleTester
{
    [Test]
    public void TestOnePlusOneEqualsTwo()
    {
        // Assert
        Assert.AreEqual(2, 1 + 1);
    }
}
```

However, if you are new to testing, you may prefer the previous approach, whereby the way you prepare, execute, and store the results, as well as the property assertions about those results, are structured clearly in a sequence of **Arrange/Act/Assert**. By storing values in meaningfully named variables, what we are asserting is very clear.

Expected value followed by the actual value

When comparing values with assertions, it is customary for the expected (correct) value to be given first, followed by the actual value:

```
Assert.AreEqual( <expectedValue>, <actualValue> );
```

While it makes no difference to the true or false nature of equality, it can make a difference to messages when tests fail with some testing frameworks (for example, "got 2 but expected 3" has a very different meaning to "got 3 but expected 2"). Hence, the following assertion would output a message that would be confusing, since 2 was our expected result:

```
public void TestTwoEqualsThreeShouldFail() {
    // Arrange
    int expectedResult = 2;

    // Act
    int result = 1 + 2; // 3 !!!

    // Assert
```

```
                Assert.AreEqual(result, expectedResult);
        }
```

The following screenshot illustrates how we will get a misleading message when the arguments are the wrong way around in our assertion method:

> TestTwoEqualsThreeShouldFail
>
> TestTwoEqualsThreeShouldFail (0.012s)
>
> ---
> Expected: 3
> But was: 2
> ---

Figure 13.19 – Confusing message due to an incorrect argument sequence in the assertion

Parameterizing tests with a data provider

If we are testing our code using a range of test data, then sometimes, there is little difference between each test apart from the values. Rather than duplicating our Arrange/Act/Assert statements, we can reuse a single method, and Unity Test Runner will loop through a collection of test data, running the test method for each set of test data. The special method that provides multiple sets of test data to a test method is known as a **DataProvider**, and we'll create one in this recipe:

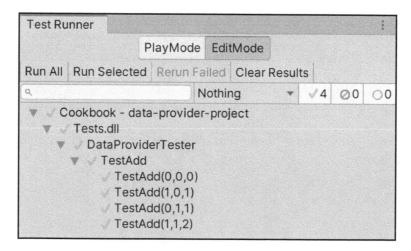

Figure 13.20 – Running the test method with many sets of values with a DataProvider method

How to do it...

To parameterize tests with a data provider method, follow these steps:

1. Create a new **3D Unity project**.
2. In the **Package Manager** window, ensure you have the latest version of the **Test Framework** package installed.
3. Display the **Test Runner** window by going to **Window | General | Test Runner**.
4. Ensure that the **EditMode** button is selected in the **Test Runner** window.
5. In the **Test Runner** panel, window the **Create EditMode Test Assembly Folder** button. You'll now see a folder called **Tests** in the **Project** window.
6. Select the **Tests** folder.
7. In the **Test Runner** window, click the **Create Test Script in Current Folder** button. Rename the script class `DataProviderTester.cs` and ensure it contains the following code:

```
using NUnit.Framework;

class DataProviderTester
{
    [Test, TestCaseSource("AdditionProvider")]
    public void TestAdd(int num1, int num2, int expectedResult)
    {
        // Arrange
        // (not needed - since values coming as arguments)

        // Act
        int result = num1 + num2;

        // Assert
        Assert.AreEqual(expectedResult, result);
    }

    // the data provider
    static object[] AdditionProvider =
    {
        new object[] { 0, 0, 0 },
        new object[] { 1, 0, 1 },
        new object[] { 0, 1, 1 },
        new object[] { 1, 1, 2 }
    };
}
```

8. Display the **Test Runner** window by going to **Window** | **General** | **Test Runner**.
9. Ensure that the **EditMode** button is selected in the **Test Runner** window.
10. Click **Run All**.
11. You should see the results of your unit test being executed. You should see four sets of results for the `TestAdd(...)` test method, one for each of the datasets provided by the `AdditionProvider` method.

How it works...

We have indicated that the `TestAdd(...)` method is a test method with a compiler attribute called `[Test]`. However, in this case, we have added additional information to state that the `[TestCaseSource(...)]` data source for this method is the `AdditionProvider` method.

This means that **Unity Test Runner** will retrieve the data objects from the additional provider and create multiple tests for the `TestAdd(...)` method, one for each set of data from the `AdditionProvider()` method.

In the **Test Runner** window, we can see a line for each of these tests:

```
TestAdd(0, 0, 0)
TestAdd(1, 0, 1)
TestAdd(0, 1, 1)
TestAdd(1, 1, 2)
```

Unit testing a simple health script class

Let's create something that might be used in a game and that can easily be unit tested. Classes that do **not** subclass from MonoBehaviour are much easier to unit test since instance objects can be created using the `new` keyword. If the class is carefully designed with private data and public methods with clearly declared dependencies as parameters, it becomes easy to write a set of tests to make us confident that objects of this class will behave as expected in terms of default values, as well as valid and invalid data.

In this recipe, we will create a health script class and a set of tests for this class. This kind of class can be reused for both the health of human players and also **artificial intelligence (AI)**-controlled enemies in a game:

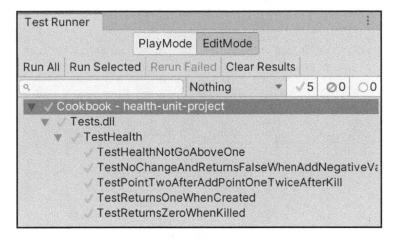

Figure 13.21 – Passing tests for our Health script class

How to do it...

To unit test a health script class, follow these steps:

1. Create a new **3D Unity project**.
2. In the **Package Manager** panel window, you have the latest version of the **Test Framework** package installed.
3. Create a new folder named _Scripts.
4. Inside your _Scripts folder, create a new Health.cs C# script class containing the following:

```
using UnityEngine;
using System.Collections;

public class Health
{
    private float _health = 1;

    public float GetHealth()
    {
        return _health;
    }
}
```

```
public bool AddHealth(float heathPlus)
{
    if(heathPlus > 0){
        _health += heathPlus;

        // ensure never more than 1
        if(_health > 1) _health = 1;
        return true;
    } else {
        return false;
    }
}

public bool KillCharacter()
{
    _health = 0;
    return true;
}
}
```

5. Since we want to test scripts in this folder, we need to add an **Assembly Definition** here. From the **Create** menu in the **Project** window, create an **Assembly Definition** and name it `HealthScriptAssembly`:

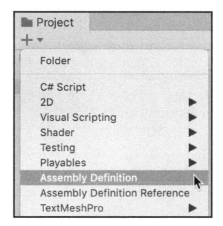

Figure 13.22 – Creating an Assembly Definition in our _Scripts folder

6. With the name `HealthScriptAssembly` selected in the **Project** window, in the **Inspector** window for the platform, select just the Editor:

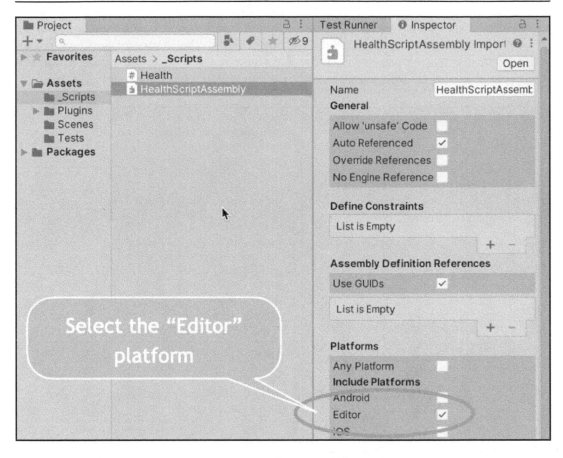

Figure 13.23 – Setting the Editor platform for HealthScriptAssembly

7. Display the **Test Runner** window by going to **Window | General | Test Runner**.

8. Ensure that the **EditMode** button is selected in the **Test Runner** window.

9. In the **Test Runner** window, click the **Create EditMode Test Assembly Folder** button. You'll now see a folder called **Tests** in the **Project** window.

10. Select the **Tests** folder. This contains an **Assembly Reference** named **Tests**. Select this asset file in the **Project** window and look at its properties in the **Inspector** window. This **Assembly Reference** already has references to two Assembly Definition
References: **UnityEngine.TestRunner** and **UnityEditor.TestRunner**.

11. Now, we need to add our `HealthScriptAssembly` to the **Tests** assembly so that we can test our `Health` script class. In the **Inspector** window, click the plus (**+**) button to add a new **Assembly Definition Reference** to the slot that was created to locate and drag the **HealthScript** Assembly Definition:

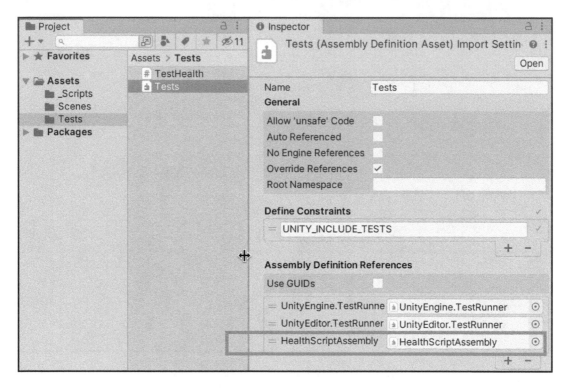

Figure 13.24 – Adding HealthScriptAssembly to the Tests Assembly Definition

12. In the **Test Runner** window, click the **Create Test Script in Current Folder** button. Rename the script class `TestHealth.cs` and ensure it contains the following code:

```
using NUnit.Framework;

class TestHealth {
    [Test]
    public void TestReturnsOneWhenCreated()   {
        // Arrange
        Health h = new Health ();
        float expectedResult = 1;

        // Act
```

```
        float result = h.GetHealth ();

        // Assert
        Assert.AreEqual (expectedResult, result);
    }

    [Test]
    public void TestPointTwoAfterAddPointOneTwiceAfterKill()
{
        // Arrange
        Health h = new Health();
        float healthToAdd = 0.1f;
        float expectedResult = 0.2f;

        // Act
        h.KillCharacter();
        h.AddHealth(healthToAdd);
        h.AddHealth(healthToAdd);
        float result = h.GetHealth();


        // Assert
        Assert.AreEqual(expectedResult, result);
    }

    [Test]
    public void
TestNoChangeAndReturnsFalseWhenAddNegativeValue()        {
        // Arrange
        Health h = new Health();
        float healthToAdd = -1;
        bool expectedResultBool = false;
        float expectedResultFloat = 1;

        // Act
        bool resultBool = h.AddHealth(healthToAdd);
        float resultFloat = h.GetHealth();

        // Assert
        Assert.AreEqual(expectedResultBool, resultBool);
        Assert.AreEqual(expectedResultFloat, resultFloat);
    }

    [Test]
    public void TestReturnsZeroWhenKilled()        {
        // Arrange
        Health h = new Health();
        float expectedResult = 0;
```

```
        // Act
        h.KillCharacter();
        float result = h.GetHealth();

        // Assert
        Assert.AreEqual(expectedResult, result);
    }


    [Test]
    public void TestHealthNotGoAboveOne()      {
        // Arrange
        Health h = new Health();
        float expectedResult = 1;

        // Act
        h.AddHealth(0.1f);
        h.AddHealth(0.5f);
        h.AddHealth(1);
        h.AddHealth(5);
        float result = h.GetHealth();

        // Assert
        Assert.AreEqual(expectedResult, result);
    }
}
```

13. Display the **Test Runner** window by going to **Window** | **Debug** | **Test Runner**.
14. Ensure that the **EditMode** button is selected in the **Test Runner** window.
15. Click **Run All**.
16. You should see the results of your unit tests being executed.

How it works...

Each of the C# script classes is described here.

Health.cs

This script class has one private property. Since it is private, it can only be changed by methods. Its initial value is 1.0 – in other words, 100% health:

- `health` (float): The valid range is from 0 (dead!) to 1.0 (100% health).

There are three public methods:

- `GetHealth()`: This returns the current value of the health float number (which should be between 0 and 1.0).
- `AddHealth(float)`: This takes a float as input (the amount to add to the health) and returns a Boolean `true`/`false` regarding whether the value was valid. Note that the logic of this method is that it accepts values of 0 or more (and will return true), but it will ensure that the value of health is never more than 1.
- `KillCharacter()`: This method sets health to zero and returns true since it is always successful in this action.

TestHealth.cs

This script class has five methods:

- `TestReturnsOneWhenCreated()`: This tests that the initial value of health is 1 when a new **Health** object is created.
- `TestPointTwoAfterAddPointOneTwiceAfterKill()`: This tests that after a kill (health set to zero), and then adding 0.1 on two occasions, that the health is 0.2.
- `TestReturnsZeroWhenKilled()`: This tests that the health value is set to zero immediately after the `KillCharacter()` method has been called.
- `TestNoChangeAndReturnsFalseWhenAddNegativeValue()`: This tests that attempting to add a negative value to health should return `false` and that the value of health should not have changed. This method is an example of a test with more than one assertion (but both are related to the actions).

- `TestHealthNotGoAboveOne()`: This test verifies that even when lots of values are added to health that total more than 1.0, the value that's returned from `GetHealth()` is 1.

Hopefully, all the tests pass when you run them, giving you some confidence that the logic that's been implemented in the `Health.cs` script class behaves as intended.

Creating and executing a unit test in PlayMode

It's a good idea to write as much of the logic for a game as isolated, non-MonoBehaviour classes that are easy to unit test in Edit Mode as possible. However, some of the logic in a game relates to things that happen when the game is running. Examples include physics, collisions, and timing-based events. We test these parts of our games in **PlayMode**.

In this recipe, we'll create one very simple **PlayMode** test to check that the physics affect a **Rigidbody** (based on an example from the Unity documentation):

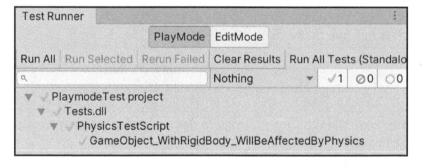

Figure 13.25 – Running a physics PlayMode test

How to do it...

To create and execute a unit test in **PlayMode**, follow these steps:

1. Create a new **3D Unity project**.
2. In the **Package Manager** window, ensure you have the latest version of the **Test Framework** package installed.
3. Display the **Test Runner** window by going to **Window** | **General** | **Test Runner.**
4. Ensure that the **PlayMode** button is selected in the **Test Runner** window.
5. In the **Test Runner** window, click the **Create PlayMode Test Assembly Folder** button. You'll now see a folder called **Tests** in the **Project** window.
6. In the **Test Runner** window, click the **Create Test Script in current folder** button. Rename the script class `PhysicsTestScript.cs` and ensure it contains the following code:

```
using UnityEngine;
 using UnityEngine.TestTools;
 using NUnit.Framework;
 using System.Collections;

 public class PhysicsTestScript
 {
     [UnityTest]
     public IEnumerator
GameObject_WithRigidBody_WillBeAffectedByPhysics()
     {
         // Arrange
         var go = new GameObject();
         go.AddComponent<Rigidbody>();
         var originalPosition = go.transform.position.y;

         // Act
         yield return new WaitForFixedUpdate();

         // Assert
         Assert.AreNotEqual(originalPosition,
go.transform.position.y);
     }
 }
```

7. Click **Run All**.

8. In the **Hierarchy** window, you'll see that a temporary scene is created (named something along the lines of **InitTestScene6623462364**) and that a GameObject named **Code Based Test Runner** is created.

9. In the **Game** window, you will briefly see the message **Display 1 No Cameras Rendering**:

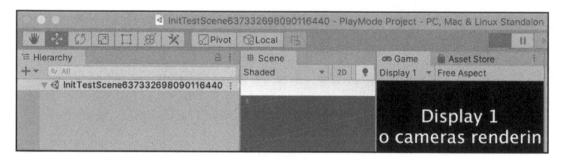

Figure 13.26 – Temporary scene and GameObject for the runtime test

10. You should see the results of your unit test being executed – if the test is concluded successfully, it should have a green tick next to it.

How it works...

Methods marked with the [UnityTest] attribute are run as coroutines. A coroutine has the ability to pause execution (when it meets a yield statement) and return control to Unity, but then to continue where it left off when called again (for example, the next frame, second frame, and so on). The yield statement indicates the statement after which, and for how long, execution of the method is to be paused. Examples of different types of yield include the following:

- Waiting until the next frame: null
- Waiting for a given length of time: WaitForSeconds(<seconds>)
- Waiting until the next fixed-update time period (physics is not applied to each frame (since the framerate varies) but after a fixed period of time): WaitForFixedUpdate()

The `GameObject_WithRigidBody_WillBeAffectedByPhysics()` method creates a new GameObject and attaches to it a **Rigidbody**. It also stores the original Y position. The `yield` statement makes **PlayMode Test Runner** wait until physics has begun at the next fixed update period. Finally, an assertion is made that the original Y position is not equal to the new Y position (after the physics fixed update). Since the defaults for a **Rigidbody** are that gravity will be applied, this is a good test that physics is being applied to the new object (in other words, it should have started falling down once physics had been applied).

PlayMode testing a door animation

Having learned the basics of **PlayMode** testing in the previous recipe, let's test something non-trivial that we might find in a game. In this recipe, we'll create a **PlayMode** test to ensure that a door opening animation plays when the player's sphere object enters a collider.

A scene has been provided with the player's sphere initialized to roll toward a red door. When the sphere hits the collider (the `OnTriggerEnter` event), some code sets the door's **Animator Controller Opening** variable to `true`, which transitions the door from its closed state to its open state, as shown in the following screenshot:

Figure 13.27 – The door will open (upward) when hit by the sphere

Thanks to the creator of the ground texture; it was designed by *Starline* and published at `Freepik.com`.

Getting ready

For this recipe, a Unity package has been provided (`doorScene.unitypackage`) in the `13_12` folder.

How to do it...

To **PlayMode** test a door animation, follow these steps:

1. Create a new **3D Unity project** and delete the default folder, called **Scenes**.
2. In the **Package Manager** window, ensure you have the latest version of the **Test Framework** package installed.
3. Import the Unity package provided (**doorScene.unitypackage**).
4. Add the **doorScene** and **menuScene** scenes to the project build (the sequence doesn't matter).
5. Ensure that the scene that's currently open is **menuScene**.
6. Display the **Test Runner** window by going to **Window | General | Test Runner**.
7. Ensure that the **PlayMode** button is selected in the **Test Runner** window.
8. Now, we have to restart the Unity Editor (just close the application and then reopen it with your project).
9. In the **Test Runner** window, click the **Create PlayMode Test Assembly Folder** button. You'll now see a folder called **Tests** in the **Project** window.
10. In the **Project** window, select the top-level folder called **Assets**.
11. In the **Test Runner** window, click the **Create PlayMode Test Assembly Folder** button. A new folder, named `Tests`, should have been created.
12. In the **Project** window, open the `Tests` folder.
13. In the **Test Runner** window, click the **Create Test Script in the current folder** button. Rename this script class `DoorTest`.
14. Edit the `DoorTest.cs` script class by replacing its content with the following:

```
using System.Collections;
using NUnit.Framework;
using UnityEngine;
using UnityEngine.SceneManagement;
using UnityEngine.TestTools;
```

```
public class DoorTest
{
    const int BASE_LAYER = 0;
    private string initialScenePath;
    private Animator doorAnimator;
    private Scene tempTestScene;

    // name of scene being tested by this class
    private string sceneToTest = "doorScene";

    [SetUp]
    public void Setup()
    {
        // setup - load the scene
        tempTestScene = SceneManager.GetActiveScene();
    }
}
```

15. Add the following test method to `DoorTest.cs`:

```
[UnityTest]
 public IEnumerator TestDoorAnimationStateStartsClosed()
 {
    // load scene to be tested
    yield return SceneManager.LoadSceneAsync(sceneToTest,
LoadSceneMode.Additive);
SceneManager.SetActiveScene(SceneManager.GetSceneByName(sceneT
oTest));

    // Arrange
    doorAnimator =
GameObject.FindWithTag("Door").GetComponent<Animator>();
    string expectedDoorAnimationState = "DoorClosed";

    // immediate next frame
    yield return null;

    // Act
    AnimatorClipInfo[] currentClipInfo =
doorAnimator.GetCurrentAnimatorClipInfo(BASE_LAYER);
    string doorAnimationState =
currentClipInfo[0].clip.name;

    // Assert
    Assert.AreEqual(expectedDoorAnimationState,
doorAnimationState);

    // teardown - reload original temp test scene
```

```
SceneManager.SetActiveScene(tempTestScene);
        yield return
SceneManager.UnloadSceneAsync(sceneToTest);
    }
```

16. Add the following test method to `DoorTest.cs`:

```
[UnityTest]
 public IEnumerator TestIsOpeningStartsFalse()
 {
        // load scene to be tested
        yield return SceneManager.LoadSceneAsync(sceneToTest,
LoadSceneMode.Additive);
SceneManager.SetActiveScene(SceneManager.GetSceneByName(sceneT
oTest));

        // Arrange
        doorAnimator =
GameObject.FindWithTag("Door").GetComponent<Animator>();

        // immediate next frame
        yield return null;

        // Act
        bool isOpening = doorAnimator.GetBool("Opening");

        // Assert
        Assert.IsFalse(isOpening);

        // teardown - reload original temp test scene
        SceneManager.SetActiveScene(tempTestScene);
        yield return
SceneManager.UnloadSceneAsync(sceneToTest);
    }
```

17. Add the following test method to `DoorTest.cs`:

```
[UnityTest]
 public IEnumerator
TestDoorAnimationStateOpenAfterAFewSeconds()
    {
        // load scene to be tested
        yield return SceneManager.LoadSceneAsync(sceneToTest,
LoadSceneMode.Additive);
SceneManager.SetActiveScene(SceneManager.GetSceneByName(sceneT
oTest));

        // wait a few seconds
```

```
        int secondsToWait = 3;
        yield return new WaitForSeconds(secondsToWait);

        // Arrange
        doorAnimator =
GameObject.FindWithTag("Door").GetComponent<Animator>();
        string expectedDoorAnimationState = "DoorOpen";


        // Act
        AnimatorClipInfo[] currentClipInfo =
doorAnimator.GetCurrentAnimatorClipInfo(BASE_LAYER);
        string doorAnimationState =
currentClipInfo[0].clip.name;
        bool isOpening = doorAnimator.GetBool("Opening");

        // Assert
        Assert.AreEqual(expectedDoorAnimationState,
doorAnimationState);
        Assert.IsTrue(isOpening);

        // teardown - reload original temp test scene
        SceneManager.SetActiveScene(tempTestScene);
        yield return
SceneManager.UnloadSceneAsync(sceneToTest);
    }
```

18. Click **Run All**.
19. As the tests run, you will see that, in the **Hierarchy**, **Game**, and **Scene** windows, a temporary scene is created, then **doorScene** running, with the sphere rolling toward the red door.
20. You should see the results of your unit test being executed – if all the tests conclude successfully, there should be green ticks (check marks) next to each test.

How it works...

In this recipe, you added two scenes to the build so that they can be selected in our scripts using **SceneManager** during **PlayMode** testing.

We opened **menuScene** so that we can clearly see when Unity runs different scenes during our **PlayMode** testing – and we'll see the menu scene reopened after testing takes place.

There is a SetUp() method that is executed before each test. The SetUp() and TearDown() methods are very useful for preparing things before each test and resetting things back to how they were before the test took place. Unfortunately, aspects such as loading our door scene before running each test, and then reloading the menu after each test, involve waiting until the scene load process has completed. We can't place yield statements in our SetUp() and TearDown() methods, so you'll see that each test has repeated scene loading at the beginning and end of each test:

```
// load scene to be tested
  yield return SceneManager.LoadSceneAsync(sceneToTest,
LoadSceneMode.Additive);
SceneManager.SetActiveScene(SceneManager.GetSceneByName(sceneToTest));

  // Arrange-Act-Assert goes here

  // teardown - reload original temp test scene
SceneManager.SetActiveScene(tempTestScene);
  yield return SceneManager.UnloadSceneAsync(sceneToTest);
```

For each test, we wait, either for a single frame (yield null) or for a few seconds (yield return new WaitForSeconds(...)). This ensures that all objects have been created and physics has started before our test starts running. The first two tests check the initial conditions – in other words, that the door begins in the DoorClosed animation state and that the animation controller's isOpening variable is false.

The final test waits a few seconds (which is enough time for the sphere to roll up to the door and trigger the opening animation) and tests that the door is entering/has entered the DoorOpen animation state and that the animation controller's isOpening variable is true.

As can be seen, there is quite a bit more to **PlayMode** testing than unit testing, but this means that we have a way to test actual GameObject interactions when features such as timers and physics are running. As this recipe demonstrates, we can also load our own scenes for **PlayMode** testing, be they special scenes that have been created just to test interactions or actual scenes that are to be included in our final game build.

There's more...

There seem to be some changes in how to enable PlayMode tests for all assemblies. The issue is that enabling PlayMode tests can increase the size of build projects – the default setting is to disable PlayMode tests for all assemblies. If your version of the Unity Editor **Test Runner** window does not offer a menu option to **Enable playmode tests for all assemblies**, then you can enable these by setting the `playModeTestRunnerEnabled` setting to `1` in the `ProjectSettings/ProjectSetting.asset` file. You can learn more about this in the Unity Test Framework documentation: `https://docs.unity3d.com/Packages/com.unity.test-framework@1.1/manual/workflow-create-playmode-test.html`.

PlayMode and unit testing a player health bar with events, logging, and exceptions

In this recipe, we will combine many different kinds of tests for a feature tha's included in many games – a visual health bar representing the player's numeric health value (in this case, a float number from 0.0 to 1.0). Although far from comprehensively testing all the aspects of the health bar, this recipe will provide a good example of how we can go about testing many different parts of a game using the Unity Testing tools.

A Unity package has been provided that contains the following:

- `Player.cs`: A player script class for managing values for player health that uses delegates and events to publish health changes to any listening `View` classes.
- Two `View` classes that register to listen for player health change events:
  - `HealthBarDisplay.cs`: This updates `fillAmount` for a UI Image for each new player health value that's received.
  - `HealthChangeLogger.cs`: This prints messages about the new player health value that's received by the `Debug.Log` file.
- `PlayerManager.cs`: A manager script that initializes player and `HealthChangeLogger` objects, and also allows the user to change the health of the player by pressing the *Up* and *Down* arrow keys (simulating healing/damage during a game).

- A scene that has two UI Images – one is a health bar outline (red heart and a black outline), while the second is the filler image, showing dark blue to light blue to green, for weak to strong health values.

This recipe allows several different kinds of testing to be demonstrated:

- **PlayMode** testing, to check that the actual `fillAmount` of the UI Image displayed matches the 0.0 to 1.0 range of the player's health.
- **Unit testing,** to check that the player's health starts with the correct default value and correctly increases and decreases after calls to the `AddHealth(...)` and `ReduceHealth(...)` methods are made.
- Unit testing, to check that health change events are published by the player object.
- Unit testing, to check that expected messages are logged in `Debug.Log`.
- Unit testing, to check that argument out-of-range exceptions are thrown if negative values are passed to the player's `AddHealth(...)` or `ReduceHealth(...)` methods. This is demonstrated in the following screenshot:

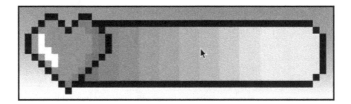

Figure 13.28 – The graphical heath bar we'll be testing in PlayMode

Thanks to *Pixel Art Maker* for the health bar image:
`http://pixelartmaker.com/art/49e2498a414f221`.

Getting ready

For this recipe, a Unity package has been provided (`healthBarScene.unitypackage`) in the `13_13` folder.

How to do it...

To **PlayMode** and **unit test** a player health bar, follow these steps:

1. Create a new **3D Unity project** and delete the default folder called **Scenes**.
2. In the **Package Manager** window, ensure that you have the latest version of the **Test Framework** package installed.
3. Import the Unity package provided (`healthBarScene.unitypackage`).
4. Open the **HealthBarScene** scene and add this scene to the project's **Build** (menu: **File** | **Build Settings ...**).
5. Display the **Test Runner** window by going to **Window** | **General** | **Test Runner**.
6. We need to enable **PlayMode** tests for all assemblies. Do this by displaying the drop-down menu in the top-right corner of the **Test Runner** window and selecting **EnablePlayMode tests for all assemblies** (click **OK** for any message concerned with restarting the editor).
7. Now, we have to restart the Unity Editor (just close the application and then reopen it with your project).
8. Since our **PlayMode** tests make use of the `Player` script class in the **Project** folder (**Assets** | **HealthBarScene** | **_Scripts**), we need to add an **Assembly Definition** there. Select this folder and from the **Create** menu of the **Project** window, create a new **Assembly Definition**, naming it `PlayerAssembly`:

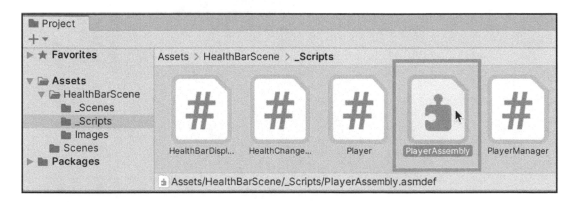

Figure 13.29 – PlayerAssembly created in the _Scripts folder

9. Now, select **PlayMode** in the **Test Runner** window.
10. In the **Project** window, select the top-level folder, called **Assets**.

11. In the **Test Runner** window, click the **Create PlayMode Test Assembly Folder** button. A new folder, named **Tests**, should have been created.

12. Select the **Tests** folder. This contains an **Assembly Reference** named **Tests**. Select this asset file in the **Project** window and look at its properties in the **Inspector** window. This **Assembly Reference** already has references to two Assembly Definition References: **UnityEngine.TestRunner** and **UnityEditor.TestRunner**.

13. We now need to add our **PlayerAssembly** to the **Tests** assembly so that we can perform our **PlayMode** tests that make use of the `Player` script class. In the **Inspector** window, click the plus (**+**) button to add a new **Assembly Definition Reference**. In the slot that's been created, locate and drag the `PlayerAssembly` **Assembly Definition**.

14. In the **Test Runner** window, click the **Create Test Script in the current folder** button. Rename this script class `HealthBarPlayModeTests` and replace its content with the following code:

```
using UnityEngine;
 using UnityEngine.UI;
 using UnityEngine.TestTools;
 using NUnit.Framework;
 using System.Collections;
 using UnityEngine.SceneManagement;


[TestFixture]
public class HealthBarPlayModeTests
{
    private Scene tempTestScene;

    // name of scene being tested by this class
    private string sceneToTest = "HealthBar";

    [SetUp]
    public void Setup()
    {
        // setup - load the scene
        tempTestScene = SceneManager.GetActiveScene();
    }
}
```

15. Add the following test to `HealthBarPlayModeTests.cs`:

```
[UnityTest]
    public IEnumerator
TestHealthBarImageMatchesPlayerHealth()
```

```
        {
            // load scene to be tested
            yield return SceneManager.LoadSceneAsync(sceneToTest,
LoadSceneMode.Additive);
SceneManager.SetActiveScene(SceneManager.GetSceneByName(sceneT
oTest));

            // wait for one frame
            yield return null;

            // Arrange
            Image healthBarFiller = GameObject.Find("image-
health-bar-filler").GetComponent<Image>();
            PlayerManager playerManager =
GameObject.FindWithTag("PlayerManager").GetComponent<PlayerMan
ager>();
            float expectedResult = 0.9f;

            // Act
            playerManager.ReduceHealth();

            // Assert
            Assert.AreEqual(expectedResult,
healthBarFiller.fillAmount);

            // teardown - reload original temp test scene
            SceneManager.SetActiveScene(tempTestScene);
            yield return
SceneManager.UnloadSceneAsync(sceneToTest);
        }
```

16. Click **Run All**.

17. As the tests run, you will see that, in the **Hierarchy**, **Game**, and **Scene** windows, a temporary scene is created, then **HealthBarScene** running, with the visual health bar.

18. You should see the results of your **PlayMode** test being executed – if the test concludes successfully, there should be a green tick (checkmark).

19. Now, let's add some unit tests to our player health feature.

20. Ensure that the **Tests** folder is selected in the **Project** window.

21. Select **EditMode** in the **Test Runner** window.

22. In the **Test Runner** window, click the **Create Test Script in the current folder** button. Rename this script class `EditModeUnitTests`.

23. Edit the `EditModeUnitTests.cs` script class, replacing its content with the following code:

```
using System;
 using UnityEngine.TestTools;
 using NUnit.Framework;
 using UnityEngine;

public class EditModeUnitTests
{

    // inner unit test classes go here

}
```

24. Add the following class and basic tests to the `EditModeUnitTests` class in `EditModeUnitTests.cs`:

```
public class TestCorrectValues
{
    [Test]
    public void DefaultHealthOne()
    {
        // Arrange
        Player player = new Player();
        float expectedResult = 1;

        // Act
        float result = player.GetHealth();

        // Assert
        Assert.AreEqual(expectedResult, result);
    }

    [Test]
    public void HealthCorrectAfterReducedByPointOne()
    {
        // Arrange
        Player player = new Player();
        float expectedResult = 0.9f;

        // Act
        player.ReduceHealth(0.1f);
        float result = player.GetHealth();

        // Assert
        Assert.AreEqual(expectedResult, result);
    }
```

```
[Test]
public void HealthCorrectAfterReducedByHalf()
{
    // Arrange
    Player player = new Player();
    float expectedResult = 0.5f;

    // Act
    player.ReduceHealth(0.5f);
    float result = player.GetHealth();

    // Assert
    Assert.AreEqual(expectedResult, result);
}
}
```

25. Add the following class and limit test to the EditModeUnitTests class in EditModeUnitTests.cs:

```
public class TestLimitNotExceeded
{
    [Test]
    public void HealthNotExceedMaximumOfOne()
    {
        // Arrange
        Player player = new Player();
        float expectedResult = 1;

        // Act
        player.AddHealth(1);
        player.AddHealth(1);
        player.AddHealth(0.5f);
        player.AddHealth(0.1f);
        float result = player.GetHealth();

        // Assert
        Assert.AreEqual(expectedResult, result);
    }
}
```

26. Add the following class and event tests to the EditModeUnitTests class in EditModeUnitTests.cs:

```
public class TestEvents
{
    [Test]
    public void CheckEventFiredWhenAddHealth()
    {
```

```
        // Arrange
        Player player = new Player();
        bool eventFired = false;

        Player.OnHealthChange += delegate
        {
            eventFired = true;
        };

        // Act
        player.AddHealth(0.1f);

        // Assert
        Assert.IsTrue(eventFired);
    }

    [Test]
    public void CheckEventFiredWhenReduceHealth()
    {
        // Arrange
        Player player = new Player();
        bool eventFired = false;

        Player.OnHealthChange += delegate
        {
            eventFired = true;
        };

        // Act
        player.ReduceHealth(0.1f);

        // Assert
        Assert.IsTrue(eventFired);
    }
}
```

27. Add the following class and exception tests to the `EditModeUnitTests` class in `EditModeUnitTests.cs`:

```
public class TestExceptions
{
    [Test]
    public void
Throws_Exception_When_Add_Health_Passed_Less_Than_Zero()
    {
        // Arrange
        Player player = new Player();
```

```
            // Act

            // Assert
            Assert.Throws<ArgumentOutOfRangeException>(
                delegate
                {
                    player.AddHealth(-1);
                }
            );
        }


        [Test]
        public void
Throws_Exception_When_Reduce_Health_Passed_Less_Than_Zero()
        {
            // Arrange
            Player player = new Player();

            // Act

            // Assert
            Assert.Throws<ArgumentOutOfRangeException>(
                () => player.ReduceHealth(-1)
            );
        }
    }
```

28. Add the following class and logging tests to the EditModeUnitTests class in EditModeUnitTests.cs:

```
    public class TestLogging
    {
        [Test]
        public void
Throws_Exception_When_Add_Health_Passed_Less_Than_Zero()
        {
            Debug.unityLogger.logEnabled = true;

            // Arrange
            Player player = new Player();
            HealthChangeLogger healthChangeLogger = new
HealthChangeLogger();
            string expectedResult = "health = 0.9";

            // Act
            player.ReduceHealth(0.1f);

            // Assert
```

```
            LogAssert.Expect(LogType.Log, expectedResult);
    }
}
```

You can see that the inner classes allow us to group the unit tests visually in the **Test Runner** window:

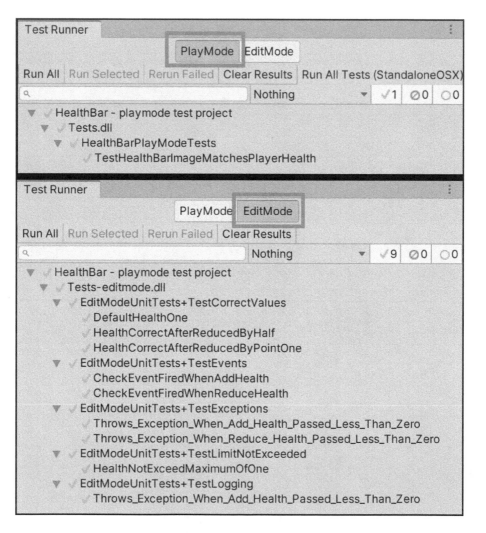

Figure 13.30 – PlayMode and EditMode test results - all of which passed (green ticks)

How it works...

Let's take a look at how this recipe works in detail.

PlayMode testing

The PlayMode test called `TestHealthBarImageMatchesPlayerHealth()` loads the `HealthBar` scene, gets a reference to the instance object of **PlayerManager**, which is a component of the **PlayerManager** GameObject, and invokes the `ReduceHealth()` method. This method reduces the player's health by 0.1. So, from its starting value of `1.0`, it becomes `0.9`.

The **PlayerManager** GameObject also has as a component that's an instance object of the C# `HealthBarDisplay` script class. This object registers to listen to published events from the player class. It also has a public **UI Image** variable that has been linked to the **UI Image** of the health bar filler image in the scene.

When the player's health is reduced to 0.9, it publishes the `OnChangeHealth(0.9)` event. This event is received by the `HealthBarDisplay` object instance, which then sets the `fillAmount` property of the linked health bar filler image in the scene.

The `TestHealthBarImageMatchesPlayerHealth()` PlayMode test gets a reference to the object instance named `image-health-bar-filler`, storing this reference in the `healthBarFiller` variable. The test assertion that's made is that the `expectedResult` value of `0.9` matches the actual `fillAmount` property of the UI Image in the scene:

```
Assert.AreEqual(expectedResult, healthBarFiller.fillAmount);
```

Unit tests

There are several unit tests that can be grouped by placing them inside their own classes, inside the `EditModeUnitTests` script class.

- `TestCorrectValues`:
    - `DefaultHealthOne()`: This tests that the default (initial value) of the player's health is 1.
    - `HealthCorrectAfterReducedByPointOne()`: This tests that when the player's health is reduced by 0.1, it becomes `0.9`.
    - `HealthCorrectAfterReducedByHalf()`: This tests that when the player's health is reduced by 0.5, it becomes `0.5`.
- `TestLimitNotExceeded`:
    - `HealthNotExceedMaximumOfOne()`: This tests that the value of the player's health does not exceed 1, even after attempts to add 1, 0.5, and 0.1 to its initial value of 1.
- `TestEvents`:
    - `CheckEventFiredWhenAddHealth()`: This tests that an `OnChangeHealth()` event is published when the player's health is increased.
    - `CheckEventFiredWhenReduceHealth()`: This tests that an `OnChangeHealth()` event is published when the player's health is decreased.
- `TestLogging`:
    - `CorrectDebugLogMessageAfterHealthReduced()`: This tests that a `Debug.Log` message is correctly logged after the player's health is reduced by 0.1 to 0.9.

- TestExceptions:
  - Throws_Exception_When_Add_Health_Passed_Less_Than_Zero(): This tests that an ArgumentOutOfRangeException is thrown when a negative value is passed to the AddHealth(...) player method.
  - Throws_Exception_When_Reduce_Health_Passed_Less _Than_Zero(): This tests that an ArgumentOutOfRangeException is thrown when a negative value is passed to the ReduceHealth(...) player method.

 These two tests illustrate one convention of naming tests that adds an underscore (_) character between each word in the method name in order to improve readability.

See also

You can learn more about the LogAssert Unity Script reference in the Unity documentation: https://docs.unity3d.com/ScriptReference/TestTools.LogAssert.html.

The method for unit testing C# events has been adapted from a post on philosophicalgeek.com: http://www.philosophicalgeek.com/2007/12/27/easily-unit-testing-event-handlers/.

The delegate-event publishing of health change events in this health bar feature is an example of the **Publisher-Subscriber** design pattern.

Reporting Code Coverage testing

A useful tool in projects with code testing is to be able to analyze how much of a C# script class is being tested. For example, is every method being tested with at least 1 set of test data? Unity now offers a Code Coverage feature, which we'll explore in this final code testing recipe. As shown in the following screenshot, Unity allows us to create a set of HTML pages for documenting the Code Coverage of tests against C# code. With this, we can see what percentage of our code is covered by tests, and even which lines of code are, and are not, covered by our tests:

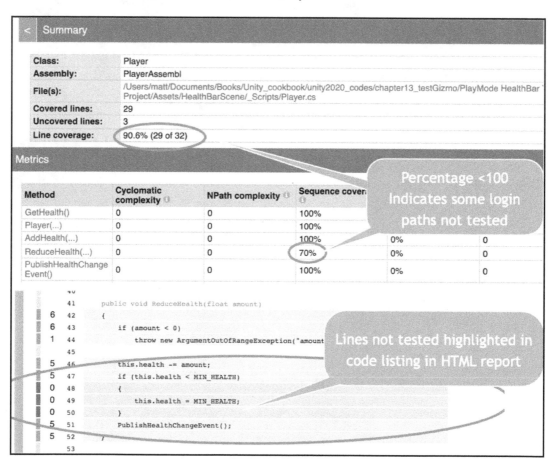

Figure 13.31 – Code Coverage HTML report for the Player script class

Getting ready

This project builds on the previous one, so make a copy of that and work on the copy.

How to do it...

To add Code Coverage reporting to a project with unit tests, follow these steps:

1. Open the **Package Manager** window (menu: **Window | Package Manager**), select the **Unity Registry** list of packages, and type **Code Coverage** into the search bar. When you see the **Code Coverage** package listed, click the **Install** button:

Figure 13.32 – Using Package Manager to install Code Coverage

2. Open the **Code Coverage** window by going to **Window | Analysis | Code Coverage**.

3. In the **Code Coverage** window, check the **Enable Code Coverage** option. Then, ensure the **Generate HTML Report** and **Auto Generate Report** options are checked:

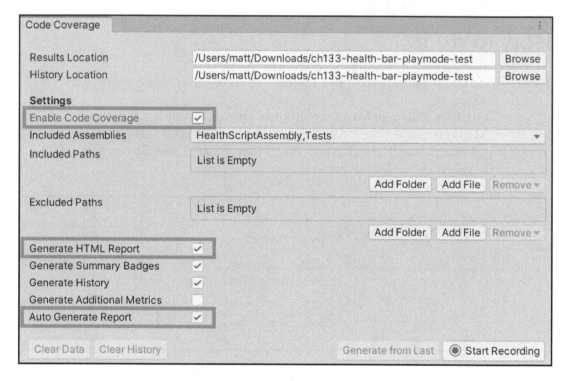

Figure 13.33 – Code Coverage window options

4. In **Test Runner**, choose **PlayMode** and click the **Run All Tests** button.
5. Once the testing is finished, an HTML code coverage report should automatically be created and opened in your computer's default web browser application. The report will be created in a new folder named **Report** inside a folder named **Code Coverage** in your Unity project folder. See *Figure 13.33*.

How it works...

The Unity debugger monitors which lines of code are being executed as the tests are run. It uses this data to compile a report on how much of each method of each class has been executed for the assemblies involved in the testing. By adding the Code Coverage package and enabling it, debugging data will be collected and reported upon when you run Unity tests.

As shown in *Figure 13.33*, the Unity **Code Coverage** tool generates a set of web pages to inform us about how much and which lines of our code are being examined with our unit tests. While even 100% coverage does not guarantee the code is "correct," a high percentage of code coverage does indicate that the behavior of most of our code is being tested to some extent.

Running simple Python scripts inside Unity

Unity Python is a package that allows Python code to be executed as part of a Unity project. In this recipe, we'll install the package, test the **Python Script Editor** window with a traditional `Hello World` Python `print` statement, and create C# scripts to run Python based on the examples provided by Unity at `https://docs.unity3d.com/Packages/com.unity.scripting.python@4.0/manual/inProcessAPI.html`.

How to do it...

To run simple Python scripts inside Unity, follow these steps:

1. Open the **Package Manager** window (menu: **Window | Package Manager**). At the time of writing, this package is still experimental, so while in the future you should be able to just search for **Python for Unity** in the **Unity Registry** list of packages, for now, you will need to choose the option to **Add package by name...** and then enter `com.unity.scripting.python`. The package should then be added to the project:

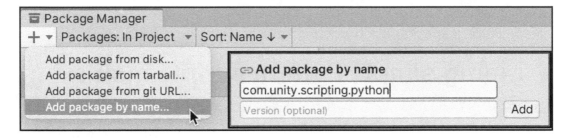

Figure 13.34 – Adding the Unity for Python package to a project

2. Open the **Python Script Editor** window by going to **Window | General | Python Console**.

3. Enter `print ('Hello World')` in the editor section (lower half) of the **Python Script Editor** window and click the **Execute** button. You should see a message stating **Hello World** appear in the output (top section) of the window:

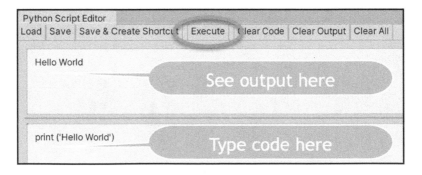

Figure 13.35 – Executing a Hello World statement in the Python Script Editor window

4. Now, let's create a C# script that can execute Python in a string using the Python API. Create a _Scripts folder in the **Project** panel. Inside it, a new C# script class file named HelloConsole.cs that contains the following code:

```
using UnityEditor.Scripting.Python;
using UnityEditor;

public class HelloConsole
{
    [MenuItem("My Python/Hello Console")]
    static void PrintHelloWorldFromPython()
    {
        PythonRunner.RunString(@"
                import UnityEngine;
                UnityEngine.Debug.Log('hello console')
                ");
    }
}
```

5. You should now see a new menu named **My Python** with an item called **Hello Console**. When you select this menu item, a message stating **hello console** should be output to the **Console** window.

6. Now, let's create a text file in our _Scripts folder containing pure Python – you may need to create this text file outside the Unity Editor by navigating to the _Scripts folder and using a text editor application to create and save this new file. Create a new text file named renamer.py that contains the following code:

```
import UnityEngine

all_objects =
UnityEngine.Object.FindObjectsOfType(UnityEngine.GameObject)
for go in all_objects:
    if go.name[-1] != '_':
        go.name = go.name + '_'
```

7. Now, let's create a C# script that offers a menu item that will execute our Python script file. Create a new C# script class file called InvokeRenamer.cs that contains the following code:

```
using UnityEditor.Scripting.Python;
using UnityEditor;
using UnityEngine;
```

```
public class InvokeRenamer
{
    [MenuItem("My Python/Underscore Renamer")]
    static void RunEnsureNaming()
    {
PythonRunner.RunFile($"{Application.dataPath}/_Scripts/renamer
.py");
    }
}
```

8. On the **My Python** menu item, there should now be a second menu item named **Underscore Renamer**. When you select this menu item, you should see that all the GameObjects in the **Hierarchy** window now end with underscore characters:

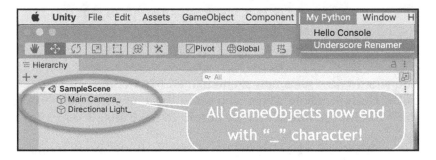

Figure 13.36 – The My Python menu items and the renamed Hierarchy window GameObjects

How it works...

The Python for Unity package adds an API (code library) that we can access through our C# code, as well as the **Python Script Editor** window for testing and running simple Python statements. We tested **Python Script Editor** with a traditional `Hello World` print statement.

Our C# script class, called `HelloConsole.cs` , demonstrated how we can use the `PythonRunner.RunString($...)` method in our C# scripts to execute a string containing Python code. Note that we must add a `using` statement to import the `UnityEditor.Scripting.Python` library for this work.

In both our scripts, we used the `[MenuItem("<menu/item>")]` Editor instruction to enable us to easily test out code from a menu item.

Our `Invoke.cs` C# script class demonstrated how we can use the `PythonRunner.RunFile($...)` method in our C# scripts to execute a text file containing Python code. We created a file called `renamer.py` containing pure Python code in order to loop through all the GameObjects. We added an underscore suffix if they didn't already have such a suffix. We followed the convention of using the `.py` file extension for files containing just Python code.

Notice how we indicated the location of the `renamer.py` file by writing `{Application.dataPath}/_Scripts/` before the file name. We could change this to indicate a different location for the Python file we wish to execute.

In both our Python string and file, we were able to make use of the UnityEngine library (assembly) by writing `import UnityEngin` before our Python statements – this works just like the C# `using` statement.

Further reading

You can learn more about unity testing at the following links:

- Unity Test Framework Manual documentation: `https://docs.unity3d.com/Manual/testing-editortestsrunner.html`
- Unity Test Framework package documentation: `https://docs.unity3d.com/Packages/com.unity.test-framework@1.1/manual/index.html`
- Unity Test Framework how-to pages: `https://unity.com/how-to/unity-test-framework-video-game-development`
- A website for the book *The Art of Unit Testing* (and lots of other learning resources associated with testing): `http://artofunittesting.com/`
- A great dual article tutorial about Unity testing by Tomek Paszek from Unity (talking about the old Unity test tools, but most of the content is still very relevant): `https://blogs.unity3d.com/2014/06/03/unit-testing-part-2-unit-testing-monobehaviours/`
- YouTube, where you can learn lots about Unity testing (and other topics) from Infalliblecode: `https://www.youtube.com/infalliblecode`
- CodeProject.com's introduction to TDD and NUnit: `https://www.codeproject.com/Articles/162041/Introduction-to-NUnit-and-TDD`

- A great tutorial about unit testing by Anthony Uccello on Ray Wenderlich: `https://www.raywenderlich.com/9454-introduction-to-unity-unit-testing`
- The Code Coverage features of the Unity Test tools: `https://docs.unity3d.com/Packages/com.unity.testtools.codecoverage@1.0/manual/`

Testing in Unity usually involves **Unity Assemblies**. This is an approach to separating the components of a game into separate modules. A great introduction to Unity Assemblies by *Erdiizgi* can be found at `https://erdiizgi.com/why-modular-game-development-and-how-to-do-it-with-unity/`.

You can learn more about Unity Python by reading the official package documentation: `https://docs.unity3d.com/Packages/com.unity.scripting.python@4.0/manual/inProcessAPI.html`.

14
Particle Systems and Other Visual Effects

Whether you're trying to make a better-looking game or you want to add interesting features, visual effects can add enjoyment and a more professional look and feel to many games:

Figure 14.1 – Multiple light sources in Coco VR by Pixar and Magnopus (featured on the Unity website Made with Unity)

At the end of the day, what we can see is the color properties of the rectangular array of pixels (picture elements) that make up the screen (or screens, for VR) that we are looking at. The Unity game engine must use the GameObjects in a scene and their properties to decide what to **render** (draw) in the **Game** window. Some GameObjects model 3D objects, with properties relating to physical **materials**, and **renderer** components for configuring how they should be displayed. Other GameObjects simulate **Light** sources. Modern computers with powerful CPUs and GPUs are beginning to support **real-time raytracing**. Raytracing involves calculating how light from light-emitting GameObjects (lights, emissive materials, and so on) bounces from surface to surface and eventually ends up arriving at the location in the scene where the camera is located.

These different lights can be customized to affect the type of light and directions where light is generated in the scene. The different materials will affect in what directions, and how much of the light hitting a surface of a simulated 3D object, will bounce off it – plus, some GameObjects can emit light themselves with **emissive materials**. The different rendering features affect how GameObjects and their materials are drawn for the user to see. There are several techniques that have been developed to reduce the amount of computation required while still producing high quality, but not quite realistic, rendering for 3D scenes. One of these techniques is the **pre-baking** (pre-calculation) of light sources and surface interactions. A second technique is the use of simulated **particle systems**, which can be customized through parameter settings and image textures to give the impression of a wide range of visual effects, including flames, smoke, rain, lightning, and so on.

Unity offers four types of lights (all of which can be added as components of GameObjects in a scene):

- **Directional Light**: For simulating a distance light source, such as sunlight.
- **SpotLight**: A simulated spotlight for projecting light in one direction, increasing in size the further it is from the light, in a cone shape.
- **Point Light**: Similar to a real-world light bulb, which means it emits light in all directions.
- **Area Light**: A processor-intensive, subtle lighting source for rectangular areas of a scene (pre-baking only, not at **runtime**).

Each light can be customized in many ways, such as its range and color. The intensity of the lights can also be customized. For the **SpotLight** and **PointLight** components, the intensity is reduced based on their distance from the location of the GameObject.

Lights can have a cookie **Texture** applied to them. Cookies are textures that are used to cast shadows or silhouettes in a **Scene**. They are produced using the cookie **Texture** as a mask between the light source and the surfaces being rendered. Their name, and usage, comes from the use of physical devices called cucoloris (nicknamed cookies), which are used in theatre and movie production to produce shadow effects for environments, such as moving clouds, the bars of a prison window, or sunlight being broken up by a jungle leaf canopy.

In addition to the **Light** components of GameObjects, a second source of local lighting in a scene can be from stationary objects that have emissive materials. We'll explore this in the final recipe in this chapter:

Figure 14.2 – Emissive material in Osiris: New Dawn by Fenix Fire (featured on the Unity website Made with Unity)

The use of processing-intensive **real-time** lighting can be reduced by pre-computing lighting for each scene. This is known as **Lightmap Baking**. Static – immovable – parts of the scene (lights and other objects) can have their lighting "baked" (pre-computed) into a **Texture Map**, based on the light sources in the scene. Then, at runtime, game performance is improved and the pre-calculated lightmaps can be used, avoiding the lighting of each frame having to be calculated at runtime. As always with computing, there is a memory-versus-speed tradeoff, so more memory is required for scenes to store the pre-computations as lightmaps. Unity currently offers the **Progressive CPU** lightmapper (and at the time of writing, a preview **Progressive GPU** lightmapper).

Another source of scene lighting is **Ambient Lighting** (global environmental lighting). This doesn't come from any locational source as it exists evenly throughout the scene. Ambient light can be used to influence the overall brightness of a scene and is achieved typically through the use of **Skybox** materials and simulated sunlight generated from a **Directional Light**. Skyboxes can be defined in the **Lighting settings** window. Such lighting can be generated at runtime or (more efficiently) pre-calculated as a baked **Lightmap** before the scene is run:

Figure 14.3 – Ambient lightning in D.R.O.N.E. by Five Studios Interactive (featured on the Unity website Made with Unity)

Unity offers two windows for managing lighting in a scene: the **Lighting settings** window and the **Light Explorer** window. The **Lighting** window (menu: **Window** | **Rendering** | **Lighting Settings**) is the hub for setting and adjusting the scene's illumination features, such as **Lightmaps**, **Global Illumination**, **Fog**, and much more:

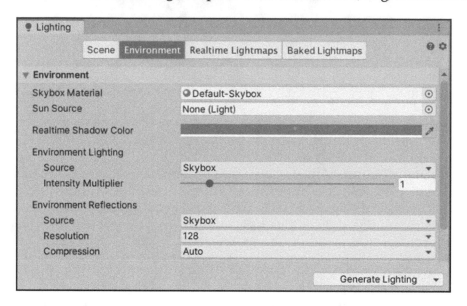

Figure 14.4 – The lighting window for adjusting the scene's illumination

Then, there's the **Light Explorer** window, for working with **Lights** in a scene. This panel allows you to edit and view the properties of **all** of the lights in the current scene. The **Light Explorer** window lists all **Lights** in a single panel, making it easy to work with each individually or change the settings of several at the same time. It can be a great time-saving tool when working with scenes involving lots of **Light** GameObjects. To display the **Light Explorer** window, go to **Window** | **Rendering** | **Light Explorer**:

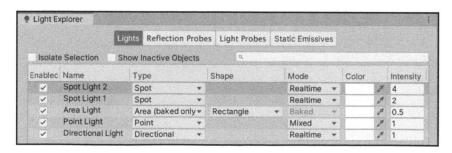

Figure 14.5 – The Light Explorer window

In this chapter, we will cover the following recipes:

- Exploring Unity's Particle Pack and reusing the samples for your own games
- Creating a simple particle system from scratch
- Using Texture Sheets to simulate fire with a particle system
- Making particles collide with scene objects
- Simulating an explosion
- Using Invoke to delay the execution of an explosion

Technical requirements

For this chapter, you will need Unity 2021.1 or later, plus one of the following:

- Microsoft Windows 10 (64-bit)/GPU: DX10, DX11, or DX12-capable
- macOS Sierra 10.12.6+/GPU Metal-capable Intel or AMD
- Linux Ubuntu 16.04, Ubuntu 18.04, and CentOS 7/GPU: OpenGL 3.2+ or Vulkan-capable, NVIDIA or AMD

For each chapter, there is a folder that contains the asset files you will need in this book's GitHub repository at `https://github.com/PacktPublishing/Unity-2021-Cookbook-Fourth-Edition`.

Exploring Unity's Particle Pack and reusing samples for your own games

Unity has published a great demonstration of particle system effects as a package on the Asset Store. While it's fine to explore the samples, by looking at the GameObjects in the scene and the asset files in the **Project** window, we can exploit these free resources and adapt them for our own projects.

In this recipe, we'll explore the sample scene and create two versions of a new scene. One will give the effect of fire on the ground, while the second will look like a flaming torch attached to a concrete wall. In both cases, we'll make use of fire prefabs from the Unity examples:

Figure 14.6 – Part of the Unity Particle System demo scene

How to do it...

To reuse Unity particle examples for your own games, follow these steps:

1. Start a new **Unity 3D project** and ensure you are logged into your Unity account in the Unity Editor.
2. Open **Unity Asset Store** in a web browser and log into your Unity account.
3. Tick **Free Assets** and search for and select the free **Unity Particle Pack** on the Asset Store (not the 5.x version, but the one that was updated in 2020):

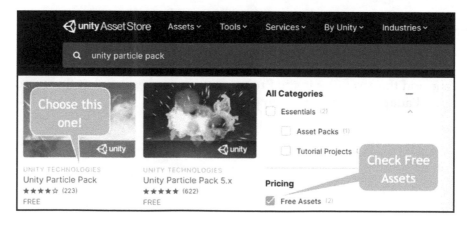

Figure 14.7 – The Unity Particle Pack on the Asset Store website

4. Click **Add to My Assets**. Then, after the button changes, click **Open in Unity**.

5. In your Unity Editor, the **Package Manager** window should open, and **Unity Particle Pack** should be selected in the list of **My Assets**. Click **Download** and, once downloaded, click **Import**. You should now see several folders appear in the **Project** window. The import folder is **EffectExamples**. There should also be a new scene named **Main** in the **Scenes** folder.

6. Open the **Main** scene from the **Scenes** folder in the **Project** window.

7. Run the game and, using **First Person Controller**, explore all the different **Particle System** examples from Unity.

8. Stop the game and create a new, empty scene. In this scene, add a 3D **Plane**. In the **Inspector** window for the **Mesh Renderer** component, select the **Concrete Floor** material (click the circle asset file selector for **Element 0** of the **Materials** property). This will act as a floor that we can create some fire on.

9. Select **Main Camera** in the **Hierarchy** window and, in the **Inspector** window, set its **Position** to (0, 3, -3) and its **Rotation** to (45, 0, 0).

10. In the **Project** window, locate the **LargeFlames** prefab (in **EffectExamples** | **Fire & Explosion Effects** | **Prefabs**). Drag this prefab into the **Hierarchy** window to add a new GameObject clone of this prefab in the scene. In the **Inspector** window, ensure the position of this **LargeFlames** GameObject is (0, 0, 0).

11. Save and run the scene. You should see some realistic animated flames in the center of the concrete floor:

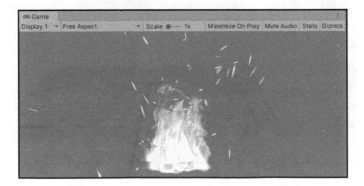

Figure 14.8 – Reusing the LargeFlames prefab on a concrete-styled 3D Plane

12. Stop the scene. Delete the **LargeFlames** GameObject.

13. Now, let's create a wall with a flaming torch attached to it.

14. To create the wall, add a 3D **Cube** to the scene named `Cube-wall` with a **Position** of (`0.5, -1, 4`), a **Rotation** of (`0, 25, 0`), and a **Scale** of (`7, 7, 2.5`). In the **Inspector** window for the **Mesh Renderer** component, set **Element 0** to **Concrete Wall** (in the **Project** window, go to **Assets** | **Shared** | **Environment** | **Materials**).

15. To create the head of the torch, add a 3D **Cube** to the scene named `Cube-torch` with a **Position** of (`0.2, 0, 1.8`), a **Rotation** of (`-1.5, 125, -33`), and a **Scale** of (`0.14, 0.06, 0.15`).

16. To create the pole of the torch, add a 3D **Cylinder** to the scene named `Cylinder-torch` with a **Position** of (`0.45, -0.97, 2.4`), a **Rotation** of (`154, -17, -20`), and a **Scale** of (`0.1, 1.15, 0.1`).

17. To see the flaming torch close up, move **Main Camera** closer by setting its **Position** to (`1, 1, 0`) in the **Inspector** window.

18. Now, let's add an animated flame to our torch. From the **Project** window, locate the **CandleFlame** prefab (in **EffectExamples** | **Misc Effects** | **Prefabs**) and drag it into the **Hierarchy** window to create a clone of it as a GameObject. Then, set the position of this **CandleFlame** GameObject to (`0.2, 0.04, 1.75`).

19. Save and run the scene. You should see your torch object with a nice animated flame:

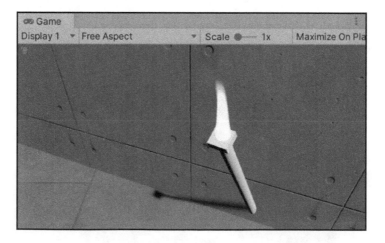

Figure 14.9 – Reusing the CandleFlame prefab for our simple wall torch object

How it works...

In this recipe, we learned how to add the Unity **Particle Pack** asset package to a new project and explored the included sample scene.

The Particle Pack package includes many prefabs for each of the sample particle systems. We were able to select one prefab, **LargeFlame**, and create our own scene with a concrete floor **Material** for a 3D **Plane**, and then make this floor look like it was on fire by adding a clone of the **LargeFlame** prefab.

Prefabs can be used for different purposes, as shown in this demo scene. So, we were able to make use of the **CandleFlame** prefab from the Unity examples and use it as the flame for a simple model of a flaming torch. We did this by using a 3D **Cube** and a 3D **Cylinder**.

Unity provides many prefabs of ready-to-use particle effects. In many cases, as in this recipe, we just need to import the pack from Unity and then create GameObjects in our own scenes using the assets provided by Unity.

Creating a simple particle system from scratch

Making use of prefabs from Unity, as we did in the previous recipe, is fine if we're happy to use such prefabs without any *tweaking*. However, we often want to adjust the look and feel of assets and particle systems so that they fit in with the style of a particular game or scene. Therefore, it is useful to learn how to create and customize particle systems from scratch, in order to learn about the different **parameters** and **modules** that make up Unity particle systems. Knowing how to adjust these values means we are able to either create what we need or customize a **Particle System** prefab from a third-party source, such as the Unity examples.

In this recipe, we'll create a **Particle System** from scratch and customize it in several ways to learn about some of the most important modules and parameters:

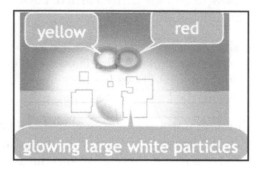

Figure 14.10 – The scene we'll create in this recipe with white, red, and yellow particles shimmering around a Sphere

How to do it...

To create a particle system from scratch, follow these steps:

1. Start a new **Unity 3D project**.
2. Let's create a floor and wall from scaled 3D Cubes to create a location where we can view our particle system.
3. Create a 3D **Cube** GameObject named Cube-wall. In the **Inspector** window, set its **Position** to (1, 0, 3) and its **Scale** to (20, 20, 1).
4. Create a second 3D **Cube** GameObject named Cube-floor. In the **Inspector** window, set its **Position** to (0, -1, 0) and its **Scale** to (20, 1, 20).
5. Create a new **Material** asset file in the **Project** window named m_grey. Set the **Albedo** property of this **Material** to a mid-gray color (halfway between white and black). Now, drag the m_grey asset file from the **Project** window onto Cube-wall in the **Hierarchy** window. The wall should now be gray.
6. Often, the visual effect of a particle system comes from a GameObject, so let's create a 3D **Sphere** at a **Position** of (0, 0, 0) so that it appears as the source of our particles.

7. Now, let's add a GameObject containing a **Particle System** component by going to **GameObject | Effects | Particle System**. You should now see a new GameObject in the **Hierarchy** window named **Particle System**. In the **Inspector** window, you'll see it has just two components: a **Transform** and a **Particle System**. Ensure the position of **Transform** is (0, 0, 0) so that the particles appear to be coming out of the sphere at that same location.

8. When the **Particle System** GameObject is selected in the **Hierarchy** window, you will see an animated preview of the particle system in the **Scene** window. You'll also have a **Particle Effect** control panel that allows you to **Pause/Restart/Stop** the particle system. You can minimize the **Particle Effect** control panel by clicking the small triangle icon in its top-left corner:

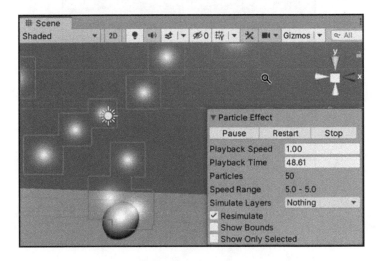

Figure 14.11 – The Scene window's Particle System previewer

9. Sometimes, we'll want to add a **Particle System** component to an existing GameObject. When we do so, there is no default setting for the renderer's material, so we'll see pink squares indicating there's no **Material**. Let's learn how to do this and assign a **Material** to get rid of the pink squares.

10. Delete the **Particle System** GameObject from the scene. Now, create a new, empty GameObject in the scene (menu: **GameObject | Create Empty**) named MyParticles. In the **Inspector** window, add a **Particle System** component by clicking the **Add Component** button and searching for **Particle System**.

11. Ensure that the **MyParticles** GameObject is selected in the **Hierarchy** window. You should see a preview of the animated **Particle System** in the **Scene** window. If you are seeing pink squares rather than white circles, then the **Particle System** component's **Renderer** module is missing the link to the **Default-Particle** material. Let's fix that.

12. In the **Inspector** window, click the **Renderer** module title bar to open the properties of this part of the **Particle System** component. Then, for the **Material** property, click the **selection** button (the small circle with the dot in the middle) and from the list of materials, select **Default-Particle**. You should now see "glowing" white circles being generated from your particle system (and no more pink squares):

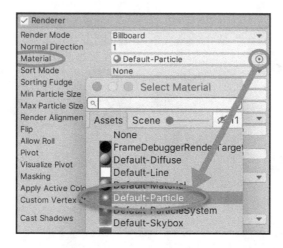

Figure 14.12 – Setting Material in the Renderer module to Default-Particle

13. Now, since we usually want particles to be initially floating upward, in the **Inspector** window, set **Rotation** to (-90, 0, 0). With that, we have recreated the same GameObject containing a **Particle System** component that Unity creates for us when we go to **GameObject | Effects | Particle System**.

14. As you can see, there are quite a few **modules** in the **Particle System** component. Particle systems are powerful components that can generate a wide range of visual effects. Click the headings of different modules to see the different properties for each module to get to know some of the customizable parameters.

15. Some of the most influential properties are in the top section of the component, under the name of the GameObject, so in this case, it will be **MyParticles**.

16. With **MyParticles** selected in the **Hierarchy** window, stop the **Particle System** preview. Then, play it again.

    You should see that when you press **Play**, there are initially no particles in the scene and that particles begin to appear from the location of the sphere. After about 3-4 seconds, as the first particles start to disappear above our **wall** GameObject, the scene settles into a steady state, with new particles appearing at the same rate as old particles disappear.

17. Now, check the **Prewarm** option in the **Inspector** window. Then, in the **Scene** window, stop and play the particle system again.

    You'll see that the scene is in the steady state, with new particles appearing at the same rate as old particles disappear. This **Prewarm** option makes Unity store the **Particle System** simulation status after running it for a little bit, so as soon as we enable **Particle System**, it will be pre-warmed into its steady state. This is useful for visual effects such as flames or fog, where we don't want the user to see the beginning of the particle system from its source. However, for visual effects such as explosions, we will want the user to see the beginning and growth of the particle system, so in those cases, we would **not** check the **Prewarm** option:

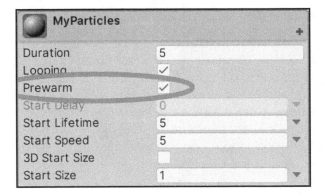

Figure 14.13 – Checking the Particle System Prewarm option

18. The initial **Start Lifetime** of a particle system is **5** seconds. Let's reduce that to **1** second. Also, let's reduce **Start Speed** from **5** to **1**. This means we now have particles that rise up slowly and die after **1** second. Finally, let's increase **Start Size** from **1** to **5**. We should now have large white glowing particles hovering around the top of our sphere - a bit like our sphere is being **haunted**:

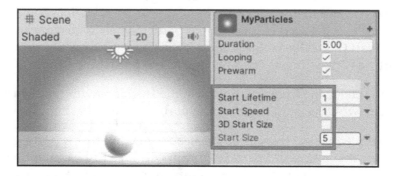

Figure 14.14 – Big, short-lived, slow-rising particles around our Sphere to produce a ghostly glowing effect

Now, let's add a nice red spot effect. We'll make the particles turn red just before they disappear, and also get smaller at the same time – so, we'll see little red dots around the top of the white glowing particle system. To achieve what we want, our particles should change color and size toward the end of their lifespan of 1 second. There are dedicated modules to customize these parameters.

19. Check the **Color over Lifetime** module in the **Inspector** window and click this module's title to reveal its **Color** parameter. Then, click the **Color** selector rectangle to open the **Gradient Editor** window. In the **Gradient Editor** window, we want particles to stay **White** until their last 10% of life. So, move the bottom left **White** color handle 9/10ths of the way to the right (**Location** 90%). Then, select the bottom-right color handle and change its color to **Red**. You should now see a gradient from **White** to **Red** in the right-hand 10% of the color gradient:

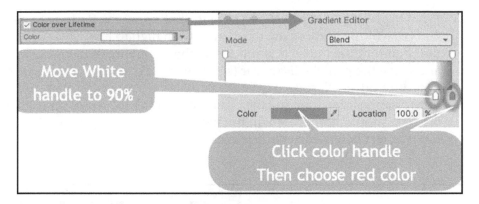

Figure 14.15 – Making particles turn red toward the end of their life

If you look in the scene, you should now see occasional large flickers of **Red** light in the particle system around our Sphere.

Now, let's make these **smaller** balls **Red** by changing the **Size over Lifetime** parameter curve.

Many parameters of particle systems are defined by curves. When a GameObject containing a **Particle System** component is selected at the bottom of the **Inspector** window, the **Particle System Curves** window will appear. This panel displays each of the active (checked) modules that are controlled by curves. Each active curve is assigned a unique color, and when it is being edited, only that curve will be displayed as a bright line (any other curves will be faintly drawn in their colors behind the current curve being edited).

20. Check the **Size over Lifetime** module in the **Inspector** window and check this module's title to enable and reveal its **Size** curve parameter. Leave the **Separate Axes** option unchecked. Click the inside **Size** curve parameter rectangle to make the **Particle System Curves** window display the curve controller of this **Size over Lifetime** module.

21. From the selection of preset curves at the bottom of the **Particle System Curves** window, choose the third one – from high to low. This should leave the beginning size at **1.0** (the full size at the beginning of the particle's life) and make the particle disappear (size **0.0**) at the end of its life. Those red dots are a bit small, so let's have the particles go no smaller than 20% before they disappear by dragging the right-hand end of the curve up from **0.0** to **0.2**. You should now see small (but not too small) red light particles flashing just before each particle dies:

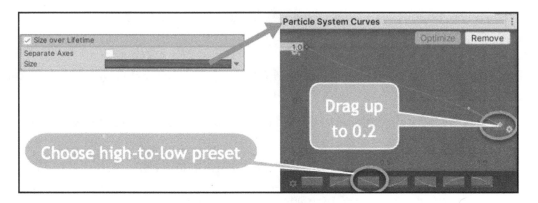

Figure 14.16 – Editing the Size over Lifetime curve to make particles smaller toward the end of their life

22. Finally, let's add some yellow dots of light as well. First, rename our particle GameObject MyParticles-red and then duplicate it, naming the copy MyParticles-yellow. With MyParticles-yellow selected in the **Hierarchy** window, in the **Inspector** window, click the **Color over Lifetime** module's title to reveal its **Color** parameter. Then, click the **Color** selector rectangle to open the **Gradient Editor** window. Click the (red) bottom-right color handle and change its color to yellow. Select both MyParticles-red and MyParticles-yellow in the **Hierarchy** window to see both of their previews at the same time.

While we can see the occasional red and yellow flash of light, we now have twice as many particles, emitting white for most of their life, so it's harder to see the colored flashes now. Let's solve this by making the particles from MyParticles-yellow mostly transparent during their lifetime, except to become yellow just before they die. We can do this easily in the **Gradient Editor** window by making use of the upper two color handles.

23. Click the top-right color handle and then use the slider (or text box) to set the **Alpha** value to 0. Now, our yellow particles will start invisible, and then become visible and yellow at the end of their lifetime:

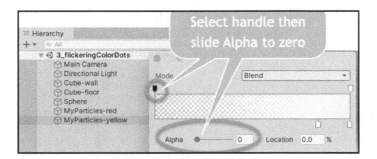

Figure 14.17 – Setting the yellow particles to start life invisible (Alpha = 0)

24. Save and run the scene. You should see large white shimmering particles around the sphere, and occasional flashes of small red and yellow lights as those particles die.

How it works...

In this recipe, we explored a range of the different modules and parameters of Unity particle systems. The core of a particle system is based on the **Material** particles they are displayed (rendered) with. By changing the material of the **Renderer** module, we can influence how the system looks – in this case, we ensured the **Default-Particle** material was being used, solving the issue of pink squares for no **Material**.

Changing the **Start Lifetime** and **Start Speed** properties of particles determines how far the particles will go from their starting point – the shorter the lifetime and the slower they move, the less distance they will travel. Changing the color and size of particles during their life allows effects such as the red glows/spots we created in the recipe to be implemented. Having multiple particle systems and varying the **Alpha** transparency of particles allows us to customize how they may interact; so, our yellow particles were only visible toward the end of the life of each particle.

Many aspects of **Particle System** module parameters are controlled by curves, as we explored with the **Size over Lifetime** parameter. So, it is worthwhile getting familiar with the **Particle System Curves** window, both for selecting preset curves and then customizing them as required.

Using Texture Sheets to simulate fire with a particle system

Much of the work of creating visual effects can be achieved if we have a multiple-image **sprite sheet**. Then, the visual form of each particle as it changes over its lifetime can be driven as a 2D animation, looping through the sequence of images from the sprite sheet.

In this recipe, we'll create a flickering blue flame effect using a particle system that animates its particles from a multiple-image sprite sheet from the Open Game Art website:

Figure 14.18 – The flickering blue flames Particle System we'll create in this recipe

Getting ready

For this recipe, we need a sprite sheet with multiple images on a black background. Either use one of your own or use the `fire2_64.png` blue flame sprite sheet from Open Game Art. Thanks to *Ben Hickling* for sharing this asset for game developers to use.

We've prepared the file you need in the `14_03` folder. Alternatively, you can download the sprite sheet image file directly from the Open Game Art website: `https://opengameart.org/content/animated-fire`:

Figure 14.19 – Downloading the blue fire sprite sheet from the Open Game Art website

How to do it...

To simulate fire using Texture Sheets, follow these steps:

1. Create a new **Unity 3D project** and import the `blue2_64.png` flame sprite sheet texture image asset file. Ensure this image asset has its **Texture Type** set to **Sprite 2D and UI** in the **Inspector** window.

2. Examine the sprite sheet, making a note of the number of columns (X-tiles) and rows (Y-tiles). We need these numbers to customize our particle system later in this recipe:

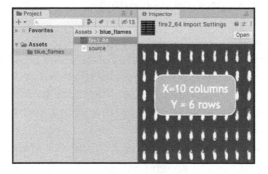

Figure 14.20 – The blue flames sprite sheet (X = 10-columns, Y = 6-rows)

3. To use sprite sheet texture images, we must create a **Material** to assign to the particle system's **Renderer** module. In the **Project** window, create a new **Material** named `m_blueFire` (menu: **Create | Material**).

4. With `m_blueFire` selected in the **Project** window, in the **Inspector** window, select the **Particles/Standard Unlit** shader, set **Rendering Mode** to **Additive**, and check the **Soft Particles** option:

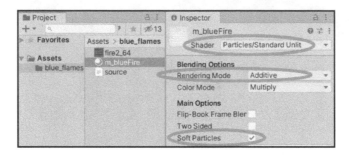

Figure 14.21 – Customizing m_blueFire for the particle system's Renderer component

5. Then, in the **Inspector** window, set the **Albedo** property of the material to the `blue2_64` sprite asset.

   First, let's create a floor and wall from scaled 3D cubes as a location to view our particle system.

6. Create a 3D **Cube** GameObject named `Cube-wall`. In the **Inspector** window, set its **Position** to (`1, 0, 3`) and its **Scale** to (`20, 20, 1`).

7. Create a second 3D **Cube** GameObject named `Cube-floor`. In the **Inspector** window, set its **Position** to (`0, -1, 0`), and its **Scale** to (`20, 1, 20`).

8. Now, let's create a new **Particle System** in the scene by going to **GameObject | Effects | Particle System**. Set **Start Lifetime** to **2** and **Start Speed** to **0** so that particles live for 2 seconds and do not move from the place they are created. Set **Start Size** to **5** and **Max Particles** to **1** so that we have just one large (size 5) flickering flame based on our animated sequence of images.

9. For the particle system's **Renderer** module, set **Material** to `m_blueFire`.

10. At the moment, we can see the **entire** sprite sheet as a particle (all 60 images!). For our final customization, we need to check the **Texture Sheet Animation** module of the **Particle System** component in the **Inspector** window and set the grid side to **X** = `10` and **Y** = `6` (since our sprite sheet has 10 columns and 6 rows):

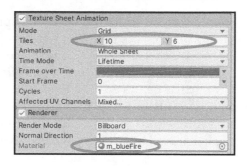

Figure 14.22 – Setting the 10 x 6 Texture Sheet grid and the Renderer material

11. Save and run the scene. You should see a nicely animated fire with blue flames.

How it works...

By creating a **Material** using one particle that's been rendered and linked to a multiple-image sprite sheet, we are able to take advantage of the **Texture Sheet Animation** module feature of Unity's **Particle System**.

The default **Render Mode** for particle systems is **Billboard**. This means that the image for each particle is always facing toward the camera. In this way, a 2D animation of a flame works very well since whatever direction the user is looking at the particle system from, they will always see the intended 2D flame animation, giving the visual effect of a 3D fire.

The particle system's **Rendered** component needs to be linked to the material for the sprite sheet, and the X- and Y-tile grid needs to match the number of columns (X) and rows (Y) in the sprite sheet file.

By having 0 for **Start Speed** and only one particle (**Max Particles = 1**), we ensure we have a single animated particle staying in one spot. The size of the particle may be limited by the pixel density of your sprite sheet images – less detailed images will only work well with smaller particles.

We selected the **Particles/Standard Unlit** shader for our **Material**. This is one of the shaders that's been designed for particles, and it is faster than the **Particles/Standard Surface** shader since it does not perform any lighting calculations. The flames of our system do not need to show any interaction with any light sources in our scene.

For our material's **Rendering Mode**, we chose the **Additive** option. This adds the particle's color and background pixel colors together, which is great for glowing effects if we wish to simulate fire, for example. We could have tweaked the way the final colors for pixels are chosen even further by trying out different **color modes**. Color modes determine how particle colors are combined with the material's text colors. The default color mode is **Multiply**, which, again, works fine for fire effects. Other texture/particle color combinations include additive/subtractive and so on. The following figure from the Unity documentation on particle shaders (`https://docs.unity3d.com/Manual/shader-StandardParticleShaders.html`) explains the different **Color Mode** options well:

Figure 14.23 – Illustration of different Material Rendering Modes (from Unity documentation)

We enabled **Soft Particles** for our **Material**, which reduces hard edges when particles are close to surfaces in the scene – again, this is good for flame effects.

While the visual effect from this recipe is rather modest, when combined with other sprite systems and 3D modules, animated particle systems with sprite sheets can speed up your scene development process. This is because a lot of the work has already been completed through the animations that were achieved in the multiple-image sprite sheets.

Making particles collide with scene objects

A great way to enhance the visual effects of particle systems is for the particles to behave as if they are a real part of the 3D world. We can easily give this impression by enabling the **Collision** module, which makes particles change their direction of movement when they "hit" the colliders of 3D objects in the scene.

In this recipe, we'll create a scene containing some 3D objects and create two particle systems – one like a fountain of ping-pong balls and another like a gun firing many small balls in a line. Both sets of particles will bounce and change direction when they collide with the objects in the scene:

Figure 14.24 – The two bouncing particle systems in the collision scene we'll create in this recipe

How to do it...

To create a particle system from scratch, follow these steps:

1. Start a new **Unity 3D project**.

2. Move **Main Camera** to **Position** (0, 1, -20) so that we can see more of the scene GameObjects.

   Now, let's create a floor and wall from scaled 3D cubes, as a location to view our particle system.

3. Create a 3D **Cube** GameObject named Cube-wall. In the **Inspector** window, set its **Position** to (1, 0, 3) and its **Scale** to (20, 20, 1).

4. Create a second 3D **Cube** GameObject named Cube-floor. In the **Inspector** window, set its **Position** to (0, -1, 0), and its **Scale** to (20, 1, 20).

5. Often, the visual effect from a **Particle System** comes from a GameObject, so let's create a 3D **Sphere** at a **Position** of (0, -0.5, 0) so that it appears to be embedded in the ground and the source of our particles. Check the **Is Trigger** setting for the sphere's **Collider** so that it will not be something our particles will bounce into.

6. Now, let's add a GameObject containing a **Particle System** component by going to **GameObject | Effects | Particle System**. Rename this GameObject `Particle System-fountain`. In the **Inspector** window, set this new GameObject's Transform **Position** to (0, 0, 0) so that the particles appear to be coming out of the sphere at that same location.

7. Let's create a circle-like **Material** for our fountain particles. In the **Project** window, create a new **Material** named `m_circleParticle` (menu: **Create | Material**).

8. Select `m_circleParticle`. Then, in the **Inspector** window, change its **Renderer** to **Particles/Standard Unit** and its **Rendering Mode** to **Additive**. Click the texture section circle for **Albedo** and choose the built-in **Knob** texture from the **Select Texture** window:

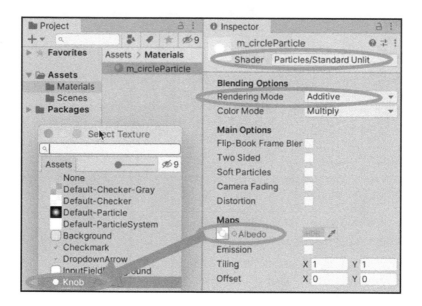

Figure 14.25 – Creating our circle particle material

9. In the **Hierarchy** window, select this **Particle System** and in its **Renderer** module, set **Material** to `m_circleParticle`. In the general particle, increase **Start Speed** to 7 and reduce **Size** to 0.3. Check the **Collision** module to enable it, and change **Type** to **World** (so particles bounce off the colliders in the scene).

If you run the scene now, it should look as if lots of small ping-pong balls are being emitted from the sphere.

10. Now, let's try to add some gravity and increase the number of particles being emitted to make it more fountain-like. In the general settings (labelled **Particle System**), set **Gravity Modifier** to 1 – these particles should now go up and then fall toward the ground. In the **Emission** module, increase **Rate over Time** to 50 – we should now see lots of particles being "sprayed" upward from our sphere:

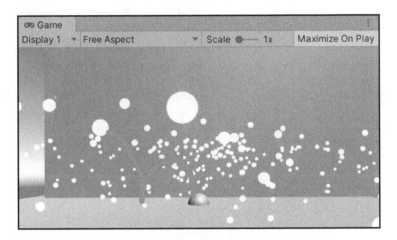

Figure 14.26 – The ping-pong ball foundation from our half-sphere

11. Save the scene.
12. Let's add a ping-pong hose/gun effect. Add a 3D **Cube** to the scene named Cube-hose. In the **Inspector** window, set its **Position** to (-4, 2, -6), **Rotation** to (-25, 0, 0), and **Scale** to (1, 1, 3) to give the effect it is pointing toward the wall. Check the **Is Trigger** setting for the cube's **Collider** so that this GameObject will not be something our particles will bounce into.
13. Create a new **Particle System** and name it Particle System-hose. Set this particle system's **Position** to (-4, 2.5, -5) and **Rotation** to (-125, 0, -180).
14. Ensure that the Particle System-hose GameObject is selected in the **Hierarchy** window. In the **Inspector** window, for the **Renderer** module, set **Material** to m_circleParticle. Increase **Start Speed** to 10 and reduce **Size** to 0.3. Check the **Collision** module to enable it and change **Type** to **World** (so that particles bounce off the colliders in the scene).

15. To get all our ping-pong ball's particles to all be fired out in a straight line, we need to set the **Shape** module of our **Particle System** to **Shape = Edge**, with a **Radius** of 0.5.

Another way to achieve a less flattened hose effect would be to use a **Cone** shape with an angle of **zero**.

16. Set the **Emission** module's **Rate over Time** to 100 so that there is a dense steady stream of ping-pong ball-type particles being emitted:

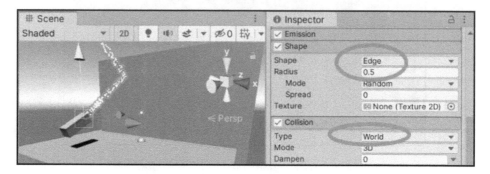

Figure 14.27 – Collision with the World GameObject and the edge-shaped Particle System emitter

When you save and run the scene, you should see many ping-pong balls being emitted as if from a hose toward the wall, and as if from a fountain from the sunken **Sphere**.

How it works...

When a 3D scene contains objects with **Collider** components, they define 3D spaces where there are surfaces that can be collided with. By enabling the **Collision** module of our **Particle System**, we are able to create more convincing visual effects since the particles "bounce" off surfaces of objects that have colliders.

We used an edge-shaped **Particle System** that emitted hundreds of particles to create a steady stream of particles, as if they had been fired from a gun or pumped out from a hose.

There's more...

Interesting effects can be achieved when a "trail" is added to some or all particles, visually marking the path the particle has followed during its lifetime. Explore this by making the following changes to the fountain scene:

1. Create a new yellow **Material** named `m_yellow`.

2. In the **Hierarchy** window, select the fountain's **Particle System**. Then, in the **Inspector** window, enable the **Trails** module.

3. You'll now see a new property for the **Renderer** module named **Trail renderer**. For this property, select the new `m_yellow` **Material**.

4. For the **Trails** module, set the following options to make every 100th particle leave a thin trail behind it:
   - **Ratio**: `0.01` (1 out of 100 get a trail)
   - **Width over Trail**: `0.1` (narrow):

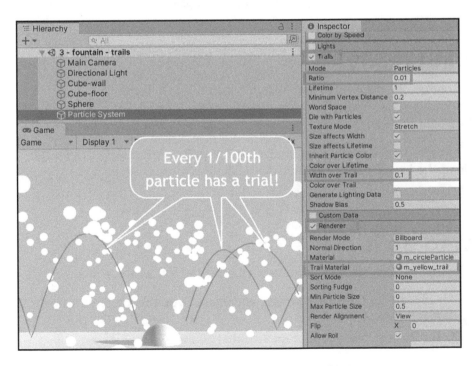

Figure 14.28 – Adding occasional Trails to particles from our fountain

Simulating an explosion

For many games, there will be events where we want to display an explosion in the scene, such as when the player's character dies or when they collide with an object that deals damage. We can quite easily create a visual explosion effect using an appropriate 2D image and a particle system that fires one with a burst of many fast-moving, short-lived particles, in all directions. That's what we'll create in this recipe:

Figure 14.29 – The explosion effect we'll create

Getting ready

For this recipe, we need an image of an explosion, so we'll use the `firecloud.png` image that's been published on the PNG-EGG website. Thanks to *GAMEKILLER48* for sharing this asset for game developers to use.

We've prepared the file you need in the `14_05` folder. Alternatively, you can download the image directly from the PNG-EGG website: `https://www.pngegg.com/en/png-ffmwo`.

How to do it...

To create a particle system to simulate an explosion, follow these steps:

1. Start a new **Unity 3D project** and ensure you are logged into your Unity account in the Unity Editor.
2. Import the provided image file; that is, `firecloud.png`.

   Let's create a **Material** for this image that can be used by particle systems.

3. In the **Project** window, create a
   new **Material** named `m_fireCloud` (menu: **Create | Material**). Drag the
   `firecloud` texture asset into the **Albedo** property of `m_fireCloud` in the
   Inspector window.

4. With `m_fireCloud` selected in the **Project** window, in
   the **Inspector** window, select the **Particles/Standard Unlit** shader and
   set **Rendering Mode** to **Additive**.

5. Open the Unity Asset Store in a web browser and log into your Unity
   account.

6. Tick **Free Assets** and search for and select the free **Stylized Crystal** on the
   Asset Store:

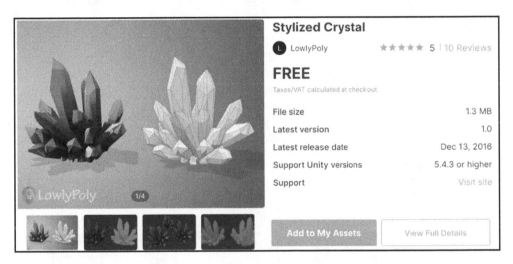

Figure 14.30 – The free Stylized Crystal asset on the Asset Store

7. Click **Add to My Assets**. Then, after the button changes, click **Open in
   Unity**.

8. In your Unity Editor, the **Package Manager** window should open, and
   the **Stylized Crystal** assets should be selected in the list of **My Assets**.
   Click **Download** and, when downloaded, click **Import**. In
   the **Project** window, you should now see a new folder called `Stylized
   Crystal`.

We are also going to need a 3D character and scene for this project, so we'll use the **Third-Person** character and demo scene from one of the free Unity **Starter Assets** package.

9. Visit the Asset Store again and search for the free **Starter Assets – Third Person Character Controller** package from Unity Technologies.

10. Click **Add to My Assets**. Then, after the button changes, click **Open in Unity**.

11. In your Unity Editor, the **Package Manager** window should open, and the **Starter Assets - Third Person Character Controller** assets should be selected in the list of **My Assets**. Click **Download** and, when downloaded, click **Import**. Say **Yes** to any popup about resetting the project to use the new input system.

12. In the **Project** window, you should now see a new folder called `StarterAssets`.

13. Open the provided **Playground** scene, which you can find in the **Project** window (menu: **Assets | StarterAssets | ThirdPersonController | Scenes**).

14. Locate **PlayerArmature** in the **Hierarchy** window and move this character near the bottom of the stairs in the scene.

15. Now, let's add a spiky crystal to this scene. From the **Project** window, drag the **crystal_17_2** prefab (**Stylized Crystal | Prefab**) to a position just in front of the **PlayerArmature** character:

Figure 14.31 – Character standing in front of the spiky Stylized Crystal GameObject

16. In the **Inspector** window, add a **Box Collider** to **crystal_17_2** and check its **Is Trigger** option. This means that `OnTriggerEnter(...)` event messages will be received by both the **crystal_17_2** and **ThirdPersonController** GameObjects when Ethan walks into the crystal.

Now, let's create an explosion-style **Particle System** that we'll then make into a prefab and instantiate from code when that collision occurs.

17. Add a new **Particle System** to the scene named `Particle System-explosion` (menu: **GameObject** | **Effects** | **Particle System**).

18. Now, let's ensure that this **Particle System** is located at the same place as **crystal_17_2**. Focus the **Scene** window on the location of **crystal_17_2** by double-clicking this GameObject in the **Hierarchy** window. Then, single-click to select the **ThirdPersonController** GameObject in the **Hierarchy** window and go to **GameObject** | **Move To View**. This moves the selected GameObject (`Particle System-explosion`) to the location the **Scene** window is focused on.

19. We want particles to be single (not looped), short-lived, and moving quickly due to gravity. So, in the **Inspector** window for the general properties of **Particle System-explosion**, set **Duration** to `0.50` and uncheck **Looping**. Then, set **Start Lifetime** to `0.5`, **Start Speed** to `10`, **Start Size** to `2`, and **Gravity Modifier** to `1`.

20. We want the explosion to go in **all** directions, so enable the **Shape** module and set **Shape** to **Sphere**.

21. We want our **Particle System** to use the `m_fireCloud` material we created at the beginning of this recipe, so in the **Renderer** module, set **Material** to `m_fireCloud`:

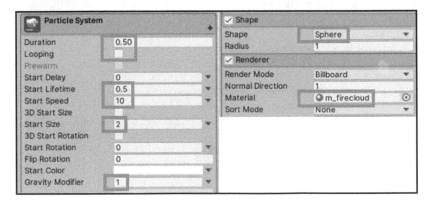

Figure 14.32 – The General, Emission, and Shape settings for our explosion Particle System

22. We want a **burst** of many particles as the particle system begins, which we can achieve in the **Emission** module. Click the plus (**+**) button to create an emission burst and set the count to `200`:

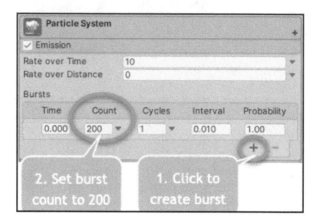

Figure 14.33 – Setting an emission burst of 200

Now that we've customized our **Particle System** in the scene to behave as the explosion we need, let's turn this into a **Prefab** that we can instantiate at runtime when the player's character dies by hitting a spiky crystal.

23. Create a folder in the **Project** window named `Prefabs`. Drag **Particle System-explosion** into this folder from the **Hierarchy** window. You should now see a new prefab named `Particle System-explosion` in the `Prefabs` folder.

24. Delete the `Particle System-explosion` GameObject from the scene.

25. Create a new C# script class called `Crystal.cs` containing the following code:

```
using UnityEngine;

public class Crystal : MonoBehaviour {
    public GameObject explosionPrefab;

    private void OnTriggerEnter(Collider other) {
        // create explosion at same location as this Crystal
        GameObject explosion = Instantiate(explosionPrefab,
transform.position,
            transform.rotation);

        // destroy particle system after 1 second
```

```
        Destroy(explosion, 1);

        // remove this Crystal
        Destroy(this.gameObject);
    }
}
```

26. Add a copy of `Crystal.cs` as a component of **crystal_17_2**.

27. With **crystal_17_2** selected in the **Hierarchy** window, drag `Particle System-explosion` from the `Prefabs` folder into the public **Explosion Prefab** slot of the **Crystal (script)** component of the GameObject in the **Inspector** window:

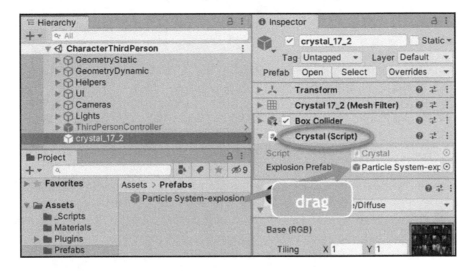

Figure 14.34 – Assigning the explosion prefab to the Crystal (Script) component

28. Run the scene. When the player's character collides with the crystal, the crystal is destroyed and an explosion takes place (before being destroyed itself after 1 second).

How it works...

Using a **Material** from a related still image is a good way to improve the visual effect of a particle system and saves us from having to do extra work, such as changing the colors of particles over time. The **Particles/Standard Unit** shader in **Additive** mode is all we needed for this example, to make the material ready to be selected by the particle system's **Renderer** module.

We were able to create the quick and striking visual effect of an explosion by changing the particle system's **Shape** to a **Sphere** so that the particles go everywhere, and also by creating a burst **Emission** set to 200. We made our particles move fast, live a short time, and be affected by a Gravity Modifier.

We only wanted the explosion to happen once, so we disabled the **Loop** option in the general **Particle System** parameters.

We were able to create a reusable **Prefab** from the particle system in the scene simply by dragging the GameObject into our **Project** window and then removing the original **Particle System** GameObject from the scene.

The Crystal.cs script class we created was quite straightforward as it was designed to have instance objects attached as components to the crystal GameObjects in the scene. When a crystal detects a collision receiving an OnEnterFrame(...) message, it creates (**instantiates**) a new GameObject instance of the explosion particle system from the Prefab asset file we created. The explosion GameObject is created at the same location and rotation as the crystal, invoking Destroy(...) on the particle system but with a delay of 1 second (so that the explosion will be completed), and then also destroying the GameObject that was collided with.

You may wish to add an audio effect to increase the impact of the explosion on the player – you learned how to add sound effects in *Chapter 4, Playing with and Manipulating Sounds*.

Using Invoke to delay the execution of an explosion

In the previous recipe, we wanted to immediately instantiate and play a particle system as soon as the player's character collided with a crystal GameObject. However, there are times where we want to delay for a few moments when we want a prefab to be instantiated. This recipe customizes the previous one, in that we'll allow our player to move around the scene while dropping bombs. 3 seconds after being dropped, that bomb will be replaced by an explosion - an instantiation of our explosion **Particle System** from the previous recipe. This recipe is inspired, although in a much simplified form, by games such as **BomberMan**:

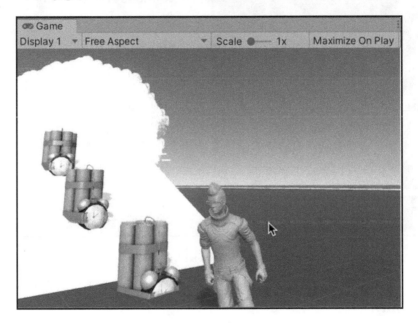

Figure 14.35 – Our Unity BomberMan

Getting ready

This recipe follows on from the previous one, so make a copy of that and work on the copy.

How to do it...

To delay an explosion using the `Invoke(...)` method, follow these steps:

1. Work on a copy of the previous recipe.
2. Ensure you are logged into your Unity account in the Unity Editor.
3. Open the Unity Asset Store in a web browser and log into your Unity account.
4. Tick **Free Assets** and search for and select the free **Free Bombs** package on the Asset Store:

Figure 14.36 – The free Yughues Free Bombs assets on the Asset Store

5. Click **Add to My Assets**. Then, after the button changes, click **Open in Unity**.
6. In your Unity Editor, the **Package Manager** window should open, and the **Free Bombs** asset should be selected in the list of **My Assets**. Click **Download** and, when downloaded, click **Import**. In the **Project** window, you should now see a new folder called **Meshes** and inside that, a folder called **Bomb Packs**.
7. Delete the **crystal_17_2** GameObject from the scene.
8. In the **Project** window, locate the **Old-time bomb** prefab file (**Meshes | Bomb Packs | Old-time bomb**) and create a GameObject in the scene by dragging the prefab from the **Project** window into the **Scene** window. Rename the new GameObject `bomb-small`.

9. With this new `bomb-small` selected in the **Hierarchy** window, make it 100 times smaller by changing its **Scale** to (`0.01, 0.01, 0.01`) in the **Inspector** window – the bomb should now be about the same size as the **PlayerArmature** character:

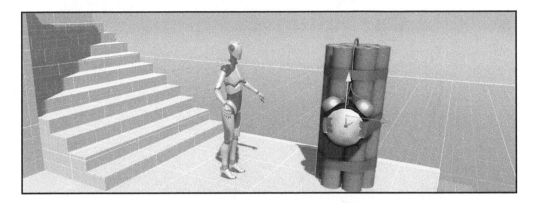

Figure 14.37 – The bomb-small GameObject in the Scene window

10. Create a new C# script class called `BombBehaviour.cs` containing the following code:

```
using UnityEngine;

public class BombBehaviour : MonoBehaviour {
    public GameObject explosionPrefab;

    void Start() {
        // after 3 seconds instantiate the explosion
        float delay = 3;
        Invoke(nameof(Explode), delay);

    }

    private void Explode() {
        // create explosion at same location as this player
        GameObject explosion = Instantiate(explosionPrefab,
            transform.position, transform.rotation);
        // destroy particle system after 1 second
        Destroy(explosion, 1);

        // destroy this bomb GameObject
        Destroy(gameObject);
    }
}
```

11. Add a copy of `BombFeature.cs` as a component to `bomb-small`. With `bomb-small` selected in the **Hierarchy** window, drag **Particle System-explosion** from the `Prefabs` folder into the public **Explosion Prefab** slot of the **Bomb Feature (script)** component of the GameObject in the **Inspector** window:

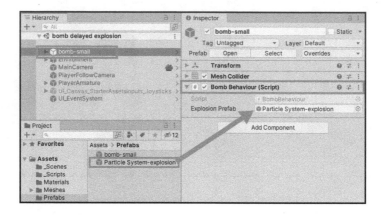

Figure 14.38 – Creating our small bomb prefab

12. Now, let's turn this into a prefab that we can instantiate at runtime so that when the player presses the *B* key, a `bomb-small` GameObject will be instantiated. Drag the `bomb-small` GameObject into the `Prefabs` folder in the **Project** window (choose **Original Prefab** when asked what type to create). You should now see a new prefab named `bomb-small` in the `Prefabs` folder.

13. Now, delete the `bomb-small` GameObject from the **Hierarchy** window.

14. Now, we need to write more C# code to detect when the player presses the *B* key. Create a new C# script class called `BombFeature.cs` containing the following code and attach an instance as a component of the `PlayerArmature` GameObject:

```
using UnityEngine;
using UnityEngine.InputSystem;

public class BombFeature : MonoBehaviour
{
    public GameObject bombPrefab;

    void Update()
    {
        if (Keyboard.current[Key.B].wasReleasedThisFrame)
```

```
            {
                // create bomb at same location as this player
                Instantiate(bombPrefab, transform.position,
transform.rotation);
            }
        }
    }
```

15. With `PlayerArmature` selected in the **Hierarchy** window, drag `bomb-small` from the `Prefabs` folder into the public **Bomb Prefab** slot of the **Bomb Feature (script)** component of the GameObject in the **Inspector** window:

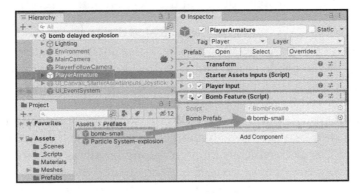

Figure 14.39 – Populating BombFeature (Script) on ThirdPersonController

16. Save and run the scene. As you walk around the scene with `PlayerArmature`, you can press the *B* key to drop a bomb. After 3 seconds, the bomb will disappear and be replaced by an explosion – this is due to our explosion prefab!

How it works...

Having imported a bomb model into our project, we used a 100-times smaller (scaled 0.01) version to create a prefab for our game. Before saving the small bomb as a prefab, an instance of the `BombBehaviour.cs` C# script class was added as a component of the GameObject, and its public **Explosion Prefab** property was linked to the explosion prefab we created in the previous recipe.

A second script class called BombFeature.cs was added as a component to **PlayerArmature**, and its public **Bomb Prefab** property was linked to our new small bomb prefab. Since the starter assets our project is based on use the new Unity input system, we needed to write if (Keyboard.current[Key.B].wasReleasedThisFrame) to detect the *B* key being pressed and released. We also needed to add a using statement to import the UnityEngine.InputSystem package.

The feature we added used BombFeature.cs in **ThirdPersonController** to detect when the player presses the *B* key. We did this using a test for GetKeyDown(...) every frame in the Update() method. When the *B* key is detected, a GameObject is instantiated from the small bomb prefab at the location of the player.

When a new bomb-small GameObject was created, its Start() method was executed. In that method, we used an Invoke() statement to create a 3-second delay before executing the Explode() method. The Invoke() statement needs just the name of the method and the length of the delay in seconds (3, in our case). Most of this work was achieved by the Explode() method of the BombBehaviour.cs script class. Just as in the previous recipe, an explosion GameObject is created from its prefab, and a delayed Destroy() statement is used to delete the explosion GameObject after 1 second, which is more than long enough for us to see the explosion effect from the particle system. Having created the explosion and its delayed Destroy() statement, we destroy the bomb GameObject itself.

There's more...

In the BombFeature.cs C# script class, we could add some logic to the Explode() method before the bomb GameObject is destroyed. Since we've displayed an explosion, we could use, for example, Physics.OverlapSphere(...) to get an array of all the colliders that are in the radius of the sphere that's centered on our bomb's location. Our logic could then loop through those colliders, sending their parent GameObjects (or scripted components) messages about how much damage has been taken, or simply Destroy() the GameObjects of all the colliders in the blast radius's sphere:

```
private void Explode() {
        // create explosion at same location as this player
        GameObject explosion = Instantiate(explosionPrefab,
transform.position, transform.rotation);
        // destroy particle system after 1 second
        Destroy(explosion, 1);
```

```
        // --- do any collision logic for bomb here -----
        Collider[] hitColliders = Physics.OverlapSphere(center,
radius);
        // loop through colliders to destroy them / send them damage
.....

        // destroy this bomb GameObject
        Destroy(gameObject);
}
```

Further reading

Here are some resources that provide more details about this chapter's topics:

- The Unity manual lighting
  page: https://docs.unity3d.com/Manual/Lighting.html
- Unity manual SkyBox component: https://docs.unity3d.com/Manual/class-Skybox.html
- Unity Lightmapping resources:
  - https://docs.unity3d.com/Manual/Lightmappers.html
  - https://learn.unity.com/tutorial/configuring-lightmaps
- Unity's **Global Illumination (GI)** pages:
  - https://docs.unity3d.com/Manual/GIIntro.html
  - http://docs.unity3d.com/Manual/GlobalIllumination.html

- Information about Unity's cookie **Textures** can be found on their manual
  page: https://docs.unity3d.com/Manual/Cookies.html
- Another source for Unity and cookie **Textures** is the *CgProgramming WikiBook* for
  Unity: https://en.wikibooks.org/wiki/Cg_Programming/Unity/Cookies
- Unity manual about choosing a color
  space: https://unity3d.com/learn/tutorials/topics/graphics/choosing-color-space
- Unity manual about the **Lighting Explorer** window: https://docs.unity3d.com/Manual/LightingExplorer.html

You can learn more about particle systems at the following links:

- Unity's particle system tutorial: `https://learn.unity.com/tutorial/visual-effects-with-particles`
- Ray Wenderlich's introduction to particle systems: `https://www.raywenderlich.com/138-introduction-to-unity-particle-systems`
- PolyToot's *Advanced Fire Effect Tutorial With Unity Particles*: `https://www.youtube.com/watch?v=G0R7MIbX3MU`

Unity offers a choice of two color spaces: **Gamma** (the default) and **Linear**. You can select your desired **Color Space** by going to **Edit** | **Project Settings** | **Player**. While **Linear** space has significant advantages, it isn't supported by all hardware (especially mobile systems), so which one you should choose will depend on which platform you are deploying on. For more information about **Linear** and **Gamma** lighting workflows, go to `https://docs.unity3d.com/Manual/LinearRendering-LinearOrGammaWorkflow.html`.

Finally, an exciting package that is now out of preview is **Visual Effects Graph**. This offers powerful ways to create stunning visual effects in Unity projects. Learn more here:

- Ray Wenderlich's Visual Effects Graph tutorial: `https://www.raywenderlich.com/9261156-introduction-to-the-visual-effect-graph`
- The Unity Visual Effects Graph samples project to download (it's over 1 GB): `https://github.com/Unity-Technologies/VisualEffectGraph-Samples`
- A Unity blog post about Visual Effects Graph samples: `https://blog.unity.com/technology/visual-effect-graph-samples`

15
Virtual and Augmented Reality (VR/AR)

In this chapter, we will present a set of recipes introducing **augmented reality** (**AR**) and **virtual reality** (**VR**) game development in Unity.

VR is about presenting an immersive audio-visual experience to the player, engaging enough for them to lose themselves in exploring and interacting with the game world that has been created. AR is the use of devices (such as smartphones and see-through headsets) to add a visual overlay on top of what we are seeing. The term **extended reality** (**XR**) is used as a catch-all term that covers both types of application and experience. As well as gaming, XR applications offer amazing experiences to help us explore graphics and videos in immersive 3D, such as **Google Earth VR** and **Oculus Quest Wander**:

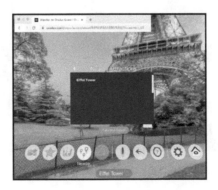

Figure 15.1 – The Oculus Wander application showing the Eiffel Tower in Paris, France

From one point of view, XR simply requires two cameras in order to generate the images for each eye to give a 3D effect. But effective XR needs content, UI controls, and tools to help create them. In this chapter, we will explore recipes that work with 360-degree videos and pre-made assets for sitting/standing XR projects.

Google Earth VR is great fun! The following screenshot, which is from a live VR session, shows the virtual hand controller and a virtual screen menu showing photos and text about six suggested locations to visit:

Figure 15.2 – Google Earth VR

AR applications are becoming more and more common. One very successful AR app is the Arts and Culture app for Android smartphones, offering interactive experiences such as putting your own face into famous paintings:

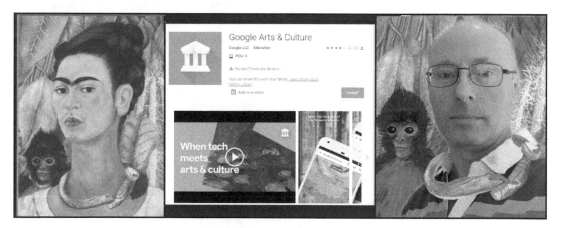

Figure 15.3 – One of the authors of this cookbook (Matt Smith) impersonating Frida Kahlo in Self-Portrait with Monkey with the Arts and Culture app

XR systems can be categorized as either desktop (tethered) or mobile. There are several types of mobile XR devices:

- **Desktop (tethered) VR**: A VR headset that's "tethered" via a high-speed cable to a computer with powerful graphics. VR examples include the Oculus Rift, HTC Vive, and Windows Mixed Reality. Some early research AR systems were tethered but these days, almost all AR systems are mobile. Some standalone devices can also work tethered, to make use of a more powerful desktop computer to run more processor-intensive VR applications, such as an Oculus Quest with the Oculus Link cable (there is also a wireless Air Link in beta – see the *Further reading* section at the end of this chapter).

- **Mounted smartphone XR**: A form of XR housing for a mobile device. These are headsets that house an Android/iOS smartphone, of which the two best known are Google Cardboard and Samsung Gear. Interestingly, some proposed AR systems link digital glasses via a cable to a smartphone, so while mobile and smartphone-based, they won't be a single head-mounted display unit. The forthcoming Ghost smartphone headset is an example of smartphone AR.

- **Standalone mobile VR/AR smartglasses**: Many recent mobile VR headsets have Android mobile devices built into them. Examples include Google Cardboard/Daydream, the Oculus Quest/Quest 2/Go, HTC Vive Focus 3, and the Pico Neo/2. Standalone AR glasses are usually called smart glasses, with the most (in)famous being Google Glass. Other examples include Microsoft HoloLens, Magic Leap, and the Vizux Blade.

- **Smartphone/tablet AR**: One way to experience AR is simply by looking at the world through the camera (and AR overlay) of your phone. While not an immersive experience, it is a quick and easy way to experience and test AR projects. In 2021, Google launched the Maps AR/Live View feature, which provides an AR experience through their mobile apps: `https://www.pocket-lint.com/apps/news/google/147956-what-is-google-maps-ar-navigation-and-how-do-you-use-it`.

Unity is perfect for creating and building XR projects since by simply changing the **Build** target to iOS or Android, a project can be created that will work on almost all the current XR devices:

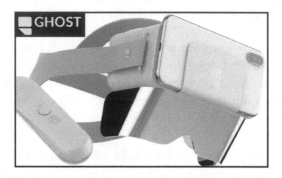

Figure 15.4 – The forthcoming Ghost AR phone-reflection-based headset

There are basically five ways to get a VR/AR application running on a device to experience it, as shown in the following diagram. They are as follows:

- **The Unity Mock HMD simulated headset**: This is probably the fastest way to test a VR/AR app, although only a limited range of VR game features can be tested when running in 2D in the Unity Editor.
- **Compiled application**: Compile the Unity project into an executable app (usually Android or iOS) and copy it via USB cable, Wi-Fi, or web download onto the device. Then, run the app and experience the VR/AR application running.
- **Tethered headset**: Desktop VR – a VR headset "tethered" via a high-speed cable to a computer with powerful graphics. Examples include the Oculus Rift, HTC Vive, and Windows Mixed Reality. You can create and run a VR project in the Unity Editor, and use a tethered (cabled) device to immediately test the application. After the Mock HMD headset Unity package, this is the fastest way to run-test a VR application.
- **Internet published WebXR project**: Build a Unity project as a WebXR/WebGL project, and then publish this build on an internet server. The AR/VR application can then be experienced when using an XR browser (such as **Firefox Reality**) on a device.

- **VR stores**: There are now VR stores, such as the Oculus Rift/Quest Stores, so publishing a built project to a store is another route from Unity development to downloading and running a VR app on a device:

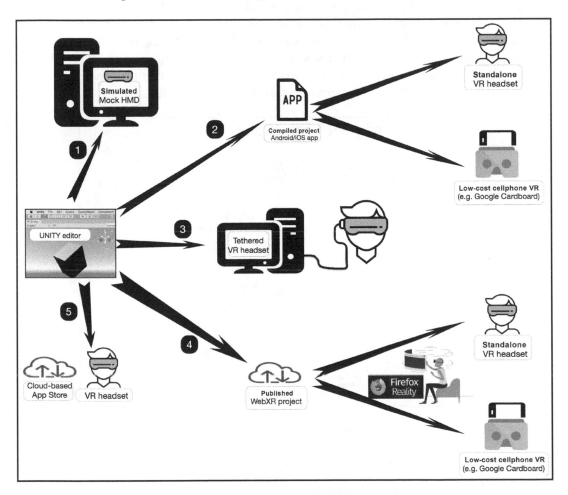

Figure 15.5 – Methods of publishing and experiencing VR/AR

There are several layers of components that make up the Unity XR framework for plugins. Unity provides the following diagram to summarize the architecture (see `https://docs.unity3d.com/Manual/XRPluginArchitecture.html`). Unfortunately, Unity has decided to charge for the **MARS** tools separately (above the cost of a Pro subscription), so we won't assume everyone has access to that. However, the XR Interaction Toolkit offers many powerful VR/AR features, and there are also hardware provider SDKs from the likes of Oculus, Valve, Microsoft, and Pico. There's also the WebXR standard and the SDKs from the open source community. So, we have lots of software libraries to help up make XR projects with Unity:

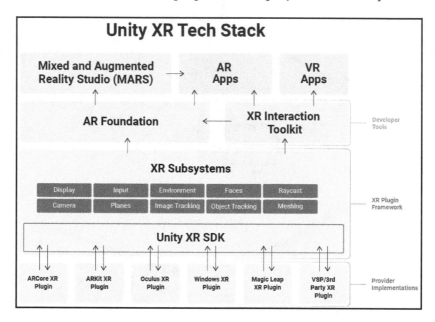

Figure 15.6 – The Unity XR plugin framework

In this chapter, we will cover the following recipes:

- Setting up Unity project for VR
- Setting up an Oculus Quest/2 in Developer Mode
- Creating a VR project for the Oculus Quest/2
- Creating a VR project using the Mock HMD device
- Working with the Mozilla demo WebXR project
- Adding 360-degree videos to a VR project
- Exploring the Unity AR samples
- Setting up Unity for AR

- Creating a simple AR Foundation project
- Detecting and highlighting planes with AR Foundation
- Creating an AR furniture previewer by detecting horizontal planes
- Creating a floating 3D model over an image target

Technical requirements

To complete the recipes in this chapter, you will need Unity 2021.1 or later, plus one of the following:

- Microsoft Windows 10 (64-bit)/GPU: DX10, DX11, and DX12-capable
- macOS Sierra 10.12.6+/GPU Metal-capable Intel or AMD
- Linux Ubuntu 16.04, Ubuntu 18.04, and CentOS 7/GPU: OpenGL 3.2+ or Vulkan-capable, NVIDIA or AMD

For each chapter, there is a folder that contains the asset files you will need in this book's GitHub repository at `https://github.com/PacktPublishing/Unity-2021-Cookbook-Fourth-Edition`.

You will also need an AR device and a VR device. For this, you can use a dedicated device such as a VR headset, or you can use mobile cell phone apps to begin experiencing AR and VR. If you wish to use a mobile cell phone for VR projects, there are many low-cost devices to choose from, such as Google Cardboard and similar: `https://arvr.google.com/cardboard/get-cardboard/`. There is also a Unity Mock HMD package that offers a simulated VR headset: `https://docs.unity3d.com/Packages/com.unity.xr.mock-hmd@1.3/manual`:

Figure 15.7 – The low-cost Google Cardboard headset for mobile cell phones

To experience WebXR publishing projects, you'll need a browser that supports WebXR:

- Desktop/laptop/VR headset users can use the **Firefox Reality** browser.
- Android phone users can use the mobile **Google Chrome** or **Samsung Internet** browsers.
- iOS phone users can use Mozilla's **WebXR Viewer**. It is likely Apple will add WebXR features to its Safari browser in 2021:

Figure 15.8 – The App Store Mozilla WebXR viewer for iOS

Setting up Unity for VR

There are some basic steps you need to perform so that your Unity editor application is set up for VR development. In this recipe, you'll learn how to add the modules you need to your editor application, install the templates, open the sample scene, and set up the Build Settings for Android development for an Oculus Quest/2 VR headset.

How to do it...

To create and set up a project for VR, do the following:

1. Open the **Unity Hub** application and choose the **Installs** tab on the left.
2. Now, select the version of Unity you wish to develop your VR projects with.
3. Next, add the **Android Build Support** modules to your application and click **Done**.
4. Ensure that both the **Android SDK/NDK Tools** and **OpenJDK** sub-modules are checked, as shown in the following screenshot:

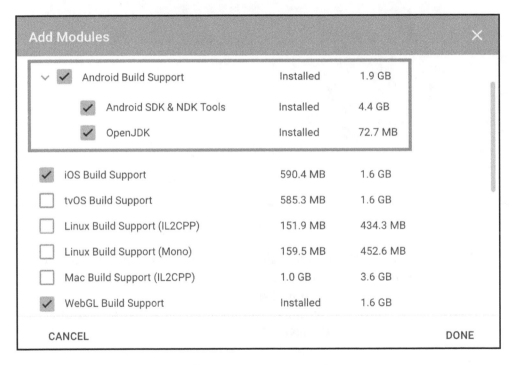

Figure 15.9 – Installing the Android modules with Unity Hub

5. In the **Unity Hub** application, choose the **Projects** tab on the left and click the **NEW** button for your version of Unity.

6. After a few seconds, additional templates should be displayed. Find the **VR** template and click the **Download** button:

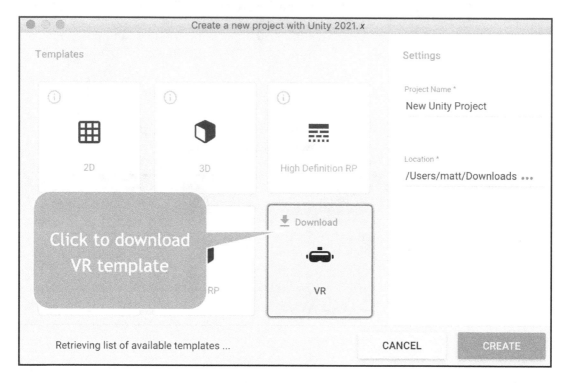

Figure 15.10 – Installing the VR project template from Unity Hub

7. Now, select the **VR** template and choose a new location for your project. Then, click the **CREATE** button.

8. After a moment, Unity should start up, with a pop-up window welcoming you to the VR project template and reminding you to select your chosen platform(s) from the **Project Settings** window.

9. In the **Project** window, you'll see a `Scenes` folder, as well as two other folders named `XR` and `ExampleAssets` – these are part of the VR template resources:

   - Open the **Project Settings** window by going to **Edit | Project Settings...**.
   - For the **XR Plugin Management** settings, choose the **Android** (robot icon) tab and then check the box for your VR plugin provider (in this example, I checked **Oculus** since I'm using the **Quest** VR headset):

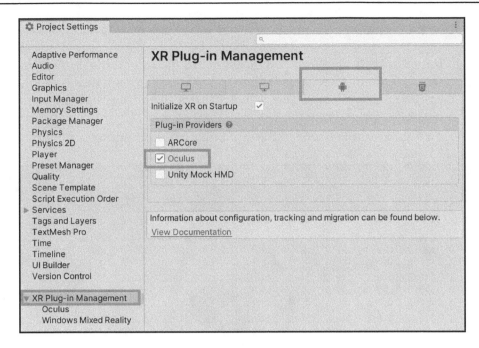

Figure 15.11 – Enabling the Oculus plugin provider for XR Plugin Management in the Project Settings window

10. Now, select your device from the **XR Plug-in Management** dropdown and ensure your device is enabled. The following screenshot shows the **Oculus** setting chosen, and both the **Quest** and **Quest 2** devices enabled:

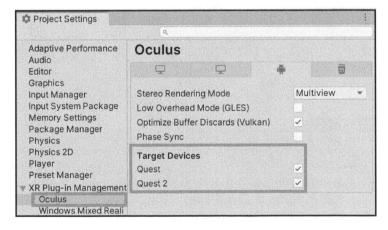

Figure 15.12 – Enabling the Quest and Quest 2 VR devices for Oculus in the Project Settings window

11. Open the **Build Settings** dialog window (**File | Build Settings...**) and switch **Build Target** to **Android**.

12. If it's not already open, open the provided **Sample Scene** (in the **Project** window, go to the **Scenes** folder). In the **Hierarchy** window, you'll see it has an XR-Rig GameObject, which has three children; that is, a camera and left and right controllers.

13. Add this **Sample Scene** to the build in the **Build Settings...** window:

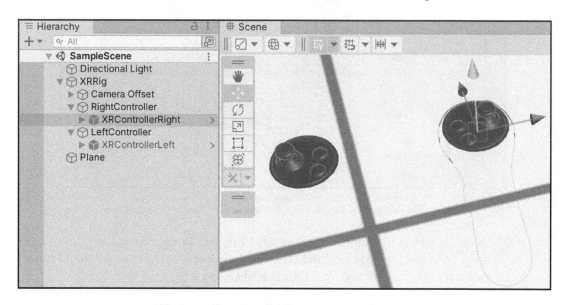

Figure 15.13 – The XR GameObjects in the provided sample scene

14. Congratulations! You have set up a project that's ready for VR project development.

How it works...

This recipe illustrated the basic steps you must follow to set up a VR project. First, you added the appropriate module (Android) to your Unity editor. Then, you downloaded the appropriate project template (VR). The target device group (Oculus) was selected in the **XR Plug-in Management** settings, and a particular device (in my case, Quest) was provided. With that, you've made all the foundational preparations to actually create and run VR projects with Unity.

Setting up an Oculus Quest/2 in Developer Mode

The most popular VR headset of 2019/2020 was the Oculus Quest and Quest 2. These are low-cost, walk-around headsets that provide a great introduction to VR for many people. It can be a bit fiddly to set up a Quest for Unity project development, so we'll go through the steps required in this short recipe. Between this and the next recipe, you'll have the satisfaction of creating VR projects and loading them onto your headset.

 These steps were performed at the time the book was being written. But things change fast, and it may be that not all the steps/screenshots are the same when you attempt this developer mode setup. However, we have included this recipe since we believe it will still be helpful to those beginning development for the Quest/2 to see the kinds of actions they'll need to take.

Getting ready

For this recipe, you'll need the following:

- A Facebook/Oculus account
- A mobile phone
- An Oculus Quest VR headset
- A USB C data communication cable (such as the Oculus Link)

Oculus has stated they intend to add a feature to allow a headset to be shared between multiple accounts, but it is not available at the time of writing. Therefore, if your headset has been paired with a different Oculus account already, you may need to perform a factory reset on the headset before following this recipe. The following web page from Oculus describes how to factory reset a Quest headset: `https://support.oculus.com/298586437740040/`.

How to do it...

To pair your Quest VR headset with the Oculus mobile phone app, do the following:

1. On a mobile phone, install the Oculus app and log in with your Facebook/Oculus account (you can create a new account if you don't have one). You may need to permit location services for your phone to link to your Oculus Quest VR headset.

2. You need to create an organization in order to work with the Quest headset in **Developer Mode**. Visit the following web page, create an organization, and give it a name (for example, I created one named `mattsmithdev`): `https://dashboard.oculus.com/organizations/create/`.

3. You'll also be asked to set up a VR profile name and image, as well as set up a PIN code for the Oculus store.

4. You will then be asked to select your headset – select **Quest** or **Quest 2** as appropriate:

Figure 15.14 – Selecting the headset type in the phone app

5. You'll be guided through powering and turning on your headset.

6. You will then be able to pair the headset by using the five-digit code that's displayed on the headset and entering it into the Oculus phone app (this may happen automatically). Once you've done this, the headset should be paired to the phone app and Oculus account. At this point, you need to complete the setup (language, Wi-Fi, and so on).

7. The headset may connect to Wi-Fi to update the headset software. Once that update is completed, the headset should be paired to your Oculus phone app, which means you are ready to start developing.

8. Choose the **Settings** tab and select your Quest device from the list. Expand the details for your Quest device and choose **More Settings**. Choose **Developer Mode** from the list.

9. On the Quest headset, you should now have a **USB Debugging** dialog window pop up. Check the option for **Always allow from this computer** and then click the **OK** button:

Figure 15.15 – Enabling USB debugging on the Quest headset

10. On your mobile phone, you should now be able to check the **Developer Mode** option on the screen.

11. Power off your Quest headset, and then turn it on again, to restart it in Developer Mode.

Now, if you connect a USB data cable (such as the Oculus Link) between your computer and the Quest headset, Android File Transfer should run, allowing you to move files between your computer and the Quest headset.

How it works...

The mobile phone app connects to your Quest headset via Bluetooth. Each Quest needs to be linked to an Oculus/Facebook account. Android devices, including Quest headsets, need to go through USB debugging/Developer Mode to allow us to load our own compiled Android applications onto them, rather than only being able to download apps from the web or Oculus Store.

Having followed the steps in this recipe, your Quest headset should now be ready to run Unity VR projects that we will develop and build ourselves.

Creating a VR project for the Oculus Quest/2

In this recipe, we'll create a simple scene and build it into an app to run on the Oculus Quest/2:

Figure 15.16 – The Quest VR app we'll create in this recipe, running on a Quest VR headset

Getting ready

You need to put your Quest headset into Developer Mode before trying this recipe. To learn how to do this, see the previous recipe, *Setting up an Oculus Quest/2 in Developer Mode*.

You will also need to have the Android modules and the VR template installed. To learn how to do this, see the first recipe of this chapter, *Setting up Unity for VR*.

How to do it...

To prepare a project for the Oculus Quest, do the following:

1. Having set your Quest/2 to **Developer Mode** and installed the **Android** modules and **VR** template, create a new VR project in Unity.
2. When Unity has loaded the new project, open the sample scene (in the **Project** window, go to the **Scenes** folder).
3. Open the **Project Settings** window by going to **Edit | Project Settings...**.
4. For the **XR Plugin Management** settings, choose the **Android** (robot icon) tab and then check the box for your Oculus VR device.
5. Open the **Build Settings** dialog window (**File | Build Settings...**) and switch **Build Target** to **Android.**
6. Connect your computer to your Quest headset using a USB-C data cable.
7. Put on the Quest headset and confirm you are happy to put the Quest into USB Debug mode and that you accept the connection from the computer.

8. Back in Unity, open the **Build Settings** dialog window. Under the **Android** settings, you should be able to click **Refresh** to update devices. Select your **Oculus** device and then **Run Device**. Your device will have a long hexadecimal serial number such as 1PASH23423423:

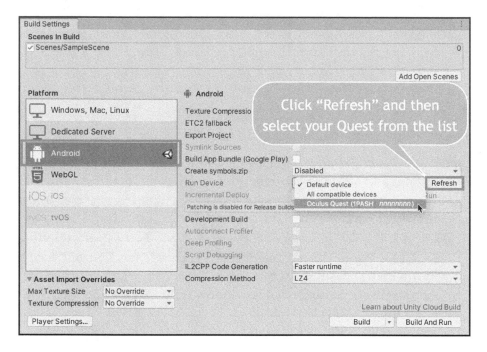

Figure 15.17 – Selecting Oculus Quest as the run device from the Android Build Settings

9. Add your scene to the build.

10. Click **Build And Run**. After a few seconds/minutes of compiling, your Unity project will run on the connected Oculus Quest headset. Put on the headset and explore!

11. While the scene is running correctly on the Quest, there is **nothing to interact with!**

   Let's add interactions with **XR Interaction Toolkit**. At the time of writing, this is still a pre-release package, so we'll need to access it for this project.

12. Open the **Project Settings** window by going to **Edit | Project Settings...**. For the **Package Manager** settings, check the **Enable Pre-Release Packages** option:

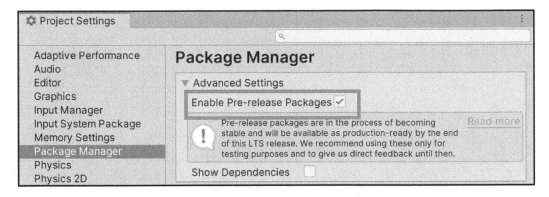

Figure 15.18 – Checking the Enable Pre-Release Packages checkbox inside Package Manager

13. Open the **Package Manager** window (menu: **Window | Package Manager**). Select **Unity Registry** from the dropdown and type XR into the search bar. Select **XR Interaction Toolkit** and install this package. Say **Yes** to the warning about the new **Input System** and when you're asked if you want to enable backends. The Unity Editor may need to restart.

14. In the **Package Manager** window the **XR Interaction Toolkit**, click the triangle widget to reveal the available samples. Import **Default Import Actions**:

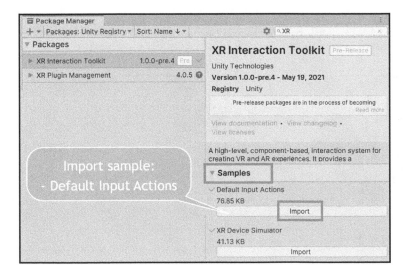

Figure 15.19 – Importing Default Input Actions from XR Interaction Toolkit in the Package Manager window

15. We need to set up the default input actions for
our **Left** and **Right** simulated controllers. In the **Project** window, select
the **XRI Default Left Controller** asset file (folder: **Assets | Samples | XR
Interaction Toolkit | 1.x.version | Default Input Actions**). Then, in the
Inspector window, click the **Add to ActionBasedController default** button.

16. Repeat this for the **XRI Default Right Controller** asset file:

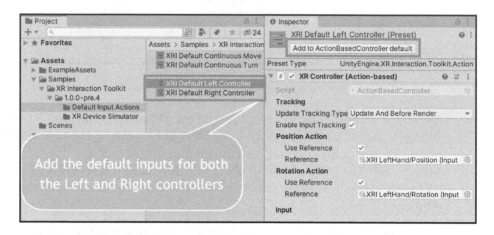

Figure 15.20 – Adding the XRI input actions to the project defaults

17. We now need to label the filters for these presets in **Project Settings**. Open
the **Project Settings** window (menu: **Edit | Project Settings...**). For
the **Preset Manager** settings, enter `Right` for **XRI Default Right
Controller** and `Left` for **XRI Default Left Controller**:

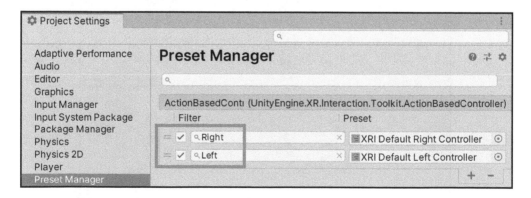

Figure 15.21 – Naming the Right/Left filters for the controller presets

18. Since we have the default input actions set up, we can remake our XR Rig GameObject so that it's automatically populated with them. Delete **XR Rig** from the **Hierarchy** window.

19. Create a new **XR Rig** (menu: **GameObject | XR | XR Rig (Action Based)**). If you select this new XR Rig in the **Hierarchy** window, you'll find a child GameObject called **Camera Offset** and in that, two children called **LeftHand Controller** and **RightHand Controller**. If you select **LeftHand Controller** in the **Inspector** window, you will see how the **XRI** input references have been automatically assigned from the defaults when this new **XR Rig** was created:

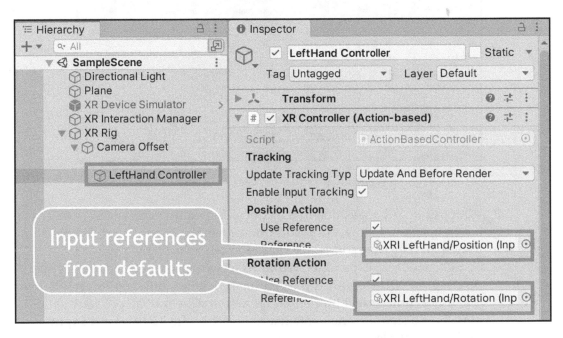

Figure 15.22 – Viewing the assigned input actions on one of the XR hand controllers

20. Let's add a VR controller model for each controller – some prefabs came with the examples that are part of the VR project template. Select the LeftHand Controller GameObject in the **Hierarchy** window. In the **Inspector** window for the **XR Controller (Action Based)** component, locate the **Model** property and for the **Model Prefab** value, drag the **XRControllerLeft** prefab from the **Project** window.

21. Repeat the preceding step for the **RightHand Controller** child of the
    Camera Offset child of **XR Rig** to add
    its **XRControllerLRight** prefab reference:

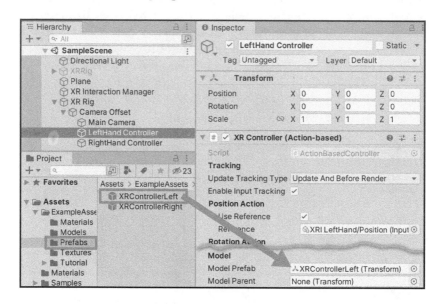

Figure 15.23 – Adding a reference to the XRControllerLeft model prefab in the XR Rig child GameObject

22. With this XR Rig selection in the **Hierarchy** window, in
    the **Inspector** window, click **Add Component** and type **Input Action
    Manager**. Once this component has been added to the XR
    Rig GameObject, expand its **Action Assets** array property (currently size
    0). Drag the **XRI Default Input Actions** asset file from the **Project** window
    into the **Action Assets** property. The **Action Assets** array property should
    now have a size of 1 and contain a reference to the **XRI Default Input
    Actions** asset file:

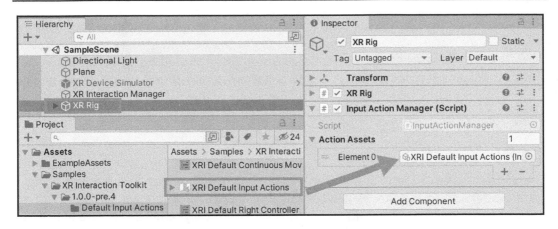

Figure 15.24 – Assigning XRI Default Input Actions to the Input Action Manager component that was added to the XR Rig GameObject

23. Open the **Project Settings** window (menu: **Edit | Project Settings...**) and, in the **Player** section, set an appropriate **Company Name**, **Product Name**, and **Version**. This **Product Name** value will be the name of the app when it is copied to your Quest headset. Set the **Product Name** to My VR Project 1:

Figure 15.25 – Setting the project's name and other details in the Player settings

24. Add to the scene **Hierarchy** a 3D Cube, named Cube-table, with a position of (0, 0, 3) and a scale of (3, 0.1, 3).

25. Add to the scene **Hierarchy** a 3D Sphere with a position of (0, 1, 4).

26. Create a black **Material** named m_black and apply it to the Sphere GameObject.

27. In the **Inspector** window, add an **XR Simple Interactable** component to the Sphere GameObject.

28. Save this updated scene.

29. Click **Build And Run** and specify the build file (just overwrite the existing one).

30. Put on your Quest headset and explore! You should now see the hand controller models firing red rays, but the rays will turn white when they hit the interactable `Sphere` GameObject.

How it works...

The build target needed to be set to Android – this is because we had previously added the Android module via Unity Hub. By connecting our Quest headset to the computer with a USB cable, and enabling USB access to the Quest, we were able to set the Android device to our specific USB connected Quest headset (choosing the device by serial number).

We imported the **XRI Interaction Toolkit**, allowing us to use those asset files to set up several sets of action presets for our project, especially those for the left- and right-hand controllers. By creating a new `XR Rig` GameObject after those defaults were set, **XR Rig** automatically assigned the default input actions, saving us the work of assigning a set of actions to the right and left controller GameObjects. We were also able to set these controller GameObjects to use the controller model prefabs from the examples provided by the VR project template – so that we can see controller objects when running the VR app – rather than having light rays starting from empty space where our hands are.

 Everyone is hoping the cumbersome manual labeling for the Right/Left filters will be automatic in future versions of Unity (see *Figure 15.21*).

The XRI Interaction Toolkit provided a set of default input actions that our app can recognize once we had added an **Input Action Manager** to our `XR Rig` GameObject and assigned the imported sample **Default Input Actions** asset file to this component.

Then, we set the name of the app as it will appear on the VR device by setting its **Product Name** in the **Player** settings. On the Quest, we chose to list **All apps**, then just apps from **Unknown Sources**. You should have seen the apps being loaded each time you clicked **Build And Run** and sent the built app to your headset – see the following Quest screenshot:

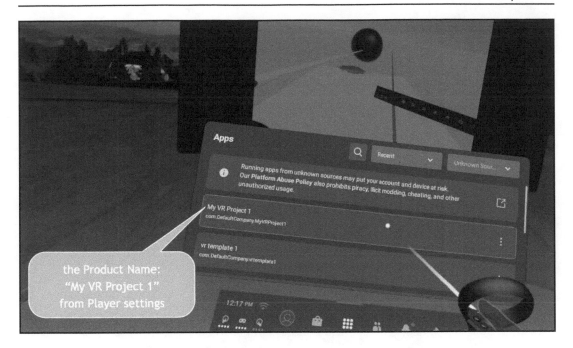

Figure 15.26 – The app's name in the headset based on the product name that was set in the Player settings

There's more...

Here are some suggestions for taking this recipe further.

Build failure due to Android version

If Unity fails to build when your Quest is set as **Run Device** in **Build Settings**, check the error message in the **Console** window. A common error is that the version of Android in the **Player** settings is too low for the version of Android on the device.

For example, the first time I tried to build for a Quest, I got this error:

```
Error building Player: Android Minimum API Level must be set to 23 or
higher for the Oculus XR Plugin.
```

It was resolved by opening the **Project Settings** window (menu: **Edit | Project Settings**) and increasing **Minimum API Level** to the number stated in the error message. You can do this in the **Player** section and by modifying the **Other Settings** values:

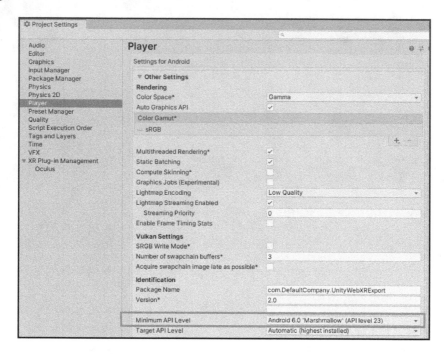

Figure 15.27 – Setting Minimum API Level of the Android version in the Player settings

Build failure due to "namespace cannot be found" error

When you are writing or using code with namespaces and assembly definitions, Unity may fail to build due to a compiler error in the following form:

```
The type or namespace name '<<someNamespace>>' could not be found
```

If this occurs, then you will need to create/edit the **Assembly Definition** file in the **Project** window folder where the scripts are located. If an **Assembly Definition** already exists, select it (otherwise, create a new one and select that). Then, in the **Inspector** window, check the **Android** option and click **Apply**:

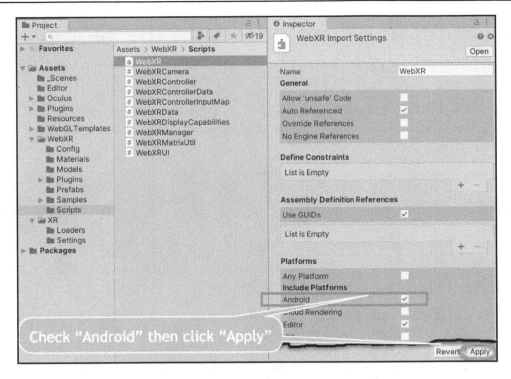

Figure 15.28 – Adding the Android platform to the WebXR settings

Sideloading APK files to an Android device (such as the Quest headset)

An alternative to **Build and Run** is to just build the APK Android app file and then **sideload** it to the Android device.

For this, you can use a USB cable and either of the following:

- The Android File Transfer app: `https://www.android.com/filetransfer/`
  `T`.
- The command-line **Android Debug Bridge (ADB)**. You can find a good ADB tutorial here: `https://androidcommunity.com/how-to-getting-adb-on-your-pc-without-installing-full-android-sdk-20180307/`.

Once you've transferred the APK file to the Quest/Android device, you can install and run the app.

Creating a VR project using the Mock HMD device

Sometimes, for speed of testing, or when we find that we want to do some VR development work without a VR headset, it can be useful to run and test scenes on our computer just within the Unity Editor. Unity provides the Mock HMD simulated device for this purpose:

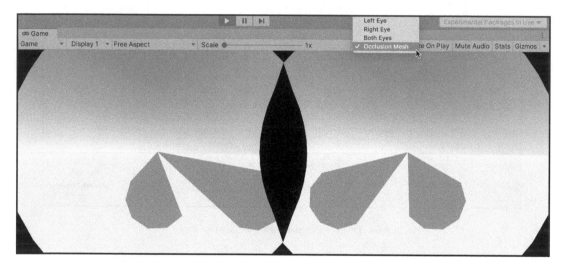

Figure 15.29 – Running the Mock HMD device in the Unity Game window

Getting ready

This recipe is for a VR project, so we'll build on the first recipe in this chapter, *Setting up Unity for VR*. So, either repeat those steps before beginning this one or make a copy of that recipe's project and work on that copy.

How to do it...

To create a VR project using the Mock HMD device, do the following:

1. Having installed the **VR** template, create a new VR project in Unity.
2. Open the **Project Settings** window (menu: **Edit | Project Settings**).

3. In the **Project Settings** window for the **XR Plugin Management** settings, select the desktop tab (on the left), and then check the box for **Mock HMD Loader**. You may see a message stating that it is installing:

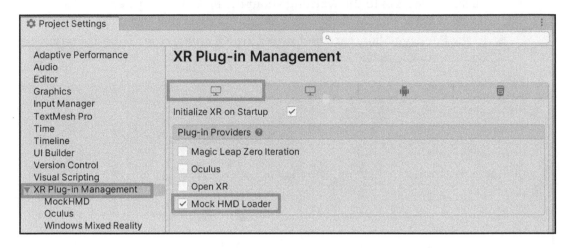

Figure 15.30 – Selecting Mock HMD Loader Plug-in Provider in the XR Plug-in Management settings

4. Open the **Project Settings** window (menu: **Edit | Project Settings...**). For the **Package Manager** settings, check the **Enable Pre-release Packages** option:

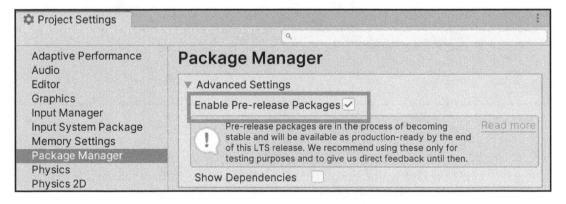

Figure 15.31 – Enabling Pre-release Packages for Package Manager

5. Open the **Package Manager** window (menu: **Window | Package Manager**). Select **Unity Registry** from the dropdown and type XR into the search bar. Select **XR Interaction Toolkit** and install this package. Say **Yes** to the warning about the new **Input System**, and asking if you want to enable backends. The Unity Editor may need to restart.

6. In the **Package Manager** window for the **XR Interaction Toolkit** entry, you will see two samples. Import both of them:

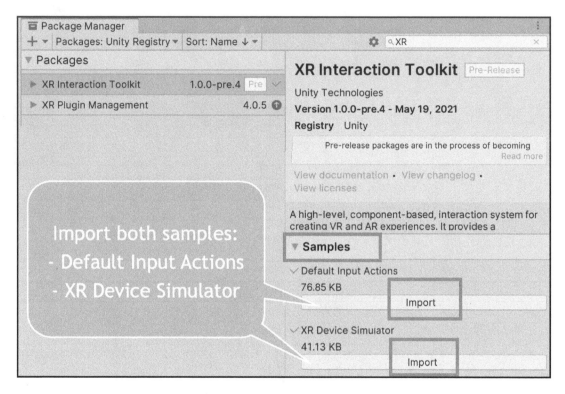

Figure 15.32 – Importing Default Input Actions and XR Device Simulator from the XR Interaction Toolkit package

7. We need to set up the default input actions for our **Left** and **Right** simulated controllers. In the **Project** window, select the **XRI Default Left Controller** asset file (folder: **Assets | Samples | XR Interaction Toolkit | 1.x.version | Default Input Actions**). Then, in the **Inspector** window, click the **Add to ActionBasedController default** button.

8. Repeat this for the **XRI Default Right Controller** asset file:

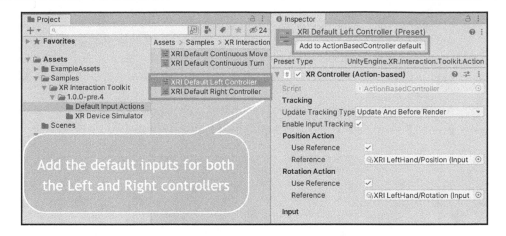

Figure 15.33 – Adding the XRI default input actions to the project presets

9. We now need to label these presets in **Project Settings**. Open the **Project Settings** window (menu: **Edit | Project Settings**). For the **Preset Manager** settings, enter `Right` for **XRI Default Right Controller** and `Left` for **XRI Default Left Controller**:

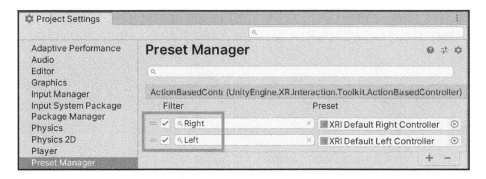

Figure 15.34 – Naming the Right/Left filters for the controller presets

10. From the **Project** window, drag the **XR Device Simulator** prefab asset file (folder: **Assets | Samples | XR Interaction Toolkit | 1.x.version | XR Device Simulator**) into the **Hierarchy** window.

11. Since we have the default input actions set up, we can remake our XR Rig GameObject to use them. Delete XR Rig from the **Hierarchy** window. Then, create a new one (menu: **GameObject | XR | XR Rig (Action Based)**).

12. With this `XR Rig` selected in the **Hierarchy** window, in the **Inspector** window, click **Add Component** and type `Input Action Manager`. Once this component has been added to the `XR Rig` GameObject, expand its **Action Assets** array property (currently size 0). Drag the **XRI Default Input Actions** asset file from the **Project** window into the **Action Assets** property. The **Action Assets** array property should now have a size of 1 and contain a reference to the **XRI Default Input Actions** asset file:

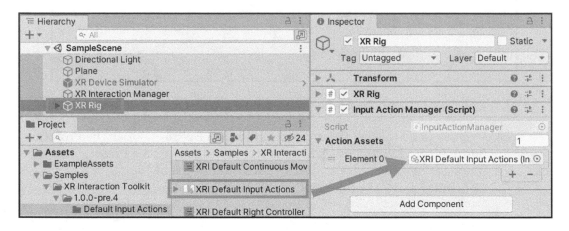

Figure 15.35 – Assigning XRI Default Input Actions to the Input Action Manager component that we added to the XR Rig GameObject

13. Run the scene. You'll see an extra drop-down menu for the **Game** window where you can choose one eye, both eyes, or an occlusions view of the simulated VR HMD device.

14. There is a range of controls you can use with the Mock HMD:

   - **Change Camera (X/Y) position**: *Mouse move + RightMouseButton*
   - **Change Camera (Z- near/far) position**: *MouseScrollWheel + RightMouseButton*
   - **Left controller only**: *Spacebar + Mouse move + RightMouseButton / Spacebar + MouseScrollWheel + RightMouseButton*
   - **Right controller only**: *Left-Shift + Mouse move + RightMouseButton / Left-Shift + MouseScrollWheel + RightMouseButton*

How it works...

This recipe illustrated how the **XRI Interaction Toolkit** offers a simulated VR device that will map keyboard and mouse movements from our computer into right/left-hand controller actions. By importing the **Mock HMD** device assets and adding a prefab GameObject to our scene, we are able to run and test our VR project on our computer, without the need for an actual VR headset. This can be useful when no headset is available, or we are testing aspects of the project that don't need full user testing in an actual VR environment. In many cases, it will be much faster to just use this simulated device and run a scene in Unity than building an app and testing on a headset, or even using a Link cable/Wi-Fi and having to put on/take off a VR headset each time some aspect of a scene needs testing.

Of course, there will be many situations that can only be tested properly by running them on an actual VR device, but this **Mock HMD** device is a useful tool to have in any VR developer's "toolbox."

Working with the Mozilla demo WebXR project

One likely future of VR is through the web – **WebXR**. The open source Mozilla Corporation has created a browser tuned for VR and AR called **Firefox Reality**. In this recipe, we'll learn how to download, customize, build, and publish the demo project based on the **WebXR Export** Unity package published by Mozilla Corporation:

Figure 15.36 – The Desert WebXR project sample from Mozilla

Getting ready

This recipe will help you create a WebXR project. To do this, you'll need the following:

- A VR headset with the Firefox Reality browser installed. You can find the Firefox Reality browser here: `https://labs.mozilla.org/projects/firefox-reality`.
- To "host" the generated folder and HTML pages on the internet, you'll need access to a web server. In the *There's more...* section, you will learn how to do this for free with GitHub Pages.
- **WebXR** is built on top of **WebGL**, so you need to ensure the version of Unity you are using can build to a WebGL target platform. This can all be installed using the **Installs** section of the **Unity Hub** application. The following is a screenshot of the **Unity Hub** screen where you can add modules to a Unity Editor version:

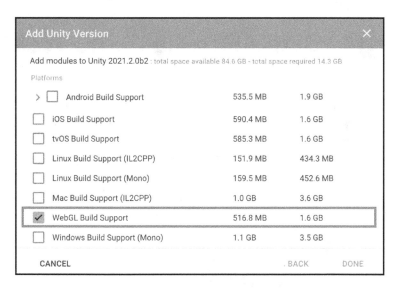

Figure 15.37 – Unity Hub WebGL Build Support for the selected Unity Editor

How to do it...

To work with the Mozilla demo WebXR project, follow these steps:

1. Start a new 3D project and ensure you are logged into your Unity account in the Unity Editor.
2. Open the **Build Settings** dialog window and switch **Build Target** to **WebGL**.
3. Open the Unity Asset Store in a web browser and log into your Unity account via **Asset Store**.
4. Search for and select the free **WebXR Exporter** via **Asset Store**.
5. Click **Add to My Assets**. Then, after the button changes, click **Open in Unity**:

Figure 15.38 – The WebXR Exporter on the Asset Store

6. In your Unity Editor, the **Package Manager** window should open, and the **WebXR** assets should be selected in the list of **My Assets**. Click **Download**; then, when downloaded, click **Import**.
7. In the **Project** window, you should now see two new folders named **WebGL Templates** and **WebXR**.
8. Open the scene file named **WebXR** in the **Project** window (folder: **WebXR | Samples | Desert | Scenes**).

9. You should now see the cartoon-style 3D Desert scene – a table, with cubes and a sphere on top of it, and two VR "hands" in front of the table:

Figure 15.39 – The core contents of the Desert scene from the WebXR package

10. Open the **Project Settings** window (menu: **Edit | Project Settings...**) and select **Player** settings.
11. Under **Resolution and Presentation**, ensure **WebXR** under **WebGL Template** is selected.
12. Under **Publishing Settings**, set **Compression Format** to **Disabled**:

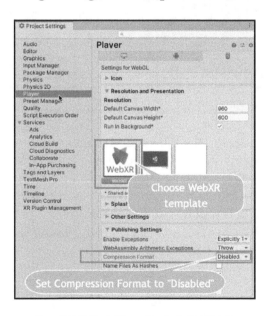

Figure 15.40 Setting the Player settings for the WebXR build

13. Now, open the **Build** dialog (menu: **File | Build Settings...**), add the current scene to the build, and build the project by clicking the **Build** button. When asked to choose a name for the build folder, enter `docs`. A folder will be created for your build containing an `index.html` web page and the associated WebXR/WebGL and Unity assets.

14. By publishing the build folder contents on the web, you will be able to interact with your WebXR project using a VR headset running a WebXR compatible browser such as Firefox Reality.

15. Now, create a new empty scene and add a **Directional Light** (there should be no **Main Camera** in this scene, since there is a camera in the prefab we are about to add...).

16. From the **Project** window (folder: **WebXR | Samples | Desert | Prefabs**), drag the **WebXRCameraSet** asset file into the scene. This creates the core GameObject for our WebXR experience.

17. Add a 3D **Cube** to the scene and scale it so that it's very large and positioned lower than the two virtual hands.

18. Add a 3D **Sphere** to the scene that's positioned by the virtual hands. Add a **Rigidbody** component to this **Sphere**. Tag this GameObject as **Interactable**:

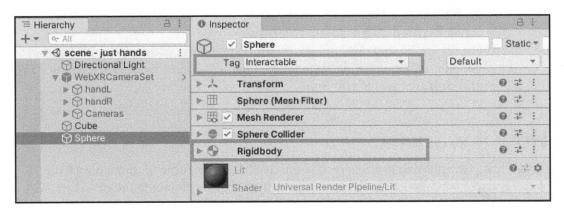

Figure 15.41 – Making the Sphere GameObject an interactable Rigidbody GameObject

19. Locate and drag the `MouseDragObject` C# script file onto the `Sphere` GameObject in the scene. You'll find this script in the **Project** window (folder: **Packages | WebXR Interactions | Runtime | Scripts**):

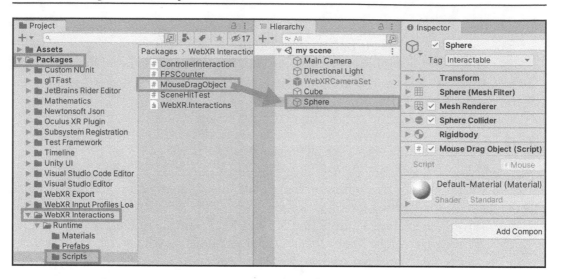

Figure 15.42 – Adding the Desert script to the virtual right hand

20. Save the current scene.
21. Now, open the **Build** dialog (menu: **File | Build Settings...**) and add the current scene to the build. Also, remove any other scenes for this build.
22. Build the project by clicking the **Build** button.
23. Finally, publish it on the web. When you visit the page with a VR headset, you should have two virtual hands, where the right hand is able to pick up and drop/throw the sphere.

How it works...

Since Unity can publish projects to WebGL, we have been able to make use of the WebXR Exporter assets to build a WebGL project that implements the new WebXR standard.

When a WebXR project is viewed on a VR headset with a compatible browser, the code within the WebXR assets detects the type of VR device and communicates with the Unity web asset.

As we saw when creating a scene from scratch, the core of the WebXR project is the GameObject combining cameras and hand models.

The `DesertControllerInteraction` C# script animates a hand's *fingers* in response to controller inputs, and also allows GameObjects to be grabbed and moved when a hand containing a component of this script collides with a GameObject that is tagged as `Interactable`. The cube for the ground was not tagged or given a rigid body, so it cannot be affected by our virtual hand. However, the sphere we created was given a **Rigidbody** (so that it has mass and can be affected by simulated physics forces). We tagged the sphere as `Interactable` so that our virtual right hand is able to pick up and move/throw the sphere.

There's more...

Here are some suggestions for taking this recipe further.

Using GitHub Pages to publish your WebXR project for free

GitHub offers us a way to publish a free website for each project with a feature called **GitHub Pages**. The simplest way to do this is to have a `docs` folder in your GitHub project. To publish your WebXR project using GitHub Pages, do the following:

1. First, create a project on GitHub and clone it to your computer. The steps for this can be found in the *Creating and cloning a GitHub repository* recipe of chapter *Chapter 8, Web Server Communication and Online Version Control*.
2. Build your Unity WebXR to a new folder named `docs` in the GitHub project folder you cloned to your computer.
3. Add all the files to the current Git snapshot by typing `git add` in the command-line terminal.
4. Create a snapshot of the added files by typing `git commit -m "created docs folder"` in the command-line terminal.
5. Push the files from your computer up to the GitHub cloud server by typing `git push` in the command-line terminal.

6. On the GitHub project **Settings** page, scroll down to the **GitHub Pages** section, and select the main branch and the `/docs` folder:

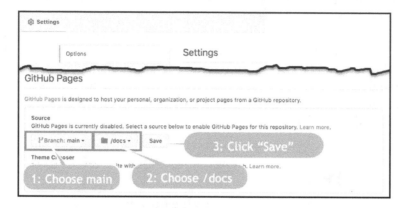

Figure 15.43 – Setting the GitHub pages to publish from the docs folder

You can see an example of a public Unity project published on GitHub with a `docs` folder (the one for this recipe) at `https://github.com/dr-matt-smith/unity-cookbook-2020-ch15-10-webxr-basic-scene`.

The GitHub Pages published docs folder URL for your WebXR browser is can be found at `https://dr-matt-smith.github.io/unity-cookbook-2020-ch15-10-webxr-basic-scene/`:

Figure 15.44 – The published build via the free GitHub Pages service

Learning more about the WebXR example project

Visit the documentation pages for the GitHub project to learn more about this WebXR project: `https://github.com/MozillaReality/unity-webxr-export`.

Fixing pink (shader/material) problems

If there is a mismatch between the Unity version that the WebXR package was created for and the version of Unity you are using, there may be an issue with some of the materials in the project. The result is a shader error and objects that look **pink** in Unity. Sometimes, this can be fixed by reimporting all assets (menu: **Assets |**
Reimport). Otherwise, you can fix the issue by selecting each **Material** in the **Project** window (usually in a folder named **Materials**) and choosing an appropriate shader –
in most cases, the **Standard** shader is fine for fixing this issue.

The community maintaining more up-to-date XR resources

The WebXR project from Mozilla wasn't working with Unity 2021 when this chapter was being written (it may have been updated since). If you need to use the official Mozilla project from 2020, then you can develop with **Unity 2019.4.13f1 LTS**.

Since the project is open source, some members of the community are working to help update the WebXR resources themselves. One version of the Mozilla Desert demo project that's kept up to date is from De-Panther. It can be downloaded as a ZIP file from `https://github.com/De-Panther/unity-webxr-export`:

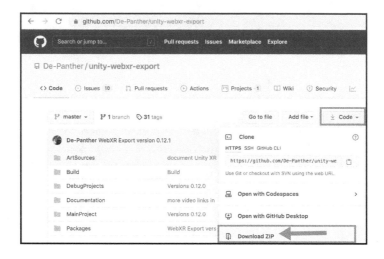

Figure 15.45 – Downloading the up-to-date De-Panther version of the Desert WebXR demo project

If you just want to install the WebXR Export package (not the whole demo project), OpenUPM has published an up-to-date package on GitHub that you can use by adding a package to Package Manager via `https://github.com/De-Panther/unity-webxr-export.git?path=/Packages/webxr`.

You can learn more at the OpenUPM site at `https://openupm.com/packages/com.de-panther.webxr/`

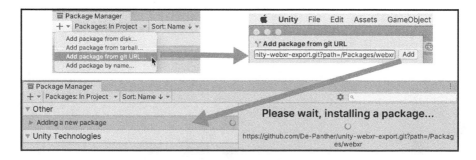

Figure 15.46 – Adding the WebXR Exporter package via its GitHub URL

Another project that contains examples of Unity WebXR can be found at `https://github.com/Rufus31415/Simple-WebXR-Unity`. Thanks to *Florent Giraud*, also known as *Rufus*, for publishing this.

Fixing obsolete code errors

At the time of writing, Unity 2021 had made some of the code in the **WebXR Exporter** package obsolete, causing errors after adding the package – this may have been fixed with a more recent release of **WebXR Exporter**. The blog post at `https://forum.unity.com/threads/xrdevice-ispresent-is-obsolete.1057556/` discusses this issue, and a solution can be found at `https://docs.unity3d.com/ScriptReference/XR.XRDevice-isPresent.html`. Basically, the `XRDevice.isPresent` expression is no longer valid in Unity. This can be resolved by following these two steps:

1. Create a C# script file called `XRDeviceUtility.cs` in the **Project** window folder called **WebXR | Scripts** and ensure it contains the following code:

```
using System;
using System.Collections;
using System.Collections.Generic;
using System.Linq;
using UnityEngine;
using UnityEngine.XR;

namespace WebXR {
    internal static class XRDeviceUtility {
        public static bool isPresent() {
            var xrDisplaySubsystems = new
List<XRDisplaySubsystem>();
SubsystemManager.GetInstances<XRDisplaySubsystem>(xrDisplaySub
systems);
            foreach (var xrDisplay in xrDisplaySubsystems)  {
                if (xrDisplay.running) {
                    return true;
                }
            }
            return false;
        }
    }
}
```

2. Replace each occurrence of `XRDevice.isPresent` with `XRDeviceUtilities.isPresent()` in the `WebXRManager.cs` and `WebXRController.cs` files.

This is the solution that's adopted in the completed recipe project, which is available in this book's GitHub repository.

Adding 360-degree videos to a VR project

Affordable, 360-degree cameras mean that it's easy to create your own or find free online 360-degree images and video clips. In this recipe, we'll learn how to add a 360-degree video clip as a Skybox to a VR project. You will also learn how the 360-degree video clips can be played on the surface of 3D objects, including the inside of a sphere – a bit like **Google Earth VR** mode when you raise the sphere to your head to view its 360-degree image contents:

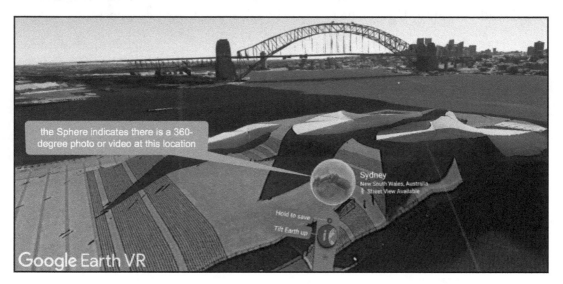

Figure 15.47 – Locating a 360-degree video in Google Earth VR

Getting ready

For this recipe, we have provided a short `Snowboarding_Polar.mp4` video in the `15_07` folder. This project builds on the previous one (a basic VR project), so make a copy of that and work on the copy.

Special thanks to *Kris Szczurowski* from TU Dublin for permission to use his snowboarding 360-degree video clip, and for his help with these VR project recipes.

How to do it...

To add 360-degree videos to a VR project, follow these steps:

1. Import your 360-degree polar format video clip into your Unity project (in our example, this is `Snowboarding_Polar.mp4`).

2. Select the video asset in the **Project** window and, in the **Inspector** window, make a note of its resolution (we'll need this later); for example, `2560 x 1280`:

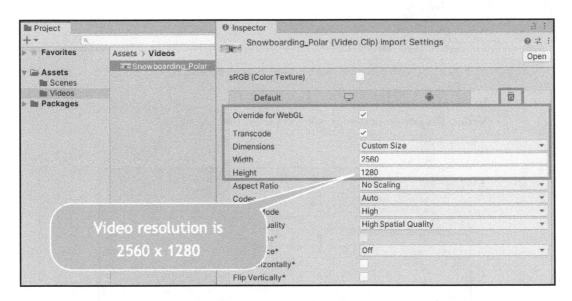

Figure 15.48 – Noting the dimensions of your 360-degree video clip from the Inspector window

3. Create a new empty GameObject named `video-player` by going to **Create | Empty**.

4. Select **video-player** in the **Hierarchy** window and, in the **Inspector** window, add a **Video Player** component by going to **Add Component | Video | Video Player**.

5. From the **Project** window, drag your video asset file – for example, `Snowboarding_Polar` – into the **Video Clip** property of the **Video Player** component in the **Inspector** window. Also, check the **Loop** property of the **Video Player** component.

6. In the **Project** window, create a new **Render Texture** asset file named `VideoRenderTexture` by going to **Create | Render Texture**.

7. Set the resolution of `VideoRenderTexture` so that it matches the video asset resolution; for example, `2560 x 1280`:

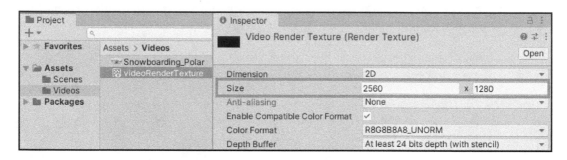

Figure 15.49 – Setting the dimensions of your Render Texture asset file

8. In the **Hierarchy** window, select the `video-player` GameObject. For the **Video Player** component, set the target texture to be `VideoRenderTexture`:

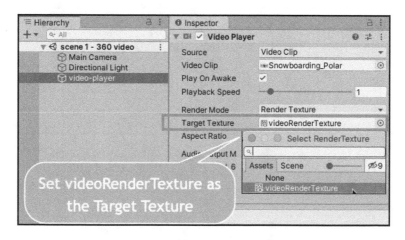

Figure 15.50 – Making the Video Player component layer send the video to videoRenderTexture

9. In the **Project** window, create a new **Material** asset file named `video_m` by going to **Create | Material**.

10. With `video_m` selected in the **Project** window, change its **Shader** to **Skybox | Panoramic**:

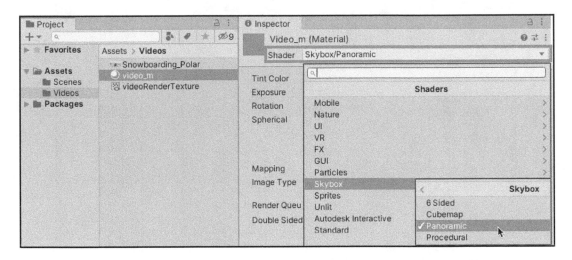

Figure 15.51 – Setting the Shader material to a Panoramic Skybox

11. In the **Inspector** window, for the **Spherical HDR** property, click the **Select** button and choose **videoRenderTexture**:

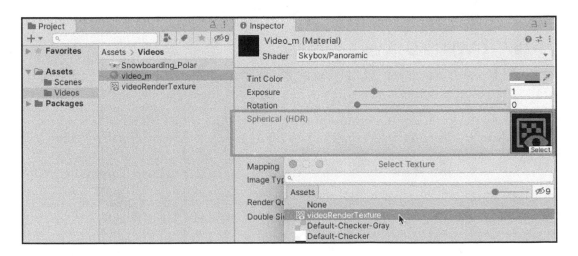

Figure 15.52 – Setting the Spherical HDR property of the material to our videoRenderTexture

[747]

12. Open the **Lighting Settings** window by going to **Window** | **Rendering** | **Lighting Settings**. In the **Inspector** window, set **Skybox Material** to `video_m`:

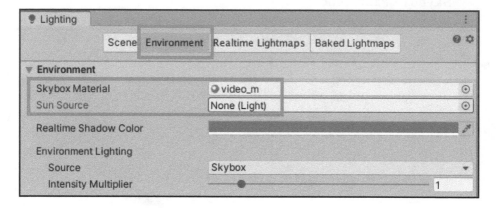

Figure 15.53 – Setting the Environment Lighting settings for the Skybox material to our video_m material

13. Choose the **Build Settings** that are appropriate for your VR device (for example, **Android** or **WebGL**).
14. Build your project and load the project onto your VR headset.
15. When you run the app, you should see the 360-degree video playing all around you.

How it works...

This recipe uses the strategy of playing a 360-degree video as the panoramic **Skybox** material in a scene.

We can use the **Lighting Environment** settings to define which **Material** is used for our **Skybox**. By creating a new material called `video_m`, we were able to set this as the material to be used as the Skybox when the scene runs. To be used as a Skybox material, we had to set the **Shader** property of `video_m` to **Skybox** | **Panoramic**.

To play a video, we need a GameObject in the scene with a **Video Player** component, and we can make this play the video at runtime in a **Render Texture** asset file. **Render Texture** needs to have the same dimensions as the resolution at which we wish to play the 360-degree video – usually, we'll set this to be the same dimensions as the video, for maximum quality. So, we set the dimensions of our **videoRenderTexture** to `2560 x 1280`.

To connect the playing video to our **Skybox** material, all we had to do was make the `video_m` material link its **Spherical HDR** property to **videoRenderTexture**, which is where the video is playing.

There's more...

Here are some suggestions for taking this recipe further.

Playing 360-degree videos on the surface of a 3D object

To play 360-degree videos on the surface of a 3D object, perform the aforementioned steps, but do not set the Skybox to `video_m`. Instead, set the material of the **Mesh Renderer** component of your 3D object to `video_m`:

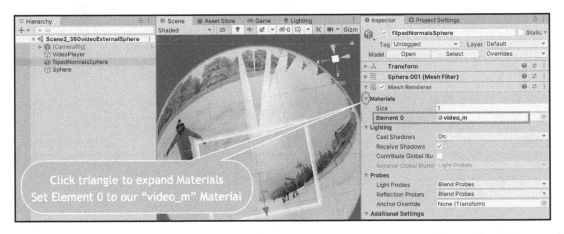

Figure 15.54 – Setting the material for a Flipped Normal Sphere

This works for 3D objects with inverted normals, for example, a hollow 3D **Sphere** that you can look at from the inside. If you wish to try working with a hollow 3D **Sphere** with flipped normals, you can import the one we have prepared in the Unity package in the `15_03` folder on GitHub.

Exploring the Unity AR samples

Unity provides an up-to-date set of sample AR scenes in a project you can download from the `github.com` website. In this recipe, we'll download the project, build an AR phone app, and try some of the samples from Unity:

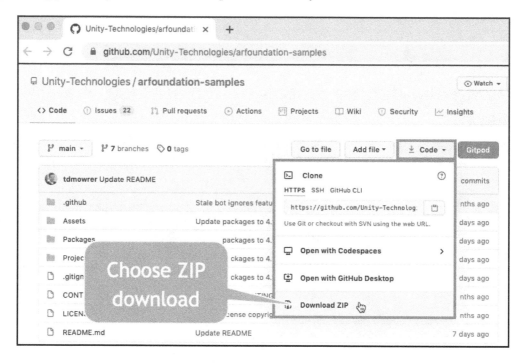

Figure 15.55 – Downloading the AR samples from GitHub

Getting ready

You'll be running your AR projects on either an Android or iOS device, so you need to ensure the version of the Unity Editor you are using has the appropriate Build Support plugin installed. For iOS development, you need the iOS Build Support module, while for Android, you need the Android Build Support plugin installed, including Android SDK and OpenJDK. This can all be installed by going to the **Installs** section of the **Unity Hub** application (it may take a while since several gigabytes need to be downloaded).

For iOS, you will also need the Xcode development tools since Unity builds an Xcode project. Then, you can use Xcode to install the app on the iOS device. In this recipe, we'll illustrate the process for **Android** phones. Then, in the *There's more ...* section, we will provide details regarding how to test and run AR apps on **iOS** devices:

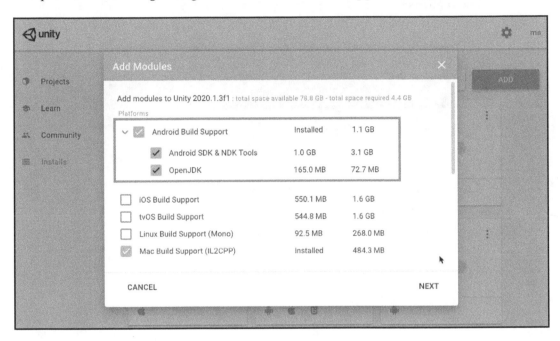

Figure 15.56 – Installing the Android SDK and OpenJDK tools with Unity Hub

How to do it...

To download and explore the Unity AR samples, do the following:

1. Go to `https://github.com/Unity-Technologies/arfoundation-samples` and download the files as a ZIP file:

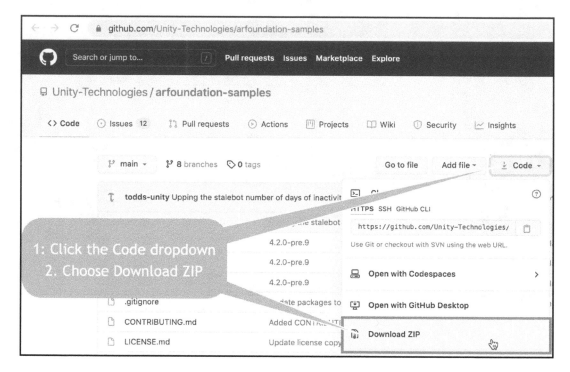

Figure 15.57 – Downloading the AR samples from GitHub

2. Unzip the project files and open them in Unity.
3. Open the **Build Settings** dialog window and switch **Build Target** to **Android** (or **iOS** if appropriate).
4. You'll see that all the scenes have already been added to the build for this project, with the AR Foundation Menu scene listed first.
5. Connect your computer to your phone/device with an appropriate USB cable and on your device, agree to permit the computer to communicate with it. Then, **Refresh** the list of devices and select your device. In the following screenshot, I've connected a Samsung S9+ Android device to test the AR samples:

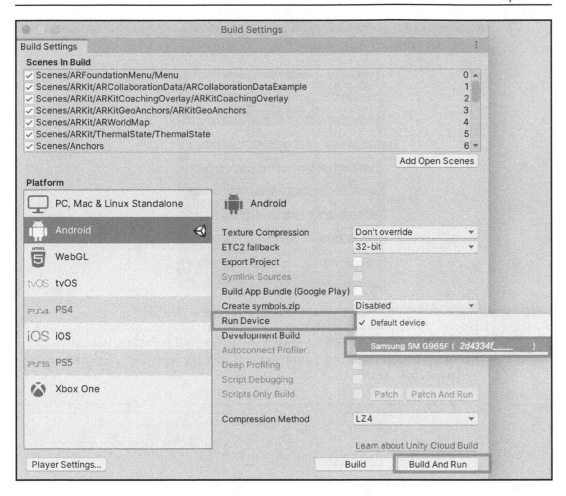

Figure 15.58 – Selecting a Samsung Android device from the list

6. Build the project by clicking the **Build And Run** button – enter an appropriate folder name for the project build, such as `Build1`.

7. Once Unity has finished building the app, you should now see a menu listing all the runnable scenes, including **Face Tracking**, **Plane Detection**, and so on.

8. Run some of the scenes to get a feel for how AR apps are able to identify faces, flat surfaces, and so on:

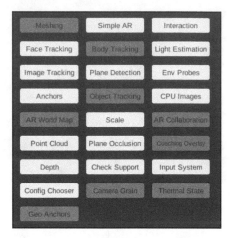

Figure 15.59 – The main menu list of scenes running on an Android phone

9. On your computer, select the **Rafflesia** image in the **Project** window (**Scenes | ImageTracking | Images**) and display its details and preview in the **Inspector** window:

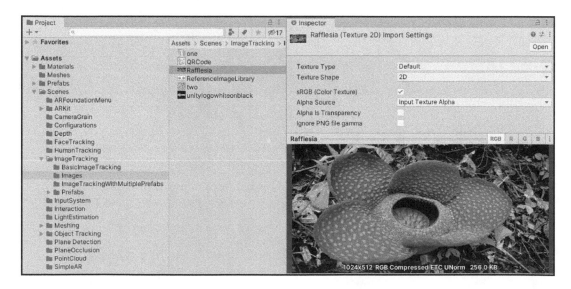

Figure 15.60 – Displaying the Rafflesia image on your computer screen

10. On your phone, choose **Image Tracking | Basic Image Tracking**. Now, when you view the computer screen through your phone, you should see annotations appear overlaid on the **Rafflesia** image:

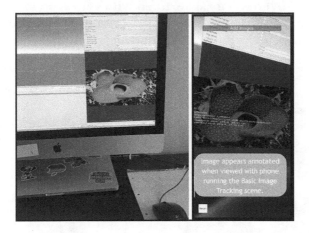

Figure 15.61 – The AR information overlay when viewing the Rafflesia flower image with the phone app

11. Load an image of a country's flag into the **Project** window (I live in Ireland, so I loaded the Irish tricolor flag).

12. In the **Project** window, select the `FaceMeshPrefab` asset file (this can be found in the `Prefabs` folder).

13. In the **Inspector** window, change the **Albedo Main Map** property to your map image (in my case, I got the **Flag_of_Ireland** image from Wikipedia and copied it into the Unity project as a `PNG` image file asset):

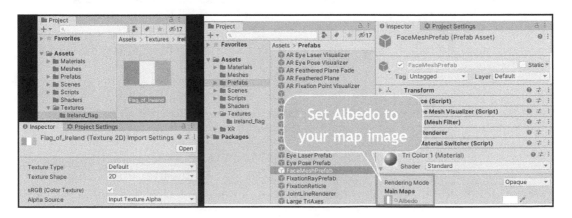

Figure 15.62 – Setting the image to texture the face mesh mask

14. Now, build the app again and load the updated app onto your phone.

15. Runt the phone app and choose **Face Tracking | Face Mesh**. The app should use the front phone camera to view your face. After a second or two, it will overlay a mask textured with your map image over your face. As you move your head around and open and close your mouth, the mask should move accordingly, as if you were really wearing a flag mask:

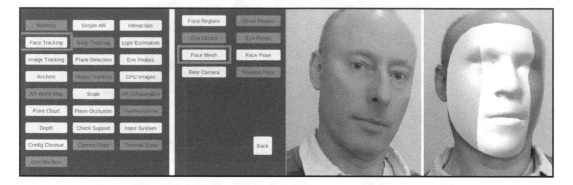

Figure 15.63 – Running the face mesh scene, which maps a flag image over your face!

How it works...

GitHub.com is a cloud storage site for files and projects (supporting the powerful **Git** file history and version control system). We used the ZIP download feature to download a complete Unity project as a single ZIP file and then decompressed it into a folder on our computer. We had to ensure the correct modules were installed by **Unity Hub** for the target device to be used for running the AR project (that is, **Android** or **iOS**). Once a project is open in Unity, the required **Build Target** must be switched to, and all the scenes that will be part of the app need to be added to the Build Settings.

The Unity project contains many (over 20) scenes, each illustrating different AR features. Once the app was built and transferred to our device, the buttons on the menu scenes allowed us to navigate to each of the sample scenes.

By changing the settings of a prefab – the **FaceMeshPrefab** asset file (in the Prefabs folder) – and rebuilding the app, we were able to see how the **Material** setting of the prefab influenced which image was dynamically drawn as a face mask overlay using Unity's **AR Foundation Face Mesh** detection and tracking.

There's more...

Here are some ways to take this recipe further.

Targeting iOS device builds

If you are targeting your AR apps for **iOS** devices such as iPhones, you'll need to adjust how you build and transfer your project to such devices:

1. First, you'll need to set up the **Xcode** editor with your Apple ID.
2. Switch the Unity project's **Build Platform** to iOS.
3. In the **Project Settings Player** window, you need to enter your chosen **Bundle Identifier** (for example, `com.your_website_name`).
4. After clicking **Build**, you'll see a file ending with the `.xcodeproj` extension. Unity does not build iOS apps – it builds Xcode projects for your iOS app.
5. Open this `.xcodeproj` file to open this project in the Xcode editor.
6. Select **Unity-iPhone** in the Xcode project settings and fix any issues.
7. You'll have to download certificates and a provisioning profile the first time you use Xcode with your Apple ID.
8. Connect your iOS device (iPhone/iPad) to your computer with a USB cable.

 It's a good idea to turn off auto-locking on your device since you don't want your phone to lock while the Xcode build is taking place.

9. Build the Xcode project (click the "run" triangle button).
10. When complete, the app will be on your iOS device, ready to run.

More details about how to build an **AR Foundation** project for iOS devices can be found in these online tutorials:

- `https://learn.unity.com/tutorial/building-for-mobile`
- `http://virtualxdesign.mit.edu/blog/2019/6/22/viewing-your-models-in-ar`

Allowing Android APK file downloads on your phone

An alternative to using a USB cable to transfer a build to your Android device is to publish the build APK file on a website, and then install it onto your device via a mobile web browser. We have provided some steps for downloading Android APK builds using a web browser app.

 Only download and install APK files you have created yourself or from sources you trust!

On **non-Samsung** devices, do the following:

1. Go to your phone's **Settings**.
2. Go to **Security & Privacy | More Settings**.
3. Tap on **Install Apps from External Sources**.

4. Select the browser (for example, Chrome or Firefox) you want to download the APK files from.
5. Toggle **Allow app installs** on.

On **Samsung** devices, do the following:

1. Go to your phone's **Settings**.
2. Go to **Biometrics and Security | Install Unknown Apps**.
3. Select the browser (for example, Chrome or Firefox) you want to download the APK files from.
4. Toggle **Allow App Installs / Allow from this source** on.

Setting up Unity for AR

There are some basic steps you need to perform so that your Unity Editor application is set up for AR development. AR projects created with Unity have, at their core, the **AR Foundation** package and **XR Plugin Manager**. In the previous recipe, things were set up for us already as part of the Unity AR samples project. In this recipe, we'll create a new Unity project and set up **AR Foundation.** As part of this recipe, we'll also be adding the appropriate plugin for the target device that the AR project is going to be developed on (**iOS/Android**).

In this recipe, you'll learn how to add the modules you need to your editor application, install the templates, open the sample scene, and set up the Build Settings for development on an Android device:

Figure 15.64 – The AR project we'll create, with just a Cube overlaid on the device camera view

How to do it...

To create and set up a project for AR, do the following:

1. Open the **Unity Hub** application and choose the **Installs** tab on the left.
2. Now, select the version of Unity you wish to develop your AR projects with.
3. Next, add the **Android Build Support** modules to your application and click **Done**.
4. Ensure both the **Android SDK/NDK Tools** and **OpenJDK** sub-modules are checked, as shown in the following screenshot:

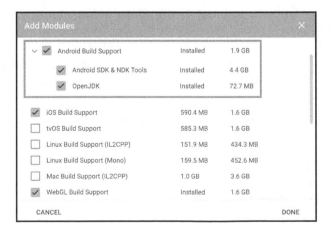

Figure 15.65 – Installing the Android modules with Unity Hub

5. In the **Unity Hub** application, choose the **Projects** window on the left and click the **NEW** button for your version of Unity.

6. After a few seconds, additional templates should be displayed. Find the **VR** template and click the **Download** button:

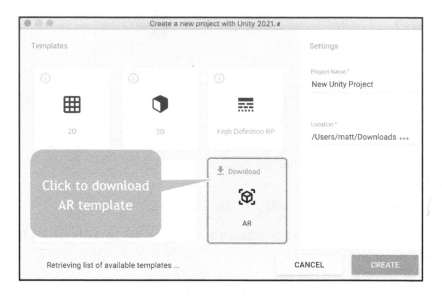

Figure 15.66 – Installing the AR project template from Unity Hub

7. Now, select the **AR** template and choose a new and location for your project. Then, click the **CREATE** button.

8. After a short time, Unity should start, with a pop-up window welcoming you to the AR project template and reminding you to select your chosen platform(s) from the **Project Settings** window.

9. In the **Project** window, you'll see a **Scenes** folder, as well as two folders named **XR** and **ExampleAssets** – these are part of the AR template resources.

10. Open the **Project Settings** window (menu: **Edit | Project Settings**).

11. For the **XR Plugin Management** settings, choose the **Android** (robot icon) tab and then select the tab for your target platform (**iOS/Android**). Then, check the plugin provider for your platform (**ARKit** for iOS or **ARCore** for Android):

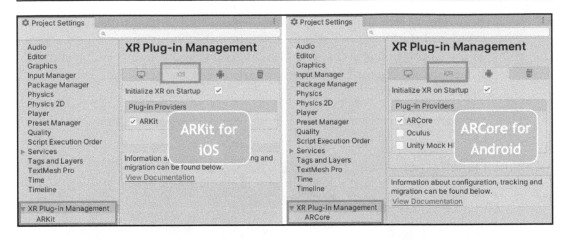

Figure 15.67 – Adding ARCore/ARKit via the XR Plugin Management plugin settings

12. If it's not already open, open the
    provided **SampleScene** (in the **Project** window, go to the **Scenes** folder). In
    the **Hierarchy** window, you'll see that it has an AR Session
    Origin GameObject, which has an AR Camera child. There is also an AR
    Session GameObject:

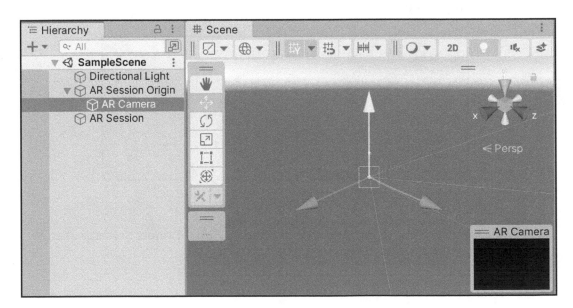

Figure 15.68 – The AR GameObjects in the provided SampleScene

13. Let's add a **Cube** to this scene so that we have something to see when we build and run this app. Create a 3D **Cube** with a position of (0, 0, 6) and a rotation of (45, 90, 45). If you select AR Camera, you should be able to see the cube in the camera preview rectangle in the **Scene** window:

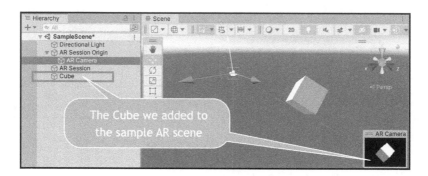

Figure 15.69 – The Cube added to our scene

14. Add this **Sample Scene** to the build in the **Build Settings** window.

15. In the **Build Settings** window, switch **Build Target** to **Android** (or **iOS**, if appropriate):

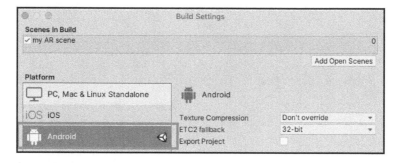

Figure 15.70 – Switching to the build target (in this case, Android)

16. Open the **Project Settings** window (menu: **Edit** | **Project Settings...**) and select the **Player** tab.

17. Insert an appropriate **Company Name**, **Project Name**, and **Version** (this **Project Name** becomes the name of the app on the device):

> If you are building for **iOS**, then also ensure that **Auto Graphics API** is **not** checked.

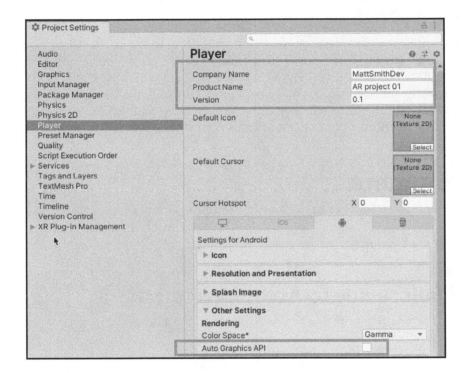

Figure 15.71 – Player settings for an AR build

18. Connect your computer to your phone/device with an appropriate USB cable. Then, on your device agree, to permit the computer to communicate with it. Then, **Refresh** the list of devices and select your device. (Alternatively, follow the *There's more...* steps for iOS from the previous recipe if you're targeting an iOS device).

19. Build the project by clicking the **Build and Run** button – enter an appropriate folder name for the project build, such as **Build1**.

20. Once Unity has finished building the app on your device, you should see a menu listing all the runnable scenes, including **Face Tracking**, **Plane Detection**, and so on.

21. Congratulations! You have set up a project so that it's ready for AR project development.

How it works...

This recipe illustrated the basic steps you must follow to set up an AR project. The appropriate module (Android or iOS) needed to be added to your Unity Editor. Then, the appropriate project template (AR) had to be downloaded. Next, you selected the plugin provider for your device by going to the **XR Plug-in Management** settings. It should be **ARKit** for iOS or **ARCore** for Android. With that, you've done all the necessary preparation to actually create and run AR projects with Unity.

There's more...

The first time we create and build a new type of project, there may be some issues. Here are some troubleshooting tips. If Unity fails to build, then check the error message in the **Console** window.

Build failure due to Android version

A common error is that the version of Android in the **Player** settings is too low for the version of Android on the device.

For example, the first time I tried to build for an Android AR project, I got the following error:

```
Error building Player: Android Minimum API Level must be set to 23 or
higher.
```

 By the time you run this project, the required Android version may be 24 or higher – read the message and follow its requirements. There may be some setting up the first time you build for Android, but once you have it working, you'll be able to develop and publish VR and AR projects on your Android devices.

This can be resolved by opening the **Project Settings** window (menu: **Edit | Project Settings**) and increasing **Minimum API Level** to the number stated in the error message, or a higher version. You can do this in the **Player** section and by going to the **Other Settings** values:

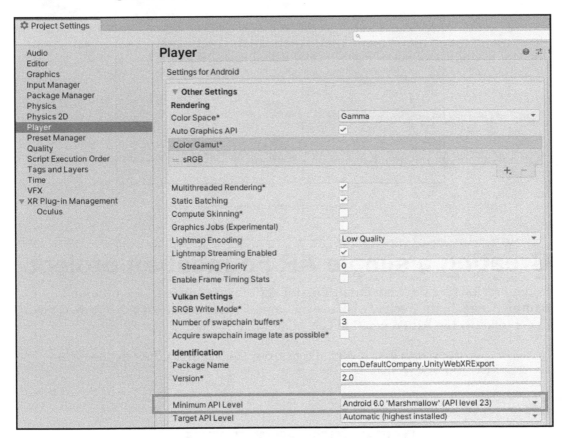

Figure 15.72 – Setting Minimum API Level in the Player settings

Build failure due to Vulkan API graphics settings

AR projects don't work with the Vulkan graphics API, so if this is listed in your **Player** settings, you'll get an error.

To resolve this error, open the **Project Settings** window (menu: **Edit | Project Settings**) and select the **Player** tab. Then, under **Graphics API**, select the **Vulkan** row and delete it by clicking the minus (**-**) button:

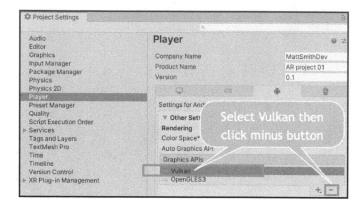

Figure 15.73 – Removing the Vulkan graphics system from the Player settings

Creating a simple AR Foundation project

In the previous recipe, we set things up for AR projects and used the provided **SampleScene**. In this recipe, we'll use the same setup, but build a scene from scratch to get to know the AR Foundation GameObjects.

 Special thanks to *Nina Lyons* from TU Dublin for helping out with the AR recipes

Figure 15.74 – Running this recipe's AR project on my Android phone – the two Cubes are floating in front of my window!

Getting ready

This recipe builds on the previous one. So, either repeat those steps before beginning this one or make a copy of that recipe's project and work on that copy.

How to do it...

To create a simple **AR Foundation** app, do the following:

1. Having installed the **Android/iOS** modules and AR template, create a new Unity project using the AR template.
2. For the **XR Plugin Management** setting, select the tab for your target platform (iOS / Android) and check the plugin for your platform (**ARKit** for iOS and **ARCore** for Android).
3. Create a new, empty scene.
4. Add a **Directional Light** to the scene.
5. Add an AR Session GameObject and an AR Session Origin GameObject (menu: **GameObject | XR**).
6. In the **Hierarchy** window, select the AR Camera child object of the AR Session Origin GameObject. In the **Inspector** window, tag this GameObject as **Main Camera**:

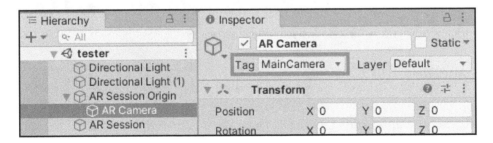

Figure 15.75 – Tagging the AR Camera child GameObject as Main Camera

7. Add the AR content to your scene. In this simple recipe, we'll add two floating cubes in front of the camera to the lower right of the view. Create two 3D Cubes (menu: **GameObject | 3D Object | Cube**) and position them at (1, -0.25, 3) and (1, -1, 4):

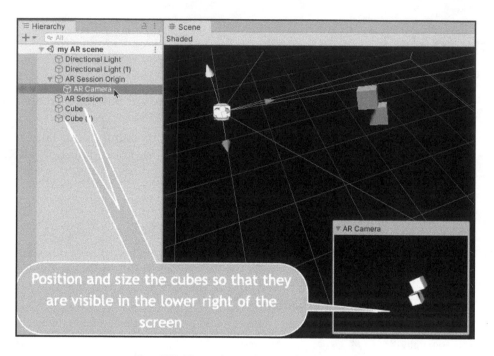

Figure 15.76 – The two cubes that will appear in our AR application

8. Save your scene, naming it **Two Cubes**.
9. Open the **Build Settings** panel (menu: **File | Build Settings...**) and add your scene to the build.
10. Set the build target to **iOS / Android** as appropriate and click **Switch Target**.
11. Now, either **Build And Run** your app on your device, or just **Build** the app and copy/install it onto your device.
12. When you run it, you should see a cube floating in front of you wherever you look. Congratulations – you've just created an augmented reality scene from scratch!

How it works...

The main difference from the normal working environment is that we have added two GameObjects called `AR Session Origin` and `AR Session` to the **Hierarchy** window. `AR Session Origin` and `AR Session` are important, so it's worth understanding a little bit about each:

- `AR Session Origin`: This is the parent for an AR setup. It contains a camera and any GameObjects that have been created from detected features such as planes and point clouds. `AR Session Origin` defines the origin of the project. If you select this object in the **Hierarchy** window, in the **Inspector** window, you will see that it has the **AR Session Origin (Script)** component. It also has a child GameObject named `AR Camera`, containing a **Camera** and other AR Script components. This is the AR camera that we see. It will be rendering what the camera sees behind it, and any AR features inside of Unity will be on top of that.

- `AR Session`: As described in the Unity documentation, `AR Session` coordinates the major processes that **ARKit/ARCore** performs on its behalf to create an AR experience. These processes include reading data from the device's motion sensor hardware, controlling the device's built-in camera, and performing image analysis on captured camera images. The session synthesizes all of these results to establish a correspondence between the real-world space the device inhabits and a virtual space where you model AR content. Another way to look at this is that `AR Session` is what *maps* our AR world.

Note that we didn't need a separate **Main Camera** GameObject in our scene since AR projects use the camera that is a child of `AR Session Origin`, which needs to be tagged as **Main Camera**.

Detecting and highlighting planes with AR Foundation

One of the features of AR is its ability to detect flat surfaces through device cameras and other sensors (such as the LIDAR sensors on some high-end iPads and iPhones). This recipe illustrates how a Unity **AR Raycast**, combined with some **AR Foundation** objects and scripts, can highlight detected planes (horizontal and vertical) with a circular highlighter image:

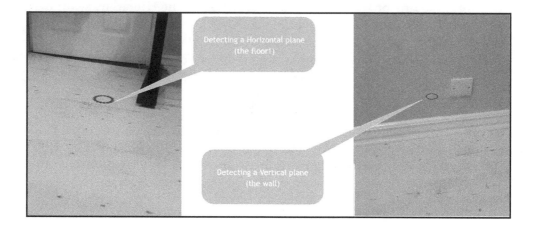

Figure 15.77 – Highlighting detected planes in our AR app

Getting ready

This recipe follows the previous one. So, make a copy of that and work on that copy.

We also need an image to display on detected planes. We have provided a suitable circular image called `plane_highligher.png` in the `15_09` folder.

How to do it...

To create an AR plane highlighter app, do the following:

1. Delete the two cubes in the **Hierarchy** window.

2. In the **Hierarchy** window, select the AR Session Origin GameObject. In the **Inspector** window, add an **AR Plane Manager (Script)** component by clicking the **Add Component** button and searching for **AR Plane** in the **Inspector** window. Ensure that **Detection Mode** is set to **Everything**.

3. Now, add an **AR Raycast Manager (Script)** component to this GameObject by clicking the **Add Component** button and searching for **AR Raycast** in the **Inspector** window:

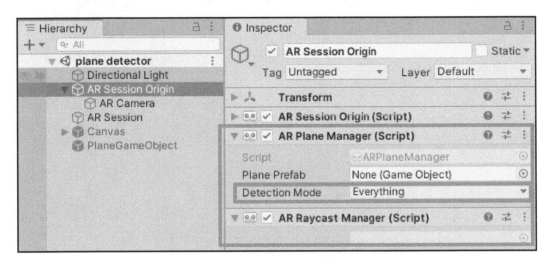

Figure 15.78 – The AR Plane Manager and AR Raycast Manager components of AR Session Origin

4. Import the provided image; that is, plane_highligher.png.

5. Add a 3D **Plane** named PlaneHighlighter to the scene. To do so, in the **Hierarchy** window, go to **Create | 3D Object | Plane**.

6. Set the position of the PlaneHighlighter GameObject to (0, 0, 0) and make it suitably small for your AR device camera by setting its scale to (0.01, 0.01, 0.01).

7. Drag the plane_highligher image asset file from the **Project** window onto the PlaneHighlighter GameObject in the scene.

8. In the **Inspector** window, set the **Shader** property of **Plane_highlighter (Material)** to **Unlit/Transparent** (we do not need to provide a value for the **Text Image Data** field – this will be set by the script class we'll create next):

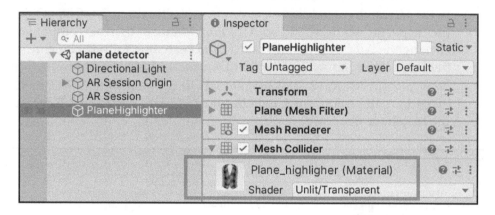

Figure 15.79 – Setting the Plane_highlighter shader to Unit/Transparent

9. In the **Project** window, create a new C# script class named `PlacementIndicator.cs` containing the following code:

```
using System.Collections.Generic;
using UnityEngine;
using UnityEngine.XR.ARFoundation;
using UnityEngine.UI;

public class PlacementIndicator : MonoBehaviour {
    public GameObject planeVisual;
    public Text textImageData;
    private ARRaycastManager _raycastManager;
    private List<ARRaycastHit> hits = new
List<ARRaycastHit>();

    void Awake() {
        _raycastManager = GetComponent<ARRaycastManager>();
    }

    private void Update() {
        Vector2 screenCenter = new Vector2(Screen.width / 2,
Screen.height / 2);
        _raycastManager.Raycast(screenCenter, hits);

        if(hits.Count >0) {
            Pose hitLocation = hits[0].pose;
```

```
                planeVisual.transform.position =
hitLocation.position;
                planeVisual.transform.rotation =
hitLocation.rotation;
                if(!planeVisual.activeInHierarchy)
                    planeVisual.SetActive(true);
                textImageData.text = "plane WAS detected - should
show highlighter!";
            } else {
                textImageData.text = "(no plane detected)";
                planeVisual.SetActive(false);
            }
        }
    }
```

10. Add an instance object of this script class to the AR Session Origin GameObject in the **Hierarchy** window by dragging PlacementHighlighter from the **Project** window onto the AR Session Origin GameObject in the **Hierarchy** window.

11. Now, in the **Inspector** window, drag the PlaneHighlighter GameObject into the **Plane Visual** public script variable for the PlacementIndicator script component:

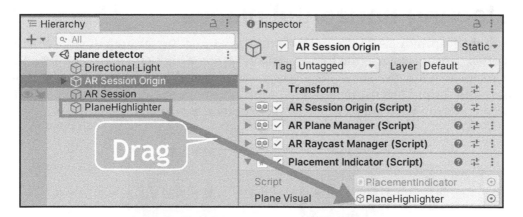

Figure 15.80 – Assigning our PlaneHighlighter GameObject to the public Plane Visual public script variable

12. Now, **Build** your app.

13. Copy and install the app onto your device.

14. When you run it, each time **AR Foundation** identifies a **Horizontal** or **Vertical** plane, the circle highlighter image should be displayed, showing how the plane is being found.

How it works...

AR Plane Manager allows the app to detect horizontal and vertical planes in the device's camera's view. **AR Raycast Manager** allows the app to identify which horizontal or vertical plane a raycast from the direction of the camera would strike. Our script fires a ray every frame via the `Update()` method.

By tagging `AR Camera` as **Main Camera**, we are able to easily get a reference to the camera using `Camera.main`.

By placing the instance object of our script class as a component of the `AR Session Origin` GameObject, we are able to get a reference to the **ARRayCastManager** sibling script component by using `GetComponent<class>()` in the `Awake()` method.

The only public variable we have to set for the instance object of our `PlacementIndicator` script class in the `AR Session Origin` GameObject is the GameObject of the plane that's displaying our circle image.

Creating an AR furniture previewer by detecting horizontal planes

One of the features of AR is its ability to detect flat surfaces through device cameras and other sensors (such as the LIDAR sensors on some high-end iPads and iPhones). This recipe will illustrate how a Unity raycast, combined with some AR Foundation objects and scripts, lets us create a basic AR furniture previewer just by tapping on the screen where we want a virtual 3D piece of furniture to be displayed:

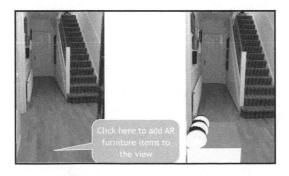

Figure 15.81 – Adding yellow sphere-cube sofa furniture at the bottom of a flight of stairs!

Getting ready

This recipe builds upon the previous recipe, *Creating a simple AR Foundation Project*, so make a copy of that and use the copy.

How to do it...

To create an AR furniture previewer, do the following:

1. Delete the two cubes in the **Hierarchy** window.
2. In the **Hierarchy** window, select the AR Session Origin GameObject. In the **Inspector** window, add an **AR Plane Manager (Script)** component by clicking the **Add Component** button and searching for **AR Plane** in the **Inspector** window. Set **Detection Mode** to **Horizontal**.
3. Now, add an **AR Raycast Manager (Script)** component to this GameObject by clicking the **Add Component** button and searching for **AR Raycast** in the **Inspector** window:

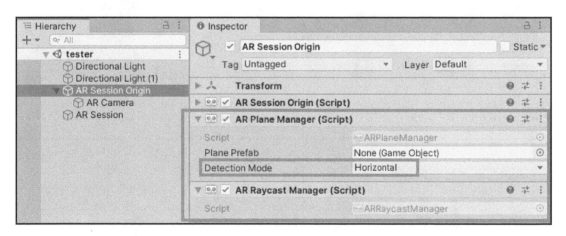

Figure 15.82 – The AR Plane Manager and AR Raycast Manager components of AR Session Origin

4. In this scene, we'll create a simple chair-like object using a cube and three spheres. You could, of course, find a free detailed 3D model of more realistic furniture on the Unity Asset Store (for example, `https://assetstore.unity.com/?free=trueq=furniture`):

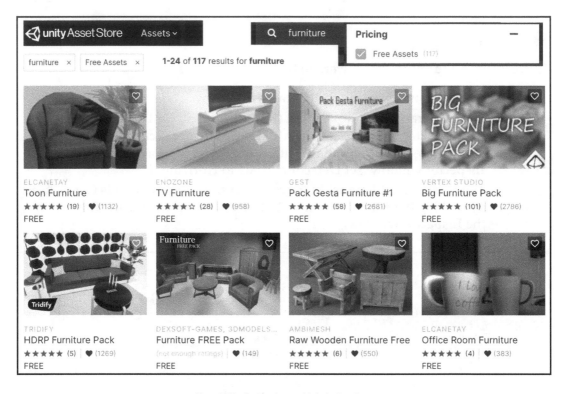

Figure 15.83 – Free furniture models in the Asset Store

5. In the **Hierarchy** window, create a new empty GameObject named `cube-ball-chair` (menu: **GameObject | Empty**). Set the position of this GameObject to `(0, -2, 5)`.

6. Create a **Cube** and make it a child of `cube-ball-chair`. Position the **Cube** at `(0, 0, 0)` and scale it to `(1, 0.4, 1)`.

7. Create a **Sphere** and make it a child of `cube-ball-chair`. Position the **Sphere** at `(-0.3, 0.25, 0)` and scale it to `(0.4, 0.4, 0.4)`.

8. Duplicate the sphere and move the duplicate's position to `(-0.3, 0.25, 0.3)`.

9. Duplicate the sphere a second time and move the duplicate's position to `(-0.3, 0.25, -0.3)`.

10. In the **Project** window, create a new **Material** (menu: **Create | Material**) named m_yellow. With the new **Material** selected in the **Project** window, in the **Inspector** window for the **Albedo** property, use the color picker to select a bright yellow color.

11. Select the **Cube** and the three **Sphere** child GameObjects of cube-ball-chair and drag the m_yellow material onto them. You should now see a yellow chair-like object in the scene:

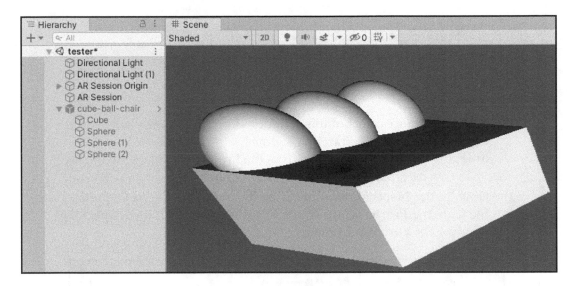

Figure 15.84 – Our yellow cube-sphere furniture prefab

12. Drag the cube-ball-chair GameObjects from the **Hierarchy** window into the **Project** window to create a prefab asset file named **cube-ball-chair**. Now, delete **cube-ball-chair** from the **Hierarchy** window.

13. In the **Project** window, create a new C# script class named FurnitureManager.cs containing the following code:

```
using System.Collections.Generic;
using UnityEngine;
using UnityEngine.XR.ARFoundation;

public class FurnitureManager : MonoBehaviour {
    public GameObject furniturePrefab;
    private ARRaycastManager _raycastManager;
    public List<ARRaycastHit> hits = new List<ARRaycastHit>();

    void Awake() {
        _raycastManager = GetComponent<ARRaycastManager>();
```

```
        }

        void Update() {
            if(Input.GetMouseButtonDown(0))
            {
                Ray ray =
Camera.main.ScreenPointToRay(Input.mousePosition);
                if(_raycastManager.Raycast(ray, hits))
                {
                    Pose pose = hits[0].pose;
                    Instantiate(furniturePrefab, pose.position,
pose.rotation);
                }
            }
        }
    }
```

14. Add an instance object of this script class to the `AR Session Origin` GameObject in the **Hierarchy** window by dragging `FurnitureManager` from the **Project** window onto the `AR Session Origin` GameObject in the **Hierarchy** window.

15. Now, in the **Inspector** window, drag the `cube-ball-chair` prefab asset file from the **Project** window into **Furniture Prefab** in the **Inspector** window for **FurnitureManager**:

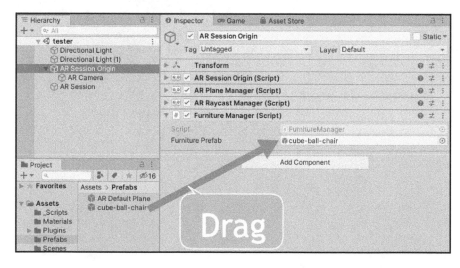

Figure 15.85 – Assigning our prefab to the Furniture Prefab public script variable

16. Now, **Build** your app.
17. Copy and install the app onto your device.
18. When you run it, each time you click the screen on a floor (horizontal) surface, a clone of the yellow cube-sphere chair model should be added to that location in the room.

How it works...

AR Plane Manager allows the app to detect horizontal planes in the device's camera's view. **AR Raycast Manager** allows the app to identify which horizontal plane a raycast from the direction of the camera would strike. Our script fires a ray each time the device screen is pressed (clicked), and the location of the first horizontal plane hit by a raycast is the location where a new clone of the prefab is created.

By tagging **AR Camera** as **Main Camera**, we can easily get a reference to the camera using `Camera.main`.

By placing the instance object of our script class as a component of the `AR Session Origin` GameObject, we can get a reference to the `ARRayCastManager` sibling script component by using `GetComponent<class>()` in the `Awake()` method.

The only public variable we have to set for the instance object of our `FurnitureManager` script class in the `AR Session Origin` GameObject is the prefab of whatever piece of furniture we want to be creating clones of in our camera's AR scene at runtime.

Creating a floating 3D model over an image target

A common way to use AR to enhance the world that's seen through the device's camera is to recognize a *target* image and either display a different or animation image in its place or to add a 3D model to the view that tracks the location of the image.

We'll do the latter in this recipe, making a 3D model appear over a book's cover image that we will add to a library:

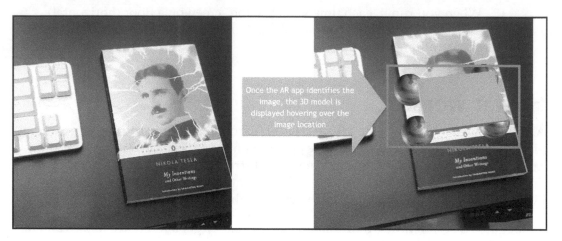

Figure 15.86 – A 3D "car" model displayed above the book cover image in our AR phone app

Getting ready

This recipe builds upon the previous recipe, *Creating a simple AR Foundation project*, so make a copy of that and use the copy.

You'll also need a target image. Either take a photo of an object in your home/office or use the provided book cover image called `tesla_book.jpg` in the `15_11` folder. You'll also need to print the image out or display the image onscreen while running the AR app on your phone.

How to do it...

To create a floating 3D model over an image target, do the following:

1. Remove the two cubes from the scene by deleting them in the **Hierarchy** window.

2. Add a new, empty GameObject to the scene named `car` (menu: **GameObject | Create Empty**).

3. Now, add a 3D **Cube** GameObject to the scene (menu: **GameObject | 3D | Cube**) and make it a child of `car`. In the **Inspector** window, set the position of the Cube to (0, 0, 0) and its scale to (0.07, 0.01, 0.1).

4. Now, add a 3D **Sphere** GameObject to the scene (menu: **GameObject | 3D | Sphere**) and make it a child of `car`. In the **Inspector** window, set the position of the sphere to `(0.03, 0, 0.05)` and its scale to `(0.03, 0.03, 0.03)`.

5. Now, texture this **Sphere** with our Tesla book image (or some other image) by dragging the image asset from the **Project** window onto the GameObject in the **Hierarchy** window.

6. Duplicate the sphere three times, setting the positions of these duplicates like so:

   - `(-0.03, 0, 0.05)`
   - `(0.03, 0, -0.05)`
   - `(-0.03, 0, -0.05)`

7. Create a **Prefab** of this `car` GameObject by dragging the `car` GameObject into the **Project** window:

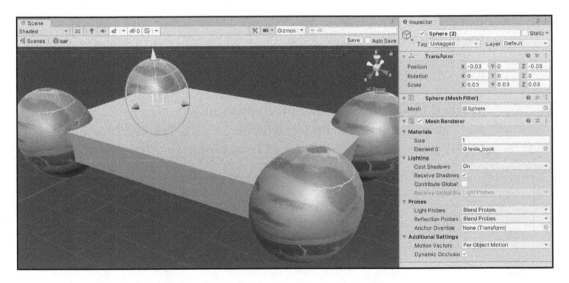

Figure 15.87 – Our cube-sphere car prefab 3D object

8. Now, remove the object from the scene by deleting the `car` GameObject from the **Hierarchy** window.

9. Import the image you are using as a target for this project – that is, `tesla_book.jpg` – or some other image you have chosen.

10. Create a **Reference Image Library** asset file named `myReferenceImageLibrary` in the **Project** window by going to **XR | Reference Image Library**.

11. With the `myReferenceImageLibrary` asset file selected in
the **Project** window, in the **Inspector** window, click the **Add Image** button.
Now, drag your image file into the image slot in the **Inspector** window:

Figure 15.88 – Adding our image to the Reference Image Library

12. In the **Hierarchy** window, select the `AR Session Origin` GameObject. In
the **Inspector** window, click the **Add Component** button and locate the **AR
Tracked Image Manager** component and add it to this GameObject.

13. Now, drag the `myReferenceImageLibrary` asset file from
the **Project** window into the **Serialized Library** property of the **AR
Tracked Image Manager (Script)** component.

14. Next, drag `car` from the **Project** window into the **Tracked Image
Prefab** property of the **AR Tracked Image Manager (Script)** component:

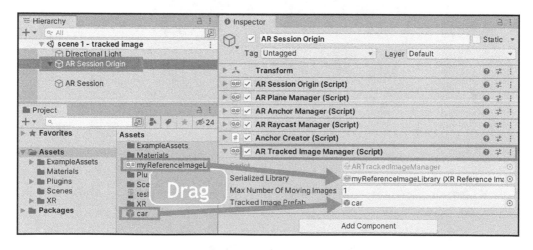

Figure 15.89 – Adding our Reference Image Library to the Tracked Image Manager component of the AR Session Origin GameObject

15. Now, save the scene and add it to the build. Remove any other scenes from the build and **Build** your app.

16. Once you've copied/installed the app onto your device, then when you run it and when the image (for example, the Tesla book cover) from your reference library is visible to the device camera, you'll see the 3D car model floating above the book on your phone screen. If you change your position or move the book, the 3D model should move (track) with the target image.

How it works...

In this recipe, we created a **Reference Image Library** asset file containing one image – the book cover. The Unity **AR Foundation** offers the scripted **AR Tracked Image Manager (Script)** component. This can use a library of images (in our case, **Reference Image Library**) to look for, identify, and track the position and orientation of the image of interest.

Further reading

The following are resources from Unity for their XR Interaction Toolkit:

- Example project: `https://github.com/Unity-Technologies/XR-Interaction-Toolkit-Examples`
- Blog: `https://forum.unity.com/threads/xr-interaction-toolkit-1-0-0-pre-2-pre-release-is-available.1046092/`

You can learn more about developing for Oculus VR headsets by going to their support pages and some third-party sites:

- `https://developer.oculus.com/documentation/unity/unity-overview/`
- `https://developer.oculus.com/documentation/native/android/mobile-device-setup/`
- `https://learn.adafruit.com/sideloading-on-oculus-quest/enable-developer-mode`
- `https://www.vrmarvelites.com/how-to-enable-oculus-developer-mode-on-oculus-quest-1-2/`
- `https://www.youtube.com/watch?v=AeQGE0ZI_Pw`

There are some great videos out there for learning Unity and XR:

- *How to Make Oculus Quest 2 Games // Introduction to Unity VR Development*, by Justin P Barnett: `https://www.youtube.com/watch?v=wnn-dzHz-tA`
- *Oculus Quest 2 Development With Unity XR Interaction ToolKit !*, by Dilmer Valecillos: `https://www.youtube.com/watch?v=Xa1h0XGWRu8`

The Google Cardboard Unity plugin can be found at `https://developers.google.com/cardboard/develop/unity/quickstart`.

A great resource for Unity VR projects is the book *Unity 2020 Virtual Reality Projects* by Jonathan Linowes, also from Packt: `https://www.packtpub.com/product/unity-2020-virtual-reality-projects-third-edition/9781839217333`.

The Oculus desktop app can be downloaded from the following links for macOS and Windows, respectively:

- `https://developer.oculus.com/downloads/package/oculus-developer-hub-mac/`
- `https://developer.oculus.com/downloads/package/oculus-developer-hub-win/`

Learn how to use an Android emulator to test AR apps: `https://developers.google.com/ar/develop/c/emulator`.

AR Core vs. AR Kit vs. Vuforia comparison: `https://bluewhaleapps.com/blog/comparing-arkit-vs-arcore-vs-vuforia-the-best-augmented-reality-toolkit`.

MIT's extended AR samples: `https://github.com/virtualxdesign/artemplate`.

Sideloading to Android devices using ADB: `https://androidcommunity.com/how-to-getting-adb-on-your-pc-without-installing-full-android-sdk-20180307/`.

To learn more about the Oculus Air Link, a wireless way to run PC VR games on an Oculus Quest 2 headset, take a look at the following links:

- `https://www.oculus.com/blog/introducing-oculus-air-link-a-wireless-way-to-play-pc-vr-games-on-oculus-quest-2-plus-infinite-office-updates-support-for-120-hz-on-quest-2-and-more/`
- `https://uploadvr.com/how-to-air-link-pc-vr-quest-2/`

The following are useful resources for learning more about WebXR development:

- The official W3C WebXR API standard (still a draft at the time of writing): `https://www.w3.org/TR/webxr/`
- Learn about XR programming in the Playcanvas web-first game engine: `https://developer.playcanvas.com/en/tutorials/webxr-ray-input/`
- A great source of WebXR information can be found at the Immersive Web website: `https://immersiveweb.dev/#unity`

To learn more about the Unity Editor's XR/VR and Unity WebGL, take a look at the following links:

- Unity blog post about this editor: `https://blogs.unity3d.com/2016/12/15/editorvr-experimental-build-available-today/`
- Unity docs WebGL: `https://docs.unity3d.com/Manual/webgl-gettingstarted.html`

Index

CPSIA information can be obtained
at www.ICGtesting.com
Printed in the USA
JSHW032309220722
28384JS00008B/3